The Urban Experience

The Urban Experience

Economics, Society, and Public Policy

Barry Bluestone
Mary Huff Stevenson
Russell Williams

OXFORD
UNIVERSITY PRESS
2008

OXFORD

UNIVERSITY PRESS

Oxford University Press, Inc., publishes works that further
Oxford University's objective of excellence
in research, scholarship, and education.

Oxford   New York
Auckland   Cape Town   Dar es Salaam   Hong Kong   Karachi
Kuala Lumpur   Madrid   Melbourne   Mexico City   Nairobi
New Delhi   Shanghai   Taipei   Toronto

With offices in
Argentina   Austria   Brazil   Chile   Czech Republic   France   Greece
Guatemala   Hungary   Italy   Japan   Poland   Portugal   Singapore
South Korea   Switzerland   Thailand   Turkey   Ukraine   Vietnam

Published by Oxford University Press, Inc.
198 Madison Avenue, New York, New York 10016

www.oup.com

Oxford is a registered trademark of Oxford University Press

Library of Congress Cataloging-in-Publication Data
Bluestone, Barry.
The urban experience : economics, society, and public policy / Barry Bluestone, Mary Huff Stevenson, Russell
Williams.
  p. cm.
Includes bibliographical references and index.
ISBN 978-0-19-531308-6
1. Cities and towns—United States.   2. Urbanization—United States—History.   3. Urban economics—
United States.   4. Sociology, Urban—United States.   5. City and town life—United States.   6. Urban policy—
United States.   I. Stevenson, Mary Huff, 1945–   II. Williams, Russell, 1951–   III. Title.
HT123.B56   2008
307.760973—dc22

                                                                          2007046158

9   8   7   6   5   4   3   2   1

Printed in the United States of America
on acid-free paper

To Seth, Elizabeth, Joshua, Alex, Michelle, Rachel, Nicole, and Brian, and all others of the next generation who will inherit both the joys and the challenges of cities and suburbs our generation helped create.

Preface

When the three of us decided to write this book, we wanted to create something that would truly address the realities of life in twenty-first-century U.S. metropolitan areas. We wanted to help readers understand the forces that continuously shape and reshape the places where they live and work.

From the beginning, our focus has been on the variety of urban experiences, perhaps reflecting the variety of our own experiences. Among the three of us, one or another has lived inside a big city, in a small town, in a suburb, and for a brief time, on a farm at the fringes of a metropolitan area. We have lived in a tenement slum, a public housing project, a tract house, a two-family house, and a single-family house on a large plot of land. We have lived in the Northeast, the Midwest, and the South. We are the children of college graduates and high school dropouts. We are black and white, male and female.

Of course, no three individuals could possibly span the full range of urban experience—for instance, none of us is disabled, none speaks English as a second language—but each of us does come with a distinctly different perspective on the question of what it means to live in a metropolitan area. Each of us cares passionately about making cities and suburbs work better—putting scarce resources to better use, spreading the fruits of prosperity more equitably, holding decision makers accountable for their choices, and helping the voiceless to make their viewpoints heard.

Because metropolitan areas are complex systems, they cannot be understood purely within the framework of a single discipline. Although all three of us were trained as economists, each of us recognizes the limits inherent in applying a narrowly defined economic approach to understanding real-world urban problems. We have strived to examine metropolitan areas through a much broader social science perspective, and have combined a historical narrative with an analytic approach that uses the tools of political science and sociology as well as those of economics.

Our narrative describing and analyzing the ways that U.S. cities have grown and changed makes a deliberate connection between events that occurred more than two centuries ago with events that may have occurred just last week. We have made a special effort to understand some of the most recent changes, particularly the impact of globalization, that make life in twenty-first-century U.S. metro areas so distinctly different from even that of the late twentieth century.

We hope that readers will gain a deeper understanding of how and why metro-politan areas function the way they do. However, we hope that they will go beyond passive acceptance and begin to question whether current practices and policies need to be revisited. Much of this book focuses on the role of public policy in shaping metropolitan areas. We hope that readers will also see the role they can play, as individuals and in concert with others, in shaping the public policies of the future.

Our book contains a wealth of data. Using the latest data available as well as historical information, we follow twenty metropolitan areas and ask a variety of questions about population, income, and educational attainment, among others. The CD-ROM accompanying this book allows the reader to ask these and many other questions about every city and town within every metropolitan area throughout the United States. If you want to know how population and income have changed in the city, town, or suburb where you were born, where you live now, or in the place you are thinking of moving to—or if you want to know other information about these places—this user-friendly CD can provide the answers to your questions. In this manner, too, we encourage more active engagement with the varieties of metro-politan experience. Once you have seen how the twenty metro areas we follow in the text are doing, check out how your city or suburb of interest stacks up.

Although this book contains many facts, these alone cannot provide a coherent explanation of metropolitan areas and how they developed. To understand and make sense of the information, it is useful to have some themes and fundamental theories around which the facts can be organized. We rely on several such themes, among which is the notion that place matters. As we demonstrate in the text, a metropolitan area can be comprised of prosperous suburbs and devastated central cities. The prospects for children growing up in such a metropolitan area depend greatly on whether or not their families' homes are located inside city limits. Other themes include opportunity cost—the sacrifice of a forgone alternative every time a choice is made—and the central importance of density as the defining characteristic of metro areas. Places where there are many people per acre are different, not just in degree but fundamentally different in kind from places that are sparsely populated. Density both allows and requires that we be more interdependent in metropolitan areas; it amplifies the effect of one person's actions on the lives of his neighbors. We borrow gener-ously from the seminal work of hundreds of economists, sociologists, and political scientists—as well as a range of keen urban observers without fancy letters after their names—to explore the theories and facts that help us understand how metro areas grow and function. We hope from all of this that readers will develop a coherent under-standing of the metropolitan areas where they live and that they will use that knowl-edge to engage in critical thinking and to question the conventional wisdom in order to help make their communities better places for them to enjoy with their neighbors.

This book has four major sections: Part I, "Introduction to Cities and Suburbs," provides the reader with a context for understanding contemporary U.S. metropol-itan areas and introduces the key issues and concepts that are the tools of the trade. It also provides a large amount of data introducing the twenty metro areas that we follow throughout the book to provide examples of key urban trends.

Part II, "Dynamics of Metropolitan Development," provides a historical narrative of how American cities and suburbs developed from colonial times to the present. The chapters in this section incorporate basic theories and formal models from economics, sociology, and political science that are used throughout the text to provide insight and analysis into the dynamics of metro areas.

Part III, "Foundations of Metropolitan Area Prosperity," examines the conditions necessary for promoting and sustaining urban prosperity. It focuses on the role of trade, labor markets, and the development of human capital through education and training.

Finally, Part IV, "Current Policy Issues in Metropolitan Areas," introduces the role of government as a response to various forms of market failure—including positive and negative externalities—and inequality in the urban setting. It proceeds in a series of chapters to examine in greater detail the public sector's responsibilities in the areas of physical infrastructure (water supply systems, waste treatment, public amenities, and transportation); social infrastructure (public health, public safety, and public welfare policy); urban housing markets, residential location, and housing policy; land-use controls, sprawl, and smart growth; and urban economic development strategies. The book concludes with a chapter on urban well-being, civility, and civic engagement.

We have many colleagues and friends to thank for helping us complete this enormous work. They include Barbara Hamilton, who prepared the amazing CD-ROM for this book. We thank Mitchell Vainshtein for his valuable research assistance, particularly with regard to Chapter 5 on the twenty-first-century city. Stein Helmrich assisted us in preparing the glossary.

We were especially fortunate to have a vast number of reviewers who helped us improve every section of this book. None provided more or better feedback than the executive director of Harvard University's Rappaport Institute for Greater Boston, David Luberoff, who read every word of the original manuscript. Individual chapters benefited from the insights of Alison Albers, Bruce Cohen, Matthew Drennan, David Fasenfest, Joan Fitzgerald, Frank Glover, Jack McDevitt, and Richard Rothstein, as well as a number of anonymous reviewers.

We also had the benefit of an enormous amount of feedback from our graduate students, who were kind enough to provide comments on the substance and readability of each chapter. We are especially indebted to Sandra Arevalo, Guy Bellino, Justin Betz, Chase Billingham, Chris Chanyasulkit, Robert DeLeo, Karen Erickson, Jill Eshelman, Thiana Ferry, Seneca Joyner, Tej Kumar Karki, Kate Maloney, Riva Milloshi, Lauren Nicoll, Lauren Pouchak, Rayn Sauvé, Vicki Schow, Mara Weibley, and Craig Welton. Thanks also to Shefali Rajpal, who sifted through the entire manuscript with a fine-tooth comb, finding all kinds of ways to improve on the text.

We also want to thank Oxford University Press and especially our acquisitions editor, Terry Vaughn, and our assistant editor, Catherine Rae, for the faith placed in us in developing this project. They truly understood the need for a new textbook that conveyed the excitement and mystery of the modern city and provided readers with a new multidisciplinary way to investigate the places where most of us live.

Contents

Part I   Introduction to Cities and Suburbs

1   The Wonder and Paradox of Urban Life   3

Urban Issues and the Social Science Lens   3
    Our Love/Hate Relationship with the City   5
    Our Love/Hate Relationship with the Suburbs   6
    The Importance of Density   8
    Urban Spillovers   8
The Dynamics of Metropolitan Development   9
    Well-Being and Public Policy   12
    The Role of Political Power and Interest Groups   13
    Paradox and Urban Inquiry   15
Key Issues in Urban Policy   16
    The Changing Role of the U.S. City in a "Flat" World   17
The Tools of the Trade   18
    Opportunity Cost   18
    The Criteria of Efficiency and Equity   20
    Externalities   20
    Unintended Consequences   21
    Other Important Economic Concepts   22
Questions and Exercises   23

2   How Metro Areas Rank   25

Cities and Their Reputations   25
Defining Metro Areas   27
    The Need for Standard Definitions   27
    New Definitions   28
Ranking Metropolitan Areas   32
    Race and Ethnicity   37
    Median Family Income   41
    Changes in Median Income over Time   45
    Poverty   48

Additional Measures of Metro Area Well-Being   50
    Purchasing Power   50
    Affordable Housing and Home Ownership   52
    Income Disparity and Inequality   53
    Education   53
    Environmental Quality   54
    Crime   54
    Transportation   55
Using Data Wisely   55
Questions and Exercises   56

Part II   **Dynamics of Metropolitan Development**

3   Urban America from the Seventeenth to the Early Twentieth Century:
    The Dynamics of City Growth   61

The Geography of Growth: Centripetal and Centrifugal Forces   62
    The Era of Water and Steam Power   63
    The Era of Railroads, Electricity, and the
        Telephone   64
Some Economic Concepts Underlying Urban Growth   65
    Trade and Transportation Costs   66
    Agglomeration Economies and Density   66
    Internal Economies of Scale   68
    Size of Consumer Markets   70
    Technological Progress   70
Transportation Costs *between* Nineteenth-Century Cities   73
    Weber's Graphical Model of Transportation Costs   76
    Other Important Ideas from Weber and from Isard   78
Transportation Costs *within* Nineteenth-Century Cities   81
Agglomeration Economies and the Growth of Cities   82
Technological Progress and Innovation   85
Demographic Growth and Change in Urban Areas   86
    Internal Migration: From Rural to Urban America   87
    Immigration and the Growth of American Cities   90
    Annexation and the Growing Size of Cities   94
The Changing Pattern of Urban Population Growth   94
Questions and Exercises   98

4   Cities and Suburbs in the Late Twentieth Century:
    The Dynamics of Metropolitan Expansion   100

Formal Models of Urban Growth and Development   101
    Understanding Urban Land Values   103
    The Basic Alonso Model   103
        How Does a Bid Rent Curve Get Established?   104

What Happens When There Is More Than One Bid
  Rent Curve? 106
Applying the Bid Rent Model to Metro Area Development 108
The Residential Paradox 110
Constrained Choice and Political Factors in Land Values and Location   112
The Evolution of Twentieth-Century U.S. Metropolitan Areas   113
    The Decentralization of Business Location   113
    Post–World War II Business Location   114
    The Rise of the Post–World War II Suburb   116
    The Impact of Federal Policies on Suburbanization   117
Class, Race, and Ethnic Segregation in the American City   121
    New Immigration and the Cities   123
Cross-Currents of the Late Twentieth Century: Sunbelt Cities,
  Edge Cities, and Gentrification   125
    The Rise of Sunbelt Cities   125
    The Rise of Edge Cities   126
    Central Cities and Gentrification   128
Classification of Twentieth-Century Cities   129
    The Changing Fortunes of Individual Cities   131
Appendix A: Expansions on the Basic Alonso Model   134
Questions and Exercises   140

5 U.S. Metro Areas in the Twenty-First Century:
   The New Dynamics of Urban Location   143

The New World Is "Flat"   143
Weber and the Twenty-First-Century City   146
    Expansions on the Basic Weber Model   146
    Weber in a World of Declining Transportation and
      Communications Costs   147
Alonso and the Twenty-First-Century City   150
    Alonso in a World of Declining Transportation
      and Communications Costs   150
What's Left for the City in the Twenty-First Century?   153
    Cities as Centers for Twenty-First-Century Business Services   153
    Cites as Centers for Twenty-First-Century Consumption   154
    Cultural Amenities versus Economic Factors   155
The Classification and Economic Functions of U.S. Metro Areas in the
  Twenty-First Century   156
    A Taxonomy of Twenty-First-Century Cities   157
Smart Growth and the New Urbanism Movement   161
The New Demographics of the Twenty-First-Century City   162
    Gentrification and Income Segregation   163
    Young Workers, Empty Nesters, and New Immigrants   164
Questions and Exercises   167

Part III   Foundations of Metropolitan Area Prosperity

6   Urban Prosperity and the Role of Trade   171

Metro Area Household Incomes   171
A Short Primer on the Economics of Trade   174
   Absolute Advantage   174
   Comparative Advantage   175
   Limitations in the Theory of Comparative Advantage   177
   New Trade Theory   178
The Theory of Competitive Advantage   179
   Trade and Prosperity   181
Export Base Theory: The Demand Side of the Metropolitan
   Area's Economy   182
The Basic/Nonbasic Approach: A Simple Measurement
   Technique   184
   Job Multipliers   184
   Location Quotients   185
   Limitations of the Basic/Nonbasic Approach   186
Input-Output Analysis: A More Complex Measurement
   Technique   187
   Limitations of the Input-Output Measurement Technique   187
   Limitations of the Demand-Side Focus   188
   Shifting the Focus from the Demand Side to the
      Supply Side   188
The Supply Side: A Long-Term Perspective   189
   Interactions between the Demand Side and the
      Supply Side   190
   Strategies for Less Resilient Metropolitan Areas   191
   Competitive Advantage in Inner-City Neighborhoods   192
Understanding Metro Area Prosperity in Light of
   Economic Theory   192
   The Case of Detroit   193
   The Case of Hartford   193
   The Case of Boston   194
   The Case of Chicago, Milwaukee, and Buffalo   195
   Newly Prosperous Metro Regions   195
Appendix A: Input-Output Calculations   199
Questions and Exercises   203

7   Urban Labor Markets and Metro Prosperity   206

Employment and Unemployment   207
   Where Are the Good Jobs?   209
Labor Market Earnings by Metro Area   211
   Occupational Wage Differentials *across* Metro Areas   214

Occupational Wage Differentials *between* Occupations
    across Metro Areas   216
Understanding Wage Differentials   218
    Human Capital   219
    Market Power and Barriers to Mobility   220
    Racial and Ethnic Discrimination   222
    Spatial Mismatch   224
    Skills Mismatch   228
    Spatial Mismatch, Deindustrialization, Education,
        and Race   230
    The Role of Unions   232
    Immigration   235
Explaining Metro Area Earnings Differentials   236
Labor Markets and Urban Prosperity   238
Appendix A: The Sources of Personal Income   239
Appendix B: The Simple Labor Market   242
Questions and Exercises   244

8   Urban Public Education and Metro Prosperity   247

The Decentralized U.S. Educational System   248
The Importance of Schooling in Modern Society   249
    Variation in Educational Attainment across Metro Areas   250
    Educational Attainment and Metro Area Income   254
Education, New Growth Theory, and the Well-Being of Cities
    and Suburbs   254
    New Growth Theory   255
    Education and Urban Economic Development   256
Education Production Functions   257
    Variation in School Spending   258
    Does Spending Matter?   261
    Where Teachers Teach   262
    School Tracking and Curriculum Choice   263
What Really Counts in School Performance   264
    An Expanded Education Production Function   264
    Educational Success: The Empirical Record   266
Challenges Facing Urban School Systems   267
    Racial Segregation and Educational Achievement   268
Urban Schools and Reform of School Structure   271
    Magnet Schools, Charter Schools, and For-Profit Schools   272
    Educational Standards and "No Child Left Behind"   275
    School Choice and Voucher Programs   276
    Do These School Reforms Work?   277
Questions and Exercises   282

Part IV **Current Policy Issues in Metropolitan Areas**

9 The Urban Public Sector 287

  Government's Economic Role in Metro Areas 287
    How the Private Market Is Supposed to Work 288
    Supply and Demand in the Private Sector 289
  Market Failure and the Public Sector 291
    Market Power 291
    Information Problems 293
    Negative and Positive Externalities 294
      Pollution: A Negative Externality 294
      Elementary and Secondary Education: A Positive Externality 295
    Pure Public Goods 296
  Government and the Distribution of Well-Being 298
    The Debate over the Scope of Government Intervention 299
  Market Failure and the Alternatives for Providing Goods
    and Services 301
    Regulated Private Markets 301
    Public Funding/Private Provision 302
    Public Provision 302
  Local Government Employment and Spending Patterns 303
    Privatization 305
  Paying for Government Services 307
    Income and Sales Taxes Levied by Local Governments 309
  Pricing in the Public Sector 309
    A Primer on the Economics of Building and Paying for Bridges 310
      *Scenario 1: Uncrowded Bridge Used by a Cross-Section of
        the Population* 311
      *Scenario 2: Uncrowded Bridge Used Primarily by Higher-Income
        Households* 311
      Scenario 3: Crowded Bridge 312
    User Fees 313
    The Tiebout Hypothesis 313
    Limitations in the Tiebout Hypothesis 314
    Metropolitanism 316
  Individuals, Interest Groups, and Values 316
    Public Choice Theory 317
    Interest Groups and Elites 317
    Incrementalism 318
    Regime Theory and Growth Machines 319
    The Challenge of Public-Sector Decision Making 320
  Appendix A: Negative Externalities 322
  Appendix B: Positive Externalities 324
  Questions and Exercises 328

10 Urban Physical Infrastructure: Water, Sewer, and Waste;
        Parks and Libraries; Transportation   331

   Combating Disease and Death   331
      Density and the Spread of Epidemics   332
   Water Supply Systems   334
      From Private to Public Operation   334
   Solid Waste Management   336
      The First Municipal Garbage Systems   336
      Coping with Mountains of Trash   338
   Urban Wastewater and Sewers   340
      Urban Sewer Systems   341
      New Challenges to Urban Sewer Systems   342
   Urban Public Amenities: Public Libraries and Pastoral
      Parks   345
      Social Unrest and the Provision of Urban Public
         Amenities   346
      A Failure of Expectations   348
   Transportation: Roads and Rails in Metro Areas   348
      What Consumers Want: The Demand Side of Metropolitan
         Transportation   350
      Travel Trends   350
      The Journey to Work   354
      Externalities and Mass-Transit Subsidies   355
      The Supply Side of Metropolitan Transportation   358
      Issues in Contemporary Metropolitan Transportation
         Policy   360
         Short-Run Issues: Getting Prices Right   360
         *Long-Run Issues: Deciding on Future Transportation
            Infrastructure Investment*   364
         Transportation Equity Issues   365
   Questions and Exercises   368

11 Urban Social Infrastructure: Public Health, Public Safety,
        and Public Welfare Policy   372

   The Provision of Public Health Services   372
      Local Public Health Departments   373
      Personal Health Care: Hospitals and Health Centers   374
      Health Care for the Poor   376
      Health Disparities in the Metro Region   377
      Why Are Health Disparities So Prevalent?   378
      Health Disparities between Neighborhoods   380
      Urban Public Health in a Global Context: Epidemics, Bioterrorism,
         and Homeland Security   381

Urban Police   382
    The Impact of Demographic Change on Police   383
    Transformation in the Structure and Responsibilities of Urban
       Police Departments   385
    Crime Prevention in Urban Settings: From Twentieth- to
       Twenty-First-Century Paradigms   386
    Community Policing versus Traditional Approaches   386
    Twenty-First-Century Public Safety Issues: Private Security,
       Internet-Based Crime, and Homeland Security   389
Fire Departments and Emergency Medical Services   390
    Emergency Medical Services   392
Urban Social Welfare   392
    Ameliorating Living Conditions in Poor Neighborhoods   394
Questions and Exercises   397

12   Urban Housing Markets, Residential Location,
    and Housing Policy   401

The Housing Consumer: The Price of an Individual Home   401
    Attributes Theory and Hedonic Prices   403
    Budget Constraints and Housing Preferences   404
Home Ownership versus Rental Housing   406
    The Role of Government Incentives for Home
      Ownership   407
    Trends in Home Ownership   408
    Household Income and the Individual's Housing Demand   409
The Urban/Metro Housing Market   411
    What Drives Metro Area Housing Prices: Supply
      and Demand   414
    Housing "Affordability"   417
    Housing Prices and Vacancy Rates   417
The Impact of Housing Prices on Local Employment and Population
    Growth   421
    Housing Prices and Employment Growth   424
    Housing Prices and Population Migration   426
Post–World War II Suburbanization and Residential
    Segregation   428
    Measuring Segregation   429
    The Causes of Housing Segregation   429
    Segregation and Social-Class Structure   431
    Concentrated Poverty in the Inner City   432
Federal Housing Policy   433
    Subsidizing Housing Demand   434
    Subsidizing Housing Supply   435
State and Local Housing Policy   436

Rent Control   438
    The Unintended Short-Run Consequences of Rent Control   438
    The Unintended Long-Run Consequences of Rent Control   439
Intervening in Housing Markets: A Word of Caution   442
Appendix A: Indifference Curves and Budget Constraints   443
Questions and Exercises   446

13   Land-Use Controls, Sprawl, and Smart Growth   451

Land-Use Restrictions and Zoning   452
    The Power of Eminent Domain   453
    The Power to Enact Zoning Regulations   454
    Houston's Alternative to Zoning   456
    Underzoning and Overzoning   458
Equity Issues in Zoning   460
Zoning and Metropolitan Sprawl   462
    What's Wrong with Sprawl?   463
    Urban Sprawl and Commuting Times   463
    The Debate about Sprawl   467
    Measuring Sprawl   468
Generating Sprawl: Market Forces and Public Policy   473
    Reducing Sprawl: Market Forces and Public Policy   474
    Smart Growth   475
    Barriers to Smart Growth Implementation   476
    Equity and Efficiency Considerations in Alternative
        Metropolitan Growth Scenarios   477
Land-Use Controls and Spatial Form   478
Questions and Exercises   481

14   Urban Economic Development Strategies   483

Deindustrialization and Firm Relocation   483
    Deindustrialization in the 1970s   485
    Continuing Deindustrialization   486
Goals of Economic Development   486
Location from the Business Perspective   488
Public Policy, Economic Development, and Firm Location   490
    Reducing Capital Costs ($r \times K$)   491
    Reducing Labor Costs ($w \times L$)   493
    Reducing Raw Materials, Natural Resources, and Transportation
        Costs ($p_n \times N$), C_s 494
    Reducing Taxes (T)   495
    Streamlining Regulations (R)   497
    Increasing Social Amenities   499
What Works?   500
    Increasing a Firm's Total Revenue   502

Reducing a Firm's Capital Costs   503
Reducing Labor Costs/Increasing Skills and Education   505
Public Provision of Transportation and Land   507
Industrial Parks and Eminent Domain   508
Reducing State and Local Taxes   508
Streamlining Regulations and Enterprise Zones   509
Building Convention Centers and Sports Stadiums   510
Why Do Cities Pursue Economic Development Strategies with Such Low
    Payoffs?   511
What Should City Leaders and Policy Makers Do to Play
    the Economic Development Game Better?   513
Appendix A: Cost-Benefit Analysis   515
Questions and Exercises   521

15 Urban Well-Being, Civility, and Civic Engagement
       in the Twenty-First Century   523

What Do We Want from Our Neighborhoods
    and How Do We Get It?   523
    The Tiebout Hypothesis and the Privatization of Public Space   524
    Gated Communities and the Avoidance of Disamenities   526
    Dissatisfied Citizens and Their Choices: Exit versus Voice   527
How Do We Create Better Communities?   529
    The Role of Social Capital and Civic Engagement   530
    Social Capital, Suburbanization, and Sprawl   532
    Social Capital and Neighborhood Form   532
    Recent Empirical Work on Communities and Social Capital   534
Neighborhood Form and Crime Reduction   535
The Effect of Social Capital on the Lives of the Most Vulnerable   536
Central City Renaissance   538
Regeneration for Whom? Rebuilding Central City Neighborhoods   541
    The Role of Community Development Corporations   542
    Demographic Change and Low-Income Communities   544
    The Perils of Success   544
Questions and Exercises   547

Glossary   549

Index   583

CD-ROM Instructions   601

INTRODUCTION TO
CITIES AND SUBURBS

The Wonder and Paradox of Urban Life

1

Place matters. Whether it's the exhilaration some of us feel when the hometown team wins the big game, or the desire to escape our surroundings and seek our fortune elsewhere (or, paradoxically, the ability to feel both sentiments simultaneously), we care passionately about the places where we live. Even when we choose to leave the places where we grew up, we are often nostalgic for "the old neighborhood" or "the old country." We carry our origins with us even as we reinvent ourselves, crafting lives that are different from those of our parents or grandparents. While the reach of technology—radio, television, and the Internet—permits us to share more in common, the place we call home still affects us in profound ways.

Where we live says a lot about who we are and what our daily lives are like. Four-fifths of Americans today live in *metropolitan* areas—in central cities or suburbs. This means that urban living, with its challenges and promises, is essential to most of us, just as the exigencies of rural life were for 95 percent of the nation's families who lived in villages or on farms at the time of the American Revolution. Moreover, understanding urban issues, from the causes and consequences of local economic development and suburban "sprawl" to the problems associated with urban/suburban income inequality and disparity in the provision of public services, helps us to better understand—and possibly find remedies for—some of the most persistent problems facing American society.

Urban Issues and the Social Science Lens

Social science looks for patterns in human behavior and tries to explain them. Each of the key social science disciplines—economics, political science, and sociology—approaches social phenomena in a different way. Economics focuses on the role of markets in understanding how people relate to each other; in a sense, dollars count. Political science examines the role of nonmarket institutions (such as political parties) that operate through an array of public institutions where votes and political influence count. Sociology analyzes human social relations beyond the bounds of the market or government institutions; social standing and the web of relationships within one's community matter.

3

Economics is divided into two broad fields: **Macroeconomics** looks at the big picture, the behavior of large aggregates of consumers or business firms, focusing on factors that determine the level of total production in a society. Essentially, macroeconomists try to understand why an economy experiences booms and busts and what can be done to smooth out the economic roller coaster of inflation and recession. **Microeconomics** studies the behavior of individual consumers and firms, how prices are set in individual markets, and how output is divided among workers and families and among firms.

Urban economics is important because it takes macroeconomic and microeconomic concerns and places them in a context—a physical space where they can be studied under a microscope. We can look at all the factors that determine the general level of output in a particular city or metropolitan area. Why is median family income in the city of Seattle nearly double (+ 92%) that in St. Louis? Why is per capita income growing rapidly in Phoenix while it is stagnant in Newark and Cleveland? Instead of looking at individual markets in the abstract, we can study specific conditions—the kind that determine the price of housing in cities and suburbs, or why the wages of janitors in San Francisco are so much higher than in Birmingham or Kansas City. The study of urban economics provides a special lens through which we can understand human behavior in the real world, in places where people really live.

By itself, though, economics cannot do justice to an understanding of urban issues and urban public policy. We need to add the perspective of other social sciences, including political science and sociology, if we are to explain both behavior and outcomes in cities and suburbs. In a thousand different ways, political decisions involving public expenditure, taxation, and direct and indirect regulation influence and often trump the pure economic calculus of the market. Cities and towns that have instituted a minimum wage or "living wage" try to change the outcome of local labor markets. Zoning determines where housing and commercial properties will be developed. Building codes alter the way our homes are constructed.

Sociology is important, too; as the scientific study of human social relations and group life, this discipline is central to understanding how large numbers of people live in close proximity to each other in cities and suburbs. By studying social class, race and ethnicity, family and community, and the social uses of power, sociology adds to the study of metropolitan regions the subtle but powerful impact of neighborhood groups, community organizations, and similar nongovernmental units that affect daily life. A "Not in My Back Yard" mentality (NIMBYism) often explains why there is an insufficient supply of new housing to meet increased demand better than anything we know about land values and real estate law. Community organizations made up of active neighborhood residents can use their power to influence how mayors and city councils implement public regulations that affect the market decisions of commercial developers.

Urban public policy thus draws on economic, political, and sociological theory and combines them to yield important insights about the well-being of various racial and ethnic groups living in central cities and suburbs; the reasons for rising or falling crime rates; the location of housing, commercial, and industrial properties within a city or suburb; and a myriad of other matters that affect where and how we live. The metro area becomes the laboratory for exploring economic, political, and social issues that affect how our communities and neighborhoods are organized.

Our Love/Hate Relationship with the City

As in the classic children's fable about the city mouse and the country mouse, some of us are energized by the bounteous offerings of the big city, while others prefer the peace and tranquility of smaller places. But our fascination with the big city is evident both in popular culture and in works of literature. New York City, often called the Big Apple or the City That Never Sleeps, is the setting for numerous TV sitcoms and dramas that shape—and distort—our image of the place. Likewise, Los Angeles, the City of Angels; Chicago, the City of Big Shoulders; Boston, the Hub of the Universe; and New Orleans, the Big Easy, have all been the settings for popular TV series and Hollywood films. In earlier times, the endless possibilities offered by the city were exuberantly celebrated in the poetry of Walt Whitman.

For many of those who live in them and others who visit, cities offer the thrill of a fast-paced life. Research by sociologist Robert Levine (1997) reveals that the pace of life varies according to where one lives. Within the United States, Levine finds important regional differences, with the cities of the Northeast having a faster pace (as measured by speed in walking, talking, banking transactions, and the proportion of people wearing wristwatches) than those of the laid-back Southwest.

Besides its quick pace, many observers of city life have celebrated its theatrical aspects. Lewis Mumford (1961), a leading urban historian of the mid-twentieth century, likens the city to a "stage," while the insightful urban commentator Jane Jacobs (1969) describes the "ballet" of daily life on a busy neighborhood street. The sociologist William H. Whyte (1989) harkens back to the "agora," or marketplace, of ancient cities, but he is less concerned with economic interchange than with the role of the city as a public meeting place. These urbanists prize the serendipity of life in the city, the unexpected delights, the chance encounters, the sheer pleasure of watching people in a place with so many people to watch.

Yet, even as the metropolis captures our imagination with its infinite offerings, there is also ingrained deep within our traditions a distrust and fear of big cities. Thomas Jefferson envisioned a nation of yeoman farmers living in small towns, far removed from the industrial cities of England with their "dark Satanic mills," as the poet William Blake described them. In *Sister Carrie,* the early-twentieth-century American novelist Theodore Dreiser (1900) tells the story of a sweet and innocent young woman from a small town who loses her virtue when she goes to the big city of Chicago; from there she travels on to New York, an even bigger metropolis, and descends into greater shame and corruption. In Dreiser's narrative, Carrie is not just corrupted *in* the city, but she is also corrupted *by* the city. On TV, we have seen not only the mischievous urban humor of *Seinfeld* and *Friends* but also the depictions of mean streets and urban violence found in *NYPD Blue, CSI Miami,* and *The Sopranos.*

Our Love/Hate Relationship with the Suburbs

The desire to avoid the crime, disease, poverty, noise, and congestion that often typified city life fueled a centrifugal movement away from the centers of large cities even before the advent of automobiles at the beginning of the twentieth century. When people left big cities, they generally did not move to rural areas, but instead settled in the quieter places just outside the city limits. Although these suburbanites no longer lived inside the city, they usually continued to identify with it. Even today, if travelers far from home are asked where they are from, they are likely to say "Chicago" or "Detroit," when they actually live in suburban communities like Evanston or Southfield. There is a good chance that people outside the Midwest will recognize the names of the two big cities, and a much smaller likelihood that they will recognize the names of the suburbs.

For many, the quintessential symbol of the American Dream is the suburban single-family house complete with lawn (white picket fence optional). In his study of Levittown, a New York suburb built right after World War II on Long Island, sociologist Herbert Gans (1967) argues that "perhaps more than any other type of community, Levittown permits most of its residents to be what they want to be—to center their lives around the home and the family, to be among neighbors whom they can trust, to find friends to share leisure hours, and to participate in organizations that provide sociability and the opportunity to be of service to others." It is much easier and much less expensive to build such communities on the cheaper, often unoccupied land at the periphery of the metropolitan area than to do so in the central city.

As Levittown and the older suburbs of the East and the Midwest began to age, a newer generation of suburbs was being created in the Southwest, on wide-open land that stretched to the horizon. The journalist David Brooks (2002) refers to these as "Sprinkler Cities," because so many of them are being carved out of the often-arid land of the Southwestern desert. He notes that "people move to Sprinkler Cities for the same reasons people came to America or headed out West. They want to leave behind the dirt and toxins of their former existence—the crowding and inconvenience.... Sprinkler City immigrants are not leaving cities to head out to suburbia. They are leaving older suburbs—which have come to seem as crowded, expensive, and stratified as cities—and heading for newer suburbs, for the suburbia of suburbia." In these newer communities, as in Levittown, people seek orderliness, cleanliness, easy friendships, leisure-time (often sports-related) activities, and rich, healthy childhood experiences for their kids.

Of course, there are many critics of the suburban lifestyle. They focus on its mass-consumption aspects: the "need" for every household to have its own lawn mower, snow blower, megasize gas grill, and, in many cases, more automobiles per household than there are drivers. Others emphasize the lack of aesthetic considerations in the design of suburban housing, and the unrelenting sameness of suburban subdivisions across the United States.

Along with the suburban housing developments themselves, there has been a growing worry about the "malling" of America, as one strip mall after another is built in suburban communities. While wonderfully convenient, these palaces of consumption look nearly identical no matter where they are located. Hence, the title of James Kunstler's (1993) critique of the suburbs, *The Geography of Nowhere*, which dwells on the undifferentiated sameness of suburbs with their nearly identical homes and identical shops as compared with the rich diversity of central city life. Even though a majority of the U.S. population now lives and works in a suburb (Hobbs and Stoops 2002), Eric Bogosian's play *SubUrbia* paints a dark vision of the sterility and boredom of such places, with their supposed conformity, materialism, and lack of drama.

To some extent, our love-hate relationship with cities and suburbs is based on stereotypes. Suburbanites may exaggerate the dangers of the big city; city dwellers may underestimate the range of people and activities that actually can be found in the suburbs. People often stereotype the racial, cultural, and/or social characteristics of city or suburban residents, but the complexity of both city and suburban life is such that any stereotype will always be more misleading than not. Life in many central cities is safe and clean, and there are suburbs that offer rich diversity in the racial and demographic composition of their residents, in their housing, and in their retail districts.

To be from New York, Los Angeles, Chicago, or any other major metropolitan area may mean one thing to the baby boomers who came of age there in the post–World War II era and quite another to young adults today. A program from the early days of television, *The Naked City,* proclaimed that there were "eight million stories" to tell (a reference to New York City's population at the time). Race, gender, ethnicity, income, and social class all have a profound influence on the way we experience our surroundings. To paraphrase Charles Dickens, "it was the best of places, it was the worst of places."

Annie Dillard (1987) wrote a well-regarded memoir, *An American Childhood*, about growing up in Pittsburgh in the 1950s. Dillard grew up in a relatively privileged, white, native-born household. However, growing up in Pittsburgh during that time would likely have been a substantially different experience for another young girl who was the child of Hungarian immigrants or for a young boy who was the great-grandchild of slaves.

Moreover, it is not just that the city will be experienced differently by *different* people but also that a large city offers the anonymity necessary for the *same* individual to explore different facets of his or her personality. Sociologists use the concept of **multiple identities** to describe a situation in which an individual may have one persona within a specific group at one time and a completely different persona with another group at another time. For example, a gay teen from a religious family background might find that the city affords sufficient anonymity to express both aspects of his personality while continuing to build a comprehensive sense of self. The anonymity of the city also allows for fresh starts; it facilitates that uniquely urban practice of "reinventing" oneself. In small towns and rural communities, this is often difficult to do. Everyone there knows everyone else and much that is private quickly becomes public.

Vibrant metropolitan areas theoretically provide a range of neighborhoods from which people can choose the physical and social environment that suits them best. But how much freedom they have in choosing where they live has always had a lot to do with income, and often with race and ethnicity. Metropolitan areas provide a magnificent economic, political, and social laboratory where we can seek to better understand the promises and challenges of society as a whole.

The Importance of Density

Large numbers of people living in close proximity to each other—what sociologists and demographers call **population density**—is the hallmark of urban areas. It provides cities and their environs with a range of activities that rural areas could never afford nor duplicate. If, for example, only one in a hundred people ever attends a professional hockey game or a ballet performance, the economic survival of a National Hockey League franchise or a dance company can only occur in a metro region where there are hundreds of thousands of people. Similarly, other businesses catering to rare or expensive tastes need to have a critical population mass and this, too, will be found only in the larger cities.

Because of density, metropolitan regions function in ways that are different in kind, not just in degree, from places where households are more sparsely settled. Residential neighborhoods are more likely to have the critical mass necessary to provide elementary schools within walking distance of their pupils, restaurants that can cater to varied tastes, and a range of recreational and cultural attractions that can please even those with unconventional preferences. Similarly, density is what allows the construction of a well-developed physical infrastructure—the road network, the mass-transit system, water and sewer systems, and power grids—at a relatively low cost per household. Density also permits a complex social infrastructure to develop based on a wide array of neighborhood and community-based organizations and formal and informal interpersonal networks for the exchange of ideas and information. If, as the saying goes, "variety is the spice of life," large cities are generally "spicier" than other places simply because they have the population density to permit it. This is also why cities are particularly good at fostering creativity, a major advantage in an era when economic success increasingly relies on the production of ideas, which flourish where there are many creative minds concentrated in one place (Florida 2002).

Urban Spillovers

With so much activity taking place, cities are littered with "spillover" effects. One can enjoy window shopping along a street filled with specialized boutiques without spending a penny. However, the exhaust from cars, trucks, and buses along the route could make a person dread such a stroll downtown. The first represents a positive spillover; the latter a negative one. The closer people live to one another and the denser the level of economic activity, the greater the number of such spillovers—or what economists call externalities—and the greater their impact. In the nineteenth century, before major reforms in public health and sanitation, the extraordinarily high densities in large cities made them centers for air- and waterborne illnesses. Today, central city residents often suffer a higher incidence of asthma and other diseases. In shifting to a less dense pattern of suburban development, though, we have also changed the way we use land, leading to current concerns about urban sprawl and environmental degradation. Because these problems are usually more prevalent in metropolitan areas than rural communities, they have become urban policy issues worthy of careful study.

As the economic activities of the dense central core of early American cities spilled over into surrounding areas, cities typically expanded their political boundaries through annexation of adjoining towns to keep pace with the geographic expansion of the area's economy. By the end of the nineteenth century, however, efforts to annex independent suburban jurisdictions met with resistance across the established metropolitan areas of the Northeast and mid-Atlantic states. From then on, as the economic boundaries of the metropolitan area expanded, the political boundaries remained unchanged, leading to a curious duality: A metropolitan area is a single economic unit—encompassing most of the residences of those who work there and most of the workplaces of those who live there—but with a set of fragmented political units containing, in some instances, dozens if not hundreds of separate municipal jurisdictions. This tension between economic integration and political fragmentation often places severe constraints on the development of area-wide public policies. Initiatives that would benefit the entire metropolitan area but adversely affect any one jurisdiction (e.g., the expansion of a major research university that would bring economic growth to the region but remove property from the tax rolls of the municipality in which it is located) will require a lengthy and often contentious process of negotiation.

The Dynamics of Metropolitan Development

Places change constantly. The sturdy, working-class neighborhood of one generation might become the dangerous slum of the next. The seedy warehouse district of a previous era might be transformed into today's trendy neighborhood of artists' lofts. The changing fortune of individual neighborhoods might also mirror the changing fortunes of entire cities, metropolitan areas, and even regions. The Sunbelt states of the South and West continue their rapid expansion, while many cities in the Snowbelt states of the Northeast and Midwest stagnate or decline. During the past thirty years, Las Vegas, Nevada, has been the fastest-growing city in America. Cities like Youngstown, Ohio, and Flint, Michigan, have seen their populations decline sharply. The fact that some places might be on the upswing while others fall on hard times has important implications for the well-being of families, businesses, and communities. While many changes might appear to be random, a well-trained eye can often spot an underlying pattern. As any accomplished sleuth would testify, recognizing the pattern is the first step in finding the solution to the mystery.

In the mystery of what we call metropolitan dynamics—the rise and fall (and sometimes the rise again) of individual cities and suburbs—the pattern is more easily recognized if we keep our eye on the factors noted in **Figure 1.1**. We want to follow **demographic shifts**, changes in the racial and ethnic composition of cities and suburbs. We need to pay special attention to **industrial transformation**, as certain industries expand and prosper while others become technologically obsolete. And, finally, we want to trace the **spatial relocation** of households and businesses from one region to another (including immigration from abroad), from one city to another, or from city to suburb and back again. These three forces, working through private-market forces, augmented by public policy, social networks, and community process, largely determine the ebb and flow of urban life across the nation.

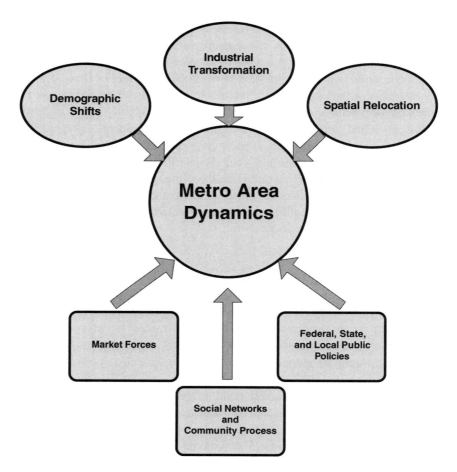

Figure 1.1 The Factors and Forces of Metropolitan Dynamics. Metropolitan areas are affected by changes in the size and composition of their populations and their business firms, along with changes in the way these households and business firms are located across the area. All of these changes are affected by the complex interplay of private markets, government interventions, and informal community practices and traditions.

In part, the individual choices made by thousands upon thousands of households and business firms determine whether places will grow and prosper or whether they will wither and decay. People might be drawn to a place for any number of reasons: a mild climate, proximity to natural beauty, or a population that shares the same ethnic or religious background, educational opportunities, or employment opportunities. But as they flock to a location, they also transform it. What was once a sleepy little town is now a bustling suburb. The places left behind are also transformed, as declining populations translate into fewer stores on Main Street and bleaker prospects for attracting new companies. Business firms, too, might be attracted to a particular location because of cheap land, superb transportation facilities, or a skilled workforce. Their relocation also transforms both the place where they came from and the place where they went.

Even as thousands of individual choices accumulate into good news or bad for specific neighborhoods, cities, and entire metropolitan areas, the well-being of these geographic entities exerts its own influence on the choices available to individuals. A prosperous community can provide safety, security, and high-quality education for its children; an area that has fallen on hard times will be far less able to do so. These feedback effects—success breeds success; failure breeds failure—make it ever more difficult for places that have fallen behind to catch up.

When the steel mills in Pittsburgh began to close down, younger and better educated residents often left to build their futures elsewhere. For a time, this made Pittsburgh even less attractive to potential new businesses. The ever-declining prospects of the city led to further rounds of destructive "selective migration." When people begin to abandon a city, the city's tax base erodes, making it more difficult to support good schools and public amenities. This leads to successive rounds of out-migration and diminished services in a downward spiral—at least until new industry springs up or existing industries undergo a renaissance. Pittsburgh and its suburbs have been able to build a new employment base and stem the city's population loss by attracting new businesses and diversifying its industrial base, in part because of its relatively depressed land costs and its highly respected universities.

Boston's heyday based on shipping came to an end by the early nineteenth century, but it was replaced by a resurgent economy based on manufacturing. Its fortunes declined sharply again after World War II until the last quarter of the twentieth century when higher education, health care, and financial services became critical to American economic success. With its more than forty universities and colleges, its rich array of hospitals and clinics, and its role as the birthplace of the mutual fund industry, Boston was poised for an economic renaissance once these industries began to grow. Now, because of its great success, the cost of living in the city is so high that it is once again challenged to retain and attract jobs and population.

But urban success or failure is not merely a matter of individual choices made by households and businesses. The various branches of government—at the local, state, and federal level—make decisions that have an impact on which places will flourish and which will languish. Early massive public investment in public works played a crucial role in catapulting New York, Chicago, and Los Angeles to the top of the charts among U.S. metropolitan regions. Intriguingly, the key public works projects in all three cities had to do with redirecting the flow of water. In the case of New York, the development of the Erie Canal in 1825 provided the impetus for growth, by creating the best route from the Atlantic Ocean to the Great Lakes. This gave the Port of New York an edge over the East Coast port cities of Boston, Philadelphia, and Baltimore, and fueled the phenomenal growth of this world-class city of commerce. In Chicago, the stupendous engineering feat of reversing the flow of the highly polluted Chicago River so that it emptied into the Des Plaines River rather than into Lake Michigan allowed the city to protect the safety of its water supply. This gave Chicago its competitive edge over such midwestern contenders as Cincinnati and Indianapolis. In Los Angeles, redirecting the rivers of northern California to flow into the parched region surrounding the city made the City of Angels what it is today. Without the water supply from these rivers passing through an elaborate system of aqueducts, the city could not have supported anywhere near its current population.

The interplay of private-sector decisions and public policy helps to explain the rise of that quintessential Sunbelt city, Houston. The development of air-conditioning made it livable and an economy based on oil and gas made it prosperous, but it was the enthusiasm and political clout of then vice president Lyndon Johnson that helped to bring the headquarters of the National Aeronautics and Space Administration (NASA) to the city, thereby aiding Houston's growth. The interplay of market forces and public policy propelled the growth of suburbs throughout the country and dramatically changed the shape of metropolitan areas in the mid-twentieth century. Federal housing programs and federal highway dollars made suburbs affordable and accessible. Successive rings of suburbs have grown and receded around many of America's major cities. Inner-ring suburbs have often seen their fortunes decline, while outer suburbs and the even farther out "exurban" regions grow rapidly. Cities and suburbs never stay the same for very long; they are always changing.

Well-Being and Public Policy

As realtors tell us, "The three things that are most important in valuing property are location, location, and location." Place is important for several reasons. A particular site might be appealing for its inherent beauty, or repugnant because of the toxic wastes it contains. Alternatively, we may be interested in a specific place because of its proximity to something else. When we choose where to live, for example, we might take into account how long it takes to commute to work, or whether friends and family are close by.

Place also may be important because each specific location ties us into a different network of opportunities and constraints. Just as communication systems and transportation networks link some places and leave others out of touch, there are neighborhood-based social networks that can provide access to important resources. Being in the right network makes a difference. A family living on one side of a district line sends its children to a school considered exceptional, while a family on the other side sends its children to a school with a poorer reputation. One town provides excellent connections to neighborhood associations and community resources while another does not. Every location offers a different mixture of advantages and disadvantages. How well individuals are connected to places, to things, and to other people will help to determine their well-being in various parts of the metropolitan area.

The economist George Galster has introduced the concept of "opportunity structures" to capture the fact that where people live has a major impact on their access to resources (Galster and Killen 1995). These opportunity structures are continuously shaped and reshaped by the interaction of individual choices, private business decisions, and government policy.

Opportunity structures vary across race, ethnicity, income, and wealth, contributing to tensions within a metropolitan area. Various groups attempt to use government to address their own needs and to expand their choices. This inevitably leads to conflict over public budget priorities, regulatory decisions, and tax policy. As a result, intersections of public policy and private decision making present some of the most complex aspects of urban life. How much should be spent on public works such as water and sewer lines, roads, and bridges? How much should be spent on public primary and secondary education, police and fire protection, and public health and sanitation?

These decisions are fraught with controversy as individuals and interest groups contest both for resources and over who should pay for them. When the commonwealth of Massachusetts spent more than $14 billion to depress Boston's Central Artery as part of its famous "Big Dig" project, the overriding question was how much the taxpayers of Massachusetts would pay for the new road and how much would be paid by the federal government. When cities face severe fiscal crises as a result of a downturn in the national economy, mayors and city councillors have to decide where to make budget cuts: Should teachers' jobs be sacrificed to avoid laying off police and firefighters, or vice versa? In either case, some jobs will be lost and some constituents will lose valuable services.

The Role of Political Power and Interest Groups

Put more generally, politics and political power count. Metro areas constantly evolve, at least in part, as the result of external pressures. Detroit's decline from its status as one of America's wealthiest cities was due in large measure to the globalization of the auto industry. The rise of San Jose, Boston, and Raleigh-Durham-Chapel Hill, North Carolina, owes much to the information revolution and the role that great research universities have played in spawning industries related to the computer, biotechnology, and nanotechnology in the late twentieth and early twenty-first centuries. Prodigious increases in agricultural productivity have sharply reduced the need for farm labor, compromising the growth of cities and towns that sprung up to serve them in the farm belt.

Yet, the quality and pace of change in the urban setting is also intimately related to the array of interest groups and political alignments within each metro area. As Logan and Molotch (1987) argue, there are powerful local interest groups who have a stake in promoting growth because of its subsequent enhancement of land values. This **growth machine** includes real estate interests and the politicians who rely on them for campaign contributions, along with the local media (such as newspapers and radio and television stations), whose power and profits depend on population growth, as well as others (like utility companies), whose fortunes are tied to a specific locality. Even if these groups disagree on other matters (e.g., even if construction companies and unions in the building trades are adversaries in wage negotiations), they would nevertheless be aligned together as part of the area's pro-growth coalition.

Businesses, labor unions, nonprofit voluntary organizations, and community groups all interact to influence the political process and the fate of cities and suburbs. Through the chambers of commerce and other business groups that exist in virtually every municipality, business leaders use their economic clout to influence the mayor and city council or town selectmen to make decisions over taxes, regulations, and spending that support the interests of business. Public-sector unions strive to use their power to increase the wages and benefits of police officers, firefighters, teachers, and other city employees and to set work rules regarding what their members can and cannot do on the job. Voluntary organizations that range from advocates for public transit, neighborhood parks, and the homeless to Parent-Teacher Associations (PTAs) and community development corporations all vie to influence political leaders to address the issues that stir their passion. Neighborhood associations work to protect the value of the homes in their communities and to serve the interests of those who live there.

Inevitably, there are conflicts—often powerful ones—that erupt among these many interest groups as they all compete to support their own interests. Businesses often fight for lower taxes, arguing that high taxes discourage investment in the city and this would cost the community jobs that are badly needed. But with lower taxes, how would the city or suburb pay for quality schools, police and fire services, and pleasant parks? Public-sector unions usually take every opportunity to push for better compensation for their members, but this often strains municipal budgets. Housing developers try to get zoning laws changed and building regulations modified in order to make it easier for them to build new homes. But neighborhood associations often battle back if they feel that the developments being planned will change the character of their communities or bring in new families that are "different" from them. Conflicts arise regarding where to place new highways and roads since these inevitably affect property values in adjacent neighborhoods. This often pits one local 'hood against another.

Every group attempts to gain political favor by contributing to local political candidates and lobbying the city council or the school board. Every group tries to mobilize its members to act in solidarity for the positions they take. In the end, given the unequal power of individual interest groups, what comes out of the political process is not always what benefits the entire community, but what serves the interests of those who are most adept at political maneuvering.

Since the 1960s, political scientists have debated whether the interest groups that exert influence on local governments are best described as a business elite united around issues like economic growth and redevelopment (as in Floyd Hunter's 1953 study of Atlanta) or a more disparate group of organizations with competing interests that require negotiation and compromise (as found in Robert Dahl's 1961 study of New Haven). More recently, this dichotomy between **elitism** and **pluralism** has been leavened by a concept introduced by Norman and Susan Fainstein (1983) and Clarence Stone (1989)—**regime theory**—broadly described as the informal channels and arrangements that influence formal government authority. According to Stone (1993), these regimes can take several different forms: development regimes that emphasize growth; middle-class progressive regimes that endorse neighborhood and environmental protections that slow growth; lower-class opportunity expansion regimes in which disadvantaged groups press for a greater share of resources; and maintenance regimes, which tend to be static caretaker governments less reliant on private-sector resources. It is less clear within these categories, but just as important, that the competition for power and influence in cities and suburbs is part of an ongoing and probably never-ending struggle.

Paradox and Urban Inquiry

Adding even more excitement to the study of metropolitan areas is an array of puzzles and paradoxes that require an understanding of urban economics, sociology, political science, and public policy. Why do poor people tend to live on the expensive land close to the center of the city, while wealthier people live on the cheaper land at the periphery? Why does rush-hour traffic seem to get even worse after a new highway is built to relieve congestion? When artists convert a marginal neighborhood into a more attractive and livable community, why do they wind up not being able to afford to live there themselves? Why are suburban subdivisions so often named for the orchards or forests they destroyed, so that the innumerable "Shady Groves" dotting the landscape offer no shade and contain no groves? Why is wine bottled in rural areas, close to where the grapes are grown, but beer is bottled close to major metropolitan areas, far away from where the barley, malt, or hops are grown? Why will a new restaurant often want to locate on a street with many other restaurants, rather than finding a street where it wouldn't have to share potential customers with its competitors?

In each of these cases, the spatial aspect of the decisions made by households and businesses forms the core of our analysis. In looking at the dynamics that affect the quality of poor inner-city urban housing, for example, we need to understand the forces that led to its deterioration. Unlike some of the housing in rural areas, which might have been poorly constructed initially, or perhaps built without indoor plumbing, housing in urban areas is more likely to have been built originally to conform to prevailing middle-class standards. However, if middle-class households decide to move elsewhere, and landlords then rent to people with less ability to pay, these property owners might decide to skimp on maintenance and repairs, assuring that these buildings will begin their descent to lower quality. The process by which we get poor-quality housing in rural areas is entirely different from the process whereby urban housing deteriorates. And it is the location decisions of households and business firms that make all the difference between the two instances.

Key Issues in Urban Policy

Metropolitan areas are where many of the hottest domestic issues of the day are being played out—issues around disparities in income and wealth, inequalities by race and ethnicity, inequities in educational resources, and the integration of new immigrants into the mainstream, to name but a few. Cities are simultaneously places of boundless opportunity for some and deadly poverty traps for others. Some cities are doing well economically, but one in three central cities of metropolitan areas have poverty rates of 20 percent or more, even when poverty rates for the nation as a whole have been at or below 15 percent since the mid-1960s. Why are some cities wealthier than others? Why have cities provided upward mobility for some, but not others? What factors contribute to the distribution of income and wealth in a metropolitan area? Why do central cities often include the metropolitan area's wealthiest families and at the same time its poorest? These are all questions of urban policy.

Understanding urban dynamics is also necessary for insightful public policy in the crucial area of education and the labor market. Among the important services provided by local governments is schooling from kindergarten through twelfth grade. Individuals need access to *effective* education, and also need to have *opportunities* to transform the education they receive into income. Providing for good schools and making them available in the inner city as well as the suburbs raises many questions. How does education relate to the economic dynamics of a metropolitan area? What determines differences in access to high-quality education? Why can some people find jobs, while others with equal training levels cannot? What particular factors distinguish urban labor markets? Why do some metro areas have higher unemployment rates than others?

Besides good schools and good jobs, a thriving metro area needs to find a way to provide all its households with decent housing at affordable prices. Yet, in numerous communities, the price of housing exceeds what many families can afford. What determines the cost of housing? Why does a house in one location cost a great deal more than an exact duplicate of that house located elsewhere in the same metro area? Why are housing prices in San Francisco and Boston so much higher than in Detroit, Albuquerque, and Boise? How, if at all, should city governments respond to problems of housing affordability? How can cities respond to problems of homelessness?

For many economic and social reasons that are discussed later in this book, housing is different from most other goods. It is more costly, more durable, and less transportable. It requires land, and consequently places those who seek housing in competition with other potential land users. Since the early 1900s, housing has been subject to zoning regulations implemented by local governments. While some zoning laws are designed to protect residential areas from noxious industrial activities, zoning has also been used to exclude households on the basis of race or income—or both.

Transportation is another vital area of public policy. The economic and social well-being of cities depends upon the ability of workers, consumers, and residents to move from one point to another within the metropolitan region. In addition to moving people, it is also necessary to have an efficient way to move goods. The repair of potholes, the design of new thoroughfares, the enforcement of parking regulations, and the creation and management of public transportation are all among the many important tasks undertaken by governments in metropolitan areas. Why do some cities have worse traffic jams than others? How have commuting patterns changed over time? Why do some metropolitan areas have a great deal of public transportation, while others have relatively little? What determines the availability of public transportation in different parts of a metropolitan area? Who should bear the cost for highways?

Other questions of public policy and quality of life surround many aspects of metropolitan growth. What conceptual tools do we need to understand the effect of metropolitan growth on environmental quality? How do activities in one part of the metropolitan area affect the well-being of other parts? How does urban sprawl affect the costs and quality of water supply and sewer lines? How does it alter our decisions about transportation planning and other components of metropolitan infrastructure?

In the chapters to come, we use the tools of economics, political science, and sociology to address the questions and issues we have just posed, as well as many others. We examine how and why particular industries grew up in specific metro-politan areas, and how that changed over time. Cities developed initially as a result of proximity to some natural resource or an advantageous feature, such as a deep harbor. With changes in transportation and communication costs and new tech-nology, those advantages declined in importance, and other factors made cities desirable or undesirable places in which to locate. Cities that came of age during different transportation eras have different configurations. Nineteenth-century cities were highly centralized, but newer cities tend to be decentralized. Some metro-politan areas have been able to reinvent themselves, as the emerging industries of one era have become the sunset industries of another. Others have had a more difficult time adapting to change. The separate political jurisdictions within a metropolitan area have an incentive to cooperate for the good of the area as a whole, but they are also in competition with each other. The prospects for the well-being of households, businesses, and communities within the metropolitan area depend on the successful resolution of these conflicting forces.

The Changing Role of the U.S. City in a "Flat" World

Just as changes in transportation and communication technologies reshaped U.S. cities in the eighteenth, nineteenth, and twentieth centuries, they continue to play a role in determining which metropolitan areas will thrive and which will fall on hard times, as well as determining changing patterns of land use within metropolitan areas. While previous eras of technological change intensified the competition between U.S. metropolitan areas, current technological developments have intensified the competition between metropolitan areas worldwide. With falling transportation costs and declining communication costs, it is feasible for an increasing amount of work to be done far afield of the initial supplier or the final customer. The most efficient location for production of any particular product or service—in economic jargon, the place that has a **comparative advantage** relative to all others—can now be selected from a vastly wider array of metro areas, both domestic and foreign.

To use Thomas Friedman's (2005) metaphor for the leveling of the playing field between potential competitors, the world is indeed becoming "flat," and in such a flat world, the key to metropolitan prosperity depends even more on developing a workforce with specialized skills, talents, and expertise that cannot easily be replicated elsewhere. This is what Michael Porter (1998) refers to as establishing a **competitive advantage**. If older metropolitan areas are able to reinvent themselves, the sturdily built factories, lofts, and warehouses that provided industrial jobs to previous generations will be recycled to provide postindustrial jobs as well as attractive living spaces for its current generation of residents.

When a wide variety of goods and services can be produced almost anywhere, does place still matter? Surely, but it matters for different reasons. As we will discuss more extensively later in the book, successful places do not necessarily offer proximity to raw materials nor do they offer especially favorable transportation costs in an era in which transportation costs are so low that they don't matter very much. Instead, successful places offer the social interactions that help people create and transmit knowledge, and they provide the amenities—recreational, cultural, and environmental—that enhance the quality of life and therefore attract workforces with needed skills.

The Tools of the Trade

To address the wide range of issues raised here, we need to rely on a battery of concepts and research tools that are the province of the economics profession, but which are important to political scientists and sociologists alike—even if they do not use the economist's jargon. We use these because they provide insight into the mysteries of how metropolitan areas operate. A few of these concepts—like *opportunity cost, the criteria of equity and efficiency, externalities,* and *unintended consequences*—appear as themes throughout the book and, because of their importance, are briefly introduced here. Additional concepts are explained as needed in later chapters.

Opportunity Cost

Who was the better economist, poet Robert Frost or baseball catcher Yogi Berra? We believe the poet Frost. Here's why. Berra, known now as much for his hilariously fractured use of English as for his legendary skills as a catcher with the New

York Yankees, once said, "When you come to a fork in the road, take it." It would be impossible, of course, to follow that advice, since you cannot travel down two roads simultaneously. You have to choose. Frost, on the other hand, understood this. In his poem "The Road Not Taken," he comes to a fork in the road and must make a choice, knowing full well that his choice has consequences—that it "made all the difference." In choosing the one, he necessarily forgoes the other.

This is the crux of opportunity cost, one of the most fundamental concepts in economics. We can't have everything, so we must make choices. And every time we make a choice, we give up the chance to follow an alternative path. The cost of choosing A is the forgone opportunity of being able to have B, if your income only permits the purchase of one. To economists, this sacrifice of the next best alternative is the "true" cost of making a choice, and it applies to time as well as money. Your out-of-pocket cost for a movie ticket might have been $8, for example, but an economist would want to know not only what else you could have done with that money but also what else you could have done with that time. The value of the next best alternative is the most important way to measure the cost of making a choice.

THE ROAD NOT TAKEN

Two roads diverged in a yellow wood,
And sorry I could not travel both
And be one traveler, long I stood
And looked down one as far as I could
To where it bent in the undergrowth;
Then took the other, as just as fair,
And having perhaps the better claim,
Because it was grassy and wanted wear;
Though as for that the passing there
Had worn them really about the same,
And both that morning equally lay
In leaves no step had trodden black.
Oh, I kept the first for another day!
Yet knowing how way leads on to way,
I doubted if I should ever come back.
I shall be telling this with a sigh
Somewhere ages and ages hence:
Two roads diverged in a wood, and I—
I took the one less traveled by,
And that has made all the difference.*

Robert Frost

In the urban setting, there are all kinds of opportunity costs. A tax dollar spent on repaving a road is a dollar that cannot be used to pay for improving a subway system. A dollar spent on public health is a dollar that cannot be spent on improving public

Source: This poem, first published in 1916, is widely available on many Web sites, including www.bartleby.com.

schools. The choices made by taxpayers and their municipal governments can sometimes "make all the difference" in whether a city or town grows or declines, whether it becomes a more attractive place to live or one that residents wish to leave.

The Criteria of Efficiency and Equity

Efficiency and equity are criteria used to evaluate economic outcomes, especially the outcomes produced as the result of public policy initiatives through laws, regulations, and judicial decisions. **Efficiency** refers to being as productive as possible with limited resources. Technically speaking, a process is efficient if it results in producing the most output (of given quality) with a given amount of input. Alternatively, efficiency occurs whenever a given output of given quality is produced in a manner that uses the least input. Implicitly, efficiency requires being mindful of the opportunity cost of using scarce resources. Because almost all resources are scarce—from basic building materials and skilled labor to natural resources like clean water—efficiency requires not only using resources in the least wasteful manner but also using those resources for the best purpose.

Equity, on the other hand, refers to fairness with respect to the distribution of resources or income. This concept can be quite elusive, since each of us might have a different idea regarding what constitutes "fairness." Many of us would argue that equity requires that all residents of a city have clean water, a decent and safe place to live, and a fair chance to get a good education and receive adequate health care. To the extent that there is great inequality in access to a clean environment and to housing and a great disparity in education and health resources, one could argue that the goal of equity has not been fulfilled.

Ideally, we would like our local, state, and federal governments to enact only those programs that are both efficient and equitable. Some of the most difficult choices occur when the criteria are in conflict and there are trade-offs that must be made: A program that is warranted on the grounds of efficiency might not be equitable, or vice versa. Efforts to reduce traffic congestion, for example, might justify subsidizing high-speed commuter rail lines to attract a ridership among high-income suburban motorists, even if those rail lines do nothing to address the transit needs of lower-income communities. When the criteria of equity and efficiency conflict, economic analysis cannot determine which of the two should take precedence; that becomes a political question, rather than a purely economic one. How much to sacrifice efficiency for equity (or vice versa) is one of the toughest issues before any mayor or city council, before any governor or state legislature, or before the U.S. president and the Congress.

Externalities

When a market functions smoothly, it automatically takes into account *all* of the costs of producing a good and *all* of the benefits of consuming it. In some instances, though, the market is incapable of doing this and some costs or benefits remain unaccounted. A transaction between a buyer and a seller leaves some third parties better off or worse off, but compensation to or from the third party cannot be easily made.

Examples of such **externalities** (or spillovers) abound. Mrs. Frisoli, for example, has a lovely rose garden that she has planted next door to Mr. Jones. She paid a good deal of money to a nursery to plant these roses and she has worked hard to keep them well fertilized and healthy. From his porch, Mr. Jones gets enormous pleasure from seeing Mrs. Frisoli's roses and smelling their beautiful aroma. Yet he doesn't pay a cent for this benefit. It is a purely positive externality to him. Perhaps he should subsidize Mrs. Frisoli to help her pay for the roses, but he has never done so and no one is forcing him to do it.

Unfortunately, Mrs. Frisoli's roses pose a severely negative externality for Mr. Jones's wife, who is allergic to the pollen and coughs and sneezes every time they bloom. Perhaps Mrs. Frisoli should compensate Mrs. Jones for the discomfort she experiences and for the cost of prescription drugs she takes that allow her to breathe more easily. But no such compensation has ever been offered or required.

In other cases, we have resorted to government to "internalize" externalities. That is, the government has stepped in to subsidize a positive externality, tax a negative externality, or regulate the production of goods that would otherwise generate huge positive or negative externalities to society at large.

Pollution is a good example of a negative externality. If a new paper mill opens up and pollutes a stream that residents had been using for fishing and swimming, the residents have been made worse off, but have no recourse to receive compensation through the normal workings of the market. Government action of some sort is required—minimally, to define property rights, impose a tax on the polluter that is used to clean up the pollution, or more forcefully, to pass strict antipollution laws.

Elementary and secondary education provides positive spillovers for others in the community, who reap the benefits of a more productive workforce and a better-informed citizenry. In the absence of government subsidies, families might not purchase enough years of education for their children, since they would not take the positive spillovers into account. As a society, we believe so strongly in the positive externalities of elementary and secondary education that we collect the necessary tax revenue to offer the service free of charge to the consumer. If that is not inducement enough, we also regulate education by making attendance mandatory for children up to age 16.

As we pointed out earlier in this chapter, although positive and negative externalities can occur anywhere, we are particularly cognizant of them in urban areas because they are more likely to occur when people live at higher densities. Playing your sound system at top volume will generate more negative externalities if you live on a street of apartment buildings than if you live 5 miles from your nearest neighbor; being inoculated against polio and thereby helping to avoid an epidemic will generate more positive externalities in the dense city than the rural town.

Unintended Consequences

Although much of this book addresses the role of public policy in trying to improve the workings of metropolitan areas and the lives of the people who reside there, it is best to approach the topic with a large dose of humility. As we shall see, many of the public policy initiatives launched with great fanfare in previous generations have ultimately failed because their full consequences were not foreseen.

Consider the case of kudzu, a plant native to China and Japan, where its growth is kept in check by natural enemies. It was used as a ground cover in the United States to protect against soil erosion, and planted across the nation by Civilian Conservation Corps workers during the Great Depression of the 1930s. With ideal growing conditions and the absence of any natural enemies in the southeastern United States, it has overrun many areas in that part of the country, engulfing cars, houses, and just about anything else in its path. The plant has been declared a weed for the past thirty years, but efforts to eradicate it have been notably unsuccessful. A seemingly good idea to make abandoned open-pit coal mines more attractive ended up having serious unintended consequences.

Other Important Economic Concepts

Concepts like supply and demand, income and price elasticities, fixed and variable costs, comparative and competitive advantage, path dependency, negative sum/zero sum/positive sum games, economies and diseconomies of scale, and specialization and the division of labor are all incredibly useful in deciphering how cities and suburbs work and how people thrive or suffer within them. We introduce these terms as we need them, not because of their intrinsic value, but because of their power to help explain the mysteries, paradoxes, and secrets of urban life. For those already familiar with such concepts, insight will be gained as to how these ideas can be used in the specialized study of metropolitan areas. For those not already familiar with these terms and ideas, we have tried to explain all in nontechnical language.

This book is also data rich. We use a large number of charts and tables to present information that helps bring the more abstract concepts and ideas of urban economics, political science, and sociology to life. With the statistics presented here, you will be able to compare metropolitan areas across the country and contrast urban outcomes whether related to family incomes, housing values, or say, crime statistics. With the accompanying CD, you will be able to compare and contrast the same types of statistics for virtually every metro area and city in the United States—including your own or one near you.

The theories, concepts, and tools of social scientists are brought together with a rich array of city and suburban data, all calculated to provide a new, exciting, and rich understanding of the urban world around us. Read on, learn, and enjoy.

References

Brooks, David. 2002. "Patio Man and the Sprawl People: America's Newest Suburbs." *The Weekly Standard*, August 12, pp. 19–29.
Dahl, Robert A. 1961. *Who Governs?* New Haven, Conn.: Yale University Press.
Dillard, Annie. 1987. *An American Childhood.* New York: HarperCollins.
Dreiser, Theodore. 1900. *Sister Carrie.* New York: Doubleday.

Fainstein, Norman I., and Susan S. Fainstein. 1983. "Regime Strategies, Communal Resistance, and Economic Forces." In Norman Fainstein and Susan Fainstein, eds., *Restructuring the City: The Political Economy of Urban Development*. New York: Longman Publishing Group, pp. 245–282.

Florida, Richard. 2002. *The Rise of the Creative Class*. New York: Basic Books.

Friedman, Thomas L. 2005. *The World Is Flat: A Brief History of the Twenty-First Century*. New York: Farrar, Straus and Giroux.

Galster, George C., and Sean P. Killen. 1995. "The Geography of Metropolitan Opportunity: A Reconnaissance and Conceptual Framework," *Housing Policy Debate* 6, no. 1: 7–45.

Gans, Herbert. 1967. *The Levittowners: Ways of Life and Politics in a New Suburban Community*. New York: Random House.

Hobbs, Frank, and Nicole Stoops. 2002. *Demographic Trends in the Twentieth Century*. Washington, D.C.: U.S. Bureau of the Census, Census 2000 Special Reports, November.

Hunter, Floyd. 1953. *Community Power Structure*. New York: Anchor Books.

Jacobs, Jane. 1969. *The Economy of Cities*. New York: Random House.

Kunstler, James. 1993. *The Geography of Nowhere: The Rise and Decline of America's Man-Made Landscape*. New York: Simon & Schuster.

Levine, Robert. 1997. *A Geography of Time*. New York: Basic Books.

Logan, John R., and Harvey L. Molotch. 1987. *Urban Fortunes: The Political Economy of Place*. Berkeley: University of California Press.

Mumford, Lewis. 1961. *The City in History: Its Origins, Its Transformations and Its Prospects*. New York: Harcourt, Brace, and World.

Porter, Michael. 1998. *Competitive Advantage: Creating and Sustaining Superior Performance*. New York: Free Press.

Stone, Clarence N. 1989. *Regime Politics*. Lawrence: University Press of Kansas.

———. 1993. "Urban Regimes and the Capacity to Govern." *Journal of Urban Affairs* 15: 1–28.

Whyte, William H. 1989. *City: Rediscovering the Center*. New York: Doubleday.

Chapter 1 Questions and Exercises

1. Land area, population, and density of all metropolitan areas in the United States can be found at the following Bureau of the Census Web address:

   http://www.census-charts.com/Metropolitan/Density.html

   + Which MSAs have a density of more than 2,000 people per square mile?
   + How does your MSA (or the one closest to your home) rank in density?
   + How does your school's MSA (or the one closest to it) rank?

2. Using the *Urban Experience* CD, create a table that displays the population of your city or town and the population of the CBSA in which you live (or the one closest to you) for the period from 1970 through 2000 (or 2005).

   To obtain these data in the *Urban Experience* CD, follow these steps:

   • Go to the "Get Data" screen.
   • In the "Choose Data Items" section, click on the arrow immediately to the right and choose "Counts."
   • Check the box next to "Counts" when it appears under "Choose Data Items" and a drop-down list of data categories will appear.
   • Check the box next to "Population."
   • Another box, labeled "Total Population," will appear. Check this box.
   • Next, go to the "Choose Locations" section of the screen.

- Double-click on "By CBSA Name" and a drop-down list of all CBSAs (metropolitan areas and micropolitan areas) will appear.
- Scroll down until you locate the CBSA in which your city or town is located.
- Double-click on the name of the CBSA and a list will appear. The first item in the list is the sum for all principal cities of the CBSA (the identifying name ends with ("CBSA-Prin Cities"). The second item in the list is the sum for all suburbs in the CBSA (the identifying name ends with "CBSA-suburbs"). The next items in the list are each of the individual principal cities in alphabetical order (there may be one or more than one). After all principal cities have been listed, the list continues with each of the individual suburbs in alphabetical order. Check the box for your city or town.
- Scroll back up to the top of the drop-down list. Note that the box for the CBSA itself is offset to the left above the drop-down list. Check that box.
- Finally, in the "Choose Years" section of the screen, check the boxes for all of the years that are available.
- Click on "Go."
- On the far left side of the screen, click on "Table."

  - In which decade did your city or town grow the fastest or decline the most?
  - In which decade did the CBSA in which you live (or the one closest to you) grow the fastest or decline the most?

3. List and describe three of the major externalities in your home city or town.

4. How do these externalities affect you and your household?

5. How does your city or town attempt to deal with these externalities?

6. In your city or town, which individuals and groups are powerful? What power do they have and how do they exercise it?

7. What types of changes do you think residents of your city/town would want to make regarding municipal agencies or programs?

8. Which organizations, city officials, and individuals in your city/town are important in making changes in education, housing, access to jobs, crime, public transportation, health care, and business growth?

How Metro Areas Rank

How well an individual, a household, or a family fares in any community can be judged by many criteria. Economists suggest that a household's well-being can be gauged by its consumption of goods and services. In turn, that household's consumption depends on its income. The more it earns, the greater its ability to consume, and thus the greater its economic well-being. Political scientists might suggest that individual well-being, as well as that of a community, is dependent on the quality of political institutions, the level of participation in the democratic process, and the extent to which human rights are guaranteed. Sociologists might rank the well-being of individuals and households on the basis of community cohesion and on the extent of social networks. Across the disciplines, well-being certainly depends on incomes and how they are distributed, but money is not everything. The quality of life in any city or suburb depends on how individuals fare and how they tend to treat each other.

Cities and Their Reputations

One way that we might rank the quality of life across cities is through their reputations. When *Travel + Leisure* magazine surveyed more than half a million travelers in 2002 about the cities they liked the most, the respondents named San Juan, Honolulu, and San Francisco the three most romantic cities in the United States. Of the twenty-five major cities in this poll, Washington, D.C., ranked twenty-second when it came to romance. Only Dallas/Fort Worth, Baltimore, and Atlanta were considered less romantic. On the other hand, travelers judged Washington, D.C.'s public transportation system the third best in the nation, with only New York City and Portland, Oregon, having better ones. Portland, Honolulu, and the Twin Cities (Minneapolis/St. Paul) are considered to be the safest, while Las Vegas was judged the easiest to navigate. San Francisco is judged to have the most interesting neighborhoods, with New York, New Orleans, and Boston not far behind. The Twin Cities ranked second on cleanliness, but dead last when it came to weather. San Francisco was judged the most "attractive" city of the lot; Los Angeles, less than 400 miles to its south, was judged the least. If you want great sights, visit Washington, D.C., or Orlando. If you want a great meal, go to New Orleans, Chicago, or

New York. According to travelers, no one is more proud of his or her city than a New Yorker and no one is friendlier than a resident of Nashville.

How one ranks cities by reputation depends very much on who is doing the ranking. The Washington, D.C.–based Partners for Livable Communities periodically produces a "Livability Index." Based on the index, the organization recognizes "America's Most Livable Places" (Partners for Livable Communities 2006). In 2004, it focused on "creative places" and defined them as "attractive places to live, work, play, visit, retire, raise a family, attend a university, grow a business, and enjoy diversity." Pulling together countless statistics that could be used to measure such attributes, Partners named what it considered to be the ten "Most Livable Large Cities":

- Charlotte, North Carolina
- Cincinnati, Ohio
- Denver, Colorado
- Ft. Worth, Texas
- Jacksonville, Florida
- Kansas City, Missouri
- Louisville, Kentucky
- San Diego, California
- San Jose, California
- Tulsa, Oklahoma

Some of these might seem obvious—San Diego comes to mind, with its mild year-round climate—but others might be surprising to those who do not live there.

The Mercer Company, a human resources firm that helps its clients determine whether they should offer a "hardship allowance" to top company executives who are relocated to a new city, has a created a "Quality of Living" index (Mercer Consulting 2007). It is based on how safe and stable a city is and whether it has a "dynamic *je ne sais quoi*" (a quality or attribute that is difficult to describe or express) like that often attributed to Paris, Tokyo, London, or New York. As of 2007, the Mercer index puts Zurich and Geneva, Switzerland, at the very top of the list of desirable places to live, followed by Vancouver, Canada; Vienna, Austria; and Auckland, New Zealand. The first U.S. cities do not show up until number 27 with Honolulu and San Francisco in a tie, followed by Boston (36), Washington, D.C. (42), New York (47), and finally Seattle (49). In evaluating the credibility of this index, it may be useful to know that the author of the Mercer report resides in Geneva, Switzerland!

Closer to home, according to a study conducted by Black Entertainment Television (BET) in 2002, the best U.S. city for African Americans is Columbus, Ohio. The ranking is based on comparing poverty and infant mortality rates, high school graduation rates, home ownership, median income and unemployment, teen pregnancy, and crime in the cities with the highest African American population percentages. Houston came in second in this study, followed by Boston, Charlotte, and Indianapolis. Larger cities like New York and Atlanta tended to be closer to the bottom of the list. Columbus ranked high due in part to its low rate of violent crime and high percentage of home ownership. Houston had the lowest rate of black infant deaths and relatively few children living in single-parent families (BET *Nightly News* 2002).

If you are a major league baseball fanatic, you probably would rank Boston, New York, and Chicago as the greatest places to live. After all, the Red Sox–Yankees rivalry is legendary, the Sox consistently sell out home games, and Red Sox "Nation" has hundreds, if not thousands, of loyal Boston fans at virtually every away game, no matter where it is played. The Chicago Cubs have few rivals when it comes to committed followers. St. Louis and Cincinnati can also lay claim to being great baseball towns.

All of these rankings, of course, are highly subjective. Social scientists continually look for more objective measures to assess cities and suburbs. In this chapter, we compare metropolitan areas across a broad range of measures, most of which are produced by U.S. government agencies. First, however, it is useful if we become a little familiar with how we define the geographic boundaries of cities and suburbs.

Defining Metro Areas

Thus far we have relied on "cognitive" maps that individuals carry around in their heads to define a city. To sports fans, for example, Detroit is the home of the Tigers, the Lions, the Pistons, and the Red Wings. For older folks, Detroit is still remembered as the automobile capital of the world. To the generation of postwar baby boomers, Detroit is "Motown"—the city that spawned a musical tradition including Diana Ross and the Supremes, Stevie Wonder, and Smokey Robinson and the Miracles. Current music fans know it as the home of rapper Eminem. Current or past residents of other cities carry their own cognitive maps about the places they call home.

To be more scientific, however, we need to complement our cognitive maps with an "economic" map of metro areas—using official federal government definitions to define the boundaries of central cities and metropolitan areas.

The Need for Standard Definitions

Until 1950, there was no uniform economic definition for metro boundaries. There were political boundaries to be sure in the form of **municipalities**—areas over which a local government exercises political authority and provides public services. But these seldom corresponded to the economic boundaries of a region. Each federal and state government agency used a map of its own to define the economic borders relevant to that agency. The U.S. Department of the Interior looked at watershed regions. Local transportation agencies used maps that included all the bus and subway transit stops in their networks. But only beginning with the 1950 census did the federal government create the first set of uniform and consistent definitions of metro areas based on the economic concept of commuting patterns. With some modification and new terminology, these census definitions have continued to evolve. Let's look at some of the key terms used for defining urban/suburban areas:

- **Urban cluster**—A geographical region consisting of a central place (or places) and adjacent densely settled territory that together contain at least 2,500 people, generally with an overall population density of at least 1,000 people per square mile.
- **Urbanized area**—An area with a total population of at least 50,000, consisting of one large central city together with adjacent areas with a population density of 1,000 or more people per square mile.

The Bureau of the Census has also defined something called the **urban population** in order to measure what share of the nation's entire population can be considered living in an urban setting as opposed to a rural community. Officially, the urban population includes all people living in official urbanized areas plus people outside of these areas who live in urban clusters (i.e., towns with more than 2,500 inhabitants). The total urban population currently comprises 80 percent of all U.S. residents.

The first official definitions issued in 1950 by the Bureau of the Budget, the predecessor to today's U.S. Office of Management and Budget (OMB), designated large metro areas as "standard metropolitan areas." In 1959, the term was changed to **standard metropolitan statistical areas (SMSAs)**. In 1983, the OMB dropped the word "standard" and just referred to them as **metropolitan statistical areas (MSAs)**, the same term used today. Seven years later, the term **metropolitan area (MA)** was adopted to refer collectively to metropolitan statistical areas, while **consolidated metropolitan statistical areas (CMSAs) was** reserved for areas around the very large cities that contain more than one MSA. Finally, **primary metropolitan statistical areas (PMSAs) was** the name given to the MSAs that were part of a large CMSA.

New Definitions

Confusing as all this may be, the OMB changed definitions again in 2003, and the terms CMSA and PMSA disappeared. Now, urban regions are divided into metropolitan and **micropolitan statistical areas** (U.S. Bureau of the Census 2003). As you might guess, metropolitan statistical areas are larger entities.

- Metropolitan statistical area—A large urban area with at least one urban cluster that has a population of at least 50,000 inhabitants.
- Micropolitan statistical area—A smaller urban area with at least one urban cluster of between 10,000 and 50,000 inhabitants.

Together, metropolitan and micropolitan statistical areas are now referred to as **core-based statistical areas (CBSAs)**. As of the 2000 census, there were 370 metropolitan statistical areas (including 8 in Puerto Rico) and 565 micropolitan statistical areas (including 5 in Puerto Rico) totaling 935 large and small CBSAs.

Determining what counts as a CBSA and what its boundaries are is a fairly complicated process. But the government begins with a general concept that has remained central to the definition of an urban area for decades and still holds for the newfangled CBSA:

- A CBSA is a core area containing a substantial population nucleus, together with adjacent communities having a high degree of economic and social integration with that core.

Under this definition, the government begins with the political unit of the county—everywhere but in New England—to define a metropolitan statistical area. The county (or counties) containing the largest city in a region becomes the "central county" (counties). Then any adjacent counties—in that state or in an adjacent state—that have at least 50 percent of their population in the urbanized area surrounding the largest city are added to the MSA. Additional outlying counties are also added to the MSA if they meet specified commuting and population density requirements. The boundaries of a particular MSA are set when it is far enough away from one of its central counties to make commuting between the periphery and the central counties unlikely. The very largest MSAs may have one or more geographically concentrated metropolitan divisions within them, each covering several counties.

Atlanta (or more correctly, the Atlanta-Sandy Springs-Marietta, Georgia metropolitan statistical area) is a good example of an MSA. It contains more than 3.7 million residents living in twenty-eight different counties with the city of Atlanta at its core. Atlanta is the largest **principal city** in the Atlanta MSA; Sandy Springs and Marietta are considerably smaller, but are still considered to be principal cities since both of these municipalities have more than 10,000 residents. Principal cities used to be known as **central cities** under the old OMB/Census definitions and we continue to use that familiar term in this book. Principal or central cities are political jurisdictions defined by municipal boundaries, not necessarily economic logic.

In the six New England states, where counties are less important units of government and where all land is part of one municipality or another, MSAs are collections of cities and towns rather than counties. The largest urban unit in the New England states is now known as a NECTA—a New England City and Town Area.

Figure 2.1 provides one map showing all the metropolitan and micropolitan statistical areas in 2000 and another limited to the metropolitan statistical areas in 1990. As the first map reveals, almost all of the country with the exception of the plains states and the interior Northwest is blanketed with MSAs. Even restricting the map to the larger metropolitan statistical areas reveals widespread urban areas throughout the East, the Midwest, the Southwest, and large parts of the South.

The Bureau of the Census also has a new definition for the largest urbanized areas in the country. They used to be called consolidated metropolitan statistical areas (CMSAs), a term introduced earlier. Now they are called **combined statistical areas (CSAs)**, which link together MSAs where there is a substantial amount of commuting between individual metropolitan areas. Hence, within the largest CSAs there can be a number of MSAs, each with one or more counties and principal cities. These combined statistical areas can cover hundreds of square miles.

2000 Metropolitan and Micropolitan Areas in the United States

(2000 coverage = 1,764 counties)

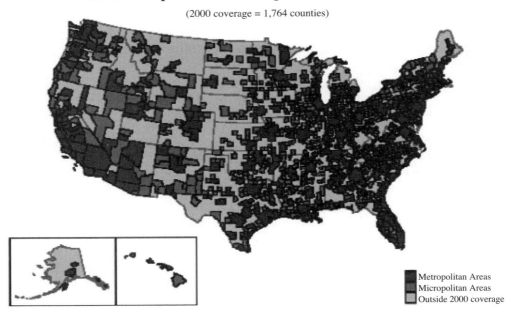

Metropolitan Areas
Micropolitan Areas
Outside 2000 coverage

1990 Metropolitan Areas in the United States

(1990 coverage = 806 counties outside New England;
578 New England MCDs)

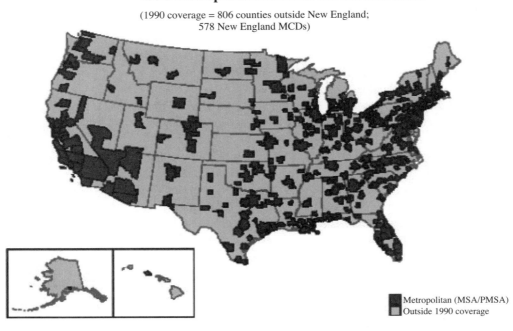

Metropolitan (MSA/PMSA)
Outside 1990 coverage

Figure 2.1 Metropolitan and Micropolitan Areas of the United States, 1990 and 2000. *Note:* Areas in New England are MCD-based under the 1990 standards but county-based under the 2000 standards. *Source*: U.S. Bureau of the Census 2003.

Of the CSAs designated by the U.S. Bureau of the Census, the largest is New York, which covers New York City and other adjacent communities in New York State, parts of northern New Jersey and eastern Pennsylvania, and a few counties in southwestern Connecticut (see **Table 2.1**). According to the 2000 census, this single CSA contained more than 21 million residents in 2000—approximately 7 percent of

Table 2.1 New York-Newark-Bridgeport, NY-NJ-CT-PA Combined Statistical Area (CSA)

Metropolitan Statistical Area	Metropolitan Division	County	Principal City
New York-Edison, NY-NJ-PA	New York-Wayne-White Plains, NY-NJ	Bergen Hudson Passaic Bronx Kings New York Putnam Queens Richmond Rockland Westchester	New York City Wayne White Plains
	Newark-Union, NJ-PA	Essex Hunterdon Morris Sussex Union Pike	Newark Union
	Edison, NJ	Middlesex Monmouth Ocean Somerset	Edison
	Suffolk County-Nassau County, NY	Nassau Suffolk	
Trenton-Ewing, NJ		Mercer	Trenton Ewing
Bridgeport-Stamford-Norwalk, CT		Fairfield	Bridgeport Stamford Norwalk Danbury Stratford
New Haven-Milford, CT		New Haven	New Haven Milford
Poughkeepsie-Newburgh-Middletown, NY		Dutchess Orange	Poughkeepsie Newburgh Middletown Arlington
Kingston, NY		Ulster	Kingston
Torrington, CT (Micropolitan Statistical Area)		Litchfield	Torrington

Source: U.S. Bureau of the Census 2003.

the total U.S. population—living in six metropolitan statistical areas and one micropolitan area spread out over thirty counties. Interstate 95, the Saw Mill River Parkway, the Long Island Expressway, the New York subway system, and commuter rail make it possible for all of these people to commute to work within the same geographically defined labor market and, therefore, this region is designated as a single combined statistical area. New York City itself, with its five boroughs, is the largest principal city in the CSA with more than 8 million inhabitants. There are also twenty other principal cities in this one CSA, including Poughkeepsie, Newburgh, and Middletown in New York State; Newark, Edison, and Union in New Jersey; and Bridgeport, Stamford, Norwalk, Danbury, New Haven, and Stratford in Connecticut. A map of the combined statistical areas in New York State is found in **Figure 2.2**. All combined statistical areas across the country are defined in the same way, their boundaries dependent on the extent to which the local transportation system permits residents to commute to work. The better the transportation system, the larger the CSA. If CSAs existed in the nineteenth century, they would have been considerably smaller than they are today simply because it was infeasible for residents to commute very far to work given horse-drawn carts, a primitive highway system, and only limited street railways.

Ranking Metropolitan Areas

With these definitions, we can rank metropolitan areas along a number of dimensions, including population growth, racial and ethnic composition, family income, income inequality and poverty, environmental quality, crime, and transportation. Some of these have to do with a metro area's demographics; others have to do with its quality of life.

We begin with population. **Table 2.2** lists the twenty-two largest combined statistical areas in the United States in 2006, including San Juan, Puerto Rico. Topping the list are New York-Newark-Bridgeport, Los Angeles-Long Beach-Riverside, Chicago-Naperville-Michigan City, Washington, D.C.-Baltimore-northern Virginia, Boston-Worcester-Manchester, and San Jose-San Francisco-Oakland, each with more than 7 million residents. Note that four of these CSAs cover more than one state, given the ability of commuters to live in one state and work in another. Rounding out the list are Charlotte-Gastonia-Salisbury, Cincinnati-Middletown-Wilmington, and Orlando-Deltona-Daytona Beach.

Another way to rank metro areas is by seeing how much each has grown over the past three decades. **Table 2.3** presents just such a comparison, where we have ranked each of 114 MSAs according to its central (or now principal) city growth and its suburban growth over three decades—the 1970s, 1980s, and 1990s. These 114 were selected from the complete set of MSAs so that they roughly represent the whole country. An MSA was considered to have a *low-growth central city* if it experienced a population loss in at least two of these three decades. It was considered to have a *high-growth central city* if it had at least two decades of 10 percent growth or better.

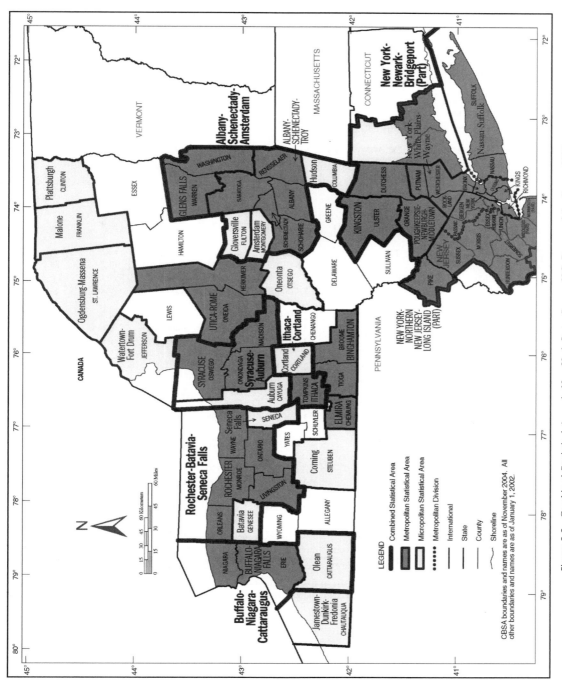

Figure 2.2 Combined Statistical Areas in New York State. *Source:* U.S. Bureau of the Census 2004.

Table 2.2 Twenty-Two Largest Combined Statistical Areas (CSAs) in the United States

Rank	Combined Statistical Area	State(s)	2006 Estimate	2000 Population	1990 Population	Percent Change, 2000–2005	Percent Change, 1990–2000
1	New York-Newark-Bridgeport	NY-NJ-CT-PA	21,976,224	21,361,797	19,710,239	2.5	8.4
2	Los Angeles-Long Beach-Riverside	CA	17,775,984	16,373,645	14,531,529	7.7	12.7
3	Chicago-Naperville-Michigan City	IL-IN-WI	9,725,317	9,312,255	8,385,397	3.8	11.1
4	Washington-Baltimore-Northern Virginia	DC-MD-VA-WV	8,211,213	7,572,647		7.3	
5	Boston-Worcester-Manchester	MA-RI-NH	7,465,634	7,298,695		1.8	
6	San Jose-San Francisco-Oakland	CA	7,228,948	7,092,596	6,290,008	1.1	12.8
7	Philadelphia-Camden-Vineland	PA-NJ-DE-MD	6,382,714	6,207,223		2.7	
8	Dallas-Fort Worth	TX	6,359,758	5,487,956		12.5	
9	Houston-Baytown-Huntsville	TX	5,641,077	4,815,122	3,855,180	11.7	24.9
10	Atlanta-Sandy Springs-Gainesville	GA-AL	5,478,667	4,548,344	3,317,380	15.4	37.1
11	Detroit-Warren-Flint	MI	5,410,014	5,357,538	5,095,695	1.3	5.1
12	Seattle-Tacoma-Olympia	WA	3,876,211	3,604,165	3,008,669	5.6	19.8
13	Minneapolis-St. Paul-St. Cloud	MN-WI	3,502,891	3,271,888	2,809,713	6.0	16.4
14	Denver-Aurora-Boulder	CO	2,927,911	2,629,980		9.1	
15	Cleveland-Akron-Elyria	OH	2,917,801	2,945,831	2,859,644	−0.5	3.0
16	St. Louis-St. Charles-Farmington	MO-IL	2,858,549	2,754,328	2,629,801	3.1	4.7
17	San Juan-Caguas-Fajardo	PR	2,694,909	2,622,876	2,429,378	2.7	8.0
18	Pittsburgh-New Castle	PA	2,462,571	2,525,730	2,564,535	−1.9	−1.5
19	Sacramento-Arden-Arcade-Yuba City	CA-NV	2,211,790	1,930,149	1,587,249	13.3	21.6
20	Charlotte-Gastonia-Salisbury	NC-SC	2,191,604	1,897,034	1,501,663	11.8	26.3
21	Cincinnati-Middletown-Wilmington	OH-KY-IN	2,147,617	2,050,175	1,880,332	3.1	9.0
22	Orlando-Deltona-Daytona Beach	FL	2,053,623	1,697,906	1,256,429	17.6	35.1

Source: U.S. Bureau of the Census, Census of the Population, July 2006.

Medium-growth central cities fell in between. Similarly, if an MSA had a suburban population that grew less than 10 percent in at least two periods, it was considered a *low-growth suburban area*. A *high-growth suburban area* was one with at least 20 percent population growth in at least two periods. The higher thresholds for sub-

Table 2.3 Central City and Suburban Population Growth among Selected Metro Areas, 1970–2000

		Central City Population Growth					
		Low or Negative		**Medium**		**High**	
Suburban Population Growth	**Low**	Akron	OH	Cheyenne	WY	Billings	MT
		Boston	MA	Columbus	GA	Fargo	ND
		Buffalo	NY	Fort Wayne	IN	Lexington-Fayette	KY
		Charleston	WV	Jersey City	NJ	Lincoln	NE
		Cincinnati	OH	Los Angeles	CA	San Jose	CA
		Cleveland	OH	Long Beach	CA		
		Dayton	OH	Lubbock	TX		
		Detroit	MI	New York	NY		
		Hartford	CT	Omaha	NE		
		Louisville	KY	San Francisco	CA		
		Milwaukee	WI				
		New Orleans	LA				
		Newark	NJ				
		Philadelphia	PA				
		Pittsburgh	PA				
		Providence	RI				
		Rochester	NY				
		St. Louis	MO				
		Shreveport	LA				
		Toledo	OH				
		Worcester	MA				
	Medium	Baltimore	MD	Baton Rouge	LA	Bakersfield	CA
		Birmingham	AL	Columbus	OH	Charlotte	NC
		Burlington	VT	Greensboro	NC	Corpus Christi	TX
		Chicago	IL	Honolulu	HI	Fresno	CA
		Columbia	SC	Knoxville	TN	Little Rock	AR
		Grand Rapids	MI	Mobile	AL	Modesto	CA
		Kansas City	MO	Montgomery	AL	Stockton	CA
		Kansas City	KS	Oklahoma City	OK		
		Oakland	CA	Tulsa	OK		
		Portland	ME	Arlington	VA		
		Washington	DC	Wichita	KS		
				Wilmington	DE		
	High	Atlanta	GA	Dallas	TX	Albuquerque	NM
		Denver	CO	Fort Worth	TX	Austin	TX
		Des Moines	IA	Houston City	TX	Boise City	ID
		Jackson	MS	Indianapolis	IN	Colorado Springs	CO
		Memphis	TN	Jacksonville	FL	El Paso	TX
		Minneapolis	MN	Madison	WI	Arlington	TX
		St. Paul	MN	Manchester	NH	Las Vegas	NV
		Norfolk	VA	Miami	FL	Virginia Beach	VA
		Richmond	VA	Nashville-Davidson	TN	Santa Ana	CA
		Salt Lake City	UT	Newport News	VA	Anaheim	CA

(continued)

Table 2.3 (*continued*)

	Sacramento	CA	Orlando	FL
	Seattle	WA	Phoenix	AZ
	Spokane	WA	Mesa	AZ
	Tacoma	WA	Portland	OR
High	Tampa	FL	Raleigh	NC
	St. Petersburg	FL	Riverside	CA
			San Bernardino	CA
			San Antonio	TX
			San Diego	CA
			Sioux Falls	SD
			Tucson	AZ

Legend (1970–1980; 1980–1990; 1990–2000): Low-Growth Central City: Experienced population loss in at least two of these three decades. High-Growth Central City: Experienced at least two decades of 10 percent growth or better. Low-Growth Suburban Area: Experienced less than 10 percent growth in at least two of these three decades. High-Growth Suburban Area: Experienced at least 20 percent growth in at least two of these three decades.
Source: U.S. Department of Housing and Urban Development, HUD User Policy Development and Research Information Service, SOCDS data set, 2007, http://socds.huduser.org.

urban communities reflect the fact that, in general, suburbs grew much faster than central cities during this three-decade period.

Of the MSAs in Table 2.3, twenty-one ranked low on both central city and suburban growth. Virtually all of these, save four, are in the Northeast or the Midwest. (The four exceptions are Charleston, West Virginia; Louisville, Kentucky; and New Orleans and Shreveport, Louisiana.) These tend to be older cities or ones with leading industries that have declined dramatically. Detroit and Pittsburgh are good examples: Detroit grew rapidly before 1950 as a result of the booming auto industry; Pittsburgh did the same, as the result of big steel. Between 1970 and 2000, Detroit's central city shrank from 1.5 million residents to 951,000, an extraordinary drop of 37 percent. Detroit's suburbs grew by nearly 20 percent over the same time period, leaving the total population of the region nearly unchanged. Pittsburgh's central city declined from 520,000 to 335,000. Along with a decline in its suburban population of 139,000, Pittsburgh's total MSA population shrank by more than 12 percent.

At the opposite end of the growth spectrum are MSAs experiencing rapid growth in both their central cities and their suburbs. These are overwhelmingly in southern and western states and include such metro areas as Austin, El Paso, Arlington, and San Antonio in Texas and Phoenix, Mesa, and Tucson in Arizona. Las Vegas holds the record, its population quadrupling to more than 1.5 million between 1970 and 2000. Its central city alone grew from 125,000 to more than 475,000 in just three decades. Air-conditioning made many of these areas comfortable for year-round living, drawing many retirees as well as younger families.

Two other growth patterns are of special interest. The first involves metro areas that lost central city population but saw a rapid expansion in their suburbs. Atlanta, Denver, and Richmond, Virginia, are typical of this small set of cities. Thousands of families left the central city for the suburbs, while nearly all newcomers to these areas chose suburban locations for their new homes.

The second involves five areas with high central city growth but low suburban expansion. Annexation, in many cases, accounts for this unusual pattern. The central city of San Jose, California, for example, has been growing in area through annexation of its suburbs since it was founded in 1850. In 1950, the city boundaries enclosed just 18 square miles. A decade later, the central city had expanded through the incorporation of previously unincorporated land to 40 square miles. In the following decade, the city added still another 100 square miles and another 20 square miles during the 1980s. Today, the central city spreads over nearly 180 square miles, ten times its original size. Between 1970 and 2000, San Jose's central city population literally doubled, from 447,000 to 895,000. Many of these new residents came from other places to take advantage of the city's booming economy. Others stayed put, but became citizens of San Jose when their community was absorbed into the central city. As a result of annexation, the remaining suburbs grew by less than 90,000, an increase of just 24 percent. In other parts of the country, annexation has occurred as well, but rarely in the same dramatic fashion as San Jose with its Silicon Valley.

In brief, the pattern of metro area growth and decline reflects a wealth of economic, demographic, and political factors. The general movement of people from the Northeast and Midwest to the South and West follows the fortunes of local industry. The aging of the population favors these same Sunbelt areas, as retirees flee the cold winters of the North. Rising family income provides the wherewithal to feed the tourism industry with the result that metro regions like Orlando, Florida, and Las Vegas have become boom towns with hundreds of thousands of jobs tied to vacationers and conventioneers. Federal government spending also plays an important role. Metro areas in California and Texas have benefited from huge defense expenditures that underwrite military bases and defense contractors.

Race and Ethnicity

Besides their growth rates, metro areas also differ significantly in terms of racial and ethnic composition. To get some idea of the variance in this demographic feature, we selected a small sample of metro areas from Table 2.3. From those MSAs with both low central city and suburban growth, we chose Detroit. From the low central city/high suburban growth cell, we selected Atlanta. From the medium-growth central city/low suburban growth areas, San Francisco and Los Angeles were singled out. Finally, from the high central city/high suburban growth MSAs, we focused on San Antonio and Las Vegas.

The Detroit MSA is one of the country's most segregated. While its central city, based on the 2000 census, was more than 80 percent black, its suburbs were almost 87 percent non-Hispanic white (see **Figure 2.3**). Its Hispanic population is quite small— less than 3 percent of the total. Of all the blacks who live in the entire Detroit metropolitan area, nearly 80 percent live in the central city. The central city of Las Vegas, on the other hand, looks demographically much like its suburbs (see **Figure 2.4**). About 58 percent of the central city population is non-Hispanic white; in the suburbs, non-Hispanic whites comprise about 65 percent of the population. While the black

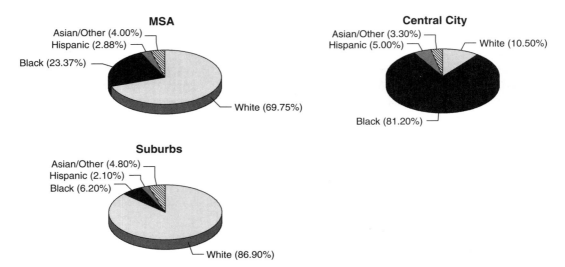

Figure 2.3 Racial/Ethnic Composition, Detroit, 2000. *Sources*: Lewis Mumford Center for Comparative Urban and Regional Research, "Census 2000 Project," www.albany.edu/mumford/; U.S. Department of Housing and Urban Development, HUD User Policy Development and Research Information Service, SOCDS data set, 2007, http://socds.huduser.org.

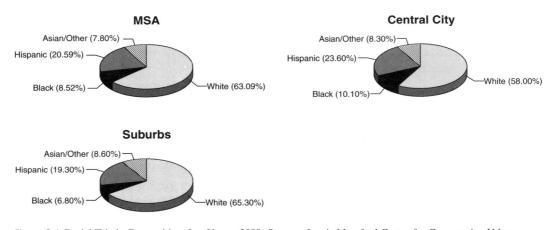

Figure 2.4 Racial/Ethnic Composition, Las Vegas, 2000. *Sources*: Lewis Mumford Center for Comparative Urban and Regional Research, "Census 2000 Project," www.albany.edu/mumford/; U.S. Department of Housing and Urban Development, HUD User Policy Development and Research Information Service, SOCDS data set, 2007, http://socds.huduser.org.

population is relatively small (less than 8 percent MSA-wide), Hispanics make up about one-fourth of the central city population and about one-fifth of the suburbanites.

Atlanta looks neither like Detroit nor Las Vegas. To be sure, its central city is 61 percent black while the suburbs are 63 percent white (see **Figure 2.5**). But unlike Detroit, a large proportion of the black population of Atlanta lives in the suburbs—

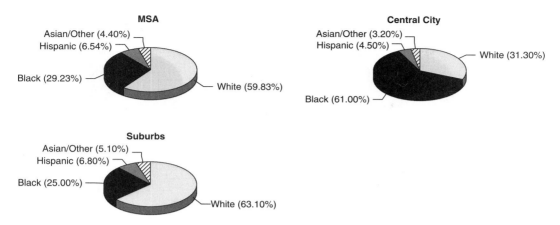

Figure 2.5 Racial/Ethnic Composition, Atlanta, 2000. *Sources*: Lewis Mumford Center for Comparative Urban and Regional Research, "Census 2000 Project," www.albany.edu/mumford/; U.S. Department of Housing and Urban Development, HUD User Policy Development and Research Information Service, SOCDS data set, 2007, http://socds.huduser.org.

close to 80 percent of the total number of blacks in the entire MSA. Part of the overall population shrinkage of this MSA's central city is due to the out-migration of black families to the surrounding suburbs. This has only recently begun to occur in Detroit.

Fast-growing San Antonio reflects the rapidly expanding Hispanic presence in the United States. More than half of the entire MSA's population (51.2%) is of Hispanic origin (see **Figure 2.6**). Less than 40 percent is non-Hispanic white and only 6 percent is non-Hispanic black. While Hispanics are somewhat concentrated in the central city, 32 percent of San Antonio's suburban population is Hispanic. It is not surprising that you hear almost as much Spanish spoken in San Antonio as English.

Asians are also becoming a significant part of America's new urban landscape. More than one in eight people who live in Los Angeles are Asian or of Asian descent; in San Francisco, the proportion is one in four (see **Figures 2.7** and **2.8**). In the city of San Francisco, famous for its Chinatown, a third of the residents are of Asian heritage—with a smattering of Native Americans making up the balance in this combined Asian/other category. There are nearly eight Asian Americans in the Golden Gate city for every ten non-Hispanic whites. In Los Angeles, where one in seven residents is of Asian ancestry, a somewhat higher proportion lives in the suburbs than in its central city. One more glance at the pie charts shows how much a city like Los Angeles (or San Francisco) has become a "prismatic metropolis" comprised of a wide array of people from different racial and ethnic backgrounds (Bobo et al. 2002).

As these charts demonstrate, there is now an enormous variation in the demographic composition of American cities. In these MSAs alone, the proportion of non-Hispanic whites runs from a high of nearly 70 percent to a low of 31 percent. Non-Hispanic blacks comprise less than 9 percent of the population in the Las Vegas MSA, but nearly 30 percent of Atlanta's. Hispanics are less than 3 percent of the

MSA

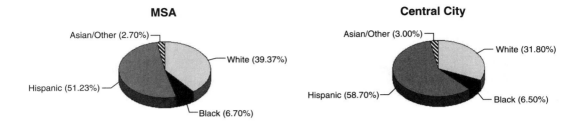

Central City

Asian/Other (2.70%)

White (39.37%)

Hispanic (51.23%)

Black (6.70%)

Asian/Other (3.00%)

White (31.80%)

Hispanic (58.70%)

Black (6.50%)

Suburbs

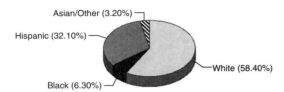

Asian/Other (3.20%)

Hispanic (32.10%)

White (58.40%)

Black (6.30%)

Figure 2.6 Racial/Ethnic Composition, San Antonio, 2000. *Sources*: Lewis Mumford Center for Comparative Urban and Regional Research, "Census 2000 Project," www.albany.edu/mumford/; U.S. Department of Housing and Urban Development, HUD User Policy Development and Research Information Service, SOCDS data set, 2007, http://socds.huduser.org.

MSA

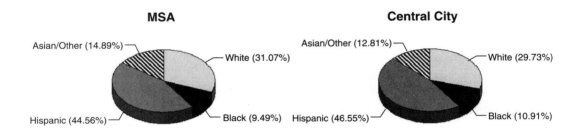

Central City

Asian/Other (14.89%)

White (31.07%)

Hispanic (44.56%)

Black (9.49%)

Asian/Other (12.81%)

White (29.73%)

Hispanic (46.55%)

Black (10.91%)

Suburbs

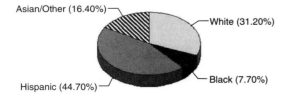

Asian/Other (16.40%)

White (31.20%)

Hispanic (44.70%)

Black (7.70%)

Figure 2.7 Racial/Ethnic Composition, Los Angeles, 2000. *Sources*: Lewis Mumford Center for Comparative Urban and Regional Research, "Census 2000 Project," www.albany.edu/mumford/; U.S. Department of Housing and Urban Development, HUD User Policy Development and Research Information Service, SOCDS data set, 2007, http://socds.huduser.org.

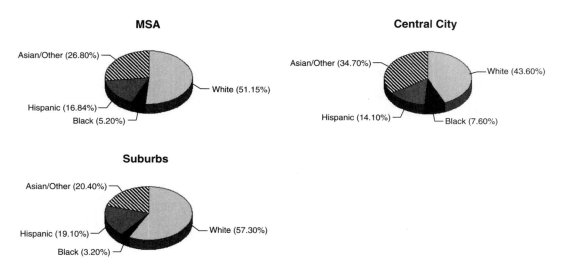

Figure 2.8 Racial/Ethnic Composition, San Francisco, 2000. *Sources*: Lewis Mumford Center for Comparative Urban and Regional Research, "Census 2000 Project," www.albany.edu/mumford/; U.S. Department of Housing and Urban Development, HUD User Policy Development and Research Information Service, SOCDS data set, 2007, http://socds.huduser.org.

Detroit MSA population, but represent a clear majority in San Antonio. It is rare to see an Asian American in San Antonio, where less than 2 percent of the population is ethnically Asian, but it is hard to miss the Asian flavor of San Francisco, where nearly a quarter of the metro region's population is of Japanese, Chinese, Indian, or Southeast Asian origin. The demographic distribution in each metro region contributes to the often unique and exciting character of each individual city, while simultaneously posing some challenges regarding the sharing of political power, equity in the provision of public services, and other types of turf battles.

Median Family Income

There are literally hundreds of ways to rank metro regions economically, but using **median family income** is particularly effective because it summarizes so much about the living standards in a particular area. If you array all the families in a city from the poorest to the richest and then take the middle one, you will have selected the family with the median income. Social scientists normally use this measure rather than mean (or average) income because a relatively few rich families in a city can make the "average" family in town seem better off than it is. The median, in most cases, represents a more "typical" family.

Generally speaking, urban areas with high median incomes tend to rank high on many other measures as well. More often than not, urban areas with high median incomes have lower poverty rates and crime rates and higher education and health levels. The housing stock is less dilapidated; more money is normally spent on parks and recreation. Hence, simply knowing something about median family income in a

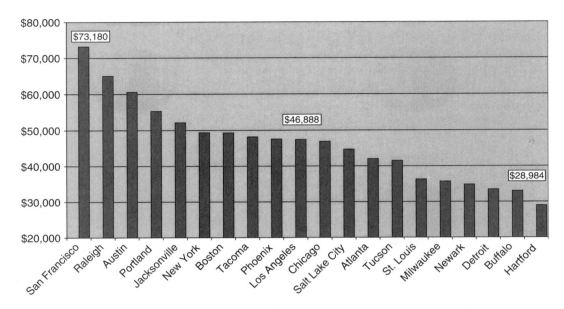

Figure 2.9 Median Family Income, Central Cities, 2005. *Source*: U.S. Department of Housing and Urban Development, HUD User Policy Development and Research Information Service, SOCDS data set, 2007, http://socds.huduser.org.

city or suburb often tells a good deal about the quality of life in those communities along multiple dimensions.

Figure 2.9 provides a snapshot of median family income in 2005 for a more or less randomly selected group of twenty of the nation's central cities—urban areas we follow for illustrative purposes throughout this book (see **Map 2.1**). Within this group, San Francisco boasts the highest median family income: $73,180. Half of the city's families live on more than $73,180; the other half live on less. At the opposite extreme is Hartford, where median family income is only $28,984—a bit less than 40 percent of San Francisco's. Somewhere in the middle of these twenty cities is Chicago, with a median of $46,888. Buffalo, Detroit, Newark, and St. Louis join Hartford at the bottom of the list. Raleigh, Austin, Portland (Oregon), Jacksonville, and New York join the Golden Gate city at the top. This simple list itself suggests a general (but not universal) geographic pattern in income. The lowest incomes are now found predominantly in the older central cities of the Northeast and Midwest. The highest median incomes are now found in the West and generally in places with warmer climes. Cities like Boston, Los Angeles, and Chicago are home to some of the wealthiest families in America. Although these families raise the average income in their cities, they do not make much of a difference in the median given that there are relatively few of them. If the income of the very richest families were to rise, the mean would go up, but the median would remain unchanged.

Not unexpectedly, median incomes are generally higher—often much higher—in the suburbs. **Figure 2.10** provides the information for the suburbs, while **Figure 2.11** shows the ratio of the suburban median to the central city median for each

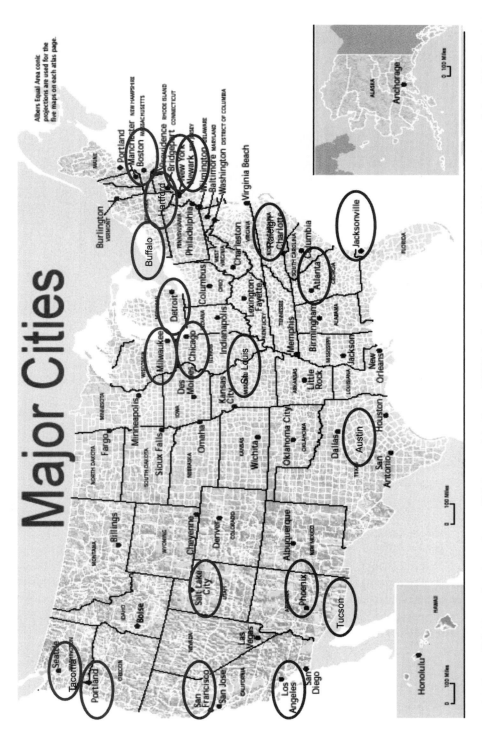

Map 2.1 Twenty U.S. Metropolitan Areas. *Sources:* U.S. Bureau of the Census, TIGER data for county lines and Census 2000 data for city populations; U.S. Geological Survey, GTOPO30 elevation data for terrain shading; Environmental Systems Research Institute, ArcData for North America map. Cartography: Population Division, U.S. Bureau of the Census.

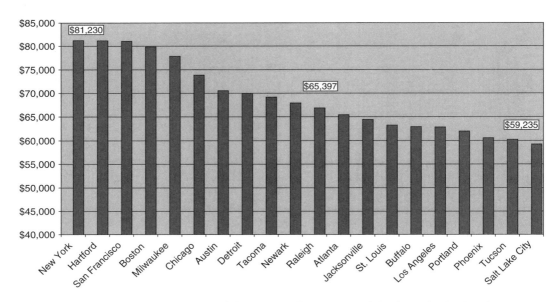

Figure 2.10 Median Family Income, Suburbs, 2005. *Source*: U.S. Department of Housing and Urban Development, HUD User Policy Development and Research Information Service, SOCDS data set, 2007, http://socds.huduser.org.

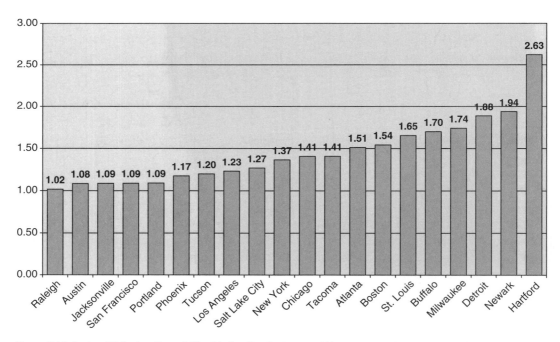

Figure 2.11 Ratio of Suburban/Central City Median Family Income, 2005. *Source*: U.S. Department of Housing and Urban Development, HUD User Policy Development and Research Information Service, SOCDS data set, 2007, http://socds.huduser.org.

metro area. In MSAs like Raleigh, Austin, Jacksonville, and Portland, the suburban medians are no more than 9 percent higher than those in their central cities. Yet in the older industrial cities of the Northeast and Midwest, the central cities have clearly been left behind. Hartford provides the extreme case, with the typical suburban family enjoying more than 2.5 times the income of the typical central city resident. In Newark, Detroit, Milwaukee, Buffalo, and St. Louis, the suburban/city income ratio is at least 1.6 to 1.

Changes in Median Income over Time

Each of the income rankings we have reviewed so far is "static." Each refers to a ranking at a single point in time—in this case, 2005. However, for a study of urban well-being, it is much more interesting to observe how metro areas change over time—in other words, an examination of urban "dynamics." There is a fascinating ebb and flow of economic success in many metro areas that often can be traced back decades and even centuries. Urban areas that once dominated the landscape are replaced in rank order by others when there is a major change in demographics or an upheaval in technology and industry. Once-proud cities fall on hard times; other regions gain new energy and become leading centers of commerce, tourism, and cultural amenities. Why this happens is discussed at length throughout this book. To prepare us for this later discussion, we look briefly here at how median family income has changed over time—a good proxy for the economic fortunes or misfortunes of metro areas across the country.

Figure 2.12 provides a graphic representation of how families have fared economically in central cities between 1970 and 2005. During this period of three and a half decades, San Francisco, Austin, and Raleigh all experienced substantial increases in real median family income. By "real," economists mean adjusted for increases in the cost of living. The typical family in the Bay Area in 2005 enjoyed nearly one-third more real income than the typical family in 1970. For a number of other central cities, including New York, Salt Lake City, Tacoma, and Atlanta, median incomes rose, but not quite as fast as inflation. The result was a slight loss in real income by 2005. Then there were some big losers; none have experienced harder times than Hartford, Detroit, Milwaukee, and Buffalo. The typical family living in the city of Hartford in 2005 was more than 40 percent poorer than the typical family in 1970. In Detroit and Buffalo, real median income fell by 17 percent or more. These cities saw their key industries substantially downsize or move away, followed by many of their wealthier residents. Left behind in these central cities was an increasingly poor population, partly comprised of families who lost good jobs and fell down the income ladder, but mostly made up of both long-term residents and new arrivals who had never enjoyed good economic times.

Those who live in suburbs have, in general, experienced a very different pattern of income growth. As **Figure 2.13** demonstrates, none of the suburbs in the MSAs we have followed experienced a decline in real family income between 1970 and 2005. Hartford is a vivid example of diverging well-being between central city and

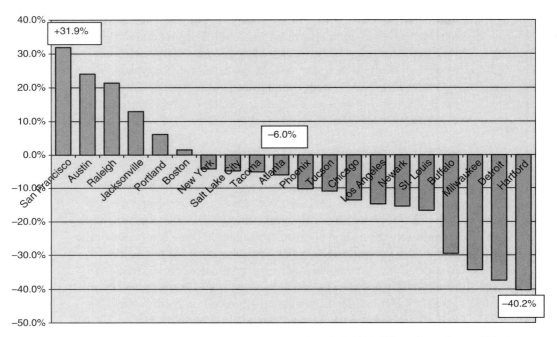

Figure 2.12 Percent Change in Median Family Income, Central Cities, 1970–2005 (2005 Dollars). *Source*: U.S. Department of Housing and Urban Development, HUD User Policy Development and Research Information Service, SOCDS data set, 2007, http://socds.huduser.org.

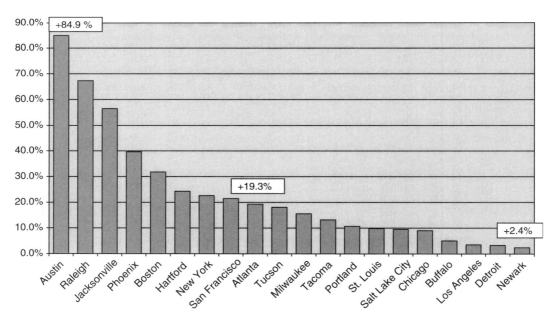

Figure 2.13 Percent Change in Median Family Income, Suburbs, 1970–2005 (2005 Dollars). *Source*: U.S. Department of Housing and Urban Development, HUD User Policy Development and Research Information Service, SOCDS data set, 2007, http://socds.huduser.org.

suburb. While real incomes in the city of Hartford were falling by more than 40 percent, suburban dwellers in the Hartford MSA were enjoying nearly a 25 percent *increase* in their incomes. Indeed, Hartford suburbanites saw their incomes rise proportionately faster than suburbanites living in such western boomtowns as Tucson, Portland, and Tacoma. The suburbanites who have fared the best, however, are found in Austin, Raleigh, and Jacksonville. In just thirty-six years, real median income in Austin has grown by an extraordinary 85 percent. That is quite an accomplishment for any region and reflects Austin's ability to create and grow companies like Dell Computer.

One last set of figures provides us with an even clearer picture of the diverging fortunes of central cities and highlights the real winners in the suburbs. **Figure 2.14** depicts the levels of real family income in central cities in 1970 and in 2005. Compared with the extraordinary variance in incomes across central cities in 2005, the picture back in 1970 was of much greater uniformity that indicated greater equality. Note, for example, that in 1970 there was a $7,000 difference in real median income between San Francisco and Hartford. By 2005, the typical central city family in San Francisco had an income more than $44,000 higher than its Hartford counterpart. In percentage terms, the typical San Francisco household in 1970 was about 14 percent better off income-wise than the typical Hartford family. By 2005, the median San Franciscan family was 152 percent better off. This trend toward inequality across cities mirrors the growth in inequality among individual families, a trend that has been ongoing since the early 1970s.

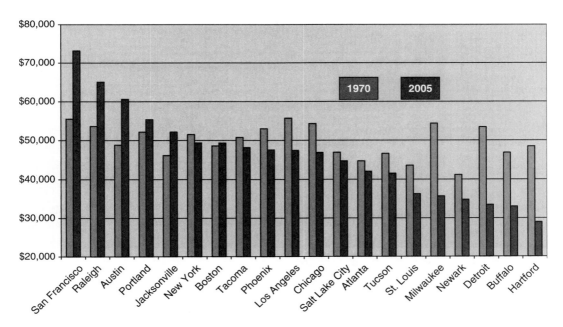

Figure 2.14 Median Family Income, Central Cities, 1970 versus 2005 (2005 Dollars). *Source*: U.S. Department of Housing and Urban Development, HUD User Policy Development and Research Information Service, SOCDS data set, 2007, http://socds.huduser.org.

Statistics on the standard deviation—a measure of variation—in real median income reveal that this growing divergence in central city incomes is not true only for San Francisco and Hartford, but holds more generally. In 1970, the standard deviation equaled just 8.5 percent of the average median income across our twenty central cities. By 2005, this variance measure had nearly tripled to 24.5 percent.

If anything, the picture in the suburbs seems to be the reverse of the central city experience (see **Figure 2.15**). With such rapid income growth in what had been lower-income suburbs like those in Austin, Jacksonville, and Raleigh, the gap between the best- and worst-faring suburbs has closed a bit. This is confirmed by using the same variance statistic we calculated for the central cities. For the suburbs, the standard deviation as a percent of the average median *declined* between 1970 and 2005, from 17 percent to 11 percent. Hence, we seem to have some convergence across suburban communities in economic well-being, while divergence seems to be the name of the game for the central cities. While some suburbs have fared better than others, the real gap in living standards has occurred across central cities, with some enjoying continued economic success or a recent renaissance while others face a deepening erosion of industry and employment opportunity.

Poverty

Closely related to how median family incomes are distributed across the country is the distribution of poverty. In 2005, a family of four was considered officially poor if

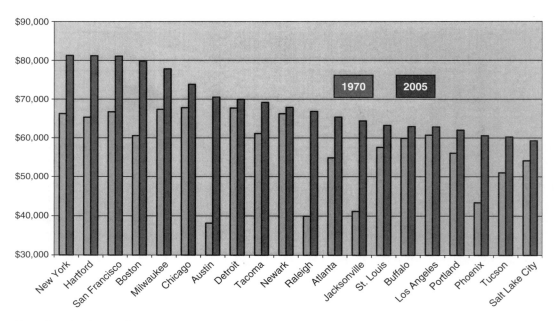

Figure 2.15 Median Family Income, Suburbs, 1970 versus 2005 (2005 Dollars). *Source*: U.S. Department of Housing and Urban Development, HUD User Policy Development and Research Information Service, SOCDS data set, 2007, http://socds.huduser.org.

its money income—income excluding the value of food stamps or rent subsidies—
fell below $19,305 for the year. That amounts to little more than $1,600 per month or
$370 per week to pay for rent, food, clothing, transportation, and everything else. In
the 2000 census, Danbury, Connecticut, had the lowest incidence of poverty among
all MSAs in the country—just 4.4 percent. Of all the metro areas across the nation,
about a third (106) had poverty rates under 10 percent. But in nineteen metropolitan areas, more than one in five residents was officially poor. These very poor metro
areas were concentrated in Louisiana, Georgia, and Texas. The McAllen-Edinburg-
Mission, Texas MSA along the Mexican border was poorest of all, with more than
one-third (36%) of its more than half a million residents in poverty.

Central city poverty rates are, in most cases, much higher than those in suburban
areas. Data from the U.S. Census Bureau's 2003 *American Community Survey*
reveals that nearly 30 percent of the population in Miami, Florida, and nearly 27
percent in Atlanta and Detroit were officially counted as poor. In New York City, the
rate was 20 percent; in Washington, D.C., 17.5 percent.

With the post–World War II migration of middle-income households, particularly white families, from the inner city to the suburbs, there was a concern that
particular neighborhoods in the central cities would become areas of concentrated
poverty—where 40 percent or more of the households are living under the poverty
line (Danziger and Gottschalk 1987; Kasarda 1993). The concern turned out to be
fully justified. By 1990, there were more than 3,400 census tracts containing 10.4
million people living in concentrated poverty, most in inner cities. A **census tract** is
a contiguous neighborhood of 2,500 to 8,000 persons who generally share similar
population characteristics, economic conditions, and living standards. These 3,400
neighborhoods represented more than a doubling from 1970 in the number of high-
poverty census tracts in the country. Across all of the high-concentration poverty
neighborhoods in the United States, 69 percent of the residents were black or non-
white Hispanic, while just 26 percent were white.

In 1990, among the twenty largest metro areas in the United States, Detroit had
the highest concentration of black poverty (Jargowsky 2003). More than half (54%)
of all poor black people in the metro area lived in census tracts where 40 percent or
more of the residents were poor. Other metro regions that had more than a third of
their poor black residents concentrated in high-poverty neighborhoods were Chicago (45%), New York (40%), St. Louis (39%), and Baltimore (35%). Among
Hispanics, Philadelphia had the highest concentration of poverty (62%), followed by
New York (41%) and Detroit (36%).

Only with the reemergence of the central city as a prime location for young
professionals and older "empty nesters" has this trend been partly arrested. Still,
most central cities today have particular neighborhoods that are dilapidated and often
crime-ridden—a function in part of the growing income inequality throughout the
nation.

In general, the proportion of the central city population in poverty is greater today
than in the 1960s and 1970s. In Boston, for example, 15.5 percent of central city
residents in 1970 were listed as poor. By 2005, the census counted 22.3 percent in

poverty. In Chicago, the rate has gone from 14.4 to 21.3 percent; in Detroit, it has exploded from 14.7 to 31.4 percent.

Additional Measures of Metro Area Well-Being

Using data from the 2000 U.S. census, researchers in the St. Louis MSA have tracked the well-being of its area households across a broad array of measures, comparing St. Louis to thirty-five "peer" metro regions across the country (East-West Gateway Coordinating Council 2002). An MSA was considered a peer region if it had a population of 950,000 or more, was within 500 miles of St. Louis, or had an economic function similar to that of the St. Louis region. The MSA peers ranged from huge metro areas like New York and Los Angeles to smaller ones like Cleveland, Nashville, and Austin.

Purchasing Power

Knowing a household's income is only part of the information needed to understand its real standard of living. The inflation-adjusted incomes used here, published by the U.S. Bureau of the Census, rely on national data and not local variation to adjust for price changes over time. Given the enormous difference in living costs across the country, the same income in, say, San Francisco and Minneapolis, confers very different purchasing power in the two cities. In almost all cases, the most important difference in purchasing power is related to the cost of housing. Generally, paying for housing absorbs 25 percent or more of a household's income.

After adjusting median household income for the cost of living in each of St. Louis's peer regions, it turns out that Baltimore—ranked ninth in income—was number one when it came to purchasing power. The ability to buy a median-priced house for less than $160,000 contributed mightily to the region's star billing in the purchasing power index. The other cities rounding out the top five in purchasing power were Minneapolis, Atlanta, Austin, and Dallas. At the very bottom of the purchasing power index were New York, San Francisco, Miami, Los Angeles, and Washington, D.C. The nation's capital might have had the second-highest median family income among St. Louis's peers (after San Francisco), but its eighth-highest housing costs helped put it thirty-first when it came to overall purchasing power. San Francisco was ranked thirty-fourth. With the median household income you would have received in either of these cities, you might have felt pretty well-off—until you had to find a place to live.

The "Family Budget Calculator," available from the Economic Policy Institute in Washington, D.C. (2005), provides an alternative measure of the cost of living in each metro area. The calculator uses a wide array of price data to estimate basic budgets for working families of various sizes. The budgets are constructed by costing out what a family needs to fulfill its basic needs for housing, transportation, food, personal items, health care, and other necessities, based on existing 2004

Table 2.4 A Tale of Two Cities

Boston		Raleigh-Durham-Chapel Hill	
Monthly Housing	$1,266	Monthly Housing	$ 779
Monthly Food	$ 587	Monthly Food	$ 587
Monthly Child Care	$1,298	Monthly Child Care	$ 866
Monthly Transportation	$ 321	Monthly Transportation	$ 358
Monthly Health Care	$ 592	Monthly Health Care	$ 368
Monthly Other Necessity	$ 500	Monthly Other Necessity	$ 369
Monthly Taxes	$ 824	Monthly Taxes	$ 350
Monthly Total	$5,388	Monthly Total	$3,677
Annual Total	$64,656	Annual Total	$44,124

Source: Economic Policy Institute 2005.

prices in each region. The difference in cost of living can be dramatic, as **Table 2.4** indicates. The overall cost of living for a family of four with two children was estimated to be $64,656 in the Boston MSA. In Raleigh-Durham-Chapel Hill, the same market basket of goods and services would cost only $44,124. Boston's housing costs, child care expenses, health care, other necessities such as haircuts and other personal services, and taxes are all higher than in the North Carolina metro region. Cost of living differences of this magnitude can affect where businesses locate and where families choose to live. If your family earns $65,000 in Boston, you are just barely making ends meet. If you can earn the same in Raleigh, you have $20,000 left over for other things—including savings—after paying for the same basic set of goods and services.

Since the cost of living can differ so much across metro areas, a family's real standard of living cannot be judged by income alone. It is important to consider the relationship between family income and living costs. **Figure 2.16** provides just such a comparison by showing the ratio of MSA median family income in 2005 to MSA living costs for a family of four with two children in the twenty metro regions we have been tracking. To make this calculation, we adjusted the 2004 living cost data from the Economic Policy Institute to 2005 using an official government price index so that we could compare median incomes with purchasing power for the same years. Even though New York and Boston rank high on median family income, after controlling for purchasing power, these two metro regions are the least affordable places to live among our twenty MSAs. In contrast, lower-income metro areas like Milwaukee and Detroit turn out to have higher real standards of living, given how far each dollar goes in the marketplace. A family of four living in New York and earning the region's median family income has just 11 percent more than what it needs to pay for its basic family budget. A lower median family income in Milwaukee will nevertheless buy 46 percent more than what the basic family budget costs. Other "best buy" metro areas include Hartford, Tacoma, and Austin. Differences in the cost of living may be so great today that they actually affect where people wish to live and where businesses seek to set up operations or expand (Bluestone 2006).

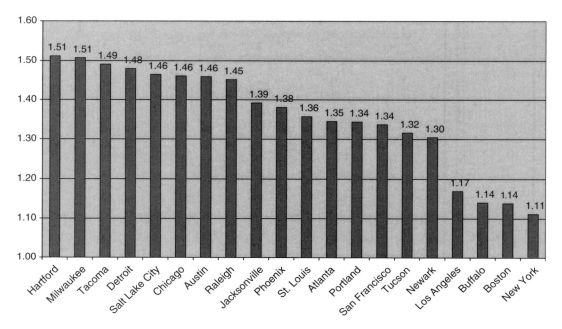

Figure 2.16 Metro Area Median Family Income versus Cost of Living, Four-Person Family, 2005. *Source*: U.S. Department of Housing and Urban Development, HUD User Policy Development and Research Information Service, SOCDS data set, 2007, http://socds.huduser.org; Economic Policy Institute 2005.

Affordable Housing and Home Ownership

Another way to judge the cost of living is to consider what percent of the homes in a region are affordable to a household with median income. **Affordable housing** in this case is defined by the U.S. Department of Housing and Urban Development as a home mortgage payment or monthly rent that takes no more than 30 percent of a household's income. Using this housing affordability measure, Indianapolis is ranked number one among St. Louis peers. There, with plenty of modestly priced housing units, more than 83 percent of homes are affordable by the median-income family. In San Diego, on the other hand, only about one in five households (22%) can find "affordable" housing. San Francisco, as you might imagine, is almost off the charts. Only 7.8 percent of the single-family homes in that region are affordable by the median-income household. This might not be a major problem for a family that moved to San Francisco years ago and bought a home when prices were more affordable. But for families who have recently arrived in the Bay Area, trying to buy a house there today is an expensive and often frustrating experience. Boston is not much better; in just five years between 2000 and 2005, the median home price rose by 60 percent (Heudorfer and Bluestone 2006).

Home ownership rates also vary tremendously across America. On average, about 65 percent of households own their own home—or, more accurately, share ownership with a bank or mortgage company. In Charlotte, North Carolina, the home ownership rate is better than 75 percent, with Detroit, Philadelphia, and Kansas City near the top of the St. Louis peer list. At the other end of the list are Los Angeles, San Francisco, and New York, where the majority of households rent rather than own.

Income Disparity and Inequality

When St. Louis set out to compare itself to other metro regions, it also investigated economic disparity using an index measure of economic inequality between central city and suburb. The measure it selected takes into account such factors as household income, poverty rates, and home ownership. The higher the index number, the greater the disparity between the economic well-being of typical households in the suburbs compared to those in the central city. The largest disparity in economic well-being was found in Milwaukee, Detroit, Cleveland, and Washington, D.C., where suburbanites did so much better than their central city counterparts. The areas with the smallest gaps between the well-being of city and suburban households were Phoenix, Oklahoma City, Charlotte, Miami, and Salt Lake City. Given that a community's tax base depends on household income and/or the value of residential and commercial property, wide differences in income between a metro region's central city and its suburbs means that the quality of public services is likely to vary substantially as well—often exacerbating differences in income per se.

Education

Economists have shown that income is highly correlated with education. Education is one form of "human capital," defined as any investment or attribute that renders a worker more productive. Other forms are training, health status, and one's willingness to migrate to areas with better economic opportunities. In general, the more education you have, the better your chances to get a good job at good pay.

Of the thirty-five metro regions in the St. Louis study, Washington, D.C., Boston, and San Francisco had the highest percentage of adults (age 25+) with master's, professional, or doctorate degrees. Almost one in five (19%) of those living in the Washington, D.C. metro region were this well educated. Charlotte, Memphis, and San Antonio were at the other end of the continuum, having no more than one in twelve (8%) of their adults with advanced degrees. Approximately two out of five adults in San Francisco, Washington, D.C., and Boston had bachelor's degrees, while in Louisville this number was less than one in seven. Minneapolis led the peer cities in terms of adults with at least a high school diploma (90%). In Los Angeles, less than 70 percent had their diplomas, owing in large measure to the great number of recent immigrants from Mexico, Central America, and Southeast Asia. New York spent the most on its public school students—nearly $12,000 per year per student. Salt Lake City spent the least, only a little more than $5,000 per student. How this affects metro area prosperity is discussed in Chapter 8, where we focus on the issue of urban education.

Environmental Quality

The quality of urban life depends a great deal on income and purchasing power, but other things matter as well. The environmental quality in a city or suburb is increasingly a factor that households take into account when considering where to live. In 2000, Los Angeles suffered through forty-five days of "unhealthy air quality"; Houston, Atlanta, and Memphis all had twenty-four such days or more. At the other end of the environmental-quality spectrum are San Francisco, Minneapolis, Chicago, San Antonio, Miami, and Portland—all of which had zero days of unhealthy air quality.

Threats to water quality, as reported by the U.S. Environmental Protection Agency, also differ significantly across metro regions. Among the St. Louis peer regions in 1999, Dallas had the best watershed conditions, followed by Denver, Nashville, and Austin. The worst watershed conditions were found in Philadelphia, Louisville, Milwaukee, and Indianapolis.

Crime

Where families want to live also depends on the level of crime and a sense of personal security. In 2000, the murder capital among the St. Louis peer regions was Memphis, where nearly 15 people per 100,000 were murder victims. Your chances of being murdered in Memphis were tiny compared with death from heart disease (252 per 100,000) or cancer (197 per 100,000), but you were still more likely to die at the hands of someone else than by suicide (10.7 per 100,000). Boston had the lowest murder rate (1.8 murders per 100,000), followed by Portland, Seattle, and San Diego. Washington, D.C., which once was considered the murder capital of the United States, had a murder rate only half that of Memphis and just slightly above the peer group average of 6.7 per 100,000.

The MSAs where you are most likely to be the victim of theft are Miami, Oklahoma City, and San Antonio. In Miami, there were 6,856 property crimes reported per 100,000 population in 2000. Perhaps surprising, New York is third *lowest* on this measure at only 2,666 per 100,000. Only Boston and Pittsburgh have lower rates than New York.

One might also want to consider the central city to suburban crime ratio as an indicator of how the central city environment differs from the usually more affluent suburbs. The highest disparity is found in St. Louis, where residents of the central city are five times as likely to be crime victims as residents in the surrounding suburbs. Detroit, Milwaukee, and Oklahoma City also have high central city to suburban crime ratios. At the bottom of the list is San Diego, where you are only 20 percent more likely to be a crime victim in the region's central city neighborhoods than in its suburbs. Denver, Miami, and Phoenix also have relatively low central city/suburban crime ratios. Such disparities in crime rates and therefore personal security ultimately affect where people would like to live. Studies have shown that cities with high and rising crime rates are among the most likely to lose population, particularly among families who have the income to relocate to what they believe are safer communities within the region (Nivola 1999).

Transportation

Commuting patterns differ across regions. Miami, Los Angeles, Portland, and Detroit have the most miles of roadway relative to the number of square miles in the MSA. There are nearly 16 miles of roadway per square mile in Miami and better than 12 miles in Los Angeles. Nashville has one-third as much as Miami. Los Angeles holds the record among St. Louis peer regions in terms of roadway congestion. Your chance of being caught in a traffic jam on the Los Angeles freeways is twice as high as in Pittsburgh or Kansas City. Commuters also need a lot of patience to drive in San Francisco, Washington, D.C., and Atlanta.

The most extensive mass-transit system in the nation is in New York; in 2000, the subways and buses in the region provided 37 billion passenger miles of public service. The next highest is Chicago, with 11 billion passenger miles, and at the bottom of the list is Oklahoma City, where buses served up only 118 million transit seat miles. In some cities, your best way to get to work is by bus or subway; in others, you are more than likely to be traveling to work by car. In some metro areas like Detroit, you have little choice but to use your car or spend hours on a mass-transit system that lacks street railways or subways.

Using Data Wisely

Data help to answer questions, but they are also quite useful for posing them. If you have been following the statistics closely, numerous questions might already have occurred to you. Why is the population of some metro areas rising rapidly while it seems to be collapsing in others? How can median household incomes be diverging so much between the central cities and suburbs of particular MSAs and among central cities across the country? Why is there a housing cost explosion in some communities, but not in others? What accounts for differences in environmental quality and the incidence of crime? These but scratch the surface of a whole array of interesting questions that are raised whenever you use the lens of urban economics to delve into a wide range of economic, social, and political issues.

Essentially, statistics provide the first step in a much longer process of inquiry. The first task is to try to decipher clear patterns in the data. Are there real differences between central cities in the old industrial Midwest and the newer central cities in the Southwest? If so, what do these differences represent and with what are they correlated? Can we trace the economic and institutional mechanisms that are responsible for the dynamic trends we see in the data? The answers to one set of questions will almost inevitably force us to dig deeper into the data to find root causes. In the chapters that follow, we will use economics, sociology, and political science to try to answer these questions and others. Hang on and enjoy the ride!

References

BET *Nightly News*. 2002. "Columbus, Ohio Tops List of Best Cities for African-American Families." October 3.

Bluestone, Barry. 2006. "Sustaining the Mass Economy: Housing Costs, Population Dynamics, and Employment." Paper prepared for the Boston Federal Reserve Bank/Rappaport Institute Conference on Housing and the Economy, May 22.

Bobo, Larry, Melvin Oliver, James H. Johnson, Jr., and Abel Valenzuela Jr. 2002. *Prismatic Metropolis: Inequality in Los Angeles*. New York: Russell Sage Foundation.

Danziger, Sheldon, and Peter Gottschalk. 1987. "Earnings Inequality, the Spatial Concentration of Poverty, and the Underclass." *American Economic Review* 77: 211–215.

Economic Policy Institute. 2005. "Family Budget Calculator." http://www.epinet.org.

Figgs, Larry W. 2002 "The Strategic Assessment of the St. Louis Region," 4th ed. St. Louis, MO: East-West Gateway Coordinating Council.

Heudorfer, Bonnie, and Barry Bluestone. 2006. "The Greater Boston Housing Report Card 2005–2006." Boston: The Boston Foundation.

Jargowsky, Paul. 2003. "Stunning Progress, Hidden Problems: The Dramatic Decline of Concentrated Poverty in the 1990s." Washington, D.C.: Center for Urban and Metropolitan Policy, the Brookings Institution.

Kasarda, John. 1993. "Inner City Poverty and Economic Access." In J. Sommer and D. A. Hicks, eds., *Rediscovering Urban America: Perspectives on the 1980s*. Washington, D.C.: U.S. Department of Housing and Economic Development.

Lewis Mumford Center for Comparative Urban and Regional Research. n.d. "Census 2000 Project." www.albany.edu/mumford/.

Mercer Consulting. 2007. "Highlights from the 2007 Quality of Living Survey." www.mercerhr.com/referencecontent.jhtml?idContent=1128060.

Nivola, Pietro. 1999. *Laws of the Landscape: How Policies Shape Cities in Europe and America*. Washington, D.C.: The Brookings Institution.

Partners for Livable Communities. 2006. "America's Most Livable Communities." www.mostlivable.org.

Travel + Leisure. 2002. "America's Favorite Cities." www.travelandleisure.com.

U.S. Bureau of the Census. 2002. *Statistical Abstract of the United States*. Washington, D.C.: Government Printing Office.

———. 2003. *Metropolitan and Micropolitan Statistical Areas*. Washington, D.C.: Government Printing Office.

———. 2004. *State-Based Metropolitan and Micropolitan Statistical Area Maps*. Washington, D.C.: Government Printing Office, November.

U.S. Department of Housing and Urban Development. 2007. HUD User Policy Development and Research Information Service. SOCDS (State of the Cities Data Systems) data set. http://socds.huduser.org.

Chapter 2 Questions and Exercises

Metropolitan and Micropolitan Areas

1. Go to

   http://www.census.gov/geo/www/maps/stcbsa_pg/stBased_200411_nov.htm

   and take a look at the map of metropolitan and micropolitan statistical areas in your state. Which three MSAs within your state are closest to where you live?

   You also might want to look at MSAs in adjoining states. Do you live in a metropolitan or a micropolitan statistical area, or in neither?

2. As mentioned in this chapter, there are 370 metropolitan statistical areas and 565 micropolitan statistical areas in the United States.

   + How many metropolitan areas are in your state?
   + How many micropolitan areas are in your state?
   + How many of the metropolitan areas in your state are part of larger CSAs?

Exploring and Comparing Important Characteristics of Metropolitan Areas

3. Using the *Urban Experience* CD, select the CBSA closest to your home, or another CBSA of your choice (other than the twenty presented in the book), and prepare charts for the racial and ethnic composition (percentages) of this CBSA, its principal cities, and its suburbs.

   To obtain these data in the *Urban Experience* CD, go to the "Get Data" screen and follow these steps:

   • In the "Choose Data Items" section, click on the arrow immediately to the right and choose "Percentages."
   • Check the box next to "Percentages" when it appears under "Choose Data Items" and a drop-down list of data categories will appear.
   • Check the box next to "Race/Ethnicity & Nativity." A drop-down list will appear. Check the boxes next to "Black," "Hispanic," "Other," and "White."
   • Next, go to the "Choose Locations" section of the screen. Double-click on "By CBSA Name" and a drop-down list of all CBSAs (metropolitan areas and micropolitan areas) will appear. Scroll down until you locate the CBSA you have selected. Double-click on the name of the CBSA and a list will appear. The first item in the list is the sum for all the principal cities in the CBSA (the identifying name ends with ("CBSA-Prin Cities"). The second item in the list is the sum for all suburbs in the CBSA (the identifying name ends with "CBSA-suburbs"). The next items in the list are each of the individual principal cities in alphabetical order (there may be one or more than one). After all principal cities have been listed, the list continues with each of the individual suburbs in alphabetical order. For this exercise, check the box next to the CBSA name (offset to the left above the drop-down list). Then check the box for the sum of all principal cities ("CBSA-Prin Cities") and the box for the sum of all suburbs ("CBSA-suburbs").
   • In the "Choose Years" section of the screen, check the box for 2005.
   • Click on "Go," and then, on the far left side of the screen, click on "Chart." (*Note:* Census data for some principal cities and some suburbs are not available for 2005. If the chart comes up blank for the areas you chose, go back to the "Get Data" screen and under "Choose Years," uncheck "2005" and check "2000.")

   Of the six metro areas for which we have described the racial and ethnic composition in the book, which comes closest to describing the racial and ethnic composition in the CBSA you have selected?

4. Using the *Urban Experience* CD, prepare tables for the median family income in the MSA, the principal cities, and suburbs that you used in question 3.

✦ Which central (principal) cities in the chapter are most similar to your principal cities?

✦ Which suburbs are most similar to the suburbs in your MSA?

To obtain these data in the *Urban Experience* CD, follow these steps:

- Go to the "Get Data" screen.
- In the "Choose Data Items" section, click on the arrow immediately to the right and choose "Counts."
- Check the box next to "Counts" when it appears under "Choose Data Items" and a drop-down list of data categories will appear.
- Check the box next to "Income and Poverty" and another drop-down list will appear.
- Check the box next to "Median Family Income (2005$)."
- Proceed with the "Choose Locations" segment of the screen as you have done in the exercises for Chapter 1.

5. Using the median family income data in the *Urban Experience* CD for 1980 and 2000 for the CBSA you selected in question 3, calculate the percentage change in income for your CBSA, for its principal cities, and for its suburbs. Choose a suburb close to your home, or another suburb in any metro area of your choice, and compare changes in median family income to the suburban data in this chapter.

   Focusing on the differences you find in the median family income of principal cities versus suburbs, which factors might be responsible for these differences?

6. Using the *Urban Experience* CD, repeat questions 3, 4, and 5 for your own city or town (if it is not the only principal city in your CBSA).

DYNAMICS OF METROPOLITAN DEVELOPMENT

Urban America from the Seventeenth to the Early Twentieth Century

3

The Dynamics of City Growth

More than 5,000 years ago, the earliest known cities on the planet arose in Mesopotamia and the Nile River valley (present-day Iraq and Egypt, respectively). Well over 2,000 years ago, they were followed by cities in the Indus Valley, in Mediterranean Europe, in the Yellow River valley of China, and in Mesoamerica (today, Central and South America). These cities of antiquity served one or more purposes: defense against invaders, places of trade, centers of religion or government, and places where such handicrafts as metalworking and jewelry making could be practiced (Brunn, Williams, and Zeigler 2003). Many early cities were surrounded by walls that provided safety for inhabitants and for the activities carried on within (Bruegmann 2005).

The rise of these early cities was roughly contemporaneous with the development of agriculture in these regions. Many anthropologists speculate that improvements in agricultural practice allowed the creation of a food surplus, which, they argue, is what allowed cities to develop by freeing up labor to move from rural areas to central locations where they could work in activities other than food production. According to conventional wisdom, without the development of more efficient agricultural methods, there would be no cities (Palen 2002). The renowned urban expert Jane Jacobs argues just the opposite, however, in *The Economy of Cities* (1969). She points to early cities as places where goods and ideas were exchanged and where innovations occurred. She posits that the ideas underlying the productivity gains in food production originated in the cities and that without these early cities, more efficient agriculture would never have developed.

We may never have the evidence to resolve this chicken-and-egg question in the case of the earliest cities. But we do know that when the first colonists traveled from the cities of Europe to the New World, they initially established towns along the eastern seaboard as outposts of their civilization; they did not scatter over the countryside. From the first villages and towns, the agricultural hinterlands then developed, allowing the small population of the colonial towns to spawn a much larger rural population. Similarly, as demonstrated in Richard C. Wade's *The Urban Frontier* (1959), the establishment of urban outposts in places like Pittsburgh, St. Louis, Cincinnati, Louisville, and Lexington, Kentucky, allowed the expansion of agriculture into the Midwest.

By the time the American colonies declared their independence from England in 1776, there were only a handful of cities along the Atlantic Coast, with the vast

61

majority of the population living in small villages or in rural outposts. The new
nation's first census, taken in 1790, revealed that only 5 percent of the population
lived in cities with 2,500 people or more. During the next two centuries, the urban
population expanded dramatically while the share living in nonurban areas declined.
As noted in Chapter 1, today more than four out of five U.S. residents live in metropolitan areas (see **Figure 3.1**), with the majority in the very largest metropolises
that have populations of more than a million.

In this chapter, we will delve more deeply into the question of how cities originated, grew, and became the dominant places for economic activity and residential
location in America. In the following chapter, we shall look at how cities themselves
expanded into the suburbs and beyond. And, finally, in Chapter 5, we will take a look
at the future of cities in an increasingly globalized world.

The Geography of Growth: Centripetal and Centrifugal Forces

One important way to conceptualize growth in American cities focuses on geography, using the concepts of centripetal and centrifugal force. **Centripetal force**
drives businesses and households to seek locations at or near the center of a region.
Centrifugal force encourages the dispersal of businesses and households to the
outskirts. To illustrate, let's take a look at early American cities and their development through the nineteenth century.

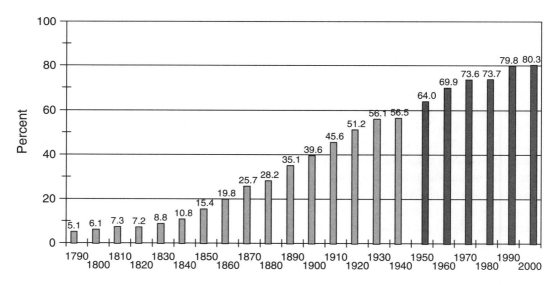

Figure 3.1 U.S. Urban Population, 1790–2000 (Percentage of Total U.S. Population). *Note*: 1950–2000 reflect new
MSA Urban Definition. *Sources*: U.S. Bureau of the Census, "Selected Historical Decennial Census, Population and
Housing Counts"; Marc J. Perry and Paul J. Mackun, "Population Change and Distribution: 1990–2000, "U.S. Bureau of
the Census, April 2001 (Washington, D.C.: U.S. Government Printing Office, 2001).

Cities like Boston, New York, Philadelphia, Charleston, and Norfolk were established by explicit decisions on the part of European colonial powers to create outposts in the New World. In an era when the most efficient form of long-distance transportation was by water, these cities were established in places with good, safe harbors. In the seventeenth and eighteenth centuries, their role was to provide raw materials to the mother country and, hence, their primary purpose was commercial. The major economic focus of urban life was the transfer of agricultural products—cotton for European manufacturing inputs, and wheat, corn, rice, tobacco, and other staples for consumption in Europe, the West Indies, and other places. The activities related to this economic focus were centered around the docks, where the transfer of raw materials to ships took place. Access to the waterfront was crucial and the competition for space there was keen.

Cities of this era were compact and dense with a radius of, at most, only 2 to 3 miles. They were pedestrian cities, where people walked to get from place to place and parcels were transported by horse and wagon. Residences were jumbled together with workplaces. Wealthy families had grand houses along the street and poor families lived in humble shelters in the back alleys. In addition to trade with the mother country, these early American cities served as centers of government and housed craftsmen who produced items needed for commerce (e.g., shipbuilders to produce seagoing vessels and coopers who made barrels and crates) or artisans who produced luxury goods for the wealthy (e.g., silversmiths like Paul Revere, whose house can still be seen in the oldest part of Boston).

The Era of Water and Steam Power

The first factories for milling grains and weaving textiles required new sources of power. Initially, the waterwheel replaced human power and horsepower. To take advantage of the waterwheel, mills had to be located at appropriate places along rivers where canals could be constructed to produce a steady flow of water. This resulted in the shift of many business locations from harbor-based cities to towns situated on rivers. Centrifugal forces began to take hold, dispersing economic activity away from the harbors that had been the centers of the colonial economy.

These new river-based factories soon developed their own centripetal forces. As the factories were built and began hiring, first hundreds and then thousands of individual workers and households moved to rooming houses or cottages built within walking distance of the factories themselves. In similar fashion, craftspersons moved to close-in locations where they could ply their products to new businesses and households.

The introduction of steam-powered manufacturing after 1800 made it possible to relocate business once again, this time away from the riverbank and canal. Freed from the constraints of rivers and streams, and eager to reduce the costs of obtaining labor, procuring raw materials, and distributing their products to markets, owners tended to establish new factories in the middle of cities. The owners of the new factories sought existing cities because there was already a potential labor force in urban centers. There was no need to move families to new locations, and in an age dominated by dense housing and foot traffic, there was less need to worry about getting workers from their existing homes to factories. Centripetal forces dominated, leading to ever-increasing density in central cities.

Manufacturing was not the only type of business vying for central locations. Expanding business in shipping and in retail trade increased the competition for centralized land. Eventually, instead of buying land right in the middle of the city where it was becoming more expensive, many manufacturers found it more profitable to buy land on the outskirts of the commercial district where they now had access to railroad lines via short stretches of track. Often the new manufacturing plants needed to buy residential land and convert it for manufacturing purposes. This forced residential developments to expand even farther outward.

The location dynamics for retail business during the nineteenth century were different. By 1850, urban retail shopping was changed by the emergence of the large department store. These new stores centralized the purchase of many goods by marketing and selling many different types of products under the same roof (Bluestone et al. 1981). The first of these stores appeared in New York in 1846 and the concept spread quickly to other cities. By providing an abundance of many types of goods in one place, department stores reduced shopping time for customers and became retail centers for the entire urban area, despite the geographic expansion that was occurring. In the years to come, city downtowns became synonymous with the presence of large stores that offered a wide array of goods. In order to have sufficient customers and be profitable, these high-volume stores needed to be at the epicenter of surrounding residential neighborhoods.

The Era of Railroads, Electricity, and the Telephone

Railroads and harbors were important to these stores because they provided the means of transportation for the products that were sold. But also important were the streetcar lines that brought customers from all parts of the city to the stores. Transportation lines that converged on downtown were a powerful centripetal force for retail trade through their ability to create the high volume upon which such stores thrived. Retail stores were able to expand vertically (i.e., construct taller buildings), unlike manufacturing plants, where heavy equipment made vertical expansion problematic. Creating taller buildings allowed them to stock more goods, offer wider variety, and maintain their high-customer-volume locations. The development of new building technology, in the form of iron-girdered construction in 1889, followed on the heels of the invention of the elevator in the mid-1800s. This created new possibilities of vertical expansion for retail buildings.

The last half of the nineteenth century was characterized by a growing spatial separation of commercial offices from production plants. The introduction of the telegraph, followed by the telephone, created new communication possibilities for offices that were not directly involved in production. Before these new technologies arrived, communication in person was necessary, either directly or indirectly through messengers. The new forms of communication allowed the transfer of information and instructions from spatially separated sites. Thus, an owner could be in the central city, where there were advantages of information transfer and proximity to a wide array of business services, and still be in communication with production supervisors at a plant in another part of the metro area. As in the case of the large department store, the creation of high-rise buildings with steel girder structures made it possible for these commercial offices to remain centralized, even while the staff devoted to such operations and the space they required increased dramatically.

The allure of downtown areas for entertainment was advanced with the introduction of electric power stations that provided a new source of lighting for evening activities. The first commercial power station, owned by Thomas Edison, began operations in 1882 and was used to provide night lighting for lower Manhattan. By the late 1880s, electric power stations existed in many U.S. cities and, in addition to lighting, were used to power electric motors for streetcars and factories.

By 1900, then, transportation, energy, and communication technologies had shifted the set of costs associated with location in ways that affected manufacturing, retail, and office functions quite differently. The interaction of railroad and related streetcar technology with the spatial needs of mass production had produced both centripetal and centrifugal forces. Retail and office functions had strong centripetal dynamics, while manufacturing increasingly located along the railroad lines that radiated from the city core and encouraged centrifugal activity. By the beginning of the twentieth century, the layout of the modern metro region was beginning to form: a dense downtown devoted to retail and office activity, residential neighborhoods surrounding the **central business district (CBD)**, and more and more factories on the outskirts of town.

Some Economic Concepts Underlying Urban Growth

To understand the dynamics of urban growth, it is helpful to keep in mind five key economic factors: (1) **trade** and **transportation costs,** (2) **agglomeration economies,** (3) **internal economies of scale**, (4) the size of **consumer markets**, and (5) **technological progress**. We will return to these over and over again to deepen our understanding of urban growth and the centripetal and centrifugal patterns that have accompanied the growth of U.S. cities. In this chapter, we use these concepts to gain insight into why economic activity became concentrated in dense central cities in the nineteenth and early twentieth centuries. In the next chapter, we see how these factors were responsible for the great migration of businesses and households to the suburbs in the post–World War II era. The relative importance of each of these five factors varies for individual cities at any given point in time. The influence of each of these factors may also change for any particular city as it evolves over time.

The implications of these five basic economic concepts are explained more fully as they are needed in this chapter. For now, however, a few thumbnail explanations will serve our purpose.

Trade and Transportation Costs

Why do some forms of economic activity concentrate at specific points on the map, and why do some places grow faster than others? On average, there are about 85 people per square mile across America's land mass of 3.5 million square miles. However, we know that the population density is many times higher than that in the largest metro areas and a fraction of it elsewhere. More than 26,000 people per square mile live in New York City. In Wyoming, on the other hand, there are only five residents per square mile (U.S. Bureau of the Census QuickFacts). What causes households and firms to gather at specific places on the U.S. map rather than spreading themselves out smoothly?

A relatively self-sufficient household may, with great effort, provide for all its needs: building its own shelter, growing its own food, weaving its own cloth, birthing its own babies, and burying its own dead. However, such a household living in an isolated area is likely to have a low standard of living, at least in terms of material goods and services. By focusing on the production of one good and exchanging it for goods and services produced by others, this household and its trading partners can enjoy the benefits of **specialization** and **division of labor**. This is the economic and social basis for trade and explains the role of the city as a marketplace—a central location where people come together to exchange goods and services.

Bringing goods to market, however, requires transporting them from one place to another. In a time when travel was difficult, dangerous, and expensive, transportation costs played an important role in determining which goods would be traded and where trading cities would be located. High transportation costs help explain why people live closer to each other than they might if travel were instantaneous and essentially free. Even if goods can be transported quickly and inexpensively between regions of the country and even globally, many services need to be close to the consumer or the transportation costs add up rapidly. Consider the cost of getting a professional haircut, in terms of time alone, if you live on a million-acre sheep station in the middle of Australia, 300 miles from the nearest town.

Agglomeration Economies and Density

As the original trading cities grew, they became large enough to support a variety of commercial specialists. A greater division of labor and increased specialization made it possible for individual firms to operate at lower cost in these locations. For example, a producer of salted cod in colonial New England who wanted to ship his product to Europe would find that he could operate more efficiently if he located near the barrel makers and trading companies he needed, virtually all of whom had set up shop in port cities. The existence of these city-based specialists meant that new firms could operate more efficiently in these places than at other points on the map, and port cities therefore increased in size. Greater density brought greater efficiency, which encouraged urban development, and greater density spawned even greater density.

Cost-saving factors that emanate from *outside* the individual firm—like the barrel makers' contribution to the success of the salted cod producer and vice versa—are known generally as **external economies** of production. In urban settings, they are also called agglomeration economies. Simply put, having your lawyer and your accountant nearby helps lower your operating costs and therefore boosts profits, or at least permits you to compete successfully against other firms that are trying to lower their costs. Technically speaking, agglomeration economies permit a firm to lower its *short-run* average cost curve—the cost per unit of output, as shown in **Figure 3.2**. The short run is defined in economics as a period brief enough that the firm does not have the opportunity to make new investments in its plant or equipment.

Conversely, **external diseconomies** are factors outside the firm that *raise* a firm's short-run average cost curve. Imagine what would happen to a firm's average costs if it relied on ferry service to transport its goods to market and the ferry company went out of business. Urban density can reach a point where congestion is so great that the

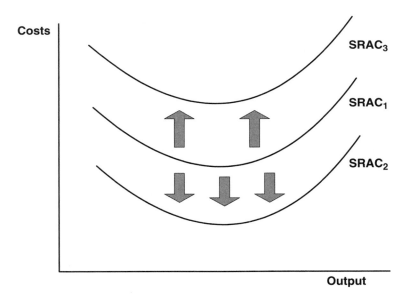

Figure 3.2 Effect of External Economies and External Diseconomies on Short-Run Average Costs. Each short-run-average-cost curve is U-shaped, indicating that (1) at low levels of output average costs are high (due to fixed costs), but fall as the amount of output increases, and (2) as a firm continues to increase output, it becomes harder to find some inputs (perhaps labor). Therefore, average costs rise as less productive or more expensive inputs have to be used. External economies lower the firm's short-run average cost curve from SRAC$_1$ to SRAC$_2$. External diseconomies raise the firm's short-run average cost curve from SRAC$_1$ to SRAC$_3$.

cost of commuting and transporting goods becomes a real disadvantage for firms in the middle of the city. In this case, the benefits from agglomeration might be more than offset by the external diseconomies. Agglomeration economies tend to favor production in urban centers; external diseconomies tend to favor more dispersed production away from central cities.

Internal Economies of Scale

Just as external economies reduce a firm's short-run average cost curve, the existence of **scale economies** internal to a firm allow it to produce more efficiently—at lower unit cost—as it moves to larger facilities. Economists refer to this as occurring in the *long run*, when the firm can increase its plants and equipment. Suppose an industry has 100 plants, each producing 1,000 units of a good at a cost of $50 per unit. If **economies of scale** exist, then it would be cheaper (perhaps $40 per unit) to produce these 1 million units in two large plants, and cheapest of all (perhaps $30 per unit) if one single large factory produces all 1 million units. Now suppose that 1 million units per factory is the most efficient scale of production possible. If the market demand for this good is 3 million units per year, there would then be room in this industry for only three very large firms. Smaller firms would disappear from the industry because their scale of operations would not permit them the luxury of the lower costs of the big firms. The big firms could easily price the smaller ones out of the market by charging a price higher than their own lowest cost per unit, but below that of the smaller firm. The combination of agglomeration economies plus internal economies of scale are part of the reason why a few cities in Massachusetts, including Lawrence, Lowell, and New Bedford, grew to be the home of the U.S. textile industry in the nineteenth century. Instead of being scattered over the entire national landscape, these industries with their very large producers were concentrated in a small number of cities, keeping their average unit costs near the bottom of their long-run average cost curve.

The long-run average cost curve is often called an "envelope curve" because it illustrates the most efficient points on a variety of short-run average cost curves, each reflecting different plant sizes and amounts of equipment. In many industries, the long-run average cost curve resembles **Figure 3.3**.

We can apply the same idea of economies of scale to the size and structure of metropolitan areas. Small places do not have a large enough population to support a wide variety of goods and services in the same way that a small factory can produce only a limited number of products. According to **central place theory**, there is a hierarchy of places within any given region. The central city of a metropolitan area with its dense population is where large office buildings, department stores, libraries, museums, and professional sports stadiums will usually be located because all of these depend on large numbers of employees or consumers who can reach the central business district from many surrounding neighborhoods. In the suburbs, one will find lower population density and, beginning in the early twentieth century,

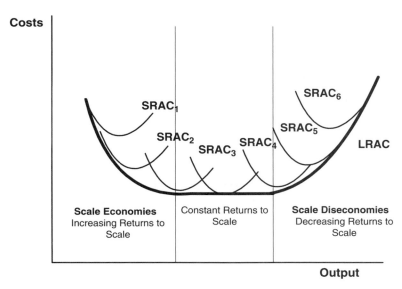

Figure 3.3 A Typical Long-Run Average Cost Curve. The long-run average cost (LRAC) curve indicates (1) the range of output over which moving to larger plant capacity would reduce average costs (economies of scale), (2) the range over which there are no advantages or disadvantages associated with size (constant returns to scale), and (3) the range over which larger plants are less efficient (diseconomies of scale). Each short-run average cost (SRAC) curve provides information about the cost of production at a given level of plant capacity. The LRAC is derived from the most efficient points on the short-run average cost curves, thereby showing the most efficient production with different amounts of plant and equipment. The LRAC curve declines initially, flattens out for a time, and often begins to rise only at very high levels of output. In the declining region of the curve, there are increasing returns to scale (scale economies), which means that moving to a larger plant size allows output to be produced at lower average cost. The flat section of the curve indicates the range of output where plants of different sizes can produce equally efficiently—in other words, a range of constant returns to scale where there are no advantages or disadvantages associated with size. The rising section indicates the range of output in which there are decreasing returns to scale (diseconomies of scale), where problems of coordination and control might make very large plants *less* efficient.

manufacturing plants. Farther out, one will find smaller towns and villages with a general store serving farm communities and mining companies.

For a time, there were efforts to define the optimum size for a city. Presumably, such an optimal-sized city would have a population large enough to benefit from scale economies in the provision of goods and services without encountering the diseconomies of scale—the congestion, pollution, and higher per capita costs for many big city public services such as education and public safety. The efforts came to naught, however, because by the time a city reached the critical mass necessary to achieve economies of scale for some services, it was already encountering diseconomies of scale for others. The ultimate conclusion was that if a nation offered a wide variety of places, each of a different scale, every household could decide for itself the trade-offs of living in larger areas versus smaller ones—each "optimal" for the residents who choose it.

Size of Consumer Markets

While transportation costs, agglomeration economies, and scale economies can help us understand the location of economic activity—why, for example, the early steel industry was so heavily concentrated in Pittsburgh on the Monongahela and Allegheny rivers—it is the strength of demand for an area's products that will determine how fast it grows. When the market for a particular product increases, the region where it is produced usually benefits, creating employment opportunities and boosting local incomes. When the demand for steel increased sharply in the second half of the nineteenth century to fulfill the needs of the burgeoning railroad industry and then for use in skyscrapers, Pittsburgh became a boomtown.

In 1910, only New York City, Chicago, and Philadelphia had populations of more than a million. But with the growth of mass-consumer markets, beginning during the first half of the twentieth century and continuing to the present, many more metropolitan areas joined the million-plus club (see **Figures 3.4** and **3.5** [Brunn, Williams, and Zeigler 2003]). If automobiles had remained toys for the wealthy, as they were at the turn of the last century, Detroit would not have grown to be among the largest U.S. metropolitan areas. If the motion picture industry had not provided entertainment for the masses by the 1930s, Hollywood might still be just a sleepy little town with lots of sun.

Technological Progress

Finally, we cannot ignore the role that technology plays in urban development. Before the introduction of the waterwheel as a means to power such equipment as textile looms, bringing together a huge number of machines in one location was neither needed nor beneficial. Weavers and craftsmen could produce goods in their own homes and only the cost of transportation suggested the need for some amount of density. But once power looms were invented, with flowing water as their source of energy, it made economic sense to bring hundreds if not thousands of looms together in one "manufactory," where the power could be distributed to each machine from a central source through an elaborate network of belts and shafts. Needed now were hundreds and sometimes thousands of workers who lived close enough to the mills to walk to work. The result was the rapid expansion of cities that had rivers running through them. As we have noted earlier, the introduction of the steam engine as the dominant source of power in late-nineteenth-century factories also encouraged density, but manufacturing cities no longer needed to be located near flowing water. Bringing workers together in a factory where they could be disciplined by managers if they slowed their pace was no doubt a benefit to the profitability of firms that came along with the establishment of large factories (Edwards 1980).

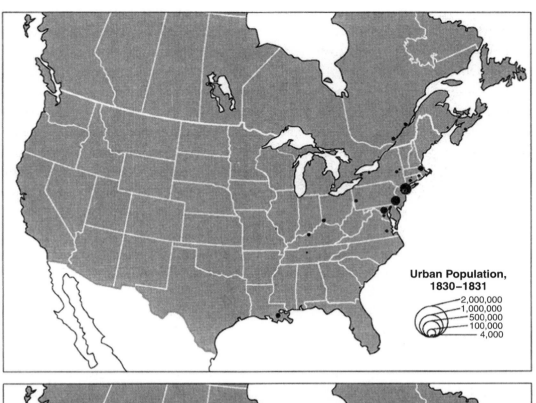

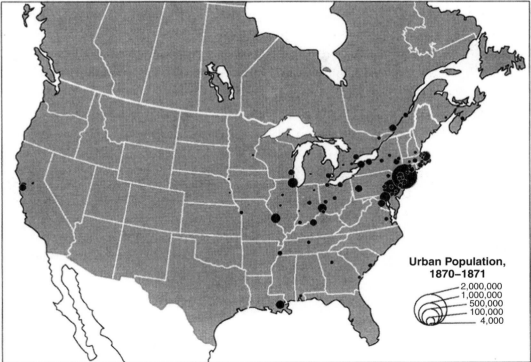

Figure 3.4 Urban Places in the United States and Canada, 1830–1831 and 1870–1871. *Source:* Brunn, Williams, and Zeigler 2003, p. 51.

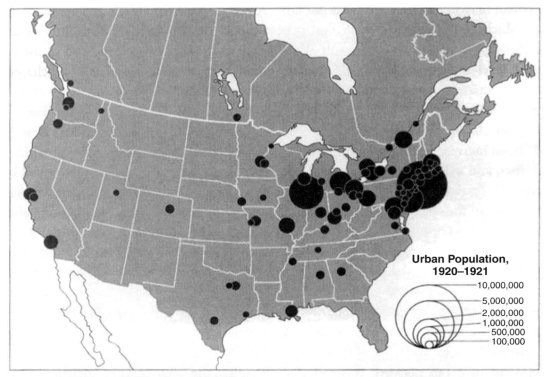

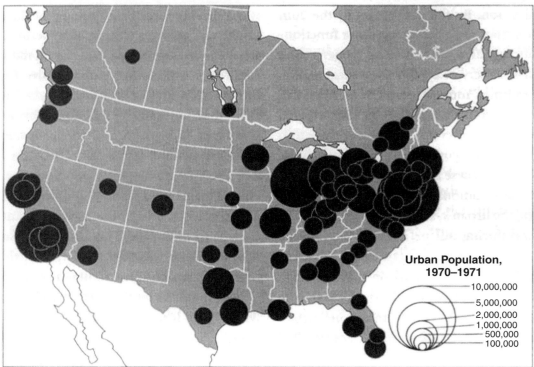

Figure 3.5 Urban Places in the United States and Canada, 1920–1921 and 1970–1971. *Source:* Brunn, Williams, and Zeigler 2003, p. 53.

Thus, the fate of individual cities and towns, central cities, and suburbs rests on the ever-changing sands of transportation costs, agglomeration economies and diseconomies, changes in scale economies, the fickleness of consumer response to old and new products, and the evolution of always newer and more productive technologies.

In order to draw out some of the more complex implications for the creation and growth of urban areas, a closer look at these location factors is now needed.

Transportation Costs *between* Nineteenth-Century Cities

When steam power replaced waterpower in factories, and railroads replaced ships as the principal way to transport goods, firms were no longer tethered to port cities and mill towns, yet they still faced constraints. In the industrial age, an economy based on manufacturing takes raw materials and turns them into finished goods to be sold to consumers. The transportation of raw materials to the factory or finished goods to their final consumer markets often involves significant cost. The desire to minimize these costs places its own set of limitations on a firm's location decision.

Consider the following development in the economic history of the United States. For the first half of the 1900s, the tire manufacturing center in the United States was Akron, Ohio. Why in Akron, instead of somewhere else? Almost all the crude rubber used in the manufacture of tires came from East Asia (the regions that have now become Malaysia, Indonesia, and Sri Lanka). Why not San Francisco, or one of the other West Coast port cities geographically closest to East Asia? Until the 1870s, practically all of the U.S. experience with working with rubber was in New England. Why not in Massachusetts or Connecticut, which together accounted for half of the rubber-using firms in 1870? Why not in Philadelphia, where Charles Goodyear discovered the important process of vulcanization of rubber in 1839, or in New York State, where B. F. Goodrich opened his first business? Part of the answer lies in the roles of transportation procurement and distribution costs. Keep Akron's tire industry in mind as we examine the impact of transportation costs on industry location.

Think of the wide variety of economic activities as arrayed along a spectrum, from those whose location choices are most constrained to those whose choices are least constrained. At one extreme are the extractive industries, along with others that are based on some natural feature. If you want to operate a coal mine, you have to go where there are deposits of coal; if you want to operate a lumber mill, it is useful to locate near forests. At the other extreme, there is the occasional poet or philosopher, who can work equally well on the highest mountain, in the deepest valley, or along the most densely populated city street. For all firms except those that mimic our poet/philosopher, location matters, either as an absolute constraint or, more commonly, as a major cost consideration.

In general, the profits of an enterprise represent the difference between revenue generated from sales and costs incurred in production. Consider a simple categorization of types of costs:

1. **Site costs**—the costs of the land and physical plant
2. **Operating costs**—the costs of materials, labor, energy, and other inputs used in the operation of the firm
3. **Transportation costs**—the costs of moving raw materials to the firm and finished products to the market

Firms for which transportation costs are the primary determinant of location are called **transportation-cost-oriented firms**. The costs of moving inputs from their source or sources to the place where they will be used to manufacture goods are called **procurement costs**. The costs of moving the final product to the places where it will be sold are called **distribution costs**. For a manufacturing firm, total transportation costs equal the sum of procurement costs plus distribution costs. The goal of the firm is to minimize total transportation cost by locating where the sum of procurement costs and distribution costs is lower than anywhere else.

Firms that produce goods or services entailing high transportation costs must locate at a site that minimizes the sum of these costs. Otherwise, they will be at a competitive disadvantage relative to firms that make cost-effective location decisions. In some cases, the location that minimizes transportation costs will be close to the source of its raw materials and in other cases, closer to its consumers.

Transportation costs are determined for the most part by the nature of the material being transported and the type of transportation being used. Suppose for the moment that the same means of transportation—say, railroads—is used for both procurement and distribution. Then the cost of transportation depends upon the weight of the material (heavier items require more fuel for the engine), the bulk of the material (more railroad cars are needed if the shipment takes up more space), and the fragility of the items (more packing material is needed for items that carry a risk of breaking). The location that minimizes transportation costs would then depend upon whether the raw materials are heavier, more bulky, or more fragile than the finished product. If the production process that transforms the raw material into a finished product involves the loss of weight, a loss of bulk, or a reduction in fragility, the finished product will be cheaper to transport. For example, sawmills are located close to forests because it is less expensive to transport finished two-by-fours or plywood sheets than to transport the logs and cut them up at their final destination near the local Home Depot or Lowe's. Similarly, fruit and vegetable canneries (and wineries) are located near the fields where the crops are grown, because fresh fruit and vegetables are more likely to be damaged or spoil en route than canned vegetables or bottles of wine. These are examples of **materials-oriented firms** in which transportation costs are minimized by locating the processing plant close to the source of raw materials.

If, on the other hand, the finished product is heavier, bulkier, or more fragile than the raw materials, transportation costs will be minimized by shipping the raw materials close to the final consumer markets before processing them. These are called **market-oriented** firms. For example, large national firms in the baking, brewing, or bottling industries use regional processing plants because it is cheaper to ship the ingredients than the final product. The bread is bulkier and more perishable than the flour and yeast. If a decent water supply is available locally, it is cheaper to ship the hops or syrup than the beer or soda. These market-oriented industries minimize their transportation costs by operating regional processing facilities. Those who prefer Heineken to Budweiser or Perrier to Poland Spring are paying a premium partly because they are paying to transport from Europe a product that is mostly water.

Similarly, the geographic expansion of consumer markets has implications for firm location because of the distribution costs to potential buyers who are relatively far away. Instead of incurring high distribution costs, it is sometimes more cost efficient for firms to establish branch plants—production centers in various cities—to lower distribution costs. Branch plants and their retail counterpart—chain stores—proliferated beyond the cities where firms were founded, both responding and con-tributing to the growth of more cities. Still, such businesses capitalized on economies of scale in certain enterprise functions—accounting, design, and so forth—by lo-cating their corporate headquarters in a single city.

To account for differences in the type of transportation used, economists refer to the **monetary weight** of transportation, which is calculated by multiplying the monetary cost of transporting a given number of units of a particular product and the weight of the product. The term "monetary weight" may sound strange at first, but it actually follows a long tradition of mathematical nomenclature. For example, in physics, one of the measurement units of energy is the foot-pound, obtained by multiplying the distance that a force moves an object by the pounds of force applied. In economics, we also use the concept of person-hours, obtained by multiplying the number of workers by the hours that they worked.

The difference in the monetary weights of procurement and distribution provides an important insight for the answer to our question about Akron. Rubber was transported to manufacturing sites in bales, packed as tightly as possible. In contrast, the tires that were produced were more bulky, since the shape of tires includes space where there is just air. Because the number of conveyances (boxcars, trucks) needed to transport bulky items is greater than the number needed to transport more closely packed items, the costs of transportation for the more bulky tires was greater than the cost of the inputs. The monetary weight of the tires was greater than the monetary weight of the inputs. Therefore, it made more sense for tire manufacturers to locate near the final market for the tires: the automobile industry based in Michigan.

In some instances, as goods are transformed from raw material to finished product, their journey is partly by water and partly by land. Processing plants often arise at these junctures. Historically, that is how the Chicago stockyards originated. Live animals were transported across the land (first on hoof, later via cattle car), slaughtered and partially disassembled in Chicago, and then sent to other cities and towns—originally by ship across the Great Lakes and down rivers, and after the mid-1800s by specially made railroad cars refrigerated with ice—where the final cutting and trimming was done in local butcher shops (Cronon 1991; Miller 1996). Simi-larly, wheat is refined into flour in Minneapolis (nicknamed the Flour City) and shipped all over the country by rail and truck.

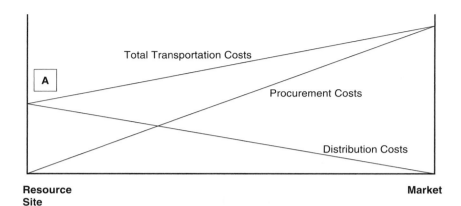

Figure 3.6 Transportation Costs for a Resource-Oriented Firm (Also Called a Materials-Oriented Firm). In the basic Weber graph, there is one resource site and one market. The horizontal axis represents the distance between these two sites, and thus, each point along the axis is a potential location for the firm. Procurement costs are represented by the upward sloping line extending from the origin at the resource site. Since it costs more to move materials longer distances, procurement costs increase as we consider potential sites moving from left to right, from the resource site toward the market. Similarly, distribution costs are represented by a line extending from the origin at the market leftward toward the resource site, indicating that the costs of moving final goods from the firm to the market increases as we move away from the market toward the resource site. The rate of increase in costs (and thus the actual costs at any point along the horizontal axis where the firm might choose to locate) depends upon (1) the characteristics of the raw materials (for procurement costs) or final goods (for distribution costs), and (2) the type of transportation used. A firm considering where to locate will take into account total transportation costs (procurement plus distribution) at each potential firm location, and, if transportation costs are the deciding factor for location, will locate at a point that minimizes total transportation costs. As shown in this graph, if the increase in procurement costs from the resource site origin is greater than the increase in distribution costs from the market origin, the lowest total transportation cost (indicated by "A") will be at the resource site and, consequently, the firm will try to locate near its source of raw materials.

Weber's Graphical Model of Transportation Costs

The standard figures used in urban economic theory to visualize the impact of transportation costs on the location decisions of firms were first developed by Wilhelm Launhardt (1885) and later refined by Alfred Weber (1909). These figures, in the form of graphs, are central to the so-called Weber model.

Weber's approach assumes that transportation costs play the fundamental role in location decisions, and that other cost factors (including the cost of labor) play a secondary role. This made sense a century ago, when transportation costs were huge and most of the modern transportation network we now take for granted did not exist at all. Weber imagined a featureless geography, with a single source of raw materials, a geographically separate single market, and a road connecting the two. Suppose that, except for the raw materials, all other inputs—such as labor and capital—were available at identical costs at every point between the resource site and the market. Where would a profit-seeking firm locate—at the site where all of the raw materials needed to make its products come from, at the market where its products will be sold, or somewhere in between? This is obviously important for understanding where cities will be located and how big they will become.

In the Weber graphs, the distance from the source of raw materials to the market is represented by the distance along the horizontal axis (see **Figures 3.6** and **3.7**). Procurement and distribution costs can be considered for each location along the road. The procurement cost of transportation will be zero if the firm is located right at the resource site. Procurement costs will be highest if the firm locates at the market site where the final product is sold, the farthest distance from the resource site. Conversely, the distribution cost of transportation will be zero if the firm is located at the market where the final product is sold, and will be highest if the firm locates at the resource site. If transportation costs are incurred at a set cost per mile (i.e., proportional to distance), procurement and distribution costs for a given weight of cargo can be represented by straight lines, where the slope of the line is the cost/distance of this weight—the monetary weight.

In Figure 3.6, the procurement costs per mile are greater than the distribution costs per mile. Accordingly, as is indicated by the "Total Transportation Costs" line—representing the vertical sum of transportation procurement and transportation distribution costs—the firm will minimize its transportation costs if it locates at the resource site, point A. This is a "weight-losing" firm, where the monetary weight of distribution is less than the monetary weight of procurement. Point A will be a

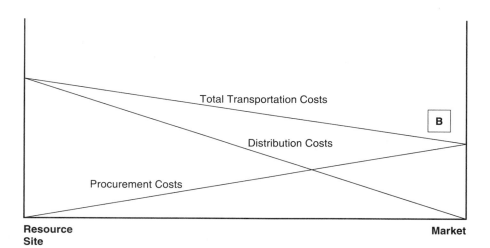

Total Transportation Costs

B

Distribution Costs

Procurement Costs

**Resource
Site**   **Market**

Figure 3.7 Transportation Costs for a Market-Oriented Firm. As in Figure 3.6, the basic Weber graph indicates that a firm considering where to locate will take into account total transportation costs (procurement plus distribution) at each potential firm location, and, if transportation costs are the deciding factor for location, will locate at a point that minimizes total transportation costs. This graph shows that if the increase in procurement costs from the resource site origin is less than the increase in distribution costs from the market origin, the lowest total transportation cost (indicated by "B") will be at the market and, consequently, the firm will try to locate near its customers.

location where economic activity takes place and at least a small urban area will begin to develop.

In Figure 3.7, the procurement costs per mile are less than the distribution costs per mile. This firm will minimize its transportation costs if it locates at the market site, point B. It is a "weight-gaining" firm, where the monetary weight of distribution is greater than the monetary weight of procurement. Point B, like point A, is where urban activity will take place and density will presumably increase.

Figures 3.6 and 3.7 are predicated on the idea that there is one site where raw materials are obtained. But what if two or more raw materials are needed, and each comes from a different location? The problem once again focuses on the minimization of total transportation costs under the assumption that other influences are the same, regardless of location. In the case of two resource sites and one market site, the optimal location for the firm—which minimizes transportation costs, and if all other things are equal, maximizes profits—may be at one of the sources of raw materials; at the market, as in the simple models depicted in the previous two figures; or somewhere within the area bordered by the triangle connecting each of these points, as shown in **Figure 3.8**. Exactly where transportation costs are minimized depends upon the same considerations—the weight of the shipment, the cost of transporting that weight given the objects being transported, and the distance transported. Cost minimization occurs at point C, which minimizes the sum of the costs of transporting the two resources to a central manufacturing plant and transporting the final product to the consumer market. It is precisely at such points that new production centers can arise with all of the related services that firms and workers need. Housing will be constructed along with retail outlets and, thus, a small urban area comes into existence. If the site proves a cost-minimizing location for an important industry like autos or steel, the emerging urban area can become a burgeoning, wealthy city and ultimately a large metro area.

Expanding on this theme, where there are multiple resource sites or multiple market sites, the transportation cost–minimizing location may be at any of the market sites, at any of the resource sites, somewhere along the path connecting any two of the sites, or within the area of the polygon created by all of the site locations. The graphical representation will become more and more complex, but the profit-maximizing business owner in a transportation-cost-intensive industry will always try to find the optimal location for his operations by minimizing the sum total of his transportation costs.

Other Important Ideas from Weber and from Isard

Let's turn back to the example of Akron and the tire industry. We have explained why the tire industry emerged in the Midwest, near Detroit, rather than in other regions of the country. But why wasn't it located *in* Detroit? Part of the answer is historical. In 1870, when B. F. Goodrich opened his rubber company in Akron, his chief vision for the company was to produce fire hoses and industrial belts for the expanding cities and manufacturing companies in the Midwest, not bicycle or au-

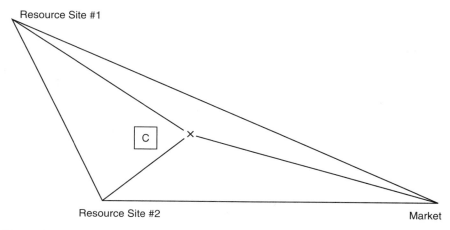

Figure 3.8   The Weber Location Polygon for Two Resource Sites and a Single Market. Often a firm does not find all of its key raw materials in the same place. In this Weber graph, there are three important locations, two resource sites, and one market. The potential locations for the firm are re-presented by the area within the triangle formed from the lines connecting Resource Site 1, Resource Site 2, and the Market. The logic remains the same as in Figures 3.6 and 3.7, but representation of costs requires visualizing the graph along three dimensions. As in the previous graphs, a firm consid-ering where to locate will take into account total transportation costs (procurement plus distribution) at each potential firm location and if transportation costs are the deciding factor for location, will locate at a point that minimizes total transportation costs. Unlike the graphs in Figures 3.6 and 3.7, the site that minimizes transportation costs may be at either one of the resource sites, at the market site, or in between, depending upon the relative procurement and distribution costs. As drawn, the graph above indicates that the lowest total transportation costs will occur at point "C," somewhere between where it procures both of its resources and where its market is located.

tomobile tires (bicycles did not become popular until the 1880s, and the auto in-dustry had not yet been born). But Goodrich and his firm were interested in taking advantage of new opportunities involving rubber, so in 1888, in response to the sudden popularity of bicycles, the Goodrich firm began to produce bicycle tires. From there it was an easy step in 1896 to becoming a pioneer in the manufacture of automobile tires (Blackford and Kerr 1996). The location of the BFGoodrich Company as a tire manufacturer was therefore tied to the original location chosen for producing hoses and belts.

This illustrates a more general point. As Jane Jacobs emphasizes in her classic book *The Economy of Cities* (1969), many new products emerge from businesses that were originally making something else, either because of insights gained during manufacture or—as was the case for BFGoodrich—because the manufacturing process of new products is similar to that of the old.

This can be partially explained by what social scientists call **path dependency**—when, in any period of time, events and characteristics are dependent upon the historical path of the past. But another part of the answer takes us to one more important insight of Weber's. While transportation-cost-oriented firms pay primary attention to the patterns of transportation costs, they cannot be totally oblivious to other costs. Weber realized that if costs other than transportation dropped sharply in areas around the market or resource site, these differences could change the cost-minimizing location for the firm. Discussing a site that might be different from the transportation-cost-minimizing site, Weber stated that even for a transportation-cost-oriented firm, it makes sense to locate at a site of lower labor costs, "if the savings in the cost of labor which this new place makes possible are larger than the additional costs of transportation which it involves" (Weber 1929, p. 103).

Weber's insight was expanded upon by Walter Isard, who considered the theoretical case of a site where labor costs are $5 per unit of output cheaper than at the transportation-cost-minimizing site, while the increase in transportation costs is only $4 per unit of output. Isard, noting the offsetting costs of labor and transportation, demonstrates that the site of cheaper labor "offers a net gain of $1 per ton relative to the optimal transport point. . . . In similar manner we can examine the pull of cheap power locations, cheap tax locations and other locations having specific advantages" (Isard 1975, p. 98). The general idea of this concept can be illustrated through the graph in **Figure 3.9**.

In fact, this insight is also part of the story of Akron. When Goodrich was exploring where to build his firm in 1870, some businesspeople in Akron wanted Goodrich to open the firm there and offered to provide some of his financing, but only if he built his rubber company in Akron. Similarly, in 1898, when Frank Sieberling started Goodyear Tire and Rubber, specifically to target the growing bicycle and auto tire business, his location of the firm in his hometown of Akron was related to the fact that he had been able to obtain an abandoned factory at a very cheap price, and that he was able to draw upon local investors for the financing to start the firm (Allen 1949; O'Reilly 1983).

One other factor is relevant to the question of how Akron became the location for the tire industry. In the late 1890s, it was not at all clear that Detroit would be the center of the automobile industry. There was still uncertainty about where automobile manufacturing would become successful, and several other cities in the Midwest, including Cleveland, were producing cars with hopes of participating in the new automobile industry (Blackford and Kerr 1996). So, uncertainty at a key point in the development of the auto industry also sheds a bit more light on the decisions that ultimately led to Akron's ultimate role.

Whether automobile manufacturing occurred in Detroit, Indianapolis, or Cleveland, the amount saved in site costs originally compensated for whatever difference in costs were incurred by moving the finished tires to those other cities. Over time, differences in costs that emerged from agglomeration economies (as firms related to tire production moved to Akron), and perhaps the importance of carving out its own local labor market rather than competing in the same local labor market as the Detroit auto manufacturers, gave reason for the tire industry to stay in Akron.

Weber's insight into the effect of the relationships between transportation costs, site costs, and operating costs for the location of firms provides a key to under-

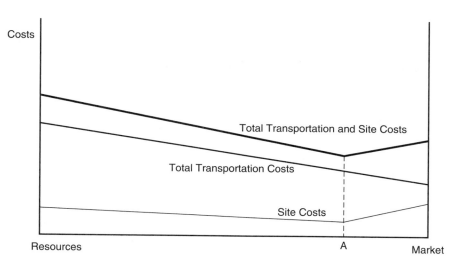

Figure 3.9   The Weber Graph with Offsetting Costs. As Weber recognized, even for a firm for which transportation costs are the most important factor for location, the spatial variation in other costs may be important. His insights were expanded upon by Walter Isard, one of the founders of modern urban economics. The basic idea is shown in this graph, where the difference in site costs offsets the optimal location from what it would be if the firm considered transportation costs alone. In this graph, as in Figures 3.6 and 3.7, the horizontal axis represents the distance between the resource site and the market, and each point along the axis is a potential location for the firm. The graph depicts a line representing total transportation costs, similar to the total transportation line in Figure 3.7. The site that minimizes transportation costs is the market and, thus, this is a market-oriented firm. However, site costs drop considerably from the market to Point A. Given this sharp drop, the optimal site when both transportation and site costs are taken into account is Point A, some distance from the market.

standing the location of firms in the nineteenth and early twentieth centuries and, therefore, the development of cities. As we shall see in Chapter 5, despite the technological marvels of the late twentieth and early twenty-first centuries, Weber's insights are still relevant.

Transportation Costs *within* Nineteenth-Century Cities

At the dawn of the twentieth century, cities still relied on the railroad to transport people and goods from one place to another and manufacturing was still the core of economic activity. Although streetcars allowed some wealthier households to move away from the hustle and bustle of the downtown, most business activity was still confined to the core, as were the majority of households. Nationwide, the proportion of the metropolitan population living in central cities reached its peak of 66 percent in 1920. This high degree of centralization meant that as urban populations grew, the bulk of that growth was still contained inside city limits. Although city populations would continue to grow, suburbs would grow more quickly after 1920.

In the late nineteenth century, a factory owner in New York who wanted to ship merchandise to Chicago would find that the most cumbersome part of the task was getting the merchandise from the factory to the railroad depot in New York and, at the other end, getting it from the railroad depot in Chicago to its final destination. As Moses and Williamson (1967) point out in their explanation for why late-nineteenth-century cities were so highly centralized, it was cheaper per mile to move goods *between* cities via the railroad than *within* cities via horse and wagon. For this reason, factories and warehouses were near the centrally located railroad depots. Although the streetcar lines radiating away from the downtowns did allow some wealthier households to escape from the center, they reinforced the center as the only place where a large labor force could be collected, since that was the only spot where the lines converged. As Moses and Williamson have observed, in the late-nineteenth-century city, it was cheaper to move people (via streetcars) than to move goods. This helps account for the growing density of the central business district in American cities in the nineteenth and early twentieth centuries.

Other technological developments of the era also contributed to the highly centralized development of the city. Because access to the downtown was so valuable, the price of centrally located land was very high. One way of counteracting the high price of land is to use it more intensively. As noted earlier, the advent of the elevator, in the middle of the nineteenth century, and steel beam construction in the 1880s, meant that buildings could rise more than four or five stories, the limit for nonsteel-reinforced masonry construction. Though these early skyscrapers are dwarfed by the heights of today's megastructures, they nevertheless multiplied the square footage of floor space that could be obtained from a plot of land by fourfold or more, making downtown commercial and production locations more affordable than they otherwise would have been. Thus, technology in the form of new energy sources, new transportation modes, and new construction materials contributed mightily to the location, size, and density of the nineteenth- and early-twentieth-century city.

Agglomeration Economies and the Growth of Cities

A business firm looking for the very lowest wage labor or the very cheapest land will not find either of them in large cities. Yet cities continued to grow throughout the nineteenth century, along with the growth of the railroads and factories. In the period from 1830 to 1860, the total U.S. population more than doubled, from 13 million to 31 million, but New York's population quadrupled (see **Table 3.1**). By 1910, fifty U.S. cities had populations of 100,000 or more (see **Table 3.2**).

If cities did not offer the cheapest land or the cheapest labor, they did offer the cost advantages that come from locating near other firms. As we learned earlier in this chapter, these advantages are called external economies or agglomeration economies because they exist outside any one individual firm, but allow all of the firms to operate more efficiently (i.e., at lower cost). Urban economists also call

Table 3.1 Populations of Principal U.S. Cities, 1830–1860

Cities	1830	1840	1850	1860
New York	202,589	312,700	515,500	813,600
Philadelphia	161,271	220,400	340,000	565,529
Brooklyn	15,396	36,230	96,838	266,660
Baltimore	80,620	102,300	169,600	212,418
Boston	61,392	93,380	136,880	177,640
New Orleans	46,082	102,190	116,375	168,675
Cincinnati	24,831	46,338	115,435	161,044
St. Louis	5,852	14,470	77,860	160,773
Chicago		4,470	29,963	109,260
Buffalo	8,653	18,213	42,260	81,130
Newark	10,953	17,290	36,890	71,940
Louisville	10,340	21,210	43,194	68,033
Albany	24,209	33,721	50,763	62,367
Washington	18,826	23,364	40,001	61,122
San Francisco			34,776	56,802
Providence	16,833	23,171	41,573	50,666
Pittsburgh	15,369	21,115	46,601	49,221
Rochester	9,207	20,191	36,403	48,204
Detroit	2,222	9,012	21,019	45,619
Milwaukee		1,712	20,061	45,246
Cleveland	1,076	6,071	17,034	43,417
Total of Urban Residents	1,127,000	1,845,000	3,543,700	6,216,500
Number of Towns over 2,500	90	131	236	392
Percent Urban	8.8	10.8	15.3	19.8
Total U.S. Population	12,866,000	17,069,000	23,191,800	31,433,300

Note: Derived from U.S. censuses in 1850, 1860, and 1910 (Washington, D.C.: U.S. Government Printing Office).
Source: McKelvey 1973, p. 37.

these **localization economies**, if the firms benefiting from locating near each other are all in the same industry and produce the same product or service.

Locating near your competitor may not sound all that appealing, but being able to draw from a common pool of specialized suppliers, skilled workers, or eager consumers reduces costs, leading in a competitive market to lower prices for consumers. For firms on the cutting edge of new technologies, **knowledge spillovers** play an important role in disseminating new advances. In a city dense with skilled workers and many firms, these can be quickly communicated through formal channels of industry symposia, but perhaps even more importantly, through informal channels as engineers and other workers from various firms get to know each other. These turn out to be especially significant localization economies, in the jargon of economists. Sociologists often refer to such relationships in terms of social network theory. A **social network** is a social structure made of "nodes" (generally, individuals or organizations) that are linked together by one or more specific types of relations, including shared expertise and skill. Social networks play a critical role in determining the way problems are solved and organizations are run.

Table 3.2 Population of Cities That Reached 100,000 by 1910

Cities	1860	1870	1880	1890	1900	1910
Albany, N.Y.	62,367	69,422	90,758	94,923	94,151	100,253
Atlanta, Ga.	9,554	21,780	37,409	65,533	89,672	154,839
Baltimore, Md.	212,418	267,354	332,313	434,439	508,957	558,485
Birmingham, Ala.			3,086	26,178	35,415	132,685
Boston, Mass.	177,840	250,526	362,839	448,477	560,892	670,585
Bridgeport, Conn.	13,299	18,969	27,643	48,866	70,996	102,054
Buffalo, N.Y.	81,129	117,714	155,134	255,664	352,387	423,715
Cambridge, Mass.	26,060	39,634	52,669	70,028	91,886	104,839
Chicago, Ill.	109,260	298,977	503,185	1,009,850	1,698,575	2,188,283
Cincinnati, Ohio	161,044	216,239	255,139	295,908	325,902	363,591
Cleveland, Ohio	43,417	92,829	160,146	261,353	381,768	560,663
Columbus, Ohio	16,554	31,274	51,647	88,150	125,560	181,511
Dayton, Ohio	20,081	30,473	38,678	61,220	85,333	116,577
Denver, Colo.		4,759	35,629	106,713	133,659	213,361
Detroit, Mich.	45,619	29,577	116,340	205,875	285,704	465,766
Fall River, Mass.	14,026	26,766	48,961	74,398	104,863	119,295
Grand Rapids, Mich.	8,085	16,507	32,016	60,278	87,565	112,571
Indianapolis, Ind.	18,611	48,244	75,056	105,436	169,164	233,650
Jersey City, N.J.	29,226	82,546	120,722	163,003	206,433	267,779
Kansas City, Mo.	4,418	32,260	55,785	132,716	163,752	248,381
Los Angeles, Cal.	4,385	5,728	11,183	50,395	102,479	319,198
Louisville, Ky.	68,033	100,753	123,758	161,129	204,731	223,928
Lowell, Mass.	36,827	40,928	59,475	77,696	94,969	106,291
Memphis, Tenn.	22,623	40,226	33,592	64,495	102,320	131,105
Milwaukee, Wis.	45,246	71,440	115,587	204,468	285,315	373,857
Minneapolis, Minn.	2,564	13,066	46,887	164,738	202,718	301,408
Nashville, Tenn.	16,988	25,865	43,330	76,168	80,865	110,364
New Haven, Conn.	39,267	50,840	62,882	81,298	108,027	113,605
New Orleans, La.	168,675	191,418	216,090	242,039	287,104	339,075
New York, N.Y.	1,174,779	1,478,103	1,911,698	2,507,414	3,437,202	4,766,883
Manhattan Borough	513,669	942,292	1,164,673	1,441,216	1,850,093	2,331,542
Bronx Borough	23,593	37,393	51,980	86,908	200,507	430,980
Brooklyn Borough	279,122	419,921	599,495	838,547	1,166,582	1,634,351
Queens Borough	32,903	45,468	56,559	87,050	152,999	284,041
Richmond Borough	25,492	33,029	38,991	51,693	67,021	85,969
Newark, N.J.	71,941	105,059	136,508	181,830	246,070	347,469
Oakland, Cal.	1,543	10,500	34,555	48,662	66,960	150,174
Omaha, Neb.	1,883	16,083	30,518	140,452	102,555	124,096
Paterson, N.J.	19,586	33,579	51,031	78,347	105,171	125,600
Philadelphia, Pa.	565,529	674,022	847,170	1,046,964	1,293,697	1,549,008
Pittsburgh, Pa.	77,923	139,256	235,071	343,904	451,512	533,905
Portland, Oreg.	2,874	8,293	17,577	46,385	90,426	207,214
Providence, R.I.	50,666	68,904	104,857	132,146	175,597	224,326
Richmond, Va.	37,910	51,038	63,600	81,388	85,050	127,628
Rochester, N.Y.	48,204	62,386	89,366	133,596	162,608	218,149
St. Louis, Mo.	160,773	310,864	350,518	451,770	575,238	687,029
St. Paul, Minn.	10,401	20,030	41,473	133,156	163,065	214,744
San Francisco, Cal.	56,802	149,473	233,959	298,997	342,782	416,912
Scranton, Pa.	9,223	35,092	45,850	75,215	102,026	129,567
Seattle, Wash.		1,107	3,533	42,837	80,671	237,194
Spokane, Wash.				19,922	36,848	104,402
Syracuse, N.Y.	28,119	43,051	51,792	88,143	108,374	137,249
Toledo, Ohio	13,768	31,584	50,137	81,434	131,822	168,497
Washington, D.C.	61,122	109,199	177,624	230,392	278,718	331,069
Worcester, Mass.	24,960	41,105	58,291	84,655	118,421	145,986

Source: McKelvey 1973, p. 73.

As places where external economies and social networks are plentiful, big cities also provide the advantage of a location where you can find whatever you need to run your business effectively and at lowest cost. Imagine a new firm, just starting out, with a newly invented product to sell. Such a firm often will not be able to afford to construct its own building at the outset. It will not be able to buy machinery designed specifically for its purpose. It will not have its own in-house fleet of delivery trucks, nor will it have its own patent lawyer to protect it if its nearest competitor sues. It might need to hire a printing company to print its business stationery and an accounting company to help keep the books. All of these business services exist outside of the firm, but it usually will be cheaper for the firm to do business if they are available within the local environment. Our new firm might need to rent loft space. It might need skilled machinists to adapt existing machinery to suit its purpose. A ready supply of such workers who are available in the local community will normally benefit the firm in the form of lower production costs. In this case of locally available resources, the agglomeration economies are called **urbanization economies**.

Firms that need face-to-face communications will also be attracted to large cities to take advantage of such economies of scale. These are the head offices of large corporations and portions of the publishing, advertising, and fashion industries, as well as specialized legal and banking services. Raymond Vernon (1972) found that it was just such factors that allowed the New York City metropolitan area to sustain a healthy rate of economic growth, even though the city had among the highest rents and highest costs of living in the nation. If it were not for agglomeration economies, there would be fewer large cities, urban areas in general would be much smaller, and more of the population would live outside of metropolitan areas altogether.

Technological Progress and Innovation

We discuss technological progress last—but it certainly is not least—because over time, it has been one of the most powerful dynamics in urban growth, affecting the geography of growth and the dynamics of trade and transportation, agglomeration economies, internal economies of scale, and the size of consumer markets. To take a deeper look at technological progress, let's first think back to the centripetal and centrifugal forces discussed near the beginning of this chapter. As our history of centripetal and centrifugal forces illustrates, a firm may be located in a particular part of a city or region because its energy requirements require that it be near necessary resources—such as a port facility, which may be available only at certain sites such as the fall line of a river—or because the firm's production process may require buildings of certain dimensions that cannot be found elsewhere.

What is so important about technological change is that it can remove or relax constraints—creating new location possibilities for businesses and for households. Technological change can also create new incentives that allow firms to find new ways to maximize profits and new ways for households to pursue their own goals. Since the seventeenth and eighteenth centuries, U.S. cities have undergone several waves of technological innovation, which have changed (1) the constraints and incentives that affect business and residential location; (2) the subsequent centripetal or centrifugal forces of urban areas; and (3) the cost of transportation, the value of agglomeration economies and economies of scale, and the dynamics of consumer markets.

Douglas Rae (2003), an urban political scientist, examines both the general process of technological change and the impact of such innovation on American cities. Building upon the idea of "creative destruction"—the replacement of older industries with newer ones—originally advanced by the economist Joseph Schumpeter, Rae states that within all cities, competition and the desire to increase profit create pressure on firms to discover new ways to do things, and thus to constantly seek out new techniques that lower costs or improve the quality and consequently the demand for their goods or services.

As Rae describes it, in different historical periods, this unrelenting "creative edge of capitalism" has forced company managers to fasten upon particular aspects of their production processes in a constant search for ways to take advantage of new production techniques, transportation modes, or communication media. When this process is successful, a series of innovations ensue, removing old constraints and creating new possibilities. In response to these technological innovations, firms and households make adjustments about the location and content of their economic activities, and new location patterns of economic activity are formed. Like the steam engine that allowed production to move away from riverbanks, new technologies make some areas hotbeds of economic activity while making others obsolete. According to Rae, the timing and characteristics of such changes vary from one urban area to another, since innovation and the subsequent adoption of new technology depend upon each city's natural resources, the financial capital available, and the acumen of the city's economic and political decision makers.

Technological progress therefore changes the cost, speed, reach, and methods of transportation and consequently the fortunes of individual cities. By changing the raw materials that firms use in production, technological change affects the types of firms that benefit from particular localization (agglomeration) economies. Advances in technology (such as transportation that allowed producers to move goods to a greater numbers of buyers, and communications technology that allowed producers to communicate with more potential buyers) have also increased the size of consumer markets.

Demographic Growth and Change in Urban Areas

A huge labor force was needed to work in the nineteenth- and early-twentieth-century factories, to drive the streetcars and lorries, and to service the new industries spawned by American technological prowess. After all, to staff an ever-greater number of larger and larger firms located within the central city, it goes without saying that you need a lot of people. Where did they come from?

In order to understand the emergence of the rapidly increasing urban labor force, we require not only an insight into market forces but also into a set of institutional factors that led to huge demographic shifts. Although some of the growth in the urban population was due to natural increase among city dwellers, there were two major flows that brought newcomers to the city: (1) the shift of U.S. households from rural to urban areas and (2) the arrival of waves of immigrants from abroad.

A combination of both **push factors** and **pull factors** has been responsible for bringing millions upon millions of immigrants to America's shores and to her cities. Like centrifugal and centripetal forces—the one pushing outward as a mass spins and the other pulling inward—these two great immigration factors explain much of the growth of urban America. Push factors refer to all the reasons people feel they must leave one place to go to another. Pull factors are all those that attract people to a particular region or city. The same factors underlie migration within the country from rural areas to central cities and, later, from central cities to the suburbs.

Internal Migration: From Rural to Urban America

The growth of U.S. cities in the late nineteenth and early twentieth centuries involved not only changes in the economic alternatives available to firms, but also consideration of lifestyles and economic possibilities for individual workers and their families. Rural life had many positive aspects. Thomas Jefferson lauded the political independence of farmers who owned their own land. The quality of agricultural life was often compared favorably against conditions in cities, but rural life also presented numerous challenges. Crops and animals need daily attention, and the demands of agricultural work could be unforgiving when the farmworker suffered illness or injury. The financial rewards to farming were highly uncertain as a result of weather, crop disease, and insect infestation.

Consequently, for families contemplating a move to a city, there was an interplay between the perceived quality of city life and the experience of life in rural areas. Push and pull factors led individuals to reexamine their physical surroundings and economic situations. Did cities offer a better alternative to the structures of opportunity in rural settings? Was it time to seek a different type of life in the city? In the late 1800s and early 1900s, there were a number of push factors, including a series of weather-related disasters, insect plagues, and economic recessions that struck agriculture. These factors brought on hunger, foreclosure, and displacement for many of those affected (see **Table 3.3**). Moving to the city seemed to be the only good opportunity for many who tried unsuccessfully to keep their farms profitable.

Among those who worked on farms but did not own them, the weather, insect plagues, and recessions were significant factors that led to migration to cities, but there were also other developments that contributed significantly to the push toward urban areas. Since the mid-1800s, various inventors had tried to develop and market steam-powered machines to aid agricultural production—with limited success. By the 1890s, these initiatives had turned to gas-powered farm vehicles, which ultimately had greater commercial success. For many farmworkers, regardless of race or

Table 3.3 Economic and Biological *Push Factors* Affecting Migration from Farms to Cities

1874–1876	Grasshopper plagues destroy crops in Western United States.
Late 1870s and 1880s	Wheat, corn, and cotton prices fall; many small farmers lose their farms.
1886–1887	Blizzards in Great Plains harm cattle ranches.
1887–1897	Drought in Great Plains states devastates farms.
1890s	Depression in the United States; cotton prices fall from 8.6 cents per pound in 1890 to 6.98 cents in 1899.
1894–1895	Double-freeze winters destroy Florida citrus crops.
1900–1910	Cotton prices rebound, rising from 9.1 cents in 1900 to 13.5 cents in 1910. But boll weevil infestation spreads east from Texas to Louisiana and Mississippi.
1904	Stem rust epidemic destroys wheat in wheat-growing states.
1910–1920	Cotton prices fall in first half of decade, reaching a low of 7.4 cents in 1914, but then rise from 11.2 cents in 1915 to 35.3 cents in 1919. But boll weevil plague spreads across Alabama, Georgia, South Carolina, and Florida.
1920–1930	Overproduction of cotton leads to an agricultural depression, creating more poverty in the South. Boll weevil problem persists through 1925. Cotton prices vary from year to year, from a low of 15.9 cents in 1920 to a high of 28.7 cents in 1923 and end the decade at 16.8 cents. Blacks migrate away from areas of heaviest depression to cities in North and South. Many white farm owners lose land and are forced into farm tenantry or migration.
1920–1930	Number of tractors in use in nine southern states increases from 25,203 to 89,016, reducing owners' need for farm laborers.
1930–1940	Cotton prices fall drastically; beginning at 9.5 cents in 1930, falling to 5.7 cents in 1931, rising only as high as 12.4 cents, and ending the decade at 9.1 cents. Use of tractors spreads east from Texas and Oklahoma, doubling in number from 89,016 to 171,431. Increased tractor use continues to reduce owners' need for farm laborers.
1932–1936	Dust bowl conditions devastate farms in Great Plains states.
1933–1939	U.S. government intervenes in cotton markets by introducing subsidies to farm owners if they restrict acreage. Resulting decrease in acreage lessens demand for labor, displacing some farmworkers. Acreage harvested falls from 42,444 in 1930 to 23,805 in 1939.

Sources: U.S. Department of Agriculture, "A History of American Agriculture: 1776–1990," http://www.usda.gov/history2; Work 1925, 1930, 1940; Agricultural Extension Service at University of Georgia, "Cotton Production and the Boll Weevil in Georgia," http://www.ces.uga.edu/pubs/PDF/RR428.pdf.

geographic region, the increasing mechanization of agriculture through the development of tractors and increasingly sophisticated weeding and harvesting machines meant wholesale displacement from farm jobs (Rasmussen 1982). The city became the only viable option for those who no longer could make a living in agriculture.

For some groups, there were additional push factors. The tenant farming system, common in the South, institutionalized some forms of economic hardship for sharecroppers and other tenant farmers, as they rented their land and tools from owners and persistently found themselves in debt to them. For African American farmworkers, economic exploitation was particularly oppressive, as they had no legal recourse if they were cheated by their bosses, and raising complaints about such situations could be life-threatening. This oppression was buttressed by the systematic political disenfranchisement that was institutionalized during the 1890s and the physical violence perpetrated upon blacks with the tacit, if not explicit, support of many white business and political leaders in the South. Between 1900 and 1914, more than a thousand African Americans were murdered, the victims of brutal lynchings, most in the South (Work 1938). For blacks, "Going to Chicago" became a euphemism, not only for the search for new job opportunities but also for an escape to places with less political and social brutality (Work 1924; Fligstein 1981).

Between 1910 and 1930, in the first wave of what has come to be known as the Great Migration, more than a million African Americans moved from the South to the North, with most going to northern cities, among them New York, Philadelphia, Chicago, Indianapolis, St. Louis, and Kansas City (U.S. Bureau of the Census 1979; Work 1938). Hundreds of thousands more moved to southern cities, such as Atlanta, Birmingham, Jackson, and Memphis.

The migration slowed during the 1930s, but during this decade, federal policies that were introduced to help farm owners (in particular, the Agricultural Adjustment Act of 1933) ultimately had the unintended consequence of intensifying the economic push factors affecting farmworkers, which led to increased migration in the decades that followed. By stabilizing the market price for cotton and other agricultural products that had suffered from low prices due to overproduction relative to demand, and by giving subsidies to farm owners if they reduced the amount of land under cultivation, hundreds of thousands of farmworkers became redundant. The reduction in farm owners' demand for labor was also augmented by another impact of the federal subsidies. Subsidies provided farm owners with an infusion of cash, making it more feasible for them to buy tractors and, after 1945, new chemical weed killers and mechanized cotton pickers. These developments reduced the need for farm labor in the South, displacing tens of thousands of sharecroppers, intensifying the economic reasons for leaving southern farm areas, and greatly accelerating out-migration. Coupled with the continuing social and political barriers in the South that kept African Americans from access to voting, schools, and other activities, these new push factors created powerful incentives for African Americans to leave the South for what they hoped would be better conditions in the North (Lemann 1991).

While awareness of these push factors is very important for understanding this internal migration, the massive relocation of African Americans and native-born whites to cities cannot be understood without contemplating the pull factors exerted by cities. In the late 1800s and early 1900s, the growth of employment opportunities in the nation's manufacturing centers, such as those presented in **Table 3.4**, was a major factor as families considered where to move. With the exception of the Depression years in the 1930s, pull factors continued to be strong in the decades from 1910 to 1970, as automobile and steel industry jobs opened up in Michigan, Ohio, Illinois, and Pennsylvania, attracting African Americans and rural whites to cities in the country's booming manufacturing belt. The allure of cities was particularly strong during World War I and World War II, as wartime industries offered wages much beyond the average paid to farmworkers. At mid-century, with the economic boom of the late 1940s and the 1950s, the employment opportunities in cities of the North and West continued to stoke internal migration, pulling large numbers of people from rural areas and small towns to city life.

Thus, the combination of push factors in rural areas and pull factors in U.S. cities created a massive flow of internal migration to the growing cities. As early as 1920,

Table 3.4 Economic *Pull Factors* Affecting Migration to Cities

1890–1910	Textile manufacturing, introduced into the South in the 1880s expands, drawing workers to southern cities. By 1910, half of all U.S. textile manufacturing is being done in the South.
1900–1910	Cities in the North and South grow rapidly.
1914–1918	Expansion of manufacturing during World War I attracts whites and blacks to cities in the North and South.
1920s	Displacement due to introduction of machinery is negligible.
1930–1940	Number of black farmers decreases by 23 percent, from 749,000 to 574,000 (a decrease of 175,000). Number of white farmers decreases by 50,000 (less than 4 percent). Reverse migration by whites from cities is substantial, as some whites leave cities and take on subsistence farming to weather the Great Depression (the number of white farm owners increased by 74,000, or 12 percent).
1940s	War industries (steel, refineries, textiles) spur city development.

Source: Fligstein 1981.

half of all native whites and a third of African Americans lived in urban areas. Between 1900 and 1940, the number of native-born whites living in urban areas increased by 30 million, doubling the total number to 59 million. The number of African Americans living in urban areas tripled, from 2 million to 6 million. Rural white families moved in all directions to cities across the nation, while black migration tended to go from the rural South to cities in the South, North, and West. In turn, the internal migration contributed to changes in the geographic size of urban areas, their demographics, and their socioeconomic dynamics.

Immigration and the Growth of American Cities

The new American city of the nineteenth century and, later, in the early twentieth century was populated not only by those who came from small villages and farms, but also by millions who came from abroad. In 1830, a year after Andrew Jackson's inauguration as the nation's seventh president, 12.5 million people lived in the United States. Just twenty years later the number had nearly doubled to 23 million, and a decade later it had grown to 31 million. Of these, more than 5 million—one in six—were immigrants. Many of those who disembarked in port cities along the East Coast quickly moved to the interior of the country to renew or take up a life of farming, mining, or working in America's vast timberlands. But many made their new home in urban America, practicing trades they had learned in the old country or learning new ones. In New York in 1850, 45 percent of the population was foreign born, with Ireland and Germany responsible for most of the new immigrants. In Philadelphia, about one in four residents had been born in Europe (Kraus 1959).

More than a million Irish men, women, and children, mostly from rural areas, came to the United States between 1815 and 1845. In the early days of this great wave of emigration, they were escaping—pushed out—of their emerald homeland, forced off their farms to make way for pasturage. Later, the trickle turned into a torrent of Irish emigration as the great potato famine struck with a vengeance in the 1840s. Trying to escape starvation, the Irish filled boats bound for the United States and Canada, their passage often paid for by the Irish government or private philanthropy. Meanwhile, the emerging factory system in Britain and Germany undermined the skills of craftsmen who saw their wages fall and their working day lengthen. Religious and social persecution added to the push away from Europe and would have done so even if the United States had little to offer.

But, indeed, it had much. In the nineteenth and early twentieth centuries, America's abundant land and the growth of jobs in its expanding cities beckoned, pulling millions of these immigrants to our shores. Guidebooks, travel accounts, and newspapers afforded prospective emigrants a vision of the better life awaiting them in the New World. Innkeepers and labor contractors helped round up emigrants for America with promises of good jobs at good pay. For as little as $5, an immigrant could make it to North America on a Canadian lumber vessel or a fishing boat. But those arriving with nothing could rarely leave the cities where they disembarked. Only about 10 percent of the Irish moved to rural areas, the vast majority staying in the cities to work in the emerging textile industry, in construction, and on the docks (Bluestone and Stevenson 2000). Those who came with some wealth began their own businesses, contributing capital and entrepreneurship to American industry.

The immortal words of Emma Lazarus inscribed on the Statue of Liberty in New York Harbor represent both of these forces—the push away from poverty and political repression, the pull toward what many saw as the golden opportunities beckoning in the United States:

> Give me your tired, your poor,
> Your huddled masses yearning to breathe free,
> The wretched refuse of your teeming shore,
> Send these, the homeless, tempest-tossed to me,
> I lift my lamp beside the golden door!

During the second half of the nineteenth century, new immigrants poured into the United States from both western and eastern Europe. By 1900, the countries sending the largest number of emigrants to America were Germany, Ireland, Canada, Great Britain, Sweden, Italy, Russia, and Poland. Between 1900 and 1920, more than 14.5 million new immigrants arrived in the United States—a number not surpassed until the last two decades of the twentieth century, 1980–2000.

In the West, immigration became a major factor as well. Between 1850 and 1880, 300,000 Chinese entered the country, most coming from Kwantang Province in southeastern China and settling in California. Nine in ten of these new arrivals were men, many recruited as contract laborers by the "forty-niners," who had come to the West to pan for riches in California's gold rush. Others were taken against their will and forced to join railway gangs to help build the transcontinental railroad. By 1860, 9 percent of California's population was Chinese. By the early 1880s, 25,000 to 30,000 people of Chinese descent lived in San Francisco, most in a single neighborhood known even today as Chinatown. Hence, by the end of the nineteenth century, you would have heard a great number of languages spoken in America's cities, whether you stood under a gas lamp on the Bowery in lower Manhattan, in the crowded precincts around the slaughterhouses in Chicago, or near San Francisco's bustling waterfront (see **Table 3.5**).

Table 3.5 Foreign-Born Americans (Includes All Places over 2,500)

Year	Urban Population	Percent of Foreign-Born Population Living in Urban Areas
1890	5,679,135	61.4
1900	6,859,078	66.3
1910	9,745,697	72.1
1920	10,500,942	75.4
1930	11,250,815	79.2
1940	9,276,707	80.0

Source: U.S. Bureau of the Census, "Nativity of the Population by Urban-Rural Residence and Size of Place: 1870 to 1940 and 1960 to 1990," Technical Paper 29, table 18.

Yet the boom in immigration had just begun. Between 1880 and 1890, according to historical statistics compiled by the U.S. Immigration and Naturalization Service (INS), nearly 9 million new immigrants reached American shores and nearly the same number in the following decade (see **Figure 3.10**). To be sure, many of those who came to America returned to their homelands or moved elsewhere. Many left because they were homesick, others because they could not find good jobs. A few who were born in the United States chose to move to other countries because of marriage or wanderlust. Times were so difficult during the Great Depression of the 1930s that more people left the United States than entered (see **Table 3.6**). Still, the net inflows—arrivals minus departures—were so great earlier in the century that by

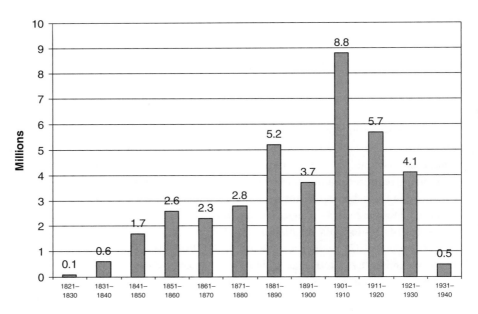

Figure 3.10 U.S. Immigration, 1821–1940 (Millions). *Source:* U.S. Department of Homeland Security, Office of Immigration Statistics 2006.

Table 3.6 Immigration and Emigration by Decade, 1901–1940 (Thousands)

Period	Immigrants to the United States	Emigrants from the United States	Net Immigration	Ratio: Emigration/ Immigration
1901–1910	8,795	3,008	5,787	0.34
1911–1920	5,736	2,157	3,579	0.38
1921–1930	4,107	1,685	2,422	0.41
1931–1940	528	649	−121	1.23

Sources: U.S. Bureau of the Census, *Statistical Abstract of the United States 2007* (Washington, D.C.: U.S. Government Printing Office, 2007), table 1; R. Warren and E. Kraly, *The Elusive Exodus: Emigration from the United States*, Population Trends and Public Policy Occasional Paper No. 8 (Washington, D.C.: Population Reference Bureau, 1985).

1910 there were 13.5 million foreign-born residents in the United States—nearly 15 percent of the nation's total population. Only in the last decade of the twentieth century did official immigration come close to matching the level reached at the beginning of the century. The 2000 census found that more than one in ten (10.4%) of those in the United States were foreign born, a total exceeding 28 million (U.S. Bureau of the Census 2001).

Immigration is not simply a matter of push and pull factors. Politics and legislation play a key role. After the massive wave of foreigners came to the United States between 1880 and 1910, the rate of immigration slowed due to World War I and congressional passage of laws in 1921 and then again in 1924 that severely restricted immigration. The new legislation reduced the overall amount of immigration allowed, while establishing immigration quota systems that strongly favored countries in the Western Hemisphere and northern and western Europe. During the Great Depression of the 1930s and then during World War II, immigration was also quite low. By 1950, the number of foreign born was down to just 6.9 percent of the total population.

During those key decades of vast immigration, however, America's cities were populated and its urban factories and commercial businesses were supplied with a workforce needed to make central city locations economically viable. The coming together of central city economic demand as a result of transportation economies, agglomeration economies, economies of scale, and mass markets with a ready supply of labor and capital produced America's great and small cities.

U.S. cities grew both in population and in geographic size. As economic activity in cities developed, both the demand for labor and the opportunities for additional businesses expanded. As people moved to cities in response to increased labor demand and expanding business opportunities, the demand for housing and for commercial and industrial space increased. With the urban population increasing, new service businesses were founded and cities became even more alluring. The explosion in the size of cities was the result of this interaction between business expansion and population growth.

Ultimately, this created new possibilities for the owners of farmlands adjacent to the growing cities: If the profits from the sale of land for residential or business purposes exceeded the profits that could be expected from agricultural use, why continue farming? Hence, the expansion of population and of commercial activity pushed the borders of cities outward, swallowing up the surrounding farms. Cities became denser at their core while expanding outward to their fringe.

Annexation and the Growing Size of Cities

Until the late nineteenth century, as economic activity expanded, the political boundaries of most cities expanded to accommodate it. For outlying areas, access to water and sewage systems and to a variety of other public services provided a strong incentive to become part of the city. Through the process of **annexation**, central cities encompassed larger and larger areas. Philadelphia, for example, expanded from just 2 square miles in 1850 to 130 square miles two decades later. The city of New York increased its geographic size sevenfold between 1890 and 1910 (from 44 to 299 square miles) by annexing Brooklyn, Queens, Staten Island, and the Bronx. Chicago expanded from 10 square miles in 1850 to 169 square miles in 1890.

However, as political discord intensified in the late-nineteenth-century city, and as states chose to provide public services to their municipalities through the creation of special water and sewer districts, many suburban communities had little need to join the central city and fought further annexation attempts. Fischel (2001) has argued that the communities' desire to maintain control over land-use decisions within their boundaries was a major motivation in their resistance to annexation attempts by the central city.

Suburban communities sought to maintain their independence from city political power, to control their own environments, and, in many cases, to maintain their economic, ethnic, or racial exclusivity. This was the case in metropolitan Boston, for example, where annexation has been successfully resisted since the late nineteenth century. Nonetheless, annexation continued well into the twentieth century in the newer cities of the South and West. Los Angeles grew from 85 square miles in 1910 to 440 square miles in 1930. In the period after 1950, Jacksonville expanded from 30 square miles to 827 square miles, while Indianapolis expanded from 55 square miles to 379 square miles.

As a result, today the proportion of the geographic area occupied by the central cities of metropolitan areas varies considerably. According to the 2000 census, only 2.8 percent of the land in the Greater Boston metropolitan area is actually in the city of Boston and the city proper contains less than 15 percent of the area's total population. In contrast, the city of Phoenix occupies nearly three-fifths of its surrounding metro area and accounts for nearly half of the MSA's population.

The Changing Pattern of Urban Population Growth

While economics and politics were transforming the boundaries of cities, technological marvels were also transforming the urban home. Thomas Edison's incandescent bulb made electric lighting common beginning in the early twentieth century. Electric lights replaced gas lamps on city streets. In the 1880s and 1890s, hot-air furnaces were first introduced, gas stoves replaced coal-burning cast iron ranges, and iceboxes were becoming standard, even before the electric refrigerator made its debut. Factory-made products replaced homemade, from breads and canned goods to clothing. As historian Foster Rhea Dulles notes, most of these new innovations were still largely confined to the city and "the traditional divergence between urban and rural ways of living was sharply accentuated. The future, indeed, belonged to the city and ultimately its culture would invade even the most isolated country areas" (Dulles 1959, p. 91).

Cities were becoming the intellectual, artistic, and literary centers of the nation. With the exception of the land-grant universities, most of the great institutions of higher education were located in cities along with the nation's most prestigious museums and libraries. America's wealthiest moved into the cities to take advantage of their great and growing amenities.

Meanwhile, members of a growing middle class were moving into their first owner-occupied homes in the city, often on quiet streets farther from the central business district. Cities like Chicago, Detroit, and Philadelphia boasted thousands of single-family homes that were built for professionals, small business owners, and increasingly even for some of the better off among the blue-collar working class.

Yet, even a century ago, the urban paradox of poverty among plenty ruled. The urban experience was truly diverse for those who populated the cities. At the beginning of the twentieth century, approximately one-tenth of the population in the largest cities lived in slums. In New York City alone, it was estimated that more than 1.5 million people were crowded into 43,000 tenements where they were closely packed together in five- and six-story buildings, hurriedly built with plumbing, heating, and lighting that was primitive at best. Deadly fires, disease, crime, and juvenile delinquency were common. Although some immigrants to the United States had been told that in this land of opportunity the streets were "paved with gold," most streets still did not even have asphalt. City populations were often divided along ethnic, racial, religious, and income lines (Chudacoff and Smith 2000). Reflecting such divisions, various interest groups exerted important influences in both market (e.g., housing, employment) and nonmarket (e.g., political and social) activities. Later, in the mid-1900s, when many in the middle class left for the suburbs, the largest cities became more polarized along the dimensions of income and race. Some of the richest and many of the poorest families in America ended up as the residents of central cities, as working-class and middle-class families sought their dream homes in the suburbs.

In the industrial age, the high concentrations of population and economic activity within the city limits allowed for the creation of many of the institutions that define our cities even today. The physical infrastructure of the city—from paved roads to lighted streets to reliable water supplies—depended on a large critical mass of people to be served. To be sure, it was the dense population of cities that contributed to the diseases associated with filth. But it was in response to these diseases that the public health movement was born, resulting in sanitation departments, health departments, and the movement for the construction of public parks in the middle of cities.

It was both the concentration of people in large cities and the great fortunes that sprang from the urban industrial age that allowed new cultural, religious, medical, and educational institutions to flourish there. Many of our finest urban facades—public libraries, museums, concert halls, railroad stations, and courthouses—date from this period.

Certainly, the positive economies of scale in the central city represent only one side of the urban coin. The flip side contains the story of vice and corruption, congestion, violence, and danger in ever more densely packed central cities. While technology was reinforcing the primacy of central locations, its need for large manufacturing workforces and the consequent gathering of huge populations that were new to industrialization and urbanization led to turmoil.

The rise of the automobile dramatically reshaped the contours of the American city beginning in the middle of the twentieth century, a topic we will explore in detail in the next chapter. Highways now linked cities across the map of the United States in ways that railroads could not. Some of the largest metropolitan areas today—like Dallas-Forth Worth (#9) and Houston (#10)—did not appear in Table 3.2 because they did not have even 100,000 residents in 1910. Metropolitan growth has spread from the Northeast and Midwest to the South and West, and this also can be seen as an interaction between market forces and public policy.

In addition to the economic and technological changes that expanded the location choices of firms and households, politics also contributed to the growth of cities in places where vacant land was cheaper and more available and where labor costs were lower. The seniority of a number of southern congressmen and senators allowed them key committee chairmanships. They used their influence to bring a disproportionate number of military facilities to southern states and to relocate large military contractors to the Sunbelt, raising the South's share of all Department of Defense prime contract awards from 7.6 percent in 1951 to 23.5 percent in 1967 (Schulman 1991). Moreover, Congress passed the Taft-Hartley Act in 1947, which made it more difficult for northern unions to follow their workers to the South and made it almost impossible for them to organize in states with right-to-work laws—most of which were in the South. Such political factors helped redirect where growth would take place and where small towns would turn into burgeoning cities.

In the newer metropolitan areas, where lower-density development was the rule, both the cities and the suburbs were more likely to be oriented around the needs of the motorist rather than those of pedestrians or public transit users. The lower density itself made these areas costly locations for public transportation, especially with the auto industry lobbying for more highways and roads. The role served by the waterfront in colonial cities and the railroad depot in industrial cities was now served by the highway interchange in the postindustrial twentieth-century metropolis, as we see in the next chapter.

References

Allen, Hugh. 1949. *The House of Goodyear*. Cleveland, Ohio: Corday and Gross.

Blackford, Mansel G., and K. Austin Kerr. 1996. *BF Goodrich: Tradition and Transformation, 1870–1995*. Columbus: Ohio State University Press.

Bluestone, Barry, Patricia Hanna, Sarah Kuhn, and Laura Moore. 1981. *The Retail Revolution: Market Transformation, Investment and Labor in the Modern Department Store Industry*. Boston: Auburn House.

Bluestone, Barry, and Mary Huff Stevenson. 2000. *The Boston Renaissance: Race, Space, and Economic Change in an American Metropoli*s. New York: Russell Sage.

Bruegmann, Robert. 2005. *Sprawl: A Compact History*. Chicago: University of Chicago Press.

Brunn, Stanley D., Jack F. Williams, and Donald J. Zeigler, eds. 2003. *Cities of the World*, 3rd ed. Lanham, Md.: Rowman & Littlefield.

Chudacoff, Howard, and Judith E. Smith. 2000. *The Evolution of American Urban Society*, 5th ed. Upper Saddle River, N.J.: Prentice Hall.

Cronon, William. 1991. *Nature's Metropolis: Chicago and the Great West*. New York: W. W. Norton.

Dulles, Foster Rhea. 1959. *The United States since 1865*. Ann Arbor: University of Michigan Press.

Edwards, Richard C. 1980. *Contested Terrain: The Transformation of the Workplace in the 20th Century*. New York: Basic Books.

Fischel, William A. 2001. *The Homevoter Hypothesis: How Home Values Influence Local Government Taxation, School Finance, and Land-Use Policies*. Cambridge, Mass.: Harvard University Press.

Fligstein, Neil. 1981. *Going North: Migration of Blacks and Whites from the South, 1900–1950*. New York: Academic Press.

———. 1983. "The Transformation of Southern Agriculture and the Migration of Blacks and Whites, 1930–1940." *International Migration Review* 17, no. 2: 268–290.

Isard, Walter. 1975. *Introduction to Regional Science*. Englewood Cliffs, N.J.: Prentice Hall.

Jacobs, Jane. 1969. *The Economy of Cities*. New York: Random House.

Kraus, Michael. 1959. *The United States to 1865*. Ann Arbor: University of Michigan Press.

Launhardt, Wilhelm. 1885. *Mathematische Begrundung der Volkswirtschafslehre*. Leipzig, Germany: W. Engleman. Trans. John Creedy (1993) as *Mathematical Principles of Economics*. Aldershot, England, and Brookfield, Vt.: Edward Elgar.

Lemann, Nicholas. 1991. *The Promised Land: The Great Black Migration and How It Changed America*. New York: Alfred A. Knopf.

McKelvey, Blake. 1973. *American Urbanization: A Comparative History*. Glenview, Ill.: Scott, Foresman.

Miller, Donald L. 1996. *City of the Century: The Epic of Chicago and the Making of America*. New York: Simon & Schuster.

Moses, Leon, and Harold F. Williamson Jr. 1967. "The Location of Economic Activity in Cities." *American Economic Review* 57 (May): 211–222.

O'Reilly, Maurice. 1983. *The Goodyear Story*. New York: Benjamin Company.

Palen, J. John. 2002. *The Urban World*, 6th ed. Boston: McGraw-Hill.

Rae, Douglas. 2003. *City: Urbanism and Its End*. New Haven, Conn.: Yale University Press.

Rasmussen, Wayne D. 1982. "The Mechanization of Agriculture." *Scientific American* 247, no. 3 (September): 76–89.

Schulman, Bruce J. 1991. *From Cotton Belt to Sunbelt: Federal Policy, Economic Development, and the Transformation of the South, 1938–1980*. New York: Oxford University Press.

U.S. Bureau of the Census. 1979. "The Social and Economic Status of the Black Population in the United States: An Historical View, 1790–1978." U.S. Department of Commerce Special Studies Series P-23, No. 80. Washington, D.C.: U.S. Government Printing Office.

———. 2001. *Selected Historical Decennial Census, Population and Housing Counts*. Washington, D.C: U.S. Government Printing Office, April.

U.S. Bureau of the Census QuickFacts. http://quickfacts.census.gov/qfd.

U.S. Department of Homeland Security. Office of Immigration Statistics. 2006. *Yearbook of Immigration Statistics*. Washington, D.C.

U.S. Department of Housing and Urban Development. 2007. HUD User Policy Development and Research Information Service. SOCDS (State of the Cities Data Systems) data set. http://socds .huduser.org.

Vernon, Raymond. 1972. "External Economies." In Matthew Edel and Jerome Rothenberg, eds., *Readings in Urban Economics.* New York: Macmillan, pp. 37–49.

Wade, Richard C. 1959. *The Urban Frontier: The Rise of Western Cities 1790–1830.* Cambridge, Mass.: Harvard University Press.

Weber, Alfred. 1909. *Ueber den Standort der Industrien.* Tübingen, Germany: J. C. B. Mohr (Paul Siebeck) Publisher.

———. 1929. *Theory of the Location of Industries.* Trans. Carl J. Friedrich. Chicago: University of Chicago Press.

Work, Monroe N. 1924. "The Negro Migration." *Southern Workman* (May): 202–212.

———. 1925. *The Negro Year Book 1925.* Tuskegee, Ala.: The Negro Year Book Publishing Company.

———. 1930. *The Negro Year Book 1930.* Tuskegee, Ala.: The Negro Year Book Publishing Company.

———. 1938. *The Negro Year Book 1937–1938.* Tuskegee, Ala.: The Negro Year Book Publishing Company.

———. 1940. *The Negro Year Book 1940.* Tuskegee, Ala.: The Negro Year Book Publishing Company.

Chapter 3 Questions and Exercises

The Economic Roles of Early U.S. Cities and Towns

1. Consider the city or town in which you live (or where you grew up). Using the official Web site of the municipality or the community's historical society, which you should be able to find using a Web browser, identify the products (goods or services) that seem to have contributed most to the early growth of this area. What connection, if any, can you make between these early economic activities and Weber's theory linking business location and transportation costs?

2. Was the city or town you studied in question 1 famous nationwide for a particular product (good or service) produced there? Were there many companies producing this product in your city or town? Does this represent agglomeration economies?

Immigration and Internal Migration

3. The Census Bureau Technical Paper #29, "Historical Census Statistics on the For-eign-born Population of the United States: 1850–1990," is available at

http://www.census.gov/population/www/documentation/twps0029/twps0029.html

It includes Table 22, which tracks the nativity of the population from 1890 to 1990 in approximately ninety cities that had at one time or another been among the fifty largest cities in the United States. The table shows the total population at the end of each decade, the total number of native-born persons in these cities in each of these years, and the number and percentage of foreign-born individuals in these cities for each of these years. Take a look at the information in this table for the city closest to your home and two other cities of your choice. For each of your selected cities, in which decade did it experience the fastest growth in population? Does the population boom for each of those cities seem to have been most strongly caused by an increase in immigration or an increase in internal migration?

4. For the three cities you chose in question 3, take a look at the city's Web site, the local historical society's Web site, or some other source giving the history of the city. Which economic pull factors stimulated migration to those cities during the periods of peak population growth?

4 Cities and Suburbs in the Late Twentieth Century

The Dynamics of Metropolitan Expansion

If you stand at the center of most large cities and look skyward, you will see high-rise office towers, some of which soar fifty stories or more—unless, of course, it is a city with explicit government-imposed height restrictions, like Washington, D.C., or Paris, France. Now, if you travel to a point 1 mile from the geographic center of the city, what do your surroundings look like? How about at 5 miles or 15 miles? The answer depends upon the particular city you are in and often on whether you travel north, south, east, or west from the city center. You may find yourself in an area of small single-family homes or large apartment buildings, in a new high-tech industrial park, or in a small business area that has existed for decades. It could be a neighborhood characterized by large, expensive mansions, a community of small bungalows, or, alternatively, a rural area of farms or forests. Depending more on politics than economics, you may still be within the city's jurisdiction, in a suburb, or in an unincorporated area. Most likely, as you move away from downtown, the average scale of the buildings will decline, although in late-twentieth-century metro areas there were, like today, places other than the geographic center where there was the equivalent of a high-rise village.

How each metro area is laid out depends upon millions of choices made by individual families and firms over time. Some of these choices are made in the marketplace, others through the ballot box. But they are almost invariably influenced by land prices, which are in turn influenced by advances in transportation and communications technology, changing social mores, and the evolution of political institutions.

It is perfectly clear, however, that the pattern is not random. To understand where businesses and families locate within metro areas, where greater density in population and economic activity occurs, how the landscape will be spiked with high-rises and office towers, and how each of these changes over time, it is useful to turn first to a set of formal models developed by economists, sociologists, and urban geographers. All of these models have a common goal—to understand the patterns of land use and the physical structure of the landscape in terms of land prices or what economists refer to as **rent**. Once we have explored these formal models, we will use them to explain the evolution of metro areas in the late twentieth century. In doing so, we also need to bring in a number of important insights from political science and sociology.

100

Formal Models of Urban Growth and Development

There are three principal descriptive models of land-use patterns in urban areas. The first, set forth by Ernest Burgess in 1925 (slightly revised in 1929) as part of the so-called "Chicago School" of urban sociology, described cities in terms of concentric rings. The inner ring (Zone 1) contained the city's central business district (CBD). The subsequent rings were (in order of proximity to the central business district): the "zone of transition" (Zone 2), which Burgess's 1929 article described as containing factories on the innermost side and "areas of residential deterioration caused by the encroaching of business and industry from Zone 1" that were populated by newly arrived immigrants in rooming houses and homeless men; the zone of workingmen's homes (Zone 3), a residential area of "skilled and thrifty" factory and shop workers; a residential zone of somewhat higher incomes (Zone 4) that included single-family homes, apartment houses, residential hotels, and "bright light areas"; and, finally, the commuters' zone (Zone 5). In Burgess's view, changes in land use proceeded from the inner ring outward, with each ring "invading" the next in a competition for use of the land as city expansion occurred (Burgess 1925, 1929).

The second major descriptive model, advanced by Homer Hoyt in 1939, is known as the "sector model." Instead of concentric rings, this model envisioned cities developing in sectors or wedges. The sector model proposed that as cities expand and wealthy families move to well-to-do suburbs, retail businesses follow, locating along the transportation routes leading to these suburbs. Subsidiary development then follows along the outskirts of transportation routes, creating wedge shapes. Topography (the characteristics of the land) can also be a factor in the development of sectors. Individual sectors associated with a specific industry may arise since (as noted in Chapter 3) some industries seek locations near bodies of water. Sectors of distinct income levels may arise because high-income families seek land with the best qualities, while poor families may not be able to afford the most desired land.

The third major descriptive model, known as the multinucleic or polycentric model, was developed by Chauncy Harris and Edward Ullman in 1945. Harris and Ullman rejected the concept that cities had just one center. "In many cities," they wrote, "the land-use pattern is built not around a single center but around several discrete nuclei. In some cities these nuclei have existed from the very origins of the city; in others they have developed as the growth of the city stimulated migration and activities and the concentration of like functions" (Harris and Ullman 1945, p. 14). They attributed the existence of distinct nuclei to four factors: (1) some activities require specific types of facilities, (2) the existence of localization economies, as discussed in Chapter 3, (3) some activities are incompatible with others, and (4) some areas are not affordable for some uses. Each of these models foretold the changes that metro areas would undergo, particularly after World War II. **Figure 4.1** provides a pictorial representation of the concentric zone, sector, and multiple nuclei models of metro area location.

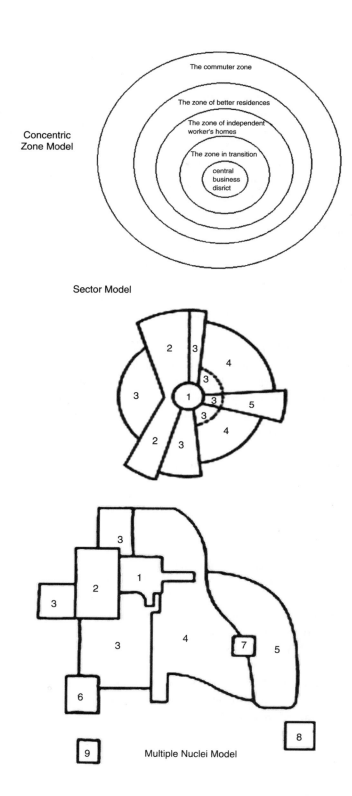

Concentric Zone Model

The commuter zone

The zone of better residences

The zone of independent worker's homes

The zone in transition

central business disrict

Sector Model

Multiple Nuclei Model

Understanding Urban Land Values

The descriptive models above can be understood more fully by studying the economic forces that contribute to the price or market value of land. Anyone who has played the game of Monopoly knows that as you travel around the board, you progress from the cheapest properties on Baltic and Mediterranean to the most expensive ones on Boardwalk and Park Place. The game was created during the Great Depression of the 1930s, and the street names refer to Atlantic City, New Jersey, when it was primarily a summer resort, long before the advent of the casinos. The land values portrayed in the game reflect the fact that people going to Atlantic City at that time wanted access to its beach and ocean. The highest values were therefore along the oceanfront; land values declined with greater distance from the shore. If you land on Monopoly's premier waterfront property, Boardwalk, and no one already owns it, you can buy this piece of undeveloped land, but it will cost you $400 of play money. If the roll of the dice lands you on Mediterranean Avenue, you can buy this back-alley property—a distance from the beach—for only $60.

The question of how urban land gets its value is far more complicated than what can be portrayed in Monopoly. Nevertheless, it is useful to begin with a stripped-down model to help us understand the underlying forces that affect the price of land. Such a model will not fully explain land use and land values in any one specific city, but it will provide a template that can then be adapted to accommodate the geographical, historical, legal, and cultural differences that have made each place unique and help us to understand how places change over time. In the course of this chapter, we begin with a simple model and add complexity as we go along. To start, we hearken back to the early twentieth century, when transportation costs were still a significant factor in business location.

The Basic Alonso Model

The economist William Alonso (1964), building on the earlier work of German economists (on the value of agricultural land), created a simple model of urban land

---

Figure 4.1 An Illustration of Concentric Zone, Sector, and Multiple Nuclei Urban Structures. The top figure above depicts the concentric model of cities, as envisioned by Ernest Burgess, one of the prominent early members of the Chicago School of Sociology. Burgess envisioned cities as composed of five concentric zones, the central business district (CBD), the zone of transition, the zone of independent workingmen's homes, the zone of better residences, and the commuter zone. The middle figure is a depiction of the sector model. In the sector model, there is a central business district with wedges of various sizes emanating from the CBD. The multinucleic model (an example of which is shown in the bottom figure) envisions cities as having multiple centers of activity, each of which can be a source of further development. In the middle and bottom figures, the numbers indicate different uses of land, as follows: (1) central business district, (2) wholesale businesses and light manufacturing, (3) low-income residential, (4) medium-income residential, (5) high-income residential, (6) heavy manufacturing, (7) outlying business district, (8) residential suburbs, and (9) industrial suburbs. *Sources:* The above depiction of the concentric zone model is adapted from a figure given in Burgess 1925, p. 55. The depictions of the sector and multinucleic models are from Harris and Ullman 1945, p. 13.

markets in the mid-1960s (von Thunen 1826; Launhardt 1885; Dunn 1954; Isard 1956). He was interested not only in explaining how land got its value but also how it was distributed across different categories of users, including business firms and households. Just as everyone in Monopoly wants access to the beachfront, everyone in the basic Alonso model wants access to the central marketplace. Although he is best known for this **monocentric (one-center) model**, Alonso did envision other possibilities (see **Appendix A**). His insights are easily adapted to situations beyond the ones sketched out in the simple framework and therefore can be used to understand the location pattern in today's metro areas.

While Alonso's ultimate goal was to understand complex *urban* land markets, he started with the simplest case of an agricultural land market in which identical farmers produce the same crop in the same way on the same amount of acreage (von Thunen 1826; Alonso 1964). The only difference between the farmers is that some have land very close to the central marketplace to which they transport their crops for sale, while others live and farm farther away. Assuming that these individual farmers actually own the land they farm and therefore need not pay rent, and that the cost of transporting goods is substantial and increases the farther one has to carry those goods, the farmers who are located nearer the market will be more profitable. Economic profit will decline as the distance to the market increases.

This is true because profitability is the result of the difference between total revenue and total cost, where total cost is comprised of production costs plus transportation costs. For example, if each farmer's acreage produces 1,000 pounds of wheat for bread production and the market price for wheat is $2 per pound, each farmer will receive $2,000 in revenue from the sale of his output. Under the assumptions mentioned in the preceding paragraph, production costs would be the same for each farmer, but transportation costs would vary with the number of miles traveled. If production costs amounted to $1,500 and transportation costs were $10 per mile, the farmer right next to the marketplace would wind up with an economic profit of $500 ($2,000 − $1,500 − $0 transportation costs) while the farmer 20 miles down the road would have an economic profit of only $300 ($2,000 − $1,500 − $200 transportation costs).

Economic profit refers to the return the farmers receive over and above what is necessary to keep them willingly in business. Therefore, according to standard economic analysis, an economic profit equal to zero is just sufficient to cover all of the farmers' costs, including the opportunity cost of paying themselves a return (or profit) equal to their next best alternative. In this example, the farmer located 50 miles from the marketplace would earn zero economic profit and any farmer trying to compete in this market farther from the central marketplace would suffer an economic loss. In this case, all of the crop would be grown within a 50-mile radius of the marketplace. It would not be financially feasible to grow it farther away. As this example illustrates, there is an essential link between market forces and patterns of land use.

How Does a Bid Rent Curve Get Established?   Let us take this initial insight further. So far, we have assumed that all the farmers own their land, but what if they have to rent the farmland from others, as tenant farmers and sharecroppers do? The farmer on the land closest to the marketplace still has the lowest transportation cost and the farmer on the land 50 miles away has the highest. Therefore, farmers working the land 50 miles away would be willing to pay up to $500 to rent the land at the center, since that is what they would save in transportation costs, but they would be willing to pay *no more* than $300 to rent the land 20 miles out. These values are called the **bid rents** and refer to what a renter or buyer would be willing to bid in order to gain access to and use of a specific parcel of land. Ultimately, then, as shown in **Table 4.1**, the landlord closest to the center can charge $500 in rent; the one 20 miles out can charge only $300. Beyond the 50-mile radius, the land would have no economic value, at least with regard to this one crop.

When every tenant farmer is paying the market-determined rent, none is better off than any other. Those closer to the center pay more for rent and less for transportation. Those farther away pay more for transportation and less for rent. The sum of rent plus transportation costs is the same for every tenant farmer, and leaves each with an economic profit (above opportunity costs) of zero. For every farm, the difference between the revenue received and the cost of production ends up with the landlord. Those landlords who are lucky enough to own land near the central marketplace make out the best; those farther away earn less and less rent, the farther their land

Table 4.1 Understanding Bid Rents

		Production costs					
Distance between farm and marketplace (miles)	Revenue from sale of 1,000 pounds of wheat	Amount farmer pays to others (for seed, fertilizer, etc.)	Minimum amount farmer pays to himself (the amount the farmer would receive from his next-best alternative to farming)	Transportation costs to take wheat from farm to marketplace	Economic profit before paying rent for farmland	Maximum amount farmer is willing to pay to rent the farmland	Economic profit after paying rent for farmland
0	$2,000	$1,300	$200	-0-	$500	$500	-0-
10	2,000	1,300	200	$100	400	400	-0-
20	2,000	1,300	200	200	300	300	-0-
30	2,000	1,300	200	300	200	200	-0-
40	2,000	1,300	200	400	100	100	-0-
50	2,000	1,300	200	500	-0-	-0-	-0-
60	2,000	1,300	200	600	−100	Farmer chooses another occupation	

Note: In a situation in which farmers rent land, they will be willing to pay any amount of rent that leaves them with a profit greater than their next-best alternative occupation. Accordingly, landowners can charge rent up to those levels. The amount of profit, however, depends upon the costs of transporting the crops to the market. Higher transportation costs leave less profit. This leads to the array of rents in the column second from the right. For example, a farmer renting land at the marketplace would pay up to $500, while a farmer at 30 miles out would be willing to pay a maximum of only $200. A farmer at 60 miles out would be operating at a loss, compared with his next-best alternative occupation, and so would choose to stop farming.

from the center. The outcome of this process is illustrated in Panel A of **Figure 4.2,** which shows how the rent the farmers are willing to pay varies inversely with distance from the marketplace.

What if the market price of the crop increases? Each producer is a small part of the whole market, so no individual producer has any influence over price. But if the demand for the crop rises, its price will also rise. Panel B of Figure 4.2 shows the effect of a rise in the market price of the crop, **ceteris paribus**—a Latin phrase used in economics to mean "holding everything else constant." If the market price of the crop rises from $2 to $2.10, total revenue would rise to $2,100 ($2.10 × 1,000 lbs. of wheat). With production costs of $1,500 and transportation costs of $10/mile, it would be feasible to incur up to $600 in transportation costs and to grow this crop up to 60 miles from the marketplace. Given the new higher price for his wheat, the farmer at the outer limit would be willing to pay up to $600 to rent the land at the center. So the effect of an increase in the price of the product is to shift the **bid rent curve** out *parallel* to its original position, making land everywhere within the 60-mile radius more valuable. Landowners would benefit from the increase in the price of the farmers' crop.

What if transportation costs fell, instead of an increase in the price of the product? Panel C of Figure 4.2 illustrates this case. If transportation costs fell to $5/mile, it would be feasible to transport this crop 100 miles. However, since the savings in transportation costs from 100 miles out would still be $500, the rent at the center would not change. The bid rent curve pivots out around its vertical intercept so that land farther from the center is more valuable than before and land has a positive value all the way out to 100 miles. Distant locations become more valuable, and the ratio of the value of distant land to central city land rises throughout the metro area. As you might imagine, during the early 1900s, when local governments in many cities extended paved roadways into suburbs, and again after World War II, when major highways were constructed and became available to suburban residents, the roads and highways made it easier to live in suburbs (Baum-Snow 2007). Accordingly, the value of the land farther from the city increased. Landowners in what were previously farm communities could sell their land to housing developers for tract housing in new suburbs and to commercial and industrial developers who were building office parks and industrial parks far from the central city.

What Happens When There Is More Than One Bid Rent Curve?   What if the land can be used to grow more than one kind of crop? What if a second group of tenant farmers comes along, growing a crop that brings in more revenue but is more difficult to transport? If our first group of farmers is growing wheat, this second group might be growing tomatoes, which are more valuable but also more perishable and require special handling when they are transported. Assume that these tomato farmers are also identical to each other except for their location. They will also be arrayed along a bid rent curve, but their bid rent curve will be steeper. They have a greater desire to avoid transportation costs, so they place a higher value on accessibility and can pay more for it. Compared with our original example, these tomato farmers might receive $3,000 in total revenue, have $2,200 in production costs, and incur

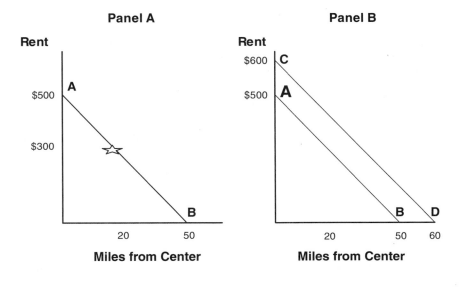

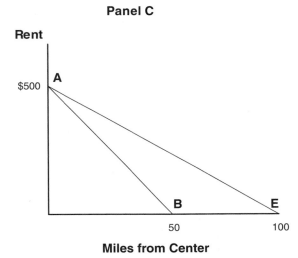

Figure 4.2 The Bid Rent Curve and the Effect of a Change in Product Price or a Change in Transportation Costs.

Panel A: Farmers face a trade-off between rent and transportation costs. If total revenue is $2,000 and production costs are $1,500, and if transportation costs are $10 per mile, it is feasible to operate within a 50-mile radius of the center. Compared with a location 50 miles away, a central location will save the farmer $500 in transportation costs, and that is what farmers would be willing to pay in rent. The sum of rent and transportation costs are $500 anywhere along the bid rent curve, line AB. At a distance 20 miles out, for example, transportation costs are $200 and rent would be $300.

Panel B: If the market price of the product increases, everything else constant, so that total revenue rises to $2,100, it is now feasible to operate within a 60-mile radius of the center. Since a central location now represents a savings of $600 in transportation costs for the farmer who is farthest away, rent at the center rises to $600. The bid rent curve has shifted out from AB to CD.

Panel C: Starting from our original situation in Panel A, if transportation costs fall from $10 per mile to $5 per mile, everything else constant, it is now feasible to operate within a 100-mile radius of the center. Since the savings in transportation costs from 100 miles out are still $500 in this example, that is still the rent that can be charged at the center. The bid rent curve pivots out from point A. The original curve is AB and the new curve is AE.

higher transportation costs of $20/mile because of the perishable nature of their crop. Thus, the tomato crop can be grown no farther than 40 miles away from the center because, at this point, the production costs ($2,200) plus transportation costs ($800) equal total revenue of $3,000. A tomato farmer, in this case, would be willing to pay $800 in rent for a site right next to the marketplace.

Now that there are two bid rent curves, there are several ways in which bidding occurs:

    a. As individuals, the wheat farmers compete against each other along their bid rent curve (Line AB in Panel A of **Figure 4.3**).

    b. As individuals, the tomato farmers compete against each other along their bid rent curve (Line CD in Panel A of Figure 4.3).

    c. The wheat farmers as a group compete against the tomato farmers as a group.

The landlord will rent to the highest bidder, so the group with the highest curve at any location will have the winning bid. Since the tomato farmers have the steeper curve, they will win the competition for the land that is closer in. The wheat farmers will outbid the tomato farmers for the land that is farther out. The land within a 30-mile radius will be planted in tomatoes; the concentric ring with a radius from 30 to 50 miles out will be planted in wheat, as illustrated in Panel B of Figure 4.3. Other uses of land can be added with additional bid rent curves.

As we shall see, this is the same type of process by which the concentric ring model of the city developed. Those with the greatest need for a central location bid up land prices in the central city, while those who could afford to be at a distance from the central city selected less expensive suburban locations to set up business.

Applying the Bid Rent Model to Metro Area Development. As Alonso realized, these insights of earlier economists about farmers and the rent they pay had direct applicability to the pattern of land use and land values in metropolitan regions. Essentially, the steeper the bid rent curve, the higher the value placed on accessibility to the center. And the higher the value per square foot of land, the more it made economic sense to use that land intensively by building multistory buildings that housed high-value operations—even if the construction cost per square foot of floor space in a skyscraper was significantly higher than the cost for a one- or two-story structure. The Empire State Building made sense in midtown Manhattan and the Sears Tower made sense in downtown Chicago because of the cost of land and the need for extensive face-to-face contact on a daily basis for core businesses that include law, financial services, and advertising. Since these enterprises were also likely to be doing business with people outside the metropolitan area, there was a need for downtown hotels. Some restaurants and venues for live entertainment were also particularly attracted to downtown locations. Uses that were more space-extensive, such as single-story factories and warehouses with flatter bid rent curves, moved to the outskirts of the metropolitan area. For many families that were priced out by the competition for land near downtown, life in high-density apartment buildings near the city center gave way to living in small single-family homes in the suburbs. If you

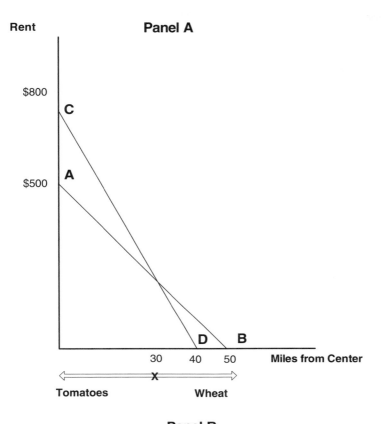

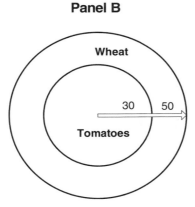

Figure 4.3 Bid Rent Curves for Two Different Uses of Land and the Resulting Land Distribution.

Panel A: Grain farmers compete against each other along bid rent curve AB. Tomato farmers, who grow a more profitable crop but incur higher transportation costs, compete against each other along bid rent curve CD. As a group, they outbid wheat farmers for the land within a 30-mile radius of the center. The grain farmers can outbid for the land in a concentric ring 30 to 50 miles away from the center.

Panel B: The resulting distribution of land is illustrated here. Tomato farmers operate within a 30-mile radius of the center, and wheat farmers operate in the concentric ring 30 to 50 miles away.

rotate bid rent curves 360 degrees around the city center, this model results in a pattern of concentric rings, as described by Burgess and illustrated in Figure 4.1, with the height of buildings declining in successive rings. Each type of land use had its own place, its own building height, and distance from the city center.

As one moved out from the center, land costs fell and lower-rise buildings were economically feasible. In the suburbs, single-story ranch-type homes were feasible, while the land costs for such housing were prohibitive closer to the city center. Flying over any large city even today provides visual evidence of this land-use pattern. The basic logic of the dynamics behind land values and land use in the Alonso model are also pertinent to sectoral and multinucleic models, as is discussed in Appendix A.

The Residential Paradox.   The parable of the wheat and tomato farmers also provides the basic framework for Alonso's resolution of the **residential paradox**—his observation that the poor often live on expensive land in the central city, while the wealthy tend to live on cheaper land in the suburbs. Metaphorically, then, the poor play the role of the tomato farmers. Unlike the tomato farmers, though, the poor do not have greater revenue with which to outbid the wealthy, so how can they afford to live there? The resolution of the paradox can be represented by the bid rent curve in **Figure 4.4**, but the explanation is a bit more complicated.

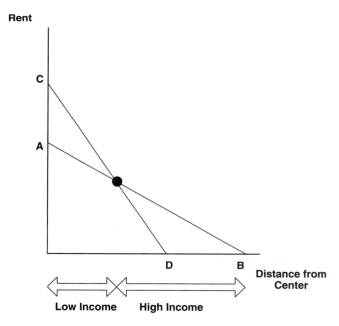

Figure 4.4 The Residential Paradox. All households prefer to live at low density. High-income households are able to absorb higher transportation costs in exchange for cheaper land and are represented by bid rent curve AB. Low-income households are unable to achieve their goal. They need to avoid high transportation costs and place a greater value on accessibility (bid rent curve CD). They pay for the more expensive land by living at higher density than they would otherwise prefer.

Alonso starts with the assumption that in the second half of the twentieth century, most U.S. families preferred to live at lower population density in the suburbs, and then shows why higher-income families were more likely to achieve that goal.

Let us assume that a low-income family and a high-income family both prefer to follow the American Dream of owning a single-family house on its own plot of land somewhere outside the city center. Assume further, for simplicity, that the low-income family has a budget for shelter and transportation of $1,000 per month, while the high-income family has a budget of $5,000 per month. Land values fall and transportation costs rise as we go farther from the center. The transportation costs are $100 per month close to the center, $200 per month 10 miles out, and $300 per month 20 miles out. Thus, as shown in **Table 4.2**, after paying for transportation costs, the rich and poor families would have left over for shelter, respectively, $4,900 and $900 near the center, $4,800 and $800 out 10 miles, and $4,700 and $700 out 20 miles. For each family, there is a trade-off between the falling price of land and the rising cost of transportation.

For the poor family, however, the transportation costs represent a large and dramatically growing percentage of their budget as they move farther out. They would be devoting 30 percent of their budget to transportation costs if they lived 20 miles out ($300/$1,000). The falling price of land does not compensate for the rate at which their budget diminishes. In the wealthy household, however, the increase in transportation cost is still a tiny portion of the family's budget. The lower price of land means the family can realize its desire to live at much lower density farther out. Alonso concludes that income and transportation costs constrain the lower-income family. As we saw in the history of the nineteenth-century suburbs, only the wealthier families could afford to commute downtown from their suburban homes.

The wealthier households outbid the poor for the land farther out. But how do the poor wind up "outbidding" the wealthy for the higher-priced land close to the center? They do so by choosing the best residential alternative available to them— living at much higher density. One four-person family in a single-family home on a half acre of land means a population density of only eight people per acre. But in

Table 4.2 Impact of Transportation Costs on Low-Income and High-Income Families

| Transportation Costs for Family | Low-Income Family: Budget $1,000 | | High-Income Family: Budget $5,000 | |
	Transportation as Percent of Budget	Amount Remaining for Shelter	Transportation as Percent of Budget	Amount Remaining for Shelter
Close to Center: $100	10%	$900	2%	$4,900
10 Miles Out: $200	20%	$800	4%	$4,800
20 Miles Out: $300	30%	$700	6%	$4,700

Note: Although a low-income family and a high-income family may have the same transportation costs, those costs represent a higher proportion of the budget for low-income families, leaving them with much less for other needs. Because high-income families are more able to absorb higher transportation costs, they are more likely than low-income families to move to suburbs with greater transportation costs.

central city tenements, there might be one hundred families per acre with a population density of 400 people per acre or more, depending on family size. The poor "outbid" the wealthy by pooling the purchasing power of many more families per acre to live at population densities that are unacceptably high to suburbanites. In fact, they are not so much "outbidding" as they are forced to accept a living situation that is often much denser than they would like if they could afford to live elsewhere.

Constrained Choice and Political Factors in Land Values and Location

The Alonso model, even extended to take into consideration travel distances and highways, focuses like all models on only a few key elements and necessarily simplifies the underlying reality. The hypothetical farmers described by Alonso looked only at the trade-off between rent and distance in their quest to maximize profits. They did not consider, for example, the quality of the soil or irrigation. Alonso's urban households had preferences only with regard to the population density where they desired to live and their willingness and ability to trade commuting costs for additional space.

In order to fully understand land use in the real world and the location dynamics underlying late-twentieth-century metropolitan areas, it is necessary to take into account a long list of physical constraints, individual preferences, social mores, and political considerations. For this reason, bid rent curves by themselves cannot tell the whole story about land values, where people live, or where businesses set up their operations. Understanding choice and constraints is important for understanding how individuals make decisions about where to live. As we will discuss more extensively in later chapters, the choices that individuals and firms can effectively make depend not just upon their individual proclivities but also upon their ability to wield various forms of power, and by the benefits they gain through actual or perceived membership in groups. The available set of choices changes over time, so these concepts are also important for understanding the consequences of changes in patterns of residential location and the development of cities.

Poor households are priced out of the market to the extent that municipalities enact laws and zoning regulations that prohibit more than one or two houses per acre, thus driving up the price of housing. The problem for a low-income family willing to accept the higher transportation costs of living in a suburb is that the multifamily housing such a household could afford is simply not available as a result of large-lot **exclusionary zoning**. Thus, political decisions over land use changes the final disposition of land and its price from what the market would otherwise establish.

Taking factors other than simple bid rent curves into account is also necessary because there are many things that individuals want when deciding where to live. The ideal home might be a place with an incredible view, with just the right proximity to work, friends, and shopping. To be optimal, it would be exactly the right size and would have precisely the features desired by the owner. It would be far from the things that people try to avoid such as pollution and crime, but would have access to outdoor activities, entertainment, or other sources of enjoyment.

Typically, however, the ideal home in the ideal location is not attainable for any but the wealthiest families. Just about everyone else is faced with a range of constraints when making choices. One constraint is simply that the ideal home in the ideal place may not exist; it is a figment of imagination. More likely, there are budget constraints; most of us cannot afford the perfect place with all the features we want. There are constraints imposed by social institutions. For example, a city may not allow the construction of housing in the most desirable location because of environmental laws. Social convention or outright discrimination may limit housing choices for particular racial or ethnic groups. Instead of being able to get everything we want, we have to consider what is feasible, examine the trade-offs contained in this more limited set of possibilities, and then select from among the available and affordable alternatives.

The Evolution of Twentieth-Century U.S. Metropolitan Areas

With the Alonso theory and some understanding of the social and political constraints placed on location as preface, we can examine the way land use in American cities changed over the course of the twentieth century. We first examine the factors that affected business location and then turn our attention to changes in residential location.

The Decentralization of Business Location

As technology opened up the possibility of new, cheaper forms of transportation, other costs of production became relatively more important. To remain competitive, company managers had to solve a more complex cost equation in which transport costs were only one item in a growing list.

Essentially, managers had to reconsider the fundamental equation for business profits:

$$\text{profits} = \text{total revenue (TR)} - \text{total costs (TC)}$$

where total revenue refers to the total value of the goods and services sold by the firm and total costs refers to all the costs a firm incurs in producing its product or service.

In our simple bid rent model, we assumed that all of the wheat farmers faced identical production costs, as did all of the tomato farmers. None of the farmers needed to take tax rates into account because our simple model did not include any role for government. Although the bid rent curve illustrates the trade-off between rent and transportation costs, we must acknowledge that production costs, site costs, taxes, and government regulatory burden can also vary at different locations throughout the metropolitan area and from one metro region to another. These factors can influence the choice of a site, once transportation is assured.

Looking more closely at the concept of costs, we can identify five broad categories:

- **Production costs** are incurred in the actual manufacture of a good or service, including the cost of labor and raw material.
- **Transportation costs** are incurred in moving inputs to business and shipping the output to points of sale.
- **Site costs** are incurred in procuring the land and buildings that the business occupies.
- **Taxes** and **fees** comprise levies imposed on business by local, state, and federal government.
- **Regulatory costs** are incurred by business in the course of complying with local, state, and federal law, including environmental protection requirements.

As this list makes evident, to maximize profits, business owners must ultimately consider a large number of location-dependent costs and array these against the economies of scale and agglomeration economies offered by any particular location.

The location decisions of firms changed in the twentieth century, as transportation constraints weakened, the composition of industry shifted from resource extraction to manufacturing to services, and new products and new techniques of production emerged. The resulting shift in the geography of work sites contributed significantly to changes in the overall patterns of land use in urban areas. We can see this historically in the ever-changing location of business activity in the metro region.

Post–World War II Business Location

As we noted in Chapter 3, early cities in the United States were built on the sea, along canals, or next to rivers because transportation costs dominated all others and water transport was the most efficient method available. In the nineteenth century, the railroad opened up the possibility of building cities away from the water and made it possible for cities to trade goods even when they did not share a common waterway. The early street railway and road systems made it possible for some people and some firms to move to the periphery beyond the central city, and thus the first inner-ring suburbs were born.

Constraints due to transportation costs continued to dissipate in the twentieth century. By 1950, fewer firms were limited by transportation, thanks to the dense web of paved highways and roads that had been constructed by local municipalities, states, and the federal government. Therefore, many locations could flourish in the production of each good and service. As we saw earlier, Detroit, still known as the Motor City because it was the center of production for the nation's three largest domestic producers—General Motors, Ford, and Chrysler—would lose its stature as the primary location for auto production throughout the last decades of the twentieth century. The corporate headquarters remained there, but production increasingly moved to other parts of the Midwest and the South, as well as to Canada and Mexico. With the ability to move parts and assemblies around the country by rail and by truck, Ford could assemble cars as cheaply in Atlanta and Chicago as in Dearborn, Michigan—a nearby suburb of Detroit. As transportation costs declined as a share of total costs, and as air-conditioning permitted comfortable living in the heat of Arizona or the heat and humidity of Florida, cities could expand almost anywhere, as long as there was a good reason for people to congregate at a particular place or region.

The post–World War II transportation revolution took many forms. The passage of the Federal-Aid Highway Act of 1956—also known as the National Interstate and Defense Highways Act—which led to the construction of 42,500 miles of super-highways crisscrossing America, provided more direct, reliable, speedy truck transportation that reduced the costs of both short- and long-distance hauling. Wider, double-barreled highways with median strips permitted longer trucks and, in many locations, tandem trailers.

Containerization transformed the way goods were transported by ship, making it easier to shift cargo from sea to rail to road, thereby reducing transshipment costs. As for rail transportation, the full adoption of powerful diesel locomotives in the 1940s and 1950s, replacing the slower and costlier steam-powered engines, made it possible to haul more container cars in a single train with fewer time-consuming stops to replenish fuel supplies. Double-stack container cars known as "trailer on flat car" (TOFC) provided more volume for cargo, further reducing transportation costs.

The introduction of the supertanker and the supercargo ship made it possible to haul huge amounts of cargo across long distances. This added to the possibility of fragmenting production processes over longer distances. By the end of the twentieth century, General Motors Corporation (GM) was producing its sporty Pontiac GTO for the American market in Australia, shipping key components from the United States for assembly Down Under and then shipping the completed vehicles back to the United States for distribution and sale. Excess assembly capacity in GM's Holden car division in Australia encouraged the company to use this production strategy for their specialized, limited-production, high-performance vehicle. Without the revolution in shipping technology and in communications that made such production coordination possible, long-distance manufacturing would not have become anywhere near as cost effective.

Satellite-linked telephone communication followed the successful launch of America's first man-made satellites in 1958, and jumbo jet aircraft—such as the Boeing 747—were introduced in 1969. Together, these technologies made it possible to ship higher-valued cargo across the globe at nearly the speed of sound, and gave corporate managers the ability to travel halfway across the earth in a single day and to coordinate worldwide production of goods and services at nearly the speed of light.

With all of the new transportation and communications technology available to business, transportation costs plummeted in the second half of the twentieth century. Glaeser and Kohlhase report that by 2001, the average cost (adjusted for inflation) of moving a ton of goods one mile by rail was only one-eighth of what it was in 1890. When all forms of transportation were taken into account (including trucking, which is more expensive than rail), the transportation costs for goods fell by more than 1 percent each year between 1960 and 1992 (Glaeser and Kohlhase 2004). The lowered transportation costs and the consequent freedom for businesses to consider locations farther away allowed firms to search widely in a bid to lower other input costs—most importantly, the cost of labor. In competitive industries, the ability to use lower-cost labor in the American South encouraged firms to take advantage of this option or to seek out highly specialized labor that added to the value of the end product. Cities like Atlanta, Miami, and Houston became powerful business centers that rivaled many in the Northeast and Midwest. The population center of the United States moved south and west.

The effect of these changes on manufacturing costs, and the subsequent decision by many manufacturing companies to move production to other geographic areas, has been called **deindustrialization**. In *The Deindustrialization of America*, Bluestone and Harrison (1982) identify four dynamics that affected cities: (1) the redirection of profits from successful plants in existing locations to build new facilities elsewhere, (2) decisions not to replace machinery that was wearing out or becoming obsolete so that the money saved could be used to build facilities elsewhere, (3) relocating some of the equipment from one facility to a new facility in a distant location, and (4) shutting down plants and moving or selling the building and equipment. As we shall see in Chapter 6, where we discuss the dynamics underlying the prosperity of cities, the relocation of key businesses and industries without their replacement by new businesses has both direct and indirect effects on the economy of metropolitan areas.

The key point is that in the decades following World War II, the viability of many older cities was placed in jeopardy as new locations vied to be production centers for their once-vaunted goods. With the revolution in transportation technology, older urban areas were threatened (e.g., Detroit, Michigan, and Akron and Toledo, Ohio), while newer urban areas in the South and West—and increasingly in Mexico, in Europe, and in Japan—became production centers for consumer products used everywhere in the country.

At the same time that lower transportation costs spread economic activity across the country and even to other countries, new roads and highways were transforming the character and location of activities *within* each individual metro region. The social role of cities and suburbs changed dramatically, challenging the very economic viability of many older central cities.

The Rise of the Post–World War II Suburb

Nothing transformed the relationship between city and suburb more than the automobile. It was the dramatic increase in automobile ownership after World War II that led to explosive growth in suburban residential development. Instead of locating within walking distance of stops along the rail lines, individuals could locate anywhere there were roads. Residential development, which had been concentrated along the rail line spokes, spread out to cover a broader area. In 1948, there were 33 million automobiles registered in the United States. By 1960, there were 61 million cars on the road and the number doubled again to 124 million by 1980. The percentage of families owning at least one automobile surged from 54 percent in 1948 to 77 percent in 1960 (U.S. Bureau of the Census 1950, 2006). While individual states built new highways that connected city to suburb and city to city, the passage of the 1956 Federal-Aid Highway Act ultimately put the national economy on wheels. The interstate highway system not only facilitated interstate commerce but also allowed workers to commute longer distances and consumers to drive to the suburban mall for convenient retail shopping within the same metro area. Living in the suburbs became feasible for tens of millions of families whose breadwinners worked in the central city or in rapidly growing office parks and shopping centers constructed adjacent to suburban highways and circumferential roads.

Suburbanization was also spurred by changes in technology associated with the construction of housing. In the early twentieth century, houses were typically built one at a time, with most contractors building no more than five houses per year. However, after World War II, new mass-production techniques—including the standardization of building components and implementation of a division of construction labor into simple, repetitive steps—were increasingly used to build suburban housing. These changes led to house building on an unprecedented scale and the development of massive suburban subdivisions. The largest of these, in Levittown, New York, comprised 17,400 houses (Jackson 1985). With such techniques, houses were built faster and were available at lower costs than before, adding to the economic incentives for families to move to suburbs.

Along with changes in residential location came a further decentralization of business locations. Corporate headquarters generally remained downtown in what became taller and taller office towers, where managers could meet face-to-face with their accountants, lawyers, and other business service providers. With prime real estate downtown escalating in price per square foot, it no longer made economic sense for manufacturers and those who operated warehouses to stay there or in the inner ring of suburbs. Cheaper and faster transportation made it cost effective to move to suburban locations farther and farther from the central business district. The rapidly increasing highway and road system that surrounded the city made it possible for employees to get to work and for their products to get to market.

The Impact of Federal Policies on Suburbanization

Not surprisingly, there was an emptying out of the residential areas in most older central cities after World War II, as the highway network expanded and autos and trucks became the primary mode of transportation. Downtown department stores and other retail outlets followed suit, moving to the suburbs to be near their customers. The federal government also reinforced this trend toward suburbanization through Internal Revenue Service (IRS) personal income tax provisions that favored home ownership and through the operations of two of its agencies, the Federal Housing Authority (FHA) and the Veterans Administration (VA). When federal income taxes were established in 1913, the provisions included a deduction for interest paid on home mortgages, which made home ownership more economically advantageous than renting. This did not help renters who lived in central city apartment buildings—at least until late in the twentieth century, when many apartments were converted to owner-occupied condominiums. For most of the post–World War II period up until then, this tax provision spurred the production of single-family homes in suburbia. The deductibility of local residential property taxes against the federal income tax made the bias in favor of home ownership even greater.

Changes in the structure of home mortgages added to the demand for home ownership and, therefore, the choice of suburbia for many families. Before the early 1930s, a five- to seven-year mortgage was typical, with a high down payment, interest rates of up to 12 percent, and a substantial final payment. The sudden economic downturn that began in 1929 created high unemployment and numerous defaults on mortgages. To stabilize the situation of both home buyers and lenders, the federal government created the Home Owners Loan Corporation (HOLC) in 1933 to provide a means for home owners in cities and suburbs to refinance their loans at low interest rates over fifteen years. A year later, the federal government created the Federal Housing Authority (FHA) to insure private bank loans used for buying or repairing homes. This made it possible for banks and other mortgage lenders to offer even lower mortgage interest rates and the extension of mortgages to as long as thirty years.

In practice, the FHA guidelines supported newly constructed single-family homes to the exclusion of other forms of new housing and to the detriment of the existing housing stock. Families who might have preferred homes in more densely populated parts of urban areas found that they often were not eligible for the new low-interest, long-term mortgages. For such families, there was a great incentive to build their new home in the suburbs. In sum, the HOLC and FHA provided another major shift in trade-offs for families' residential decisions, not only by reducing the cost of moving but also by reducing the forgone benefits of staying.

Meanwhile, in efforts to reduce housing shortages for veterans returning from World War II, the Veterans Administration created a mortgage program under the Servicemen's Readjustment Act of 1944, which allowed veterans to buy houses with no down payment. The mortgage loans were guaranteed by the federal government—if the person who took out the loan defaulted, the government would pay the lender the amount remaining on the loan—so that lenders incurred no risks (Jackson 1985; Palen 1995). The FHA and VA programs, together with the highway transport revolution, led to a mushrooming of suburbs at the end of World War II, when wartime restrictions on residential construction were removed.

By 1950, the population of suburbs was growing ten times faster than the population in central cities. After 1950, central city populations began to decrease sharply in many metro areas, as the number of people leaving cities for suburbs surpassed the number of people moving to the central cities. We can see this general trend by

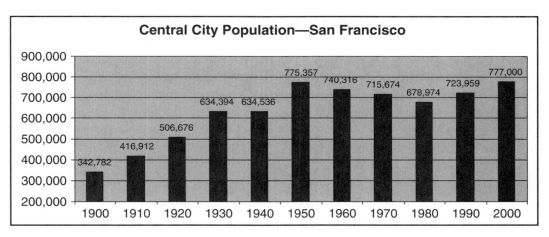

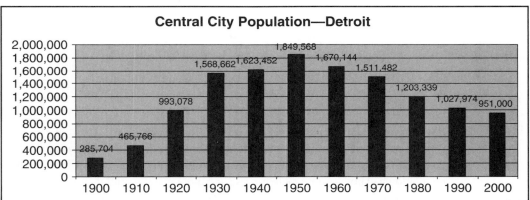

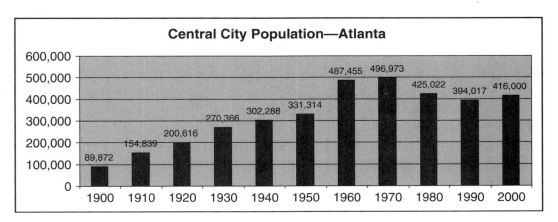

Figure 4.5 Central City Population, 1900–2000. *Sources:* Gibson 1998; U.S. Department of Housing and Urban Development, HUD User Policy Development and Research Information Service, SOCDS data set, 2007, http://socds.huduser.org.

Table 4.3 Percent of Metropolitan
Population Living in Central
Cities

Year	Percent in Central Cities
1910	64.6
1920	66.0
1930	64.6
1940	62.7
1950	58.6
1960	51.4
2000	37.4

Note: As this table shows, the percentage of the
metropolitan population living in central cities has
declined through most of the twentieth century,
from 66 percent in 1920, to under 59 percent in
1950, to just above 37 percent in 2000.
Sources: McKelvey 1973, p. 126. Data for 2000
come from U.S. Bureau of the Census 2005.

looking at just a few cases—San Francisco, Detroit, and Atlanta—illustrated in
Figure 4.5. This figure presents the decennial central city population living in San
Francisco from 1900 through 2000. Note that the population more than doubled
through mid-century, but from 1950 through 1980, it declined. Only after 1980 was
there a movement back into the central city, and it took until 2000 for the Golden
Gate City to regain the population peak it had a half century earlier. Detroit's
population had both a more meteoric rise and more meteoric fall than San Francisco.
As Figure 4.5 reveals, Detroit's population grew six times over in the first half the
twentieth century only to see its population fall by 50 percent in the next half
century. Indeed, Detroit's central city population at the turn of the twenty-first
century was smaller than it was in 1920, just after the end of World War I. Atlanta
was somewhere between these two cities, as Figure 4.5 demonstrates; its population
kept rising right through 1970, but has declined since.

Among all metro areas in the United States, the percent of the metropolitan
population living in central cities remained roughly constant at 63 to 66 percent
between 1910 and 1940, as **Table 4.3** shows. But just twenty years later in 1960, it
was down to half (51.4%) of the total metro population. The suburbs were burgeoning. In the next forty years, the central city population continued to decline so
that by 2000, only 38 percent of the U.S. metro population was living there. More
than three-fifths of metro area residents lived in the suburbs, which were spreading
farther and farther over the landscape.

With residential funding focused on suburban areas and in the new cities of the
South and the West, the housing stock in central cities deteriorated, particularly in
the older industrial cities of the Northeast and the Midwest. Older housing in need
of repair suffered from a lack of viable financing alternatives. Abandoned buildings
became common in many cities. This generated another incentive to move to suburbs

for those who had the choice. In many metro areas, this resulted in the juxtaposition of increasingly wealthy suburbs surrounding increasingly dilapidated central cities, a phenomenon we still see in many metro regions today.

In summary, during the past two hundred years, innovations in transportation and housing construction, and a changing set of economic and political constraints have shifted the balance of centripetal and centrifugal forces. This has changed the decision framework of possibilities and opportunity costs and has transformed the location decisions of families as well as the uses of both central and more distant land. As we shall discuss further in Chapter 5, this change continues, as digital technology has created opportunities for some workers to pursue productive work at home through their connection to computer networks to workplaces miles away.

Class, Race, and Ethnic Segregation in the American City

While the combined impact of technological change and public policy decisions led to changes in the spatial form of metropolitan areas, each successive wave of foreign immigration in the late nineteenth and early twentieth centuries held the possibility for tension between newcomers and those descended from earlier immigrants. This contributed to major changes, not so much across cities as within them. Residential segregation along social class and ethnic and racial lines ensued; many cities had their "Chinatowns," "Greektowns," and "Poletowns," where families of one or another ethnic group congregated.

In those cases where proximity to work was an important factor in residential location, recruitment and hiring dynamics also contributed to the creation of segregated neighborhoods with relatively homogeneous populations. Some employers chose to recruit among certain ethnic groups; other employers found that hiring individuals referred by existing workers was worthwhile, thereby reinforcing ethnic segregation. For other firms, word of vacancies quickly spread within ethnic neighborhoods, even if the employer was not consciously seeking to recruit certain groups. To some extent, segregation was also a matter of personal choice, as many families chose to live near their co-ethnics for various forms of networking support. Thus, within the overall contours of centrifugal and centripetal forces, social and market forces existed for the clustering of individual groups.

Until World War II, the greatest urban disparities in job opportunities and living standards were found among white ethnic groups, especially in northern cities. But after World War II, with the full mechanization of the cotton harvest, newly unemployed black farmworkers and sharecroppers from the Mississippi Delta and other parts of the Cotton Belt came North in search of blue-collar jobs. Whites from depressed communities in West Virginia, Kentucky, and Tennessee also followed the trail to manufacturing jobs in midwestern cities. These workers sought jobs in the burgeoning auto, steel, and other manufacturing industries in cities like Detroit; Chicago; Gary, Indiana; Newark, New Jersey; and Cleveland, Ohio. As **Table 4.4** indicates, more than 1.5 million black Americans migrated out of the South between

1940 and 1950, followed by similar numbers in the 1950s and 1960s. The overwhelming majority came to the northeastern and north central states.

The demographic patterns within metropolitan areas during this period reflect a history of discrimination. Racism manifested itself in labor and housing markets. Many employers refused to hire African Americans or relegated them to the lowest-paying menial positions. This helped to create what became in the following decades an increasing gulf between a rapidly rising standard of living for a predominantly white middle class in the suburbs and an overwhelmingly black "underclass," increasingly concentrated in the central city (Wilson 1987, 1996).

Before 1920, racially motivated violence in a number of cities had led to the destruction of African American homes, the forcible removal of families from white neighborhoods, and, in some instances, even loss of life. African American businesses were destroyed in Chicago, Philadelphia, Tulsa, and Wilmington, North Carolina. Anti-Chinese riots occurred in Los Angeles, Denver, and Seattle. Just as proximity to work was a major historical constraint in residential decision making for many families, discrimination and violence operated as a major constraint for some groups, affecting the possibilities and opportunity costs involved in their location decisions.

From 1930 on, however, the most influential discriminatory influences were the same federal government programs discussed earlier in this chapter that helped many white families move to the suburbs—the Federal Housing Authority and the Home Owners Loan Corporation. The FHA and the HOLC advocated both residential segregation and "redlining"—the explicit classification of African American neighborhoods as the least desirable areas for financial institutions to make

Table 4.4 Estimated Migration of Black Americans from the South

Year	Net Migration from South	Migration Regional Destinations		
		Northeastern States	North Central States	Western States
1880–1890	70,000	46,000	24,000	NA
1890–1900	168,000	105,000	63,000	NA
1900–1910	170,000	95,000	56,000	20,000
1910–1920	454,000	182,000	244,000	28,000
1920–1930	749,000	349,000	364,000	36,000
1930–1940	347,000	171,000	128,000	49,000
1940–1950	1,599,000	463,000	618,000	339,000
1950–1960	1,473,000	496,000	541,000	293,000
1960–1970	1,380,000	612,000	382,000	301,000

Note: This table enumerates the Great Migration, discussed in Chapters 3 and 4. The period from 1910 into the 1930s was characterized by what historians call the first wave of the migration. The peak of the first wave that lasted from about 1914 into the 1930s occurred during the 1920s, when 749,000 black Americans from the South moved to other regions. The second wave of the migration, between 1940 and 1970, was much larger. During this period, nearly 4.5 million black Americans moved from the South to other parts of the United States. In the 1940s, migration reached almost 1.6 million. As shown in the three columns farthest to the right, the most common destinations before 1940 were the northeastern and north central states, but the western states were a very significant migration destination after 1940.
Source: U.S. Bureau of the Census 1979, table 8, p. 15.

mortgages and other loans. From 1930 to 1950, the official code of ethics of the National Association of Real Estate Boards, the professional group representing real estate brokers, stated that selling homes in white neighborhoods to African Americans would be a violation of professional standards. Racially restrictive covenants that barred both current and future sale of housing and land to nonwhites became common. Even in the absence of such documents, refusal to sell to nonwhites was typical in new post–World War II suburban communities, including the affordable communities filled with mass-produced housing, such as Levittown, New York. The resulting demographic geography of metropolitan areas came to reflect distinct racial patterns in the period between 1920 and 1970. The discrimination visited on black families would have repercussions on their children and grandchildren.

With jobs moving to the suburbs and most African Americans trapped by residential segregation in central cities, the employment opportunities for inner-city residents deteriorated. With a growing gap between the wealth of the suburbs and the poverty of the central cities, anger spilled over into the streets of many cities. Major urban riots scarred Detroit, Newark, Washington, D.C., Los Angeles, and a host of smaller cities in the mid-1960s.

Segregation, especially with regard to race, still dominates virtually all cities in the United States. Nevertheless, from 1970 to the present, as a result of the passage and enforcement of antidiscrimination laws in employment, housing, and lending, as well as changing racial attitudes, there has been a movement of African Americans, Asian Americans, and Latinos to suburban areas. Today's metropolitan areas are demographically different from those of fifty years ago, just as those of 1950 were different from those of 1900.

In 2000, there was no single pattern that described every metro area. According to studies of the 2000 census, in 24 of the 102 largest metro areas, African Americans constitute 10 percent or more of suburban residents. Hispanic and Asian suburban residents are found in large numbers in 35 of these largest metro areas—specifically, in those metro areas that were major centers of immigration during the 1990s. But, as discussed further in Chapter 12, considerable segregation remains in many metropolitan areas (Frey 2001; Glaeser and Vigdor 2001; Logan et al. 2001; Frey and Myers 2005). The history of migration flows and differences in economic opportunity still play a crucial role in the demographic patterns of U.S. metropolitan areas.

New Immigration and the Cities

Until the mid-1960s, the labor force in cities grew mainly through internal migration, since immigration had been restricted for the previous four decades. After 1965, however, the United States experienced a new wave of immigration from abroad. Congress passed the Hart-Cellar Act in 1965, with the intent of removing discrimination against Southern and Eastern Europeans by eliminating the national origins quotas that had favored Great Britain, Germany, and Ireland. The act placed new emphasis on family unification, which should have favored European nations, but when it passed, it also removed quotas on residents in former British colonies, including Jamaica and Trinidad and Tobago. With Great Britain limiting immigration itself, far more immigrants came to the United States from these Caribbean countries than expected.

The new law also permitted political refugees from other countries to enter without quota and allowed immediate family members of U.S. citizens (spouses, parents, and minor children) to be admitted outside of quotas. As a result, during the 1970s and 1980s, a new wave of immigrants came to the United States, many coming to cities in the West and Southwest. War refugees from Vietnam and Cambodia came to California and Texas. Political refugees from El Salvador, Guatemala, and Nicaragua came north to escape civil war and civil strife. On the East Coast, a flood of Cubans settled in Miami. Haitians and Jamaicans, fleeing political and economic strife immigrated to cities like New York and Boston. Ethiopians, fleeing civil war, came to Washington, D.C. In the course of all this in-migration, the combination of powerful push factors that emanated from political and economic repression and the pull factors of American jobs and a better standard of living helped repopulate many U.S. cities.

Like those who came before them, today's immigrants tend to settle in the largest metropolitan areas in the country. Indeed, more than half (54.5%) of all the foreign-born people now living in the United States live in the largest nine metropolitan areas of the country, those with populations of 5 million or more. In contrast, only 27.3 percent of the native born population lives in these large urban centers. Immigrants make up nearly 30 percent of the population in the Los Angeles metro area, more than 28 percent of San Francisco's inhabitants, and nearly 23 percent of New York's (see **Table 4.5**). The concentration of immigrants is particularly high within the central cities of large metropolitan regions, where more than one in four residents (26%) is now foreign born. Across metro regions in the United States in 2000, first-generation immigrants accounted for nearly one in six residents (16%) as compared to one in ten (10%) in the suburbs alone.

Combined with the native born, who come to these same central cities, often as college students and young professionals, the composition of many of these cities has undergone a dramatic transformation. To take one extraordinary example, as late as 1950, the city of Boston's population was 95 percent white, with large numbers of first-, second-, and third-generation Irish and Italian families. A decade later, the "minority" population, mostly African American, made up nearly 10 percent of the central city's residents. Just two decades later, in 1980, nearly one in three residents was black, Hispanic, or Asian. In just another two decades, in 2000, Boston's booming economy was anchored in a central city "majority minority," with just over half of the residents reporting they were black, Asian, Hispanic, Native American, or multiracial.

Indeed, without the increased flow of immigration into America's twenty-five largest cities during the 1990s, these cities would have seen their combined population decline in size. In seven of these cities—San Diego, San Jose, New York, San Francisco, Chicago, Los Angeles, and Boston—the central cities grew only because of the presence of new immigrants (Sum and Pond 2002).

Table 4.5 Foreign-Born Population in Metropolitan Areas with 5 Million or More People, 2000
(Civilian Noninstitutional Population Plus Armed Forces Living Off-Post or with Their Families On-Post)

Metropolitan Area	Percent of Total Metro Population
New York-Northern New Jersey-Long Island, NY-NJ-CT-PA CMSA	22.8
Los Angeles-Riverside-Orange County, CA CMSA	29.6
Chicago-Gary-Kenosha, IL-IN-WI CMSA	12.3
Washington-Baltimore, DC-MD-VA-WV CMSA	11.9
San Francisco-Oakland-San Jose, CA CMSA	28.3
Philadelphia-Wilmington-Atlantic City, PA-NJ-DE-MD CMSA	5.1
Detroit-Ann Arbor-Flint, MI CMSA	7.4
Boston-Worcester-Lawrence, MA-NH-ME-CT CMSA	12.5
Dallas-Ft. Worth, TX CMSA	12.8

Note: As this table shows, immigration plays a significant role in the populations of many metropolitan areas. More than one-quarter of the population in the Los Angeles metro area and the San Francisco metro area are foreign-born, while the New York metro area is only slightly under one-quarter. The Chicago, Washington, D.C., Boston, and Dallas-Ft. Worth metro areas all have foreign-born populations above 10 percent.
Source: U.S. Bureau of the Census 2001, table 5-2A.

Cross-Currents of the Late Twentieth Century: Sunbelt Cities, Edge Cities, and Gentrification

Toward the end of the twentieth century, further changes in transportation and communications as well as a new source of demographic change—the aging of the U.S. population—contributed to the rapid growth of new cities in the South and West that were organized around recreation and retirement. In addition to the growth of these new metropolitan areas, existing metropolitan areas found that more and more of the traditional functions of the central city were now being replicated in the suburbs. Yet, even as these phenomena seemed to reduce the importance of established central cities, other changes led to the resurgence in the desirability of central city living among a self-selected group of higher-income households. We examine each of these phenomena in turn.

The Rise of Sunbelt Cities

As the core of the U.S. economy shifted away from **primary sector industries** (agriculture and mining) to **secondary sector industries** (manufacturing and construction) and then to the **tertiary sector industries** that are composed of wholesale and retail trade and business and personal service industries, the size and location of metropolitan areas came to depend less heavily on satisfying the need for transportation and more on the growth of mass consumer markets for an array of goods and services that were once only affordable by the affluent.

Tourism and retirement communities provide good examples. While tourism *contributes* to the economies of cities like New York, Boston, and San Francisco (which have long economic histories based on trading and manufacturing), it became an important *foundation* of economic growth for places like Orlando and Las Vegas. In 1960, before Walt Disney World was built in Orlando, the Orlando metropolitan area had a total population of 395,000. By the end of the century, the Orlando metro area held almost 1.65 million residents, its growth fueled largely by its emergence in the last decades of the century as one of the foremost vacation and convention destinations in the world. Similarly, the Las Vegas metro area had fewer than 275,000 residents in 1970; three decades later, due to economic growth based mainly on tourism, it too had ballooned, to 1.6 million residents.

Important changes in consumer spending made these developments possible. Through the course of the twentieth century, airplane travel ceased to be the province of the wealthy, as it had been before mid-century. Similarly, the paid vacation became a common job benefit during World War II, when unions could not easily negotiate wage increases because of wartime wage and price controls. Cheaper, quicker travel and more leisure time made tourism a skyrocketing industry. The growth in the number of relatively affluent retirees contributed not only to the demand for tourism but also for year-round retirement communities. These trends, augmented by the introduction and spread of air-conditioning, were responsible for propelling the boomtown cities of the South and Southwest as tourist destinations, convention locales, and places for northern retirees to leave their winter homes behind.

The Rise of Edge Cities

The term **edge city** was coined by the journalist Joel Garreau (1991) to describe a pattern of urban growth where there are multiple urban cores in the outer rings of metropolitan areas. Edge cities are often built around large retail malls or the intersection of two or more major highways located well beyond the central city. They are sometimes called suburban business districts, suburban cores, mini-cities, urban subcenters, or even superburbia, technoburbs, peripheral centers, urban villages, or suburban downtowns. An edge city, according to Garreau's criteria, must have a minimum of 5 million square feet of leasable office space and at least 600,000 square feet of retail space. Using these criteria, there were approximately 250 edge cities in North America by the end of the twentieth century, with southern California, the metro area of Washington, D.C., and metro New York having the largest concentrations. These edge cities contained two-thirds of all the office space in the United States, up from just 25 percent in 1970 (Soja 2001). With the rise of edge cities where both jobs and housing are located, cross-commuting between suburbs increased dramatically (Judd and Swanstrom 2004).

The archetypal edge city is Tysons Corner, Virginia, outside Washington, D.C. It is located near the junctions of Interstate 495, Interstate 66, and Virginia 267 (the route from Washington, D.C., to Dulles International Airport). Until a few decades ago, Tysons Corner was little more than a small village, but by the end of the 1990s, it was home to the largest retail area on the East Coast south of New York City, with 6 anchor department stores and more than 230 stores in all, more than

3,400 hotel rooms, more than 100,000 jobs, and more than 25 million square feet of office space.

Going back to the Alonso model, we can see how the rise of edge cities changes the shape of bid rent curves. The bid rent curves we presented earlier in this chapter were drawn on the basis of **monocentrism** or **mononuclearity**—one central city with land values that decline the farther away one moves from the center. Until the massive relocation of firms and households after World War II, this was an emi-nently reasonable model that described reasonably well the evolving pattern of metro areas. With the development of new centers of commerce and with residential com-munities located farther and farther away from the central city, monocentrism no longer prevailed. Nonetheless, the general implication of the bid rent curve analysis still applies: The places to which people want access will increase in value. In the final chapter of *Location and Land Use*, Alonso (1964) considered several types of polycentric metropolitan forms, one of which has two independent centers of un-equal size. This model is similar to the notion of edge cities.

If the bid rent curves used to decline monotonically, we can now replace those bid rent curves with ones that decline with distance away from the center, but have up-ticks as the distance to an edge city or a circumferential highway interchange de-clines (see **Figure 4.6**).

In some metropolitan areas, such upticks occur in a radius around an inner-ring circumferential highway and again around an outer-ring circumferential highway. It is no coincidence that many of the newer edge cities are in just such places. Thus, although we need to recognize the limitations of the bid rent curve analysis,

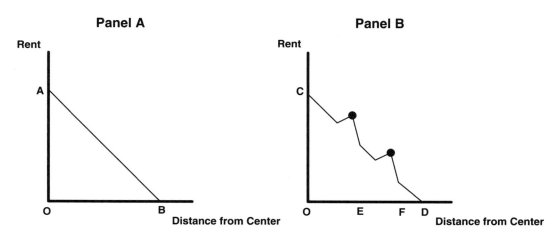

Figure 4.6 A Monocentric Bid Rent Curve versus a Bid Rent Curve for a Region with Edge Cities.

Panel A: In a monocentric city, the bid rent curve declines steadily the farther away form the center one travels because the center is the only point to which people desire access.

Panel B: With the advent of edge cities, there is more than one place to which people want access. If there is significant economic activity in edge cities along an inner-ring circumferential highway OE miles from the center and an outer-ring circumferential highway OF miles from the center, access to these sites will raise their land value, as reflected in upticks on the bid rent curve.

we can also acknowledge that the fundamental ideas contained in this formulation provide a helpful tool in understanding the dynamics of urban land markets, even in this new era of edge cities and the dense suburb.

Since 1980, there have been new centrifugal forces emerging from developing technology. Information retrieval through the Internet, videoconferencing, and other advances has made possible virtually instantaneous communication from remote locations. With this has come an even greater expansion in edge cities, which rely upon continuing advances in transportation technology to allow firms and customers to locate even farther out from central city locations.

Central Cities and Gentrification

Even as edge cities continued to grow, many central cities experienced a renaissance as they became more attractive to some higher-income households. Given all of the reasons discussed earlier for why higher-income households moved to the suburbs, and the continuing overall shift of jobs and population growth to suburban areas, what accounts for this ebb tide of wealthier households choosing to move in the other direction?

Decisions get a lot more complicated when transportation costs rise sharply because of highway congestion. "Free" highways may exist, and during much of the post–World War II era, gasoline was fairly cheap—with the exception of the period immediately following the 1973 oil embargo. What became expensive was the time spent in commuting along increasingly crowded roadways. In a growing number of cities, highways were no longer able to accommodate the heavy load of commuting traffic. Since "time is money," the increase in commuting time took its toll on suburban dwellers. In this case, some richer suburbanites began to reconsider their location decisions. Moving downtown—especially given all variety of close-by amenities including restaurants, museums, music venues, and boutique shopping—became a desirable option for an increasing number of households. Many of these were empty nesters, who preferred the suburbs while raising school-age children, but for whom the central city now provided the preferred place to live. Young professionals—usually without children—were also attracted to the central city for the same amenities.

In some cities, this form of relocation gave way to a new model of residential land use: high-rent apartments and townhouses at the center for the well-to-do, a ring of low-income tenants in the city around the central core, and middle-income families in the suburbs. This process, called **gentrification**, can also be illustrated using Alonso's bid rent curves. Our earlier discussion of the residential paradox was based on the assumption that everyone wanted to live at low density. However, if we acknowledge that there are some groups who prefer high density and that these groups, albeit small in number, are growing, we can introduce a third bid rent curve into the analysis. **Figure 4.7** illustrates this case by adding another bid rent curve to the previous figure that reflects the preferences of those who choose high density.

This group behaves analogously to the tomato farmers in our earlier agricultural example. The households in this group place a high value on access to the center and

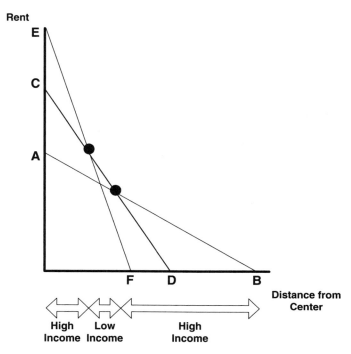

Figure 4.7 Gentrification. There is a small group of high-income households, represented by bid rent curve EF, who prefer high density and can outbid lower-income households for the land near the center. In places where this has happened, it is more difficult for low-income households to find affordable housing.

they have the ability to outbid other groups. Many lower-income households find themselves squeezed out of some central areas but still not able to compete for places in more expensive suburbs. Instead, in many metro areas, there has been a movement of lower-income households to some of the less sought after older industrial suburbs, just beyond the central city boundary. In some metro areas where this possibility does not exist, or where the supply of housing in such suburbs is insufficient for those being displaced, the problems of homelessness and the lack of affordable housing have reached crisis proportions. The poor are forced to accept even greater overcrowding in the central city or leave the metro area altogether.

Along with the growth of Sunbelt cities and edge cities, gentrification helps us to understand some of the changing patterns of location that affected U.S. metropolitan areas toward the end of the twentieth century.

Classification of Twentieth-Century Cities

The economic and social forces that shape city functions are, of course, not static; they change constantly. As a consequence of this dynamism, the economic specialization of each city may exhibit considerable change from one decade to the next. Moreover, as the economic output of the entire nation changes—for example, from the production of farm goods and timber to traditional manufacturing to the production of business and personal services—the fortunes of individual cities rise and fall.

Amid all of these transformations, we can classify twentieth-century cities and the metropolitan areas that surrounded them into five categories. Each represents the income-generating activities that drove the economy of the city. Of course, some cities had more than one of these activities, but each city had a reputation for at least one.

1. **Natural resource cities** produce and export products related to the extraction of minerals, the cutting of timber, and the growing of farm products. Cities in the Midwest such as Des Moines, Iowa; Omaha, Nebraska; and Peoria, Illinois became centers for the farm and livestock industry, while cities like Denver, Colorado; Wheeling, West Virginia; and Duluth, Minnesota became famous for their contributions to the mining industry. Timber provided an economic base for cities like Seattle, Washington.

2. **Manufacturing cities** produce finished consumer goods or components for use as inputs in further manufacture elsewhere. These range from textiles and apparel to steel and autos to computers and chemicals. As described by Meinig (2004), the Manufacturing Belt, extending from Pittsburgh and Buffalo to the east—through Cleveland, Youngstown, and Detroit, and other cities in Ohio and Michigan—to Chicago and St. Louis in the west contained the most important industries of the mid-twentieth century. From the early part of the twentieth century until at least the 1960s, many of these cities became extraordinarily prosperous, as their manufacturers churned out the steel, glass, tire, auto, aircraft, and machine tool products to satisfy nationwide demand.

3. **Transportation hubs** are cities where major transportation lines converge, where goods are switched from one mode of transportation to another—for example, from ships to trains—and where large shipments of goods are broken down into smaller shipments for delivery to specific locations. Transportation hubs play a crucial role in providing manufacturers, commercial businesses, and households throughout the United States with products from distant cities and regions. During much of the twentieth century, Chicago, Atlanta, and Tacoma, Washington, were among the cities whose growth was indispensably linked to that role. Chicago's location and the convergence of many transportation networks in that city made it possible to send and receive goods by rail and road from cities to the east, west, and south, and by ship around the Great Lakes. Atlanta was originally formed as a transportation hub for the South and Southeast, serving as a site where railroads from Birmingham and other southern cities to the west converged with rail lines from cities in the Midwest, mid-Atlantic states, and the Northeast. In Tacoma, the depth of the harbor right up to the shore provided excellent access for ships from other North American cities and countries across the Pacific, and this important attribute led railroad owners to select it as the western terminus for the Northern Pacific Railroad. Adopting the motto, "when rails meet sails," Tacoma became an important site for transferring raw materials and finished goods from ships to high-capacity

railroad lines bound for Denver, St. Louis, and Chicago. By the end of the twentieth century, Tacoma was the seventh-largest container port in the country (Tacoma Historical Society 2007).

4. **Finance cities** provide the access and expertise to link companies with potential investors and sources of loans, provide a venue in which owners of stocks and bonds can resell them to other buyers, link companies and individuals to financial experts to handle the management of their wealth, and provide a range of insurance vehicles. Such activities typically involve many agglomeration incentives, since they require expertise in numerous areas, frequent communication, and ongoing transfers of information about activity in the United States and other countries. During the twentieth century, New York, San Francisco, and Charlotte were among the cities best known for providing these services. New York's Wall Street has long been synonymous with financial markets serving the nation and the world. San Francisco has been home to huge banking empires including the original Bank of America, while Charlotte emerged as the financial center of the Southeast in the latter decades of the twentieth century, serving as headquarters for Nations Bank, among other financial giants.

5. **Innovation cities** provide new ideas and new products to the overall economy. While innovation has occurred to some extent in every city and in every time period, cities *specializing* in innovation emerged in the last half of the twentieth century. As the locus of invention moved from places like the Wright Brothers' bicycle shop in Dayton, Ohio, and Henry Ford's garage in Detroit to the sophisticated laboratories of great research universities, innovation almost became an industry itself. Boston, San Jose, Seattle, and Raleigh-Durham-Chapel Hill have become important innovation centers for the overall economy, utilizing the expertise and creativity of highly educated workforces, private and public investments in research and development, and the presence of universities and medical facilities engaged in cutting-edge exploration.

The Changing Fortunes of Individual Cities

As the importance and location of particular industries have changed, so have the fortunes of their cities. The extraction of minerals and the production of other natural resources, including agricultural products and timber, continued to fuel the growth of many cities in the twentieth century, as it had in the nineteenth century. Cities such as Butte, Montana, near sites of newly valued natural resources like copper—so important to the electrical and electronic industries—expanded rapidly. In contrast, cities like Charleston, West Virginia, decreased in importance relative to places like Tulsa, Oklahoma, and New Orleans, as dependence on "King Coal" gave way to reliance on oil.

Similarly, the location of key manufacturing industries—including autos, tires, glass, and machine tools—dispersed from Detroit and other midwestern cities to rural towns in Tennessee and Kentucky, as well as to other countries including Japan, Sweden, Germany, and Korea. The interstate highway system and national rail networks made it possible to move assemblies, parts, and finished products over longer distances at cheaper prices, contributing to the decentralization of manufacturing.

As transportation modes switched from canal and railroad to truck and airplane, individual cities saw their fortunes rise or fall. Access to interstate highways and airports could help stimulate local business trade with other regions and could also attract new businesses, while the absence of such infrastructure could lead to a city's economic deterioration. Some cities were better able than others (because of differences in financial resources and political power) to finance, build, and support such infrastructure. Other cities exercised greater creativity and sought new ways to integrate air traffic and economic growth. Atlanta, for example, integrated its emergence as a hub for Delta and Eastern Airlines into a larger economic development plan to become a leading city for conventions and corporate offices (Altshuler and Luberoff 2003). Even the center of financial activity changed with the times; southern cities like Charlotte, Atlanta, and Miami became banking hubs for much of the country. Advances in communications led to changes in the markets for stocks and bonds, and in the locations of the businesses that handled such financial instruments. The development of major research universities, including Stanford in California and Duke in North Carolina, challenged the great Ivy League schools of the Northeast, such as Harvard, Columbia, and Princeton, as innovation centers.

As technology advances, no city is assured of continued prosperity or dominance. Those that can adapt and change have a much greater chance of survival and economic success, while those that cannot see their economic vitality sapped. The ranks of the top 100 cities in terms of population provide just one indication of how important this is. With the value of steel for skyscraper production, auto manufacturing, and railroads skyrocketing at the beginning of the twentieth century, Birmingham, Alabama, went from the ninety-ninth-largest city in 1900 to thirty-fourth in 1930—only to fall back to seventy-sixth by 2000, as the U.S. steel industry lost out to other building materials and to steel produced in Japan and Korea. Duluth, Minnesota, the home of the iron range where taconite for steel production is mined, went from the ninety-second-largest city in 1890 to the sixty-ninth by 1920. But already by 1940, it had fallen back to ninetieth (U.S. Bureau of the Census, 1998).

In manufacturing, Detroit went from the thirteenth-largest city in 1900 to the fourth-largest in the country in 1930; today, it ranks eleventh. Cleveland, home to the steel industry as well as auto manufacturing, has gone from the fifth-largest city in 1920 to thirty-sixth in 2004. Meanwhile, Long Beach, California—home to the aircraft industry and tourism—has moved up from fifty-seventh in 1930 to thirty-fourth in 2004, and San Jose—home to Silicon Valley and high technology—has skyrocketed from the fifty-seventh-largest city in 1960 to the tenth largest in America today. Back in 1900, the tenth-largest city was Cincinnati, Ohio, famous as the headquarters for Proctor and Gamble, one of the nation's premier producers of personal care products. Just as Cincinnati was eclipsed by San Jose, some of today's largest cities are likely to be eclipsed by the cities now at the cutting edge of twenty-first-century technologies.

The only thing certain about metro areas is that they will constantly and inevitably change, which, of course, is true of most things. Some of this change will be advantageous, as when new products and services evolve and their production is concentrated in certain regions. Some of this change causes great disadvantage, as when old products and services lose their luster and their markets; the cities where these goods and services were produced find themselves challenged to remain prosperous.

Now, in the twenty-first century, new technologies and global relations seem to be evolving faster than ever. We now turn our attention to how they will affect cities and suburbs.

Appendix A

Expansions on the Basic Alonso Model

As he continued his theoretical work, William Alonso considered how several other aspects of urban geography might influence land-use patterns. In addition to introducing polycentric models, he incorporated more realistic elements, including street layouts; high-speed highways, expressways, and circumferential beltways; and specific "sectoral" growth areas scattered throughout the city.

Street Layout

In his initial work, Alonso developed models in which distance was measured in straight lines from any point in the periphery to the city center, as though there were direct straight roads from any point in a metro area to the city center. Obviously, this is an unrealistic abstraction. As a result, later in his research, Alonso complicated his abstract model by introducing the concept of **travel distance**, the measurement of distance along existing routes rather than as the crow flies. Anyone who has searched MapQuest or Expedia for driving directions on the Internet knows that the shortest route in miles is not necessarily the quickest route in terms of time. It all depends on whether the route is along city streets or an expressway and may depend on congestion conditions as well. Instead of concentric rings in Alonso's pure abstract model, the route-based measurement of distance leads to a set of **iso-access lines** that form a square pattern. **Figure A4.1** provides a view of a standard city street grid with an overlay of iso-access lines. The iso-access lines are square-shaped such that the travel distance from any point on a single iso-access square to the city center is identical. Note, for example, that the travel distance from point A to the city center is equal to four segments. Similarly, the travel distance from point B is equal to four segments—one segment going west and then three going south (or three south and then one west). Each set of concentric iso-access squares represents points equidistant in travel distance from the city center given the grid form of actual city streets.

Housing and business location patterns and bid rent curves will be based on these travel distances rather than simple concentric rings. Even though point B is physically closer to the city center, it takes the same travel time to get there as it would a resident who lives at point A and, therefore, the rent at the two locations, ceteris paribus, will be the same.

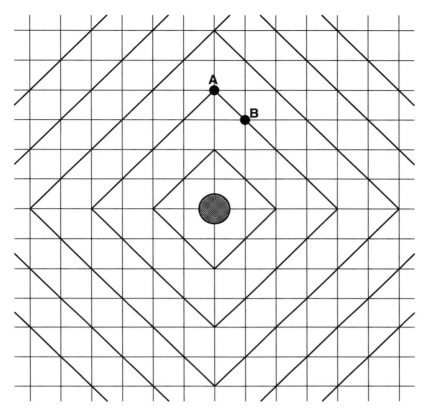

Figure A4.1 Travel Distance Iso-Access Diagram. In the above figure, the horizontal and vertical lines represent city streets. If measured by a straight line from the city center, point B is closer than point A, but to travel from point B to the center, one has to travel one block to the left, and three blocks down—a total of four blocks, the same distance as would be traveled from point A to the center. Thus, in terms of travel distance, point A and point B, and other points along the bolded square are points of equal access (iso-access). In this figure, each bolded square represents a set of iso-access points— locations with equal travel distances to the city center. *Source:* Alonso 1964, figure 36, p. 131.

Travel Speed

As commuters know, access is dependent not only upon distance along routes but also upon the speed at which one can travel those routes. Accordingly, Alonso also discussed a model in which the iso-access lines are influenced by highways along which commuters can drive at higher speeds. The simplest model, shown in **Figure A4.2**, shows a grid formation of streets where there also exist two highways crossing perpendicularly at the city center. The effect of the highways is to increase the iso-access distance from the city center along the north-south and east-west highways, suggesting in this figure that traveling along one of these highways permits one to cover twice the distance in the same amount of time as one who travels on regular city streets. The result is a star-shaped iso-access diagram, where the travel time to the city center is equal at all points on a given iso-access star. Thus, with higher-speed transportation, areas farther from the central city gain in value simply as the result of faster commute times. It is, therefore, not surprising that when a new highway interchange opens or a new subway stop is constructed, nearby land rises in value—often dramatically.

Alonso's diagrams can become even more complicated and intricate if you add a circumferential beltway to the highway and road system, so that the shortest travel time between any point in the periphery and the center may include driving to a beltway, following the beltway to a major north-south or east-west highway, and then

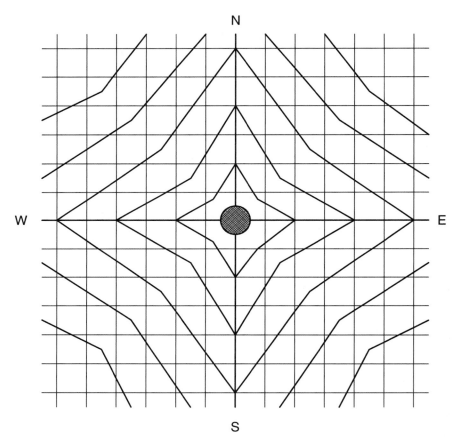

Figure A4.2 Traffic Distance Iso-Access Diagram with Expressways. Alonso recognized the impact of travel time on land values, and included this figure in his book to show how expressways can impact the iso-access diagram shown in Figure A4.1. Here, the horizontal and vertical lines again represent city streets, but two high-speed expressways are also included—one extending from south to north, and a second extending from east to west. These expressways change the iso-access points, to those shown in the bolded star shapes. As shown in this figure, points on and near the expressway can be reached as quickly as other points on the bolded stars, even though they are farther away (in terms of travel distance). This phenomenon explains why both the existence of expressways, and the specific locations of expressways, are important for the values that residents and businesses are willing to bid for particular pieces of land within a metropolitan area. *Source:* Alonso 1964, figure 37, p. 132.

taking this highway to the city center. Obviously, once you include the possibility of highway congestion, the iso-access lines may change again. In the case of a major highway accident in which the road is closed, the quickest way downtown might be to take the normal city grid streets. Ultimately, a bike may be faster than a car!

In general, the models that incorporate street layout and travel speed demonstrate the importance of access, as opposed to just distance, in the determination of prices for land. The relevance of this to modern metropolitan areas as they have expanded is indicated by a question asked by many individuals when they consider buying a piece of land: "How long does it take me to get from here to there?"

Polycentric Cities with Income-Differentiated Neighborhoods

The case of edge cities is shown earlier in Figure 4.6. Edge cities are a particular manifestation of the more general case of the **polycentric city form**. It is possible to have multiple centers in an edge city that appear to have similar features. However, more commonly, the individual centers in an edge city serve different economic functions, attract different types of workers, and provide for different household needs. Alonso provides two models to show how bid rent curves can help us understand how such centers can lead to distinct residential patterns based on income stratification. In each of these models, he posits that upper-income residents of the metropolitan area—who are assumed to be employed disproportionately in centers typified by office work—may be more attracted to housing near their work than low-income residents, who, according to the model, work disproportionately in manufacturing firms located away form the office work center and tend to shop in retail districts located away from these centers as well. It is possible that these dynamics may result in an island of high-income population near the office work center due to the ability of the high-income population to outbid low-income households for land near the downtown office and retail district. Thus, we get the gentrification of inner-city locations, particularly by young professionals without children and empty nesters, whose children are no longer of school age.

Still another possibility is that high-income residents can outbid low-income residents for some of the land close to the downtown office/shopping center, but live nearby an island of low-income households. These close-by centers result from circumstances where the residential paradox applies. The advantages of proximity to the office/shopping center for low-income residents is great enough that some are willing to live in very high-density housing, so that in the aggregate, their small living units effectively "outbid" the offers of higher-income residents for some of the downtown land.

Sectoral Growth Patterns

Sector-shaped patterns of land use can occur from the location of various activities along different routes out of the city. To illustrate how bid rent dynamics could lead to residential patterns that reflect areas of high land prices *distant* from the city center, Alonso draws upon the possibility that some high-income residents may make locational choice on the basis of status-seeking behavior. High-income residents might seek the prestige of locating with other high-income residents along a particular route, such as Philadelphia's Main Line commuter rail route or Long Island's Gold Coast, the elite North Shore area immortalized in F. Scott Fitzgerald's *The Great Gatsby*, where land values were far higher than those on the South Shore, even though both areas were equidistant from New York City. The bid rent curves reflect this dynamic, showing higher offers for property in that specific area. The result is that while most of the city has concentric land prices, a high-income wedge develops in the area along the high-status road.

Once you take into account all of these factors—street grids, expressways, and household preferences mitigated by income differences and status needs—metro areas can be found with bid rent curves that have large anomalies in them at various distances from the city center. Hence, the concentric circle bid rent curve provides only a rough approximation of the land prices that one would find in various neighborhoods in real cities.

References

Alonso, William. 1964. *Location and Land Use: Toward a General Theory of Land Rent*. Cambridge, Mass.: Harvard University Press.

Altshuler, Alan, and David Luberoff. 2003. *Mega-Projects: The Changing Politics of Urban Public Investment*. Washington, D.C.: Brookings Institution Press.

Baum-Snow, Nathaniel. 2007. "Did Highways Cause Suburbanization?" *Quarterly Journal of Economics* 122, no. 2: 775–805.

Bluestone, Barry, and Bennett Harrison. 1982. *The Deindustrialization of America*. New York: Basic Books.

Boyer, M. Christine. 1994. *Dreaming the Rational City: The Myth of American City Planning*. Cambridge, Mass.: MIT Press.

Brakman, Steven, Harry Garretsen, and Charles van Marrewijk. 2001. "Geography and Economic Theory." In *An Introduction to Geographical Economics*. Cambridge: Cambridge University Press, chap. 2.

Burgess, Ernest. 1925. "The Growth of the City." In Robert Park, Ernest Burgess, and Roderick McKenzie, *The City*. Chicago: University of Chicago Press, pp. 47–62.

———. 1929. "Urban Areas." In T. V. Smith and L. D. White, eds., *Chicago: An Experiment in Social Science Research*. Chicago: University of Chicago Press, pp. 113–138.

Chudacoff, Howard, and Judith Smith. 2000. *The Evolution of American Urban Society*, 5th ed. Upper Saddle River, N.J.: Prentice Hall.

Dear, Michael, ed. 2002. *From Chicago to L.A.: Making Sense of Urban Theory*. Thousand Oaks, Calif.: Sage.

DiPasquale, Denise, and William C. Wheaton. 1996. *Urban Economics and Real Estate Markets*. Englewood Cliffs, N.J.: Prentice Hall.

Dunn, Edgar. 1954. *The Location of Agricultural Production*. Gainesville: University of Florida Press.

Fishman, Robert. 1987. *Bourgeois Utopias: The Rise and Fall of Suburbia*. New York: Basic Books.

Frey, William, and Dowell Myers. 2005. "Racial Segregation in U.S. Metropolitan Areas and Cities, 1990–2000: Patterns, Trends, and Explanations." Research Report 05-573. Ann Arbor: Population Studies Center, Institute for Social Research, University of Michigan.

Frey, William H. 2001. "Melting Pot Suburbs: A Census 2000 Study of Suburban Diversity." Washington, D.C.: Center on Urban and Metropolitan Policy, the Brookings Institution.

Garreau, Joel. 1991. *Edge City: Life on the New Frontier.* New York: Doubleday.

Geyer, H. S., ed. 2002. *International Handbook of Urban Systems: Studies of Urbanization and Migration in Advanced and Developing Countries.* Cheltenham, England: Edward Elgar.

Gibson, Campbell. 1998. "Population of the 100 Largest Cities and Other Urban Places in the United States: 1790 to 1990." Washington, D.C.: U.S. Bureau of the Census, Population Division, June.

Glaeser, Edward, and Janet Kohlhase. 2004. "Cities, Regions and the Decline of Transport Costs." *Papers in Regional Science* 83, no. 1 (January): 197–228.

Glaeser, Edward, and J. Vigdor. 2001. "Racial Segregation in the 2000 Census: Promising News." Washington, D.C.: Center on Urban and Metropolitan Policy, the Brookings Institution.

Harris, Chauncy. 1990. "Urban Geography in the United States: My Experience of the Formative Years." *Urban Geography* 11: 403–417.

Harris, Chauncy, and Edward Ullman. 1945. "The Nature of Cities." *Annals of the American Academy of Political and Social Science* 242, no. 1: 7–17.

Harris, Richard, and Robert Lewis. 1998. "Constructing a Fault(y) Zone: Misrepresentations of American Cities and Suburbs, 1900–1950." *Annals of the Association of American Geographers* 88, no. 4: 622–639.

———. 2001. "The Geography of North American Cities and Suburbs, 1900–1950: A New Synthesis." *Journal of Urban History* 27, no. 3 (March): 262–292.

Hoyt, Homer. 1939. *The Structure and Growth of Residential Neighborhoods.* Washington, D.C.: Federal Housing Administration.

———. 1941. "Forces of Urban Centralization and Decentralization." *American Journal of Sociology* 46, no. 6: 843–852.

———. 1964. "Recent Distortions of the Classical Models of Urban Structure." *Land Economics* 40, no. 2 (May): 199–212.

Hylton, Joseph Gordon. 2000. "Prelude to Euclid: The United States Supreme Court and the Constitutionality of Land Use Regulation, 1900–1920." *Washington University Journal of Law and Policy* 3, no. 1: 1–37.

Isard, Walter. 1956. *Location and Space-Economy: A General Theory Relating to Industrial Location, Market Areas, Land Use, Trade, and Urban Structure.* Cambridge, Mass.: Technology Press of MIT; New York: Wiley.

Jackson, Kenneth. 1985. *Crabgrass Frontier.* New York: Oxford University Press.

Judd, Dennis R., and Todd Swanstrom. 2004. *City Politics: Private Power and Public Policy.* New York: Pearson Education.

Launhardt, Wilhelm. 1885. *Mathematische Begrundung der Volkswirtschafslehre.* Leipzig, Germany: W. Engleman. Trans. John Creedy (1993) as *Mathematical Principles of Economics.* Aldershot, England, and Brookfield, Vt.: Edward Elgar.

Logan, John, Deirdre Oakley, Polly Smith, Jacob Stovell, and Brian Stults. 2001. "Separating the Children." Albany, NY: The Lewis Mumford Center.

Matthews, Fred L. 1977. *Quest for an American Sociology: Robert E. Park and the Chicago School.* Montreal, Canada: McGill–Queens University Press.

McKelvey, Blake. 1973. *American Urbanization: A Comparative History.* Glenview, Ill.: Scott, Foresman.

Meinig, David W. 2004. *The Shaping of America: A Geographical Perspective on 500 Years of History,* vol. 4: *Global America.* New Haven, Conn.: Yale University Press.

Mohl, Raymond. 1997. "The Second Ghetto and the Infiltration Theory in Urban Real Estate, 1940–1960." In June Manning Thomas and Marsha Ritzdorf, eds., *Urban Planning and the African American Community: In the Shadows.* Thousand Oaks, Calif. Sage, pp. 58–74.

Palen, J. John. 1995. *The Suburbs.* New York: McGraw-Hill.

———. 2002. *The Urban World,* 6th ed. New York: McGraw-Hill.

Pursell, Carroll W., Jr. 1969. *Early Stationary Steam Engines in America: A Study in the Migration of a Technology.* Washington, D.C.: Smithsonian Institution Press.

Rose, Mark H. 1990. *Interstate: Express Highway Politics, 1939–1989,* rev. ed. Knoxville: University of Tennessee Press.

Scott, Mel. 1969. *American City Planning since 1890.* Berkeley: University of California Press.

Seely, Bruce E. 1987. *Building the American Highway System.* Philadelphia: Temple University Press.

Silver, Christopher. 1997. "The Racial Origins of Zoning in American Cities." In June Manning Thomas and Marsha Ritzdorf, eds., *Urban Planning and the African American Community: In the Shadows.* Thousand Oaks, Calif.: Sage, pp. 23–42.

Soja, Edward W. 2001. *Postmetropolis: Critical Studies of Cities and Regions.* Oxford: Blackwell.

Sum, Andrew, and Nathan Pond. 2002. "The Contributions of Foreign Immigration to the Demographic Revival of America's and the Northeast Region's Big Cities in the 1990s." Boston: Center for Labor Market Studies, Northeastern University, July.

Tacoma Historical Society. 2007. Telephone conversation with Russell Williams, August 9.

U.S. Bureau of the Census. 1950. *Statistical Abstract of the United States.* Washington, D.C.: U.S. Government Printing Office.

———. 1979. "The Social and Economic Status of the Black Population in the United States: An Historical View, 1790–1978," Department of Commerce, Current Population Reports Special Studies Series P-23, no. 80. Washington, D.C.: U.S. Government Printing Office.

———. 1998. "Population of the 100 Largest Cities and other Urban Areas in the United States: 1770–1990." Population Division Working Paper #27. http://www.census.gov/population/www/documentation/twps0027.html.

———. 2001. *Statistical Abstract of the United States, 2001.* Washington, D.C.: U.S. Government Printing Office.

———. 2005. *Statistical Abstract of the United States, 2005.* Washington, D.C.: U.S. Government Printing Office.

———. 2006. *Statistical Abstract of the United States, 2006.* Washington, D.C.: U.S. Government Printing Office.

U.S. Department of Housing and Urban Development. 2007. HUD User Policy Development and Research Information Service. SOCDS (State of the Cities Data Systems) data set. http://socds.huduser.org.

von Hoffman, Alexander, and John Felkner. 2002. "The Historical Origins and Causes of Urban Decentralization in the United States." Cambridge, Mass.: Joint Center for Housing Studies, Harvard University, January.

von Thunen, Johann Heinrich. 1826. *Der Isolierte Staat in Beziehung auf Landwirtschaft und Nationalokonomie.* Dusseldorf, Germany: Verlag Wirtschaft und Finanzen. Trans. Peter Geoffrey Hall (1966) as *Isolated State: An English Edition of Der Isolierte Staat.* Oxford: Pergamon Press.

Walton, Judy, and Larry Ford. 2003. "Cities of the United States and Canada." In Stanley Brunn, Jack Williams, and Donald Zeigler, eds., *Cities of the World: World Regional Urban Development,* 3rd ed. Lanham, Md.: Rowman & Littlefield, pp. 47–91.

Wilson, William Julius. 1987. *The Truly Disadvantaged: The Inner City, the Underclass and Public Policy.* Chicago: University of Chicago Press.

———. 1996. *When Work Disappears: The World of the New Urban Poor.* New York: Vintage.

Wright, Richard A. 1996. "A Brief History of the First 100 Years of the Automobile Industry in the United States." Detroit: Wayne State University, Department of Communications.

Wunsch, James L. 1995. "The Suburban Cliché." *Journal of Social History* 28, no. 3 (Spring): 643–658.

Zeigler, Donald, Stanley Brunn, and Jack Williams. 2003. "World Urban Development." In Stanley Brunn, Jack Williams, and Donald Zeigler, eds., *Cities of the World: World Regional Urban Development,* 3rd ed. Lanham, Md.: Rowman & Littlefield, pp. 1–45.

Chapter 4 Questions and Exercises

Land Values and Land Use in Metropolitan Areas

1. In the metropolitan area closest to you, or another one of your choice, where are the largest manufacturing firms located? How about the largest financial industry firms

and the largest retail businesses (for food, clothes, and for other goods bought by families)? How, if at all, can you relate the patterns you find to the Alonso model of land costs and land use? How, if at all, do the patterns you find reflect the location of the markets for the industries? How, if at all, do they reflect access to railroads, highways, airports, or harbors? How, if at all, do they reflect agglomeration economies?

2. American Factfinder, one of the census-related Web sites, has some mapping capabilities. To investigate the geography of poverty in your MSA, go to

http://factfinder.census.gov/servlet/TMGeoSearchByList
Servlet?ds_name=DEC_2000_SF3_U&_lang=en&_ts=219056048761

and follow the steps below:

- Under "Select a geographic type," click on the arrow and a drop-down list will appear.
- Select "Metropolitan Statistical Area/Consolidated Metropolitan Statistical Area." A list of all MSAs will appear in the box labeled "Select a geographic area." Pick one MSA and click on "Next."
- A list of themes (data categories) will appear. Scroll down the list and click on "TM-P069—Percent of Families Below the Poverty Level in 1999:2000." Click on "Show Result."
- A map outlining the MSA will appear. Just above the map, click on the arrow to the right of "Display Map by...." A drop-down list will appear. Click on "Census Tract."
- A new map will appear showing the poverty rates by census tract in the MSA.
- Use the "+" icon to zoom in to get a closer look at particular parts of the MSA.

To interpret the colors in the map, see the legend on the left. If you want to adjust the map to show particular percentages, click on "Data Classes" under "Change" above the legend. Under "Classing method," click on "User Defined," and put in the percentage intervals that you want displayed.

- ✦ Where are the high-poverty-level census tracts located?
- ✦ Why do you think that they are located in those specific areas?
- ✦ What connection, if any, do you think the locations have with Alonso's explanation of the "residential paradox"?

The Rise of the Suburbs

3. This chapter discusses the construction of highways that connected cities to suburbs and suburbs to other suburbs. Go to the following Web site:

www.mapquest.com

Type in the name of a city of your choice and look at the road map MapQuest provides. Identify the major routes used by commuters traveling by automobile. How many of these routes are interstates (identifiable by a red, white, and blue shield)?

How do you think access to interstate roadways has affected the growth of communities in your area?

The Relocation of Industry and Workforces to Other Metro Areas

4. The Bureau of the Census has data on the mean and median center of population of the United States. Go to the following Web address:

   http://www.census.gov/geo/www/cenpop/cntpop2k.html

   How has this center of population changed since 1900? Which factors caused this movement?

5. Using the *Urban Experience* CD, compare the change in manufacturing jobs in the Flint metropolitan area between 1970 and 1990 with the change in manufacturing jobs in Detroit; Charleston, West Virginia; San Diego; Phoenix; and another metropolitan area of your choice. What similarities and/or differences do you find?

Metro Areas and Immigration after World War II

6. Using the *Urban Experience* CD, select any five principal cities in the United States and develop a chart indicating the percentage of foreign-born individuals from 1970 through 2005. Taking the city with the largest foreign-born population, consider what factors might have attracted these immigrants to this city.

U.S. Metro Areas in the Twenty-First Century

The New Dynamics of Urban Location

5

For more than three decades, social scientists and journalists have been chronicling the **globalization** of business and world commerce. Of course, trade and production processes involving interaction across continents are not new. As we mentioned in Chapter 3, the major function of early U.S. cities was to transfer raw materials to Europe. Trade between continents was an important part of economic dynamics in many parts of the world. However, it is generally recognized that since the 1970s, there has been an acceleration of many developments that have changed both the volume and the characteristics of today's global transactions.

Social scientists have been studying the repercussions of this trend, including the rising influence of multinational corporations and the enhanced role of particular cities in the world economy (Friedmann 1995; Storper 1997; Taylor, Walker, and Beaverstock 2002; Schaeffer 2003; Sassen 2006). The specific focus of this chapter is not on international politics or on the overall characteristics of a worldwide economy, but instead on understanding how the underlying dynamics that contribute to globalization are shaping U.S. cities. As the twenty-first century began, the context for trade, production, and investment was considerably different from the context that had existed just a few decades before, and the implications of this change were being felt by cities across the United States.

The New World Is "Flat"

With the revolution in transportation technologies ushered in with the introduction of the jumbo jet, the supertanker, and the container ship, manufacturing firms have been able to move their operations farther and farther away from where their products are actually consumed. Now, with such revolutionary telecommunications technology as high-speed Internet, mobile phones, and satellite links, all kinds of business services—from banking services, teleconferencing, and online technical assistance—can be coordinated and delivered from nearly anywhere on earth. The result, according to *New York Times* journalist Thomas Friedman (2005), is that the world is becoming "flat." As shown in **Figure 5.1**, by 2004, imports of goods and services equaled 15 percent of gross domestic product (GDP), up from 12 percent in 1990, 10 percent in 1980, and just 5 percent in 1967. Indeed, the import share in 1967

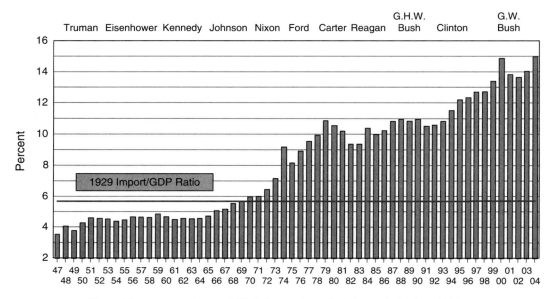

Figure 5.1 Imports as Percent of GDP. *Source:* Council of Economic Advisers 2006.

was no different than the share back in 1929 just before the Great Depression began, which suggests just how recently and how incredibly quickly the world has changed in terms of trade and globalization.

As Friedman notes, "It is now possible for more people than ever to collaborate and compete in real time with more other people on more different kinds of work from more different corners of the planet and on a more equal footing than at any previous time in the history of the world—using computers, e-mail, fiber-optic networks, teleconferencing, and dynamic new software" (Friedman 2005, p. 8). In this context, the "flattening" of the world entails connecting all the knowledge centers around the globe into a single network of producers and consumers. Not just firms but also individuals can now connect to each other in ways not imaginable even a decade ago. Cities are leading the latest advances in communications infrastructure because they house the largest information producers: banks, law offices, insurance companies, financial service providers, corporate headquarters of national and international manufacturing enterprises, and retailers (Moss 1999). All of this new technology is radically changing the role and function of cities and suburbs.

The twenty-first-century technology revolution permits the unprecedented expansion of two forms of global enterprise. **Outsourcing** involves the moving of specific limited functions originally performed within a company—a call center or a research lab—to another firm that performs the function and then sells parts or services to the original company. General Electric, the publisher Simon & Schuster, and Texas Instruments were early adopters of foreign outsourcing, finding companies that could produce parts or services for them in China, India, and other countries that offered some combination of lower wages, appropriate skills, English-speaking workers, and fewer regulations. Circuit design is being accomplished in India for Texas Instruments, while Simon & Schuster uses Indian computer operators to convert manuscript drafts into electronic formats for publishing. A company in Bangalore does medical transcriptions for U.S. doctors and hospitals, which reduces the transcription time from weeks to two hours and the cost by 80 percent (Friedman 2005, p. 130).

The more dramatic new form of global business is **offshoring**, where companies move an entire factory or production center to another country, using a U.S. central office simply to coordinate production and distribution. With its enormous supply of unskilled and semiskilled labor, and now increasingly a pool of highly skilled labor, China has become the prime location for offshoring activity. If you want proof of this, check out where your cell phone was manufactured, your home television, your computer, or nearly any electronic device you own. With China so successful at attracting U.S. companies to its shores for production purposes, other countries— including Thailand, Malaysia, Ireland, Mexico, Brazil, and Vietnam—have offered low wages for increasingly high-skilled labor hoping to attract the offshore activity of American firms. The result: In 1995, 90 percent of the manufactured goods consumed by Americans were produced in the United States; less than a decade later, the proportion was already down to 75 percent and falling fast.

As outsourcing and offshoring have increased, American firms—as well as those of Europe and increasingly elsewhere in the world—have become truly multinational, buying companies in other countries. Ford bought Jaguar and Land Rover of the United Kingdom (in 1989 and 2000, respectively), half of Volvo of Sweden (acquired in 1998), and one-third of Mazda of Japan (acquired in 1999). General Motors is the parent company to Sweden's Saab (half of which it acquired in 1990, and the other half in 2000) and Germany's Opel (which it has owned since 1931). From 1998 to 2007, Chrysler was actually owned by the German company Daimler Benz. Sony Corporation of Japan bought Columbia Pictures of the United States in 1989 and 20 percent of the U.S. media company MGM (Metro-Goldwyn-Mayer) in 2005. The Tata Group, one of the largest firms in India, bought the U.S. firm Tyco's international network of underwater cables in 2005, and acquired Corus, a large English and Dutch steel firm, in 2007.

With so much multinational activity, managing the **supply chains** across far-flung operations has become a major activity of business executives. When done efficiently, these supply chains—linking together innovative research and development (R&D) activities, the actual production of parts and final assemblies, and the distribution of final products to customers across many suppliers—result in companies like Wal-Mart, Home Depot, and IKEA being able to offer a wide array of consumer goods at very low prices to their customers. In the process, however, the ability to source parts and labor from all over the world eliminates large numbers of traditional jobs in the United States and exerts downward pressure on American workers' wages and benefits. The result for many cities in the late post–World War II period was a continuation of the **deindustrialization** we discussed in Chapter 4, the wholesale loss of factories and jobs to other parts of the country or to other nations

(Bluestone and Harrison 1982). In the twenty-first century, these same pressures are bubbling up in more highly skilled fields and have invaded all kinds of services, as well as manufacturing.

At the same time that the transportation and communications revolutions have allowed outsourcing and offshoring, computers have permitted more and more skilled people to do their work by **telecommuting** and **teleconferencing.** Instead of coming to a central workplace—an office or retail shop—individuals can perform their work from home, reading and writing reports, meeting electronically with co-workers to coordinate production, or selling goods and services over the Internet or by telephone. The exact extent and growth of telecommuting is not known, but a recent study of commuting data between 1990 and 2004 indicates that the category that encompasses such work, "working at home," is one of the fastest-growing categories in commuting patterns (Pisarski 2006). This is providing new—or at least different—forms of employment for an increasing number of workers and new and different opportunities and challenges for cities and suburbs.

Before turning to some of the current characteristics and outlooks for cities, let's examine the globalization dynamics we have discussed thus far in terms of the important models of location introduced in Chapters 3 and 4.

Weber and the Twenty-First-Century City

What we have just discussed in terms of the flat world and its implications for where production takes place can be understood by tinkering with the Weber model we first encountered in Chapter 3.

In the location models of the twentieth century, transportation costs and communication costs were so important that they were seen as the prime determinants of where firms located. In the Weber models, transportation costs are the key determinant of firm location over *long* distances. A resource-oriented firm will locate near the source of its raw materials, while a consumer-oriented firm will locate near where its consumers live. Copper for electronic devices will not only be mined from deep deposits and open pits in Arizona, but also smelted and refined near the mines to reduce the weight of the product to be shipped to electronics producers. Haircuts, on the other hand, will be provided in barbershops near where the consumers live or work, in order to cut down on the transportation costs of getting the barber to the customer or vice versa. If transportation costs are high in terms of the dollar cost of getting from point A to point B or high in terms of the opportunity cost of the time needed to traverse this distance, it makes sense for the producers of services to be near their customers.

Expansions on the Basic Weber Model

The basic Weber graphs were reasonably appropriate as descriptive approximations of firm location decisions for most of the twentieth century, but as the turn of the current century approached and transportation and communication costs decreased dramatically, their direct applicability to location decisions in the real world became more tenuous. The Internet and related technological developments particularly revolutionized the relationship between communication and physical proximity. By the end of the century, it was possible to communicate with coworkers instantaneously via e-mail at virtually no cost, whether they were located next door, across the city, across the state, across the nation, or across the globe. Videoconferencing makes it possible to have real-time meetings even though the participants are separated by thousands of miles. A person in downtown Denver, another in suburban Denver, a third in Miami, and a fourth in Singapore can videoconference—all without leaving their buildings. The cost of transportation also continued to decline with the proliferation of business jets for corporate executives and overnight delivery services such as FedEx. As the twenty-first century began, factors other than transportation and communication costs were coming to dominate the location decisions of firms.

Weber in a World of Declining Transportation and Communications Costs

As you will recall, under the Weber model, if transportation costs played the dominant role in firms' location decisions, the relative costs of transportation for the purpose of resource procurement and for product distribution determined whether the firm would be resource-oriented (locating near the source of raw material) or market-oriented (locating near the firm's customers).

To modify this model to represent the effect on location decisions of declining transportation and communication costs, it is important to recall that, as Weber recognized, these costs are not the only factors in the firm's location decision. Labor costs are another, and site costs, including the cost of buildings and physical infrastructure, are still a third. If labor costs decline with distance from the customer, then as transportation costs become less important, labor costs will become more important in determining location. The trick for corporate leaders, of course, is not to minimize any one cost, but to minimize total cost.

Expanding on the dynamics introduced in Chapter 3 (Figure 3.8), we can see three different kinds of location outcomes depending on the relative importance of three different cost items: site cost, the cost of transportation and communications, and the cost of labor. In **Figure 5.2**, site costs are relatively low and decline the farther away a producer moves from a given metro area. Construction costs, for example, are cheaper in the South than in the North and still cheaper in Asia and Latin America. Similarly, labor costs decline the farther one gets away from the original metro location. But, in this particular example, transportation costs (and communication costs) rise steeply as the distance from the original metro area to more far-flung locations increases. In this case, firms will choose to maintain their location in the original metro region in order to avoid high transportation and communication costs. This is point A on the diagram.

Now consider **Figure 5.3**, where site costs are substantially higher in the original metro area and decline the farther away one is located. Transportation costs, as

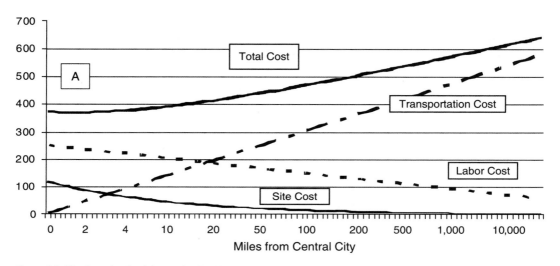

Figure 5.2 The Location Decision under Conditions of Steeply Rising Transportation and Communication Costs. Transportation costs rise steeply the farther away that a firm is from the central city. Site costs and labor costs decline with distance from the central city, but not as steeply as the rise in transportation costs. The optimal location for such a firm is near the central city, as designated by A.

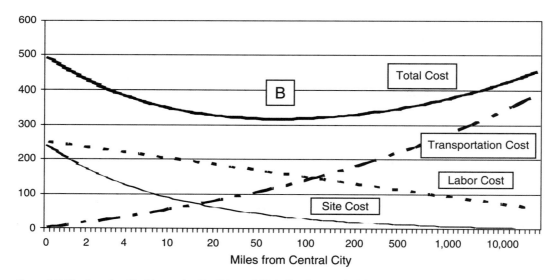

Figure 5.3 The Location Decision under Conditions of High Site Costs and Rising Transportation Costs. Transportation costs rise as a firm locates farther away from the central city; however, site costs fall precipitously, while labor costs fall steadily. Reflecting the decline in site costs and labor costs, which overshadow the rise in transportation costs, the point at which total costs are minimized is at point B, at the far edge of the metro area.

before, are low near the metro area but rise the farther one moves away. Labor costs, like site costs, also decline as one establishes production farther and farther away. Under these circumstances, total costs are lowest at point B. This dynamic is reflected in the case where firms initially operating in northern and midwestern cities moved their operations to the lower-cost states throughout the South.

Finally, consider **Figure 5.4**, where site costs decline as before, but transportation and communication costs are assumed to be zero. What dominates here is labor cost. As a result, producers will move to wherever labor costs are lowest. This could be anywhere in the world, but developing countries are especially attractive. Total cost is obtained at point C.

While reduction of transportation and communication costs to zero may seem like an extreme assumption, something close to this is, in fact, happening in some industries. Due to advances in communication technology, much information that in earlier times was carried from place to place and delivered as documents or as face-to-face conversation, can now be transferred virtually without cost around the globe. This has fueled the relocation not only of manufacturing plants but also call centers, accounting services, and other information-based services to countries where labor costs and site costs are lower than in the United States.

Some services, of course, must be located near the customer almost regardless of site costs or labor cost. McDonald's may be able to find cheaper labor to fry ham-

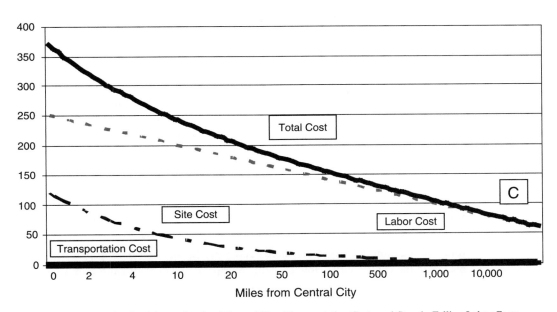

Figure 5.4 The Location Decision under Conditions of Zero Transportation Costs and Steeply Falling Labor Costs.
 Transportation costs have fallen to zero, while site costs and labor costs are higher near the central city and fall as distance from the central city increases. Under such conditions, the minimizing point for total costs is completely determined by site and labor costs, and the optimal location for the firm (the point where total costs are minimized) is at point C, thousands of miles away from where the product or service is consumed.

burgers and french fries in Bangladesh than in Boston, but even if jumbo jet service were nearly free, the increased cost of flying in Big Macs to Boston-area customers exceeds the labor cost savings of putting their franchises in Boston neighborhoods. On the other hand, the ordering functions can be spun off to distant locations using electronic transmission. When you pull up to the drive-up window at your local McDonald's, your order may be received by someone hundreds of miles away, who then transmits it electronically to the person who is actually preparing your food (Friedman 2005).

Taken together, these three figures show that as transportation costs decrease, a firm that chose to move from Chicago to Lexington, Kentucky, in 1980 due to offsetting labor costs may find it optimal to move to Mexico City in 2010. This is not because Lexington and, later, Mexico City have been newly discovered, but decreasing transportation and communication costs have changed the relative importance of other types of costs, and now the geographic variation in labor cost is the decisive factor for cost minimization. Even though the firm's transportation and communication costs may still be minimized in Chicago, the cost savings from this minimization are now outweighed by the savings in labor costs from locating in Mexico City.

Alonso and the Twenty-First-Century City

Let us turn to the Alonso model—a model of land use *within* a metropolitan area. In the most basic Alonso model, proximity to the city center is highly valued by commercial businesses, industry, and residents, in large part because proximity reduces travel costs to the important city center. In the early to mid-twentieth century, this was an important factor. But as transportation and communication costs fall for many products and services, it becomes less important to locate at the city core, and consequently, the distribution of city activity in the early twenty-first century may be different than was the case when Alonso initially produced his models. As we noted in Chapter 4, Alonso was aware of some ways in which cities were changing in terms of transportation access; thus, he produced a few models where iso-access (equal accessibility) was the key factor rather than distance.

But it is appropriate now, in the early twenty-first century, to revisit the questions: What determines land value within metro areas? How is the pattern of land values changing within metro areas? As transportation costs decrease, exerting a centrifugal force on location decisions, are there centripetal factors that tend to pull activities back into the central city? How do both centripetal and centrifugal forces affect the location decisions of business, residences, and other key decision makers today?

Alonso in a World of Declining Transportation and Communications Costs

One initial conclusion that can be made about declining transportation and communications costs is that, to the extent that such costs made proximity to the city core valuable, a reduction in these costs will reduce competition for land at the city core, as all actors take advantage of lower land prices farther out. Correspondingly, we can expect that the costs of land in other parts of the metro area will go up relative to the costs in the central city.

But what about the patterns with which land values away from the city core will increase? It is important to note here that the simplest Alonso models are explicitly based upon the concept of "a featureless plain." In other words, it is assumed that there are no distinguishing characteristics of land that might determine land values other than proximity to the city core. This made reasonable sense when transportation costs were the overwhelmingly decisive factor for city shape, but as transportation costs decrease, it becomes less descriptively appropriate. Just like declining transportation costs made other costs more salient in the Weber model, they make other characteristics of a given location more important for land values within a city in the Alonso model.

We might expect that there would still be a substantial centripetal inclination in cities simply because municipal government buildings are typically located in or near the city core. Businesses that are dependent on working with government may choose to locate close to City Hall. Businesses may also wish to take advantage of proximity to mass transit so that their employees can get to work quickly on subways or buses, avoiding long, time-consuming commutes. This certainly helps to explain why central cities continue to provide a powerful market for skyline-defining office towers.

However, as transportation and communications costs decrease, many businesses may choose to relocate from the city core to other parts of the metro area. Among the important factors that help to determine their location decisions are the size of available parcels of land, appropriate commercial zoning, the quality of water and sewer infrastructure, proximity to parks and other amenities, environmental or brownfield issues related to central city locations, and access to intercity highways. As transportation and communication costs decrease, therefore, the **morphology**— the form and structure—of cities becomes determined by a wider variety of factors, some that are market based, some that depend upon the historical path of development, and others that are strongly tied to current public policies. These factors are at the root of the growing multinucleic pattern of land use in metropolitan areas.

In a study of the changing patterns of office space location in the thirteen largest metro areas in the United States, Lang (2000) suggests that twenty-first-century metro areas are changing their development patterns away from both centralized locations as well as edge city locations and moving toward a new morphology—dispersion throughout the metro area (see **Table 5.1**). Instead of geographically distinct areas for office location where boundaries of office land use are clearly visible, according to Lang, there is a new "significant trend in the nation's office economy, which seems to be a relentless march towards decentralization. . . . People increasingly commute from dispersed locations to dispersed locations. Even the concept of well-defined suburban edge cities seems out of date, as metropolitan areas become post-polycentric or edgeless" (Lang 2000, p. 2). He concludes that because of this dispersal, currently "there is no one pattern of metropolitan development" (p. 7).

Table 5.1 Office Space Distribution by Location in Metro Areas, 1999

Metro Area and Dominant Pattern of Office Location	Percent within Central Business Districts	Percent within Secondary Business Districts	Percent within Edge Cities	Percent within Edgeless Locations
Core-Dominated Office Locations				
Chicago	53.9	N/A	19.5	26.6
New York	56.7	7.2	6.2	29.9
Balanced Office Locations				
Boston	37.4	4.6	18.8	39.2
Washington	28.6	12.5	27.1	31.8
Denver	30.4	4.2	29.4	35.9
Los Angeles	29.8	7.8	25.4	37.0
San Francisco	33.9	8.8	13.9	43.4
Dispersed Office Locations				
Dallas	20.5	4.5	40.3	34.6
Houston	23.0	N/A	37.9	39.1
Atlanta	23.6	9.9	25.3	41.2
Detroit	21.3	N/A	39.5	39.2
Edgeless				
Philadelphia	34.2	3.2	8.9	53.6
Miami	13.1	4.5	16.6	65.8
Average for Thirteen Largest Metro Areas	37.7	6.0	19.8	36.5

Note: Lang's study found that only two of the thirteen largest cities, Chicago and New York, had the majority of their office space within a single centralized business district. Five cities—Boston, Washington, Denver, Los Angeles, and San Francisco—had a balance between a central business district and other areas. Four cities—Dallas, Houston, Atlanta, and Detroit—had two-thirds or more of their office space in edge cities or "edgeless" locations (areas where offices are so dispersed with other uses that there are no visible boundaries of land use for offices). Two cities, Philadelphia and Miami, had the majority of their office space within edgeless locations.
Source: Lang 2000, "Table 3: Typology of Metropolitan areas by Core vs. Edgeless Office Space, 1999."

In addition to the changes in the business use of land, there are new dynamics of residential location. While the overall movement of population continues its shift to the suburbs, significant changes are occurring in many central cities. Increasingly, city centers are characterized by consumption-oriented upper-income housing—condominiums, for example—where young professionals and older empty nesters have chosen to live in order to be near city museums, restaurants, and entertainment venues. These areas are frequently called "downtowns," a term that has no official definition, but is used unofficially to denote particular areas of the central city where there are many locations for entertainment and other amenities for consumption. A study of such areas in forty-four cities by Eugenie Birch found that between 1990 and 2000, the number of residents in downtown areas increased by more than 10 percent. This was a striking change compared to the period covering the previous two decades (between 1970 and 1990), when the downtown population in these same cities decreased by more than 10 percent. This change in downtown residential patterns in the 1990s, led by an inflow of single individuals, unrelated individuals living together, and couples without children, resulted in downtowns that had a higher percentage of young adults and of college-educated individuals than in the surrounding city or the larger surrounding metropolitan area (Birch 2005). The demand for living in the central city has driven up rents and condominium prices dramatically in many cities, particularly on the East and West coasts. This shift has driven out not only low-income households but many middle-income households as well.

Just as Alonso's original models were not meant to depict every city exactly, it is hard to generalize about the experiences of specific cities in different parts of the country. For individual cities, local dynamics have to be kept in mind. Values will depend upon the types and sizes of businesses located in each city, local laws, zoning regulations, access to transportation, crime rates, the quality of local amenities, and the influence of past construction within each city. One needs to take into account all of these factors to understand why some older cities continue to deteriorate while others have experienced an urban renaissance.

What's Left for the City in the Twenty-First Century?

Writing in 1990, the social critic George Gilder argued, "Cities are leftover baggage from the industrial era" (Gilder 1990, p. 166). According to Gilder, cities are no longer needed for production or to access cultural and information resources. Telecommunications can bring libraries, concert halls, and business meetings to anyone anywhere. Technology permits individuals to enjoy the amenities of the city without the crime, congestion, and commuting. Gordon and Richardson (1997) make very much the same argument, suggesting that rapid advances in telecommunications are responsible for accelerating the decentralization trends that were first set in motion by the automobile. As a result, they argue, cities will continue to be less and less compact and will spread out over more and more territory—just as the Alonso model might suggest in the case of zero transportation costs.

In fact, however, since Gilder first wrote about cities as leftover baggage, other authors have argued that just the opposite seems to be taking place in many metro areas. They note that many cities are once again becoming vital and vibrant places, with rising populations and skyrocketing land costs the closer you get to the epicenter of the metro region. How can this be?

Cities as Centers for Twenty-First-Century Business Services

Moss (1999) suggests that the "leftover baggage" view of cities is based on three untested hypotheses: (1) that all information activities are conducted more efficiently electronically than in person, (2) that people do not value very highly the social/psychological attributes of the workplace and therefore would just as soon work individually by telecommuting, and (3) that the physical setting where work takes place is irrelevant or even counterproductive to the worker and organizational performance.

There is good reason, Moss says, to believe that none of these hypotheses is valid. The growth of downtown office towers, a sharp increase in the number of meetings and conventions, and the continued increase in business travel all give testimony to the desirability and productivity-enhancing attributes of face-to-face interactions. In contrast to the theory that technology reduces interpersonal interactions, an alternative school of thought regarding the impact of technology on location suggests that telecommunications provide a *complement* to—and not a substitute for—face-to-face contact. The Internet and e-mail provide additional high-speed ways for people to make plans to gather, thus fostering face-to-face meetings. These new electronic tools provide an efficient means for social networking at work, as well as a way for friends to meet and plan get-togethers.

Krugman (2006) squares the "leftover baggage" theory with this alternative view in explaining what he calls the "New York Paradox." Using data on New York's leading sector—financial services—he notes that lower transportation and communication costs have allowed banks and insurance companies to relocate their back-office operations (their lower-paying activities such as check clearing, call centers, and filing) to distant sites, while concentrating their top executives in new, highly wired and wireless downtown office towers. These towers are increasingly built in such a way as to maximize the chance that executives and office staff will meet up with each other during the day, increasing the **bump rate** at which company staff interacts. In the information age, firms use high-speed communications all the time, but in concert with face-to-face personal relations. The existence of new technology does not eliminate the benefits from agglomeration—having people working together in teams, in close proximity to each other.

It is also true that highly paid executives have a high opportunity cost of time. Every hour wasted in commuting has a much higher cost for someone worth $500 an hour than for someone who earns the minimum wage. Thus, living close to work rather than commuting in from the suburbs is quite valuable to high-income individuals, making central city residential locations highly desirable once again.

Cities as Centers for Twenty-First-Century Consumption

Along with its advantages in the production of ideas, the modern central city is an important locus of consumption. Glaeser (2000, p. 11) notes, "As important as the production side is, the future of most cities depends on their being desirable places to live. As consumers become richer and firms more mobile, location choices are based as much on their advantages for workers as their advantages for firms." Expanding on this idea of the twenty-first-century city as the locus for consumption, Joseph Cortright (2005, p. 7) argues that in a "global economy, physical inputs and outputs and financial capital can easily be moved to places where they may be most productively used . . . but talented people obey a different calculus, choosing places to live based not solely on productive considerations, but on amenities and consumption opportunities, community, social and family considerations." Turning the location decision on its head, instead of having workers move to where business has set up operations, businesses increasingly look for locations where highly skilled workers want to live and set up operations there. Cities like San Francisco that are attractive to consumers will continue to draw new residents and enjoy high property values. Business will consider settling in such cities—even if the location costs are high—in order to have access to this workforce.

Taking this argument to an even higher level, Richard Florida (2002) describes the emergence of a new social class in America, a **creative class** comprised of scientists, engineers, architects and designers, writers, artists, musicians, and the like, who are increasingly responsible for the prosperity of modern society through their development of innovations in technology, art, and culture. Essentially, over the past two centuries, the most essential workers in highly developed societies have shifted from working as farmers to manufacturing production workers to those whose main task is to generate new ideas, new products, and new services—what Florida calls the "purveyors of creativity." Because the creative class values a lifestyle built around creative experiences, its members naturally gravitate to places like New York City, Boston, San Francisco, Chicago, and Seattle, where there are plenty of cultural and recreational amenities and lots of like-minded, creative people. These are cities in which there is, in Florida's words, an "underlying eco-system or habitat in which the multidimensional forms of creativity take root and flourish" (Florida 2002, p. 55).

According to Florida, members of this class value individuality, the chance to gain reward for accomplishment and merit, and diversity and openness. Instead of fearing differences in race, ethnicity, or sexual preference, members of this class generally embrace multiculturalism. Cities that nurture such an "ecosystem" are destined to grow and prosper. The rapid growth in median family income (see Chapter 2) in metro areas such as San Francisco, Raleigh-Durham-Chapel Hill, Austin, and Portland, Oregon—in contrast to much slower growth or actual decline in older industrial cities like Detroit, Buffalo, and Hartford—presumably provides evidence of just how successful "creative class" cities have become.

Cultural Amenities versus Economic Factors

The popularity of the Florida thesis notwithstanding, there is a powerful debate over just how much cities can rely on providing an ecosystem responsive to the preferences of the creative class. Robert Weissbourd and Christopher Berry (2004) argue that too much emphasis has been placed on cultural amenities as drivers of successful cities. No matter how much young professionals of the creative class might wish to live in the hippest cities with the greatest variety of amenities, basic economic factors such as wages and the availability of jobs are far more important in determining the location decisions of college graduates. As we shall demonstrate more fully in Chapter 12 on urban housing markets, it turns out that those metro areas responsible for attracting creative industry and creative workers in the 1990s—cities like Boston, San Francisco, San Jose, and Stamford, Connecticut—found their living costs so high by 2004 that employment growth had slowed and young workers were moving to cities with lower living costs, even if they did not have quite the same cultural milieu (Bluestone 2006).

In testing Florida's model of city success, Weissbourd and Berry used a statistical model to see just how much amenities were correlated with the size of the college-educated population across cities. They found that a "Bohemian Index" measuring the social environment as well as a "Recreation Score" had only a negligible correlation with the growth rate of college graduate residents across cities, after controlling for the initial level of educational attainment. Weather had a negligible effect as well, with some evidence that the mild climate of Sunbelt cities actually was a greater attraction for the non-college-educated population. Houston, as well as both Bakersfield and Long Beach, California, experienced significant population growth between 1990 and 2000, but below-average growth in college-educated workers.

The research of Weissbourd and Berry as well as the research on cost of living suggests that to be successful in terms of employment and population growth, cities of the twenty-first century need to provide not so much the cultural ecosystem for the creative class as the economic foundation for business investment and job growth. As we shall see in Chapter 14 on development policy, this requires investment in education and training, research institutions that support innovation, and venture capital for new start-ups. It requires ensuring safe streets and good schools for the children of those who work in the city, as well as affordable housing and other necessities. Ultimately, the dichotomy between attracting firms and attracting the creative class through investments in cultural and recreational amenities may be quite misleading. A city that can do both will be better off than a city that can do neither, because there will be positive feedback between attracting firms and attracting people. But if a city manages to attract the new base industries related to information technologies, then local industries that provide the creative class ecosystem may well follow—including restaurants, bars, theaters, and recreational outlets. The result is a **virtuous cycle** of employment and population growth with more and more cultural amenities.

The Classification and Economic Functions of U.S. Metro Areas in the Twenty-First Century

During the last three decades of the twentieth century, several major changes occurred that had implications for the functions of twenty-first-century metropolitan areas. Information technology revolutionized communications within firms, between firms, and between firms and potential customers—shifting the relationship between business location and communication needs. Continued reductions in transportation costs allowed firms to shift production to areas with lower-cost labor and other cheaper inputs, and to further expand the geographic scope of markets. Trade agreements between the United States and other countries reduced governmentally imposed barriers to the movement of goods between countries, further facilitating the movement of firms to low-cost areas. The widespread use of the U.S. dollar as an internationally accepted medium of exchange further facilitated trade. Moving goods over long distances was much less an uphill battle; the world was becoming more "flat."

These changes had numerous implications for U.S. cities. Saskia Sassen (2006) states that changes in the economy near the turn of the new century established a "new set of criteria for valuing and pricing economic activities," which effectively created new criteria for economic rewards for metropolitan areas. According to Sassen, the key aspects of this new value system for economic activities included heightened value accorded to management activities for transnational corporations— corporations operating in more than one country—and increased value associated with businesses supplying professional services such as accounting, legal, computer system design, and management consultants that help firms gather and process information, and make continuous adjustments to economic changes around the world. William Beyers (2002, 2005), an economic geographer, also emphasizes the importance of the buying and selling of professional services between businesses. In addition, he notes the growth in other portions of the service economy. He estimates that in 1997, $418 billion was spent on the consumption of cultural and recreational activities. Others have emphasized the growth of metro areas serving retirees.

The economy of the twentieth century saw the emergence of a new type of specialized city—the innovation city. At the beginning of the twenty-first century, the U.S. economy also manifests some new roles for cities. In addition, as we would expect from a dynamic economy, many of the economic functions that carry over from century to century are centered in a different collection of cities. Within this framework of change, the challenge of economic health for many metropolitan areas includes **repurposing**—adapting their buildings, workforces, transportation facilities, and other productive resources so that they can fit into the changing national economy in new ways.

A Taxonomy of Twenty-First-Century Cities

Natural resource cities (centers) continue to play an important part in the national economy. However, they are less likely now to be related to mining, agricultural production, or logging activities. Instead, it is the proximity to recreational activities that counts: access to skiing or to beaches, for instance. Examples include Aspen, Colorado; Park City, Utah; and Tampa, Florida.

Manufacturing cities (centers) continue to constitute a significant part of the economic structure in many metro areas, and are a key factor in economic growth for some. In the automobile industry, the Toyota plant in the Evansville, Indiana metro area (opened in 1995) and the BMW and Michelin plants (and national headquarters) in the Greenville-Spartanburg, South Carolina metro area (opened in the mid-1990s) have been important sources of growth. However, in many metropolitan areas, manufacturing is a less secure part of the economy, as businesses are more subject to failure in world competition or to relocation as firms search for lower costs. Between 1970 and 2005, U.S. employment in manufacturing firms decreased by 20 percent, from 17.8 million to 14.3 million (Sassen 2006). Many U.S. manufacturing cities, most centered in the Northeast and Midwest, faced decline as work shifted to Mexico, India, China, and other countries.

Transportation hubs of the early twenty-first century attract economic activity because of their proximity to regional, national, and international production sites and markets. Finished products, intermediate inputs (products or substances to be used for further manufacture), passengers, and communications are channeled through these transportation hubs. But as transportation has changed, the location of hubs and the tasks related to transportation shipments have also changed. Today, airline hubs near the middle of the country, like the FedEx hub in Memphis, Tennessee, and the UPS hub (Worldport) in Louisville, Kentucky, are among the primary sites for swiftly delivering packages to cities across the United States (Friedman 2005).

The importance of this function is shown in part by employment figures for those firms—FedEx and UPS are the largest employers in their cities, with 30,000 and 18,000 employees, respectively (in 2006). The volume and speed of activity in the transportation hubs—Worldport can sort 304,000 packages per hour—has had several spin-off activities, evincing what Jane Jacobs referred to as "creating new work out of old." Memphis and Louisville are not only expediting the movement of material but they are also becoming centers for repair of appliances—consolidating the location of parts and expertise in repair to handle high-volume work that otherwise would be spread among many diffuse locations. In addition to the airline hubs, other cities serve as hubs for surface transportation lines. For example, Dallas is developing plans to expand its "Inland Port" railway and highway facilities to capitalize upon its location between Atlanta and Los Angeles (along an east-west axis) and between Mexico and Chicago/Detroit (along a northeast-southwest axis) (Urban Land Institute 2006).

Finance cities (centers) of the twenty-first century remain among the metropolitan areas with the most lucrative economic activities, as the removal of barriers to international financial investing and the financial returns to companies that correctly interpret information about economies in other countries have led to high profitability. The New York metro area has retained its role as the foremost financial industry site in the United States. It is one of the two most important financial centers in the world (along with London). It is particularly well known for its trading and financial expertise associated with buying firms—or building new firms—in other countries as part of global economic activities (Sassen 2006).

Like other finance centers of the twenty-first century, New York's financial industry has experienced increasing consolidation of firms due to mergers reflecting economies of scale (taking advantage of information technology) and efforts to expand the types of expertise available in teams within financial companies. Recently, Chicago and Charlotte have grown as finance centers. In October 2006, two previously rival financial companies in Chicago, the Chicago Mercantile Exchange and the Chicago Board of Trade, announced plans to merge. If approved by regulators, this merger is expected to create the largest single market location in the world for trade of financial instruments related to grain, livestock, and other agricultural products, executing as many as 9 million contracts per day (Timmons 2006). Meanwhile, Charlotte, North Carolina, has grown as a major financial center throughout the final years of the twentieth century and the early years of the twenty-first century. In 1998, Charlotte-based NationsBank purchased Bank of America, and moved the Bank of America headquarters from San Francisco to Charlotte to merge with NationsBank. Consequently, Charlotte became the home of both Bank of America (the largest consumer and small business bank in the United States) and Wachovia Bank (the fourth-largest bank in the United States). According to the U.S. Chamber of Commerce, the financial industry in Charlotte now employs more than 55,000 people.

Innovation cities (centers) play a valued role in the economy of the early twenty-first century because such cities attract and support creativity that will extend the ongoing technological revolution of recent decades into new products and new production technologies. Many of the recent technological advances in microprocessors, optical technology, biotechnology, and other areas will be further developed, as insight and creativity transform laboratory research into useful products and services. Cities like Austin, Boston, San Diego, Seattle, Raleigh, Washington, D.C., and Denver are important not only for the innovation that occurs within the research and development departments of established firms like Microsoft (Seattle), Dell Computers (Austin), Qualcomm (San Diego), and Biogen (Boston), but also for the new products and services that emerge from the many start-up businesses that flourish in these areas.

In *Rise of the Creative Class*, Richard Florida suggests that within the increasingly important "creative class," there are two tiers of people who provide innovation—a "super-creative core" of individuals who provide path-breaking insights and produce "new forms or designs that are readily transferable and broadly useful," and "creative professionals," who are not path breakers in the same sense, but who are problem solvers "drawing on complex bodies of knowledge to solve specific problems" and who "apply or combine standard approaches in unique ways to fit the situation" (Florida 2002).

Successful innovation centers are characterized by an educated workforce, the presence of universities and hospitals, a high-quality telecommunications infrastructure, a number of employment opportunities that provide both lateral and upward mobility, and a quality of life that attracts and retains highly skilled creative people. Harkavy and Zuckerman (1999) have argued that the presence of institutions of higher learning and medical facilities—"Eds and Meds"—are particularly important as a part of the infrastructure that helps to anchor creativity in a specific metro area. These institutions generate large numbers of jobs, continuously engage in research, and disseminate knowledge to their students and workers. Moreover, because they are inherently immobile, they are not likely to be lured away to other places.

Cultural/tourism/recreation centers have developed in many parts of the country, reflecting the fact that the increased speed of transportation has not only made the world a smaller place for delivery of products and business services but has also made sites of historical importance, recreation areas, and other culturally significant venues more accessible to vacationers. Nearly 30 percent of the workers in the Las Vegas metro area, which markets itself as "The Entertainment Capital of the World," are employed in leisure and hospitality industries; and in 2005, the 39 million visitors to Las Vegas spent a total of nearly $37 billion during their visits (UNLV Center for Business and Economic Research 2006). With the expansion of casinos and resorts fueling economic growth, Las Vegas attracts many new residents and is currently one of the fastest-growing metro areas in the United States, having more than doubled in size between 1990 and 2005, from 797,142 to 1,710,551.

Similar dynamics are occurring in the Orlando metropolitan area, home of Walt Disney World, Sea World, and other attractions. The thriving Orlando area experienced a 58 percent increase in population between 1990 and 2005, from 1.2 to 1.9 million. In 2005, metro Orlando's nearly 50 million visitors spent nearly $30 billion during their visits (Orlando/Orange County Convention and Visitors Bureau 2006). Reflecting the importance of tourism, approximately 188,000 (more than one-sixth) of metro Orlando's jobs are within the leisure and hospitality industry, with 57,000 of these workers employed at Walt Disney World alone (Metro Orlando Economic Development Commission 2006a, 2006b).

Las Vegas and Orlando may be unique among U.S. cities for the scale of their entertainment sites, but many other metro areas have smaller-scale attractions that contribute substantially to the area's economic activity. Philadelphia—the city in which both the Declaration of Independence and the Constitution were written, the capital of the United States from 1790 to 1800, and home of the Liberty Bell—has a unique historical legacy that brings many visitors to the city. Attracted by this rich history, visitors are also drawn to art museums on the Avenue of the Arts, recreational activities, restaurants, and retail stores. Since 2000, Philadelphia has enhanced its appeal to visitors by improving the Independence National Historic Park, opening a family entertainment complex on the waterfront, and building a 5,000-seat Regional Performing Arts Center.

Retirement centers have emerged as a significant force in the U.S. economy, and the attraction of retirees has become part of the economic development plans of many areas. Retirees may be classified as one of three types—individuals who have lived in an area for much of their lives and choose to stay there, individuals whose health leads them to migrate to other locations near caregiving family members, and individuals who seek to migrate to a pleasant environment. Because travel and communication costs are much lower than they were in the past, retirees can live in a new location while still keeping in frequent touch with family.

Retirement centers target this last group, reasoning that amenity-seeking retirees often have sources of income that are not dependent upon local economic conditions and thus can contribute to the stabilization of a local economy. This relatively affluent group has good health and high education levels, they add to the number of volunteers in an area, and they pay more in local taxes than they use in locally supported services—largely because they do not have school-age children attending local schools. Their relatively high levels of discretionary income can be spent in the local economy.

In addition to their immediate effects on the local economy, retirees are seen as potentially valuable to a local economy over the long haul because their relatively stable incomes generate public-sector tax revenue and private-sector spending that can "prime the pump" for future economic development activities in a community. As the numbers of migrant retirees increase, so does the overall spending from that cohort, stimulating the growth of service-based businesses, and the in-migration of younger cohorts to fill the new jobs. This, in turn, can stimulate the growth of a wider range of businesses (Graff and Wiseman 1990; Fagan and Longino 1993; Skelley 2004).

Retirees often want locations with quality health care, warm climates, a low cost of living (including decent, affordable housing), safe neighborhoods, and convenient routine shopping. But they also often value being near cities that offer cultural events, recreation, and other attractions that would not be possible in a more distant small town.

Smart Growth and the New Urbanism Movement

The reemergence of the healthy central city as well as the growth of the new sub-urban edge cities (see Chapter 4) comport well with the **Smart Growth** movement that gained adherents in the late 1990s and continues to grow in importance today. The central idea behind this movement is to increase density through planned development so as to limit further suburban sprawl. According to Smart Growth disciples, quality planned development improves blighted central city areas, promotes environmental quality, lowers energy consumption through the substitution of mass transit for the private automobile, saves public resources by concentrating public infrastructure investment, and preserves rural land and open space.

The **New Urbanism** movement is tied to Smart Growth in that it promotes physical design of urban and suburban space that favors reducing dependence on the private automobile. The Charter of New Urbanism, which evolved out of the Congress for New Urbanism organized in 1994, stresses that individual architectural projects should be seamlessly linked to their surroundings and that the promulgation of graphic urban design codes can enhance the economic health and harmonious evolution of neighborhoods, districts, and land corridors. New Urbanism also promotes the construction of civic buildings and public gathering places that reinforce community identity and the culture of democracy (Judd and Swanstrom 2004).

By 1995, the New Urbanism movement was so strong that *Newsweek* magazine devoted the better part of an issue to outlining the key principles of what it predicted would be the hallmark characteristics of the twenty-first-century city (Adler 1995), including:

- Shrink building lot sizes and reduce the distance between the street and homes in order to conserve land and improve the streetscape.
- Bring back the corner store within a walkable distance of most residents.

- Make the streets skinny to force drivers to slow down and to improve the street-scape for pedestrians.
- Drop the cul-de-sac so that individual homes are not artificially separated from each other.
- Draw growth boundaries to keep sprawl from spreading ever farther into green space.
- Hide the garage to make neighborhoods look people-friendly rather than car-friendly.
- Mix housing types including single family homes and rental apartments to create a more heterogeneous community by income and family type.
- Plant trees curbside to humanize the city and suburb.
- Plan for increased mass transit to get people out of their cars voluntarily.
- Put new life in old retail malls so that the malls themselves can become the nucleus for real neighborhoods.
- Link work to home, making it possible for more people to walk or bicycle to work.
- Create real town centers with plazas, squares, and parks.
- Shrink parking lots in order to eliminate asphalt deserts that are empty for much of the evening and nighttime.
- Turn down the lights where safety is not an issue in order to cast a gentler glow in the community at night.
- Preserve green space wherever possible.

While such a list may seem utopian, more and more communities are considering and debating parts of the New Urbanism credo as they try to remake themselves into places that are more inviting to new residents and new businesses in the twenty-first century. We will take another look at these issues in Chapters 13 and 15.

The New Demographics of the Twenty-First-Century City

As the growth of New Urbanism and the redevelopment of the central city proceed, there are consequences that many observers do not see in as sanguine a light as the new urban ecosystem theorists seem to suggest. In most of the older cities that are experiencing an economic renaissance, housing prices have tended to rise much faster than wages. Glaeser notes that between 1980 and 1990, the elasticity of wages with respect to metro area population increased from .051 to .082, while the elasticity of housing costs with respect to population shot up from .114 to .225. This means that for every 10 percent increase in population, average wages rose by just 8.2 percent, while housing costs increased by nearly three times as much—22.5 percent (Glaeser 2000). Young professionals in many of these cities bid up housing prices because housing production does not keep pace with demand. This is particularly true of those neighborhoods closest to downtown where the array of cultural amenities beckons higher-income households. Low- and moderate-income families are increasingly priced out of such downtown areas and are forced to move to presumably less desirable neighborhoods in the city, the first tier of older, less expensive suburbs, or sometimes distant communities where they face long commutes to work. When entire neighborhoods rise in value to the point where existing residents can no longer afford to live in them, the neighborhood has experienced **gentrification**.

Gentrification and Income Segregation

According to Booza, Cutsinger, and Galster (2006), in 1970, 45 percent of the central city neighborhoods in twelve of the largest metro areas in the United States had a middle-income profile—including Atlanta, Baltimore, Chicago, Denver, Indianapolis, Los Angeles, Louisville, Oakland, Philadelphia, San Antonio, San Francisco, and Washington, D.C. By 2000, only 23 percent of the neighborhoods in these cities could be considered middle class. Some of these neighborhoods became poorer, while others became richer with fewer and fewer occupied by middle-income families. The share of families in the very highest income group increased the most—by 4.5 percentage points. The share of families in the very low income group increased by 3.4 percentage points, which reflects the growing bifurcation of central cities into very rich and very poor neighborhoods with fewer middle-class neighborhoods remaining intact. **Table 5.2** provides a summary of these results. Note the sharp decline in both middle-income families and middle-income neighborhoods across metro areas.

Table 5.2 Family and Neighborhood Income Profile, 100 Largest Metro Areas, 1970–2000 (Percentage Shares)

Family Income Type	1970	1980	1990	2000
Very Low Income	17.2	19.7	20.1	20.6
Low Income	18.5	17.5	17.7	17.8
Moderate Income	14.8	12.7	12.0	11.4
High–Moderate Income	13.2	12.0	10.9	10.1
High Income	12.6	14.0	13.1	12.1
Very High Income	23.6	24.1	26.3	28.1
Middle Income	28.0	24.7	22.9	21.5
Neighborhood Type				
Very Low Income	3.5	7.5	9.1	8.2
Low Income	20.8	21.2	21.3	24.0
Moderate Income	31.7	26.3	24.2	22.5
High–Moderate Income	26.6	23.6	20.2	18.4
High Income	12.6	14.5	15.4	15.1
Very High Income	4.9	6.8	9.7	11.8
Middle Income	58.2	49.9	44.4	40.9

Notes: Very Low Income Families: Below 50 percent of metro area median family income. Very Low Income Neighborhoods: Median family income under 50 percent of metro area family median. Other Income Classes: Low Income (50–80%); Moderate Income (80–100%); High–Moderate Income (100–120%); High Income (120–150%); Very High Income (over 150%); Middle Income combines the moderate and high–moderate categories.
Source: Booza, Cutsinger, and Galster 2006.

Neighborhoods like the South End in Boston, for decades comprised of rooming houses and low-rent apartments, now are home mostly to wealthy professionals who have taken deteriorating brownstones and converted them into upscale condominiums and single-family homes. In Brooklyn, New York, formerly low-income neighborhoods like Fort Greene and Bedford-Stuyvesant have become new urban villages that only higher-income households can afford. Such a transformation in neighborhoods increases the tax base and brings wealthier families back into the city, but in the process forces lower-income households to move because they can no longer afford the new higher rents.

Essentially, many of the cities of the twenty-first century are becoming resegregated, now along income and wealth lines rather than simply by race and ethnicity. Such income polarization, according to some social scientists, is eliminating the social glue that bonds lower- and higher-income areas together (Berube 2006).

Young Workers, Empty Nesters, and New Immigrants

While many cities are polarizing along income and wealth lines, they are also undergoing a demographic revolution. Cities are becoming magnets for young people, empty nesters, and new immigrants. Richard Florida's creative class is comprised heavily of young professionals who have come back to the central city for all-the reasons mentioned earlier in this chapter. Many older couples, having launched their children, no longer see the need to hold on to their large four- and five-bedroom, single-family homes in the suburbs. They are coming back to the central city, renting smaller apartments or buying condominiums—in the process, reducing their need to care for lawns or maintain houses. New immigrants coming from Asia, Central America, Africa, and the Caribbean are populating the central city, bringing much greater diversity to the life of the city. Somalis have fled their war-torn country and have settled in cities like Minneapolis-St. Paul, where nearly 9,000 were living as of the 2000 U.S. Census.

In a new twist of urban settlement patterns, many new immigrant groups are bypassing the major cities, settling in smaller cities like Lawrence, Massachusetts, where now close to 70 percent of the population is of Latino descent. The older suburbs of Long Island, New York, are now home to large numbers of Japanese, Koreans, Vietnamese, Indians, Pakistanis, Iranians, and Guatemalans. As of 2000, 58 percent of Asians and 49 percent of Latinos were living in suburbs rather than central cities, with the highest proportion in Sunbelt metro areas. Between 1980 and 2000, the percentage of minority residents—non-Hispanic blacks, Asians, and Hispanics—living in Boston suburbs increased to 13.3 percent from just 3.7 percent in 1980. Portland, Oregon's minority suburban population increased threefold to 14.3 percent. Milwaukee, Hartford, Tacoma, Salt Lake City, Chicago, and Atlanta all saw their suburban minority populations more than double over this period, with more than 36 percent of Atlanta's minority population settling in the suburbs. By

2000, more than 60 percent of the minority population of Los Angeles lived outside the central city (U.S. Department of Housing and Urban Development 2007).

Even small towns like Beardstown, Illinois, near the Mississippi River are being transformed as manufacturing continues to leave metro areas for more distant, cheaper locations. A large meat-processing plant in that area has transformed the community from a sleepy rural town to a bustling Mexican-immigration center, as Mexicans have come en masse to find work (Judd and Swanstrom 2004).

As such, the city and the entire landscape of the twenty-first century is changing dramatically in terms of age, income, wealth, and ethnicity. How this all plays out over the next twenty-five years will be interesting to follow. But one thing is perfectly clear. Cities are constantly changing with all kinds of new dynamics that shape their evolving form.

All in all, the transportation and communications revolutions have provided much greater flexibility in terms of the location decision for both households and businesses. With the decline in transportation cost as the defining element in location, the utility of the basic Alonso model pales in significance. Yet it still provides a good starting place for any discussion of location with a panoply of other factors now responsible for divergence from the strict bid rent curves of yesteryear. The future of the central city and the suburb will rely less on minimizing transportation costs and more on how well each can provide all of the amenities that households and businesses crave. The future physical form of the metro region is therefore much in flux.

References

Adler, Jerry. 1995. "Bye, Bye Suburban Dream." *Newsweek*, May 15, p. 40.

Berube, Alan. 2006. "The Middle Class Is Missing." *New York Daily News*, July 8.

Beyers, William B. 2002. "Services and the New Economy: Elements of a Research Agenda." *Journal of Economic Geography* 2: 1–29.

———. 2005. "Services and the Changing Economic Base of Regions in the United States." *Services Industries Journal* 25, no. 4: 1–16.

Birch, Eugenie. 2005. "Who Lives Downtown." Living Cities Census Series. Washington, D.C.: Metropolitan Policy Program, the Brookings Institution.

Bluestone, Barry. 2006. "Sustaining the Mass Economy: Housing Costs, Population Dynamics, and Employment." Paper prepared for Boston Federal Reserve Bank/Rappaport Institute Conference on Housing and the Economy, May 22.

Bluestone, Barry, and Bennett Harrison. 1982. *The Deindustrialization of America*. New York: Basic Books.

Booza, Jason C., Jackie Cutsinger, and George Galster. 2006. "Where Did They Go? The Decline of Middle-Income Neighborhoods in Metropolitan America." Living Cities Census Series. Washington, D.C.: Metropolitan Policy Program, the Brookings Institution.

Cortright, Joseph. 2005. "The Young and Restless in a Knowledge Economy." Report prepared for *CEOs for Cities* (December).

Council of Economic Advisers. 2006. *The Economic Report of the President, 2006*. Washington, DC: U.S. Government Printing Office.

Fagan, Mark, and Charles F. Longino Jr. 1993. "Migrating Retirees: A Source for Economic Development." *Economic Development Quarterly* 7, no. 1: 98–106.

Florida, Richard. 2002. *The Rise of the Creative Class*. New York: Basic Books.

Friedman, Thomas. 2005. *The World Is Flat: A Brief History of the Twenty-First Century.* New York: Farrar, Straus and Giroux.

Friedmann, John. 1995. "Where We Stand: A Decade of World City Research." In Paul Knox and Peter Taylor, eds., *World Cities in a World System.* Cambridge: Cambridge University Press, pp 21–47.

Gilder, George. 1990. *Life after Television: The Coming Transformation of Media and American Life.* New York: Whittle Books.

Glaeser, Edward L. 2000. "Demand for Density? The Functions of the City in the 21st Century." *The Brookings Review* 18, no. 3 (Summer): 10–13.

Gordon, Peter, and Harry W. Richardson. 1997. "Are Compact Cities a Desirable Planning Goal?" *Journal of the American Planning Association* 63, no. 1 (January): 95–105.

Graff, Thomas O., and Robert F. Wiseman. 1990. "Changing Pattern of Retirement Counties since 1965." *Geographical Review* 80, no. 3: 239–251.

Haas, William H., and William J. Serow. 2002. "The Baby Boom, Amenity Retirement Migration, and Retirement Communities." *Research on Aging* 24, no. 1: 150–164.

Harkavy, Ira, and Harmon Zuckerman. 1999. "Eds and Meds: Cities Hidden Assets." Washington, D.C.: Center on Urban and Metropolitan Policy, the Brookings Institution.

Judd, Dennis R., and Todd Swanstrom. 2004. *City Politics: Private Power and Public Policy,* 4th ed. New York: Pearson Education.

Krugman, Paul. 2006. "The New York Paradox." *New York Times,* July 10.

Lang, Robert E. 2000. "Office Sprawl: The Evolving Geography of Business." Washington, D.C.: Center on Urban and Metropolitan Policy, the Brookings Institution.

Metro Orlando Economic Development Commission. 2006a. "Employment by Industry, Metro Orlando." http://www.orlandoedc.com/core/file.php?loc=/Documents/EDC%20Documents/Data%20Center/workforce/Workforce_EmpbyInd1990-2006.pdf.

Metro Orlando Economic Development Commission. 2006b. "Metro Orlando Major Employers." http://www.orlandoedc.com/core/file.php?loc=/Documents/EDC%20Documents/Data%20Center/major _industry/Industry_MajorEmp_2006.pdf.

Moss, Mitchell. 1998. "Technology and Cities." *Cityscape: A Journal of Policy Development and Research* 3, no. 3: 107–127.

Orlando/Orange County Convention and Visitors Bureau. 2006. "State of the Market, November 2006." http://www.orlandoinfo.com/b2b/research/population.cfm.

Pisarski, Alan E. 2006. *Commuting in America III.* Washington, D.C.: Transportation Research Board.

Sassen, Saskia. 2002. "Introduction: Locating Cities on Global Circuits." In Saskia Sassen, ed., *Global Networks, Linked Cities.* New York: Routledge, pp. 1–36.

———. 2006. *Cities in a World Economy,* 3rd ed. Thousand Oaks, Calif.: Pine Forge Press.

Schaeffer, Robert. 2003. *Understanding Globalization: The Social Consequences of Political, Economic, and Environmental Change,* 2nd ed. Lanham, Md.: Rowman & Littlefield.

Skelley, B. Douglas. 2004. "Retiree-Attraction Policies: Challenges for Local Governance in Rural Regions." *Public Administration and Management* 9, no. 3: 212–223.

Storper, Michael. 1997. *The Regional World.* New York: Guilford.

Taylor, Peter, David Walker, and Jon V. Beaverstock. 2002. "Firms and Their Global Service Networks." In Saskia Sassen, ed., *Global Networks, Linked Cities.* New York: Routledge, pp. 93–115.

Timmons, Heather. 2006. "Reverberations of a Chicago Merger." *New York Times,* October 20.

UNLV Center for Business and Economic Research. 2006. "Metropolitan Las Vegas Tourism Statistic." http://cber.unlv.edu/tour.pdf.

Urban Land Institute. 2006. "Southern Dallas County Trade Corridor: ULI Advisory Services Panel, June 25–30, 2006." http://www.dallas-edd.org/images/corporate_expansion/uli.ppt.

U.S. Department of Housing and Urban Development. 2007. *State of the Cities Data Systems (SOCDS).* http://socds.huduser.org.

Weissbourd, Robert, and Christopher Berry. 2004. "The Changing Dynamics of Urban America." Report prepared by RW Ventures for CEOs for Cities.

Chapter 5 Questions and Exercises

Cities and Suburbs: The Location of Economic Activity within Metro Areas in the Early Twenty-First Century

1. As this chapter discusses, the location of some business activity shifted from central cities to suburbs in the twentieth century, but many analysts say that cities maintain considerable economic importance within metropolitan areas. One theme emphasized throughout the book, however, is that the experiences and situations of particular cities may vary. One way of comparing central city economic activity to suburban economic activity is to compare the number of people coming into the city to work against the number of people leaving the city to work in the suburbs. A table with such information from the 2000 U.S. Census can be found at

   http://www.census.gov/population/www/socdemo/daytime/daytimepop.html

   Using Table 1 from this Web site, take a look at the information for the city closest to your home and three other cities of your choice. For each of your selected cities, what was the *numeric amount* of the net change in population due to commuting (column G in the table)? What was the *percentage* change in the daytime population due to commuting?

2. Sort the table mentioned above by the size of the total resident population. Among the fifty largest cities, which ones had a negative daytime population change (more people commuting out of the city than commuting in)? Which ones had the highest percentage increase in daytime population? (See column H.)

   Sort the table by the size of the total resident population. To sort the table, follow these steps:

   - On the far left of your screen, click on the indicator for row 12 and hold down as you move the cursor down through row 215, so that all rows of data are included in the selection.
   - Release the cursor and move back up to the beginning of the table. (Rows 12–215 should still be highlighted as you reach the top of the table again.)
   - In the menu near the top of your computer screen, move your cursor to "Data." A drop-down list will appear.
   - Click on "Sort" and a "Sort" box will appear.
   - In the box under "Sort by," click on the arrow and then click on "Column C."
   - Immediately to the right of the "Sort by" section, make sure that the circle for "Descending" is selected.
   - Skip down to near the bottom of the "Sort" box, and just above "OK" you will see a circle for "No header row." Make sure that this circle is selected.
   - Click on "Go."

       + Among the fifty largest cities (in rows 12 through 61 after the sort), which ones had a negative daytime population change? (More people commuting out of the city than commuting in—see column H.)
       + Which ones had the highest percentage increase in daytime population?

Classification of Cities

3. Using the *Urban Experience* CD for three MSAs of your choice, identify for the year 2000 the percentage of employees in each of the following industry categories:

   - Agriculture and mining
   - Construction
   - Manufacturing
   - Wholesale and retail trade
   - Transportation, communications, and utilities
   - Business and repair services
   - Finance, insurance, and real estate
   - Professional services
   - Personal services
   - Public administration

   Which industries employ the most people? Using this information, try to categorize each of these MSAs according to the taxonomy presented in Chapter 5. (*Note:* For instructions on how to use this CD, see examples in the exercises for Chapter 1.)

4. In September 2007, the U.S. Bureau of Economic Analysis began releasing estimates of each metropolitan area's gross domestic product—the market value of final goods and services produced within the metropolitan area in a given year. The data can be found at

   http://www.bea.gov/newsreleases/regional/gdp_metro/
   gdp_metro_newsrelease.htm.

   Click on "Tables only."

   - Sort the data in Table 1 by the percent change in 2004–2005. Which ten metropolitan areas had the highest percent change in GDP? In which states are these metro areas located? Can you determine any reason why these areas had especially high growth? Note that a number of metro areas had negative growth (GDP decreased). According to these data, which ten metro areas had the greatest decrease in GDP? Can you determine why these areas had negative growth? For each of these metro areas, how does the growth in 2004–2005 compare to the growth in the previous three years?
   - Take a look at Table 2. This table shows the contributions of each of thirteen economic sectors to the 2004–2005 change in the metropolitan area's GDP. Refer to your findings from question (a) above and choose any five of the ten metro areas with the highest growth percentage and any five of the ten metro areas with the greatest decrease in GDP. For these metro areas, which sector positively contributed the most to the overall percentage change of GDP in the metro area? Which sectors negatively affected growth in the metro area's GDP?

FOUNDATIONS OF METROPOLITAN AREA PROSPERITY

Urban Prosperity and the Role of Trade

6

When the U.S. economy is doing well, new college graduates have their choice of good jobs, households have more income to spend, and the future looks rosy. When the nation's economy turns sour, newly minted BAs take jobs behind the counter at Starbucks, households rein in their spending, and prospects look bleak. Like the well-being of individuals and households, the well-being of metropolitan areas is linked to the vicissitudes of the national economy and reflects its good or bad times. Yet, just as some individuals and households fare better than others, some cities and suburbs outperform other metro regions. When the nation's unemployment rate is 6 percent, more than 12 percent of the workforce might be jobless in some metro areas, while only 3 percent are unemployed in others. Some cities experience buoyant growth and rising incomes for decades, while others have their day in the sun and then see other cities and regions pass them by. Some undergo an economic renaissance, while others fall from economic grace.

Metro Area Household Incomes

One way to trace a region's well-being is to consider the household incomes of its residents and how these change over time. According to the U.S. Bureau of the Census, a household includes all related family members and all unrelated people, if any, who live in a single housing unit. A household can be as small as a single individual living alone or as large as an extended family with unrelated lodgers, foster children, wards, or even employees who share the same housing unit. Household income refers to the sum total of all income from household members, including wages and salaries, transfer payments (including unemployment benefits, Social Security income, and public assistance), interest and dividends, pension and retirement income, rents, royalties, alimony, and child support. It is therefore a broad measure of the income received by each household in a city or metro area. **Median household income** (MHI) refers to the income of the middle household in an area—the one midway between the very poorest and the very richest. As such, it is a pretty good measure of the economic well-being of the typical household in a city or suburb, although it tells us nothing about how equally or unequally income is distributed.

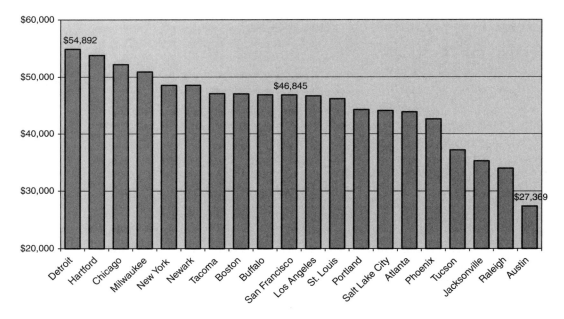

Figure 6.1 Median Household Income, Metro Areas, 1969 (2005 Dollars). *Source:* U.S. Department of Housing and Urban Development, HUD User Policy Development and Research Information Service, SOCDS date set, 2007. http://socds.huduser.org.

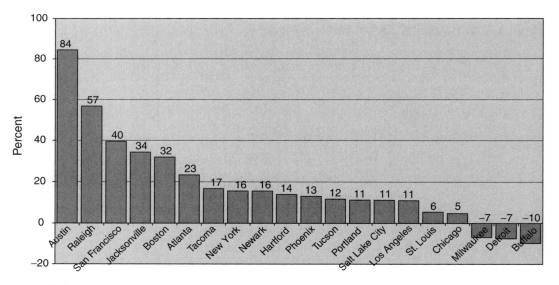

Figure 6.2 Percentage Change in Median Household Income, Metro Areas, 1969–2005 ($2005 Dollars). *Source:* U.S. Department of Housing and Urban Development, HUD User Policy Development and Research Information Service, SOCDS date set, 2007. http://socds.huduser.org.

Figure 6.1 displays real median household income in 1969 (in 2005 dollars) for the same twenty representative metro areas we explored in Chapter 2. In this case, however, we present median household income for the entire metro area rather than for the central city versus the suburbs, for here we address the relative prosperity of entire economic regions rather than parts of each region.

The metro area—including all central city and suburban households—with the highest median household income in 1969 was Detroit, the "auto capital" of the United States. Its median household income (MHI) was $54,892 (in 2005 dollars). The other metro areas with the highest MHIs were, in descending order, Hartford, Chicago, Milwaukee, and New York. There was not a southern or western metro region in the top six. At the bottom of the list of twenty metro areas were Austin, Raleigh, Jacksonville, Tucson, and Phoenix. Indeed, Austin's MHI ($27,369) was only *half* that of Detroit. Put another way, the typical household in Detroit had twice the income of the typical household in Austin. Based on the incomes of its residents in 1969, Detroit was an extraordinarily wealthy metropolitan area.

Between 1969 and 2005, however, changes in median household income reflect a dramatic redistribution of metro area prosperity. As **Figure 6.2** demonstrates, the typical resident of Austin—the metro region at the very bottom of the MHI list in 1969—experienced the largest percentage increase (84%) in real median income. Detroit, which had been at the top of the median household income list in 1969, fell to eleventh after experiencing an actual 7 percent decline in median income over this

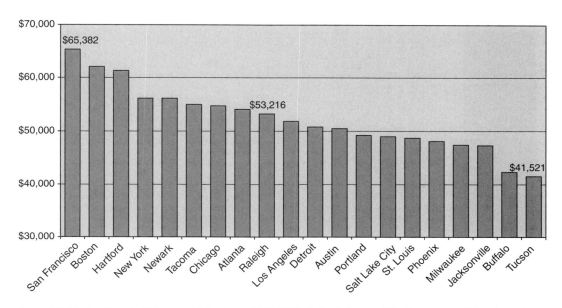

Figure 6.3 Median Household Income, Metro Areas, 2005 (2005 Dollars). *Source:* U.S. Department of Housing and Urban Development, HUD User Policy Development and Research Information Service, SOCDS date set, 2007. http://socds.huduser.org.

period of three and half decades. The residents of poor Buffalo went from ninth place to dead last—suffering a 10 percent loss in median household income.

The new top metro areas still included Hartford and Newark, but by 2005, San Francisco was at the top of the list—up from the very middle of the pack in 1969 (see **Figure 6.3**). Boston made it from eighth spot to second. Austin went from dead last to twelfth, while Raleigh moved up from nineteenth to ninth. On the other hand, Milwaukee went from fourth from the top to fourth from the bottom.

What accounts for these extreme differences in household income and these stunning changes over time? Why are the residents of some metropolitan areas able to prosper, while others experience steep declines in income? Of the five major colonial cities from the eighteenth century, why are New York, Philadelphia, and Boston still the nuclei of top-ten metropolitan areas, while Newport (Rhode Island) and Charleston (South Carolina) have been eclipsed by the growth of other areas? What allows some U.S. cities to maintain their economic viability for centuries, while others only have a moment in the sun before fading into relative obscurity? To answer these questions, we need to understand the role of trade in the metropolitan economy and how it affects the economic base of metropolitan areas—those activities that bring income and employment to an area and provide the foundation for further expansion and growth.

A Short Primer on the Economics of Trade

As we saw in Chapter 3, specialization and the division of labor are the basis for trade. In the same way that households can enjoy a higher standard of living if they focus on helping to produce only one or a few goods or services and purchase the rest from their earnings, entire metropolitan areas gain from specialization and trade. Although this sounds like a simple proposition, it is more complex than you might think. To understand how trade actually works, we will start with the easiest case that appeals to common sense, and then move on to instances that may seem to be counterintuitive. Economic theory can help explain why trade is advantageous under a much broader range of circumstances than first comes to mind, and why cities and suburbs can thrive—at least for a while—when they only specialize in the production of a few goods and services.

Absolute Advantage

People have different skills and abilities, partly because of natural talents and partly because of training. For example, consider two teenage cousins, Thelma and Louise, who live on opposite sides of town. Each has a paper route. Louise, the elder of the two, already has her driver's license; Thelma covers her route on bicycle. Louise has a weak throwing arm, while Thelma is an ace at throwing. Separately, each takes two hours to cover her route, a total of four hours of work. But if they team up to cover both routes with Louise driving and Thelma throwing, they find they can now cover *both* routes in two hours—in effect doubling their productivity and, potentially, their income. In this case, the benefits of specialization and trade are clear. When one party can do something better than another, that party is said to have an **absolute advantage**. One person is better at driving, the other is better at throwing. Their strengths and weaknesses are complementary, so by joining forces, they can accomplish things together that neither could accomplish alone. A similar argument could be made for why Norway might want to trade its sardines for pineapples grown in Honduras, why Washington State should specialize in growing apples and trade with California for oranges, and why Houston should specialize in oil refining and trade for coal from Wheeling, West Virginia.

Comparative Advantage

Starting with David Ricardo in the early nineteenth century, economists have long argued that the case for specialization and trade can often be made even in those instances where one party does *not* hold an absolute advantage in *any* of the endeavors. If that party is *less disadvantaged* in one task than in another, that is enough to justify specialization and trade, and the result will be beneficial to *both* parties. We can use a simple example to illustrate this more elusive concept of **comparative advantage**.

Consider Ellwood and Jake, the former a lawyer with a specialty in immigration law. He worked his way through college and law school doing yard work, at which he became extraordinarily adept. Jake is a recent immigrant who is earning his living doing yard work and taking courses as a paralegal at a local community college. He is very good at yard work, but not quite as good as Ellwood. Moreover, with his limited paralegal training, it takes him much longer than Ellwood to complete a standard legal document. Therefore, Ellwood has the absolute advantage in both occupations. However, Jake is at less of a disadvantage in yard work than in the preparation of legal documents, and this is the basis for mutually beneficial specialization and trade. Holding the quality of the work constant, it might take Ellwood twenty hours to do the yard work, while it would take Jake twenty-five. It would take Ellwood two hours to prepare a legal document, while it takes Jake five (see **Figure 6.4**). Ellwood is quicker at both tasks, but while it would take Jake two and a half times as long as Ellwood to prepare the document (five hours versus two), it would take him only one and a quarter times as long to do the yard work (twenty-five hours versus twenty). Therefore, Jake has a comparative advantage (he is less disadvantaged) in doing yard work. The economic principle that underlies comparative advantage is none other than opportunity cost.

Look at it this way and carefully follow the logic. Jake's opportunity cost for the five hours of work he would need to complete one legal document is equal to the time needed to complete one-fifth of the yard work (five hours of effort out of the twenty-five hours to complete the work on the yard). Ellwood's opportunity cost for completing the same legal document is that in the two hours it took him, he could have

	Do the Yard Work	**Prepare a Legal Document**
Ellwood	20 hours	2 hours
Jake	25 hours	5 hours
It takes Jake	1¼ times as long as Ellwood	2½ times as long as Ellwood

Ellwood's Opportunity Cost to Do the Yard Work (20 hours) = 10 Legal Documents
Jake's Opportunity Cost to Do the Yard Work (25 hours) = 5 Legal Documents

Ellwood's Opportunity Cost to Do a Legal Document (2 hours) = 1/10 of the Yard Work
Jake's Opportunity Cost to Do a Legal Document (5 hours) = 1/5 of the Yard Work

If Ellwood is paid $50 per hour and Jake is paid $25 per hour:
Ellwood's choice: Do yard work himself—opportunity cost = $50 × 20 = $1,000
Hire Jake $25 × 25 = $625
Jake's choice: Prepare legal document himself—opportunity cost = $25 × 5 = $125
Hire Ellwood $50 × 2 = $100

Each is better off hiring the other rather than doing the job himself.

Figure 6.4 An Example to Illustrate the Concept of Comparative Advantage

gotten one-tenth of the yard work done. So Ellwood can complete the document at lower opportunity cost: sacrificing one-tenth of the yard work, rather than one-fifth. On the other hand, if Ellwood had decided to complete the yard work, the twenty hours devoted to this task would have cost him the equivalent of finishing ten legal documents, while Jake's opportunity cost for completing the yard work in twenty-five hours is the forgone time he would have needed to finish five legal documents. So Jake can complete the yard work at lower opportunity cost: five documents rather than ten. If one party can produce something at a lower opportunity cost than another, that party is said to have a comparative advantage. Ellwood has the comparative advantage (as well as the absolute advantage) in producing legal documents; Jake has the comparative advantage (even though he does not have the absolute advantage) in doing yard work.

Given the existence of comparative advantage, we can show how trade benefits both parties. Even if Ellwood's hourly wage is twice as high as Jake's, they will *both* benefit from specializing and trading. Say, for example, that Ellwood earns $50 an hour and Jake earns $25. If Ellwood did the yard work himself, his opportunity cost is $1,000 ($50 × 20 hours); if he hires Jake, it costs him $625 ($25 × 25 hours). If Jake prepared his own documents, his opportunity cost would be $125 ($25 × 5 hours); if he hires Ellwood, it costs him $100 ($50 × 2 hours). Each is better off hiring the other. If a comparative advantage can be identified, both parties benefit from specialization and trade.

In the same way that individuals benefit from comparative advantage, so can metropolitan areas and nations. For example, call centers have become an important source of employment for cities such as Albuquerque (Uchitelle 2002). Wives of men working at military bases form a readily available workforce of people who can respond to free "800" calls on behalf of companies located far away. A hotel in

Manhattan that is part of a chain might use a call center to handle reservations. Formerly, the on-site clerk might have booked the reservation and also fielded prospective guests' questions. The clerk might have known whether room windows could be opened for fresh air, whether rooms facing the street were noisy, and whether the express train to the Bronx ran on weekends. The operator in Albuquerque can book the room, but is not likely to be able to answer these questions. Nevertheless, if work space in Manhattan hotels is scarce and expensive, booking reservations will be spun off to other places, even if it is more productive when done on-site. The same is true for similar jobs, while others—like cleaning rooms and making beds—obviously must be done on-site.

The distant call center workers have a comparative advantage, even if they are not as productive, in that their work *can* be moved, while the work of the cleaning staff cannot. The movement of back-office functions from a company's midtown skyscraper to the metropolitan area's suburban office park or to a claims processing site in a different state or even a different country is another illustration of comparative advantage because it shows the opportunity cost of using expensive real estate for functions that could be spun off to cheaper land. With improvements in transportation and communications, a firm's various functions that formerly needed to be under the same roof can now be spun off to different sites. Only those functions still reliant on agglomeration economies need to remain centrally located.

Limitations in the Theory of Comparative Advantage

If we want to know how two individuals (or metropolitan areas or nations) can maximize their well-being given a fixed amount of resources that each has available, comparative advantage tells us the answer. If one has the lower opportunity cost for producing X and the other has the lower opportunity cost for producing Y, they will maximize total output and both parties will be better off if they each specialize in just one product or service and trade for the other. This way of looking at the situation—**constrained maximization** or "maximization subject to constraint"— takes the starting situation as a given that cannot be changed. Once we accept those assumptions, the conclusion—the merits of comparative advantage and free trade— inevitably follows. Given their natural resource endowments and the quality of labor their residents possess, cities and regions will begin to specialize according to their comparative advantage. Towns in the Napa Valley in California will produce wine; cities like Houston will produce natural gas and oil; metro regions like Greater Boston, with its powerful universities, will produce biotech products.

As compelling as this may seem, the value of this approach has come under serious reconsideration (Ohlin 1967; Vernon 1966; Krugman 1990; Porter 1990; Fallows 1994). One major problem with comparative advantage is that it is essentially static. It tells you the best that can be done under the circumstances at a given point in time. It does not address the question of where the constraints—the fixed resources and the fixed opportunity costs—came from or what might be done to change them. It does not address the question of how an individual, a metropolitan area, or a nation could work to improve the quantity and/or quality of productive resources. These are questions about the dynamics of the situation: What causes things to change over time? What do those changes imply for the human ability to foster prosperity by augmenting resources and therefore changing the terms of trade? Who has what comparative advantage?

Let's go back to Jake and Ellwood. If Ellwood remains a lawyer and Jake remains in yard work, comparative advantage tells us how they can do the best under the circumstances. What happens if we do not take this static analysis as a given? Jake might complete his paralegal training and become adept at preparing legal documents. Ellwood might decide to leave his law practice and start a landscaping business because of his love of the outdoors. Over the years, Jake's and Ellwood's initial occupations might take each of them down unexpected paths, perhaps unrelated to their original specialized line of work. Comparative advantage switches in this case, so that Jake is now spending most of his time doing legal work, while Ellwood is spending his productive time doing yard work. In a dynamic context, the question is not the one raised by comparative advantage: How do you make the best of a given amount of resources? Instead, it is: What can you do to improve the quality and quantity of the resources at your disposal?

Changing comparative advantage is not easy for cities and regions to do, but it often becomes necessary when technological change or new competitors reduce a metro area's ability to successfully continue to specialize in one product or service. Chicago had to switch from meatpacking, Detroit has had to try to switch from auto production, Cleveland and Pittsburgh have had to switch from steel. Instead of blindly accepting the dictates of comparative advantage, nations, regions, and cities are constantly trying to find ways to specialize in new goods and services rather than accept the fate comparative advantage would ascribe to them.

Those cities that prove adept at marshaling the resources to gain comparative advantage in the production of new goods and services are the ones in which median household income generally rises. Those less adept see their positions erode, and the common consequence is slowly rising or actually declining median household income. Note the 40 percent or greater increase in real MHI between 1969 and 1999 in Figure 6.3 for Austin, Raleigh, and San Francisco in comparison to actual declines of 7 percent or more in Milwaukee, Detroit, and Buffalo.

New Trade Theory

Several new ideas have emerged that provide an expanded framework for understanding trade, each of which provides a more dynamic explanation, and new insights into the relationship between trade and the prosperity of geographic areas.

New trade theory emphasizes the effect of economies of scale in production and the barriers that existing large-scale production pose for the entry of new firms to an industry (Krugman 1990). According to this theory, if market demand is not sufficient to support many sites of large-scale production, the product will be produced in only a few locations. In such cases, a country, a region, a metropolitan area, or a city may benefit from **first-mover advantage**, where firms and the areas in which they are located are able to establish economies of scale or other benefits by being early entrants into the market for a new good or service. Here, the early bird gets the worm. For example, when the early auto industry got its start in Detroit, there were no areas that could effectively challenge the city's dominance in this industry—at least until after World War II.

In contrast, **product life cycle theory** postulates that the location of production for a particular good may change over time as differing production and marketing needs arise in the course of moving from initial product introduction to widespread use (Vernon 1966). When Jane Jacobs described how the economy of a metropolitan area develops over time, she used the metaphor of "adding new work to old" to capture such a process (Jacobs 1969). In the initial stage of the product's life, the site of production may be solely determined by the location of the creative insight. In Stage 2, as the product catches on and its demand from other areas increases, the initiating firm exports more of its output. As this occurs, firms in other locations begin to attempt to copy its success by producing the same or similar products. In Stage 3, competition from other firms increases, buyers have more alternatives from where to procure the product, and the initial firm's exports decrease. Eventually, the initial region may become an importer of that good.

Today, Detroiters *import* most of their cars from other regions of the country and from foreign producers. The product life cycle theory illustrates that geographic patterns of trade may reflect dynamic processes of innovation, the growth of interest in the product by consumers, export decisions, and competition from other firms. Laptop computers are a good example; when first introduced, they were manufactured by Toshiba in Japan and by companies like Dell in the United States. But as production ramped up, both companies built laptops or components in Taiwan, Malaysia, and China.

The Theory of Competitive Advantage

The most recently introduced conceptual framework for the explanation of trade and prosperity, **competitive advantage**, has emerged from business economics. In contrast to the concept of comparative advantage, which focuses on a region's gains from trade that involves different goods, the concept of competitive advantage focuses on the success of a firm in a particular industry against its rivals that produce the *same* good or service. Competitive advantage takes on locational significance, becoming relevant to nations, regions, and metropolitan areas because of the connections between place and the ability of specific firms in particular locales to initiate and maintain successful strategies against rivals.

According to Michael Porter, competitive advantage can be gained either through low-cost production or through product differentiation. Low-cost production allows a firm to underprice its competitors to obtain and keep a greater share of the market, or to gain higher profits from goods sold at the same price as a competitor. Product differentiation gives competitive advantage if it leads potential buyers to choose the firm's products over its competitors' at the same price, or if it leads the buyer to pay extra for the good because of the perceived "unique and superior value to the buyer in terms of product quality, special features, or after-sale service" (Porter 1990, p. 37).

Like the product life cycle theory, the competitive advantage approach emphasizes that industry and firm characteristics change over time. Extended periods of economic prosperity for a geographic area rest on the ability of its firms to constantly innovate in order to sustain competitive advantage against their rivals. This is called **sustained competitive advantage**.

Advantages gained through low-cost production are relatively difficult to sustain, because lower cost sources for labor or materials are often found. Textile production, once a New England industry, moved to the South early in the twentieth century in search of ever-cheaper labor. By the 1960s and 1970s, many textile firms had relocated to Mexico to reduce their costs. And now the location choice is rapidly shifting to China where labor costs are lower still.

Product differentiation strategies may be easier to sustain because they are often built upon things that are harder to duplicate, such as unique technology, brand name recognition, expertise in repair or service, durability, access to unique inputs, or other features valued by customers. Yet, since rivals can be expected to also seek competitive advantage from product differentiation, sustained advantage from such sources requires constant research and development, innovation, and creation of new resources.

Porter also emphasizes the role of **industry clusters** by which he means the external economies that occur from the agglomeration of firms operating in the same industry or in closely related industries. Regional clusters provide several important advantages to firms and therefore to the metropolitan areas in which they are located. The firms in a regional cluster can benefit from sharing labor pools, exchanging knowledge, and utilizing common infrastructure and other agglomeration economies. In the process, they give a city or region a competitive advantage over other locations trying to produce similar goods.

The geographic concentration of specialized expertise is particularly helpful in making these industry clusters successful. Knowledge spillovers allow scientists and engineers to quickly and easily share information, often in informal settings. While the Internet makes it possible for professionals to share information even if they live on opposite sides of the globe, the argument goes that face-to-face contact is even more valuable. If a metro area can build a monopoly or near monopoly in a particular type of expertise, it can specialize in an industry or industry cluster that utilizes those skills and thus become prosperous.

Detroit gained competitive advantage in auto production and all the related design, manufacturing, and service industries that belong to this industrial cluster by attracting more auto engineers than anywhere on earth. Hollywood, which had an early comparative advantage in movie production—in relation to many other parts of the United States—thanks to its year-round mild climate and large number of sunny days, attracted more producers, directors, set designers, and actors, creating an industry cluster around the silver screen. Boston, based on its huge array of universities and colleges, attracted more hardware and software engineers than most anywhere else, giving it a competitive advantage in the information and biotech sectors. Each of these cities became a boomtown rooted in building successful industry clusters and specializing in them. Today, Cambridge, Massachusetts, has become a center for cutting-edge biotechnology firms anchored by the city's two premier universities, Harvard and the Massachusetts Institute of Technology.

Attaining and sustaining a competitive advantage for a differentiated high-valued product, thereby contributing greatly to an area's prosperity, requires the full deployment of high-quality resources. Porter groups these resources into the following categories:

- *Human resources*—the size and quality of the labor force
- *Physical resources*—the amount and quality of natural resources, including location and proximity to other markets
- *Knowledge resources*—scientific and technical know-how produced by universities, government agencies, and private research and development firms
- *Capital resources*—the amount and cost of finance capital, including the availability of venture capital to fund new enterprises
- *Infrastructure*—the quality and cost of the transportation, communication, delivery, and banking systems, as well as institutions that affect the quality of life

As these five categories indicate, the resources for sustained competitive advantage typically involve the work of businesses, government, and educational institutions. Those regions that can put all or many of these resources together are destined for real prosperity that can endure over time.

Trade and Prosperity

The approaches to trade and prosperity represented by comparative advantage, new trade theory, product life cycle theory, and competitive advantage are perhaps best seen as complementary tools for understanding the economies of metropolitan areas. The essential idea of comparative advantage—that areas trade to take advantage of their different opportunity costs—is still a very important prescriptive notion for increasing production and describes much of the trade that actually occurs between cities, metro areas, and regions. New trade theory gives us the insight that economies of scale and industry structure are important aspects of trade for firms, cities, and regions. The product life cycle theory calls attention to the dynamic quality of product creation and the implications for firms and regions of the product's acceptance into widespread use. Finally, the theory of competitive advantage highlights the rivalry that occurs within market economies, and the significance of rivalry between firms and regions for investment and jobs.

We have emphasized the distinction between static and dynamic concepts. One of the major differences between the initial comparative advantage approach and the three more recent approaches is the difference between insights that are focused on the short run (when a producer's decisions are constrained by the need to operate with an existing plant and equipment) and those focused on the long run (when a producer can choose to move to a different-sized plant or change the type and amount of equipment he uses). In the context of a metropolitan area, it can also be expressed as a shift in focus from the demand side to the supply side of the area's economy. As we shall see below, a focus on the demand side—what each party brings to the table for exchange—fits into the framework of the short-run, static analysis. A focus on the supply side—the development of new capabilities for trade—generates a more dynamic, longer run perspective.

Export Base Theory: The Demand Side of the Metropolitan Area's Economy

No metropolitan area is entirely self-sufficient in the sense of being able to produce within its boundaries all the goods and services its residents want to consume. Currently, there are no automobile assembly plants in metropolitan Boston (or, for that matter, anywhere in New England). The area's drivers must buy cars produced somewhere else—Jeep Grand Cherokees from Detroit, Saturns from Tennessee, Hondas from Ohio, and imports from Japan or Germany. Similarly, Chicagoans who want orange juice or Seattle residents who want grapefruits need to bring them in from places with warmer climates. If the residents of a metropolitan area want to *buy* products from the outside, they will need to have something to *sell* to the outside in order to afford them. They must have a comparative advantage in the production of *something* if they are to remain economically viable.

Metaphorically, when areas "import" automobiles, orange juice, or grapefruits from beyond their boundaries, they need to pay for those purchases with income that has been earned by "exporting" products to the outside. In this sense, metropolitan Los Angeles exports motion pictures not only to moviegoers on other continents but also to those in northern California; metropolitan Seattle exports software not only to countries around the world but also to other places in the Pacific Northwest.

What makes a product an export is that it brings income into an area that was earned elsewhere. That is easy to see when a worker in Atlanta uses some of her income to buy a new Honda manufactured in Ohio. The funds leave the place where they were earned and provide income to another place hundreds or thousands of miles away. What if that worker decided to spend her vacation in Orlando? If she leaves home with a fat wallet and returns with a thinner one—or a larger balance on her credit card—it is the same underlying principle: the funds leave the city where they were earned and provide income elsewhere. Indeed, tourism is an important part of the economic base of many metropolitan areas, including Las Vegas, New York, and San Francisco.

The idea behind **export base theory** *is that the demand for an area's exports is the key to understanding its prosperity.* If outsiders are eager to buy what the metro area produces, income will flow to that area and it will provide the funds not only to pay for the area's imports but also to support the metro area's local service sector—those items that are produced and consumed within the region.

Think of Pittsburgh in the mid-twentieth century, the heyday of the domestic steel industry. As the demand for steel increased, more steelworkers were hired. They spent part of their new earnings on products imported from elsewhere, but some of those new earnings stayed within the local economy to be spent in luncheonettes, barbershops, or bowling alleys. Hence, the increased demand for steel meant more income initially for the new workers hired in the steel industry, but it also meant more demand for local goods and new employment in those luncheonettes, barbershops, and bowling alleys. These service workers also spent some of their new income on imports and some on local services, fueling another round of spending in the local economy. Each new round is smaller because the income spent on imports departs the area, leaving only the portion spent on local services to generate more income in the next round.

Thus, for every new job created in an export industry, there is additional employment created in the local service sector. These local jobs include not only private-sector jobs like barber or movie usher but also public-sector jobs like teacher or firefighter. An increase in the demand for a city's exports will initially fuel employment growth in its export industries and, subsequently, job growth in the area's local public and private sectors.

This phenomenon works in forward gear as the demand for exports grows, but it also works in reverse gear. If the demand for steel produced in Pittsburgh declines, steelworkers get laid off, followed by layoffs in the area's luncheonettes, barbershops, and bowling alleys. As local tax revenue declines, some teachers and firefighters might also lose their jobs. Here again, for every one hundred jobs lost in the export sector, there will be many jobs lost in the local service sector, including public and private services.

The 1989 documentary film *Roger and Me* provides vivid examples of the consequences of a decline in an area's export base. It depicted the vacant downtown storefronts that resulted from the decision by General Motors to shut down many of the automobile assembly plants in the company's birthplace, Flint, Michigan. It also included a portion of a grim local TV news report documenting that the rat population of the county outnumbered the human population, both because households were moving away to places with better employment opportunities and because the county could no longer afford to collect the trash as often.

When people move away from a depressed area in search of better opportunities elsewhere, the movers are not just a general cross-section of the population. They tend to be those who are younger, more educated, and more energetic. Demographers call this **selective migration.** When this occurs, it becomes even more difficult for an area to recover because the most economically attractive portion of its workforce has left for greener pastures.

We can summarize the key elements of export base theory in the following way:

- An export is a product that brings income earned elsewhere into a metro area.
- The demand for a metro area's exports is the driving force in determining an area's prosperity.
- Income from exports is crucial: It pays for a metro area's imports and supports the area's local service sector, including both private and public services.
- An increase in a metro area's export industries will cause a multiplied increase in the area's local service sector.
- A decrease in a metro area's export industries will cause a multiplied decrease in the area's local service sector.
- A sustained contraction will cause selective migration and will make it even more difficult for the metro area to recover.

The Basic/Nonbasic Approach: A Simple Measurement Technique

To better understand the power of export base theory, it is useful to see how economists measure the impact of exports on the prosperity of a region. The most widely used technique is known as the **basic/nonbasic approach** which measures the impact on a metro area's economy as a result of a change in export demand by estimating the size of a **job multiplier**. The technique begins by categorizing all jobs in the area as either part of the export base (basic) or part of the local service sector (nonbasic). Even if the jobs look similar, the basic/nonbasic approach treats them differently depending on whether they are part of the export sector or part of the local sector. For example, a janitor answering help-wanted advertisements might be indifferent between a job with a publishing company and a similar job at the public library. Both might offer the same wages and fringe benefits and both places have lots of books. But even though the jobs might be interchangeable from the viewpoint of the worker, they play very different roles in the basic/nonbasic approach. The *basic* job has a multiplier effect associated with it since it brings in income from outside the area; the *nonbasic* job does not. Part of the income earned by employees of the city's export sector is spent on other export goods like automobiles, but part is spent on local products and services—restaurant meals, haircuts, rent—thus generating local jobs in the local economy.

Job Multipliers

When every job in the area has been categorized as either basic or nonbasic, the job multiplier can be calculated. For example, a small metropolitan area might contain 50,000 jobs, 25,000 of which might be basic (export) and the other 25,000 nonbasic (local services). The ratio of export jobs to total jobs is 25,000:50,000, or 1:2; the ratio of export jobs to local service jobs is 25,000:25,000, or 1:1. Assuming that new jobs are like existing jobs, we conclude that when the demand for the area's exports rises, each new export job will support, on average, one new local service job. Ultimately, the increased demand for exports has created two new jobs in the area—one in the export sector, and another in the local service sector.

The simple basic/nonbasic approach implicitly assumes that the ratio of basic employment to total employment remains constant as the area grows. However, we know that larger areas are more self-sufficient than are smaller ones. As an area grows, it will be able to substitute local production for some of the items it imports. This is referred to as **import substitution**. Therefore, in larger metropolitan areas, every additional one hundred export jobs will generate even more local service jobs because there will be fewer leakages from the spending stream in the form of imports.

If, as we have seen, the ratio of export jobs to total jobs changes as an area grows, it would make more sense to calculate a multiplier based on *changes* in export employment and *changes* in total employment, rather than *levels* of export and total employment. In either case, though, calculating the job multiplier requires that the area's jobs be categorized as either export or local service—and this is easier said than done. In our earlier example of Pittsburgh, it was easy to assume that most of the steel was exported and that all of the barbers served local clientele. But what about more complicated situations where some of the steel is used locally and some of the "local" services are exported—for example, consumed by tourists? This is where we need to consider location quotients.

Location Quotients

How would we categorize restaurant workers in New York City? Some of the Big Apple's restaurants cater primarily to tourists, others serve a local clientele, and some have a mixture of locals and visitors. We need some way to apportion the jobs in this industry into those that are part of the export base versus those that are not. Presumably, we could place interviewers with clipboards at the door of each New York restaurant and ask the exiting patrons for their zip codes, but that would be prohibitively expensive. So, instead, we use a more indirect strategy—calculating a **location quotient**.

The location quotient is the proportion of the area's workers employed in a given industry divided by the proportion of the U.S. workforce employed in that industry. The location quotient measures the degree to which an industry is overrepresented (or underrepresented) in the local economy. We infer from this the degree to which each industry is part of the area's export base. For example, if 2 percent of the nation's workforce is employed in an industry but 6 percent of a given metropolitan area's workforce is employed in that industry, the location quotient for that metro area would be three (6% divided by 2%), and we would infer that one-third of the workers are producing for local needs, while the other two-thirds are producing for export. If the industry had 60,000 jobs within the metropolitan area, 40,000 of these jobs would be counted as basic (export), the other 20,000 as nonbasic (local).

A location quotient greater than one implies that an industry is producing more than enough to meet local need and is exporting the excess. A location quotient less than one suggests that a community must import some of this industry's product to satisfy local demand. A location quotient equal to one would imply that the area is producing enough to satisfy local needs, without having to import anything from this industry. We would expect the location quotient for the dry cleaning industry to be just about one in every metropolitan area, since people rely on local providers for this service. Hotels in Las Vegas or any large convention city would have location quotients well above one, indicating they are largely part of the export base.

Limitations of the Basic/Nonbasic Approach

While data on employment by industry is easily available, the basic/nonbasic approach, with its use of job multipliers and location quotients, is far from precise. In fact, it often tends to overstate the size of the job multiplier, because of an inherent tendency to understate the size of the export sector due to some questionable assumptions. Implicit to its construction, the location quotient assumes that an industry's product is homogeneous, meaning that the output of one producer is no different from the output of another. The underlying model assumes that households will always consume the output of local producers to save on transportation costs, since this product is indistinguishable from the output of producers outside the area.

That may not be such a bad assumption in the case of dry cleaners, where a location quotient equal to one would be an accurate indicator of self-sufficiency. In other instances, however, a location quotient equal to one would lead to the *mistaken* conclusion that the product was neither imported nor exported. For example, let's say that a metropolitan area had a location quotient of one for the recording industry. The assumption of product homogeneity would imply that there is no difference between one compact disc and another, and therefore that all the compact discs produced in that area were consumed there. Such an outcome is highly unlikely. The underlying reality is that compact discs produced in Nashville are sold in New York, and vice versa. By not recognizing this "cross-hauling," our location quotient would have failed to identify the recording industry in Nashville and New York as export industries, and mistakenly labeled it part of the local service sector. In this case, the location quotient would have failed to identify some export jobs, thereby underestimating the export sector and consequently overestimating the job multiplier—the number of local jobs generated as the result of the export sector.

Another limitation of the basic/nonbasic approach is that it cannot distinguish the impact of a change in demand in one part of an area's export base from a change in demand in another. The Los Angeles export base includes the aerospace industry, the motion picture industry, and several other industries. An expansion in aerospace might play out very differently from an expansion in motion pictures in terms of its specific impact on local area jobs. The basic/nonbasic approach cannot distinguish between these two scenarios because although it divides jobs into export versus local service, it does not make any distinction among different industries within the export sector.

Input-Output Analysis: A More Complex Measurement Technique

Just as scientists and physicians use tracer dyes to follow the path of fluids through a system—to identify leakages from a sewage treatment plant or diseased tissue in the human body—social scientists can use **input-output analysis** to follow the impact of a change in demand for exports as it wends its way through the economy of the metropolitan area. Unlike the basic/nonbasic approach, input-output analysis allows us to disaggregate the export sector into its component parts and to distinguish the impact of a change in demand for one export from a change in demand for another. It allows us to see the specific ways in which each industry interacts with the rest of the metropolitan economy—for example, how an increase in demand for the output of the biotechnology industry would raise the demand for its inputs, some of which would be imported from outside, some provided by local suppliers. As more income is earned by households employed in that industry, it would be spent on additional goods and services. Here again, some will be imported and some will be provided by local suppliers. By specifying the complete set of relationships between all industries on the input side (what each industry requires as inputs from every other industry to produce its output) as well as the output side (where the output of each industry goes), we have the equivalent of a tracer dye for the area's economy. (To learn more about input-output calculations, see **Appendix A**.)

Limitations of the Input-Output Measurement Technique

Although input-output models provide a far more sophisticated method than the basic/nonbasic approach for understanding the impact of a change in an area's export demand, this technique also has some important limitations. It requires vast amounts of data, delivered in an accurate and timely manner. While such requirements are met at the national level, they are far more difficult to achieve at the metropolitan level.

Moreover, the resulting model is only as accurate as the input matrix allows it to be. If we start with an accurate recipe at a given point in time, why wouldn't it be accurate later? One reason is that our recipe for producing small batches of output might not be the same as the recipe for producing larger batches, if there are some scale economies in production. Another is that over time, technological change brings us not only new products but also new processes to produce existing products more efficiently.

Yet another reason is that relative prices might change. Although our recipes would still be valid if, say, all prices doubled (in that case, a dollar's worth of output would just represent half as many physical units), our recipes would be worthless if the price of one input went up by 15 percent while the price of another fell by 5 percent. Therefore, the input matrix would need to be recalculated to account for technological change or a change in relative prices, meaning that it is valid only for relatively short periods of time. The recipe can also change, often dramatically, when a previously supplied input is imported from another region or foreign country.

Limitations of the Demand-Side Focus

Quite apart from the limitations of the measurement techniques, there are limitations to focusing so intensely on the demand side of the area's economy. Knowing the comparative or competitive advantage of a particular city or suburb does not, by itself, provide the necessary information to accurately gauge the metro area's level of prosperity. Dalton, Georgia, for example, might be the carpet production center of the United States, but the demand for carpets depends on household incomes, tastes, alternative floor covering options, and a host of other factors about which Dalton has little influence in the short run.

Moreover, even though it is indisputable that at any given moment, the well-being of the area depends on the health of its export industries, cities that rely on a single export industry are often more vulnerable than cities with a more diversified set of export industries. The old proverb, "don't put all your eggs in one basket," turns out to be good advice. Moreover, smaller cities are much more dependent on exports than larger ones, since larger areas can provide for more of their needs internally through import substitution, producing some items locally rather than importing them from outside. Detroiters can buy a Ford Mustang built in the nearby Ford Rouge plant in Dearborn, whereas residents of Wyoming need to import their cars no matter what brand they buy.

Shifting the Focus from the Demand Side to the Supply Side

Earlier in this chapter we described comparative advantage as a static analysis with greatest relevance for the short run. At any given moment, an area's exports will be comprised of industries in which the area currently has a comparative advantage. Its existing plant and equipment and other human and physical resources will be well suited to produce its current mix of output. Over time, however, the demand for an area's exports will change, and the area will need to adapt. Resources well suited to today's export industries may not be well suited to the economy of tomorrow. Before it became the motor city, Detroit was known as the nation's premier manufacturer of cast iron stoves, a consumer product that became obsolete with the introduction of the modern gas range. Fortunately for Detroit, just as the demand for cast iron stoves was drying up, the demand for cars was taking off.

Because demand is so fickle and technological change so pervasive, we need to take a closer look at how a city, suburb, or metro area deploys its resources. Using the framework of input-output analysis, we need to know more about how the area creates value added, and whether it has the resources to sustain a competitive advantage in high-value-added production. For example, the input-output table for one area might reflect the fact that its export industries are low-value-added assembly plants: components are imported from other places and are turned into finished products in a few simple steps. High-quality physical and human resources are not required for this operation, so they are unlikely to be nurtured and developed in the area. Although the area might temporarily possess a competitive advantage based on low cost—at least until a lower cost location can be found—it will be stymied in its attempt to create sustainable competitive advantage in the absence of its ability to nurture high-value-added product differentiation.

In contrast, an area rich in the variety of resources described by Porter will have an input-output table in which the difference in value between imported inputs and final output is large. These high-value-added export industries are more likely to be the basis of sustainable comparative advantage through product differentiation and the beneficial effects of industry clusters, rather than through low-cost production. For this reason, it is time to take a closer look at the supply side of the metropolitan area's economy.

The Supply Side: A Long-Term Perspective

In the late nineteenth century, the price of silver was high and there was great prosperity in the silver mining towns of Colorado. Grand avenues, fancy stores, and fine opera houses were built, befitting the families of the wealthy mine owners. When the price of silver fell, those once-prosperous places became ghost towns as their export base crumbled. In contrast, the Boston area has remained economically viable for more than 300 years, although it has gone through long periods of economic drought. Its original export bases of fishing, whaling, and shipping are long gone, but it has found new export industries to replace older ones for more than three centuries. Why are some areas more resilient than others? Why is the loss of an export base a death sentence for some communities, but only a temporary setback for others? Aside from the fact that the Colorado mining towns had only one export and were therefore more vulnerable to changes in their demand than places with a more diversified set of exports, what determines an area's economic staying power?

As we have seen, at any given moment, an area's well-being depends on the health of its export industries. However, over the long term, export industries come and go. Products might become obsolete, consumers might change their tastes, or producers might relocate in response to lower costs elsewhere.

Over the long term, the key to an area's viability is its ability to attract, invent, or otherwise create new export bases to replace the old by being a place that is inherently attractive to firms. *It is the quality and quantity of an area's productive resources—the supply side of the area's economy—that ultimately determines the viability of the area.* In shifting our emphasis from the demand side to the supply side, we have also shifted the focus away from an area where local policy makers have very little control to one where they have much more. Indeed, local policy makers can choose to improve the area's human and physical resources by investing in social infrastructure such as education and training programs, and physical infrastructure that includes transportation and communication networks.

Our shift in focus from the demand side to the supply side holds very different policy prescriptions for an area wanting to improve its well-being. It turns the key assumption of export base theory on its head: no longer does only the export sector matter, with events in the local service sector being merely a passive consequence of changes in exports (Blumenfeld 1960). Now, what happens inside the local service sector matters most in maintaining the area's attractiveness as a place to do business. Metropolitan areas with the most dynamic economies are those whose industries depend most heavily on the creativity of their workforce. Therefore, the metropolitan areas with a competitive advantage in this realm are best at providing the environments that "creative workers" seek. Florida's (2002) research shows that these are places that tend to score high on tolerance and acceptance of diversity, including not only ethnic and racial diversity but also an acceptance of alternative lifestyles like homosexuality, venues where live music is performed, and access to active recreation in places of natural scenic beauty.

Interactions between the Demand Side and the Supply Side

If the quantity and quality of the area's resources—its social and physical infrastructure—matter most over the long term, why do some areas have better resource endowments than others. Does the nature of an area's existing export industries affect the way its supply side evolves? In a classic 1961 article, the economist Benjamin Chinitz describes the *contrasts in agglomeration* that distinguish Pittsburgh from New York City. Chinitz argues that Pittsburgh's export base was characterized by oligopoly—an industry structure such as the steel industry, in which the bulk of the output is produced by a few large firms, often called a shared monopoly—while New York City's export base was comprised of more competitive firms. He argues that places in which the export base is oligopolistic are areas where the social and physical infrastructure is stunted. There is less entrepreneurship and therefore less innovation; there are fewer business services since large corporations provide for more of their needs internally—with in-house legal, printing, and shipping departments, for example. We can infer from Chinitz's arguments that places like Pittsburgh, Detroit, and Flint are less resilient, and have a more difficult time overcoming the loss of their oligopolistic export bases than New York City, Boston, or San Francisco, where entrepreneurship and innovation find more fertile soil.

In work that focuses on the nature of knowledge spillovers in metropolitan areas, Glaeser et al. (1992) distinguish between three hypotheses. The first emphasizes the role of knowledge spillovers *within* industries, and argues that they are most effective when the industry is able to use its market power—its oligopoly status—to capture the gains. The second, represented in the work of Michael Porter, also emphasizes the value of knowledge spillovers *within* industries, but argues that local competition is more effective for its dissemination. The third, represented by the work of Jane Jacobs, shares with Porter the emphasis on local competition, but argues that the most important knowledge spillovers occur *across* industries, rather than *within* them. In testing these hypotheses with data from the 170 largest U.S. metropolitan areas spanning the period 1956 to 1987, Glaeser and his colleagues find support for Jacobs's view—that knowledge spillovers across industries in a competitive environment are the most effective in generating innovation and employment growth.

Thus, while a high level of human capital is critical to the prosperity of any metro region, those areas with interlocking industries—what Porter calls industry clusters—apparently do best in taking advantage of knowledge spillovers to generate high levels of income for their regions. In the twenty-first century, Austin, Raleigh-Durham-Chapel Hill, San Jose, Seattle, and Boston are typical of metro areas well suited to compete in the new industry clusters in biotechnology, nanotechnology, pharmaceuticals, and state-of-the-art information technology hardware and software.

Strategies for Less Resilient Metropolitan Areas

While the future looks rosy for places like Austin and San Jose, it looks relatively bleak in Detroit, Pittsburgh, and Flint. As Glaeser and Saiz (2004) point out, the U.S. population has been shifting to the Sunbelt states ever since the advent of air-conditioning in the mid-twentieth century. Cities with average January temperatures above 50 degrees Fahrenheit have grown far more quickly than cities with average January temperatures below 30 degrees Fahrenheit. Among the cold-weather cities (with their relatively less attractive climates), the key distinction between those that have prospered and those that have not is the education level of the population. Glaeser and Saiz argue that investing in education is therefore especially important for the older industrial cities of the Northeast and Midwest.

How to do this is no simple matter, however. While investing in human capital will make the area more attractive to potential business firms and new residents, it also requires large expenditures. Paying for quality education requires high tax rates, which can deter new businesses and residents from locating in the area. One way for metropolitan areas to resolve this dilemma would be for the states and the federal government to play a larger role in funding education. In addition, Glaeser and Saiz emphasize the need to reduce crime rates and to offer an attractive and affordable housing stock.

In a similar vein, a recent study from the Brookings Institution (Vey 2007) argues that many older industrial cities have assets that are worth preserving—such as distinctive architecture, potentially scenic waterfronts, and a host of educational, medical, and cultural institutions. With changing demographic and economic trends, including the growth of immigration and the aging of the U.S. population, as well as the increased economic importance of urban-based institutions like universities, medical centers, and cultural institutions, these cities might be able to reverse their misfortunes. Like Glaser and Saiz, the Brookings study emphasizes the need for state governments to assist cities in their efforts to improve education, reduce crime, provide affordable housing, and promote an economic climate that is attractive to new businesses and residents.

Competitive Advantage in Inner-City Neighborhoods

While strengthening export base industries is a valid short-term focus for local policy makers, many economists believe that a longer term strategy of investing in social and physical infrastructure should guide policy. Both Michael Porter and Richard Florida look at the elements of an area's economic environment that give it particular strength—an area's competitive advantage, the basis on which it can build attractiveness that is unique and therefore more difficult for other areas to imitate.

Although Porter has written about the competitive advantage of nations, he has also applied his insights to an understanding of how the concept would work for disadvantaged inner-city neighborhoods. Porter (1995) notes that as a result of prior demographic and industrial change, many low-income ghettos depend heavily on such transfer payments as welfare benefits and food stamps. However, these areas are often near the prosperous downtowns of successful cities. This proximity offers a hard-to-duplicate competitive advantage for firms that provide services to downtown clients. Training inner-city residents to work in a range of services could make residents less dependent on transfer payments and better able to raise their living standards through employment. Porter uses the growing number of laundry and catering firms in the Roxbury section of Boston as an example of this competitive advantage—enterprises that are well positioned to provide for the needs of downtown hotels and restaurants, while providing decent job opportunities for Roxbury's residents.

Porter also makes a persuasive case for retail investment in the inner city. He notes that while residents there often earn much less per household than in the richer suburbs, higher housing density in the inner city means more consumer dollars *per acre.* His theory has been borne out by numerous instances in which the inner-city locations of retail chain stores outperform those in the suburbs (Boston Consulting Group and Initiative for a Competitive Inner City 1998).

Porter's critics note, however, that his prescriptions may apply only to some inner cities, where crime rates are relatively low and business can expect to operate in a normal fashion. They also point out that while he emphasizes the power of market forces to improve conditions in the inner city, Porter has neglected the role that market forces played in their deterioration. A third criticism is that his prescriptions emphasize the importance of investing in places, but they ignore the parallel need to invest in people as well (Boston and Ross 1997; Glasmeier and Harrison 1997).

Understanding Metro Area Prosperity in Light of Economic Theory

Using all the trade theory we have reviewed, we can take a second look at some of the metro regions we examined at the beginning of this chapter. Each has a story to tell that helps us better understand the forces that work either to help nurture prosperity or to foster economic decline.

The Case of Detroit

Recall that in 1969, Detroit was at the very top of the list on the basis of median household income. Detroit's fortunes were built on having a tremendous comparative advantage in automobile production. Before the onrush of imported cars following the oil crisis of 1973 that made large gas-guzzling American-built automobiles obsolete, Detroit was able to parlay its dominance in auto design and production into literally hundreds of thousands of high-paid jobs for both white-collar and blue-collar workers. General Motors, Ford, and Chrysler provided the export base for Detroit, while thousands of independent local manufacturing plants in the area churned out parts that the "Big 3" bought to put into their automobiles. Well-paid auto executives and unionized assembly workers had the income to spend on locally supplied goods and services that provided job opportunities in everything from restaurants and dry cleaners to golf courses and movie theaters. As long as Detroit could export huge numbers of cars and trucks to the rest of North America—and some even abroad—the city's economy boomed. Its residents, on average, were among the richest in the nation, and the good jobs in the auto industry made it possible for both white and black families to afford a middle-class standard of living. In 1969, black families in Detroit had the highest median income among African Americans in the country.

The Case of Hartford

Hartford was a booming metropolis based on two key industries: insurance and jet aircraft engines. As insurance became a national industry rather than simply local, Hartford became a leading "exporter" of insurance services. Its forty major insurance companies were responsible for selling policies throughout the nation and abroad. While The Hartford, Aetna, and Travelers had local offices throughout the country, their central headquarters hired thousands of workers to coordinate all this activity from downtown Hartford. Pratt & Whitney, located in East Hartford, became one of the world's three largest aircraft jet engine manufacturers, along with General Electric in the United States and Rolls Royce in England. Like Detroit's auto industry, Hartford's sprawling jet engine plants employed tens of thousands of highly paid workers, while the surrounding towns in the metro area housed scores of small shops that turned out high-value specialized parts, often from exotic metals, for assembling in Pratt & Whitney's plants. Thus, in 1969, Hartford had two powerful export industries, one that employed legions of white-collar insurance workers and another that provided thousands of jobs for blue-collar craftsmen, machine operators, and assembly workers. Like Detroit, the export base made it possible to have a prosperous local economy that ranged from luncheonettes and taverns near the engine plant to theaters and boutiques downtown within a short walk of Hartford's office towers.

Today, Hartford claims only nineteen of the nation's largest insurance companies, half the number of 1969. International competition from Canada and elsewhere has taken some of the insurance industry away from Hartford, while new information technologies have made it possible for central processing to be distributed to other parts of the country. As for its aircraft industry, the end of the cold war had a devastating impact on Pratt & Whitney's defense industry. In the first half of the 1990s, the Hartford area lost 200,000 jobs, about half of which were defense related. Given that nearly a quarter of the region's export base was comprised of military hardware, the decline in the U.S. Department of Defense budget for aircraft reverberated throughout the region.

Unable to provide good schools and safe streets, a large number of middle-class families fled the central city of Hartford beginning in the 1970s, and those left behind have experienced almost no increase in real median income. Nonetheless, while Hartford's central city has fallen on bad times, the overall metro area is still ranked in the top three in our list of twenty in terms of median household income. The region has benefited from being a crossroads between New York City and Boston and boasts a highly educated and skilled workforce that has held on to the top-level jobs in the remaining insurance companies, in higher education, and in the remaining specialized manufacturing industry in the area.

The Case of Boston

Boston has experienced a roller-coaster existence. More than a hundred years ago, it was among the richest metro areas in the country based on its strong export base in shipping, textiles, and shoes. When these industries moved elsewhere, usually to the South, Boston's fortunes went downhill. By the 1970s, Boston was considered one of the most depressed and distressed cities in the nation. On a scale running from −4 to +4, a 1982 Brookings Institution study rated the city of Boston −4 in terms of city decline. On its urban distress scale, it ranked a −5, the lowest score attainable (Bradbury, Downs, and Small 1982).

Since 1980, Boston has undergone a virtual economic renaissance. Its new wealth is based on high tech and biotech, higher education, sophisticated medical care, and financial services. All of these, including even higher education and medical care, are major export industries. Boston's forty-two universities and colleges attract tuition-paying students from all over the United States and the world, generating "export" earnings. Similarly, its teaching hospitals attract patients from all over the world, seeking the best in hospital and health care when state-of-the-art medical services are deemed necessary. The growth in 401(k) pension plans and the fact that more than half of Americans now own at least some shares of stock or shares in a mutual fund has fueled the rise of Boston's financial services sector. Indeed, the mutual fund industry was founded in Boston with the establishment of Massachusetts Financial Services (MFS) in 1924.

In answering the question of what has allowed Greater Boston to be economically resilient for over 300 years, Glaeser (2003) points to the following: (1) *innovation—*

the ability to shift from one set of export industries to another, (2) *diversity*—the existence of a range of industries so that smaller ones might be poised for growth as circumstances change, (3) *desirability* of the area as a place to live—making the metropolitan area attractive to young and creative workers, and (4) *investment in human capital*—the resourcefulness and ingenuity of a well-educated workforce has been the key to Boston's success for centuries. Today, Boston ranks second in terms of median household income in our list of twenty metro areas.

The Case of Chicago, Milwaukee, and Buffalo

Chicago, Milwaukee, and Buffalo have prospered because of powerful export industries particular to each metro area. Chicago was and still is the transportation hub of the Midwest. Historically, it was home to the steel industry, to meatpacking, to food processing, and to a range of other export-based industries. In the food processing industry alone, it is headquarters to Best Kosher Foods, the Quaker Oats division of PepsiCo, Royal Crown Cola, Tootsie Roll Industries, and the Wrigley chewing gum companies. Its location in the middle of the country, close to major consumer markets and a crossroads for farm products, made food processing one of the city's powerful industries. It ranks seventh on our list of twenty.

Milwaukee, of course, has long been known as one of America's beer-making centers. During its heyday in the 1950s and 1960s, four of the six largest breweries in the nation were in Milwaukee, a legacy of the beer-making craft that many of its German immigrants brought with them to the city. Pabst, Schlitz, and Blatz were national brands made in Milwaukee and exported throughout the country. Today, with Americans drinking more wine and enjoying imported brew, many of Milwaukee's famous breweries have merged, gone out of business, or moved to other parts of the country. Partly as a consequence, Milwaukee has fallen from fourth to seventeenth place in our ranking.

Buffalo is perhaps the poster child for deindustrialization. Linked to the Great Lakes, Buffalo was the quintessential steelmaking town. As late as 1969, Buffalo's manufacturers exported more than $1.25 billion in steel and various metal-related products. By 1988, total exports were down to just $200 million. The replacement of steel with other materials—for example, plastics and aluminum—plus a surge in steel imports spelled doom for this area's key industry. In another blow to its economy, its functions as a port city were eclipsed by the opening of the St. Lawrence Seaway in 1959. Today, about one-quarter of Buffalo's local economy is based on education, health, and social services. The big state university in Buffalo, SUNY-Buffalo is one of its greatest exporters, with students coming from all over the state and elsewhere. Nevertheless, the loss of its greater post–World War II industries have jettisoned Buffalo from the middle of the pack on MHI to near the bottom.

Newly Prosperous Metro Regions

The real winners today are metro regions like San Francisco, Austin, and Raleigh. If Buffalo is the poster child for deindustrialization, Austin is the poster child for the new economy. Recall that Austin was dead last among our twenty areas in terms of median household income in 1969. But high tech slowly began to form a presence in the area during the 1960s, partly as a result of the University of Texas being located there and partly as a result of IBM opening a facility nearby in 1963. In 1966, Texas Instruments moved to town, and Motorola opened operations there in 1974. The real watershed for Austin came in 1982, when young Michael Dell began Dell Computers in the area. From then on, Austin became a magnet for high-tech industry. During the 1990s, the region added 1,000 new businesses and 280,000 jobs. Today, it boasts 85 bioscience companies, and the University of Texas has become one of the largest research universities in the nation, behind only the University of California and the Massachusetts Institute of Technology (MIT) in new patents issued annually. Austin is home to 98 large semiconductor and electronics-related businesses that contribute 17,000 jobs. Along with hardware, the area now claims a booming software industry that averaged 22 percent annual growth in revenues from 1990 to 1996. Today, there are more than 500 software companies located in the metro area. Getting into high tech early and being the birthplace of companies like Dell has been the key to Austin's economic success. Not surprisingly, its real median household income has increased faster than any of the other twenty metro regions we have followed.

Raleigh, North Carolina, is not far behind. The area was predominantly farm country until the 1970s. During the 1980s, income from farming was declining at a 30 percent annual rate. But based on its strong university base in Duke and in the nearby University of North Carolina at Chapel Hill and North Carolina State, Raleigh has become one of the top five biotech and life sciences regions in the world. Fearful of losing their well-trained college graduates, a consortium of state and local government, business, and academic institutions created Research Triangle Park in 1959 to provide employment opportunities for these highly skilled professionals. Today, the "research triangle" metro area of Raleigh, Durham, and Chapel Hill has more than 140 biotech firms and 65 contract research companies within its bustling pharmaceutical and biotech, computer software and hardware, and telecommunications industries. More than 250 companies now have their headquarters in the region. Lower wages than in the North have contributed to Raleigh's ability to attract firms, but incomes are rising quickly—at a rate only second to Austin's. A lower cost of living and pleasant weather year-round has contributed to Raleigh's ability to attract workers.

Newark, New Jersey, is often maligned for its desperately poor inner city. But the metro region as a whole was actually tied for fifth place with New York among our twenty metropolitan statistical areas (MSAs) in 1969, and moved up to a tie for forth place in 1999. What accounts for its success? Many of Newark's MSA households work in New York City, but their incomes are counted for census purposes on the basis of where they live. Despite the fact that it is considered a separate MSA from New York, it is part of the official combined New York-New Jersey-Pennsylvania metropolitan area based on the commuting patterns of area workers. Thus, the Newark MSA actually contains many of the affluent New Jersey suburbs of New

York City. Newark also boasts the fact that it is the pharmaceutical capital of North America. No other metro area has a larger share of the total pharmaceutical industry than this northeastern region. Chief among the employers in the area are Johnson & Johnson, Hoffman-LaRoche, Merck & Co., Novartis, Wyeth, and a number of U.S. affiliates of international drug companies that include Daiichi Pharmaceutical and Eisai, both of Japan. Newark's long-term competitive advantage in this growing industry helps keep it near the top of the list of metro areas in the country.

Finally, there is the San Francisco success story. Many industries have helped contribute to this highly diverse metro region. Silicon Valley, located just to the south of the city, has proven to be one of the most successful high-tech capitals of the world. The area is home to more than 4,100 firms that employ more than 200,000 high-tech workers. During the 1990s, the region's top 100 companies tripled their sales and their profits increased sixfold. San Francisco is also the financial center of the West Coast and home to the region's Federal Reserve Bank, the Federal Home Loan Bank Systems, and the Pacific Stock Exchange. The area has the highest density of venture capital firms in the world, boasting by investment volume 35 percent of all venture funds in the nation. Bioscience has also played a key role in its recent success, with San Francisco often credited as being the birthplace of the industry. About fifty bioscience and medical-device firms are located in the Bay Area, many tied to the University of California in Berkeley and Stanford University in Palo Alto.

San Francisco is also home to the third-largest apparel and design region in the country, with more than 200 local companies producing their own lines and 300 contract manufacturers. Levi's has its international headquarters in the city, as does The Gap, Esprit, and Jessica McClintock. As Americans have become aficionados of wine, the Napa and Sonoma valleys have prospered, adding to the wealth of the region. More than 400 wineries are now located in the area.

Added to all of this is the fact that tourism is a leading export industry for San Francisco and its environs. More than 13 million visitors come to the metro area each year, generating billions of dollars in export earnings and creating a ready market for local restaurants, hotels, and amusements.

Why San Francisco? The answer lies in its magnificent beauty, its diverse population, its universities, and its rich array of amenities, from Chinatown and the waterfront to lush valleys and nearby outdoor activities for sportsmen of all types. In addition, AnnaLee Saxenian (1994) has argued that the culture of Silicon Valley, in which there is a high degree of collaboration between firms as well as a high degree of worker mobility between them, is particularly valuable in generating knowledge spillovers, their subsequent innovations, and the ability to adapt quickly to changing economic and technological conditions. The close proximity of firms in the area means that workers can change jobs without disrupting their informal social and professional networks. Recent research by Marx, Strumsky, and Fleming (2007) suggests that strong enforcement of postemployment noncompete covenants (restrictions on a worker's ability to join a competing firm) reduces worker mobility. The absence of these covenants in California may have facilitated the high degree of hopping between firms. Fleming and Marx (2006) argue that interfirm knowledge spillovers are becoming a more important ingredient for innovation across a wide span of industries.

The San Francisco area has been a magnet for innovative young entrepreneurs and brilliant engineers and scientists. Few places have been as successful in parlaying natural beauty and lifestyle into economic success. As a result of all of these factors, the Golden Gate MSA has moved up since 1969, from tenth place to first place in household income.

The areas that have been the most successful—the ones that make it to the top of the charts and stay there for decades and even for centuries—have fortunately had a desirable natural feature such as a deep harbor or a good climate. They have then had the wisdom to use their good fortune to develop the social and physical infrastructure to keep the area attractive not only to new firms and new industries but also to young and well-educated workers. These are the metropolitan areas where new enterprises continue to be born. The newer metro regions joining them at the top are ones that have learned how to encourage innovative new industries, attract highly skilled workers, and trade their goods and services to the rest of the world.

Appendix A
Input-Output Calculations

The Input Matrix

According to input-output analysis, one can model a metropolitan economy beginning with an input matrix, which is a set of "recipes" for producing the output of each industry in the region. However, while the cookbook recipe for a cake specifies the ingredients in physical units—number of eggs, cups of flour, pounds of butter, ounces of water, teaspoons of vanilla—the input matrix specifies the ingredients in dollar terms. Our recipe for cake would be translated as follows: to get a dollar's worth of cake, we need x pennies' worth of eggs, y pennies' worth of flour, z pennies' worth of butter, and so forth, adding up to a dollar's worth of input. One of the basic tenets of input-output analysis is that all transactions have been taken into account and, therefore, a dollar's worth of input is always equal to a dollar's worth of output—including the profit each firm makes in supplying its inputs. The use of monetary values rather than physical units is dictated by the need to find a common denominator by which to measure the output of industries as disparate as steel, publishing, biotechnology, and tourism. Each of these industries will have its unique recipe for a dollar's worth of output.

A Bare-Bones Example of Input-Output Analysis

To understand the fundamentals of input-output analysis, it may be helpful to walk through a highly simplified example.

Step 1

Let's say that a particular city has two export sectors, A and B, and a household sector, H, that provides the export sectors with their labor input (and by which the households earn their income). The following table gives the "recipes" for one dollar's worth of output for sectors A and B; the analogous column for households represents their pattern of spending from each dollar of income.

Input Coefficients	A	B	H
A	.1	.2	.3
B	.4	.1	.2
H	.3	.4	.1
Imports	.2	.3	.4
Total Input	1.00	1.00	1.00

Thus, the table tells us that for every dollar of A produced, the A sector requires an input of 10¢ from the A sector itself (for example, the computer industry requires some computers as input to making more computers), 40¢ from the B sector, 30¢ of labor input from households, and 20¢ worth of imports. The recipe for a dollar of B output is 20¢ from the A sector, 10¢ from the B sector itself, 40¢ of labor from the household sector, and 30¢ worth of imports. The column for the household sector, H, may be interpreted as households spending 30¢ of each dollar's income on A, 20¢ on B, 10¢ on labor from other households (for example, a home child-care provider) and 40¢ on imports.

Step 2

Since the export demand for a good is not subject to the area's control, it can be considered "exogenous." It is determined elsewhere, outside the workings of the metropolitan area economy itself. Therefore, we can simply assume the following level of export demand for sectors A and B (there is no direct export demand for the household sector):

$$\text{Export demand for Sector A} = \$90 \text{ million}$$

$$\text{Export demand for Sector B} = \$30 \text{ million}$$

Step 3

We can specify the following equations that represent the total output required from each sector to satisfy all sources of demand for that sector's output:

$$A = .1A + .2B + .3H + 90$$

$$B = .4A + .1B + .2H + 30$$

$$H = .3A + .4B + .1H$$

We now have three equations and three unknowns. Using the technique for solving simultaneous equations, we can solve for the values of A, B, and H.

Step 4

After cranking through the mechanics of solving the simultaneous equations, we find that the values for A, B, and H are as follows:

$$A = \$168.2 \text{ million}$$

$$B = \$133.8 \text{ million}$$

$$H = \$115.5 \text{ million}$$

In other words, given the demand for A as an input to the A sector, the B sector, the H sector, and the export demand of $90 million, it will take $168.2 million of output from the A sector to satisfy the total demand for A from all sectors in the economy—A, B, H, and export demand.

Step 5

Given the information in steps 1–4 above, we can construct the input-output table as show below in **Table A6.1**.

Step 6

Reading down column A of the table, we can say the following: In order to obtain $168.2 million of A output, we need $16.82 million of A input (.1A), $67.28 million of B input (.4A), $50.46 million of H input (.3A), and $33.64 of imports (.2A), adding up to $168.2 million of A input.

Reading across row A of the table, we can say the following: Of the $168.2 million of A that is produced, $16.82 million (.1A) goes back to the A sector as an input, $26.76 million (.2B) goes to the B sector as an input, $34.65 million (.3H) goes to the household sector, and $90 million is exported to other regions of the country and around the world.

Thus, we can see how the A sector is linked to the other sectors on the input side (what it needs from the other sectors for each dollar of output it produces) and on the output side (the destination of A output to all the places that have a demand for it).

Step 7

What would happen if the export demand for A fell by half, from $90 million to $45 million? Looking back at the cells in Table A6.1, it means that cell AE would change by $45 million, but then this change would reverberate throughout all other sectors. The change in total A output would change the amount of total A needed as an input, as well as change the amount of inputs needed from cells AA, BA, HA, and IA. In turn, those changes affect the B and H sectors, so each of those cells would also change, causing further changes in cells AA, BA, HA, and IA. Ultimately, to figure out the final impact on all sectors, we would have to return to Step 3, change the A equation to reflect the new export demand for A, solve the new set of simultaneous equations, and fill in the blanks on a new input-output table. In doing so, we would

Table A6.1 Input-Output Table

		Input			Exports	Total Output
		A	**B**	**H**	**Exports**	
Output	A	AA .1A=16.82	AB .2B=26.76	AH .3H=34.65	AE 90	168.2
	B	BA .4A=67.28	BB .1B=13.38	BH .2H=23.1	BE 30	133.8
	H	HA .3A=50.46	HB .4B=53.52	HH .1H=11.55	HE 0	115.5
	Imports	IA .2A=33.64	IB .3B=40.14	IH .4H=46.2	120	
	Total Input	168.2	133.8	115.5		

have the equivalent of that tracer dye to see how a change in demand for an export good affects all other segments of the metropolitan economy. It is a bit complicated, but it reveals how all parts of a metro area can be affected by the change in demand for just one of its products or services. In a dynamic economy, demand is shifting all the time, boosting the output and incomes in some sectors and depressing them in others. In the process, the prosperity of some metro areas rises while that of others declines.

Going back to the example of the steel industry in Pittsburgh, we can see that when the demand for steel fell, orders for coke, limestone, and iron ore also fell. Since these industries, as well as the steel industry itself, all use steel as an input, there were further reverberations that reduced the demand for steel even more, and generated another round of reductions for coke, limestone, and iron ore. Cascading rounds of layoffs reduced spending by the household sector. Each round of reductions was of smaller magnitude than the previous one, until the system finally settled down at a new and lower equilibrium level.

References

Blumenfeld, Hans. 1960. "The Economic Base of the Metropolis." In R. W. Pfouts, ed., *The Techniques of Urban Economic Analysis,* West Trenton, N.J.: Chandler-Davis, pp. 229–277.

Boston, Thomas D., and Catherine L. Ross, eds. 1997. *The Inner City: Urban Poverty and Economic Development in the Next Century.* Edison, N.J.: Transaction Publishers.

Boston Consulting Group and Initiative for a Competitive Inner City. 1998. "The Business Case for Pursuing Retail Opportunities in the Inner City," June. http://imaps.indygov.org/ed_portal/studies/bcg_inner_city_retail.pdf.

Bradbury, Katherine, Anthony Downs, and Kenneth Small. 1982. *Urban Decline and the Future of American Cities.* Washington, D.C.: Brookings Institution.

Chinitz, Benjamin. 1961. "Contrasts in Agglomeration: New York and Pittsburgh." *Papers and Proceedings of the American Economic Association* 51 (May): 279–289.

Fallows, James. 1994. *Looking at the Sun: The Rise of the New East Asian Economic and Political System*. New York: Pantheon Books.

Fleming, Lee, and Matt Marx. 2006. "Managing Creativity in Small Worlds." *California Management Review* 48, no. 4 (Summer): 6–27.

Florida, Richard. 2002. *The Rise of the Creative Class*. New York: Basic Books.

Glaeser, Edward L. 2003. "Mother of Reinvention: How Boston's Economy Has Bounced Back from Decline, Time and Time Again." *CommonWealth Magazine* (Fall): 15–20.

Glaeser, Edward L., Heidi D. Kallal, Jose A. Scheinkman, and Andrei Schleifer. 1992. "Growth in Cities." *Journal of Political Economy* 100, no. 6 (Centennial Issue, December): 1126–1152.

Glaeser, Edward L., and Albert Saiz. 2004. "The Rise of the Skilled City." *Brookings-Wharton Papers on Urban Affairs* 5: 47–94.

Glasmeier, Amy K., and Bennett Harrison. 1997. "Response: Why Business Alone Won't Redevelop the Inner City: A Friendly Critique of Michael Porter's Approach to Urban Revitalization." *Economic Development Quarterly* 11, no. 1: 28–38.

Jacobs, Jane. 1969. *The Economy of Cities*. New York: Vintage Books.

Krugman, Paul. 1990. *Rethinking International Trade*. Cambridge, Mass.: MIT Press.

———. 1991. *Geography and Trade*. Cambridge, Mass.: MIT Press.

Marx, Matt, Deborah Strumsky, and Lee Fleming. 2007. "Noncompetes and Inventor Mobility: Specialists, Stars, and the Michigan Experiment." Harvard Business School Working Paper No. 07-042.

Ohlin, Bertil. 1967. "Reflections on Contemporary International Trade Theories." Appendix II in Bertil Ohlin, *Interregional and International Trade*, rev. ed. Cambridge, Mass.: Harvard University Press.

Porter, Michael. 1985. *Competitive Advantage: Creating and Sustaining Superior Performance*. New York: Free Press.

———. 1990. *The Competitive Advantage of Nations*. New York: Free Press.

———. 1995. "The Competitive Advantage of the Inner City." *Harvard Business Review* (May/June): 55–71.

Saxenian, AnnaLee. 1994. *Regional Advantage: Culture and Competition in Silicon Valley and Route 128*. Cambridge, Mass.: Harvard University Press.

Uchitelle, Louis. 2002. "Answering '800' Calls Offers Extra Income but No Security." *New York Times*, March 27, p. A1.

U.S. Department of Housing and Urban Development. 2007. HUD User Policy Development and Research Information Service. SOCDS (State of the Cities Data Systems) data set. http://socds.huduser.org.

Vernon, Raymond. 1966. "International Investment and International Trade in the Product Cycle." *Quarterly Journal of Economics* 80, no. 2 (May): 190–207.

———. 1975. "The Location of Economic Activity." In John Dunning, ed., *Economic Analysis and the Multinational Enterprise*. New York: Praeger, pp. 89–114.

Vey, Jennifer S. 2007. "Restoring Prosperity: The State Role in Revitalizing America's Older Industrial Cities." Washington, D.C.: Brookings Institution.

Chapter 6 Questions and Exercises

1. Using the *Urban Experience* CD, for three metropolitan areas of your choice, use the industry information from 1970, 1980, and 1990 to ascertain how the number of employees changed between 1970 and 1990 for each of these industry categories:

   - Agriculture and mining
   - Construction
   - Manufacturing
   - Transportation, communication, and public utilities

- Wholesale and retail trade
- Finance, insurance, and real estate
- Business and repair services
- Personal services
- Professional services
- Public administration

(*Note:* You need to produce this table for one metro area at a time.)
Did these metro areas have a major change in their industry sectors' employment during this period? If so, what was the nature of this change? (*Note:* For instructions on how to use this CD, see examples in the exercises for Chapter 1.)

2. In the metropolitan area in which you live (or the one closest to you), what goods do the largest manufacturers produce?

3. What types of goods do households in your city/town rely on to be imported? How, if at all, does the importing of these goods relate to the Weberian theory of the role of transportation costs in business location?

4. The most recent data on each metro area's employment by industry can be found at the Census Bureau's Metro Business Patterns Web page at

    http://censtats.census.gov/cgi-bin/msanaic/msasect.pl

In the drop-down menus for metro areas, select the metro area in which you live, or another metro area of interest to you. In the drop-down menu for year, choose the most recent year available. Click on "Go" and a table will appear with broad categories of industries (two-digit industry codes). For the metro area you selected, which industries had the largest number of employees in this most recent year?

5. Among the items in your home, identify five items that you think were produced in your metro area and five that you believe were produced in other metro areas and then imported to your metro area. Approximately what proportion of all the things in your home do you think were produced in your metro area?

6. Suppose that a business with 500 employees moved to your city or town. What type of businesses would you expect to benefit from the spending done by the new employees and their households? Explain how this new spending relates to the dynamic of "job multiplier" for your city/town.

7. Location quotients for metropolitan areas can be found using the Location Quotient Calculator at the U.S. Bureau of Labor Statistics Web site found at

    http://data.bls.gov/LOCATION_QUOTIENT/servlet/lqc.ControllerServlet

Go to this site and
- Choose the latest year on the drop-down menu under "Step 1."
- Under "Step 2," for the Base Area choose "U.S. Total"; for "Analysis Areas," scroll down to the bottom of the drop-down list to find the list of all metro areas and choose three metro areas of interest to you.
- Under "Step 3," for the Base Industry choose "Total, all industries," and for the "Analysis Industry" check the box for "SuperSector."

• Then click on "Get Results." A table will appear giving employment levels, percentage of employment for each industry group, and location quotients for each industry group for each of the metro areas you selected.

  ✦ Within each metro area, which industry groups have the largest location quotients? Which industry groups have the smallest location quotients?
  ✦ Compare the location quotients across the three metro areas you chose. How do the location quotients compare?
  ✦ According to the discussion in this chapter, how are these numbers related to the concept of "export base"?

7 Urban Labor Markets and Metro Prosperity

In Chapter 6, we used household income as a measure of a metro area's prosperity. The fact is, nearly 70 percent of all household income in the United States comes in the form of wages and salaries or from job benefits that include employer-paid health insurance and pensions. The proportion of household income generated in the labor market is even higher for the more than nine out of ten households that have annual incomes under $100,000. More than 80 percent of their income is comprised of wages and benefits earned by family members who work as employees of corporations, private companies, or some federal, state, or local government agency. The remaining 20 percent is made up of interest, dividends, proprietors' and self-employment earnings, rent, and transfer payments such as Social Security and unemployment benefits. (**Appendix A** provides more detail on the sources of total personal income in the United States, taking into account wages, interest, dividends, and other sources.)

Not surprisingly, then, how most individuals and their families fare across metro areas is heavily dependent on how they fare in the labor market. Even the standard of living of those who are older and retired from the workforce depends primarily on how much they worked, how much they earned, and how generous their pension benefits are.

As we will learn, the specific employment opportunities available to individuals depend on a wide array of factors, some of which have to do with where those individuals live. Residing in one metropolitan area rather than another can make a big difference in how much one works and how much one earns. Working in a metro area's suburbs can provide different job opportunities—often better, sometimes worse—than working in the central city. The industry composition of a metro area—the range of mining, manufacturing, construction, trade, and service sectors, along with government enterprise in a region—can affect employment and earnings as well, and the composition varies dramatically across metropolitan statistical areas (MSAs). A generation ago, living in a city where the auto industry was king meant you had a chance at a better paying job than if you lived in a city where textiles or apparel were the leading industries. Today, living in a metro area still dominated by the U.S. auto industry yields a greater likelihood of unemployment.

To understand the earnings prospects that face workers in different places, we need to delve into the dynamics of the U.S. labor market. We shall do this by considering a number of theories about what determines earnings and by applying these theories to urban labor markets. But first we will take a look at how your chances of getting and keeping a job vary across metro regions, and what jobs pay once you secure employment.

Employment and Unemployment

Whether you can expect to work full-time all year long, year after year, depends on many phenomena. Some occupations, like construction worker or ski lift operator, have a seasonal pattern to them. Others, particularly in manufacturing, are highly susceptible to the national **business cycle**, the pattern of rapid growth in output and employment interrupted by periodic slowdowns in the economy. In contrast, some seem better insulated from seasonal fluctuations and the business cycle. Public schoolteachers and nurses are less likely to suffer layoffs than workers in most other occupations.

An individual's chances of unemployment also depend on his or her education and skill level. Workers who have less education or training have been subject, at least until quite recently, to more unemployment than those with college degrees or postgraduate training (Mishel, Bernstein, and Allegretto 2004).

Because of differences in industrial and occupational composition, the incidence of unemployment also varies across metro regions. Relying on the same twenty representative metro areas we have been highlighting, **Figure 7.1** demonstrates that in the year 2005, the annual average **unemployment rate** varied from 5.1 percent in the Raleigh-Durham-Chapel Hill MSA and 5.3 percent in Salt Lake City to 8.1 percent in Buffalo and 9.8 percent in Detroit. In general, higher unemployment rates are found in older industrial metro areas (Milwaukee, Chicago, Buffalo, and Detroit), with the lowest rates in metro areas that have new information-age industries, financial services, and health services (Austin, Boston, and Raleigh), as well as in MSAs that have become important destinations for retirees (Jacksonville, Phoenix).

The variance in central city unemployment rates tends to be even greater than the variance of rates among metro areas. Some older industrial cities experience **jobless rates** three to four times as high as some of the newer western and southern cities (Detroit, Hartford, and Buffalo versus Salt Lake City, Phoenix, Raleigh, and Jacksonville). Despite the fact that 2005 was a year of relatively low unemployment nationally, jobless rates in excess of 10 percent could be found in a range of central cities; in our sample, these include Chicago, Newark, St. Louis, Milwaukee, Buffalo, Hartford, and Detroit (see **Figure 7.2**).

Moreover, as **Figure 7.3** reveals, the *trend* in unemployment rates has been quite different across central cities. In Newark and Hartford, the jobless rate has generally risen since 1970; in San Francisco, it has been roughly constant at a relatively low rate, and it has actually declined in Salt Lake City.

Such high unemployment rates as those found in the central cities of Newark, Hartford, St. Louis, and Detroit suggest that life in those urban centers is quite precarious for many households. With the decline of the manufacturing sector in

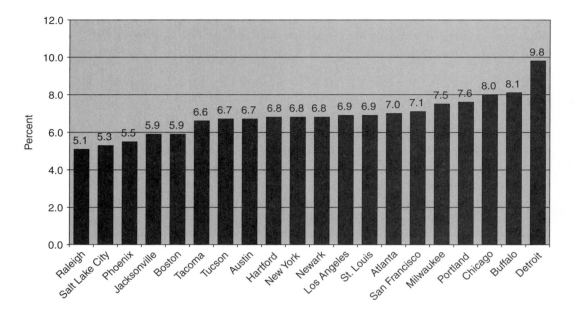

Figure 7.1 Metro Area Unemployment Rates, 2005.
Source: U.S. Department of Housing and Urban Development, HUD User Policy Development and Research Information Service, SOCDS data set, 2007, http://socds.huduser.org.

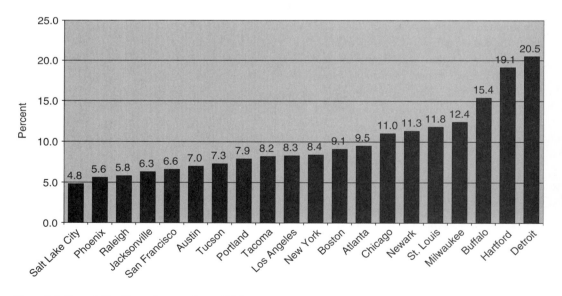

Figure 7.2 Central City Unemployment Rates, 2005.
Source: U.S. Department of Housing and Urban Development, HUD User Policy Development and Research Information Service, SOCDS data set, 2007, http://socds.huduser.org.

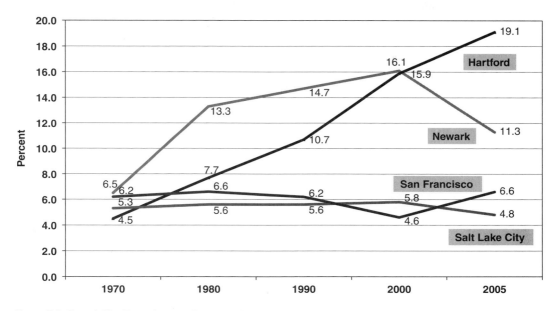

Figure 7.3 Central City Unemployment Rates, 1970–2005.
Source: U.S. Department of Housing and Urban Development, HUD User Policy Development and Research Information Service, SOCDS data set, 2007, http://socds.huduser.org.

these cities, steady work is often hard to find. Incomes fluctuate based on the ability of household members to find and keep jobs in a weak economy. Not surprisingly, many of these central cities have declined in population, as discouraged workers pull up stakes to seek new job opportunities in other cities or regions across the country. The lure of jobs in expanding cities and the lack of jobs in others are key reasons for the redistribution of population across metro regions in the United States.

Where Are the Good Jobs?

Presumably, workers not only want to find jobs, but they also want to find "good" jobs. Let's say you are beginning to think about the type of job you would like to have. No doubt one of the considerations will be how much the job pays. If you are really after a lucrative paycheck, your best prospects require a medical degree. In 2006, anesthesiologists were the best-paid workers in America, earning an average wage of $88.63 per hour. On an annual basis, they earned $184,340, the highest of any of the 820 detailed occupations tracked by the U.S. Department of Labor's Bureau of Labor Statistics (U.S. Department of Labor 2007). Indeed, physicians of one type or another are members of nine of the ten highest-paying occupations in the United States. Outside of the medical sector, chief executives, airline pilots, lawyers, air traffic controllers, and engineering managers are all on the top-twenty list of best-paid occupations (see **Table 7.1**). Financial advisers would have been high on this

Table 7.1 Top Twenty Occupations by Annual Earnings, 2006

1	Anesthesiologists	$184,340
2	Surgeons	184,150
3	Obstetricians and gynecologists	178,040
4	Orthodontists	176,900
5	Oral and maxillofacial surgeons	164,760
6	Internists, general	160,860
7	Prosthodontists	158,940
8	Psychiatrists	149,990
9	Family and general practitioners	149,850
10	Chief executives	144,600
11	Physicians and surgeons, all other	142,220
12	Pediatricians, general	141,440
13	Dentists, general	140,950
14	Airline Pilots, copilots, and flight engineers	140,380
15	Podiatrists	118,500
16	Lawyers	113,660
17	Air traffic controllers	110,270
18	Engineering managers	110,030
19	Dentists, all other specialties	108,340
20	Natural science managers	107,970

Source: U.S. Bureau of Labor Statistics 2007.

Table 7.2 Bottom Twenty Occupations by Annual Earnings, 2006

1	Combined food preparation and serving workers, including fast food	$15,930
2	Cooks, fast food	15,960
3	Dishwashers	16,190
4	Dining room and cafeteria attendants and bartender helpers	16,320
5	Hosts and hostesses, restaurant, lounge, and coffee shop	16,860
6	Counter attendants, cafeteria, food concession, and coffee shop	16,950
7	Gaming dealers	17,010
8	Shampooers	17,050
9	Waiters and waitresses	17,190
10	Ushers, lobby attendants, and ticket takers	17,500
11	Amusement and recreation attendants	17,530
12	Farmworkers and laborers, crop, nursery, and greenhouse	17,630
13	Cashiers	17,930
14	Personal and home care aides	18,180
15	Lifeguards, ski patrol, and other recreational protective workers	18,410
16	Food preparation and serving-related occupations	18,430
17	Parking lot attendants	18,450
18	Pressers, textile, garment, and related materials	18,470
19	Food preparation workers	18,480
20	Bartenders	18,540

Source: U.S. Bureau of Labor Statistics 2007.

list as well, but much of their compensation comes in the form of bonuses and stock options, not the wages and salaries measured by the Labor Department.

If you could help it, you would want to avoid the poorest paid occupations, at least when considering a permanent job. Among the twenty worst-paid occupations out of the 820, half are related to the food service industry—fast-food restaurants, cafeterias, and the like. Home-care workers, parking lot attendants, ushers, and farmworkers also fall into this lowest wage category (see **Table 7.2**). On average, a surgeon earns almost twelve times what the typical cook in a fast-food outlet makes. Put another way, before the end of January, a surgeon has earned more than what a full-time fast-food cook will earn all year long.

Most of us work in jobs somewhere in the middle of the occupational earnings distribution. If you are a political science major and end up becoming a professional political scientist, you will be rewarded pretty well. In 2006, you would have ended up at #49 out of the 820 occupations, earning an average of more than $86,000 per year—about half of what the typical orthodontist would earn, but double the salary of a member of the clergy. Economists were ranked #55 at $83,500, sociologists #121 at $68,300, and urban and regional planners #187, earning $58,940. Farther down the list are paralegals (#325) earning $45,460, tractor trailer drivers (#469) at $36,320, police dispatchers (#549) at $32,590, and electrician's helpers (#705) at $25,050.

Labor Market Earnings by Metro Area

The occupation you choose does not simply determine how much you earn; where you live also matters a great deal. Average hourly earnings differ significantly across regions. **Figure 7.4** reveals that earnings, taking into account all 820 occupations, averaged $26.33 an hour in San Francisco in 2006. Boston, New York, Newark, Hartford, and Detroit had hourly wage rates greater than $22. At the other end of the earnings spectrum, the typical worker in Tucson earned less than $18 per hour. Jacksonville, Phoenix, Buffalo, Salt Lake City, and St. Louis all were gathered near the low end of the wage distribution. The average wage in San Francisco exceeded the average in Tucson by more than 50 percent. Assuming workers spend about 2,000 hours a year in the labor market if they work full-time and work all year long, the typical employee in San Francisco is going to earn in excess of $17,600 more per year than the typical employee in Tucson.

Yet, before you pack your bags and head out to the Bay Area, you might want to consider living costs in both of these cities. By at least one estimate, the cost of living in San Francisco is more than 70 percent higher than in Tucson (CNN Money 2007). According to Cable News Network's (CNN) calculation, if you earn $60,000 in San Francisco, you would need to earn only $34,800 in Tucson to live comparably in terms of the cost of housing, food and groceries, transportation, utilities, and health care. Housing costs are the critical factor here. In 2006, you would have had to pay more than $736,000 for the median-priced home in San Francisco. If you lived in Tucson instead, you would have paid only about $245,000 to get the median-priced

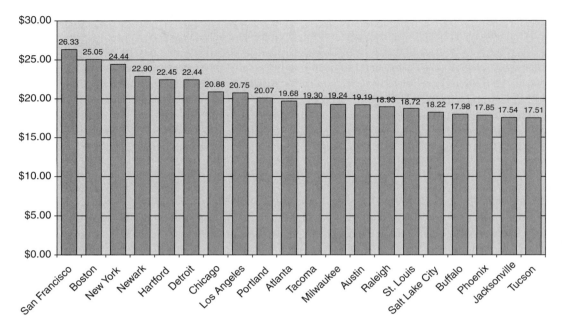

Figure 7.4 Nominal Mean Hourly Earnings—Metro Area, All Occupations, 2006. *Source:* U.S. Department of Labor, Bureau of Labor Statistics, "May 2007 Metropolitan Area Occupational Employment and Wage Estimates," http://www.bls.gov/bls/blswage.htm.

home there (National Association of Realtors 2007). Transportation would also cost you a third more in the Bay Area, taking into account the price of car insurance, gas, and repairs. Health care is also a third more expensive in northern California than southern Arizona, and you would even have to pay a bit more (9%) for food and groceries.

Once the cost of living is factored in, San Francisco moves from being the highest-wage MSA among the twenty we are following to third from the bottom, which demonstrates the important difference between **nominal wages** and **real wages**. Nominal wages are what you see on your pay stub. Real wages are what your earnings are worth once you calculate a cost of living adjustment (COLA) to take into account what you can buy with that paycheck. **Figure 7.5** adjusts the average hourly wages we saw in each of the metro areas in the previous figure using the CNN COLA adjustment.

Given the relatively high nominal wage in the Detroit MSA and its relatively low cost of living, Detroit becomes the highest real wage metro area among the twenty in the figure. In the Motor City, you need only about $36,100 to pay for the goods and services that would cost $60,000 in the Bay Area. You can buy the median-priced home in the Detroit metro area, according to the National Association of Realtors, for about $151,000—an absolute steal by San Francisco standards. Health care, food, and transportation are also cheaper in Detroit. In general, older industrial cities seem to benefit from lower costs—mainly housing—conferring on these metro areas

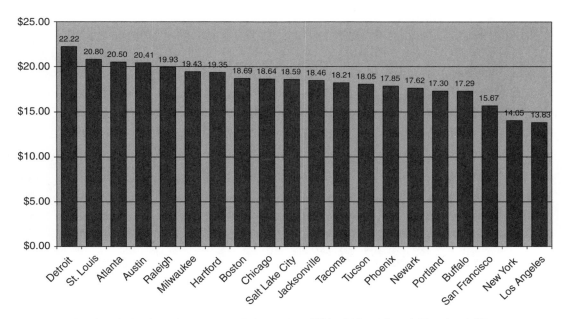

Figure 7.5 Mean Hourly Earnings—Metro Area, All Occupations, 2006—COLA Adjusted (Phoenix = 1.00).
Source: U.S. Department of Labor, Bureau of Labor Statistics, "May 2007 Metropolitan Area Occupational Employment and Wage Estimates," http://www.bls.gov/bls/blswage.htm.

a relatively high living standard, at least when it comes to simple material welfare among those who actually have jobs. Rounding out the top six MSAs with COLA-adjusted earnings are St. Louis, Atlanta, Austin, Raleigh, and Milwaukee. This might help explain why not everyone is moving to places like San Francisco, New York, and Boston to take advantage of higher nominal wages.

The higher nominal wages in places like San Francisco, New York, and Boston reflect the fact that employers in these metro areas often are forced to offer higher pay or better employment benefits to attract a sufficient number of skilled employees to work for them in the face of high living costs. According to these real-wage calculations, it would seem that employers in these high-cost locales would have to pay even higher nominal wages to compensate for their lofty housing prices. Presumably, it is only because these cities have so many natural amenities and cultural and recreational activities that workers are willing to flock there, live in smaller homes or apartments, do without a car, or give up other material possessions in order to survive on low COLA-adjusted wages. Even so, the high nominal wage and highly touted Boston metropolitan area experienced a net out-migration of more than 100,000 younger workers (ages 20–34)—16 percent of the area's total between 1990 and 2000—apparently much of this in response to a near doubling in the price of housing in the second half of that decade (Boston Foundation 2004). Employers were not willing or able to offer a large enough nominal wage differential to keep young people from seeking jobs in other metro areas where wages might not be quite as high, but where the cost of living is substantially lower.

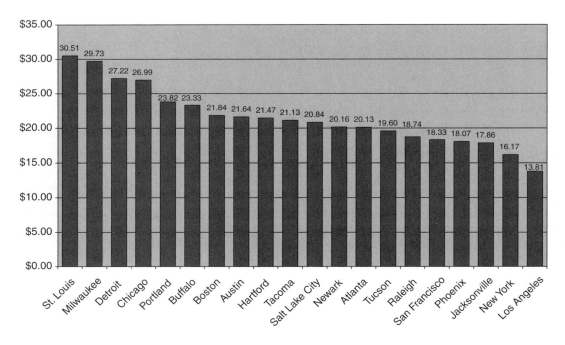

Figure 7.6 Mean Hourly Earnings—Metro Area, All Plumbers, 2006—COLA Adjusted (Phoenix = 1.00). *Source:* U.S. Department of Labor, Bureau of Labor Statistics, "May 2007 Metropolitan Area Occupational Employment and Wage Estimates," http://www.bls.gov/bls/blswage.htm.

Occupational Wage Differentials across *Metro Areas*

Such large wage differentials across urban regions, before and after controlling for the variation in living costs, could be explained in part by differences in the industrial or occupational composition in each metro area. In theory, cities with a concentration of hospitals, clinics, and highly skilled medical personnel or with corporate head-quarters housing a large number of executives and managers would presumably enjoy higher average wages than areas or regions where there is a greater concentration of lower-wage industries and occupations that are often found in vacation destinations, such as restaurants and fast-food outlets with their cooks, waiters, and waitresses. But, curiously, large wage differences prevail among those who work in the *same* occupation but live in different cities. Take plumbers, for example. Before accounting for living costs, the best-paid plumbers are in San Francisco, where they made almost $31 an hour in 2006. This was nearly twice as high as plumbers in Jacksonville, where they earned less than $17. Sales managers in New York earn almost $70 an hour, while those in Tucson earn less than $40. Surgeons in Atlanta made nearly $200,000 a year, on average in 2006, $45,000 more than those in Portland, Oregon.

Once we control for living costs, the earnings differentials are, if anything, even larger. According to **Figure 7.6**, plumbers in St. Louis earn the highest COLA-adjusted wage across the twenty metro areas we have been following. At an adjusted

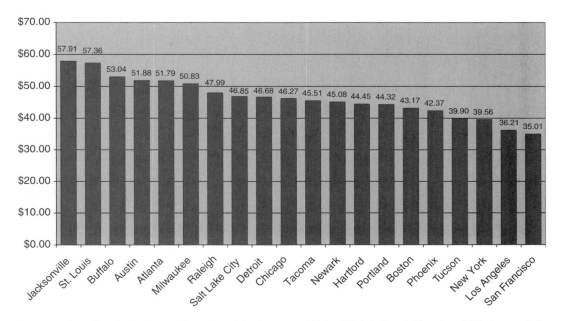

Figure 7.7 Mean Hourly Earnings—Metro Area, Sales Managers, 2006—COLA Adjusted (Phoenix = 1.00). *Source:* U.S. Department of Labor, Bureau of Labor Statistics, "May 2007 Metropolitan Area Occupational Employment and Wage Estimates," http://www.bls.gov/bls/blswage.htm.

rate of $30.51 per hour in 2006, they received almost two and a quarter times what plumbers (presumably doing the same tasks) earn in San Francisco and twice what Raleigh, North Carolina, plumbers make. These differentials are so large that it is hard to believe they reflect merely different plumbing skills. Something peculiar to each of these cities must explain what is happening here.

Similarly, large differentials are found in the hourly wages of sales managers that are adjusted for cost of living, as shown in **Figure 7.7**. Yet the cities offering the highest wages to sales managers are not quite the same as those where plumbers do well. Jacksonville, Buffalo, Austin, and Atlanta pay their sales managers best. In contrast to the relatively "rich" plumbers of Detroit, sales managers in that city are closer to the middle of the metro area wage distribution for this occupation. On the other hand, plumbers working in Raleigh do rather poorly relative to their colleagues in other MSAs, but sales managers do not.

Even the COLA-adjusted annual earnings of surgeons vary across the country (see **Figure 7.8**). Those in St. Louis, Atlanta, and Raleigh receive incomes double those in New York and San Francisco. Interestingly, while plumbers and sales managers are paid relatively poorly in Phoenix, surgeons are not. The point here is that even among workers in the same occupation, after controlling for the cost of living, where you live can make a big difference in your hourly wage. These differentials pose a labor market mystery that we need to investigate.

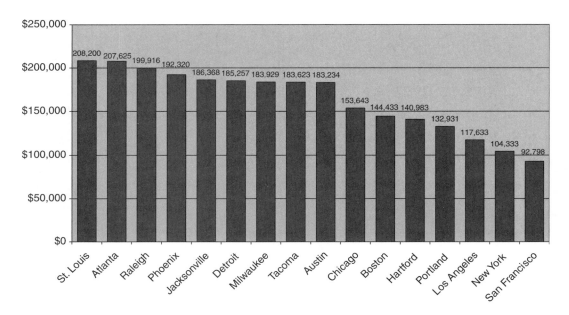

Figure 7.8 Mean Annual Earnings—Metro Area, Surgeons, 2006—COLA Adjusted (Phoenix = 1.00). *Source:* U.S. Department of Labor, Bureau of Labor Statistics, "May 2007 Metropolitan Area Occupational Employment and Wage Estimates," http://www.bls.gov/bls/blswage.htm.

Occupational Wage Differentials between *Occupations* across *Metro Areas*

Wage differentials can be even more of a mystery when we look at relative wages between occupations across metro areas. In general, workers with highly specialized skills will earn more than those with more mundane ones. But an examination of the ratio between the average wages paid in any two occupations can be markedly different depending on where one works. An example is provided in **Table 7.3**, where the nominal average hourly wage of registered nurses is compared to that of plumbers in our twenty selected metro areas. Given the skills needed for each of these occupations, one would expect the relative wages to be approximately the same—but they are not, at all.

Registered nurses need a college degree. Plumbers need to go through a highly rigorous training program and apprenticeship, and need to be licensed in most cities, just like nurses. In Milwaukee, the two occupations earn almost exactly the same hourly wage—$28.40 for nurses versus $29.43 for plumbers. But this is not true in other cities. In Los Angeles, Phoenix, and Jacksonville, nurses outearn plumbers by 50 percent or more. A clue as to what might explain these large differences in relative earnings is found in Table 7.3. Note that plumbers earn a little more than nurses in three metro labor markets—St. Louis, Chicago, and Milwaukee—and are generally within 25 percent of nurses in Buffalo, Detroit, Portland, and Hartford. For the most part, these are all older industrial cities. Plumbers do not earn anywhere near as much in southern and southwestern metro areas. Something about older

Table 7.3 Mean Hourly Wages by Occupation across Metro Areas, Registered Nurses versus Plumbers (2006 Dollars)

	Registered Nurses	Plumbers	Ratio, Registered Nurses/Plumbers
St. Louis	$25.98	$27.46	0.95
Chicago	28.90	30.23	0.96
Milwaukee	28.40	29.43	0.97
Buffalo	25.90	24.26	1.07
Detroit	29.67	27.49	1.08
Portland	31.62	27.63	1.14
Hartford	31.06	24.90	1.25
Boston	36.59	29.27	1.25
New York	35.98	28.14	1.28
San Francisco	39.83	30.80	1.29
Newark	34.10	26.21	1.30
Salt Lake City	27.04	20.42	1.32
Austin	27.44	20.34	1.35
Atlanta	27.09	19.32	1.40
Tacoma	31.93	22.40	1.43
Tucson	27.55	19.01	1.45
Raleigh	26.39	17.80	1.48
Jacksonville	25.69	16.97	1.51
Phoenix	28.31	18.07	1.57
Los Angeles	34.83	20.71	1.68

Source: U.S. Department of Labor 2007.

Table 7.4 Mean Hourly Wages by Occupation across Metro Areas, Plumbers versus Assemblers (2006 Dollars)

	Plumbers		Assemblers	Ratio, Plumbers/Assemblers
Jacksonville	$16.97	San Francisco	$23.51	0.72
Raleigh	17.80	Atlanta	21.74	0.82
Phoenix	18.07	Tacoma	16.88	1.07
Tucson	19.01	Newark	16.77	1.13
Atlanta	19.32	Detroit	16.12	1.20
Austin	20.34	Portland	15.76	1.29
Salt Lake City	20.42	St. Louis	15.15	1.35
Los Angeles	20.71	Hartford	14.98	1.38
Tacoma	22.40	Chicago	14.70	1.52
Buffalo	24.26	Boston	13.90	1.75
Hartford	24.90	Milwaukee	13.39	1.86
Newark	26.21	Raleigh	12.84	2.04
St. Louis	27.46	New York	12.66	2.17
Detroit	27.49	Salt Lake City	12.36	2.22
Portland	27.63	Phoenix	11.81	2.34
New York	28.14	Los Angeles	11.19	2.51
Boston	29.27	Buffalo	11.02	2.66
Milwaukee	29.43	Tucson	11.02	2.67
Chicago	30.23	Jacksonville	10.87	2.78
San Francisco	30.80	Austin	9.52	3.24

Source: U.S. Department of Labor 2007.

industrial cities versus newer cities in the South and Southwest might explain these large differences.

Nearly the same story can be told in terms of skilled plumbers versus lesser skilled assembly-line workers. According to **Table 7.4**, assemblers in Detroit, Newark, Tacoma, Atlanta, and San Francisco earn in nominal terms almost as much or more than skilled plumbers in Jacksonville, Raleigh, Phoenix, or Tucson. On the other hand, assemblers in Austin, Jacksonville, and Tucson earn only about a third of what San Francisco, Chicago, Milwaukee, and Boston plumbers make. Some of this may be due to differences in the cost of living, but that is only one part of the story. The standard economic analysis of supply and demand along with knowledge about the **industrial composition** in each metro area can help explain these urban wage patterns. In addition, a number of **institutional factors**, such as the existence of local minimum wage regulations and the rate of unionization, can be important in determining these urban wage patterns.

Understanding Wage Differentials

In the simplest economic model of the labor market, workers are paid according to their **marginal product.** That is, the wage for all workers of the same skill level will be equal to the value of output produced by the last worker hired. If a firm would see its output increase by $25,000 a year by hiring one additional worker, all workers who do the same work for the firm and have the same skill would be paid this amount. Competition *among workers* keeps the wage no higher than the additional output or marginal product of that last worker. Competition *among firms* for workers will keep the wage no lower than marginal product. If the wage paid workers at a particular firm was below their marginal product, another firm would be willing to hire those workers at a higher wage. If workers demanded a wage higher than their marginal product, no firm would hire them. Thus, the wage tends to settle at a particular level that simply reflects marginal productivity. (**Appendix B** provides a simple graphical treatment of why, in a competitive labor market, wages will tend to equal the workers' marginal revenue product.)

This simple model rests on five key assumptions:

1. *The labor force for any particular type of job is homogeneous.* For the same job, there are no differences between workers in skill level or in motivation.
2. *There are no barriers to labor mobility.* Workers are free to move between firms, offering their services to the highest bidder, no matter where the firm is located.
3. *The product market is competitive.* There are many firms producing exactly the same product at the same price so that consumers are perfectly indifferent between buying the same product from firm 1, firm 2, or any number of other firms.
4. *Transportation costs are negligible.* A product produced in one region can be shipped at minimal cost to other regions.
5. *Firms are in business with the simple objective of maximizing profit.*

Under this set of assumptions, firms will be forced to pay exactly the same wage for workers in a particular occupation, no matter where they are located. Auto assembly-line workers in Detroit will be paid exactly the same as assembly-line workers in Oklahoma City. If the wages in Detroit were higher for some reason, auto companies would close down these operations and move them to Oklahoma City. If they did not close down in Detroit, assembly-line workers in Oklahoma would have an incentive to leave their lower-wage jobs and move to Detroit where they would compete for jobs with the workers already in the Motor City, driving those wage rates down. The key point is that under the assumptions of the simple marginal productivity model of the labor market, all similar workers are paid the same, no matter where they live or work.

Human Capital

The model becomes a little more complicated if we relax the assumption of homogeneous labor and permit workers to have different skills. Now wages will differ among workers, but the wage differentials will reflect different skill levels. A skilled plumber will make more than an unskilled assembly-line worker because the plumber presumably generates a higher marginal product than does the worker on the assembly line. In this case, wage differentials will exist, but they will reflect differences in the **human capital** investment that workers have made in themselves. Those who are better educated or have specialized skills will earn more than those who are less educated and have only general skills that are presumably easy to acquire. Skilled plumbers are like backhoes while assembly-line workers are more like shovels. Since a worker with a backhoe can dig more trench per hour (i.e., have a higher marginal product) than one with a shovel, the better equipped worker is better paid.

However, since the other four assumptions still hold, the wages of identically skilled workers would be the same, no matter where they work or where they live. Any differences in wages between workers would be due only to differences in human capital investments that in turn affect marginal productivity. Given the assumption of unlimited mobility and minimal transportation costs, skilled plumbers would still be paid more or less the same whether they work in New York or Phoenix.

Formal schooling, vocational education, and on-the-job training are all types of human capital investment. In the specific occupation "professional baseball player," an investment in batting practice is a human capital investment, although it has little monetary value for another occupation, say, the professional accountant—even if taking batting practice may help in the company's Saturday morning softball tournament.

A simple model of earnings can be captured in an equation, as follows:

$$\text{Earnings}_i = a_0 + b_1 * \text{Years of Education}_i + b_2 * \text{Vocational Education}_i$$
$$+ b_3 * \text{On-the-Job Training}_i + b_4 * \text{Health Status}_i$$
$$+ b_5 * \text{Other Human Capital Investments}_i$$

where Earnings_i = the wage rate of individual I, a_0 = return to unskilled, uneducated labor, and b_j = return to an extra unit of a given form of human capital j.

Put in simple English, the earnings (e.g., hourly wage) of individual i are equal to some base wage rate a_0 plus the sum of the increments in earnings due to each human capital investment times the "units" of human capital that individual i has accumulated. The increment in earnings—or rate of return—to an additional year of schooling, for example, is b_1. If we were to statistically estimate b_1, we might find, for example, that it is equal to $2.50 per hour. In this case, for two workers who were identical in all other respects, except that one completed college (sixteen years of school) while the other did not go beyond high school (twelve years of school), the college-educated worker would earn $10 ($2.50 × 4) more per hour. This equation would presumably help to explain the difference in earnings between occupations such as surgeon and registered nurse, since the two require different amounts of investment in schooling. Nonetheless, if we maintain the assumption of no barriers to geographic mobility, one would expect the wages of surgeons to be just about the same everywhere. We would have a similar expectation for nurses.

Note that in this model, the return to each human capital investment (b_j) is determined in the labor market and is the same across workers. Workers differ only in the amount of human capital investment they have made. An extra year of vocational education in a specific field is worth the same across all workers who have made that investment, no matter where they work. All differences in wages reflect differences in human capital investments, pure and simple. Factors like gender, race, or ethnicity, for example, should have no effect on earnings if they are determined by the pure human capital model.

By most standards, one of the most important human capital variables is education level. Over time, the return to education has increased because the productivity of skilled workers has climbed, along with an increase in demand for such workers. **Figure 7.9** provides the real average hourly wage for workers with different levels of schooling in 2005. Those with less than a high school degree averaged just $10.53 per hour. High school graduates earned, on average, $14.14—in excess of a third more than those who had not completed high school. College grads earned over $10 per hour more than high school graduates, and those with advanced degrees earned more than $30 per hour, almost three times more than those who had not gone as far as the secondary school diploma. Such a progression in earnings with respect to schooling is precisely what human capital theory would predict.

Market Power and Barriers to Mobility

However, if we relax the assumptions of perfectly competitive firms and perfectly competitive labor markets, we begin to see that, after controlling for human capital, where someone lives and works actually can make a difference in earnings. Barriers to mobility between firms or between locations can produce wage differentials among workers with identical human capital.

This is the general case of **labor market segmentation**, where specific groups of workers are restricted by spatial immobility: by discrimination on the basis of race, gender, sexual orientation, or age; by occupational licensing requirements; or by

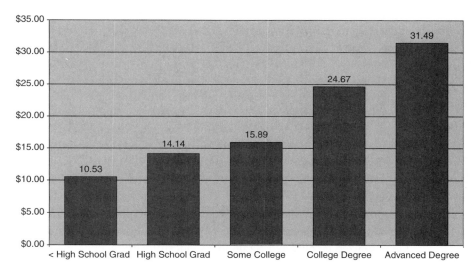

Figure 7.9 Mean Hourly Wage by Education Level, 2005. *Source*: Derived from Mishel, Bernstein, and Allegretto 2007, table 3.17, p. 150.

union rules (Edwards, Reich, and Gordon 1973; Piore 1973; Stevenson 1973; Harrison and Bluestone 1988). One variant of this model suggests that where there are barriers to entering certain labor market segments, a **dual labor market** can arise with a primary sector composed of higher wage, more secure jobs with certain career paths (often in industries that enjoy some form of monopolistic advantage) and a secondary sector, usually comprised of low-wage, temporary, and/or dead-end jobs (often in highly competitive industries).

Outside of economic activity in the formal economy, firms that pay regular taxes and are tracked in government statistics undertake an **informal, shadow,** or **underground economy** (Fields 2005). This part of the economy consists of both legal activities (with the exception that taxes are usually not paid on their proceeds) and a range of illegal activities, from unsanctioned gambling and prostitution to the sale of illicit drugs. Estimates of the size of the underground or informal economy range from 6.2 to 19.4 percent of U.S. gross domestic product (Tanzi 1999). There are employees in each of these sectors (primary, secondary, and informal)—wages are paid and incomes earned—but the level of compensation and the security of the income flows vary substantially across these segments of the labor market.

When firms enjoy a **monopoly** (or **oligopoly**) advantage in a particular market—whether in the formal or informal sector—they are not subject to the same kind of price competition that perfectly competitive firms face. These firms have **market power**, which allows them to increase their prices without losing all their customers to another firm. Depending on the **price elasticity of demand** for their products, they may be able to raise their prices without losing many customers at all. This will be true in the case of **inelastic demand**, where a commodity (e.g., a life-saving medication for which there is no substitute) is considered so valuable or necessary that consumers will continue to buy it even when its price rises. How can this affect wages?

If the labor market were still perfectly competitive, then the wages paid for a specific type of labor in the monopoly firm would still be the same across all firms using the same kind of labor, regardless of industry. But if there were barriers to mobility so that some workers could not find employment in the monopoly firm, then the workers in this firm could win a wage premium without having other workers compete it away. There are many examples where this occurs.

Consider the case of labor unions. If a firm faces little market competition and thus can charge higher prices for its products, then workers in that firm can form a union, bargain for higher wages, and, if successful, get them and keep them. A wage gap will develop between identically skilled workers who differ only by reason of union membership. If some cities are highly unionized and others are not, it would not be surprising to see that the workforce in the highly unionized city is better paid, at least if the unionized employers operate in an industry with monopoly or oligopoly advantage. This helps to explain the high wages of assembly workers in the Detroit and St. Louis metro areas, where the United Auto Workers (UAW) have organized a good share of the auto industry. It also explains the relatively low wages of assembly workers in Tucson and Los Angeles, where the manufacturing base is made up of small shops in such highly competitive industries as apparel, where unions are either weak or nonexistent, and in which the labor force is heavily comprised of Latino workers with limited education, many of whom are recent immigrants. The oligopoly power of the auto industry before the onset of foreign competition plus the bargaining power of the UAW explain a good deal of why, in 1969, Detroit had the highest median household income of the twenty metro areas we have been following.

Geographic regions that have trouble attracting new workers to them may also be forced to pay higher wages as a result of imperfect mobility between locations. If a lot of people want to move to Phoenix, Jacksonville, or Salt Lake City, even those employers with considerable market power may not need to pay a premium wage to satisfy their labor needs. Getting workers to move to Buffalo or Hartford may be more difficult. As we mentioned earlier, the high cost of housing in Greater Boston forces many employers to pay top dollar to get workers to remain in the area or to get new workers to move in. Thus, we begin to understand the importance of the spatial dimension in explaining wage differentials once we enter a world of imperfect competition between firms and barriers to mobility among workers.

Racial and Ethnic Discrimination

Still another form of labor market barrier can occur in the form of racial or gender discrimination. When otherwise similar workers are treated differently in the labor market, the assumption of perfect labor mobility is violated and wage differentials can result. At the level of the firm, this can occur when a significant number of companies discriminate on the basis of race or gender when hiring or promoting workers. In this case, those who are discriminated against are harmed by reason of

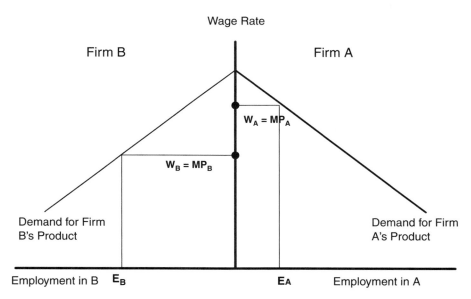

Figure 7.10 Labor Market Discrimination. Firm A and Firm B produce an identical product with the same technology and face identical demand curves. Firm A's demand curve is shown on the right; Firm B's demand curve (rotated to fit on the same diagram) is on the left. Firm A discriminates and will only hire certain workers (e.g., white men) even though other workers with identical human capital are available. Firm B will hire any such workers. As a result, Firm A must pay a higher wage (W_A) because it has artificially limited the supply of workers it is willing to employ (E_A). Firm B will hire any qualified individual and, therefore, faces a larger supply (E_B) and thus can pay a lower wage (W_B). In a perfectly competitive market, Firm A will go out of business because its average cost is higher than Firm B's and, therefore, Firm B can charge a lower price for the identical product. In this case, the firm that discriminates fails; the firm that does not discriminate prospers.

being "crowded" into the limited number of firms willing to hire them. This increases the supply of workers to these businesses, driving down the wage for those in the group being discriminated against. Meanwhile, those who are favored by employers face less competition for jobs and therefore find their wages driven up. The result is a wage gap between two groups of workers who have the same skills, but differ by skin color, ethnicity, or gender.

The effect of such discrimination can be seen in **Figure 7.10**, where we have two firms, A and B, with identical demand curves for their products. To make it easy to compare the two firms, we use the same Y axis for both firms, but have rotated the X-axis for Firm B so it is the mirror image of Firm A. Let us assume for the sake of argument that Firm A refuses to hire anyone with the exception of white men, while Firm B will hire anyone, regardless of race or gender. As a consequence, the supply of workers to Firm A is limited and the intersection of supply and demand is at wage, W_A. All the remaining workers are "crowded" into Firm B, which drives the wage down in this company to W_B. The result is the wage differential W_A–W_B favoring white men (Bergmann 1971).

As Becker (1957) demonstrated nearly half a century ago, this type of discrimination will disappear if firms have no market power and must compete in the product market. His reasoning was quite straightforward. If the owners of Firm A indulge their "taste" for discrimination, they will be forced to pay higher wages, which will force up the firm's **average total cost curve**. Firm B will benefit from not discriminating because its average total cost curve will be lower. This company will be able to lower its price below what the discriminating Firm A must charge, driving the discriminating firm out of business. This is one of those cases where the free market rewards ethical behavior.

Of course, if Firm A is a **monopolist** or **oligopolist**, it can indulge its taste for discrimination without paying the price of going bankrupt. Given that many firms have at least a modicum of market power because their products are unique or are sufficiently differentiated to garner consumer demand, the discrimination wage gap can be sustained. Thus, in the days before global competition made even the largest U.S. firms compete for consumers, discrimination could be rampant without its perpetrators paying a price for their behavior.

A more subtle form of bias is found in what economists call **statistical discrimination**, a practice in which employers judge an individual not on his or her own credentials—which may be difficult, time-consuming, or expensive to ascertain—but on beliefs about the characteristics of the typical or average member of the demographic group to which the individual belongs (Bluestone and Stevenson 2000). If employers experience better performance from a certain demographic group—or even if they just *perceive* or *believe* they will get better performance—then it is likely that the employer will choose from this demographic group again and again when new employees are needed. Similarly, employers who have a bad experience with a number of members of a particular demographic group—or hear about the experiences of other employers—may tend to shy away from other members of this group in future hiring decisions. Interviews with Chicago-area employers by Joleen Kirschenman and Kathryn Neckerman (1991) in the late 1980s revealed that many employers there did practice statistical discrimination, judging individual job applicants according to what they believed to be true of the demographic group to which the individual belonged. Many employers surmised that a black applicant, particularly from the central city, would not make as good an employee as, for example, a white immigrant. As such, many refrained from hiring blacks whenever other applicants were available. Sociologists Pager and Quillian (2005), using matched pairs of white and black job seekers with equivalent resumes, found that Milwaukee-area employers called back to interview 34 percent of white applicants without a criminal background, 17 percent of white applicants with a criminal background, and only 14 percent of blacks who had *no* criminal record—suggesting that even more information about employees, such as criminal record, did not change the cognitive map of many employers.

Spatial Mismatch

Labor market barriers need not emanate from the explicit discriminatory behavior of firms. Instead, they can be the product of **residential segregation**—where households of different races or members of particular ethnic groups live in separate neighborhoods within a city or metro area—combined with the deindustrialization of central cities. In this case, the barrier is erected not in the firm's employment office, but somewhere between where people live and where the firm is located. The concept of a **spatial mismatch**, where those trapped in inner-city neighborhoods could not easily access jobs in the suburbs, was first advanced by the Harvard economist John Kain in a seminal paper that appeared in 1968 (Kain 1968). The topic once again gained currency in the 1990s, with a flurry of academic research devoted to testing how much of the unemployment rate differential and the wage gap between blacks and whites could be explained by residential segregation (Ihlanfeldt and Sjoquist 1998).

At least until World War II, manufacturing operations were often located in central cities or suburbs close to their company's corporate headquarters. The steel mills in Pittsburgh were not far from the city along the Allegheny and Monongahela rivers; Ford and Chrysler had massive multistory assembly plants in the middle of Detroit; and the stockyards of Chicago were not far from the residential neighborhoods where their employees lived. Unskilled and semiskilled immigrant workers and African Americans who had come from the South were able to find jobs in these factories that paid reasonably well.

After the war, many U.S. firms closed operations in central cities and moved to the suburbs, often beyond the reach of mass transit (see Chapter 4). Cheaper land in the suburbs made it cost effective to keep production on a single floor rather than having to move parts and assemblies up and down a multistory building on huge freight elevators, as the Chrysler Corporation had done at its enormous six-story Dodge Main auto assembly operation in downtown Detroit. Improved intracity and intercity trucking made it feasible to be farther away from centralized port facilities and parts depots. As for the workforce, the interstate highway system made it possible for suburban-based residents to get to their jobs in suburban-based firms along circumferential highways and north-south and east-west freeways.

For black workers and new immigrants, however, leaving the central city when the jobs moved out was not always an option. As we will see in Chapter 12 where we examine housing markets, a variety of practices led to residential segregation, with whites moving to the suburbs, while minorities were often trapped in the neighborhoods where they had originally come to live in the central cities. For those unable to move to the suburbs, a spatial mismatch evolved whereby the cost and distance of commuting served as a barrier that blocked job opportunities for the central city population (Ellwood 1986).

While the actual quantitative impact of spatial mismatch has been a matter of dispute, there are a range of credible studies that have found inner-city blacks disadvantaged in terms of both income and employment. Ihlanfeldt (1996) concluded that geographic barriers to suburban jobs explained between 24 and 27 percent of the gap in employment rates between black and white workers and between 29 and 34 percent of the Hispanic/white gap. Not unexpectedly, spatial mismatch was found to be especially important in larger metro areas, where the commuting distances from central city to suburb are greater.

Other researchers have found equally strong evidence of the impact of spatial mismatch, particularly in metro areas in the Northeast and the Midwest (Jencks and Mayer 1990; Holzer 1991; Moss and Tilly 1991; Cutler and Glaeser 1997). Wyly (1996), for example, investigating the impact of an increase in spatial mismatch between 1980 and 1990 in the Minneapolis/St. Paul metropolitan area, concluded that as high-wage manufacturing jobs left the central city, black workers who could not move to the suburbs were often left with low-wage service jobs and consequently a decline in their incomes. In more recent work, Glaeser and Kahn (2003) and Stoll (2005) have added to the literature by measuring "job sprawl" as a factor in exacerbating spatial mismatch. Stoll, in particular, finds that metro areas with higher levels of employment decentralization exhibit greater spatial mismatch and this particularly affects black workers.

So it is not simply that jobs have moved to the suburbs, but the fact that they are moving farther and farther away from the central city that adversely affects workers who still live there. The cities, Stoll finds, with the highest "Mismatch Index" are generally the ones with the highest "Job Sprawl Index." Detroit, Chicago, Newark, and Philadelphia lead his list. Cities in the South and West generally have less job sprawl and less spatial mismatch.

Figure 7.11 provides some evidence of such a mismatch for two metro areas and compares these with two other metro areas where such a mismatch does not appear to be acute (U.S. Department of Housing and Urban Development 2007). Detroit is the poster child for mismatch according to this figure based on 2000 U.S. Census data. A mere 3.2 percent of all white residents in the Detroit MSA live in the central city. In contrast, more than three-quarters (76.4%) of African Americans and more than a third of Hispanics appear to be trapped there. The problem is that less than 16 percent of all the jobs and less than 12 percent of manufacturing employment in the metro region are still located inside the central city. That means that white workers are closer to the jobs, while blacks and Hispanics have to find a way to get from the central city to suburban job locations. Detroit does not have a functional mass-transit system, so most blacks must commute over long and time-consuming distances on crowded highways to get to work. For those who cannot, including those who are too poor to own cars, the number of midlevel jobs in the city is limited and many of these are in lower-wage protective and personal services. As a result, a wage gap opens up between those who have the ability to move closer to suburban jobs and those who do not, even if both groups have similar human capital.

The situation we find in Detroit is also found in metro areas like Chicago, although the mismatch there is not as pronounced. Chicago has managed to keep more than 30 percent of its total jobs and 20 percent of its manufacturing jobs in the central city.

In contrast, there is little indication of spatial mismatch in Phoenix or Los Angeles. In these two cities, the proportions of blacks and Hispanics in the central city do not far exceed the proportion of total jobs or even manufacturing employment. This pattern of

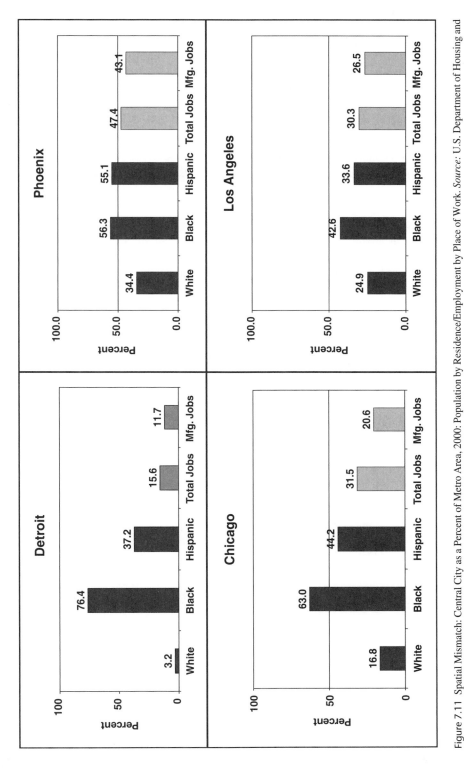

Figure 7.11 Spatial Mismatch: Central City as a Percent of Metro Area, 2000: Population by Residence/Employment by Place of Work. *Source:* U.S. Department of Housing and Urban Development, HUD User Policy Development and Research Information Service, SOCDS data set, 2007, http://socds.huduser.org.

spatial mismatch in older midwestern MSAs with fewer mismatches in the West reflects the higher incidence of plant closings in older areas, the larger size of central cities in newer areas, and the ability of African Americans and Hispanic families to find housing outside of the central city in metro areas like Los Angeles.

How does spatial mismatch affect the labor market and earnings? The association between the degree of mismatch and the earnings gap between central cities and suburbs is by no means perfect, but there does seem to be a tendency for the high mismatch metro areas to have a greater discrepancy in central city/suburban unemployment rates and household incomes. Of the four cities we looked at in Figure 7.11, **Table 7.5** reveals that the central city/suburban unemployment rate ratio is substantially higher in Detroit and Chicago and much lower in Los Angeles and Phoenix. In 2000, the same year for which we have employment data, the 13.8 percent jobless rate in the city of Detroit was nearly 3.4 times higher than the 4.1 percent unemployment rate in the Motor City's suburbs. The typical household in Detroit's central city had just half (53%) the income of the typical suburban household. In Chicago, the comparable unemployment rates were 10.1 percent in the central city and 4.5 percent in the suburbs, for a central city/suburban ratio of 2.2. Residents inside Chicago's central city earned only two-thirds (67%) as much as those in the suburbs. By way of contrast, in the two western metro regions (Los Angeles and Phoenix) where there is little spatial mismatch, the central city/suburban unemployment rate ratios are significantly lower (1.4 and 1.2, respectively) and there is a somewhat smaller intraregional income gap. Residents of these central cities are not as penalized as they are in cities where the spatial mismatch is more severe.

Skills Mismatch

Not all of the intrametropolitan unemployment rate differential or the difference in incomes can be attributed to spatial mismatch per se. As **Table 7.6** demonstrates,

Table 7.5 Central City/Suburban Unemployment Rates and Median Household Income, Selected Cities, 2000

	Unemployment Rates			
	Detroit	**Chicago**	**Los Angeles**	**Phoenix**
Central City	13.8%	10.1%	9.3%	5.6%
Suburbs	4.1%	4.5%	6.5%	4.6%
Ratio	3.37	2.24	1.43	1.22
	Median Household Income			
	Detroit	**Chicago**	**Los Angeles**	**Phoenix**
Central City	$34,612	$45,279	$43,007	$48,306
Suburbs	$65,272	$67,463	$60,788	$55,434
Ratio	0.53	0.67	0.71	0.87

Note: Median household income in 2005 dollars.
Source: U.S. Department of Housing and Urban Development, HUD User Policy Development and Research Information Service, SOCDS data set, 2007, http://socds.huduser.org.

Table 7.6 Central City/Suburban Educational Attainment, Selected Cities, 2000 (Highest Education Level Attained—Age 25 or Older)

	Less Than High School	High School Graduate	Some College	College +
Detroit				
Central City	30.4%	30.0%	28.6%	11.0%
Suburbs	14.1%	29.3%	31.2%	25.4%
Ratio	2.16	1.02	0.92	0.43
Chicago				
Central City	28.2%	23.0%	23.3%	25.5%
Suburbs	14.7%	27.0%	28.7%	29.7%
Ratio	1.92	0.85	0.81	0.86
Los Angeles				
Central City	33.4%	17.4%	23.7%	25.5%
Suburbs	25.3%	19.5%	29.5%	25.7%
Ratio	1.32	0.89	0.80	0.99
Phoenix				
Central City	23.4%	25.6%	31.1%	22.7%
Suburbs	16.7%	24.9%	34.6%	13.2%
Ratio	1.40	1.03	0.90	1.72

Source: U.S. Department of Housing and Urban Development, HUD User Policy Development and Research Information Service, SOCDS data set, 2007, http://socds.huduser.org.

there are significant differences in the educational attainment of central city and suburban residents, particularly in high spatial mismatch metro areas. In Detroit, according to the 2000 Census, more than 30 percent of central city residents (age 25 and older) had failed to graduate from high school, more than double the rate in the surrounding suburbs. More than 60 percent of central city adults had no more than a high school diploma and only about one in nine (11%) had completed college, less than half the suburban rate.

Even if there were no spatial barriers to suburban jobs, one would expect that many central city workers would have difficulty qualifying for higher-wage jobs. Thus, a significant share of both the intrametropolitan unemployment rate differential and the income differential is likely due to differences in human capital and cannot be attributed solely to a spatial mismatch between where firms and workers are located. A similar story can be told with respect to Chicago.

Not surprisingly, those metro areas with the least central city/suburban discrepancy in unemployment rates and household incomes are those where there is little difference in educational attainment within the region. The best examples are Los Angeles and Phoenix. In the Arizona MSA, central city residents appear to have a bit more education than those who live in the suburbs.

Of course, education is only one form of human capital. Differences in "soft skills," such as work attitudes and work ethic, problem-solving skills, technological competencies, and interpersonal skills and attitudes are important as well, although they are difficult to measure. Nonetheless, if these differ between those who live in central cities and suburbs, differences in formal schooling may explain only some of the central city-suburban unemployment gap or wage differential (Moss and Tilly 2001).

Statistical studies have attempted to determine the share of central city/suburban labor market differences that can be attributed to spatial versus skills mismatch. Most of this research tries to decipher the extent to which black workers are at a disadvantage because of their central city location. One of the most important early studies in this field found that 56 percent of the average wage difference between black and white workers was due to the latter's better human capital characteristics, including education and experience (Price and Mills 1985). So the *skills* mismatch was found to be the dominant factor. The remaining 44 percent of the black/white earning differential was found to be split between outright employer discrimination and spatial mismatch. In estimating how much black workers would boost their earnings by moving from the central city to the suburbs, Price and Mills concluded that about a third of the remaining wage gap was due to housing segregation.

Over time, one might expect the spatial aspect of employment and earnings differentials to decline, if the degree of housing segregation diminishes and if new technology induces a skill upgrading, even in traditional manufacturing jobs. In this case, space will become even less important relative to skill (Zhang and Bingham 2000). Some evidence of a narrowing during the 1990s in the spatial mismatch between blacks and jobs has been found in recent research (Raphael and Stoll 2002).

There is one caveat to this argument, however. If housing segregation based on race is the reason for the spatial mismatch on the employee side, deliberate relocation to the suburbs by employers to escape the racial composition of the central city should also be considered a form of spatial mismatch. Some circumstantial evidence from a 1995 employer survey in Boston seems to indicate such a motivation on the part of at least some employers. Moss and Tilly argue from their qualitative survey data that "racial composition figures prominently in employers' cognitive maps of space" (Moss and Tilly 2001, p. 347). They argue that information about race combines with the perception of concentrated poverty, crime, and congestion in central city locations to induce some employers to move to the suburbs, exacerbating spatial mismatch.

Spatial Mismatch, Deindustrialization, Education, and Race

We do know from statistical analysis that spatial mismatch was particularly harsh for one demographic group from the early 1960s through the late 1980s, when the deindustrialization of central cities was accelerating. Young black men just getting started in the labor market with no more than a high school degree and who, for one reason or another, were trapped in central cities, suffered disproportionately high unemployment and depressed annual earnings. Bluestone, Stevenson, and Tilly (1992) studied how the change in a metro area's manufacturing employment level interacted with a region's overall job growth to determine the labor market prospects of twenty- and twenty-five-year-old white and black men and women who had no more than a high school education. Using ninety-three MSAs, the researchers divided their sample into nine categories. Of these, Category 1 included metro areas that experienced a sharp decline in manufacturing employment and a decline or sluggish growth in overall employment in such sectors as retail and wholesale trade and business services, and in finance, insurance, and real estate. Typical of the cities in this category were Detroit, Buffalo, Chicago, Newark, Pittsburgh, St. Louis, and Youngstown, Ohio—all older industrial cities in the Northeast and Midwest. At the other end of their continuum, the set of MSAs in Category 9 experienced only mild deindustrialization and very rapid overall employment growth. Albuquerque, Atlanta, Ft. Lauderdale, Phoenix, and San Antonio were typical of this set of cities—virtually all in the South or Southwest. In the middle of their taxonomy were cities that experienced modest deindustrialization and modest overall job growth. Baton Rouge, Louisiana; Grand Rapids, Michigan; Houston, Texas; and Oakland, California, fell into this category.

The differences Bluestone, Stevenson, and Tilly found regarding one's race and where one lived were quite striking. Among twenty-year-old white men, of whom less than 30 percent lived in central cities, the differences in labor market outcomes between Category 1 and Category 9 MSAs were modest. Of those living in rapidly deindustrializing cities with slow job growth—and who reported they were not in school, ill, or disabled—only 4.1 percent were found to be jobless for the entire year in which they were surveyed. The group as a whole averaged $10,952 in annual earnings. For those in the least deindustrialized cities with the fastest job growth, the jobless rate dropped to 1.5 percent and annual earnings rose to $12,161.

But the same analysis for young black men, of whom nearly half lived in central cities and 36 percent in rural areas—leaving only small numbers in the rapidly expanding suburbs—revealed a jobless rate in the Category 1 MSAs to be 42 percent, virtually ten times higher than the white rate. Annual earnings averaged only $3,751, just a third of what comparable white men were making. Trapped in central cities where manufacturing jobs were rapidly disappearing and few new jobs in other sectors were being created had disastrous consequences for these young black men. One indication of the impact of deindustrialization and job loss on this particular demographic group is that in those Category 9 MSAs where manufacturing losses were modest and overall job creation was brisk, the jobless rate fell to 18 percent and annual earnings increased to $8,729. The gap between whites and blacks remained large, but those young black men living in the southern and southwestern cities where jobs were plentiful were less than half as likely to be jobless as young black men in northeastern and midwestern MSAs and their annual incomes were more than twice as high.

A similar analysis for twenty-five-year-olds showed the same general trends, but not nearly as severe. When Bluestone, Stevenson, and Tilly repeated the analysis still a third time for young women, they found only modest support for the spatial mismatch hypothesis. Their conclusion was that spatial mismatch and deindustrialization affected all workers, but especially hammered young black men. Thus, the urban riots, growing crime rates, increased drug use, and increased "underground" and illegal economic activity that we were beginning to see during the late 1960s and

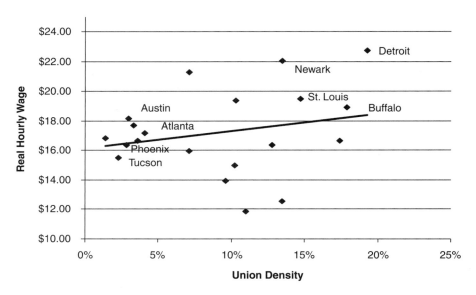

Figure 7.12 Real Wage versus Union Density for Selected MSAs, 2003. *Sources:* U.S. Department of Labor, Bureau of Labor Statistics, "May 2003 Metropolitan Area Occupational Employment and Wage Estimates" (Washington, D.C.: U.S. Government Printing Office, 2003); Barry Hirsh and David McPherson, *Unionstats.com Data Base* (http://www.unionstats.com).

throughout the 1970s, especially among young black men with limited education, could be linked to the deteriorating employment conditions in older central cities. The connections between the urban labor market and urban social conditions were clearly in evidence, according to this analysis.

The Role of Unions

Your job opportunities and your earnings appear to be affected by whether you live in the central city or the suburb, whether you are black or white, or whether you live in a deindustrializing MSA. Being a member of a union where you can negotiate collectively for wages and benefits also plays a role in labor market outcomes. After controlling for differences in the experience, education, region, industry, occupation, and marital status of the working population, it has been estimated that the average union wage premium was close to 16 percent in 2003 (Mishel, Bernstein, and Allegretto 2004). That is, nationwide, members of unions earned 16 percent more than comparable workers who were not represented by a union. The union advantage varies by race, ethnicity, and gender, with unionization being particularly important for minority workers. Overall, the union premium varies from 9.1 percent for white women and 13.8 percent for white men to 18.2 percent for black women and nearly 24 percent for black men. The union wage premiums for Hispanics are slightly larger still—19.5 percent for women, 25.5 percent for men.

It is also true that the rate of unionization—or **union density**—varies substantially across metro areas. Union density in the private sector is very low in MSAs such as Tucson (2.3%) and Austin (3.0%), along with such cities as Raleigh (1.4%), Salt Lake City (2.8%), Jacksonville (3.3%), Phoenix (3.6%), and Atlanta (4.1%). At the other end of the union density spectrum are two of the most traditionally highly unionized MSAs: Detroit (19.3%), home of the United Automobile Workers union, and Buffalo (17.9%), much of its steel industry organized by the United Steel-workers Union. Also with reasonably high private-sector unionization rates are St. Louis (14.7%), Newark and New York (both at 13.5%), and Chicago (12.8%).

As **Figure 7.12** demonstrates, MSAs that are more heavily unionized, such as Detroit, Newark, St. Louis, and Buffalo, are those in which metro area COLA-adjusted (real) wages are generally higher. Overall, the fitted trend line suggests that MSAs that are only 5 percent unionized in the private sector tend to have an average wage of about $16.75 per hour. Those with a unionization rate closer to 20 percent average about $18.50 per hour. This suggests about a 10 percent union wage differential between MSAs. In explaining the metro area wage differentials shown in earlier tables and figures, unionization cannot be ignored as a contributing factor.

The metropolitan pattern of union density found on the horizontal axis of Figure 7.12 has historical roots. Before the 1930s, only about 10 percent of the total non-agricultural workforce consisted of union members. Most of these were organized into craft unions that were the direct descendents of the medieval guilds in Europe. These were skilled blue-collar professionals, including carpenters, electricians, plumbers, and "teamsters"—those who drove horse-drawn delivery wagons. With the passage of the National Labor Relations Act (the NLRA, or Wagner Act) in 1935,

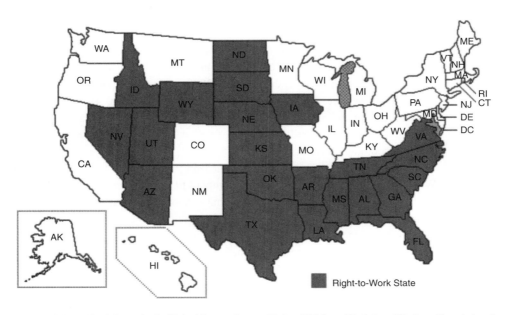

Figure 7.13 Right-to-Work States in the United States. *Source:* National Right to Work Legal Defense Foundation, http://www.nrtw.org.

workers had new protections from "unfair labor practices" that employers had used to keep their employees from joining unions.

The NLRA provided the legal support for massive union drives among unskilled and semiskilled workers in key manufacturing industries. Thus, by the end of the 1930s, as the result of new union activism, millions of auto, tire, glass, steel, and electrical machinery workers were organized. The percent of the American nonfarm organized workforce nearly tripled to 29 percent by 1939. Given that the overwhelming majority of traditional manufacturing plants were in the Northeast and the Midwest, these regions and the metro areas within them became unionized. Unionization rates in the South and Southwest were particularly low, with rates in between prevailing on the West Coast, where the aircraft industry and the movie industry became bastions of union organizing.

Meanwhile, particularly in the South, there was a business-led movement to make union organizing more difficult. The so-called "Right-to-Work" movement was successful in twenty-two states in passing laws that banned the **union shop,** which the NLRA had sanctioned. Under the union shop, if a majority of workers in an NLRA-approved bargaining unit within a firm vote to join a union, all workers in that bargaining unit are required to join the union and pay dues. In that way, no workers benefit from union representation without helping to pay for it. Essentially, the union shop borrows from the theory of taxation that everyone should pay for the services that are provided to the community. When the NLRA was amended by the Taft-Hartley Act of 1947, however, each state was given permission to opt out of this portion of the federal law. Virtually, the entire South from Virginia to Texas did so, along with Arizona, Utah, Nevada, Idaho, and Wyoming in the Southwest and West. The wage gaps we find between many metro areas in the Northeast and Midwest on the one hand and in the South and Southwest on the other continue to reflect this history, despite the weakening of the trade union movement throughout the country. **Figure 7.13** provides a map of the "Right-to-Work" states as of 2004. Not surprisingly, the union membership rates in 2000 in states like North Carolina, South Carolina, Tennessee, Virginia, Louisiana, Idaho, Oklahoma, Texas, Arizona, and Utah are all in the single digits. Non-Right-to-Work states like Alaska, Hawaii, Michigan, New Jersey, and New York are all at least 20 percent unionized (Hirsch, Macpherson, and Vroman 2001).

Today, however, unionization is something of a mixed blessing for workers. While unionized workers are better compensated, many of the private industries with strong unions have been subject to huge layoffs. The sharp cuts in employment in such industries as auto, steel, and electrical goods as well as in apparel and textiles have come as the result of automation and globalization. To the extent that union wage gains and other negotiated benefits have encouraged firms to substitute new technology for workers and to seek cheaper sources of labor in less unionized regions of the country and abroad, many unionized workers have been displaced from their jobs. Heavily unionized cities like Detroit, Pittsburgh, and Youngstown, Ohio, have been devastated by plant closings, some of which may have been related to the higher labor costs associated with a heavily unionized workforce.

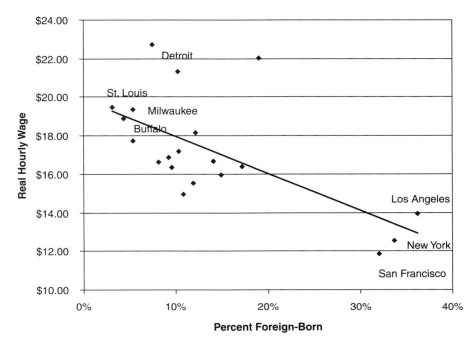

Figure 7.14 Real Wage versus Percent Foreign-Born for Selected MSAs, 2000. *Sources:* U.S. Department of Labor, Bureau of Labor Statistics, "May 2003 Metropolitan Area Occupational Employment and Wage Estimates" (Washington, D.C. U.S. Government Printing Office, 2003); U.S. Department of Housing and Urban Development, HUD User Policy Development and Research Information Service, SOCDS data set, 2007, http://socds.huduser.org.

The one bright spot in what remains of the union movement is taking place primarily in central cities, where service-industry unions like the Service Employees International Union (SEIU) and UNITE HERE (a merger of the former United Needletrades, Industrial, and Textile Employees union and the Hotel Employees and Restaurant Employees international union) have been aggressively organizing low-wage workers in janitorial services, airport concessions, industrial laundries, and food services. By 2007, SEIU boasted 1.9 million union cardholders, while the newly merged UNITE HERE union claimed more than 450,000 active members (SEIU 2007; UNITE HERE 2007).

Immigration

Unionization affects wages through labor-management negotiation rather than by permitting the free flow of labor into a firm to set wages according to the laws of supply and demand. Immigration, in contrast, can affect wages simply by increasing the supply of labor in a particular labor market. One would expect, ceteris paribus, that wages will be particularly low in metro areas that have been destinations for large flows of less skilled or less educated foreign workers. **Figure 7.14** demonstrates just such a pattern. Generally, in MSAs with a small percentage of foreign-born residents, metro-adjusted COLA wages tend to be higher than those where recent immigration has been prevalent. According to 2000 Census figures, the foreign-born population in the Detroit, St. Louis, Milwaukee, and Buffalo MSAs represented no more than 7.5 percent of the total population. In contrast, in San Francisco, New York, and Los Angeles, more than a third of the residents were foreign born, many of Hispanic and Asian background. The fitted trend line suggests that the average real wage in a metro area with a third of its population foreign born is likely to be more than 25 percent lower than an MSA with just 5 percent of its population made up of immigrants. The lower wages in the metro areas with larger foreign-born workforces may be due to any number of factors that include a higher percentage of workers with limited education, limited job skills, limited English proficiency, or simply the ability of employers to pay lower wages to undocumented workers.

One might expect the impact of immigration to be particularly acute for less skilled workers—those who end up with jobs like team assembler in the manufacturing sector. This is precisely what is found. Using the same fitted trend line method as in Figure 7.14, an assembler in an MSA with just 5 percent foreign born will earn more than twice the metro area COLA-adjusted wage of an assembler in a metro area with a third of its population comprised of immigrants. Once again, Los Angeles, New York, and San Francisco, with their large Hispanic and Asian immigrant populations, end up at the bottom of the real wage distribution. Detroit, with its small population of recent immigrants, rewards its assemblers with a metro area COLA-adjusted wage of $18.29 per hour, more than three times the COLA-adjusted wage in New York ($5.46) and 2.5 times the adjusted wage in Los Angeles ($7.13).

Explaining Metro Area Earnings Differentials

With all this information, we can take a stab at explaining the large wage differences between metro areas as shown in Figure 7.2. MSAs such as Detroit, Newark, and St. Louis were found to have the highest COLA-adjusted wages among the metro areas we have been tracking. What do they have in common? All of these are highly unionized cities with relatively little immigration. Cities like Los Angeles, New York, and San Francisco have relatively low COLA-adjusted wages. All of them have been destinations for a large number of foreign-born immigrant workers.

Why do registered nurses make less than what plumbers earn in Chicago, but in excess of 50 percent more than plumbers in such MSAs as Los Angeles, Phoenix, and Jacksonville (recall Table 7.3)? The answer has to do with both unionization and immigration. Plumbers do very well in highly unionized cities where there is little competition from nonunion immigrant workers. They fare much worse in MSAs where there has been a large influx of immigrant workers, some of whom come with the skills of plumbers. Registered nurses, on the other hand, are in great demand in southern and southwestern retirement communities like Jacksonville, Phoenix, and Los Angeles, while largely protected from immigrant competition by the education and certification requirements in this profession.

Plumbers in Chicago make nearly three times the wage of assemblers in Jacksonville (recall Table 7.4) as a result of their higher skills, their high rate of unionization, and their relative insulation from immigrant competition. Assemblers in Phoenix and Tucson suffer because they are only weakly unionized and face stiff competition from foreign-born workers.

Black, and to some extent Hispanic, workers suffer lower wages because they have less human capital, because they are often trapped in deindustrializing central cities, and because of "crowding" due to outright discrimination.

We have learned that when product markets are not perfectly competitive and mobility within labor markets is constrained, large wage differentials can occur even for workers in the same occupation but who live in different labor markets.

Race and location of residence remain critically important variables even in the twenty-first century. In a detailed study of annual earnings of black, Hispanic, and non-Hispanic white men in the Greater Boston metro region, all of whom had no more than a high school education, Bluestone and Stevenson (2000) found that black men earned only 55 percent of what white men made, and Hispanic men 63 percent. Using a statistical simulation technique, they were able to estimate how the black/white and Hispanic/white earnings ratios would change if blacks and Hispanics had different characteristics. Assigning these two groups the same human capital attributes as white men (i.e., age, education level, word recognition test scores, number of years of specific job experience, health status, and veteran status), they found that the earnings gap for these workers with no more than a high school degree totally disappeared for Hispanic men, but black men still earned only a little more than two-thirds (69%) of white men.

In an alternative simulation, Bluestone and Stevenson assigned the same metro area residential location to everyone and gave black and Hispanic men the same job

Table 7.7 Factors Affecting Racial and Ethnic Annual Earnings Differentials: Individuals with No More Than a High School Degree in Greater Boston

Men	Black/White Ratio	Hispanic/White Ratio
Original Earnings Ratio	.55	.63
Equal Human Capital	.69	1.01
Same Residence/Same Job Characteristics	.92	.87

Women	Black/White Ratio	Hispanic/White Ratio
Original Earnings Ratio	.65	.94
Equal Human Capital	.77	.96
Same Residence/Same Job Characteristics	.79	.84

Notes: Equal Human Capital assigns black and Hispanic workers the same average years of education as white workers, the same health status, the same median age, the same proportion of armed forces veterans, and the same mean score on a simple ten-word vocabulary test. Same Residence/Same Job Characteristics assigns black and Hispanic workers to residence in a neighborhood in which white households are a majority, assigns them the same number of second jobs as whites, the same average years of job experience, the same proportion working in sales and service jobs, and equal use of computers on the job.
Source: Adapted from Bluestone and Stevenson 2000, figure 8.12, p. 247.

characteristics as white men. Now the Hispanic/white ratio reached only 87 percent, but the black/white ratio reached 92 percent. They concluded that within at least this one metro area, closing the human capital gap was all that was necessary to bring earnings parity for Hispanic men. But this would not solve the problem for black men; trapped in the inner city and unable to gain admittance to the same jobs as white men because of various forms of discrimination, they were placed at a considerable disadvantage. To close most of the earnings gap, it would be necessary to overcome spatial mismatch and eliminate racial prejudice (see **Table 7.7**).

For women who had no more than a high school degree in the Boston study, the annual earnings gap between Hispanics and whites was found to be extremely modest. This turned out to be true because Hispanic women have become the new manufacturing workforce in that metro region and are more likely to have full-time jobs with union benefits. As in the case for men, however, the earnings gap between black and white women was large and could not be closed through infusions of human capital. Indeed, for all women, the key factor that explained annual earnings was related to marital status and the presence of children. Single women with children, no matter their race or ethnicity, were trapped in low-wage, part-time jobs and experienced higher unemployment. As a result, their earnings fell far below those of single women without children and below those of married women with and without children.

Labor Markets and Urban Prosperity

As we have seen, for almost all households, economic well-being is tied closely to how well their breadwinners do in the labor market. At one time, how well they did in the labor market was a function of many factors that included whether they were members of trade unions and how much discrimination they might face in the search for employment. While both of these factors are still important, human capital has become increasingly important in a global economy based on sophisticated new information technologies.

What holds for individuals also holds for cities and suburbs; prosperity is now tied increasingly to the human capital of their residents. At one time, a city's location on a key waterway or its proximity to a valuable natural resource was critical to its well-being. While physical location is still important, global competition is now based less on location per se and more on the ability of a metro area to retain and attract the talent that its industries need to remain competitive.

But it is also clear that a combination of disparities in human capital and discrimination in labor markets are responsible for the continuing gap in earnings and household incomes across racial and ethnic groups. Because of housing segregation, the pattern of racial and ethnic gaps in labor market earnings is replicated in many metro areas in the disparity of economic well-being between central cities and suburbs. To assure growing prosperity that is more equally shared, we need to explore public policies that help urban areas compete for talent and programs that help equalize individual economic opportunity. These are explored in later chapters.

Appendix A

The Sources of Personal Income

The total amount of personal income earned by individual households in the United States can be disaggregated into seven major categories:

- *Wages and salaries disbursements*: The amount of income earned by individuals in the form of paychecks from corporations, companies, or government agencies
- *Supplements to wages and salaries:* The amount of in-kind income earned in the form of employee benefits such as health insurance premiums and contributions to private pensions
- *Proprietors' income:* Income earned by individuals from self-employment, their own privately owned businesses, or their own privately owned farms
- *Rental income of persons:* Income receipts from the ownership of real property such as buildings and land
- *Personal interest income:* Income earned in the form of interest on savings accounts, bonds or other interest-bearing assets
- *Personal dividend income:* Income earned in the form of dividends distributed by corporations based on the ownership of stock shares
- *Net personal current transfer receipts:* Income from government programs, primarily social insurance benefits (e.g., social security, unemployment benefits, food stamps) less contributions made by individuals to government social insurance programs

In 2003, total personal income in the United States amounted to $9.162 trillion. It was comprised of the following amounts:

Source	Amount (Billions)	Percent of Total
Wages and Salaries	$5,103.6	64.0
Wage and Salary Supplements	1,185.5	4.6
Proprietors' Income	834.1	10.5
Rental Income of Persons	153.8	1.9
Personal Interest Income	929.9	11.7
Personal Dividend Income	392.8	4.9
Net Personal Transfer Receipts	562.2	7.0

Source: Council of Economic Advisers 2004.

Of the total, 64 percent of personal income came in the form of wage and salary paychecks with another 4.6 percent in the form of supplemental benefits paid to employees by their employers. Another 10.5 percent is in the form of earnings from privately owned and operated businesses or self-employment income. Together, these three sources represent nearly four out of five dollars that come into American households each year in the form of dollar income or in the form of employer-paid benefits.

Together, interest from savings and from stock dividends represent another 16.6 percent of dollar income each year—the equivalent of one in six dollars that households can use to buy goods and services. Only 7 percent of personal income takes the form of government transfer payments such as social security, food stamps, housing vouchers, and the like.

Of course, for individual households, the proportion of income from each of these sources can differ dramatically. As the table below indicates, households reporting between $15,000 and $30,000 of income to the Internal Revenue Service received nearly 80 percent of their income from wages and salaries. Those reporting income of $50,000–$100,000 received more than 84 percent of their income from paychecks, while those households that reported more than $200,000 received only about half their income from employment earnings. For the purposes of measuring personal income, the federal government does not count income from capital gains—income that is the result of appreciation in an asset such as stock. But, these represent a significant portion of the income of high-end households and are reported on the statistics of income generated by the Internal Revenue Service.

Sources of Income by Household Income Class

	$15–30K	**$50–100K**	**$200+ K**
Wages and Salaries	79.7%	84.3%	53.8%
Interest	3.0%	2.2%	4.9%
Dividends	1.1%	1.1%	3.0%
Net Business/Professional Income	3.8%	2.6%	4.2%
Net Capital Gains	0.7%	1.1%	14.3%
Taxable Pensions	9.2%	6.9%	1.5%
Net Rent	0.7%	0.1%	1.5%
Net Partnership and S Corp Income	0.1%	0.7%	16.5%
Taxable SS and UIB	2.4%	3.1%	0.6%

Source: Balkovic 2004.

Those in the low-income category received more than 9 percent of their income from taxable private pensions, indicating that this income group has a disproportionate number of older households. The highest income group, by contrast, received more than 30 percent of its income from capital gains and from the ownership of partnerships or closely held private businesses.

The importance of wage and salary income for most households is understood once it is clear that of the more than 130 million individual IRS returns filed in 2002, all but 8 percent were from individuals or families who reported no more than $100,000 of adjusted gross income. These households, representing more than 90 percent of American households, reported that from 80 to 84 percent of their income came from labor market wages and salaries.

Appendix B

The Simple Labor Market

Figure A7.1 illustrates the simple labor market, where all labor is homogeneous and is infinitely mobile between firms and locations, and in which companies are fully competitive with each other and seek to maximize profit:

The final wage W* occurs where the wage that workers are willing to accept in order to work for a company intersects the marginal revenue product (MRP) curve for the firm—where the MRP curve reveals the additional value generated for the firm by the last worker it hires. The MRP curve traces out the labor demand curve of the firm. At a wage higher than W*, such as W_H, the quantity of workers supplied (at A) will exceed the quantity of workers demanded (at B), driving the wage down

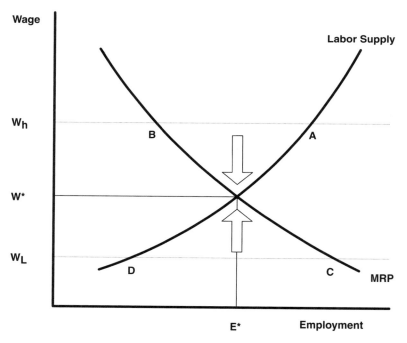

Figure A7.1 The Simple Labor Market

242

toward W*. At a wage lower than W*, such as W_L, quantity of workers demanded (at C) will exceed the quantity of workers supplied (at D) and firms will bid the wage up in order to attract enough workers to squeeze out the last bit of value for the firm.

References

Balkovic, Brian. 2004. "Individual Income Tax Returns, Preliminary Data, 2002." Internal Revenue Service. Washington, D.C.: U.S. Government Printing Office.

Baron, Harold M. 1973. "Racial Domination in Advanced Capitalism: A Theory of Nationalism and Divisions in the Labor Market." In Richard C. Edwards, Michael Reich, and David M. Gordon, eds., *Labor Market Segmentation*. Lexington, Mass.: D.C. Heath, pp. 173–216.

Becker, Gary S. 1957. *The Economics of Discrimination*. Chicago: University of Chicago Press.

Bergmann, Barbara. 1971. "The Effect on White Incomes of Discrimination in Employment." *Journal of Political Economy* 79, no. 2: 294–313.

Bluestone, Barry, and Mary Huff Stevenson. 2000. *The Boston Renaissance: Race, Space, and Economic Change in an American Metropolis*. New York: Russell Sage.

Bluestone, Barry, Mary Huff Stevenson, and Chris Tilly. 1992. "An Assessment of the Impact of 'Deindustrialization' and Spatial Mismatch on the Labor Market Outcomes of Young White, Black, and Latino Men and Women Who Have Limited Schooling." Occasional Paper. Boston: John W. McCormack Institute of Public Affairs, University of Massachusetts, Boston.

Boston Foundation. 2004. "Boston Indicators." www.bostonindicators.org.

CNN Money. 2007. "How Far Will Salary Go in Another City: 2006–2007?" www.cnnmoney.com.

Council of Economic Advisers. 2004. "Economic Indicators." Washington, D.C.: U.S. Government Printing Office, July.

Cutler, David M., and Edward M. Glaeser. 1997. "Are Ghettos Good or Bad?" *Quarterly Journal of Economics* 112, no. 3: 827–872.

Edwards, Richard C., Michael Reich, and David M. Gordon, eds. 1973. *Labor Market Segmentation*. Lexington, Mass.: D.C. Heath.

Ellwood, David T. 1986. "The Spatial Mismatch Hypothesis: Are There Teenage Jobs Missing in the Ghetto?" In Richard B. Freeman and Harry Holzer, eds., *The Black Youth Employment Crisis*. Chicago: University of Chicago Press, pp. 147–190.

Fields, Gary S. 2005. *A Guide to Multisector Labor Market Models*. Social Protection Unit, Human Development Network. Washington, D.C.: The World Bank.

Fitzgerald, Joan, and Nancy Green Leigh. 2002. *Economic Revitalization: Cases and Strategies for City and Suburb*. Thousand Oaks, Calif.: Sage.

Giloth, Robert. 1998. "Jobs and Economic Development." In R. Giloth, ed., *Jobs and Economic Development*. Thousand Oaks, Calif.: Sage, pp. 1–18.

Glaeser, Edward L., and Matthew E. Kahn. 2003. "Sprawl and Urban Growth." National Bureau of Economic Research, NBER Working Paper No. W9733, May.

Harrison, Bennett, and Barry Bluestone. 1988. *The Great U-Turn: Corporate Restructuring and the Polarizing of America*. New York: Basic Books.

Hirsch, Barry T., David A. Macpherson, and Wayne G. Vroman. 2001. "Estimates of Union Density." *Monthly Labor Review* 112, no. 7 (July): 51–55.

Holzer, Harry. 1991. "The Spatial Mismatch Hypothesis: What Has the Evidence Shown?" *Urban Studies* 28, no. 1: 105–122.

Ihlanfeldt, Keith. 1996. "The Spatial Distribution of Black Employment between the Central City and Suburbs." *Economic Inquiry* 34: 693–707.

Ihlanfeldt, Keith, and David L. Sjoquist. 1998. "The Spatial Mismatch Hypothesis: A Review of Recent Studies and Their Implications for Welfare Reform." *Housing Policy Debate* 9, no. 4: 849–892.

Jencks, Christopher, and Susan Mayer. 1990. "Residential Segregation, Job Proximity, and Black Job Opportunities." In Laurence E. Lind and Michael McGeary, eds., *Inner City Poverty in the United States*. Washington, D.C.: National Academies Press, pp. 187–222.

Kain, John. 1968. "Housing Segregation, Negro Employment, and Metropolitan Decentralization." *Quarterly Journal of Economics* 82: 175–197.

Kirschenman, Joleen, and Katherine Neckerman. 1991. " 'We'd Love to Hire Them, But...': The Meaning of Race for Employers." In Christopher Jencks and Paul E. Peterson, eds., *The Urban Underclass*. Washington, D.C.: The Brookings Institution, pp. 203–234.

Mishel, Lawerence, Jared Bernstein, and Sylvia Allegretto. 2004. *The State of Working America 2004–05*. Ithaca, N.Y.: Cornell University Press.

———. 2007. *The State of Working America 2006/2007*. Ithaca, N.Y.: ILR Press.

Moss, Philip, and Chris Tilly. 1991. "Why Black Men Are Doing Worse in the Labor Market: A Review of Supply-Side and Demand-Side Explanations." Working Paper. New York: Social Science Research Council.

———. 2001. *Stories Employers Tell: Race and Hiring in America*. New York: Russell Sage Foundation.

National Association of Realtors. 2007. "Median Sales Price for Existing Single Family Homes for Metropolitan Areas." http://www.realtor.org/Research.nsf/files/MSAPRICESF.pdf/.

National Right to Work Legal Defense Foundation. http://www.nrtw.org.

Pager, Devah, and Lincoln Quillian. 2005. "Walking the Talk? What Employers Say versus What They Do." *American Sociological Review* 70, no. 3: 355–380.

Piore, Michael. 1973. "Notes on a Theory of Labor Market Stratification." In Richard C. Edwards, Michael Reich, and David M. Gordon, eds., *Labor Market Segmentation*. Lexington, Mass.: D.C. Heath, pp. 125–150.

Price, Richard, and Edwin Mills. 1985. "Race and Residence in Earnings Determination." *Journal of Urban Economics* 17: 1–18.

Raphael, Steven, and Michael A. Stoll. 2002. "Modest Progress: The Narrowing Spatial Mismatch between Blacks and Jobs in the 1990s." Washington, D.C.: The Brookings Institution, December.

SEIU. 2007. Service Employees International Union, www.seiu.org.

Stevenson, Mary. 1973. "Women's Wages and Job Segregation." In Richard C. Edwards, Michael Reich, and David M. Gordon, eds., *Labor Market Segmentation*. Lexington, Mass.: D.C. Heath, pp. 243–255.

Stoll, Michael A. 2005. "Job Sprawl and the Spatial Mismatch between Blacks and Jobs." Washington, D.C.: The Brookings Institution, February.

Tanzi, Vito. 1999. "Uses and Abuses of Estimates of the Underground Economy." *The Economic Journal* 109, no. 456: F338–F347.

UNITE HERE. 2007. www.unitehere.org.

U.S. Bureau of Labor Statistics. 2007. Occupational Employment Survey, "May 2006 National Cross-Industry Estimates." Washington, D.C.: U.S. Government Printing Office.

U.S. Department of Housing and Urban Development. 2007. HUD User Policy Development and Research Information Service. SOCDS (State of the Cities Data Systems) data set. http://socds.huduser.org.

U.S. Department of Labor. 2007. "May 2006 Metropolitan Area Occupational Employment and Wage Estimates." Washington, D.C.: U.S. Government Printing Office.

Wyly, Elvin K. 1996. "Race, Gender, and Spatial Segmentation in the Twin Cities." *Professional Geographer* 48, no. 4: 431–444.

Zhang, Zhongcai, and Richard D. Bingham. 2000. "Metropolitan Employment Growth and Neighborhood Job Access in Spatial and Skills Perspective: Empirical Evidence from Seven Ohio Metropolitan Regions." *Urban Affairs Review* 35, no. 3 (January): 390–421.

Chapter 7 Questions and Exercises

1. Using the *Urban Experience* CD, find the unemployment rates for the metro area closest to you and two other metro areas of your choice for 1970, 1980, 1990, 2000, and 2005. Taking *each metro area* one at a time, how would you describe the change

in the unemployment rates from decade to decade in that metro area over the period from 1970 to 2005? Do the unemployment rates stay about the same, increase, decrease, or display some other pattern? Next, comparing *across* the metro areas, which of the metro areas had the greatest changes in unemployment rates over this period? (*Note:* For instructions on how to use this CD, see examples in the exercises for Chapter 1.)

2. Repeat the exercise in question 1 above for those "out of the labor force."

3. The BLS Web page at

    http://www.bls.gov/opub/gp/pdf/gp03_28.pdf

    provides unemployment rates by educational level for fifty metropolitan areas for the year 2003. Take a look at this table. In which metro areas was the unemployment of people with less than a high school degree most severe? Which metro areas had the highest unemployment rates for people with high school degrees but no college? What about people with some college or an associate's degree? What about people with bachelor's degrees or higher? Which factors mentioned in Chapter 7 might help you explain the differences you found across metro areas?

4. As Chapter 7 notes, the composition of industries within a metropolitan area (and the change that occurs in this composition) affect residents' employment and income prospects. Using the *Urban Experience* CD, choose three metropolitan areas and take a look at the industry data for manufacturing, professional services, and personal services in each of these metro areas in 1980, 1990, and 2000.

    For each metropolitan area, how did the percentage of jobs in manufacturing, professional services, and personal services change from one decade to the next? (*Note:* You need to produce this table for one metro area at a time.)

    Next, choose one central city within each of the metropolitan areas you have just explored and take a look at the change in the composition of jobs within that central city. How do they compare with the changes for the metropolitan area as a whole? How do they compare with the industry composition of jobs in the suburbs?

5. The wage for a given occupation can vary considerably across metropolitan areas (as discussed in this chapter). Estimates of wages for occupations by metro area can be found through the U.S. Bureau of Labor Statistics Web site:

    http://www.bls.gov/bls/blswage.htm

    Go to this Web site and under "Metropolitan Area Wage Data" click on the link that begins "For 375 metropolitan statistical areas." Click on a metro area of your choice (other than the twenty we follow in the charts in this chapter). Find the wage estimate ("mean annual") for the following four occupations:

    - Registered nurses (located under "Health Care Practitioner and Technical Occupations")
    - Civil engineers (located under "Architecture and Engineering Occupations")
    - Elementary school teachers—except special education (located under "Education, Training and Library Occupations")
    - Machinists (located under "Production Occupations")

Next, find this information for three other metropolitan areas of your choice. In which metro areas is the average wage/salary of each of these occupations the highest? In which metro areas is the average wage/salary the lowest? How would you explain these differences?

6. Research published in the *American Economic Review* ("Are Emily and Greg More Employable Than Lakisha and Jamal?" by Marianne Bertrand and Sendhil Mullainathan, September 2004) involving two urban areas (Chicago and Boston) found that resumes with names that were more common among whites (for example, Emily and Brendan) received more call-back responses from employers than identical resumes with names that were more common among blacks. How would the "taste for discrimination" and "statistical discrimination" theories presented in this chapter explain this outcome?

Urban Public Education and Metro Prosperity

"Go west, young man!" was the advice proffered American pioneers in the mid-1800s. Yet, for most Americans—both men and women—and certainly for most immigrants to the United States after 1860, "seeking one's fortune" is based on investing in one's own skills every bit as much as in forging ahead into the new territories. By the nineteenth century and surely by the twentieth, those skills brought the highest return in the nation's cities, where most of the good jobs could be found. To gain a competitive advantage in getting those good jobs increasingly required personal investments in human capital, and most often that took the form of education and training. In the modern era, the very prosperity of cities and suburbs depends more and more on the education of those who live there.

As cities grew during the 1800s, the political, economic, and social impact of education was a focus of considerable discussion. Mandatory education laws spread in response to increased immigration and internal migration. A common primary school education was promoted as a force for social cohesion that brought together immigrants from diverse backgrounds who lived in the burgeoning U.S. cities of the late nineteenth century. By the early twentieth century, comprehensive secondary education was being advocated by an increasing number of influential civic leaders, particularly those associated with the Progressive movement (Wraga 2006). The resulting workforce, highly educated in comparison with other industrial nations, strengthened the U.S. economy (Goldin 1998, 2001).

Today, perhaps more than ever given global competition, critics are questioning the effectiveness of America's public schools, particularly those in inner cities. The traditional public school model itself is under attack from competing institutions such as charter schools, pilot schools, and voucher systems. If inner cities are increasingly dominated by minorities, and if the education of inner-city schoolchildren diverges in quality from the schools in the suburbs, what kind of society are we building? Of all the challenges facing cities today, assuring quality education is one of the most important and most vexing. It also turns out to be crucial for sustaining the competitive advantage of individual cities and metro areas.

The Decentralized U.S. Educational System

If the subject of this book was urban dynamics in France, there probably would not be a chapter or even a section covering urban education. France has a centralized educational system, so there is little that distinguishes education in one French city from another. A curriculum set centrally means that pretty much the same math lesson is being taught in every eighth-grade classroom throughout the country, usually on the same day.

What distinguishes the U.S. school system is its high degree of decentralization. Legal authority for the provision of elementary and secondary education does not rest with the federal government, but with state governments that have traditionally delegated the actual provision of schooling to local governments. Local school boards, most elected like other municipal officials, are responsible for setting kindergarten through twelfth grade (K–12) policy, working within broad regulations set by the state, the federal government, and, in some cases, court orders issued by the state or federal judiciary.

School funding, physical resources, staffing, assignment of students to specific schools, and other important matters are still determined largely at the local level, even as the share of total primary and secondary school funding supplied by local government has declined. As shown in **Table 8.1**, local authorities provided more than 80 percent of K–12 school funding before 1930, about 50 percent in 1973–1974, and nearly 44 percent in 2003–2004 (U.S. Department of Education 2007). Following the dictum that he who pays the piper calls the tune, the still-substantial role that local communities play in funding education means they have a large degree of discretion in setting curriculum and school pedagogy—although their control is somewhat diminished with increased state funding and, to some extent, federal aid.

As of 2002, there were more than 13,500 individual school districts in the United States—down from nearly 35,000 in 1962 and almost 109,000 in 1942, due to the merger of very small school districts into regional or consolidated districts (U.S. Bureau of the Census 2002a, 2002b). How they are structured varies enormously from state to state, as does the state's financial contribution. Hawaii has essentially a state system with the state paying 87 percent of total local school costs, the federal government another 11 percent, and local communities picking up only 1 percent of total costs. But this system of finance is quite unique. In Connecticut, Illinois, Maryland, Massachusetts, Missouri, Nevada, New Jersey, Pennsylvania, Rhode Island, and Virginia, local districts are responsible for anywhere between 50 and nearly 60 percent of total K–12 spending. In many other states, there is a more equal sharing of funding responsibility between state and local government; in some, the state picks up the majority of costs. In most cases, the share from the state takes the form of state aid to local communities based on a formula for individual city and town allocations and comes with only limited strings as to how the revenue is to be used in the schools.

There are several significant consequences of having a decentralized educational system. It allows for a wide range of choice by local decision makers about the needs

Table 8.1 Public Funding for Primary and Secondary Schools by Source, Selected Years, 1919–2004

School Year	Total (Millions of Dollars)	Local Share (%)	State Share (%)	Federal Share (%)
1919–1920	970	83.2	16.5	0.3
1929–1930	2,088	82.7	16.9	0.4
1939–1940	2,261	68.0	30.3	1.8
1949–1950	5,437	57.3	39.8	2.9
1959–1960	14,747	56.5	39.1	4.4
1969–1970	40,267	52.1	39.9	8.0
1979–1980	96,881	43.4	46.8	9.8
1989–1990	208,548	46.8	47.1	6.1
1999–2000	372,944	43.2	49.5	7.3
2003–2004	462,016	43.9	47.1	9.1

Source: National Center for Education Statistics 2007, table 158, "Revenues for Public Elementary and Secondary Schools, by Source of Funds: Selected Years, 1919–20 through 2003–2004."

and goals of education in their particular economic and social environment. For families who can consider moving to different school districts, it allows them to consider differences in educational systems, and to include those differences in their choice of residential location. Decentralized systems also offer teachers a greater choice about where to work.

Such a decentralized system, however, can lead to great disparities in schooling. The available resources for schooling may vary considerably from one school district to the next, the quality and integrity of the decisions made by local authorities may differ from one location to another, and the employment decisions of teachers may also have consequences for the quality of the education that is provided.

The Importance of Schooling in Modern Society

Presumably, the goal of education is to produce individuals with the ability to compete in and contribute to the economy, to engage in civic life, and to enjoy society's cultural gifts. The education provided in elementary and secondary schools plays a particularly important role. It provides essential tools for participation in the economy at the most basic level. It is a key ingredient in creating and sustaining social and political cohesion. Elementary and secondary education provide the **option value** of laying the base for higher levels of education. By completing elementary school, one has the option to go on to high school. By completing high school, one has the option of going on to college. Secondary school education also frequently serves as the foundation for subsequent vocational opportunities, increasing the possibility for on-the-job training, since the high school diploma is often used as a screening device—an indicator of ability to learn—by employers.

Through the nineteenth century and the early part of the twentieth century, an elementary education or some high school was sufficient for jobs in the manufacturing and construction sectors. As late as 1939, 37 percent of the U.S. workforce was employed in goods-producing industries—farming, forestry, fishing, mining, construction, and manufacturing—as compared to about 16 percent today (U.S. Bureau of Labor Statistics 2007). Access to relatively well-paying jobs as assemblers or machine tenders in factories and as laborers, bricklayers, and carpenters was one of the major lures of migration for individuals from farms in the Midwest and South, workers from Appalachia, and immigrants from other countries. Given the demand for manual labor during this period of U.S. history, many newly arrived individuals could find work in the city with the skills they had, while proceeding to build greater competence in English, civic participation, and other aspects of urban life. These workers would be critical to the construction of the cities themselves—from the skyscrapers and apartment buildings to the roads, sidewalks, and, of course, the water and sewer systems that run below the surface.

Today, most employers demand greater skill from their job applicants. Many look for a high school degree as a minimum, either because of the skills required on the job or because they are using the high school degree as a screening factor for their applicants' motivation or ability to learn new things on the job. For individuals with less than a high school degree, the urban employment experience is no longer what it was in the first half of the twentieth century. Instead of being places of potential economic promise for individuals, many urban areas have become economic quagmires.

Since the labor market has changed to emphasize the obtaining of higher levels of education, one might expect that individuals would seek greater levels of learning, and that elementary and secondary school systems would respond by producing more high school graduates. Indeed, this is the case; there are more high school graduates today than there were in 1970. According to the 2000 Census, 80.4 percent of U.S. adults age 25 and older had high school degrees or higher, compared to 52.3 percent in 1970. The percentage with bachelor's degrees or higher grew from 11 percent in 1970 to 24.4 percent in 2000. The percentage with less than ninth-grade education was just 7.5 percent.

Variation in Educational Attainment across Metro Areas

However, as with many other socioeconomic characteristics, place matters when it comes to schooling. In the nation as a whole, the percentage of adults 25 and older with more education than a high school degree is slightly higher in metropolitan areas (81.3%) than the U.S. average (80.4%). However, the high school educational attainment statistics for individual metropolitan areas in the year 2000 ranged from 93.7 percent for the Iowa City, Iowa MSA to a low of just 50.5 percent in the McAllen-Edinburg-Mission, Texas MSA. Similarly, while nationally aggregated statistics show that in metropolitan areas the percentage of adults 25 and older with bachelor's degrees or higher (26.6%) is above the U.S. average (24.4%), the figures for individual metro areas vary considerably—ranging from a high of 52.4 percent in Boulder-Longmont, Colorado, to lows of 11 percent in Merced, California, and 11.3 percent in Danville, Virginia.

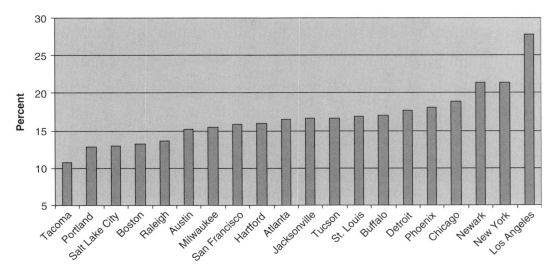

Figure 8.1 Percent with Less Than High School Degree, Persons Aged 25+, Metro Areas. *Source:* U.S. Department of Housing and Urban Development, HUD User Policy Development and Research Information Service, SOCDS data set, 2007, http://socds.huduser.org.

Figure 8.1 demonstrates this variation across the twenty MSAs we have been following in this book. The metro areas of Tacoma and Portland, Oregon, have the lowest proportion of their populations (age 25 and older) who have left school before completing the high school degree. In Tacoma, the proportion is just a little over 10 percent. The Salt Lake City, Boston, and Raleigh, North Carolina MSAs also benefit

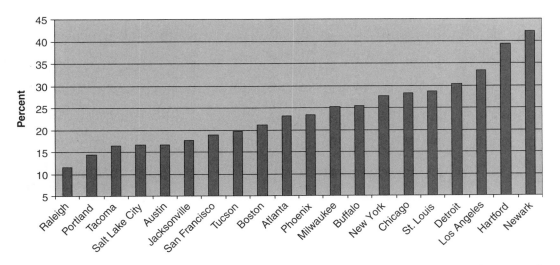

Figure 8.2 Percent with Less Than High School Degree, Persons Aged 25+, Central Cities. *Source:* U.S. Department of Housing and Urban Development, HUD User Policy Development and Research Information Service, SOCDS data set, 2007, http://socds.huduser.org.

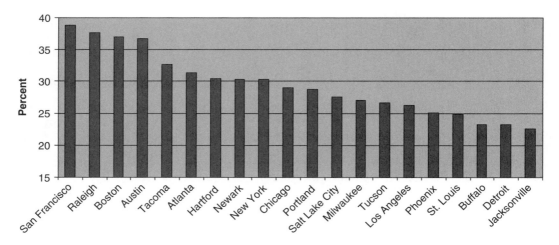

Figure 8.3 Percent with BA Degree or More, Persons Aged 25+, Metro Areas. *Source:* U.S. Department of Housing and Urban Development, HUD User Policy Development and Research Information Service, SOCDS data set, 2007, http:// socds.huduser.org.

from having adult populations in which more than 85 percent have at least completed high school. Note that even in the metro areas with the highest proportion of persons not completing high school, the percentage with a high school degree is still close to 80 percent—and in Los Angeles, with its large immigrant population, it is still nearly 75 percent.

Across central cities, the variation in those who did not complete high school is much greater. As **Figure 8.2** demonstrates, in the central cities of Raleigh and

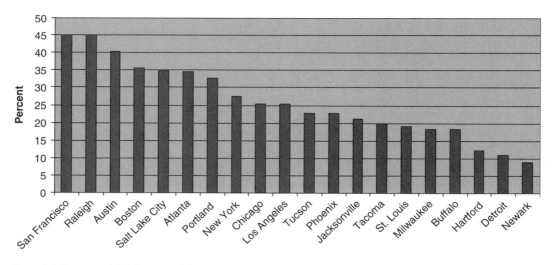

Figure 8.4 Percent with BA Degree or More, Persons Aged 25+, Central Cities. *Source:* U.S. Department of Housing and Urban Development, HUD User Policy Development and Research Information Service, SOCDS data set, 2007, http:// socds.huduser.org.

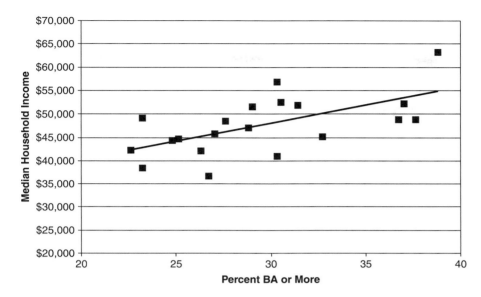

Figure 8.5 Median MSA Household Income versus Percent of Adults with BA Degree or More. *Source:* U.S. Department of Housing and Urban Development, HUD User Policy Development and Research Information Service, SOCDS data set, 2007, http://socds.huduser.org.

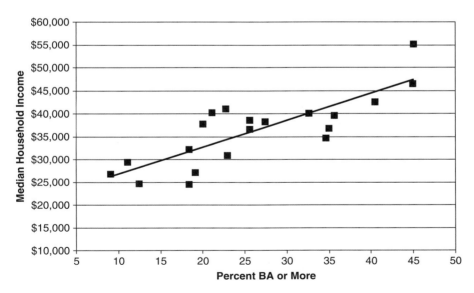

Figure 8.6 Median Central City Household Income versus Percent of Adults with BA Degree or More. *Source:* U.S. Department of Housing and Urban Development, HUD User Policy Development and Research Information Service, SOCDS data set, 2007, http://socds.huduser.org.

Portland, Oregon, less than 15 percent of the adult population is without a twelfth-grade education. In sharp contrast, more than 40 percent of Newark's adults lack the high school degree. The same is true for 30 percent or more of the population in Detroit, Los Angeles, and Hartford. With so much of the workforce lacking even this basic educational credential, it is not surprising that these central cities have high poverty rates and stagnating or declining incomes. While many of the immigrants who have come to the United States in recent years arrived with advanced education and skill—working in fields such as engineering, medical care, and computer technology—some central cities house a disproportionate share of new immigrants who arrive in the United States with less than a high school diploma.

At the high end of the educational spectrum are such metro areas as San Francisco, Raleigh, Boston, and Austin. In each of these, well over a third of the adult population has a minimum of a college degree. In their central cities, the well-educated comprise, if anything, even a higher proportion of the population. Indeed, in both San Francisco and Raleigh, 45 percent of the adults have completed college or done postgraduate studies. Not surprising, these are regions with a high proportion of universities and research centers, where much of the pathbreaking work in such emerging fields as biotechnology and nanotechnology is being done (see **Figures 8.3** and **8.4**).

Educational Attainment and Metro Area Income

Figures 8.5 and **8.6** clearly demonstrate that higher education pays off, not only for individual households but also for entire metro areas and cities. In the first of these charts, we have created a scatter plot of median household income in each of the twenty metro areas we are tracking against the percentage of adults 25 and older who have at least a bachelor's degree. The trend line confirms that those metro areas with more college graduates have significantly higher median incomes. San Francisco, with nearly two out of five (38.8%) of its adults having a college education, had a median household income of over $63,000—more than 64 percent higher than the typical household income in Buffalo, where only a little more than one out of five (23.2%) adults is comparably educated. In central cities, the relationship appears even stronger, given the steeper trend line. With 45 percent of its central city adults having at least completed college, median household income in Raleigh is more than double that of Newark ($55,221 versus $26,913), where only 9 percent have completed four or more years of college.

Education, New Growth Theory, and the Well-Being of Cities and Suburbs

To understand why education has become such an important factor in the well-being of cities and suburbs, it is useful to consult what now is known as **new growth theory**. Pioneered by Paul Romer (1986, 1994, 1996) and Robert Lucas (1988), new growth theory considers education to be one of the central factors that determines economic growth at both the metropolitan and national levels, not only because of its direct effect on the productivity of individual workers who receive advanced schooling but also because of the spillover effects that enhance the productivity of others who work with them.

New Growth Theory

To explore the impact of education as seen by new growth theory, follow a fictional chemist, Julie, who is in the early stages of her career. She has just been hired by a biotech firm in Boston and given several initial assignments that she executes well, using the skills and knowledge that she has acquired through her formal education and training. Her existing human capital, which partially consists of what she learned in high school and college, has made her a productive worker and her value to the firm has been clearly demonstrated.

But existing skill levels are not the only consideration here. More highly educated workers are also more valued because they may have gained the advantage of learning *new* things on the job faster than those with less education. Consequently, when employers invest in on-the-job training for their workforce, those individuals who are more highly educated may acquire additional knowledge and skills more quickly and thoroughly. For example, if the employer provides Julie with details about the organizational structure of the firm or about current research going on in the firm, Julie may be able to absorb this information faster because she has become adept at learning through her many years in the school classroom.

As Julie continues to settle into her new job, she is assigned to a group working on a new prototype for a product. The team to which she is assigned consists of several workers with different skills and training, including a physicist and an engineer. As they discuss their ideas, the engineer proposes a design and the physicist exclaims, "That's a very novel idea, but there is a better way to achieve the same result." Julie chimes in, saying, "Yes, and we can also modify the chemical structure of the input using some new techniques that I have just learned." In short, in situations where individuals work together, an employee with a larger amount of knowledge and skills may complement the knowledge and skills of coworkers, leading to better products and/or increased productivity for the entire group.

The effect of education on coworkers is only one aspect of knowledge spillovers. As new growth theory emphasizes, the potential role of education on economic well-being extends beyond the firm. Knowledge can also spread between firms and between industries. Julie and her coworkers may get together with friends from other firms after work, discussing both the theories they learned in school and specific ideas from their workplaces. Visitors to Julie's firm and customers buying its products might also come away with new ideas. Members of Julie's work team might be offered new jobs by competitors. The insights that she and her coworkers have adduced may be distributed within their industry and others through manuals, trade magazines, and other written records.

In contrast to the emphasis that human capital theory places on knowledge embodied directly in individuals, new growth theory highlights the role of written knowledge, calling it **disembodied knowledge**. The combination of embodied and disembodied knowledge, creative ideas, and their application to old and new endeavors can lead to innovation, new skills, new technology, new products, new firms, and new ways of organizing production throughout a geographic area and beyond.

The important point is that cities are particularly important and powerful settings for these dynamics, since the numerous interactions among people in dense urban areas and the rapid spread of written material can facilitate the adoption of these new developments and their diffusion across firms. The Internet and other forms of long-distance communication increasingly make it possible for researchers to collaborate in "virtual" laboratories, but much of the best research still relies on face-to-face interaction in real ones. Those who study this type of activity sometimes refer to the **bump rate** in a community—the number of times workers "bump" into each other at work or during leisure time and exchange ideas and new ways to solve problems (Krim et al. 2006). Dense areas are places where the bump rate is unusually high and, therefore, unusually productive. That is why places like Silicon Valley in California; the Boston area, with its rich array of universities, colleges, and teaching hospitals; Raleigh-Durham-Chapel Hill, with its "Research Triangle"; and Austin, Texas, with its great university, have become prosperous metro areas with equally prosperous central cities.

Education and Urban Economic Development

Clearly, the educational level of the workforce is critical to the economic and social success of a city or metro area. But the quality of local schools also has an independent effect on the well-being of urban regions for another very important reason. Blair and Premus (1987) have demonstrated that while in the early to mid-1900s, U.S. firms were particularly drawn to sites that minimized transportation costs (as depicted in the Weber graphs of Chapter 4), the educational environment of metropolitan areas has become an increasingly important factor in location decisions since 1960. Indeed, a study of business location dynamics by Natalie Cohen (2000) concludes, "Corporate real estate executives' litany has changed from 'location, location, location' to 'education, education, education.' "

Why is local education playing such an important role in the modern economy of metropolitan areas? Let's explore this question by returning to that young chemist, Julie. Because of the skills she has acquired, she is highly sought after by a variety of firms in a number of industries, each engaged in research and development of new product lines. The young chemist receives offers from firms in several different metropolitan areas, including the one in which she was raised.

What enticements can the firms in each area offer to get her to join their company? How does the young chemist decide which offer to accept? Certainly, wages and benefits will weigh heavily in her decision. She also may have some attachment to the area where she grew up and, if she is a rational actor, she will consider the local cost of living, including the cost of housing. But another important consideration is the quality of the elementary and secondary education that will be available to her young children. Prospective employees make decisions about where to work and live not only considering their salaries but also the overall interests of their families. In situations where highly educated workers are the source of a firm's competitive advantage, its continued success might depend upon whether those workers find the firm's location attractive along many dimensions. Consequently, successful recruitment of a talented staff may depend in part upon the quality of schools available to the families of potential employees.

According to Harvard University economist Edward Glaeser, this is especially true of "cold weather cities," which increasingly have trouble competing for young professionals who seek out municipalities with warmer climes. "Cities with average January temperatures under 30 degrees Fahrenheit grew in population only one-third as quickly from 1960 to 1990 as did cities with average January temperatures above 50 degrees" (Glaeser 2005, p. 1). To counteract this population shift, cold-weather cities need to focus on recruiting a high-skilled workforce, and Glaeser argues that highly skilled individuals who are concerned about their children will look for communities with good public schools.

There is good evidence for this conjecture. The U.S. Department of Education reported that in 2003, nearly one in four students (24%) in grades 1–12 had parents who moved to their current neighborhoods for the quality of the school system. This suggests that where employers are competing for highly skilled employees, the firm may choose to locate in a community with a well-regarded public school system. Conversely, a poor school system may be a serious hindrance to the recruitment of skilled young workers. Metropolitan areas that cannot provide high-quality educational facilities might even experience a "brain drain," as talented employees leave in search of a more suitable environment in which to raise their families.

Education Production Functions

Since education has such great significance to metropolitan areas in the twenty-first century, it is important to understand the forces that shape its production. What are the economic, political, and social factors in metropolitan areas that affect the quality and quantity of education? How do the urban dynamics of race, social class, and housing segregation interact to influence—positively or negatively—the production, distribution, and accumulation of schooling?

In Chapter 7, we discussed human capital, the idea that individuals pursue education hoping to receive higher wages in the future. In that initial discussion, we did not discuss variations in the *quality* of education received, just the quantity of education as measured by years of schooling. Yet, this is an important issue. Families who seek the best schools for their children, businesses that extol the academic reputations of nearby schools, and school system officials who compare test scores or other measures of their students' achievement against test scores from schools in other cities and metro areas all recognize that the quality of education varies from one place to another. School quality is determined by a number of different inputs that go into the process of education.

If we recognize that these inputs comprise (1) school system characteristics, (2) individual student characteristics, and (3) geographically specific socioeconomic environments, it is clear that no two educational outcomes have precisely the same inputs. However, we can try to identify the factors that are most important.

Economists and other social scientists often try to do this using the form of an **education production function**. Expressed in mathematical terminology, an education production function is like any other production function that tries to explain how inputs are converted into some output. In this case, we are interested in the overall process that turns education inputs into educational outcomes measured by, say, graduation rates or test scores.

The ideal school output is presumably an individual equipped with the knowledge and social skills to compete and contribute successfully in the modern economy, to engage intelligently in civic life, and to enjoy the many cultural gifts society has to offer. A simple education production function might be written as follows (King, Swanson, and Sweetland 2003):

$$O = f(C, R, I)$$

where O = Educational Outcome (e.g., graduation rate, test scores) for a single cohort of students, C = Student Characteristics (e.g., family income, parents' education), R = School Resources (e.g., per-student spending, pupil/teacher ratio), and I = Instructional Processes (e.g., type of curriculum); and where (f) stands for "a function of."

This simple function states that a measured educational outcome such as the tenth-grade reading scores across tens of thousands of students in perhaps hundreds of different schools or school districts is related to the socioeconomic background of the students in each district as measured by such factors as parents' income and education; the school resources available to students in each particular school or district; and the type of instructional program or processes used in each school or district.

The goal of such research is to reveal how much of the variance in educational outcomes across students is related to each of these factors. This is a critical question for cities and metro areas across the country, for it greatly influences the types of policies that might be used to improve educational outcomes in their school districts. For example, if statistical analysis reveals that the amount of school spending per child is the critical factor in educational outcomes, then one might advocate for boosting spending in the school districts where children are performing poorly on standardized tests. If the pupil-teacher ratio in each class is important to educational outcomes, then this information might inform school reform.

Variation in School Spending

To be sure, because of the decentralized school system in the United States, spending per student can vary dramatically from school district to district, both within states and across states. Rothstein (2004) identifies no less than five types of school resource inequality:

Type I: Disadvantaged children live disproportionately in *states* that spend less money on education than other states.

Type II: Within any state, disadvantaged children may attend schools in *districts* that spend less on education.

Type III: Within any district, disadvantaged children may attend *schools* that command fewer resources than others.

Type IV: Within any school, disadvantaged children may be placed in *classrooms* that have fewer resources at their disposal.

Type V: Within any classroom, disadvantaged children may be offered less adequate *assistance* than others.

Rothstein finds that the *interstate* gap in state and local government school spending (Type I) is where the greatest variance lies. Using data for 1996–1997, he finds that actual school spending per pupil ranges from 159 percent of the national average in New Jersey ($9,667) and 143 percent in Connecticut to only 61 percent in Mississippi ($3,704), 74 percent in Alabama, Arkansas, and Louisiana, and 75 percent in Oklahoma and South Dakota. That means that New Jersey spends, on average, more than 2.6 times as much on education per student as Mississippi. Of course, the cost of providing education varies across states because of differences in cost of living and teachers' salaries. But even after controlling for these factors, New Jersey spends twice as much as Mississippi, and Connecticut spends 1.45 times as much as Alabama.

These differences reflect, at least in part, variations in each state's ability to pay. Using state personal income per student (PIPS) as a measure of school spending capacity, Rothstein finds that, on average, an additional $1,000 in PIPS corresponds to approximately a $25 difference in annual per-pupil spending. Adjusted for regional cost differences, New Jersey had $172,816 in personal income per student in 1996–1997, while Mississippi could claim only $104,813. Accordingly, just on the basis of funding capacity, New Jersey could have spent 64 percent more than Mississippi on its public school students, but it spent nearly 100 percent more than Mississippi, which suggests that it was also willing to spend a higher *proportion* of its income on its schoolchildren.

Supposedly, federal spending on K–12 public schools should redress some of these imbalances in spending and spending capacity. But, given that federal funds represent only about 7 percent of total school expenditures, the federal government's ability to equalize spending is severely limited. Mississippi receives more federal funds per student than New Jersey, but even the local, state, and federal funds combined per pupil (after controlling for regional cost differences) leaves the typical student in New Jersey with 75 percent more school resources than his or her counterpart in Mississippi. Not surprisingly, with such differences, cost-adjusted per-pupil spending in New Jersey's cities and suburbs far outpaced those in Mississippi's urban communities.

Type II inequalities—*interdistrict* gaps within each state—are driven by the common reliance on the local property tax to fund schools. Because of differences across cities and towns in property wealth, in the amount of nonresidential industrial and commercial property available to be taxed, and differences in **tax effort**—the tax rate per dollar of assessed property value—differences in per-pupil spending vary within states. These gaps persist despite state funding designed to offset the effect of local property tax differences. For each state in 2005, the Education Trust (2006) has compared the average state and local revenues per student in the highest-poverty school districts—those in the top 25 percent statewide in terms of the percent of students living below the federal poverty line—to per-student revenues in the lowest-poverty (highest-income) school districts, after controlling for differences in district cost of living. The Trust concludes that in twenty-seven of the forty-nine states studied (no comparable data for Hawaii), the highest-poverty school districts receive fewer resources than the lowest-poverty districts. Nationwide, $907 less is spent per pupil in the poorest districts. Using a similar analysis for low- versus high-minority school districts, the Trust finds a discrepancy of $614 in favor of districts with the lowest minority enrollments.

The largest interdistrict gaps in spending by income are found in New York State ($2,280), Illinois ($2,065), and Wyoming ($1,149). Large gaps by race/ethnicity are found in New Hampshire ($1,892), North Dakota ($2,046), and South Dakota ($1,617) in addition to New York, Illinois, and Wyoming. Other states have used state funds to equalize spending across districts and, in some cases, to offset the higher costs of schooling disadvantaged students. Thus, in Massachusetts, spending in high-poverty districts averages $8,416, versus $7,946 in cities and towns with the fewest poor children. Likewise, New Jersey spends more in poor districts than in wealthier districts, as do Alaska, Minnesota, and Nevada.

One might think that such differences favoring either rich districts or poor would violate the U.S. Constitution, but in a famous 1973 U.S. Supreme Court case (*San Antonio Independent School District v. Rodriquez*), the justices ruled in a 5–4 decision that education was *not* a fundamental right and that states were therefore free to balance the values of local control and equality of educational resources. According to Rothstein (2004), there have been no indications that the federal court is prepared to reconsider the *San Antonio* decision.

Litigation in individual states has often led to a different conclusion. While equal educational opportunity may not be guaranteed by the Constitution, according to the U.S. Supreme Court, some state courts have ruled that extreme inequality across districts violates their state constitutions. As such, in at least nineteen states, the courts have invalidated a school finance system that disadvantaged poor cities and towns. Cases are pending in at least another dozen states.

Michigan provides one of the most extraordinary examples of disparity leading to state action (Rothstein 2004). Because of the growing disparity in wealth between rich suburbs and poor inner cities and rural communities, by 1993, property-rich districts in Michigan—mostly in the suburbs—were spending nearly $11,000 per student, while poor, rural districts spent barely $3,000. After a small, rural, poor district in the northern part of the state voted to close its public schools rather than raise local property taxes further, Republican governor John Engler, with both Democratic and Republican support, agreed to a radical system of state financing for public schools. Increasing the state sales tax and tripling taxes on cigarettes, the state took over nearly 80 percent of the financing of K–12 education. The new system immediately increased per-pupil spending in poor districts by a third. Accordingly, by 2005, the gap in spending between rich and poor districts had been reduced to under $750 (Education Trust 2006).

Does Spending Matter?

Despite enormous differences in spending per student across school districts—and one presumes, therefore, differences in the quality of teachers, the size of the average class, the number of high school electives, and the number of extracurricular activities offered through the school—how much these school resources matter in terms of student outcomes is still a matter of empirical analysis.

One of the first and most cited studies of the impact of school inputs on educational outcomes—as measured by standardized tests—was undertaken for the federal government in 1966 by James S. Coleman, a leading education expert from Johns Hopkins University. With President Lyndon Johnson pursuing his declared war on poverty, there was the need to demonstrate that spending additional money on public schools would improve the educational outcomes of poor children, especially those in inner-city schools. Coleman administered tests to thousands of students across the country, collected data on school resources in hundreds of school districts, and gathered data on the demographic and economic characteristics of the students' families (Coleman 1966).

Having analyzed the data and then reanalyzed them over and over again, Coleman concluded, to his own consternation, that variations in school resources—including teacher/pupil ratios, the number of books in the school library, and the amount of spending per student—had almost nothing to do with explaining the gap in test scores between black and white children, after controlling for such family background variables as parents' education and income (Rothstein 2004). Most of the difference in test scores was attributable to family background and the social and economic conditions of the neighborhoods where students lived.

Since the Coleman report, a plethora of studies have addressed the question of how much school resources matter. The results are extraordinarily mixed, depending on the type of sample and the statistical methods used. Take class size as an example. Alan Krueger (1997), using data from Tennessee, finds that smaller classes matter, especially for poor and minority children, with kids educated in smaller classes performing significantly better on standardized tests than kids who are in classes with twenty to twenty-five children. Eric Hanushek (1997a, 1997b), in summarizing the results of many studies, comes to nearly the opposite conclusion. He finds that class size generally has no effect on test scores. Caroline Hoxby (2000), using data from Connecticut, agrees with Hanushek that class size does not appear to affect students' performance in school. This disagreement regarding the effect of something that should be so simple to measure—class size—is because there are so many variables that affect test performance and no two studies using different data sources hold constant the same set of factors.

If it is not funding or class size that matters, are there other school variables that can explain the difference in student performance? How about the quality of teachers?

Where Teachers Teach

The ideal teacher is knowledgeable about the subject matter being taught, well-versed in the learning process for students in the classroom, skilled and experienced in the ability to convey ideas and maintain a classroom environment that is conducive to learning, relates well to students, and has a sincere interest in the educational development of his or her students. While this is the ideal, teacher quality in fact varies considerably and, as with many other variables that affect metropolitan areas, place matters.

Unlike other inputs for the production of education, teachers have some choice about where they look for work, which job offers they will accept, how much effort to put forth on the job, and whether or not to seek a change in employment after they have been in the job for a while. While there is great variation in the quality of teachers within cities and within suburbs, the overall quality of teachers may differ between central city and suburban schools. For example, a principal in New York City interviewed by education specialist Jonathan Kozol (1992) complained that his school got only the "tenth-best" tier of qualified teachers. This viewpoint has been advanced in other, more recent studies from researchers who have contributed to a growing literature attesting that schools in central cities may have more trouble recruiting and hiring highly qualified teachers, on the whole, than do suburban schools (Lankford, Loeb, and Wyckoff 2002; Buckley, Schneider, and Shang 2004).

Boyd and his colleagues (2005) find that applicants for teaching positions generally search in the school district in which they were raised and in others that they perceive as being similar. This limits their job search to a relatively small geographic area. In fact, Boyd et al. find that, in the state of New York, more than one-third of new teachers were hired by the same school districts where they attended high school, while in Pennsylvania, 40 percent of new teachers found jobs in their own high school districts. While the "draw of home" may also apply to prospective teachers from central cities, Boyd found that central city school districts in New York have more job openings than they have qualified applicants who were raised in the city. Consequently, New York City school districts have to import teachers who come from suburban backgrounds. However, the preference of suburban-raised teachers for teaching in schools like the ones they attended may mean that there are fewer applicants from whom central city school districts can choose, resulting in the hiring of poorer-quality teachers.

A second problem is that teachers who begin their careers in central city schools are more likely to leave than teachers who begin in suburban schools (Boyd et al. 2005). While there is some evidence that those who leave central city schools are not more qualified than those who stay, the effect of high turnover is that the teachers who leave are replaced (on both a temporary and permanent basis) by less experienced teachers—leaving central city schools with a high proportion of teachers with limited experience (Hanushek, Kain, and Rivkin 2004). Attrition rates in at least some central cities appear to be fueled by an insufficiency of classroom resources and by the poor quality of school buildings themselves. Two-thirds of Washington, D.C., schoolteachers complained about the poor air quality in their buildings, with 70 percent stating that their teaching is impaired by noise in hallways and classrooms. Thus, the level of school budgets and the priorities set by school administrators are ultimately reflected in the quality of the teaching force.

School Tracking and Curriculum Choice

Other scholars believe that educational attainment is influenced greatly by curriculum issues. Bowles and Gintis (1976) argue that students are funneled into different educational experiences that correspond to the larger society's perception of the expected future work roles of students. Accordingly, we need to be sure we have enough workers who can be lawyers, doctors, and engineers, but we also have to assure a sufficient quantity of laborers, retail clerks, and janitors. According to this **correspondence principle**, the school system acts as a giant sorting machine, doing its best to prepare just the right number of workers for each occupation—equipping each student with an appropriate set of skills and social norms for the labor market.

In a given school system, this may be accomplished by establishing different "tracks" for students that reflect preparation for different occupations. In the vocational education track, students whose race or class are deemed indicators of a lesser role in the hierarchy of occupations are taught rote memorization, rule-following, and other behavioral and thinking patterns that are considered appropriate for future low-skill workers. On the other hand, students whose race or class are seen as indicators of higher-status occupations are taught in a college preparatory track the analytical, creative, and leadership skills appropriate for future high-skill workers and decision makers (Bowles and Gintis 1976, 2001). Such differences presumably engender boredom and frustration for those who are designated for lower hierarchy occupations, leading to higher dropout rates and lower educational attainment (Perry 1988, 2004). Even without explicit tracking within each school, the objective of the correspondence principle can be obtained by differences in the curriculum in inner-city schools versus suburban schools.

This seems like a subtle form of class warfare or even racism, but some scholars argue that "detracking" also has its risks when students who are not prepared for the rigors of the college preparatory track are thrown in with those who have been trained for this trajectory during much of their school career (Loveless 1999). Because many metropolitan areas are geographically divided along racial and/or income lines, these curricular issues can greatly impact central city schools and can contribute to the urban-suburban disparity.

Still other scholars believe that the disparities are connected to the expectations of teachers about their students, rather than the curriculum itself. Because of racial or class prejudice, some teachers may believe that their students are destined to be low achievers, and consequently put less effort into teaching than they otherwise would, while also communicating the expectation of low achievement to their students.

What Really Counts in School Performance

Rothstein (2004) has reviewed virtually all of the major studies that have tried to measure the impact of school variables on student performance and comes to the conclusion that nearly all of them confirm Coleman's results of more than forty years ago. None of the research ends up attributing more than one-third of the variation in student achievement, no matter how measured, to school-related variables. Certainly, the amount of money spent per student and the quality of teachers makes a difference in the relative success of students. But, overall, other factors that include socioeconomic background are substantially more important.

On reflection, this finding is not as strange as it might seem. After all, up until they leave high school, kids spend only about one-sixth of their time in school. Most children spend no time in school until they reach the age of 5. Thereafter, they might spend up to seven hours a day in school on an average of 180 school days a year. A quick calculation indicates that between the ages of 5 and 18, youngsters might spend a maximum of 17,640 hours in school (7 hours per day × 180 days per year × 14 years). During their full 18 years, they are alive for (24 hours a day × 365 days per year × 18 years) = 157,680 hours. By these calculations, they are in school for only about 11.2 percent (17,640/157,680) of their young lives. Even if you subtract sleep time at an average of 8 hours a day, the percentage of waking time spent in school during one's childhood is only about 17 percent.

An Expanded Education Production Function

With children spending more than four-fifths of their lives *outside* of school, there is a great deal of time for factors other than formal schooling to affect their "education"— primarily, the effects of family, peer, and neighborhood. Reflecting these "other" factors, a slightly more complex specification for the education production function is in order:

$$O_t = f(C, R, I, N, P, Z)$$

where outcome O = Educational Outcome (e.g., graduation rate, test scores) for a single cohort of students, C = Student Characteristics (e.g., family income, parents' education), R = School Resources (e.g., per-student spending, pupil/teacher ratio), I = Instructional Processes (e.g., type of curriculum), N = Neighborhood Characteristics (e.g., crime rate, after-school activities), P = Peer Influences, and Z = Student Effort; and where (f) stands for "a function of."

Sociologists and psychologists have confirmed that parents of different socioeconomic status—defined by parental education, income, and wealth—tend to raise children somewhat differently. Better-educated parents read to their young children more often and read differently, tending to ask their children questions from the readings that make them think more deeply about the themes of the books. Cross-national studies show that the number of books in a household varies substantially by social class and affects later school performance. Poor students who go to schools with a large number of middle-class students tend to perform better in school than equally poor students who are segregated in poor inner-city schools. Peer pressure, as subtle as it might seem, makes a difference in a young student's motivation toward learning, homework, and earning good grades. Health makes a difference, too, and poorer kids in inner cities tend to be in poorer health and receive poorer medical care. Studies have shown that 50 percent or more of minority and low-income children have vision problems that interfere with their academic performance (Gould and Gould 2003).

A higher incidence of hearing problems, poor oral health, and lead exposure also disproportionately disadvantage children from poor inner-city households. Homes with poor ventilation and mold tend to contribute to higher levels of asthma, which can reduce significantly the number of days a child spends in school. Poor nutrition due to low income or parental neglect can make kids listless in class. Parents who themselves have little education may be hampered in their efforts to help their children learn.

Housing itself can make a big difference as well. Overcrowded housing means that students often do not have a quiet, undisturbed place to do their homework. A lack of affordable housing leads to a great deal of relocation among poor families. According to one government report, 30 percent of the poorest children have attended at least three different elementary schools by third grade, compared to only 10 percent of middle-class kids. Black children were more than twice as likely as white children to change schools (Government Accounting Office 1994). This can obviously disrupt the learning process. A recent statistical analysis concludes that if the rate of household mobility of black students was reduced to the average level for white children, the improvement in housing stability itself would eliminate 14 percent of the black-white test gap (Hanushek, Kain, and Rivkin 2004).

The level of crime in a neighborhood may also affect school performance. Kids are more likely to skip school if they are afraid of being attacked on their way there. Worrying about the danger of the street where you live can only make it more difficult to concentrate on your studies. Neighborhoods with lots of clubs, youth sports teams, and other forms of constructive extracurricular activities provide children with the opportunity to be mentored by adults other than their parents or teachers. A good neighborhood basketball coach or dance instructor can do wonders for building the confidence of young people and provide them with good role models.

Hence, the difference between a poor central city and a rich suburb, between a safe neighborhood and a crime-ridden one, and between a home environment that is devoted to reading and learning and one in which there are few adults to engage young minds is the difference that comprises 83 percent of the waking hours of children. Against this, it is perhaps not surprising at all that inner-city schools in poor neighborhoods, no matter how good they are and no matter how devoted their teachers, can have only a limited impact on reducing the performance differential between poor and middle-class kids and between white children and children of color. Only the truly extraordinary inner-city school can compensate for the multiple disadvantages that poor inner-city children often experience.

Recent research into neuroscience and developmental psychology provides still another reason why schools can only partially compensate for the performance differential between advantaged and disadvantaged children. Shonkoff and Phillips (2000) have shown in a pathbreaking study that "virtually every aspect of early human development, from the brain's evolving circuitry to the child's capacity for empathy, is affected by the environments and experiences that are encountered in a cumulative fashion, beginning in the prenatal period and extending throughout the early childhood years." This means that early learning—well before the child enters kindergarten—has a disproportionate impact on acquired skills and leads to self-reinforcing motivation to learn. Once a young child falls behind, there is a tendency for **circular causation with cumulative effect** to set in. This means that a small differential in early childhood education tends to be amplified throughout primary and secondary school and beyond. Small differences when one is young (up to age 4) can lead to large differences when one is an adult. No matter how many resources are devoted to inner-city schools, they simply cannot fully compensate for preschool inequality.

Educational Success: The Empirical Record

It is not surprising, then, that preschool is found to have an extremely high benefit-cost ratio. According to research on the Perry Preschool Program, a two-year intensive early intervention program for disadvantaged African American three- and four-year-olds, spending time each morning in a preschool with follow-up afternoon visits to the child's home led to increases in measured IQ by age 10, higher achievement scores on standardized tests, higher rates of high school graduation, higher salaries in adulthood, a higher rate of home ownership, a lower probability of being dependent on welfare, and fewer arrests, as compared with a control group that was followed until the young children reached age 40 (Schweinhart et al. 2005). In measuring benefit/cost ratio of this program, Barnett (2004) finds that the total cost of the program averaged $16,514. But the net present value of the benefits was nearly $128,000. Of this total, there were additional earnings in excess of $40,000, a savings in remedial K–12 education of more than $9,000, and a savings to society of $94,000 due to a lower incidence of crime. Altogether, the benefit-cost ratio is 8.74 to 1. Thus, this particular program returned nearly $9 for every $1 invested in these disadvantaged kids. With such a high payoff, it is especially unfortunate that so few children benefit from intensive preschool experiences like these.

Similar strong effects were found in a recent twenty-five-year follow-up study of participants in the Brookline Early Education Project (BEEP), a 1972–1979 program that provided health and family-centered assistance—including discussions, playgroups, visits to libraries—to the families of young children from Brookline, a

Boston suburb, and to those from part of the central city of Boston. BEEP specifically focused on the relationship between early health—from just before birth to five years old—and subsequent outcomes. The designers of BEEP believed that "health and education are linked intimately. Healthy children learn better than those who are not well, either physically or emotionally. . . .The program's essential goal was to ensure that children in the project would enter kindergarten healthy and ready to learn" (Palfrey et al. 2005, p. 145). In evaluations during second grade, low-income BEEP participants had school outcomes comparable to those of higher-income families, and the central city BEEP participants demonstrated higher abilities in reading, planning, organizing and task completion than their central city nonprogram comparison group (Hauser-Cram et al. 1991).

A twenty-five-year follow-up study found that the preschool interventions had long-lasting benefits. As young adults, BEEP participants from the central city not only completed more years of schooling than did a central city comparison group but there were also great differences in the percentage with incomes less than $20,000 (28 percent for inner-city BEEP participants versus 72 percent for a non-BEEP comparison group), in the number who reported themselves to be in very good or excellent health (64 percent among the BEEP participants versus 42 percent among the comparison group), and in voter registration (75 percent among BEEP participants versus 58 percent among the central city comparison group).

Challenges Facing Urban School Systems

For all the reasons just enumerated, as well as others, it is not surprising to find strong confirmation of large test score gaps between rich kids and poor, and between the average white child and the average black or Hispanic. The National Assessment of Educational Progress (NAEP) provides an indication of just how big those gaps are. NAEP is a national test of fourth and eighth graders used to assess reading and math proficiency. "Reading Proficient" students at the eighth-grade level should be able to show an overall understanding of the text, including inferential as well as literal information. "Math Proficient" students at the eighth-grade level are expected to have a thorough understanding of basic-level arithmetic operations and be able to solve math problems in practical applications (Standard & Poor's 2006).

In 2005, 29 percent of all eighth graders who took the NAEP scored at the proficient level on the reading exam. White and Asian students scored nearly equally, with 39 percent of Asians and 37 percent of whites scoring as proficient. In contrast, only 11 percent of black students and 14 percent of Hispanics scored this well. Girls did much better than boys overall, with more than a third of the girls scoring as proficient (34%) and less than a quarter of the boys (24%). Only 15 percent of economically disadvantaged kids were judged proficient, compared with 38 percent of those who were not disadvantaged.

In math, the scores were similar in rank, but the gaps were even larger. Overall, 28 percent of eighth graders were "math proficient," with boys this time doing slightly better than girls (30% versus 27%, respectively). Asians led the pack at 46 percent, followed by whites at 37 percent, Hispanics at 13 percent, and blacks at only 8 percent. Economically disadvantaged kids were only one-third as likely to test proficient on the math test as those who were not disadvantaged (13% versus 39%, respectively).

The gaps in school performance hold true for high school graduation rates as well. According to a 2004 Urban Institute study, the estimated graduation rate for suburban school districts in the United States was nearly 73 percent, while the graduation rate for the nation's central city school districts was only 58 percent (Swanson 2004). A gap of five percentage points or more between suburban and central city school districts exists for thirty-three of the forty-six states for which the Urban Institute calculated estimates, with this gap exceeding ten percentage points in twenty-four of those thirty-three states (see **Table 8.2**). The largest gaps between central city and suburban graduation rates were found in New York, Ohio, Maryland, Pennsylvania, and Illinois. In each of these states, the suburban graduation rate is at least twenty-five percentage points higher than the central city rate. At the other end of the spectrum are five states (Oregon, Kentucky, West Virginia, New Mexico, and Nevada) where central city graduation rates are actually higher than suburban graduation rates.

Racial Segregation and Educational Achievement

In many cases, graduation rates are highly correlated with the racial composition of the student enrollment (Orfield et al. 2004). Among twenty of the largest school districts in the nation, as shown in **Table 8.3**, the high school graduation rate in 2000 ranges from just 30.4 percent in Oakland, California and 32.4 percent in Cincinnati, Ohio to 70 percent or more in Sacramento, California; Tucson and Mesa, Arizona; and Portland, Oregon. Of these twenty districts, the predominant racial group for the thirteen districts with the lowest graduation rates is black or Hispanic. Of the remaining seven districts with the highest graduation rates, none are predominantly black, one is Asian/Pacific, two are Hispanic, and the other four are predominantly white. We find that school performance gaps have a distinctly geographic dimension due to housing segregation by income and wealth, housing location outcomes—both imposed and self-imposed—and differences in local governments' abilities to fund local schools.

As Table 8.3 demonstrates, many of the largest school districts across the nation have high proportions of minority enrollment and, in some cases, more than 90 percent of the students are members of minority groups. The reformers of the 1950s did not envision that things would turn out this way. Before the landmark 1954 Supreme Court decision in the case of *Brown v. Board of Education,* states from Maryland and west through Indiana, encompassing the entire South as well as Texas and Oklahoma, had laws mandating that black and white children were required to attend separate public schools (Ogletree 2004). This example of legally mandated and legally enforced segregation—called **de jure** segregation—had been considered in compliance with the U.S. Constitution based on the 1896 Supreme Court case of

Table 8.2 High School Graduation Rates for Urban and Suburban School Districts by State, 2003–2004

States	Urban District Graduation Rate (%)	Suburban District Graduation Rate (%)	Suburban-Urban Graduation Rate Gap (% points)
Nation	**57.5**	**72.7**	**15.2**
New York	39.8	80.0	40.2
Ohio	41.9	77.6	35.7
Maryland	47.9	79.2	31.3
Pennsylvania	52.2	83.2	31.0
Illinois	55.3	83.9	28.6
Georgia	40.0	63.4	23.4
Massachusetts	55.3	77.8	22.5
Michigan	55.7	77.8	22.1
Connecticut	60.6	81.8	21.2
Kansas	59.6	79.7	20.1
Virginia	62.3	79.9	17.6
Oklahoma	59.0	76.3	17.3
Wisconsin	68.1	85.0	16.9
Tennessee	47.5	63.9	16.4
Vermont	59.4	75.7	16.3
Missouri	61.5	77.0	15.5
Indiana	61.1	75.8	14.7
California	61.0	74.7	13.7
Mississippi	45.4	59.1	13.7
Arkansas	62.1	74.7	12.6
South Carolina	46.1	58.7	12.6
Texas	58.6	70.4	11.8
Colorado	60.6	71.9	11.3
Washington	55.6	66.8	11.2
Nebraska	69.1	78.8	9.7
Maine	66.1	75.4	9.3
Utah	71.6	80.9	9.3
Minnesota	70.8	80.1	9.3
Iowa	70.3	79.0	8.7
South Dakota	71.4	78.1	6.7
Montana	81.0	87.2	6.2
Delaware	57.2	63.2	6.0
Rhode Island	69.3	75.3	6.0
Alabama	57.8	62.8	5.0
North Dakota	74.6	79.1	4.5
North Carolina	65.0	68.2	3.2
Idaho	85.7	88.0	2.3
New Hampshire	70.8	72.4	1.6
Florida	51.6	53.1	1.5
Louisiana	63.8	64.6	0.8
Nevada	55.2	51.7	−3.5
New Mexico	60.1	56.1	−4.0
West Virginia	71.8	67.4	−4.4
Kentucky	67.8	61.1	−6.7
Oregon	79.0	71.4	−7.6
New Jersey	—[1]	86.8	—
Hawaii	—[2]	66.0	—
Wyoming	66.9	—[3]	—
Alaska	69.4	—[3]	—

(continued)

Table 8.2 (*continued*)

States	Urban District Graduation Rate (%)	Suburban District Graduation Rate (%)	Suburban-Urban Graduation Rate Gap (% points)
District of Columbia	65.2	—[3]	—
Arizona	—[4]	72.4	—

1. Reliable urban graduation estimate could not be calculated.
2. No urban districts.
3. No suburban districts.
4. Data for urban not reported.

Plessy v. Ferguson, which sanctioned segregated accommodations on passenger railroad trains.

When Oliver Brown sued the Board of Education of Topeka, Kansas, for forcing his daughter to travel past several white schools in order to attend a more distant black school, the Court overturned the precedent established in *Plessy* and required school districts to integrate their schools. Although de jure segregation was now illegal, many of the places in which it was practiced actively resisted, or at the very least were slow to make the necessary changes, even though the Court directed them to act "with all deliberate speed."

Table 8.3 High School Graduation Rates for Selected Large School Districts, 2000

School District	Enrollment	Minority Enrollment (%)	Largest Racial Group	Graduation Rate (%)
Oakland, CA	54,863	94.4	Black	30.4
Cincinnati, OH	46,562	74.3	Black	32.4
Columbus, OH	64,511	62.9	Black	34.4
New York City, NY	1,066,516	84.7	Hispanic	38.2
Atlanta, GA	58,230	93.2	Black	39.6
Houston, TX	208,462	90.0	Hispanic	40.2
Denver, CO	70,847	78.0	Hispanic	40.5
Philadelphia, PA	201,190	83.3	Black	41.9
Los Angeles, CA	721,346	90.1	Hispanic	46.4
Baltimore County, MD	99,859	89.2	Black	47.9
Chicago, IL	435,261	90.4	Black	48.8
Dade County, FL	368,625	88.7	Hispanic	52.1
Minneapolis, MN	48,834	72.8	Black	63.8
Seattle, WA	47,575	60.0	White	66.6
San Francisco, CA	59,979	88.9	Asian/Pacific	66.7
Anchorage, AK	49,526	36.6	White	69.4
Sacramento, CA	52,734	75.1	Hispanic	70.0
Tucson, AZ	61,869	58.5	Hispanic	70.6
Mesa, AZ	73,587	32.2	White	71.7
Portland, OR	53,141	37.8	White	71.9

Source: Orfield et al. 2004.

Most of the states outside of the South did not practice de jure segregation and some along the northern tier from Massachusetts to Minnesota, including Michigan, outlawed it. In many northern cities, however, schools were segregated even in the absence of legal mandates, as a result of segregated housing patterns. In contrast with de jure segregation, this was called **de facto** segregation.

By the late 1960s, schools in the Detroit metropolitan area were overwhelmingly black inside the central city and overwhelmingly white in the surrounding suburbs. Any meaningful effort toward racial integration of the schools would have required a solution for the entire metropolitan area. However, when the Detroit metropolitan area desegregation plan was brought before the Supreme Court in 1974 in the case of *Milliken v. Bradley*, the Court ruled against integration plans that would cross central city school district boundaries unless it could be shown that suburban jurisdictions or state action contributed to de jure segregation within the central city (Friedman 2002).

This decision made it far more difficult, and often impossible, to implement metropolitan plans for desegregation. As demographic change concentrated higher proportions of minorities inside central cities, the result was a high degree of racial segregation of schoolchildren, even in the absence of laws mandating that outcome.

In the absence of any effective tools to overcome de facto segregation, the big question is: What can be done to address the substantial racial gaps in educational success that are illustrated in Tables 8.2 and 8.3? This has led many education experts and policy advisors to urge basic reform in the U.S. school system, particularly in central cities where so many students appear to perform poorly (Waldrip 1998).

Urban Schools and Reform of School Structure

The call for school reform is hardly new. By 1970, several concerns about the purpose of education and about the quality of education were converging to shape new school reform initiatives. Greater equity in the distribution of educational resources was being pursued through increased state and federal aid. The level of educational achievement became a critical issue because of the fear that competing nations were doing a better job of educating their citizens. There was growing consensus that a high school diploma was a necessary minimum for participation in most labor markets, with a college degree or more needed in an increasing number of them.

Despite the increased attention devoted to education in the 1960s and early 1970s, by the 1980s, it seemed that America's schools—and particularly its inner-city schools—were failing along with their students. In *A Nation at Risk*, which became a best-selling report, the National Commission on Excellence in Education (1983) warned that the United States was falling behind Japan and Europe in its economic prowess and that this was directly related to the quality of our public schools. It concluded that:

- Out of nineteen academic tests administered to students in dozens of countries, American students were never first or second in comparison with other industrialized nations and came in dead last seven times.
- Some 23 million Americans were functionally illiterate by the simplest tests of everyday reading, writing, and comprehension.
- Average achievement of high school students on most standardized tests were now lower than in the 1950s.
- College Board Scholastic Aptitude Test (SAT) scores had suffered a virtually unbroken decline from 1963 to 1980.
- The number and proportion of students who demonstrated superior achievement on the SATs also had declined.

In trying to explain these discouraging trends, the Commission noted that part of the blame could be traced to the fact that too many teachers were being drawn from the bottom quarter of graduating high school and college students; too much teacher training focused on "educational methods" rather than on the subjects to be taught; too few highly qualified individuals went into primary and secondary school teaching because of low average salaries; too little homework was being assigned to high school students; and the school day and school year were too short. School reformers latched on to the Commission report, calling for all kinds of changes in the schools.

Advocates for the public schools claimed that the "school crisis" could be dealt with by increasing teacher salaries in order to attract better teachers to traditional public schools. Others argued for more money to extend the school day or school year. Still others stressed the need for boosting the number of teachers who were qualified to teach math and science.

A growing cadre of critics went farther, suggesting that the public school system was essentially broken and could not be fixed without at least being subject to greater competition for students. These reformers called for the creation of magnet schools, charter schools, and voucher systems—alternatives to the traditional public school. Many of these new initiatives try to loosen the link between residential location and school assignment, alter the power of particular interest groups (e.g., teacher unions), boost accountability, and through their impact on school staff, try to address low expectations or low skills of teachers and administrators.

Almost all of these innovations in K–12 education are based on the theory that competition in markets for any good or service leads to improved quality at a reasonable price. Local public schools are seen as virtual monopolies. Without competition, they have little incentive to improve quality or become more efficient in their supply of educational services (Peterson 2005). By injecting competition into the K–12 local school market, traditional public schools presumably will have to improve if they are not to lose most of their students to these new types of schools.

Magnet Schools, Charter Schools, and For-Profit Schools

Historically, students were assigned to specific schools based on their residence within distinct school districts (which may or may not have coincided with municipal boundaries) and these were divided into smaller geographic units. Children generally went to the school nearest their homes—with the exception, of course, of those school districts that practiced de jure segregation and might send black children to a distant school to keep them from integrating a white school. In contrast to neighborhood schools, **magnet schools** are public schools with a specialized curriculum or a distinctive approach to learning and open to students throughout a school district, regardless of the school to which they would normally be assigned. The first schools with this approach were begun in Tacoma in 1968, in Boston in 1969, and in Minneapolis in 1970, and were sometimes referred to as "pilot schools" because they served as laboratories for new approaches to education. The term "magnet school" caught on after Houston opened its performing arts school, stating that it acted like a magnet for interested students (Waldrip 1998).

Magnet schools became widespread because they offered the opportunity to experiment with new learning techniques, a racially integrated environment that often was not achieved in the normal school assignment plans, and a promise of high-quality education to attract families who otherwise might leave the city in search of better educational opportunities for their children in the suburbs. In addition, by broadening the area from which students were normally drawn, many magnet schools were able to offer career-related instruction, such as schools for the arts, that may not have had an adequate number of interested students in normal school assignment schemes. Magnet schools were recognized by federal courts as a suitable way to address the impact of residential segregation on the segregation of schools, and most major cities had magnet schools by the early 1980s.

Charter schools are established by private groups that provide publicly funded education under contracts (charters) with designated government authorities, usually at the state level (Finn, Manno, and Vanourek 2000; Ladd 2002). The first charter school in the United States opened in St. Paul, Minnesota, in 1992. By school year 2005–2006, there were more than 3,600 charter schools in forty-one states (and the District of Columbia), with more than half of all charter schools (51.4%) located in central cities (National Center for Education Statistics 2006). By 2005, 30 percent of the public school students in Dayton, Ohio, were attending charter schools, while nearly a quarter (24%) of the Washington, D.C., K–12 students were in such schools. By 2006, more than 1 million students were attending charter schools nationwide (Zimmer and Buddin 2006).

While magnet schools are a modification of the traditional school assignment practices, charter schools are designed to change the management structure and behavioral incentives within schools. The advocates of charter schools perceived several problems with the traditional system of public education. They argued that entrenched interests of administrators and teachers made public schools resistant to improvement, that the practices of school employees were calcified by the gradual buildup of various agreements and regulations to the detriment of education, that schools were not being held accountable for the student outcomes they produced, and that a more decentralized system would provide better academic results.

Charter schools were seen as a solution to all of these problems. Because issues involved in public-sector decision making can be particularly complex and potentially problematic in urban settings, the charter school movement was embraced in many cities. Cutting through all the bureaucratic red tape of the public school system while still relying on public funding seemed a way to improve public schools without privatizing them. Often, charter school proposals received considerable support from poor communities, from African Americans, and from Hispanics, who were frustrated by existing inner-city public schools and were seeking new solutions to raise the quality of schooling available to their children.

Charter schools are not without their critics, however, who charge that, on average, they do not perform any better than traditional public schools and may harm traditional schools by draining them of needed resources (Carnoy et al. 2005). Since state aid to local public schools is usually tied to the number of students who attend district schools, every time a family chooses to send a child to a state-chartered school, the district loses revenue. If enough students in a district transfer to charter schools, the revenue loss to the local public school district can be severe enough to further undercut the quality of the traditional schools, which makes it even more difficult for them to offer a quality education to their students. This effect might be exacerbated if charter schools "skim off" high-achieving students from the traditional public schools with adverse social and academic effects on the students remaining behind (Wells 1998; Cobb and Glass 1999).

Another reform aimed at addressing the issue of school management has been to contract out the actual operation of public schools to for-profit **education management organizations** (EMOs). In contrast to charter schools, EMOs typically do not hire their own teachers; they simply replace the management structure of the schools, using the existing teachers and other school staff (Molnar et al. 2006). In Philadelphia, twenty-two public schools that enroll more than 12,000 students are run by Edison Schools—the nation's largest EMO—while another six Philadelphia public schools, enrolling 3,900 students, are run by Victory Schools. Las Vegas contracted with Edison to manage seven schools with a combined enrollment of approximately 5,900 students. Baltimore contracts with Edison to manage three schools with approximately 2,200 students.

Proponents of EMOs argue that the profit incentive of such firms will lead to the efficient management of staff and other resources, while the fixed-length renewable contract given only for a set number of years provides incentive to produce successful students. In 2005–2006, there were approximately fifty such companies. While most served as subcontractors for charter schools, seven EMOs held direct contracts for the management of traditional public schools. Nationwide in 2005–2006, EMOs directly provided management for seventy-six public schools, with Edison Schools accounting for fifty-eight of these.

Other urban school systems have focused on reforming incentives for teachers. The Houston public school district, the seventh-largest school district in the United States, adopted a **merit pay** system in 2006, providing bonuses to teachers whose students' test scores significantly improve from one year to the next. The Denver public schools initiated a merit pay system in late 2005, awarding bonuses to teachers whose students' test scores improve, who agree to work in schools that have had poor test scores or high teacher turnover, or who take additional training to improve their teaching skills.

Educational Standards and "No Child Left Behind"

What began as an issue of merit pay for teachers that was tied to the measurable progress of their students has become part of what is now known as the **standards movement**. According to the standards movement, one of the fundamental problems with traditional schools is their lack of accountability for student outcomes (Peterson and West 2003). Whether students test well or not, no one is penalized. In 2002, the Congress enacted legislation that amended earlier federal school aid programs by adding a requirement that states impose test score standards for public schools.

The legislation authorizing these changes is named the **No Child Left Behind Act** (NCLB). Under NCLB, states are required to develop test-based criteria for measuring student progress and to annually assess each school's performance in terms of those criteria. States are required to take steps to ensure that students are taught by qualified teachers. States are also required to identify individual schools that need improvement and to take specified action in schools that fail to improve within given timelines. If schools in need of improvement fail to boost their test scores, states are required to impose specific sanctions that include providing students from such schools the option to attend other schools and changing the management of the school, or risk losing federal funds.

Critics of NCLB, however, argue that test-based standards do not adequately reflect the types of learning needed within schools, and that expected funding to implement the mandates of NCLB was not included in future federal budgets (National Education Association 2006; Karp 2007). The heads of many city school systems argue that because expenditures for the implementation of NCLB mandates have had to come from already strained budgets, their school systems are forced to cut school offerings. Putting more money into the basic subjects covered in standardized tests means less money for art classes, athletics, and other parts of the school curriculum. Another common complaint is that a number of the test criteria are harder to meet in cities with high poverty levels, substantial immigration, and other conditions that impact school performance. The performance standards instituted by states as part of NCLB have led to court cases in which cities have argued that, in light of the socioeconomic characteristics of their school population, their funding is not adequate to meet the mandated standards.

The No Child Left Behind Act is revolutionary for the decentralized U.S. school system because it centralizes many rules and sanctions under which local public school education is provided. At the same time, it enhances the possibility for school choice by encouraging the establishment of charter schools, magnet schools, and voucher programs.

School Choice and Voucher Programs

Broadly speaking, **school choice** includes any system in which parents can choose the school their children will attend, rather than having the schools assigned by residence or other criteria. As noted earlier, magnet schools and charter schools are usually open to students from throughout a school district. Many urban school districts have some form of "controlled choice," where families can designate their top choices and enrollment is determined by taking these choices and other factors, such as racial diversity, into account.

However, some advocates of school choice argue that all schools should be open to all families, without any restrictions, and that adequate accountability for results would be best achieved through such a system. They believe that such a system can function through marketlike dynamics similar to those described under perfect competition, where individual consumers (families) make decisions about the services (schools) they will buy (utilize). Invoking analogies of perfect competition, they argue that consumer choice will eventually weed out bad schools and lead to the replication of good schools, while maximizing the liberty of families to make decisions (Friedman 1962; Chubb and Moe 1990; Howell and Peterson 2006).

Critics of this argument disagree with the applicability of the theoretical world of perfectly competitive markets to education, noting that education involves many externalities, economies of scale, information problems, and interdependent utility functions (Aoki and Feiner 1995; Ladd 2002). Some critics note that research indicates that parents often choose schools for their social milieu rather than their academic rigor, asking more questions about the racial composition of schools than about data on student outcomes (Schneider and Buckley 2002). Others argue that in choosing schools, parents have to take into account the availability of transportation, parental workplaces and work schedules, the location and availability of after-school child care, and other factors. Still others believe that school choice can undermine the civic value of "common schools."

There are three basic forms of choice systems. **Intradistrict choice** allows families to select any public school within the boundaries of the school district in which they reside. **Interdistrict choice** allows families to select public schools in school districts other than the ones in which they reside. For example, a student living in a poor neighborhood in Chicago would be able to choose a school in the upper-income suburb of Winnetka, and vice versa. Such a program in Minnesota, in fact, allows families to choose any public school in the state.

Voucher programs extend choice not only to public schools but also to private schools. Vouchers are essentially entitlements to a certain amount of public funding for a child's education, regardless of whether the child attends public, private, or parochial (religiously oriented) schools. Parents of school-age children receive a voucher check that can be used to pay tuition at any school in the voucher system.

Milwaukee is the city most noted for implementing a voucher program (Euchner and McGovern 2003). Following a failed desegregation plan, black parents decided to support a school choice program that provided $2,500 vouchers for each student. The program was targeted to families who earned less than 1.75 times the poverty level. By 2001, 11,000 children in Milwaukee were receiving vouchers that permitted them to choose between public and private schools, including religious ones.

Cleveland followed Milwaukee in implementing a taxpayer-funded voucher plan with more than 4,500 children from poor neighborhoods taking advantage of it. Florida adopted a statewide voucher program in 1999, such that students in any underperforming public school are eligible for vouchers worth up to $4,000 per year to attend schools of their choice (Euchner and McGovern 2003). However, the Florida State Supreme Court decided in January 2006 that the program violated the state constitution.

One problem, of course, is that with private schools charging tuitions well above the value of the voucher, only those parents willing and able to make up the difference between tuition and the voucher check can take advantage of the plan. Indeed, about the only private schools that charge low tuition are religious-affiliated parochial schools, where the question of church-state relations remains cloudy.

The debate about school choice and its relationship to civic values and to urban dynamics has continued in the early twenty-first century, as legislation at the federal and state levels has encouraged states and municipalities to consider choice-based systems. Debate on the impact of test-based standards continues as well. Metropolitan areas are not only the cauldrons in which many school reform initiatives were born but also have been the context in which many of their complexities and perplexities have become apparent and have been hotly debated.

Do These School Reforms Work?

With all of the school reforms and experiments under way, one would have expected by now to see some real improvement in school performance and a significant decline in the test score gap between wealthier and poorer students and across racial and ethnic groups. But the results are mixed, at best.

In a well-publicized study of charter schools across the country, Caroline Hoxby (2004) compared reading and math scores of fourth-grade students in charter schools with fourth graders in neighboring traditional public schools. On average, she found that the charter school students were 3.8 percent more likely to be proficient on their state's reading exam compared to the children who attended the local district elementary school. On math tests, the charter school students were 1.6 percent more likely to be proficient. This seems to suggest that charter schools were doing a slightly better job of educating children.

Yet, other studies using the same data as Hoxby came to the conclusion that even this small charter school advantage completely vanishes when you control for the income of the children's families, as well as their race (Carnoy et al. 2005; Roy and Mishel 2005). Because the families who select charter schools for their children tend to be higher income and presumably provide more educational benefits to their kids at home, it is not surprising that they perform somewhat better in school.

Miron and Horn (2002) come to a somewhat more nuanced conclusion about the success of charter schools. They conclude that there is a slight improvement in average test scores in some states, while research in other states finds a negative impact. Most studies report both positive and negative impacts, so that many experts caution against any definitive conclusion for or against charter schools. Clearly, there are some successes where administrators, teachers, and parents are heavily involved and resources are adequate, but there seem to be at least this number, if not more, where students in charter schools fall behind those in traditional public schools on test scores, after controlling for family background and neighborhood effects.

The claims for charter schools seem to be somewhat overblown, not just on test scores but also on their claims to be more innovative and responsive to parental pressure. A study of charter schools in Arizona concludes that the actual innovation in these schools was less than anticipated by charter school advocates (Gresham et al. 2000). Accountability, which should be the hallmark of the charter school, was also found lacking (Maranto et al. 1999; Finn, Manno, and Vanourek 2000). State oversight and parental involvement was supposed to take the place of the local school board. The evidence suggests that in many cases, once the school board was out of the picture, there was no one stepping in to assure quality or innovation.

Zimmer and Buddin (2006) provide perhaps the best overall analysis of charter schools in their study of the California system. They conclude that charter schools perform about the same as regular public schools and therefore have done little to close the achievement gaps for minorities. They do, however, provide a different education model that often emphasizes non-core subjects (e.g., art, music, language study) and often uses fewer public resources than traditional schools. As a result, charter schools do not provide a "silver bullet" for school improvement, but represent a reform initiative that Zimmer and Buddin consider worth continuing, at least in California.

Pretty much the same conclusion seems to be valid for voucher programs. While voucher systems give students more school choice and therefore should contribute to greater educational achievement, evaluation studies show little more support for this proposition than the studies of charter schools. Studies of the Milwaukee system found that parents were "more satisfied" with the private schools their children attended, but there was little evidence that voucher students did any better on reading and math tests (Witte 2000). A RAND Corporation study (Gill et al. 2001) that surveyed many choice systems found only modest gains for African American children after one to two years in voucher schools, but none for Latino students. Martin Carnoy (2001) finds even less.

By 2003, after much more experience with charter schools and voucher systems, the effect of these reforms on school performance appeared to be no better. In a large-scale study that compared reading and math test scores for fourth- and eighth-grade students in nearly 7,000 public schools and more than 530 private schools, the National Center for Education Statistics—a division of the U.S. Department of Education—found that children in regular public schools generally performed as well as or better than comparable children in private schools, after controlling for race, ethnicity, income, and parents' educational background (Schemo 2006). That is, children in private schools do test better than children in public school, but only because they usually come from wealthier families where the parents are better educated and provide educational opportunities outside the school environment. Once these demographic factors are held constant, the alleged superiority of private schools largely disappears.

What are we left to conclude? The evidence seems to suggest that parental background and community factors play the pivotal role in how kids perform in school and ultimately, how they do in the labor market and in life more generally. Differences between the environments in many central cities and suburbs are critical. Because education now plays such a critical role in the labor market and in the earning potential of workers, gaps in central city/suburban school achievement can only lead to greater income and wealth inequality as education becomes more important in determining income. We need to better understand the impact of decent housing, safe neighborhoods, preschool programs, after-school programs, and health disparities to better understand why the achievement gaps by family income, race, and ethnicity are so hard to overcome. As the saying goes, "It takes a village to raise a child." The evidence seems to confirm this conjecture. Essentially, we need to change a lot about cities and suburbs to make a difference in the success of the children growing up there.

References

Aoki, Masato, and Susan Feiner. 1995. "The Economics of Market Choice and At-Risk Students." In William E. Becker and William J. Baumol, eds., *Assessing Educational Practices: The Contribution of Economics*. Cambridge, Mass.: MIT Press.

Barnett, W. S. 2004. "Benefit-Cost Analysis of Preschool Education." National Institute for Early Education Research. http://nieer.org/resources/files/BarnettBenefits.ppt.

Blair, John P., and Robert Premus. 1987. "Major Factors in Industrial Location: A Review." *Economic Development Quarterly* 1, no. 1: 72–85.

Bowles, Samuel, and Herbert Gintis. 1976. *Schooling in Capitalist America: Educational Reform and the Contradictions of Economic Life*. New York: Basic Books.

———. 2001. "Schooling in Capitalist America Revisited." University of Massachusetts, Amherst. http://www.umass.edu/preferen/gintis/soced.pdf.

Boyd, Donald, Hamilton Lankford, Susanna Loeb, and James Wyckoff. 2005. "The Draw of Home: How Teachers' Preferences for Proximity Disadvantage Urban Schools." *Journal of Policy Analysis and Management* 24, no. 1: 113–132

Buckley, Jack, Mark Schneider, and Yi Shang. 2004. "The Effects of School Facility Quality on Teacher Retention in Urban School Districts." National Clearinghouse for Educational Facilities. http://www.edfacilities.org/pubs/teacherretention.pdf.

Carnoy, Martin. 2001. *School Vouchers: Examining the Evidence*. Washington, D.C.: Economic Policy Institute.

Carnoy, Martin, Rebecca Jacobsen, Lawrence Mishel, and Richard Rothstein. 2005. *The Charter School Dust-Up: Examining the Evidence on Enrollment and Achievement*. Washington, D.C.: Economic Policy Institute.

Chubb, John E., and Terry M. Moe. 1990. *Politics, Markets and America's Schools*. Washington, D.C.: Brookings Institution Press.

Cobb, C. D., and G. V. Glass. 1999. "Ethnic Segregation in Arizona Charter Schools." *Education Policy Analysis Archives* 7, no. 1.

Cohen, Natalie, 2000. "Business Location Decision-Making and the Cities: Bringing Companies Back." Report. Washington, D.C.: Brookings Institution Center on Urban and Metropolitan Policy.

Coleman, James S. 1966. *Equality of Education Opportunity*. Washington, D.C.: U.S. Government Printing Office.

Education Trust. 2006. "The Funding Gap 2005: Low-Income and Minority Students Shortchanged by Most States." Special Report. Washington, D.C.

Euchner, Charles, and Steven J. McGovern. 2003. *Urban Policy Reconsidered*. New York: Routledge.

Finn, Chester E., Jr., Bruno V. Manno, and Gregg Vanourek. 2000. *Charter Schools in Action: Renewing Public Education*. Princeton, N.J.: Princeton University Press.

Friedman, Lawrence M. 2002. *American Law in the Twentieth Century*. New Haven, Conn.: Yale University Press.

Friedman, Milton. 1962. *Capitalism and Freedom*. Chicago: University of Chicago Press.

Gill, Brian, et al. 2001. *Rhetoric versus Reality: What We Know and What We Need to Know about Vouchers and Charter Schools*. Santa Monica, Calif.: RAND Education.

Glaeser, Edward. 2005. "Smart Growth: Education, Skilled Workers, and the Future of Cold-Weather Cities." Cambridge, Mass.: Harvard University, Rappaport Institute for Greater Boston Policy Briefs, PB-2005-1, April.

Goldin, Claudia. 1998. "America's Graduation from High School: The Evolution and Spread of Secondary Schooling in the Twentieth Century." *Journal of Economic History* 58, no. 2 (June): 345–374.

———. 2001. "The Human Capital Century and American Leadership: Virtues of the Past." *Journal of Economic History* 61, no. 2: 263–292.

Gould, Marge Christensen, and Herman Gould. 2003. "A Clear Vision for Equity and Opportunity." *Phi Delta Kappan* (December): 324–328.

Government Accounting Office (GAO). 1994. "Elementary School Children: Many Change Schools Frequently, Harming Their Education." GAO/HeHS-94-95. Washington, D.C.

Gresham, April, et al. 2000. "Desert Bloom: Arizona's Free Market in Education." *Phi Delta Kappan* (June): 751–757

Hanushek, Eric A. 1997a. "Assessing the Effects of School Resources on Student Performance: An Update." *Educational Evaluation and Policy Review* 19, no. 2: 141–164.

———. 1997b. "Outcomes, Incentives, and Beliefs: Reflections on Analysis of the Economics of Schools." *Educational Evaluation and Policy Analysis* 19, no. 4: 301–308.

Hanushek, Eric, John F. Kain, and Steven G. Rivkin. 2004. "Disruption versus Tiebout Improvement: The Costs and Benefits of Switching Schools." *Journal of Public Economics* 88, no. 9: 1721–1746.

Hauser-Cram, Penny, Donald Pierson, Deborah Walker, and Terrance Tivnan. 1991. *Early Education in the Public Schools: Lessons from a Comprehensive Birth-to-Kindergarten Program*. San Francisco: Jossey-Bass.

Howell, William G., and Paul E. Peterson. 2006. *The Education Gap: Vouchers and Urban Schools*, rev. ed. Washington, D.C.: Brookings Institution Press.

Hoxby, Caroline. 2000. "The Effects of Class Size on Student Achievement: Evidence from Population Variation." *Quarterly Journal of Economics* 115, no. 4: 1239–1285.

———. 2004. "Achievement in Charter Schools and Regular Public Schools in the United States." Cambridge, Mass: Harvard University, December. http://www.posteconomics.harvard.edu/faculty/hoxby/papers/charters_040909.pdf.

Karp, Stan. 2007. "Exit Strategies." *Rethinking Schools* 21, no. 4 (Summer).

King, Richard, Austin Swanson, and Scott Sweetland. 2003. *School Finance: Achieving High Standards with Equity and Efficiency*, 3rd ed. Boston: Allyn and Bacon.

Kozol, Jonathan. 1992. *Savage Inequalities: Children in America's Schools*. New York: Perennial Books.

Krim, Robert, David Bartone, Marti Frank, and Colin Rowas. 2006. *Innovate Boston: Shaping the Future from Our Past*. Boston: Boston History & Innovation Collaborative.

Krueger, Alan B. 1997. "Experimental Estimates of Education Production Functions." National Bureau of Economic Research Working Paper 6051. Cambridge, Mass.: National Bureau of Economic Research.

Ladd, Helen F. 2002. *Market-Based Reforms in Urban Education*. Washington, D.C.: Economic Policy Institute.

Lankford, Hamilton, Susanna Loeb, and James Wyckoff. 2002. "Teacher Sorting and the Plight of Urban Schools: A Descriptive Analysis." *Educational Evaluation and Policy Analysis* 24, no. 1: 37–62.

Loveless, Tom. 1999. *The Tracking Wars: State Reform Meets School Policy*. Washington, D.C.: Brookings Institution Press.

Lucas, Robert E. 1988. "On the Mechanics of Economic Development." *Journal of Monetary Economics* 22, no. 3: 3–42.

Maranto, Robert, Scott Milliman, Frederick Hess, and April Gresham. 1999. "In Lieu of Conclusions: Tentative Lessons from a Contested Frontier." In Robert Maranto et al., eds., *School Choice in the Real World: Lessons from Arizona's Charter Schools*. Boulder, Colo.: Westview Press, pp. 237–247.

Miron, Gary, and Jerry Horn. 2002. *What's Public about Charter Schools? Lessons Learned about Choice and Accountability*. Thousand Oaks, Calif.: Corwin Press.

Molnar, Alex, David Garcia, Margaret Bartlett, and Adrienne O'Neill. 2006. "Profiles of For-Profit Education Management Organizations: Eighth Annual Report, 2005–2006." Tempe: Arizona State University, Education Policy Studies Laboratory, College of Education.

National Center for Education Statistics. 2006. "Parental Choice of Schools." Washington, D.C.: U.S. Department of Education.

———. 2007. *Digest of Education Statistics: 2006*. Washington, D.C.: U.S. Department of Labor, June.

National Commission on Excellence in Education. 1983. *A Nation at Risk*. Washington, D.C.: U.S. Government Printing Office.

National Education Association. 2006. "It's Time for a Change." July. http://www.nea.org.

Ogletree, Charles. 2004. *All Deliberate Speed: Reflections on the First Half Century of* Brown v. Board of Education. New York: W.W. Norton.

Orfield, Gary, Daniel Losen, Johanna Wald, and Christopher Swanson. 2004. "Losing Our Future: How Minority Youth Are Being Left Behind by the Graduation Rate Crisis." Cambridge, Mass.: The Civil Rights Project at Harvard University.

Palfrey, Judith S., Penny Hauser-Cram, Martha B. Bronson, Marji Erickson Warfield, Selcuk Sirin, and Eugenia Chan. 2005. "The Brookline Early Education Project: A 25-Year Follow-up Study of a Family-Centered Early Health and Development Intervention." *Pediatrics* 116, no. 1 (July): 144–152.

Perry, Imani. 1988. "A Black Student's Reflection on Public and Private Schools." *The Harvard Educational Review* 58, no. 3.

———. 2004. "Holistic Integration: An Anniversary Reflection on the Goals of *Brown v. Board of Education*." In Dorinda J. Carter, Stella M. Flores, and Richard J. Reddick, eds., *Legacies of Brown: Multiracial Equity in American Education*. Cambridge, Mass.: Harvard Educational Review Reprint Series.

Peterson, Paul E., ed. 2005. *Choice and Competition in American Education*. Lanham, Md.: Rowman & Littlefield.

Peterson, Paul E., and Martin R. West. 2003. *No Child Left Behind? The Politics and Practice of School Accountability*. Washington, D.C.: Brookings Institution Press.

Romer, Paul. 1986. "Increasing Returns and Long-Run Growth." *Journal of Political Economy* 94, no. 5: 1002–1037.

———. 1994. "The Origins of Endogenous Growth." *Journal of Economic Perspectives* 8, no. 1: 3–22.

———. 1996. "Why Indeed in America? Theory, History and the Origins of Modern Economic Growth." *American Economic Review* 86, no. 2: 202–206.

Rothstein, Richard. 2004. *Class and Schools: Using Social, Economic, and Educational Reform to Close the Black-White Achievement Gap*. Washington, D.C.: Economic Policy Institute.

Roy, Joydeep, and Lawrence Mishel. 2005. "Advantage None: Re-examining Hoxby's Finding of Charter School Benefits." Washington, D.C.: Economic Policy Institute Briefing Paper No. 158, April.

Schemo, Diana Jean. 2006. "Public Schools Perform Near Private Ones in Study." *New York Times*, July 15, p. 1.

Schneider, Mark, and Jack Buckley. 2002. "What Do Parents Want from Schools? Evidence from the Internet." Occasional Paper No. 21, National Center for the Study of Privatization in Education. New York: Teachers College, Columbia University.

Schweinhart, Lawrence J., et al. 2005. *Lifetime Effects: The High/Scope Perry Preschool Study through Age 40*. Ypsilanti, Mich.: High/Scope.

Shonkoff, J. P., and D. Phillips. 2000. *From Neurons to Neighborhoods: The Science of Early Child Development*. Washington, D.C.: National Academies Press.

Standard & Poor's. 2006. "School Matters." NAEP Proficiency Scores for 4th and 8th Graders. www.schoolmatters.com/app/printfriendly/q/stid=1036196.

Swanson, Christopher. 2004. *Projections of 2003–04 High School Graduates*. Washington, D.C.: Urban Institute Education Policy Center.

U.S. Bureau of Labor Statistics. 2007. "Employment by Industry." www.bls.gov.

U.S. Bureau of the Census. 2002a. "Government Units in 2002." GC02-1(P), *Census of Governments, 2002*. Washington, D.C. U.S. Government Printing Office. http://ftp2.census.-gov/govs/cog/2002COGprelim_report.pdf.

———. 2002b. "Government Organization, 2002." *Census of Governments* 1, no. 1. GC02(1)-1, U.S. Department of Commerce, Economics and Statistics Administration. Washington, D.C.: U.S. Government Printing Office.

U.S. Department of Education. 2007. *Digest of Education Statistics: 2006*. Washington, D.C.: National Center for Education Statistics, June.

U.S. Department of Housing and Urban Development. 2007. HUD User Policy Development and Research Information Service. SOCDS (State of the Cities Data Systems) data set. http://socds.huduser.org.

Waldrip, Donald. 1998. "A Brief History of Magnet Schools." Washington, D.C.: Magnet Schools of America. http://www.magnet.edu/modules/content/index.php?id=36.

Wells, Amy Stuart. 1998. *Beyond the Rhetoric of Charter School Reform: A Study of Ten California School Districts*. Los Angeles: UCLA Graduate School of Education and Information Studies.

Witte, John F. 2000. *The Market Approach to Education: An Analysis of America's First Voucher Program*. Princeton, N.J.: Princeton University Press.

Wraga, William G. 2006. "Progressive Pioneer: Alexander James Inglis (1879–1924)." *Teachers College Record* 108, no. 6 (June): 1080–1105.

Zimmer, Ron, and Richard Buddin. 2006. "Making Sense of Charter Schools: Evidence from California." Occasional Paper. Santa Monica, Calif.: RAND Corporation.

Chapter 8 Questions and Exercises

1. As this chapter discusses, educational attainment within metropolitan areas, and the cities and towns that comprise metropolitan areas, has changed over the years. Using the *Urban Experience* CD, find out how educational attainment has changed since 1970 in two CBSAs (metropolitan area or micropolitan area) of your choice (other than the twenty MSAs in our charts in this chapter).

   To obtain these data in the *Urban Experience* CD, follow these steps:

   • Go to the "Get Data" screen.
   • Click on "Percentages."
   • Then double-click on "Educational Attainment," and check each box in the drop-down list that appears.
   • In the "Locations" segment, choose one CBSA from the list.
   • Finally, check all of the years that are available and click on "Go."

How have the percentages of the population with "less than 12 years," "high school diploma," "some college," and "bachelor's or more" changed between 1970 and 2005?

2. Repeat this process for a second CBSA of your choice. Educational attainment within metro areas may vary, with possible gaps between the attainment levels found in principal cities and suburbs. Use the *Urban Experience* CD to explore this for the two CBSAs you selected for the previous exercise.

   • Go back to the *Urban Experience* CD's "Get Data" screen.
   • In the "Year" segment of the screen, check only the year 2005.
   • In the "Locations" segment, double-click on the name of one of the CBSAs you chose for the previous exercise. A drop-down list of all principal cities and all suburbs in the CBSA will appear. Note that in the drop-down list, totals for all principal cities are at the top, followed by totals for all suburbs, a list of each separate principal city, and a list of each separate suburb.
   • Check the box for "CBSA-principal cities" and the box for "CBSA-suburbs."
   • Then go to the second CBSA you chose, double-click on it, and choose the same boxes for that CBSA. Then click on "Go."

Within each CBSA, what differences, if any, do you find between the educational attainment in the principal cities and the educational attainment in the suburbs? Comparing the two CBSAs, what similarities or differences do you see in the patterns? (*Note:* There may be some geographic areas where 2005 data was not available. If the table that results from your selection is blank, go back to the main screen and select the year 2000 instead of 2005.)

3. There may also be major differences between individual principal cities within the same CBSA and between individual suburbs within the same CBSA. To explore this, return to the *Urban Experience* CD's "Get Data" screen and look once again at the drop-down menu of principal cities and suburbs within the CBSA you chose. This time, for each of the CBSAs you selected, pick one or two of the separate principal cities (some CBSAs have only one principal city) and one or two of the suburbs (principal cities are listed alphabetically; they are followed immediately by an alphabetical listing of the suburbs). Change the year to 2000, because data is not available for many individual suburbs for 2005. Then click on "Go."

   ✦ For those CBSAs with more than one principal city, what differences, if any, do you find between the two principal cities you chose?
   ✦ What differences, if any, do you find between the suburbs?
   ✦ If you were asked to do further research on the differences/similarities within the CBSA, what ideas from Chapter 8 would you draw upon in your investigations?

4. The Department of Education's annual *Digest of Education Statistics* can be found at the following Web site:

http://nces.ed.gov/programs/digest

In the drop-down menu on the left choose the most recent year available, and when the next screen comes up click on "Elementary and Secondary Education" and then choose "Schools and School Districts." Scroll down just a bit and choose the table titled "Selected statistics on enrollment, teachers, dropouts, and graduates in public school districts enrolling more than 15,000 students." This table is sorted by state (found in column 2).

Find the school districts that you identified in question 1 above and answer the following questions for the most recent year available:

- ✦ What is the enrollment for that school district?
- ✦ What is the racial composition of the district?
- ✦ What is the teacher/pupil ratio?

5. Go back to the *Digest of Education Statistics* Web site and, as you did for question 3, choose the most recent year available, "Elementary and Secondary Education," and "Schools and School Districts." This time choose the table titled "Revenues, expenditures, poverty rate, and Title I allocations of public school districts enrolling more than 15,000 students." Once again, find the school districts that you identified in question 1 above and answer the following questions for the most recent year available:

- ✦ What percentage of the school district's revenues come from local government?
- ✦ What percentage comes from state government?
- ✦ What percentage comes from the federal government?
- ✦ What is the poverty rate among five- to seventeen-year-old students who attend the school?
- ✦ What is the current expenditure per pupil?

CURRENT POLICY ISSUES IN METROPOLITAN AREAS

The Urban Public Sector

9

The biggest news stories about the public sector often focus on the federal government—the decisions made by the president, the U.S. Congress, or the U.S. Supreme Court. Our daily lives, however, are profoundly affected by the ordinary activities of state and local governments, whose decisions shape our existence in myriad ways, from the time we turn on our water faucets in the morning until the time we turn off our lights at night. Decisions at the state and local level govern the regulation of public utilities like electricity, water, and cable TV; the provision of health and safety services like police and fire protection, garbage collection, sewage treatment, and building inspections; the operation of a network of paved and lighted streets and sidewalks, traffic signals and mass transportation; and the offering of educational and recreational services like schools, libraries, parks and playgrounds.

From the workers who repair potholes in the streets to the city councillors who deliberate over whether to build a new convention center, public-sector decisions affect our lives in a variety of ways both large and small. If we are to have a full understanding of how metropolitan areas work, we must understand the operation of the urban public sector. To do that, we must first step back and ask a more fundamental question: What is the economic role of government in metropolitan areas?

Government's Economic Role in Metro Areas

As we pointed out in Chapter 1, population density is the central distinguishing characteristics of metropolitan areas. A large population mass is necessary to support cable TV, municipal trash collection, or public transportation. At low population densities, children might have a short school bus ride to the local elementary school, but they would need to travel much longer distances to attend a regional high school. At very low population densities, fire protection services might rely on volunteers, or might even be sold through the market. Street lighting and paved sidewalks would be rare or nonexistent, and a visit to the nearest public library might entail a long journey. While the higher population densities of cities and towns make it *possible* to provide a wider array of public goods and services because of economies of scale, they also make it *necessary* to provide some of these goods and services through the public sector because of externalities like those we discussed in Chapter 1 and because of other ways in which private markets fail.

At the local level, the major economic task of government is to change the level of output of certain items from what the market would otherwise produce, that is, to increase the output of some items and decrease the output of others. We need, for example, more schooling but less traffic congestion and more fire protection and less pollution than the private market on its own would normally produce. Under ideal circumstances, a private-market economy will produce the right items in the right amounts. If these ideal circumstances do not apply, however, the market will produce too little of some goods and too much of others. Correcting these malfunctions comes under the **allocation role of government**, which is an important function of local governments everywhere. The denser the population of an area, the more likely parts of the private market will fail and require public intervention.

How the Private Market Is Supposed to Work

To understand the critical role of the public sector in the local economy, it helps to begin by understanding how the private sector is supposed to operate. Markets provide a mechanism for exchanging goods and services in a modern economy. The prices that consumers are willing to pay serve as signals to producers, guiding them in their decisions about what to produce and in what quantities.

Ideally, this would lead to an economic system that produces the right items in the right amounts for people who need and want them, without wasting resources, and in such a way that the items are channeled to the consumers who value them the most. The focus of **allocative efficiency** is on the maximization of each consumer's satisfaction through the market, given the consumer's initial endowment of purchasing power. If resources are not being used in this way, the prices of some goods or services demanded by consumers will rise while others will fall, signaling to business that reallocating resources to fill consumer demand will result in higher profits. In theory, this process of constant reallocation of resources in response to changes in demand and price is an elegant, self-regulating system. Adam Smith, the eighteenth-century founder of modern economics, called this "the invisible hand" of perfect competition, in which the coordination of the activities of many individuals is achieved without any one of them taking control of the market.

This idea of allocative efficiency under perfect competition requires a bit more elaboration before we can use it to fully understand the circumstances in which market failure occurs and allocative efficiency is not achieved. Specifically, the ideal world of perfect competition rests on a number of key assumptions:

1. *No one has market power.* For every good and service in the market, there are many buyers and many sellers.
2. *Output is homogeneous.* For each particular good or service, each seller produces output indistinguishable from that of all other sellers of the same good or service.

3. *There is perfect information.* All buyers are perfectly informed about the price and quality of each product so they can make a rational choice about what to buy.

4. *There are no barriers to entering or exiting the industry.* New producers are free to enter any market for a particular good or service without impediment, and existing producers are free to leave.

5. *There are no externalities.* Sellers take into account all of the costs of producing a particular good or service and only the buyers themselves receive the benefits from purchasing the particular good or service.

As we explain below, under this set of circumstances, the price at which every good and service is sold will just equal its marginal cost (the cost of producing one additional unit) and firms will produce the precise mix of goods and services that conform to maximum allocative efficiency.

Assuming there are *no* collective goals in society, but only individual ones, the market *price* for each good and service can be viewed as a proxy for **social benefit** (how much consumers really value each good and service), while *marginal cost* can be viewed as a proxy for **social cost** (the cost to society of using up the resources to produce an additional unit of each good and service rather than using the resources for some other purpose). Under these conditions, the marginal cost is the full opportunity cost of getting the last unit of any given good or service produced.

Supply and Demand in the Private Sector

Let us use one of the purest examples of a perfectly competitive market in an urban setting—street vendors. In many large cities, you can find vendors who sell everything from handbags to hot dogs. In the busiest parts of the city, there might be a hot dog vendor on nearly every street corner. The National Hot Dog and Sausage Council (2007) estimates that 15 percent of the 20 billion hot dogs Americans consume each year are bought from street vendors. Although the product is not entirely homogeneous—several brands that vary in taste or quality might be available in any given city—the conditions in this market are nevertheless very close to those of textbook perfect competition. Lunchtime strollers can choose to buy pretty much the same hot dog from many different vendors. This assures that the price of a hot dog will not vary very much, if at all, from one vendor to the next.

But how many hot dogs will be prepared and sold in this city? To answer this question, let us say that each vendor's marginal cost of purchasing hot dogs, preparing them, and selling them on the street—including a normal profit of 50 cents a dog—is initially $2 (see **Figure 9.1A**). If the initial price that consumers are willing to pay to consume all the hot dogs prepared by the vendors is greater than the marginal cost, say $2.50 per dog, vendors could raise their price and make an even greater profit. More likely, in a competitive market, some vendors would prepare more hot dogs to satisfy the demand at a price of $2. But as that happens, marginal cost will normally begin to rise because resources will have to be lured away from other industries and the scarcity of these resources will cause their prices to increase.

The vendors will find that their marginal costs are rising as they increase output to satisfy the demand. They can no longer maintain a price of $2 and thus the price will ultimately settle at something above that amount, say $2.25, where the amount supplied, Q_2, just equals the amount demanded and the new (higher) price equals the new (higher) marginal cost.

What if the initial price that vendors could charge to get rid of all the hot dogs they prepared was less than marginal cost? In this case, consumers value a hot dog at, say, $1.50, but it uses up $2 worth of resources to produce one more (see **Figure 9.1B**). If hot dogs are such a low priority for consumers, resources should leave hot dog production in search of better opportunities elsewhere. As hot dog output declines, marginal cost will fall until it equals the price that consumers are willing to pay. Again, at some point, price and marginal cost will balance, let us say at $1.75 at output Q_2.

Accordingly, when the market price is greater than marginal cost, resources generally flow into that use and output will expand. If price is less than marginal cost, resources will normally flow out of that use and output contracts. If price is equal to full marginal cost, hot dog vendors are producing just the right amount of output consistent with consumer preferences. If every good and service is produced so that price equals marginal cost, there would be no way for some businesses to grow or others to shrink that would make consumers any better off. We would be, at least temporarily, in a condition of **Pareto optimality**, where resources are so

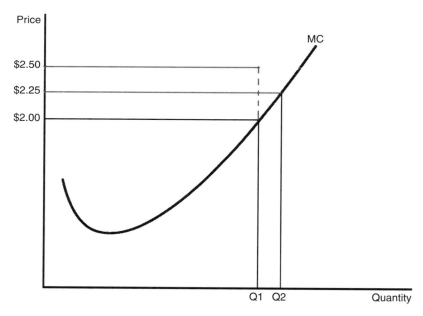

Figure 9.1A Marginal Cost Curve for Hot Dog Stand. If consumers are willing to pay a price greater than marginal cost, each vendor will want to increase his output. However, if all hot dog vendors try to produce a larger quantity, their costs for raw materials will increase and the marginal cost of a hot dog will rise for each vendor as he expands output from Q1 to Q2. At Q2, price will equal marginal cost and the vendor will not want to expand output any further.

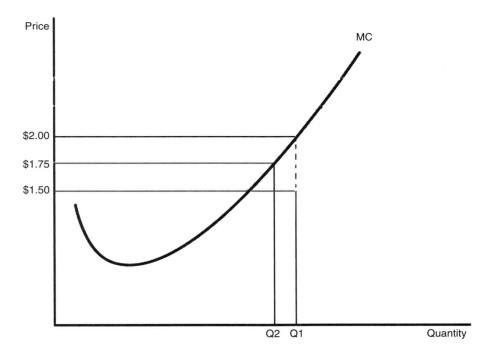

Figure 9.1B Marginal Cost Curve for Hot Dog Stand. If consumers are not willing to pay a price at least as great as the marginal cost, each vendor will want to reduce his output. However, when all vendors produce less, their costs for raw materials will decrease and the marginal cost of a hot dog will fall for each vendor as he reduces output from Q1 to Q2. At Q2, price will equal marginal cost and the vendor will not want to reduce output any further.

perfectly allocated that no shift of resources is possible without reducing the satisfaction of at least one consumer.

Market Failure and the Public Sector

In the real world, however, conditions for Pareto optimality are rarely attained. Indeed, under many normal conditions, markets fail to achieve allocative efficiency because one or another of the five assumptions of the perfectly competitive market enumerated above is violated. Indeed, there are four broad conditions under which this is true: market power, information problems, negative and positive externalities, and pure public goods. In each of these cases, government intervention may be warranted for society to get closer to an outcome more consistent with Pareto optimality.

Market Power

Perfect competition requires large numbers of buyers and sellers, just like in the hot dog vendor example. In some markets, however, there is only a handful of producers and, in some cases, only one. Patent protection, access to raw materials, or brand name identification can severely limit the number of producers of a given commodity. In these circumstances of **monopoly** or **oligopoly**—one or only a few producers in the industry, respectively—producers seeking to maximize their profit will artificially restrict output, sending prices higher than marginal cost. The purpose of government-imposed antimonopoly laws—better known as antitrust laws—is to reduce the market power of individual producers in order to expand total output and thereby lower price. Since this kind of market power often exists on a nationwide level, antitrust laws are federal laws and it is the federal government that enforces them. Using government regulation to break up monopolies and oligopolies in order to allow competing firms to enter the market normally moves the economy closer to the ideal of allocative efficiency.

But one particular form of market power arises strictly from economies of scale, where the larger the firm the lower its cost. In this case, it is more efficient in the sense of lower cost per unit—**productive efficiency** rather than allocative efficiency—for a single large firm to produce all of the output in a particular industry because only the single largest firm can produce at lowest cost. This situation is called **natural monopoly**, and it makes little sense to break up such a monopoly because this will only increase cost per unit and ultimately increase price.

In this special case, it is better for government to allow the monopoly to exist and regulate the price the monopolist can charge rather than break it up into smaller, less efficient units. **Figure 9.2** depicts a natural monopoly. Unlike the traditional U-shaped cost curve where average costs rise after a point, this cost curve declines continuously. That means the larger the firm, the lower its costs. All other firms will be run out of business if the largest firm lowers its price below the minimum point on every other firm's average cost curve. The largest firm will still make a profit as long as its price is above its own minimum average cost. Here, the large firm makes a profit of AB at the price it sets, while the smaller firm takes a loss of CD. Any small firm trying to compete with the large one will quickly go bankrupt. Knowing this, there is likely to be no upstart to challenge the acknowledged position of the natural monopolist. Note that the average total cost for a small firm in the natural monopoly industry would be higher than for the large firm. Since only one firm can be the largest and, therefore, the lowest-cost producer, this industry will ultimately have only a single firm.

Generally, natural monopolies exist where there is a large fixed cost for providing a particular service to a community but very low marginal cost of extending the service to each additional customer. Public utilities like the natural gas company fall into this category. The natural gas company needs to make an extensive investment in laying gas mains throughout a city. The marginal cost of attaching one more house to the main pipeline is trivial compared to the cost of the original main line. It makes no economic sense for a competitor to spend the enormous resources needed to construct a complete new structure of natural gas mains. Unregulated, the natural gas company could, in the short run, charge relatively high prices and customers would have no choice but to pay the price if they wanted the service. For this reason,

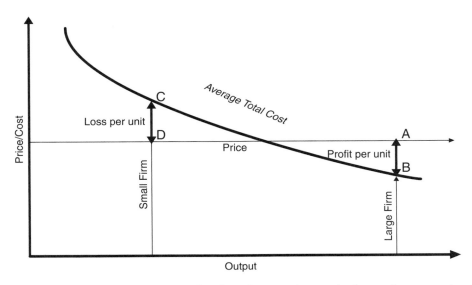

Figure 9.2 Natural Monopoly Long-Run Average Cost Curve. In a natural monopoly, there are huge economies of scale. Therefore, one large firm can produce a given level of output at lower average cost than if the same amount of output were distributed among several smaller firms. If 150,000 units of output are to be produced, for example, it would be cheaper to produce it all in one large firm than to produce it in three smaller firms, each of which could produce 50,000 units. With its lower average cost, the larger firm can be profitable at a price that causes the smaller firm, with its higher average cost, to operate at a loss. Thus, the cost shown at B for the large firm is lower than the cost C for the small firm. If the large firm charges price D, it still makes a profit equal to AB per unit, but at this price the small firm would have a loss equal to CD per unit of output.

state agencies regulate the prices that natural gas companies can charge. Over time, technology might reduce the power of such natural monopolies. The introduction of satellite-based TV, for example, provides a competitor to cable and Digital Subscriber Line (DSL) landlines, keeping prices from rising precipitously even if there is no local government regulation.

Information Problems

The model of perfect competition also assumes that the many buyers and many sellers of a particular good or service have all the information necessary to make a rational choice. This, however, is not always the case. Federal truth-in-lending, truth-in-labeling, and truth-in-advertising laws are aimed at improving information as a way of improving consumer decision making when it comes to banking services and all kinds of consumption. The detailed labeling on prepared foods is regulated right down to the font type used in the ingredients and nutrition information mandated by the federal government so that consumers can presumably make a more rational choice among products. At the city and town levels, some local newspapers routinely carry listings of restaurants cited for violating sanitary laws, along with the nature of the violation. Since consumers themselves are not always able to inspect a restaurant's kitchen, they might want to know which restaurants have been cited, and whether the violation is for improper disposal of bacon grease or for evidence of rodent infestation.

The federal government's Home Mortgage Disclosure Act of 1975 is still another example of requiring full disclosure. Banks must report the geographic location of the mortgage loans they make in a city or metro area. In this way, communities gain the information they need to determine whether banks that accept deposits within a neighborhood also make mortgage loans within that neighborhood in a fair and unbiased manner. Subsequent passage of the Community Reinvestment Act in 1977 requires that this information be taken into account when banks apply for permission to merge or acquire other financial institutions.

Negative and Positive Externalities

The model of perfect competition also assumes that all of the costs of production are borne by the producer and that all of the benefits from the consumption of a given good or service are captured by those who choose to buy it. This is the basis for our previous assertion that price is a proxy for social benefit and marginal cost is a proxy for social cost. In some cases, however, there is a discrepancy between individual and social benefit, or between individual and social cost. If price measures individual but not social benefit, or if marginal cost measures individual but not social cost, then a price equal to marginal cost will no longer represent full allocative efficiency. There will be benefits or costs not accounted for in the price of the good or service. These particular benefits and costs are called **externalities.**

Externalities can be illustrated with two examples: the case of pollution, in which there are negative externalities, and the case of elementary and secondary education, in which there are positive externalities.

Pollution: A Negative Externality.   In the late 1970s, more than a thousand households had to be evacuated and relocated from the Love Canal area of Niagara Falls, New York, because dangerous toxic wastes from chemicals dumped there in the 1940s by the Hooker Chemical Corporation had begun seeping into their basements. Love Canal alerted many cities and towns to the problem of toxic waste and, since then, thousands of other urban toxic waste sites have been discovered. While some, like Love Canal, date back to industrial processes of the mid-twentieth century and before, others, like those in Silicon Valley, are a product of more recent times and new industries. With twenty-eight hazardous waste sites within a 15-square-mile area, the semiconductor industry of Silicon Valley once had the highest concentration of Environmental Protection Agency Superfund sites in the country. Many have now been cleaned up as a result of government action.

When the owner of a semiconductor plant produces output, he must take into account the cost of capital, labor, and raw materials, along with any other expenses he pays "out of pocket" in order to calculate his total costs. In a perfectly competitive semiconductor market, price will adjust to the point where it just equals the marginal cost of these inputs. But, in the absence of government intervention, some of the costs of production are not counted in this calculation if the company is not forced to pay for remediating the contamination to the soil or water in the surrounding community. In the absence of government intervention, no individual producer will voluntarily take these costs into account because he needs to compete with the other producers and, consequently, he needs to keep his costs low. Therefore, the community bears these costs rather than the semiconductor firm.

In a sense, the consumers of the semiconductors gain as a result of lower prices because the cost of environmental remediation does not have to be included in the price. Essentially, the residents of the community and not the consumers of the semiconductors pay for the cost of the toxic waste. Allocative efficiency is not achieved because real resources (i.e., water and soil) are used up in production but not counted as a cost. What is more, equity considerations are violated since the consumers of semiconductors essentially pass on the social cost of production to others who do not purchase them.

Put another way, even if the semiconductor industry were perfectly competitive, and even if the market price were equal to private marginal cost, allocative efficiency would not be achieved because there is a discrepancy between private costs (those the owner takes into account) and social costs (private costs plus the cost of the negative externality). Because price covers only private costs and not social costs, it is too low, and the output of this industry is too high. The purpose of government intervention is to raise the price of the company's product and reduce the output until allocative efficiency is achieved with all costs of production borne by the consumer— in this case, the ultimate consumer of the semiconductors. This can be done by having the government prohibit the release of pollutants, require antipollution devices to be installed, mandate the company cleanup of the waste site, or require the company to purchase a pollution permit that provides the government with the revenue needed to clean up the site itself. (A graphical analysis of a negative environmental externality is provided in **Appendix A**.)

Elementary and Secondary Education: A Positive Externality.   In other cases, government intervenes because of a positive externality. Households have a stake in the education of their children. The private benefits of another year of education might include the ability of their children to obtain better jobs and perhaps an enhanced ability to contribute toward the support of their parents in old age. However, the benefits of elementary and secondary education also accrue to others outside the household. Educated citizens presumably can make better informed choices at the polls, improving the democratic process. Better educated individuals are less likely to be involved in crime, reducing the costs of robbery, burglary, and assault on others. Better educated workers are more likely to invent goods and services like cancer treatments that benefit all of society. If government did not intervene in this market, households might purchase enough education for their children to cover the private benefits, but not enough to cover the positive externalities. The price in the private market would be too high and output would be too low. The purpose of government intervention in this instance is to expand total output of education by subsidizing it.

As we pointed out in Chapter 1, in the United States, public elementary and secondary education is fully subsidized. The price to the consumer of public K–12 schooling is essentially zero. The costs are absorbed by taxpayers, including those who do not have children or whose children do not attend public schools. As Fischel (2001) argues, local property taxpayers without children in the public schools still have a pecuniary motive for supporting good-quality schools because it enhances the value of their homes, usually a major component of their wealth.

Because the positive externalities are considered to be so important, not only do we reduce the price to the consumer to zero, we also pass mandatory attendance laws that say a child must attend until he reaches a certain age—usually 17 or 18. The same logic of positive externalities applies to local public libraries, but we do not force people to use them. (A graphical analysis of education as a positive externality can be found in **Appendix B**.)

Pure Public Goods

The final category of market failure includes a very small number of goods that have some unusual characteristics. Most goods are **excludable**—if you do not pay the price, you cannot get the good. Most goods are also **rival**, Meaning that my consumption reduces what is left for you. **Pure public goods**, on the other hand, are neither; households that do not pay for a public good nevertheless receive the benefit of it, and one household's consumption of such a good does not reduce the amount left over for other households.

To illustrate the difference between pure public goods and ordinary private goods, imagine that you are at a Fourth of July celebration in a municipal park. There are vendors selling hot dogs, ice cream, and soda. These goods are ordinary private goods. You cannot get the hot dog unless you pay for it, and if there are lots of folks lined up ahead of you, the vendor might run out of hot dogs before you get to the front of the line. The hot dogs, therefore, are an excludable and rival good.

In contrast, the fireworks display later in the evening is neither excludable nor rival; once they are set off, they are there for everyone to see. An additional viewer can see the display without using any additional resources. The fireworks display is a pure public good; it would be difficult to charge the consumer a price to see the display, since the consumer knows he can see it whether he pays the price or not. If we tried to charge a price based on how much the consumer enjoyed the show, he would have every reason to conceal how much he really enjoyed it. By not revealing his true preferences for fireworks, he presumably would have to pay little or nothing for viewing them. When it comes to ordinary private goods, we automatically reveal our preferences every time we buy something. If we choose to spend $14 on a paperback book, we are saying, in effect, that we prefer that particular book to any other we could have bought at that price or less, and that we prefer spending the $14 on a book rather than anything else we could have spent it on.

For pure public goods, it is difficult or virtually impossible to get people to reveal their preferences. As a result, there is a **free rider problem**. Those who refuse to pay for a pure public good receive its benefits just as much as those who are willing to pay for it. Knowing this, however, no rational individual would contribute, and a good or service that many would want is not produced at all. In this case, it falls to government or some other nonmarket entity to provide these special goods. In Boston, for example, the Fourth of July fireworks are paid for by a wealthy philanthropist. In most other places, they are paid from the city or town budget. Other examples of pure public goods in metropolitan areas include public health, sanitation, sidewalks, and street lighting. Free or highly subsidized municipally provided WiFi (wireless fidelity) networks, currently a topic of heated debate, would also fall into this category.

A good that has the characteristics of a pure *private* good in low-density communities can become a pure *public* good as density increases. This is why the concepts of externalities and pure public goods both take on more significance in urban areas. Take fire protection, for example. Tennessee's Blount County Fire Protection District (2008) states that it receives no tax money for fighting fires and that it has served county residents since 1948 through its subscription program. For $110 a year, a household can buy fire protection for its single-family residence; a nonsubscriber would have to pay $2,200 to hire the company in the event of a fire. It operates seven fire stations and has fifty-five firefighters, some of whom work part-time. This good is excludable: If you have not paid $110 for a subscription and your house is on fire, your choice is to pay $2,200 or watch your house burn down. It is also rival: The company has a total of twenty-nine fire and emergency vehicles, but of these, only ten are engines and only one is a ladder truck. Its capacity to fight multiple fires is limited.

In a rural Tennessee county where houses are far apart from each other, this privatized firefighting service works reasonably well. If your house burns down, mine is presumably safe. But in densely packed cities in most metropolitan areas, a company that is called to protect apartment 4D, which has paid for its subscription, will most likely end up protecting apartments 3D and 5D as well, whether or not their owners have paid. The service that was excludable at low density is no longer excludable at high density. Thus, selling subscription fire protection through the private market is not viable in cities and most suburbs. Moreover, given the destruction that fire can cause in densely populated areas, municipalities often have reciprocal agreements with each other so that neighboring fire departments will be called in when necessary, substantially improving their ability to fight multiple fires and reducing the problem of rival goods.

While we can think of goods that fall at either end of the excludable/rival spectrum as pure public goods or pure private goods, there are also some goods that fall into a gray area in between. One example are goods that themselves are excludable and rival, but for which some consumers might have only a "standby" demand—they do not use the good regularly, but place some value on knowing it will be there should they want or need to use it in the future. In essence, the demand for the continued availability of a good on the part of nonusers makes it a public good. This so-called **option value** is the pure public good aspect of a good that is otherwise excludable and rival. Consumers who have never been to Yellowstone National Park, never used a public hospital emergency room, or never traveled on their city's buses still likely have a stake in making sure these entities continue to exist, should they want or need to avail themselves of them in the future (Weisbrod 1964). This option value bestows on such services the characteristics of a pure public good. All kinds of urban services fall into this category, from police services to public-sector emergency medical technicians.

Motorists in cities with good public transportation might use the bus or subway only when road conditions are dangerous, if their car is in the shop for repairs, or if they are going downtown where parking is very expensive—or perhaps not at all. While actually using public transportation is excludable (you must pay the fare) and rival (if the trolley is too crowded, you might have to wait for the next one), the continued availability of the service, especially if it would be difficult to start up again once it has been shut down and the tracks have been paved over, is non-excludable and nonrival. The implication of this is that the revenue collected from the fare box does not represent the entire demand for the good, since it does not include the option value or standby demand for the good on the part of nonusers. This option value of keeping the system available even when not fully used is just one reason for subsidizing the public transportation system. You may never need the entire array of urban public services, but having them available if you ever do gives greater security of mind. For this reason, most people will be willing to pay taxes to make sure these public goods are available.

In Chapter 10, where we discuss urban transportation, we shall see that there are at least two other reasons for public subsidies of mass transit—one that has to do with reducing congestion on highways and the other with the negative externalities from automobile exhaust fumes.

Government and the Distribution of Well-Being

While governments within a metropolitan area are primarily concerned with their role in allocation and dealing with market failure, differences in spending patterns from one jurisdiction to another can carry important implications for household well-being. One municipality might subsidize marinas for yachts, while another subsidizes adult literacy programs. The Parks Department in one city might focus on the centrally located facilities visited by tourists, while another emphasizes services within the neighborhoods that are located far off the tourist routes. Likewise, the public library budget might be skewed in favor of the main research library in one city, but emphasize the children's rooms in the branch libraries in another. Any given expenditure made for the purpose of allocation will almost invariably have consequences for how the costs and benefits of public services are distributed.

A similar argument can be made at the state level. For example, one state might subsidize higher education primarily through supporting a prestigious flagship campus with its research and graduate programs, while another focuses its support at the community college level. Since students from poorer households are likely to attend community colleges and those from wealthier households are likely to attend the flagship campus, the impact of higher education on income inequality will be very different in these two states.

Although the pattern of state and local spending on goods and services has an impact on the distribution of household well-being, most of the programs that are primarily redistributive in nature are the responsibility of the federal government. While markets do some things very well—for example, conveying consumer tastes and preferences to producers—they cannot guarantee that every household will have an income sufficient to support itself. Incomes earned in the market depend primarily on the quantity and quality of productive resources each household owns. A household in which everyone is disabled, old, or poorly educated is not likely to command many economic resources and will therefore have low (or no) income. As a society, however, we do not expect elderly disabled people to rely solely on income they have earned. We transfer additional income to them through a number of federal programs, from supplementary security income to food stamps and housing vouchers. The distribution role of government is to change the distribution of well-being that the market would otherwise produce.

The Debate over the Scope of Government Intervention

Economists often emphasize the degree to which competitive forces influence markets, but most would also agree that market failure occurs in the case of market power, imperfect information, externalities, and pure public goods. Economists do not agree about what should be done, whether government intervention is always necessary, or what the nature of that intervention should be. Similarly, there is great disagreement as to how much the government should be involved in "redistributing well-being" through the provision of free or low-cost public services that are funded out of tax revenues.

In this hotly contested area, a few economists believe it is better to suffer some loss in allocative efficiency and higher consumer prices than to resort to the red tape of government bureaucracy. Some believe that strict market regulation is needed, and still others think that carefully constructed regulation, tax, and subsidy programs can deal best with market failure and the distribution of well-being.

Conservative economists, following the lead of the late Nobel Laureate Milton Friedman (2002), concede the need for government intervention on allocative grounds, but only in the case of extraordinarily large externalities or in the rare case of such pure public goods as national defense, local police, and local fire protection. Even when they deem it necessary for government to act, Friedman and others favor reliance on private market forces as much as possible.

Consider the case of elementary and secondary education. Friedman agreed that there are strong positive externalities and that the market left to its own devices will produce too little. He agreed that government needs to subsidize the consumption of education as a way of lowering its price to consumers and expanding the amount of schooling consumed. He did not, however, believe that government needs to or should produce education services itself through public schools. Instead, he recommended that families with school-age children be given education vouchers by local school districts that can be used to purchase the education of their choice from what he expected would be a growing cadre of private schools. His goal was to preserve the private-market mechanism in the production of education, even as he acknowledged the need for government intervention in the financing of elementary and secondary schooling.

While conservatives generally endorse strict limits on the scope of government activity, liberals tend to argue that there is an imbalance between the relative affluence we see in private consumption and the relative deprivation we see in the public sector: fancy new cars riding over potholed streets; well-equipped campers staying overnight in poorly maintained national and state parks; and the failure of our society to deal with the chronic problems of poverty, hunger, and homelessness. An eminent liberal scholar like the late John Kenneth Galbraith (1998), a contemporary of the conservative Friedman, often endorsed an expanded role for government, and one that was more actively committed to the redistribution of well-being. He would want to ensure, for example, that public schools are well financed, that school resources are equitably shared across school districts, that police and fire services are equally provided in rich and poor neighborhoods, and that other forms of inequality be rectified by appropriate government spending. Liberals like Galbraith strongly favor universal programs funded by government, such as national health insurance.

Another controversial area of government intervention involves those instances in which government decision makers substitute their judgment for the judgment of consumers. Forcing people to put aside money for their retirement through the Social Security system is just one example; another is prohibiting consumers from doing something they otherwise would do, like using marijuana for medicinal or other purposes. Those, like Friedman, who criticize intervention in this category call it **paternalism**, and argue that adults of sound mind should be free to make their own decisions. Those who endorse intervention in this category call it **merit wants**, and argue that people do not always know what is good for them, are not always rational actors, and will sometimes choose something that gives them short-term pleasure over long-term prudence.

Recently, for example, New York City, Philadelphia, and several other municipalities have banned restaurants from using the trans fats (partially hydrogenated oils that contribute to obesity and other serious health problems) that are often an easy way to enhance the flavor of food. Other items in this category include local or state laws that mandate the use of helmets for motorcyclists or a local ordinance that prohibits the sale of alcohol within a municipality. Not too long ago, some cities and towns had "blue laws" that prohibited stores from opening on Sundays in order to give workers the day off to observe the Christian Sabbath.

Although there is disagreement about the scope and nature of government intervention, and although the preferred size of government might vary according to the political predilections of different economists, it is nevertheless true that even the minimalists would acknowledge the need for government to absorb some tasks that the market is incapable of doing. Moreover, conservatives argue that if government is to be involved in the production of goods or the regulation of markets, it is best to have this occur at the local level rather than state or federal. The argument here is that with tens of thousands of municipal governments, the local public sector is more like the private market. With local governments providing variations in the specific range and extent of public goods, consumers can "vote with their feet" for the public services they want by moving to towns or cities that offer the combination of services they prefer. With only fifty states, there is less variation in state policies and, of course, there is only one at the federal level. Conservatives would therefore argue that the public sector should be strictly limited and, where necessary, production or regulation should occur at the lowest possible level of government. With the exception of national defense, a national currency, and perhaps a national highway system, conservatives want to see cities and towns as the focus for whatever services need to be supplied by the public sector.

Market Failure and the Alternatives for Providing Goods and Services

As we have seen, if the competitive market mechanism is operating correctly—meaning that no firm has any power to set price, that there are no information problems, no externalities, and that these are pure private goods (excludable and rival)—unregulated private markets will operate effectively. However, in the case of market failure, there are alternatives for how government should intervene. These include:

- allowing a private market to operate, but under regulations set by government;
- providing public funding for goods and services produced by the private sector; and
- having the public sector produce the output itself.

Regulated Private Markets

In the case of natural monopoly, where it is more efficient to have one firm produce the entire output because of economies of scale, it is typical for U.S. cities to grant a franchise to a private firm but then place limits on the firm's behavior. Your local natural gas company, for example, would need to seek government approval if it wanted to raise its prices or expand its operations. Earlier in the twentieth century, other public utilities—such as the electric and telephone companies—were also natural monopolies subject to regulation. As the technology changed, however, it was possible to introduce competition into the markets for local and long-distance telephone service.

The market for electricity is in the midst of a transition: The firm that delivers electricity to your home is still a publicly owned company or natural monopoly subject to regulation, but increasingly these distribution monopolies purchase their electricity from numerous private companies that generate the electricity and supply it to the single company in town that owns the electric power grid. While regulation of private companies has been the norm in the United States, public provision of these services has been more common in Europe. Even in the United States, though, 251 cities and towns still have municipally owned electric companies, including Anaheim, California; Braintree, Massachusetts; Chattanooga, Tennessee; and San Antonio, Texas (Utility Connection 2007).

Public Funding/Private Provision

As we have seen, even most "free market" economists who follow in the tradition of Milton Friedman believe that primary and secondary education should be subsidized because of the substantial level of positive externalities they offer. The private market, left to its own devices, would not produce enough education. But Friedman and others believe that households should receive **education vouchers** that they can use to purchase education from private companies rather than relying on the public sector itself to produce the educational services. Other instances where we use vouchers of one sort or another to expand the consumption of goods with positive externalities include: the food stamp program to subsidize good nutritional practices and housing voucher programs such as Section 8, which permit low-income households to purchase better housing than they could on the basis of their own income. In these instances, the role of government is to subsidize some form of desired behavior while still allowing consumers to make their choices in the context of competitive markets.

Public Provision

For most of the twentieth century, many municipal services were seen as natural monopolies that should be owned and operated by the city itself. This was true of sanitation workers, teachers, and social workers, just like police and firefighters. It was also seen as natural and normal that government was responsible for building, operating, and maintaining highways. Recently, however, the notion of "privatization" (which we discuss more fully later in this chapter) has been gaining ground. In many cities, the government has signed contracts with private sanitation companies; in a few cases, such as the Chicago Skyway and the Indiana Toll Road (Poole and Samuel 2006), governments have granted long-term leases to private companies who then operate and maintain these highways. Nonetheless, while the ranks of municipal workers might shrink as privatization takes hold, it is difficult to imagine a time when most elementary and secondary schoolteachers, librarians, police, and firefighters would not be employees of local governments. While highways might be operated by private companies that charge tolls, it is unlikely that cities or towns would sell off their local streets and roads—at least until a time when technology might allow every car and truck to have a Global Positioning System (GPS)–

enhanced transponder that could keep track of mileage and charge for the use of these public goods.

Local Government Employment and Spending Patterns

To get some idea of the size of the municipal sector needed to provide the local public services we enjoy, one can look at the number of workers that local governments directly employ. As **Table 9.1** demonstrates, in 2004, the number nationwide was more than 10 million. Approximately one out of every thirteen workers in the United States works for a municipality. Of this total number, more than 60 percent work in local schools as teachers, counselors, principals, janitors, and secretaries. On this measure, public education is clearly the number-one task of local governments (U.S. Bureau of the Census 2007). Employment-wise, the other top local government services are police protection, general government administration, and public hospitals.

Information on local employment is only part of the picture, however. In addition to those public-sector functions that are largely provided by workers employed by cities and towns, local governments also purchase an extensive array of services from the private sector. This is illustrated in **Table 9.2**, which lists the major categories of local government spending. Altogether, between their direct production of services and their purchases from the private sector, city and town expenditures equal about 10 percent of the nation's gross domestic product (GDP)—about $1.3 trillion out of a nearly $13 trillion GDP in 2004–2005.

By far, the largest single expenditure of municipal government is for public education. Across all cities and towns, nearly 39 percent of the budget is spent on public schools, with close to 1 percent going for public libraries. Almost 11 percent is spent on social services and specific income maintenance programs for low-income residents. Public safety expenditures take about 9 percent of local budgets,

Table 9.1 Local Government Full-Time Equivalent Employees by Selected Function, March 2004

Elementary and Secondary Education	6,422,900
Higher Education	316,400
Public Welfare	272,500
Health	249,900
Hospitals	513,300
Highways	303,000
Police Protection	789,500
Fire Protection	319,000
Corrections	241,500
Parks and Recreation	227,360
Government Administration	690,100
Total	**10,345,400**

Source: U.S. Bureau of the Census 2007, table No. 454, "State and Local Government Full Time Equivalent Employment by Selected Function and State: 2004."

Table 9.2 Local Government Direct General Expenditure by Function, 2004–2005 (Thousands of Dollars)

Function	Local Expenditure	Percent
Total direct expenditures	**1,313,749,897**	**100.0**
Education services	**506,821,644**	**38.6**
Education	497,426,812	
Capital outlay	57,121,286	
Libraries	9,394,832	
Social services and income maintenance	**141,512,479**	**10.8**
Public welfare	44,712,587	
Cash assistance payments	9,278,172	
Vendor payments	4,539,917	
Other public welfare	30,894,498	
Hospitals	60,989,787	
Capital outlay	3,789,141	
Health	35,804,607	
Employment Security Administration	5,498	
Transportation	**69,271,086**	**5.3**
Highways	48,112,256	
Capital outlays	18,106,383	
Air transportation (airports)	17,031,470	
Parking facilities	1,387,197	
Sea and inland port facilities	2,740,163	
Public safety	**122,208,856**	**9.3**
Police protection	64,662,110	
Fire protection	30,738,976	
Corrections	20,885,203	
Capital outlay	1,131,626	
Protective inspection and regulation	4,790,941	
Environment and housing	**87,954,105**	**6.7**
Natural resources	7,441,012	
Capital outlay	1,740,668	
Parks and recreation	27,393,496	
Capital outlay	7,275,971	
Housing and community development	35,037,331	
Sewerage	35,254,120	
Capital outlay	13,616,183	
Solid waste management	18,082,266	
Capital outlay	1,527,127	
Government administration	**108,037,829**	**8.2**
Financial administration	15,504,700	
Judicial and legal	18,380,144	
General public buildings	8,932,466	
Other governmental administration	18,603,055	
Interest on general debt	46,617,464	
General expenditure	**230,527,369**	**17.5**
Utility expenditures (water, electricity, gas)	134,510,376	
Insurance trust expenditures (unemployment, pensions, etc.)	27,567,072	
Miscellaneous commercial activities	2,796,868	
Other and unallocated	65,653,053	

Source: U.S. Bureau of the Census 2006, table 1, "State and Local Government Finances by Level of Government and by State: 2004–2005."

with more than half of this amount slated for police protection. A little more than 8 percent is for general government administration. The rest is scattered across a range of services that include transportation (5.3%) and environment and housing (7%), and a large general expenditures category that includes spending on utilities and various local commercial activities (17.5%).

Note that in Table 9.2, about 12 percent of local government spending on education—more than $5.7 billion out of $497 billion—was for capital outlay. This was for the construction of new schools and major renovations of older ones. Six percent of local government hospital expenditures—$3.8 billion out of $61 billion—was spent on capital projects, as were portions of the expenditures on corrections, natural resources, parks and recreation, sewerage, and solid waste management. This investment in new or updated infrastructure is usually contracted out to private construction companies.

Privatization

As noted earlier, local governments play three roles in relation to the market—as direct service providers, as regulators of private-sector activity to adjust the quantity of some good or service and assure its quality, and as purchasers of services provided by private firms. The last of these—contracting out—can be economically appealing if a local government can achieve the same quantity and quality of services at lower cost, draw upon specialized experience, or benefit from scale economies in conjunction with bulk purchases along with other local governments. The recipients of contracts might include other government agencies (including regional agencies), private for-profit firms, or private nonprofit firms.

According to data collected by the International City/County Management Association (ICMA) (2002), approximately 52 percent of local services are provided entirely by local government employees. Among the remaining 48 percent, 23 percent are provided by a mix of local public employees who work with employees from private firms or public employees who work for a regional, county, state, or federal agency. The remaining 25 percent of "public" services are provided by private firms directly or by federal, state, county, or regional government agencies. The most common contractors in 2002 were private for-profit firms, used alone or in concert with local public employees for 18 percent of local services. Next were intergovernmental contracting firms at 17 percent and private non-profit firms at 8 percent. Other forms of service provisions, including franchises, vouchers, and volunteers, accounted for the remaining 4 percent of local services.

Beginning in the late 1980s, there was increased advocacy for **privatization**, under which operations once carried out by public agencies are transferred to the private sector. Along with other economists and political scientists, David Osborne and Ted Gaebler, in their influential book *Reinventing Government* (1992), argued that there are actual incentives for inefficiency in public bureaucracies. For example, an agency that is able to reduce its costs might not do so because it fears that its budget would then be reduced. Therefore, Osborne and Gaebler argue that at least some public services could be produced at lower cost by private firms in a competitive market, and that the size of government in general should be reduced.

Privatization can take several forms that include not only contracting out for services but also eliminating regulations that effectively prevent private firms from competing, subsidizing vouchers for private citizens to use as an alternative or replacement for publicly provided services, eliminating some public-sector service provision so that those who want it must turn to private providers, and selling or leasing public sites to private companies (Starr 1988).

In an analysis of the ICMA data for 1992, 1997, and 2002, Warner and Hefetz (2004) find that the use of private for-profit firms for services has increased slightly from 16 percent of local services in 1992 to 18 percent in 2002. Private firms are now being used for waste collection, street repair, tree trimming and planting, vehicle towing, the disposal of hazardous materials, legal services, and building and grounds maintenance. The use of private non-profit organizations has increased from 7 percent of local services in 1992 to 8 percent in 2002, with the most common areas of service being transit, health, arts and culture, and museums. Mixed public/private provision showed the greatest increase, growing from 17 percent in 1992 to 23 percent in 2002. Primary areas were street repair, programs for the elderly, tree trimming and planting, arts and culture, and fleet management/vehicle maintenance.

The areas least likely to be contracted out were administrative support functions, crime and fire prevention, traffic control, snow plowing and sanding, water treatment and distribution, and the operation of recreation centers. Notably, however, over this same period, 22 percent of local governments reported that they brought services back in-house that they had previously contracted out. The major reasons were poor quality of service rendered under private contracts, failure of anticipated cost savings to materialize, and improvements in the internal efficiency of the local government.

The choice and success of service delivery mechanisms appear to be influenced by several factors. In many cases, market competition did not exist because of the small number of possible providers. This indicates that the possibilities for privatization depend upon local-market-specific conditions, including the presence of competition in the private market and the degree of expertise that is available there.

The choice of service delivery mechanism also depends upon the degree of in-house expertise and available technology. Warner and Hefetz note that some governments privatize services that involve new skills or the need to supply a high volume of goods or services beyond the capacity of the local government. They contract out initially and then bring the service delivery in-house when the expertise, technology, or staff training becomes available internally.

Contracting out, as opposed to cessation of service delivery altogether, requires local government contract management and monitoring, the costs of which need to be weighed against anticipated savings from the service delivery itself. While there is some theoretical justification for privatization, the actual experience has been mixed.

Paying for Government Services

As we have seen, local governments provide an array of essential services. How do they pay for these services? Generally speaking, local governments receive revenue from two sources: (1) taxes and fees levied by the local government itself, and (2) revenues transferred to city and town coffers from either state or federal sources. As **Table 9.3** reveals, in fiscal year 2004–2005, a little more than a third of local revenue (34.5%) came from intergovernmental transfers, with the bulk of that local aid coming from the state rather than the federal government (U.S. Bureau of the Census 2006). The other two-thirds (65.5%) was raised from local sources with 54.2% coming from general revenues and 11.3% coming from specific revenue streams related to unemployment insurance, employee retirement funds, and workers' compensation programs.

Of all own-source general revenue (taxes and fees levied by the municipality itself), 63 percent came from various local taxes, while the remainder came from charges and fees paid by students in local community colleges, patients in city-owned hospitals, passengers using city-owned airports, and commuters using municipal parking garages.

Table 9.3 Local Government General Revenue, 2004–2005 (Thousands of Dollars)

	Local Government Revenue	As Percent of Total Revenue	As Percent of Own-Source Revenue	As Percent of Own-Tax Revenue
Total revenue from all sources	$1,307,002,281	100.0		
General revenue (total)	1,160,395,873			
Intergovernmental revenue	451,494,652	34.5		
From federal government	52,128,887	11.5		
From state government	399,365,765	88.5		
General revenue from own sources	708,901,221	54.2	100.0	
Taxes	448,273,481		63.2	100.0
Property	324,328,967			72.3
Sales and gross receipts	71,830,490			16.0
Individual income	20,675,556			4.6
Corporate income	4,446,941			1.0
License taxes	1,433,269			0.3
Other taxes	25,558,258			5.7
Charges and miscellaneous fees	260,627,740		36.8	
Current charges	185,454,628			
Miscellaneous	75,173,112			
Nongeneral (specific-use) revenues	151,901,994	11.3		
Utility revenue	99,164,647			
Insurance trust revenue	46,571,768			

Source: U.S. Bureau of the Census 2006, table 1, "State and Local Government Finances by Level of Government and by State: 2004–2005."

By far the most important source of tax revenue is generated from residential, industrial, and commercial property. Nationwide, revenue from the local property tax comprises nearly three-fourths (72.3%) of locally raised taxes. Local sales and gross receipt taxes make up pretty much the rest of the tax revenue stream for cities and towns, with local individual income taxes making up less than 5 percent of municipal tax revenue given that only a few major cities levy this form of tax. The remaining 7 percent come from a mix of restaurant taxes, hotel room taxes, licensing fees, and, in a few cases, a small corporation income tax. In contrast, most state governments rely heavily on sales taxes and income taxes, while the federal government relies heavily on the federal income tax, corporation income taxes, and taxes related to Social Security and Medicare.

In the last decades of the twentieth century, the proportion of local general revenue received through the property tax has declined, as has the proportion received through federal aid. The proportion received through state aid has grown slightly nationwide, and there has been an increased reliance on user charges (fees that vary according to the quantity used by each consumer, like water bills based on meters that gauge actual consumption). This is illustrated in **Figure 9.3.**

Tannenwald (2001) offers several reasons to explain why the proportion of general revenue received from property taxes has fallen. One is the success of **tax revolt** referenda such as California's Proposition 13 in 1978 and Massachusetts's Proposition 2½ in 1980, which limited the tax rates and amount of revenue that local areas could collect through property taxes. Another is the shift in the composition of business assets, as the economy continues not only to evolve away from the production of goods to the production of services but also to evolve within industries

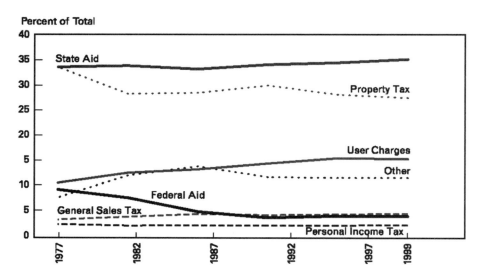

Figure 9.3 The Mix of Local General Revenues, 1977–1999. *Note:* The "Other" category consists of selective sales tax, corporate income tax, motor vehicle license tax, other taxes, and miscellaneous revenue. *Source:* Tannenwald 2001, figure 3, p. 30.

toward knowledge-based production. As a result, intangible assets (e.g., patents, databases, software, formulas, and trademarks) are growing both in importance and as a proportion of all business assets. However, intangible assets like these are not subject to property taxation. Thus, this shift in the mix of business assets has hampered growth in the property tax base. Finally, when municipalities offer location incentives for the purpose of stimulating economic development, they are often in the form of property tax relief. In fiscal year 2000, New York City estimates that the property tax relief it offered to spur economic development amounted to 7 percent of citywide property tax revenue—hardly an insignificant amount in a city filled with skyscrapers (Tannenwald 2001).

Income and Sales Taxes Levied by Local Governments

Whether a municipality will be allowed to use income taxes or sales taxes is a matter for each state to determine. Some states, including Michigan, New Jersey, New York, and Pennsylvania, allow local governments to employ property taxes, income taxes, and sales taxes. Others, including Arizona, California, Florida, North Carolina, and Washington, do not allow local governments to employ income taxes, but they do allow them to use property taxes and sales taxes. A third group, including Connecticut, Massachusetts, New Hampshire, and Rhode Island, limits local government almost exclusively to the use of property taxes (Bluestone, Clayton-Matthews, and Soule 2006). Cities and towns are chartered by the state government, which normally has the right to decide what types of taxes and sometimes even the tax rates that local governments may charge.

If a municipality can employ income or sales taxes, not only does it have more options for the manner in which to collect taxes, but it can also take advantage of other potential benefits. In periods of economic growth, receipts from income and sales taxes will rise automatically, while property tax receipts might respond more sluggishly or be dependent on periodic reassessments. Using sales or income as a tax base allows the municipality to tax nonresidents who work or shop within its boundaries and thereby benefit from some of the public-sector services it provides. However, if a municipality enacts a local income or sales tax when its neighbors do not, it risks driving residents and business firms to those neighboring jurisdictions (Peterson 1981).

Pricing in the Public Sector

As we have seen in this chapter, the economic role of government in a market economy is often in response to one form of market failure or another. When the private sector finds it difficult to supply particular goods and services—or to provide them in the right amounts—the responsibility for their provision often falls to the public sector. The ability of the public sector to solve the inherent problems in providing these goods and services is neither easy nor automatic.

What criteria should be used in determining an appropriate pricing strategy for publicly provided goods and services? It is a complicated question. We will use the example of whether to charge cars a toll for crossing a bridge under three different scenarios to illustrate the kinds of economic questions that must be resolved. But first we need to understand the economics of building the bridge.

A Primer on the Economics of Building and Paying for Bridges

Several years ago, Robert Redford directed a movie called *A River Runs Through It.* That title is an apt description of many major cities worldwide, especially those that developed during the centuries of water-based transportation. Some bridges might span relatively narrow channels and be easily crossed on foot, like many of the picturesque bridges in the centers of European cities. Others might traverse wider distances, such as the famed Golden Gate Bridge in San Francisco or the Verrazano Narrows Bridge between the boroughs of Brooklyn and Staten Island in New York City.

When a bridge is to be built, the expectation is that it will last for many generations. It is therefore appropriate to raise the revenue to pay for its construction by issuing bonds—that is, by borrowing the money now and paying it back with interest over many decades. The reason bond financing is appropriate in this instance is that if the bridge will be rendering service to future generations, it is only fair to have future generations shoulder some of the costs. In contrast, such financing would be inappropriate as a way for a city to pay for treating itself to a lavish two hundredth birthday bash. If the only ones who benefit from this celebration are those currently alive, it would be unfair to ask future generations to pay for any of those costs. This illustrates the notion of **intergenerational equity** or fairness with respect to how the costs of providing a service are divided across different generations. Costs imposed on future generations should be commensurate with benefits received by them. Municipal bonds are an appropriate way to finance long-term capital projects, but they are not an appropriate way to finance short-term consumption.

Let us assume we have issued bonds to pay for the bridge, and now we need to raise funds each year to pay for the debt service. What are our choices? Do we raise the money by charging a toll? Do we just take it out of general tax revenue? The conventional wisdom, often seen expressed in letters to the editor, is that tolls are justified when there are bonds to be paid off, but unjustified otherwise. As we will see, the conventional wisdom is wrong. Economic theory tells us that under some circumstances, even if there are bonds to be paid off, it would be better to raise the revenue from general taxation than to charge a toll. Conversely, under other circumstances, it would be desirable to charge tolls even on bridges whose bonds have been paid off long ago. This applies not only to bridges but also, of course, to tunnels and highways.

To get a better understanding of why the conventional wisdom is wrong, we will describe three different scenarios with regard to the circumstances that affect an automobile about to cross a bridge. In the first scenario, the bridge is not crowded and is used by a cross-section of the population. In the second scenario, the bridge is again not crowded, but it is used primarily by higher-income households. In the third scenario, we look at crowded bridges, a familiar situation in many metropolitan areas.

Scenario 1: Uncrowded Bridge Used by a Cross-Section of the Population. As we saw earlier in this chapter, the criterion for allocative efficiency is that price should equal marginal cost. If the cost of allowing one more car to cross the bridge (marginal cost) is zero—ignoring the trivial amount added to the wear and tear on the bridge's road surface—then it follows that the toll (price) should be zero. The rationale is that if the presence of a toll deters even one motorist from crossing the bridge when it does not actually diminish any of society's resources to allow the crossing, a misallocation has occurred. The misallocation might occur because the motorist takes a less direct route, thereby diminishing society's resources by using up more gasoline and putting more pollutants into the air. The misallocation might also occur if the motorist's response to the toll is not to make the trip at all. For example, students with limited resources might decide on less frequent visits to their great-grandmothers, who live in nursing homes on the other side of the bridge. Again, the allocation (efficiency) criterion would say not to charge a toll and pay the debt service on any outstanding bonds out of general tax revenue.

Scenario 2: Uncrowded Bridge Used Primarily by Higher-Income Households. On pure allocation (efficiency) grounds, the story remains the same, even if all the cars crossing the bridge are those of wealthy families: If an extra bridge crossing does not use up any of society's resources, the toll should be zero and any debt service should be paid from general tax revenue. However, the story now becomes more complicated because one might want to take into account how the bridge affects the distribution of well-being. In Michigan, for example, the Mackinac Bridge connects the state's Upper and Lower Peninsulas. The Upper Peninsula is a place of great natural beauty, and many of the Lower Peninsula motorists who cross the bridge are vacationers with incomes above the state's median. To pay for the debt service from general tax revenue would mean that lower-income households who do not use the bridge would wind up subsidizing the vacations of the higher-income households who do. In effect, the real distribution of income would become even more unequal, since taxes would be collected from all segments of the income distribution, but benefits would be concentrated at the high end of the distribution.

The quandary for policy makers is that on allocation/efficiency grounds, the toll should be zero, but on distribution/equity grounds, to pay the debt service from general tax revenue would be inequitable. This is just one of many examples in which the criteria of equity and efficiency conflict. Economic theory gives no guidance here about which criterion should be a higher priority. It becomes a matter of judgment on the part of policy makers, and they are the ones who must decide which of the two criteria is more important in each instance. In the case of the Mackinac Bridge, the Michigan state legislature chose equity over efficiency and imposed a hefty toll.

This lesson does not apply solely to bridges, tunnels, and highways. How much should an individual pay to check out a library book, go to a public college or university, or pay for a rescue service? Often, we think that government redistributes benefits mainly from richer families to poorer ones, but that is not always the case. Take public higher education, for instance. Most of the students who go to public universities and colleges in the United States come from middle- and upper-income families. Yet we subsidize all in-state residents who go to these schools by having the government pay for a large share of higher education costs. This means that many poor people who never take advantage of public universities and colleges end up paying for them through state sales or income taxes or through local property taxes. Similarly, the U.S. Coast Guard rescues thousands of stranded boaters a year, including some on million-dollar yachts. We all pay for this service through our taxes, but only a fraction of us own boats. What is fair? Economics alone does not provide an adequate answer.

Scenario 3: Crowded Bridge.   Distribution issues aside, there is still another scenario we need to consider and, here, economists are a bit more helpful. For those of us who live in large metropolitan areas, the idea of an uncrowded bridge conjures up a certain quaintness outside of our own everyday experience, but applicable perhaps to the beautiful covered bridges of rural New England. In contrast, our own experience is more likely to include bridges so crowded that traffic generally moves very slowly, except for those times when it comes to a complete standstill. How does our analysis change when the bridge is crowded?

First of all, it is no longer true that a car can cross the bridge without using any of society's resources. Once the bridge approaches its capacity—defined here as the number of cars per hour that can travel across the bridge while maintaining some minimum rate of speed, say 25 miles per hour—another car trying to cross will slow things down further. As traffic slows to a crawl, individual motorists experience higher costs, including the rush-hour wear and tear on themselves and their vehicles, the value of the extra time spent in traffic, and the extra gasoline used up while idling or driving at very low speeds.

In addition to the costs borne by the individual motorist, there are also external costs imposed on others. Nearby residents may suffer higher rates of respiratory disease because of the impact of highly concentrated auto emissions on deteriorated air quality. Employers and coworkers may suffer reduced productivity because of the tardiness of the worker delayed by traffic or the distracted state of mind of the one who arrives after a particularly difficult commute. To the extent that the rush-hour motorist imposes costs on others, the additional cost to society of allowing an extra car to cross the bridge is far above zero, and the price (toll) should be commensurate with that cost. The justification for a congestion toll is that motorists should confront the actual cost of their choices. If the toll deters some motorists from driving during rush hour, it is having its intended impact. Whether the bonds for the bridge have been paid off is entirely irrelevant. Explicit congestion tolls have been implemented successfully in Singapore and in central London (Transport for London 2006).

User Fees

In two of the three bridge scenarios sketched above, there was an economic justification for charging a toll. However, the justifications were very different in Scenarios 2 and 3. In the former, the toll was employed to address equity concerns; in the latter, it addressed efficiency criteria. Tolls are one category of **user fees**. Other examples of user fees are metering the use of water and charging on the basis of usage or structuring trash collection fees on a per-bag basis, rather than a flat household fee. As a growing number of communities find it politically more difficult to increase tax rates to pay for public services, there is greater interest in the employment of user fees.

Pioneers in the field of urban economics such as Wilbur Thompson (1976) and William Vickrey (1963) have long argued that price should play a greater role in the provision of public-sector services. Of course, there are some limits: User fees cannot be employed for pure public goods. For example, we cannot pay for national defense through user fees because, as we saw earlier in this chapter, it would be difficult to charge a price for this nonexcludable and nonrival good. Nor can we employ user fees for programs that have a primarily redistributive purpose. We would not want to pay for Supplementary Security Income by charging a price to the elderly poor, since the whole point of the program is to transfer additional income to them.

There are many other instances, though, where the employment of user fees can ameliorate existing income inequalities, promote a better allocation of resources, or do both (Starn 1994). At the local municipal level, most large cities and towns have installed parking meters to ration the number of parking spaces on city streets. Many cities impose a user fee whenever a building permit is issued, presumably to help cover the cost of building inspections. In some states, local communities collect an annual excise tax on the value of automobiles, in part to defray the cost of maintaining city streets and roads. Some local airports charge a departure fee on every ticket to help pay for airport services. The list goes on.

The Tiebout Hypothesis

As we saw in Chapter 2, a metropolitan area describes the boundaries of a labor market, an area that is viewed as a single social and economic entity. However, that same metropolitan area may be comprised of a hundred or more different cities and towns, each with its own local government. Is this situation economically desirable or undesirable? If 100 separate municipalities within a metropolitan area are good, would 200 be even better? If 100 are too many, would the right number be fifty, twenty-five, ten, or even one? The continuing debate over a hypothesis first proposed in 1956 by Charles Tiebout (pronounced *Tee*-bo) sheds some light on these questions, even though it does not offer definitive answers.

In "A Pure Theory of Local Expenditure," Tiebout argues that it is difficult to get people to reveal their preferences for pure public goods at the national level. Why, for example, should I be forthright in saying how much I value a strong national defense if, as a result, I might be asked to pay more than others to achieve a given level of national security? At the local level, however, he argues that people reveal their preferences for locally provided pure public goods all the time. They do so by "voting with their feet"—that is, by moving from a jurisdiction whose taxing and spending programs are not a good match for a family's preferences to another jurisdiction, where the match is closer. Ideally, households would keep moving until each found exactly what it was looking for in a jurisdiction's taxing and spending policies. Families seeking high-quality public schools would move to jurisdictions known for their educational excellence, and presumably they would be willing to pay the higher local taxes required to support those schools. Those interested in municipal recreation facilities would move to a place with that emphasis in the municipality's spending pattern. Some households would choose places with higher tax rates to get a larger and better array of public services, while others seeking to minimize their local tax payments would find places with low tax rates, albeit with more limited public services.

Tiebout argues that the more jurisdictions there are within a metropolitan area, and the more different they are from each other, the more likely it is that a household will be able to maximize its satisfaction by choosing where to live from among a large variety of jurisdictions. Essentially, access to a large number of diverse cities and towns mimics the array of choices we seem to like so much when it comes to selecting goods and services in the private market.

In addition to Tiebout's economic arguments, others who argue in favor of a large number of small jurisdictions point to the greater likelihood that local government will be more accessible and more accountable to the average citizen. It is the contrast between the traditional New England town meeting that takes place in its smallest villages—perhaps the purest form of direct democracy—versus the complex bureaucracies of large cities, best reflected in that cynical and essentially hopeless phrase, "you can't fight city hall."

Every time you hear someone saying that they moved someplace because the public schools were good or the streets were kept clean, it is confirmation of Tiebout's notion that people do, indeed, vote with their feet.

Limitations in the Tiebout Hypothesis

The controversial aspect of the hypothesis is not that public-sector services have an impact on people's decisions about where to live, but that having a large array of different municipalities within a metropolitan area is therefore desirable. It turns out that for Tiebout's conclusion to be universally true—the more municipalities the better—he needed to make several rather major assumptions, some of which have been roundly criticized by his opponents.

A number of Tiebout's assumptions are standard fare in economics. For example, he assumes that people are knowledgeable about the array of choices that are available to them, and that there are many different jurisdictions from which to choose. Because he wants to abstract from other influences on the choice of jurisdiction, he assumes away the need to consider workplace location. In the real world, of course, the commute to work is a major factor that affects where households choose to locate.

Tiebout assumes that households have complete mobility and are free to move to the jurisdiction whose public-sector package best matches their preferences. As we saw in our discussion of fiscal and exclusionary zoning in Chapter 4, this is an unlikely outcome, especially for minority households and those at the lower end of the income distribution. If the means, motives, and opportunities to practice fiscal zoning and exclusionary zoning are greater in metropolitan areas with many small jurisdictions, the Tiebout solution may exacerbate inequities based on race, ethnicity, or income. This is particularly true if, in the interest of allowing municipalities the right to offer different packages of services and taxes, they are also granted local control that permits them to impose such criteria as one- or two-acre minimum zoning for single-family homes that has the effect of excluding households of modest income from moving into them.

Finally, for the hypothesis to hold, Tiebout must assume that there are no externalities between communities and no economies of scale larger than what can be captured within a single community. If there are externalities, people consume public services in several jurisdictions but express their preferences in only one. Moreover, if there are externalities between communities, rational decision making becomes more difficult to achieve.

For example, imagine that a town was considering damming up a river that routinely flooded each spring. By damming up the river, an artificial lake could be created and floods could be controlled downstream. The recreational benefits of the lake could easily be limited to town residents—only those who live in the town would be eligible to receive permits to use the lake. However, the flood control benefits could not be limited to town residents. Once the dam is built, all the other towns downstream are also protected. The flood control benefits are a pure public good. Once the dam is built, no one can be excluded.

The problem is that in deciding whether to build the dam, the town acting rationally will take into account only the costs and benefits to its own residents. The flood-control benefits to the other towns downstream are irrelevant to its decision. It therefore may decide not to build the dam, because the benefits accruing to the town do not justify the costs. In that case, it would take a higher level of government to account for all of the costs and all of the benefits. What is "external" at the level of the town may be "internal" at the level of the county or the state. The proper geographical scope for rational decision making would encompass an area large enough to "internalize the externalities." Mancur Olson (1969) calls this the "principle of fiscal equivalence," suggesting that for rational decision making at the local level, the appropriate governmental unit must be large enough to contain all the costs and all the benefits associated with the project.

Hence, the smaller the jurisdiction, the more likely it is that there will be externalities, and the shorter the list of projects for which the jurisdiction alone can make rational decisions. Also, the smaller the jurisdiction, the less likely that it will have the critical mass of people necessary to achieve economies of scale. As is currently the case with many small towns, it may have a student population sufficient to support its own elementary school, but it may have to give up its autonomy and join with other towns to achieve the critical mass of students necessary to support a regional high school.

Thus, there is a tension between the desire to maximize citizen satisfaction by having many jurisdictions and the sacrifice of efficiency when the proliferation of jurisdictions within a metropolitan area increases the likelihood that externalities will be an impediment to rational decision making and that it will be more difficult to achieve economies of scale in the provision of public services. A 1999 study by the National Research Council concludes that small-scale local governments are more efficient for services that are heavily labor-intensive and that consolidation is more efficient for the highly capital-intensive services that are the most likely to be subject to economics of scale (Altshuler et al. 1999).

Metropolitanism

The realization that jurisdictions in a metropolitan area may have more to gain from cooperating with each other (Orfield 1997; Katz and Bradley 1999) than competing with each other—as in the Tiebout model of competition—has led to a spate of proposals for ways that central cities and their surrounding suburbs could work toward common goals. This has been called **metropolitanism.** While relatively few places in North America have a metropolitan area level of government—metro Toronto and Miami-Dade County are two of the best examples—others have sought to promote greater cooperation, even while preserving traditional units of local government. The Minneapolis-St. Paul area has engaged in tax base sharing for more than two decades. In this framework, some of the tax revenue generated by new economic growth goes to the municipality in which the growth occurred, but some goes into a pool to be distributed among all the other municipalities. By this method, the benefits of growth are more evenly spread throughout the region.

In a similar manner, cities and towns have gotten together to form regionwide mass-transportation districts, regional water districts, and multijurisdictional sewerage systems. The goal is to link the utility gains from Tiebout's multiple jurisdictions with the efficiency gains from operating large public works projects and rationally internalizing various regional externalities. In this vein, the 1999 National Research Council study argues against metropolitan area government consolidation and recommends instead that state governments play a larger role in redressing issues like economic inequality and racial segregation within metropolitan areas (Altshuler et al. 1999).

Individuals, Interest Groups, and Values

Once we leave the realm of private markets, where outcomes are presumably the result of the "invisible hand," decisions about production, allocation, and equity need to be made explicitly. Therefore, we need to examine the realm of public decision making more closely.

This becomes particularly complex because cities and suburbs contain a variety of social classes, racial and ethnic groups, and individuals with a range of political agendas. Further complexity exists because among these social classes, groups, and individuals, there are differences in the power to affect public policy outcomes, stemming from economic might or political clout. How public decisions are made under such circumstances is the province of political scientists.

We are often taught in high school civics class that public decision making is fundamentally a democratic process, at least in the United States. Residents of a municipality elect their own mayor and city council, who presumably carry out the will of the majority. This may be generally true, but political theorists find many reasons why the ideal of democratic decision making diverges from the actual practice.

Public Choice Theory

One of the most widely known theories that question the democratic nature of public-sector decision making is known as **public choice theory**. First developed by James Buchanan (1949, 2003) and Buchanan and Musgrave (1999) and further refined by subsequent writers, public choice theory was designed to provide an alternative to the notion that all public-sector decision making is done in the interest of the public. Instead, the theory argues, public-sector decisions and other non-market decisions could be understood through the assumption that all individuals (including public employees) seek to maximize personal utility—the same set of behavioral assumptions that characterize many economic theories.

Although, public employees ostensibly serve the public interest, it can be difficult for citizens to adequately monitor the behavior and choices of civil servants because the citizens who have an interest in the outcomes—who are also seen as personal utility maximizers—face opportunity costs. The time and cost spent monitoring could be spent doing other important things. Consequently, there is a likelihood that a number of decisions will be made to benefit public employees' own personal interests and not the interests of the overall public. Examples of the possible effect of the divergence of personal utility from public benefit are: a school principal who hires his friends in preference to better qualified job candidates, a school district purchasing agent who buys supplies from a firm that gives him free tickets to the area's professional football games, a superintendent who transfers a good teacher as punishment for having asked a difficult question at a meeting, or a custodian who takes time off to watch the end of a baseball game. Without a good local newspaper or TV station with a mission to investigate possible abuses of public authority, there is every reason to believe that at least some abuse will take place.

Interest Groups and Elites

While public choice theory focuses on individual utility, other theorists argue that public-sector decisions can be most accurately understood by thinking about the effects of interest groups. David Truman (1951) and Earl Latham (1952), two of the pioneers of interest-group theory, believe that people tend to think of themselves as members of groups, and that groups have more power to influence public-sector decision making than individual citizens. As stated by Latham, groups "concentrate human wit, energy, and muscle . . . for the achievement of ends common to the members, and the means of achievement is the application of the power of the association to the obstacles and hindrances which block the goal." Interest-group theory perceives public-sector decision makers as subject to the competing pressures and demands of many formal and informal groups of individuals, with each group trying to persuade the decision maker to make decisions in their group's interests.

Another group of public-policy theorists argue that the best way to understand metro area public-sector decision making is through the study of local elites. While there may be many interest groups, only a few have the power to compel mayors, city councils, and town officials to make decisions consonant with the elite's interests. As articulated by Thomas Dye and Harmon Zeigler (1996), two of the principal proponents of elite theory, "Elites control more resources: power, wealth, education, prestige, status, skills of leadership. . . . Elitism implies that public policy does not reflect demands of 'the people' so much as it reflects the interests and values of elites. . . . Elitism contends that the masses have at best only an indirect influence over the decision-making behavior of elites."

Still other social scientists believe that neither individual interests nor group interests sufficiently explain decision making in the public sector or private sector. They urge a greater awareness of moral, normative, and ideological influences on public-sector decision making. In *The Moral Dimension*, economist Amitai Etzioni (1988) argues that the goals that people pursue are determined by a combination of individual interest, group interest, and partially internalized norms acquired from their surrounding communities.

Emphasizing that individuals undergo both moral and emotional development, Etzioni focuses on the ways that such ideas shape and constrain decision making. In *Studying Public Policy*, political scientists Michael Howlett and M. Ramesh (2003) also emphasize such influences: "Although efforts have been made by economists, psychologists, and others to reduce these sets of ideas to a rational calculation of self-interest, it is apparent that traditions, beliefs, and attitudes about the world and society affect how individuals interpret their interests." The key aspect of moral input into decision making, as articulated by still other social scientists is that, in contrast to a focus on individual or group well-being, moral values and norms that provide input into decision making are "held as applicable to everyone" (Kalt and Zupan 1984).

Incrementalism

Finally, two theories of public decision making emphasize the role of existing policy and the role of nonagreement in constructing policy. Charles Lindblom (1959, 1979) argues that because individuals involved in policy making typically have neither the time nor money to explore all possibilities, policies emerge from "successive limited comparisons," in which policy makers may disagree about the ultimate ends but agree about particular means or steps to be taken in the short term. Therefore, actual public policies often emerge from incrementalism "building out from the current situation, step-by-step and by small degrees." Carol Weiss (1980), on the other hand, emphasizes that policy can be shaped by numerous small decisions from different offices in an organization without full communication and analysis of the implications of decisions—a process of decision accretion. "A lot of different people, in a lot of different offices, go about their work, taking small steps without consideration of the total issue or the long-term consequences. Through a series of seemingly small and uncoordinated actions, things happen. Precedents are set, responses are generated, and over some period of time these many steps crystallize into a change in direction."

Regime Theory and Growth Machines

Each of the theories covered so far describes possible decision-making dynamics in urban areas. Furthermore, these dynamics are not all mutually exclusive. The importance of one factor relative to others may vary from one jurisdiction to another, with one municipality being more deeply affected by interest-group dynamics ("this is what would be good for *my* group") and another municipality strongly affected by normative influences ("this is the way we should treat each other"), and still another municipality greatly affected by decision accretion ("this is the way we've always done it"). Variations in the specific ways in which public policy is formulated contribute to differences among cities and suburbs in tax and budgetary priorities.

Political scientists who specifically focus on urban public-sector decision making have sought to analyze and describe ways in which these theories combine to influence the growth and well-being of urban areas. During the 1980s, Norman and Susan Fainstein and Clarence Stone developed the concept of regime theory as an explanation of decision-making patterns in metropolitan areas (Fainstein and Fainstein 1983; Stone 1989, 2005). Regime theory incorporated awareness of the potential influence of interest groups, elites, public choice theory (self-interested decision making), and norms.

As conceptualized by these theorists, regimes are coalitions of interest groups, dominated by powerful private-sector interests, elected officials, and key public-sector administrators. Regimes form because public-sector officials and private-sector groups need each other to advance their interests. A powerful business may need waivers of various regulations to build a facility; or it may want the public sector to pay for roads, water, or other infrastructure so that the business does not have to incur these costs; or it may want help to control public outcry about a contentious issue (such as damage to the environment). Public officials may need powerful private-sector support for campaign contributions, for favorable news stories in the media, or for employment after leaving office.

After recognizing opportunities for mutual gain, and forming the nucleus of a regime, the initial members of the coalition may widen the coalition to other groups, using the organizational or financial power of the initial members to gain cooperation. Regimes might affect the interests of potential groups or individuals, for example, "through the distribution of selective incentives such as contracts, jobs, facilities for a particular neighborhood, and so on" (Mossberger and Stoker 2001), or by "providing established and familiar ways of getting things done" (Stone 2005). As mentioned by Altshuler and Luberoff (2003), the regime theory literature has "observed that not all cities are governed by cohesive regimes, that regimes can fall apart, and that regimes vary in the degree to which business must share power with other local interests."

Other political scientists studying urban public-sector decision making focus more narrowly on groups with real estate development interests. Introduced by John Logan and Harvey Molotch in 1987, the concept of "growth-machines" highlights the actions of "place entrepreneurs," businesses with significant resources that stand to benefit from real estate development, and who in pursuit of this goal form alliances with others who would also benefit from the process of development (such as construction unions), or from the outcome (such as smaller businesses and property owners who would benefit from increased property values). According to Logan and Molotch, such coalitions are often able to apply significant sustained pressure on public-sector decision makers to shape decisions about the use and development of urban land, often to the detriment of less powerful residential residents and neighborhood groups (Logan and Molotch 1987).

The Challenge of Public-Sector Decision Making

Overall, public-sector decision making is the process through which needs and wants are transformed into actual public-sector goods and services. The interplay of the decision-making dynamics discussed here affect public-sector goods and services by shaping how needs are identified, how responses are designed, how taxes are determined, and how resources are channeled to specific uses in the physical and social infrastructure of the urban environment. In the end, these outcomes contribute to the uncontroversial core within Tiebout's outlook—that public-sector services have an impact on people's decisions about where to live.

Public-sector roles and specific outcomes are shaped by needs associated with market failures, but also by debates about the appropriate roles of government, by the resources available to pay for government services, by the mobility of households, and by the ways in which public decisions are made.

As we have seen, local governments play a critical role in the everyday life of virtually every individual and household in a city. And the denser the municipality in terms of population and business, the greater the number of externalities and the greater the gain from economies of scale. It is no wonder, then, that as cities grew, more and more services were supplied by the public sector, the number of public agencies expanded, and the number of public employees increased. The modern city owes as much to the public sector as to the private.

But in a highly competitive global economy, city and town officials are faced with more than simply offering services to meet the needs of households and local businesses. Increasingly, they must find a way to maintain economic activity in their jurisdictions and attract business investment in order to keep their citizens employed and public services well financed. In the chapters to come, we turn to the role of the local public sector in promoting economic development and providing for the physical and social infrastructure of cities and suburbs.

Appendix A
Negative Externalities

In 1969, the U.S. government identified Chattanooga, Tennessee, as the city with the worst air pollution in the country. Chattanooga at that time was a manufacturing city, where iron foundries and other manufacturers produced a variety of goods and shipped them out by train. While these firms produced jobs for local workers, they created numerous problems for Chattanooga-area residents. The production and distribution activities released high levels of pollutants into the air, which led to heavy smog and a high incidence of pollution-related illnesses that included tuberculosis, bronchitis, and emphysema. While firms paid for the manufacture and distribution of goods, residents paid the additional costs of these spillover effects: the medical bills, the loss of income due to illness and/or early death, the sacrifice of pollution-free vistas, and the costs of all other deleterious effects caused by the air pollution.

The graph in **Figure A9.1** depicts such a situation of divergence of private costs (the costs paid by the firms) and social costs (the sum of the firms' costs and the costs incurred by individuals who experience the firms' production externalities). At each level of output, the marginal social costs are higher than the marginal private costs paid by the firm.

A profit-seeking firm would produce at price P1 and output level Q1, where profits for the firm are maximized. That is where marginal private costs equal marginal revenue. However, at this profit-maximizing level of output for the firm, the marginal social costs are much greater than the marginal private costs that form the basis for the firms' output decisions.

Spurred by the social costs of the worsening pollution and the unflattering national recognition, local and state officials created the Chattanooga/Hamilton County Air Quality Control Bureau, which was empowered to enforce existing regulations, create new guidelines, and take other steps to improve the air quality. One of the steps taken was to confront firms with the likelihood of fines, which essentially raised the firms' costs of production if they continued to produce as they had before. Graphically, this is shown as an upward shift of the marginal private cost curve toward the marginal social cost curve.

Firms would find that their profit-maximizing output level was now lower than the initial Q1. Suppose that fines were imposed at rates such that the marginal private cost curve was brought into correspondence with the marginal social cost curve.

Then, the new profit-maximizing level of output would be Q2 at a price of P2, the point of intersection of the marginal social cost curve and the marginal revenue curve. With the full social costs paid for by the firm, the marginal private cost curve would now coincide with the marginal social cost curve.

The goal of imposing fines is often not limited to reducing production. Fines also make it relatively more profitable to introduce pollution-control devices or to substitute cleaner technology altogether. This would reduce negative externalities, which would be reflected in a downward shift of the marginal social cost curve, and a new maximizing output greater than Q2.

In Chattanooga, firms rapidly introduced filters and scrubbers, and several firms sought out new technology. Chattanooga was in compliance with Environmental Protection Agency (EPA) standards by 1981, and now prides itself on being a city where many companies have adopted and promoted low-emission technologies.

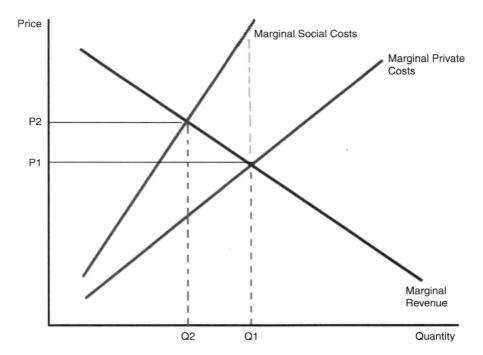

Figure A9.1 The Negative Externalities of Pollution

Appendix B
Positive Externalities

In colonial America, education was typically private, conducted within families or by a private tutor. After independence, however, many of the nation's leaders believed that effective civic participation depended upon the ability of citizens to read existing and proposed laws. These leaders became strong advocates for publicly provided schools and for compulsory attendance. This position placed them in opposition to some families and industry leaders for whom mandatory school attendance was problematic. In preindustrial times, even the youngest school-age children were old enough to be helpful in the numerous chores and income-producing activities within the home, so the opportunity costs of formal schooling for the family were high. At the dawn of the industrial age, children were often used to work in factories. Taking children out of the textile mill for compulsory schooling limited this source of cheap labor for the early industrialists. Nevertheless, public schools were established and compulsory attendance laws were passed in New England in the mid-1800s. Subsequently, laws were passed by Congress that required the western territories—and ultimately the rest of the country—to establish elementary schools. The social benefits were seen as large enough to warrant using tax dollars to pay for public education.

The divergence between private benefits and social benefits is easily visualized in **Figure A9.2** For all quantities of education, the private benefit of education is less than the social benefit, which is the sum of the private benefit plus the added benefit to society. If left to private decision making alone, the quantity of education would be Q1, obtained at a cost to families of P1. At this level, the private benefits that ensue from that level of education match the private costs that persons acting in their individual interests would be willing to pay. However, because of education's positive social externalities, the private benefit of education is less than the social benefit, as indicated in the graph. Taking into account the social benefits of schooling, public provision moves the quantity of education received out to Q2.

Externalities from education were again a major public policy focus in the late 1800s (particularly in urban areas) as immigration from southern and Eastern Europe accelerated. As noted in Chapter 3, cities were sites where people from different cultures and social allegiances came together. In this context, education held the hope not only of fulfilling the demand for expanding skills but also of influencing

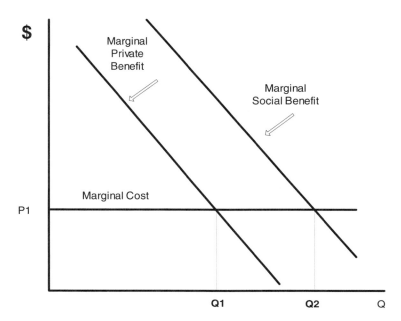

Figure A9.2 The Positive Externalities of Education

behavior, creating a base of common expectations, promoting greater cohesion, and thereby reducing social conflict. In the wake of this wave of immigration, compulsory school attendance laws were strengthened and laws banning child labor—the main source of the opportunity costs that led parents to withhold their children from school—were enacted by many city and state governments.

The depiction of this development in the graph may not be immediately apparent, but remember that economists are concerned not just with direct out-of-pocket costs but also with the relationship of those costs to opportunity costs. The increased enforcement of school attendance laws and the new bans on child labor meant that families would not benefit as much from keeping their children out of school. In effect, this meant that once these statutes were in place, the cost of school attendance (the amount given up when a child was sent to school) was less than it had been before, since now the child could not work. This can be represented as in **Figure A9.3** by a downward shift of the marginal cost curve, leading to an even greater increase in the level of education, Q3.

Currently, the rising skill requirements of a postindustrial labor force imply that the positive externalities associated with primary and secondary education are related to the need for metropolitan areas—and the nation as a whole—to have a productive workforce that is capable of competing in a worldwide economy. Increasingly, the prosperity of entire metropolitan areas depends on the skills embodied in each of their workers.

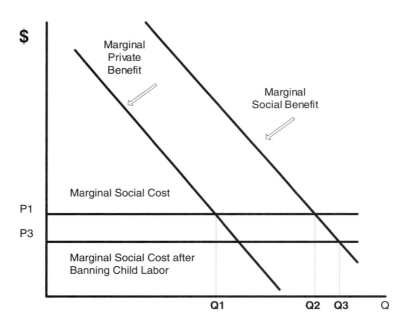

Figure A9.3 Positive Externalities of Education after Banning Child Labor

References

Altshuler, Alan, and David Luberoff. 2003. *Mega-Projects: The Changing Politics of Urban Public Investment.* Washington, D.C.: Brookings Institution Press.

Altshuler, Alan, William Morrill, Harold Wolman, and Faith Mitchell, eds. 1999. *Governance and Opportunity in Metropolitan America.* Washington, D.C.: National Academy Press.

Blount County Fire Protection District. 2008. "Subscription Form." Blount County, Tennessee. http://www.blountfire.org/.

Bluestone, Barry, Alan Clayton-Matthews, and David Soule. 2006. "Revenue Sharing and the Future of the Massachusetts Economy." Report. Boston: Center for Urban and Regional Policy, Northeastern University, January.

Buchanan, James M. 1949. "The Pure Theory of Government Finance: A Suggested Approach." *Journal of Political Economy* 57, no. 6: 496–505.

———. 2003. "Public Choice: Politics without Romance." *Policy Magazine.* Centre for Independent Studies. http://www.cis.org.au/Policy/spr03/polspr03-2.htm.

Buchanan, James M., and Richard A. Musgrave. 1999. *Public Finance and Public Choice: Two Contrasting Visions of the State.* Cambridge, Mass.: MIT Press.

Dye, Thomas R. 2002. *Understanding Public Policy,* 10th ed. Upper Saddle River, N.J.: Prentice Hall.

Dye, Thomas R., and Harmon Zeigler. 1996. *The Irony of Democracy: An Uncommon Introduction to American Politics,* 10th anniversary silver edition. New York: Harcourt.

Etzioni, Amitai. 1988. *The Moral Dimension.* New York: Free Press.

Fainstein, Norman, and Susan Fainstein. 1983. "Regime Strategies, Communal Resistance and Economic Forces." In Susan Fainstein, Norman Fainstein, Richard Hill, Dennis Judd, and Michael Smith, eds., *Restructuring the City.* New York: Longman, pp. 245–282.

Fischel, William A. 2001. *The Homevoter Hypothesis: How Home Values Influence Local Government Taxation, School Finance, and Land-Use Policies.* Cambridge, Mass.: Harvard University Press.

Friedman, Milton. 2002. *Capitalism and Freedom*, 40th anniversary edition. Chicago: University of Chicago Press.

Galbraith, John Kenneth. 1998. *The Affluent Society*, 40th anniversary edition. Boston: Houghton-Mifflin.

Howlett, Michael, and M. Ramesh. 2003. *Studying Public Policy: Policy Cycles and Policy Subsystems*, 2nd ed. Ontario, Canada: Oxford University Press.

International City/County Management Association. 2002. *Municipal Year Book 2002*. Washington, D.C.: International City/County Management Association.

Kalt, Joseph, and Mark Zupan. 1984. "Capture and Ideology in the Economic Theory of Politics." *American Economic Review* 74, no. 3: 279–300.

Katz, Bruce, and Jennifer Bradley. 1999. "Divided We Sprawl." *Atlantic Monthly* (December): 26–42.

Latham, Earl. 1952. "The Group Basis of Politics: Notes for a Theory." *American Political Science Review* 46, no. 2 (June): 376–397.

Lindblom, Charles E. 1959. "The Science of Muddling Through." *Public Administration Review* 19, no. 2: 79–88.

———. 1979. "Still Muddling, Not Yet Through." *Public Administration Review* 39, no. 6: 517–526.

Logan, John R., and Harvey Molotch. 1987. *Urban Fortunes: The Political Economy of Place*. Berkeley: University of California Press.

Mossberger, Karen, and Gerry Stoker. 2001. "The Evolution of Urban Regime Theory: The Challenge of Conceptualization." *Urban Affairs Review* 36, no. 6: 810–835.

Musgrave, Richard. 1959. *The Theory of Public Finance*. New York: McGraw-Hill.

National Hot Dog & Sausage Council. 2007. "Hot Dog Primer." Washington, D.C. http://www.hot-dog.org.

Olson, Mancur. 1969. "The Principle of 'Fiscal Equivalence': The Division of Responsibilities among Different Levels of Government." *American Economic Review* 59, no. 2: 479–487.

Orfield, Myron. 1997. *Metropolitics: A Regional Agenda for Community and Stability*, rev. ed. Washington, D.C.: Brookings Institution Press.

Osborne, David, and Ted Gaebler. 1992. *Reinventing Government: How the Entrepreneurial Spirit Is Transforming the Public Sector*. Reading, Mass.: Addison-Wesley.

Peterson, Paul. 1981. *City Limits*. Chicago: University of Chicago Press.

Poole, Robert, and Peter Samuel. 2006. "The Return of Private Toll Roads." U.S. Department of Transportation, Federal Highway Administration, *Public Roads* 69, no. 5 (March/April). http://www.tfhrc.gov/pubrds/06mar/06.htm.

Starn, Michael. 1994. "User Fees: When Given the Choice, Most Citizens Prefer Service Charges and User Fees over Property Taxes to Fund Municipal Services." *Maine Townsman* (January). http://www.memun.org/SchoolsProject/html/Resources/Budget/user_fees.htm.

Starr, Paul. 1988. "The Meaning of Privatization." *Yale Law and Policy Review* 6: 6–41.

Stone, Clarence. 1989. *Regime Politics: Governing Atlanta*. Lawrence: University Press of Kansas.

———. 2005. "Looking Back to Look Forward: Reflections on Urban Regime Analysis." *Urban Affairs Review* 40, no. 3: 309–341.

Tannenwald, Robert. 2001. "Are State and Local Revenue Systems Becoming Obsolete?" *New England Economic Review* no. 4-2001: 27–43.

Thompson, Wilbur. 1976. "The City as a Distorted Price System." In Harold Hochman, ed., *The Urban Economy*. New York: W.W. Norton, pp. 74–86.

Tiebout, Charles M. 1956. "A Pure Theory of Local Expenditures." *Journal of Political Economy* 64, no. 5 (October): 416–424.

Transport for London. 2006. *Central London Congestion Charging: Impacts Monitoring*. London, June.

Truman, David B. 1951. *The Governmental Process: Political Interests and Public Opinion*. New York: Alfred A. Knopf.

U.S. Bureau of the Census. 2006. *Government Finances*. Washington, D.C.: U.S. Government Printing Office.

———. 2007. *Statistical Abstract of the United States 2007*. Washington, D.C.: U.S. Government Printing Office.

Utility Connection. 2007. http://www.utilityconnection.com.

Vickrey, William S. 1963. "Pricing in Urban and Suburban Transit." *American Economic Review, Papers and Proceedings* (May): 452–445.

Vidich, Charles. 1976. *The New York Cab Driver and His Fare.* Cambridge, Mass.: Schenkman.

Warner, Mildred, and Amir Hefetz. 2004. "Pragmatism over Politics: Alternative Service Delivery in Local Government, 1992–2002." In *Municipal Year Book 2004.* Washington, D.C.: International City/County Management Association.

Weisbrod, Burton A. 1964. "Collective-Consumption Services of Individual-Consumption Goods." *Quarterly Journal of Economics* 78, no. 3: 471–477.

Weiss, Carol H. 1980. "Knowledge Creep and Decision Accretion." *Knowledge: Creation, Diffusion, Utilization* 1, no. 3: 381–404.

Zodrow, George R. 2001. "The Property Tax as a Capital Tax: A Room with Three Views." *National Tax Journal* 54, no. 1: 139–156.

Chapter 9 Questions and Exercises

1. One of the main sources of data about municipal governments is the U.S. Census Bureau's Census of Governments, conducted once every five years (in years ending in "2" and "7"). The amount of revenue collected by municipal governments within each state and the sources of this revenue are published in the Census of Governments' report "Finances of Municipal and Township Governments." The latest version (released in 2005) can be found at

   http://www.census.gov/prod/2005pubs/gc024x4.pdf

   Go to this report and then scroll down to Table 3, "Revenue of Municipal Governments by Source and State." Pick four states.

   + Within each of those states, what are the total amounts of intergovernmental transfers to municipalities from the federal government (column 4)?
   + What are the total amounts of intergovernmental revenue received by the municipalities from state government (column 5)?
   + For what purposes was the revenue from state government provided (columns 6 through 11)?
   + Why do you think the pattern might vary from one state to another?

2. Continuing with the report "Finances of Municipal and Township Governments," proceed to Table 5. This table gives the percent distribution of municipal government revenue from each source.

   + For each of the four states you selected for the previous question, what is the percentage of municipal government revenue obtained from the federal government (column 4) and from state government (column 5)?
   + Then, concentrating on locally generated revenue, what percentage of municipal government revenue comes from property taxes (column 8)?
   + What percentage of municipal government revenue comes from taxes from sales and gross receipts (columns 9 and 10)?
   + Do the states you selected allow municipalities to impose local income taxes (column 11)?
   + What percentage of revenue comes from current user charges (column 12)?

◆ Consult Table 4 of this report, which lists the various types of current user charges. Which three types of user charges generate the most revenue for the states you selected? Why do you think the pattern might vary from one state to another?

3. Scroll down to Table 18, "Finances of Municipal and Township Governments with a Population of 25,000 or More." The population of the municipality (as of the year 2000) is given in column 1 and the expenditures are grouped according to various categories, with total expenditures in column 10, capital outlay in column 12, and specific functions of local government in columns 13 through 22. Choose six municipalities, including three municipalities with a population over 100,000 and three with a population under 100,000.

◆ Looking first at each municipality separately, which four functions receive the highest levels of expenditures?
◆ Among the six municipalities you chose, do you find any differences between the functions receiving the largest expenditures in the larger municipalities and the functions receiving the largest expenditures in the smaller municipalities?

4. As discussed in Chapter 9, metropolitanism and other dynamics have led to the creation of government entities that provide services to one or more cities or towns but are independent from municipal and county governments. The Census of Governments provides data on these "special district" governments. You can find these data at

http://www.census.gov/prod/2004pubs/gc023x1.pdf

In "Employment of Major Local Governments," scroll down to Table 4, "Employment, Payrolls, and Average Earnings in Individual Special Districts Having 100 or More Full-Time Employees by State: March 2002." Ninety percent of the special districts have a single function and, as you will see, many of the functions are obvious from their titles. Pick two states and briefly scan twenty or thirty of the special district names.

◆ For what types of functions were the special districts in each of those two states created?
◆ Why do you think these functions were assigned to special districts rather than being provided by individual cities and towns?

5. As we saw in Chapter 8, public education is provided by local school districts. The Census of Governments states that 90 percent of these local school districts are independent from municipal governments. Data on these school districts can be found in the Census Bureau report "Public Education Finances," available on the Web at

http://www.census.gov/govs/www/school.html

Go to this Web site and select the most recent year from "Years Available." When the next screen comes up, look under "Available Data" and click on "Public Education

Finances." Go to Table 15 of this report, "Finances of Individual Public Elementary-Secondary School Systems with Enrollments of 10,000 or More: 2004–05," and select three school districts (you may want to use the same ones you used for the end-of-chapter exercises in Chapter 8).

Calculate the percentage of the school districts' total revenue (second column on first page of data for each school district) that comes from property taxes (fifth column of the second page of data for each school district). What might account for this variation?

Urban Physical Infrastructure

Water, Sewer, and Waste; Parks and Libraries; Transportation

10

Many of the physical features we now take for granted as part of city life—readily available clean safe water; paved roads and highways; subways, buses, and other public transportation systems; public libraries and parks—simply did not exist in the early cities of the United States. Investments in the urban physical infrastructure, particularly water and sewer systems, were made in response to the potentially dangerous health conditions that existed in densely populated areas. Improvements to roads and the creation of mass-transit systems were undertaken to deal with the increasing difficulty of moving people and goods through cities as congestion increased along with population growth. The construction of public libraries and pastoral parks was a response to a different sort of threat, that of social upheaval in cities rife with inequality and labor unrest. As the late nineteenth century gave way to the twentieth, new inventions such as electric street lighting, motorized streetcars, and automobiles facilitated the expansion of transportation networks that allowed cities to become larger and more productive. Each of these required enormous investments in physical infrastructure. Because of the need to deal with urban density, economies of scale, and mounting externalities, this infrastructure has been supplied and managed mostly by municipalities (or by private firms licensed and regulated by municipal governments).

In our current information age, where so much seems to be "virtual," it is important to remember that cities and suburbs are built environments with "real" roads, highways, and sidewalks and "real" water mains and sewer pipes. The physical infrastructure of the city that is made up of "bricks and mortar," steel, and concrete provides services so critical that if they did not exist, cities would be virtually uninhabitable. The provision of basic transportation, clean potable water, and waste treatment systems may not seem like the most scintillating subjects to study, but how these basic services are provided and allocated, and how they are paid for, involves some of the most engaging issues in the field of urban public policy.

Combating Disease and Death

Through the early decades of the 1800s, obtaining clear, safe, potable water was regarded as a private matter—not something provided through the public sector.

Most commonly, city residents had to obtain their own water for drinking and bathing by digging wells or by carrying water in buckets and other containers from ponds, streams, lakes, and rivers. In larger cities, some residents hired people to deliver water to them for a fee and these private-sector "water peddlers" often had thriving businesses. Residents were also expected to dispose of their own wastes. This task typically involved digging privy vaults in the ground to dispose of bodily waste or digging trenches to transport such waste to nearby bodies of water. Residents usually threw garbage into the streets to be eaten by roaming pigs and dogs. Similarly, businesses were expected to dispose of their own manufacturing by-products, a task usually carried out by simply discharging untreated by-products into nearby streams, lakes, and rivers.

Density and the Spread of Epidemics

These practices and others associated with water, garbage, and waste grew more hazardous as urban populations rose. The population dynamics of urban areas in the 1800s were characterized not just by foreign immigration, internal migration from rural areas, and high birthrates but also by high death rates. Disease, much of it related to polluted water and unsanitary living conditions, caused a massive loss of life. It is not surprising that disease spread like wildfire, given both the density of big-city tenement districts and the overcrowding of each dwelling unit.

While *density* refers to the number of people per square mile, *overcrowding* refers to the number of people in each housing unit. According to the current U.S. government definition, overcrowding occurs when there is more than one person per room in an apartment or home (Baer, Choi, and Myers 1996). Four people living together in a three-room apartment—excluding bathrooms—are considered to be living in overcrowded quarters. While it is possible for a household to live in a place that is overcrowded but not dense (a family of four in a rural two-room shack, a mile from their nearest neighbor) or dense but not overcrowded (two people in a four-room apartment, one of 120 such apartments in a thirty-story luxury residential building on a one-acre footprint), poor people in the nineteenth century often lived both in extremely dense city neighborhoods and also in overcrowded buildings.

The typical New York tenement apartment, with its $11' \times 12'\ 6''$ "parlor," small kitchen, and one tiny bedroom, had a total area of about 325 square feet—the equivalent of two $10' \times 16'$ rooms. In this small space lived households of seven or more people and, in some cases, as many as eighteen. Many apartments were dark and airless because interior windows faced narrow light shafts, if there were interior windows at all. Measles, mumps, cholera, influenza, diphtheria, and tuberculosis could hardly be contained in such an environment. The spread of disease in cramped quarters provides a classic case of a negative externality, where the actions (or inactions) of some have dramatic effects on the well-being of others.

In various years, as noted in **Table 10.1**, epidemics killed 10 percent or more of the population in such cities as Philadelphia, St. Louis, Cincinnati, and New Orleans. In many cases, epidemics returned to a city frequently. New York City suffered serious outbreaks of cholera in 1832, 1847, and 1849 (Rosenberg 1962), and the city experienced seven serious smallpox outbreaks between 1851 and 1875 (Duffy 1990; Melosi 2000). New Orleans experienced yellow fever epidemics thirteen different times between 1832 and 1905 (Humphreys 1992; Bloom 1993). Due to the high death rates experienced in cities, the fear engendered by an epidemic could change city life almost overnight. Over the course of just ten days in 1878, yellow fever caused two-thirds of the population of Chattanooga to flee the city. In Memphis, business and government activity came to a halt as three-quarters of all firms and the entire city government shut down.

Illness and death affected the economy in many ways. To avoid epidemics, individuals shut down their businesses, cities barred trade with areas that were known to harbor infection, and whole families were quarantined if a person in their household became ill. Spouses were lost and children were left without parents. Sick workers lost wages. In addition, epidemic disease was a potential impediment in the competition for economic growth. If they had any choice in the matter, people and businesses were less likely to locate in a city that was known for severe endemic and epidemic disease. This provided a competitive advantage to cities perceived as relatively "healthy" with fewer risks of environmentally caused illness and death.

Table 10.1 Major National or Regional Epidemics

1793–1806	Yellow fever hits coastal cities from New Orleans to Boston, with particularly strong outbreaks in 1793, 1798, and 1805. In Philadelphia in 1793, it kills more than 5,000 people (one-tenth of the population) in less than four months. In 1805, it strikes hard at New York; one-third of the city population flees the city.
1832–1834	Cholera hits every large city in the United States with the exception of Boston and Charleston, South Carolina. At the same time, yellow fever runs through cities in the South. In New Orleans in 1832, 12 percent of the population (6,700 of the 55,000 residents) is killed by either cholera or yellow fever.
1849–1854	Cholera epidemic again strikes cities across the United States with Cincinnati, St. Louis, New York, and New Orleans suffering the most. In 1849 alone, the epidemic kills more than 5,000 in New York City, more than 7,000 in St. Louis (10 percent of the population), and approximately 10 percent of the population of Cincinnati.
1853	Yellow fever hits coastal cities in the South, killing 8,100 in New Orleans, and 1,200 in Mobile. Two years later, it kills more than 2,800 in Norfolk, Virginia.
1866	Cholera returns to many cities. In St. Louis, more than 3,500 are killed.
1867	Yellow fever is epidemic in southern coastal cities; 3,100 die in New Orleans and more than 1,100 in Galveston, Texas.
1870s	Smallpox kills approximately 1,000 people per year in New York.
1878	Yellow fever again devastates cities in Mississippi Valley. Kills 5,000–6,000 in Memphis, and 5,000 in New Orleans.
1906	Polio kills 2,500 in New York, which remains the city hardest hit by polio until the 1950s.
1916	Polio outbreak causes 2,400 deaths in New York, and a total of 7,000 deaths across the United States.
1918–1919	"Spanish Flu" kills more than 550,000 across the United States.

Sources: Rosenberg 1962; Crosby 1989; Duffy 1990; Humphreys 1992; Bloom 1993; Melosi 2000.

Successfully addressing the problem required breakthroughs in science and the subsequent education of city residents about the role of microorganisms as causes of disease. The advances in science occurred gradually in the nineteenth century, with accelerated acceptance of the "Gospel of Germs" in the scientific and health professions after 1870, and major efforts to educate the populace in the following decades (Duffy 1990; Tomes 1998). But insights without action would not provide solutions to the epidemics. Ultimately, the problem of disease in urban areas could be controlled only by public investment in water and sewer systems and by public regulation of waste disposal.

Water Supply Systems

In 1801, Philadelphia, the second largest city in the United States at the time, built the first city waterworks. Reasoning that severe yellow fever in the city in 1793 and 1798 might have been caused by polluted water, the city built a system that pumped water from the Schuylkill River to a central reservoir from which it was released to the city through a system of pipes. New York also acted early after the yellow fever outbreaks of the 1790s, giving a charter to a private company for construction of a reservoir-based system of water supply.

The idea of central water reservoirs dispensing water through pipes was gradually adopted by other cities. By 1860, all of the sixteen largest U.S. cities and many smaller ones had either constructed publicly owned water systems, or had granted charters to private waterworks companies (Tarr 1984; Melosi 2000). Though charters to privately owned companies were common through the mid-1800s, over time there was a gradual movement toward public ownership. As early as 1870, nearly half of the waterworks were publicly owned. By 1924, the proportion was up to 70 percent (Melosi 2000; Cutler and Miller 2006).

From Private to Public Operation

The movement from private to public ownership of waterworks was due to the presence of massive fixed costs and huge economies of scale. As cities expanded in the nineteenth century, the costs borne by private water companies in providing service to additional customers was relatively small, given excess capacity in the original reservoirs, aqueducts, and water mains. With such low marginal cost, provision of water became a **natural monopoly**, akin to the provision of natural gas today, as we discussed in Chapter 9. Any new competitor to an existing supplier would have to invest huge sums to build an additional set of waterworks in order to supply water to the residents and businesses in the city. With few customers to begin with, these high fixed costs would drive the average cost of the newcomer well above the average cost of the existing supplier. This condition worked to limit competition to established companies.

As the population of many cities expanded rapidly at the end of the nineteenth century and the beginning of the twentieth as a result of immigration, existing private water companies became increasingly incapable of keeping up with demand for water. When it became necessary to seek additional water sources and build more aqueducts, filtration plants, and water mains, the initial fixed costs often exceeded the scope of what was possible for private firms, even those enjoying a monopoly status. Only the public sector had the resources to build the needed water systems and purification plants. In cases like this, some of the private firms sold their existing systems to municipal governments. Other firms tried to continue to operate, but went out of business. According to Schultz and McShane (1978), by the beginning of the 1900s, forty-one of the fifty largest cities in the United States had publicly owned water systems.

Some cities moved to create municipally owned water supplies because of poor service by the private companies. The failure to provide adequate water at a reasonable price is related to what economists term the **principal-agent problem**—a phenomenon that occurs when the interests of an agent acting on behalf of a client (the principal) diverges from the interests of his or her client. A common example is a CEO (the agent) whose compensation package is written in such a way that it prompts behavior benefiting the CEO but not necessarily the stockholders (the client). Normally, in a competitive market, this problem is solved by the ability of the client to simply choose another agent or to revise the nature of the compensation package so the interests of the agent and the client are aligned. To mitigate the principal-agent problem, top management is often offered appropriately designed profit sharing plans tied to the firm's stock price.

But where there is **asymmetric information**—where information possessed by the agent is not available to the client—a market malfunction can occur such that the interests of the client are harmed. In the situation we have been discussing, although charters issued by cities to private companies to provide water and sewer were supposedly granted in the interests of the city's residents, the grantees often acted in their own interests and instead kept crucial information about the costs of operation from city officials. In one of the most notorious cases, profits from the initial New York charter were used to finance the owners' banking interests, at the expense of adequate water service to residents. In order to have all the information they needed to run and benefit from the city water service, the city built its own municipally owned system in 1842. Between 1890 and 1920, efforts to stamp out corruption and graft involving private companies led many residents and activists to support publicly owned systems.

The ability of local governments to sell municipal bonds also contributed greatly to the growth of publicly owned waterworks. As Cutler and Miller (2006) note, after the economic Panic of 1893, investors were more willing to buy municipal bonds that were backed by the faith and credit of the local government than private-sector bonds, which had no such assurance.

Finally, the move to municipally owned systems was also fueled by a shift in perspective about the responsibility for water. As cities learned more about how disease was spread, and recognized the beneficial effects of water and sewer systems on public health, clean water was increasingly seen as a public good with profound spillover effects that *should be* the responsibility of the public sector. By the 1950s, based on the conclusive evidence of the benefits of fluoride for reducing tooth decay, cities began to add small amounts of this chemical to their water supplies. The result has been a dramatic decline in the incidence of tooth decay and greatly improved dental health, although there are still pockets of opposition to the practice.

Solid Waste Management

Of course, wastewater is only part of the problem in large dense regions. Metropolitan areas produce millions of tons of garbage (food waste), trash (paper, plastic, and other lightweight items), dead vegetation, leftover debris from building construction and repair, and other thrown-away materials—collectively known as **solid waste**.

The removal of solid waste (or **refuse**, as it is sometimes called) from residential, commercial, and industrial areas is important because, if left uncollected, it poses severe problems for metro areas. Uncollected solid waste is a health hazard that provides growth material for harmful microorganisms and breeding grounds for rats, flies, mosquitoes, and other carriers of disease. When waste builds up, it can block alleys, sidewalks, streets, and other thoroughfares. If nothing else, it is an annoyance to residents, producing putrid odors and unsightly streets and byways. In 1968, when sanitation workers went on strike in New York City for just one week, a 10-foot wall of garbage grew on many of the city's sidewalks (Wikipedia 2006). Twenty-three years later, when private solid waste haulers in the city went on strike for seventeen days, the city's Public Works Department took over hauling away garbage from the businesses that had contracted for private service. In less than two weeks, the department responded to more than 7,600 emergency calls certified by the Health and Fire Departments and collected a total of nearly 12,000 tons of refuse (Finder 1991). The crisis became so severe that some people wrapped their garbage with gift wrapping and left it on park benches, hoping it would be stolen!

The First Municipal Garbage Systems

Picking up the garbage may seem like a simple operation, but the provision of solid waste management is not simple or straightforward at all. The management of municipal solid waste actually involves a complex process of collection, transportation, and disposal—in which population density, externalities, marginal costs, land use, transportation costs, cost/benefit considerations, political dynamics, and tax incidence all play a role.

To appreciate some of the complexity, imagine that you are camping on a deserted island with some supplies that you brought with you. How would you dispose of the unwanted materials during your stay on the island? Campers often burn their flammable leftover material. You might throw some of your edible waste into the woods to be eaten by other creatures on the island. Refuse that serves as a breeding ground for harmful molds and bacteria might be buried. You might throw waste that was not decomposable into the sea—thinking that it would not present any harm in the vastness of the ocean. If the island was large enough, and you had enough land on one side for the purposes that were important to you, you might throw much of your refuse onto the other side of the island. If you expected to be there for a long time and needed to grow some of your own food, you might compost some of your leftover organic materials, creating an area where natural biological processes convert the material into nutrient-rich soil.

Now, suppose that someone else occupies the other side of the island. In this new situation, if you throw waste on the other side of the island, it affects your neighbor and if your neighbor throws waste onto your side, it affects you. There are several things that you might do. You could resign yourself to using only your side of the island for your waste, and feel a bit more cramped, or you could collaborate with your neighbor to designate one common area for waste disposal on the border between the two sides of the island. Alternatively, you might strike a deal with him. You might be willing to accept his waste along with your own, if he grew extra food and supplied you with it, so that you did not have to spend as much time growing your own. In effect, you would be involved in trade—exchanging the use of your land for food.

But now suppose that the population on the island grows larger. Space is more limited and there are more people generating externalities that affect each other. Now waste may appear on your land and it may be difficult or impossible to determine who placed it there. The amount of material thrown into the sea increases, and you begin to find that it is washing back onshore during high tide. New forms of coordination with your fellow island residents and new methods of waste disposal may be needed.

This hypothetical example captures many of the realities of the history of urban waste management in the United States. In the early nineteenth century, collection of solid waste in cities was handled by individual families, who either dumped it onto streets, onto unused land, or into rivers, lakes, and streams. Because there was a great deal of land available, people did not think as much as they do today about the externalities of this behavior. But as cities grew during the nineteenth century, so did related problems of waste management. Competing uses of land—for homes, businesses, and roads—reduced the availability of vacant dumping areas within easy carrying distance from homes.

In response, some nineteenth-century cities focused mainly on the issue of ensuring mobility within the city. They hired at public expense municipal street cleaners to periodically clear streets of debris and dead animals. Other cities focused on household waste, hiring municipally paid workers or entering into contracts with private companies to collect waste from households and carry it away to more remote disposal sites. By 1880, as documented in the Census Bureau's "Report on the Social Statistics of Cities," 60 percent of the 149 cities that provided information had some municipally sponsored collection of garbage, either directly or through contracts with private firms (U.S. Bureau of the Census 1886). By 1915, municipally sponsored collection had been adopted in virtually all U.S. cities (Melosi 2000).

Municipally sponsored collection offered some distinct advantages. Centralized collection represented a division of labor within communities. Instead of every family taking time and effort to remove waste, the task was now done by specific workers who specialized in this task. With centralized collection, dumping could be concentrated into specifically designated areas, which aided efforts to control the use of land. The use of vehicles specifically designed for compacting and transporting waste meant that the disposal of solid waste was more cost- and time-efficient than would have been the case if each household was required to dispose of its own. The resulting efficiencies in the use of labor and transportation became more and more important, as cities continued to expand and the amount of solid waste to be collected increased dramatically.

Coping with Mountains of Trash

Disposing of solid waste posed additional problems. Many cities turned to covering the waste with soil or setting controlled fires to burn it. Burning solid waste reduced the volume of the waste and thus made it possible for cities to use a particular site longer. The smell and smoke that accompanied the fires were perceived (at that time) as a nuisance, but not as a health hazard. Soon, cities began to adopt a European technological innovation, the incinerator, where wastes were burned in a large enclosed furnace before the ashes were transported to a disposal site. Municipal incinerators could be located closer to population centers than open dumps, and the combination of nearby incinerators and more remote dumps could lower the total transportation costs of solid waste management. Incinerators provided a weight-losing process (see Chapter 3), where the material collected from households and businesses was heavier and more bulky before incineration than the ashes that remained after incineration. As a result, locating incinerators near the solid waste collection sites and transporting the lighter ash to more remote disposal sites minimized transportation costs. Both city-owned and private incinerators became common in metro areas. By the mid-1960s, incinerators were handling 40 percent of New York City's refuse (Walsh 2002).

Another way that cities dealt with solid waste involved exporting it to landfills in rural areas, under agreements with those communities. This is equivalent to our hypothetical island residents, who traded dumping rights for food. Essentially, areas of the United States that have a lot of land with low population density—and, therefore, where fewer people will be affected by the externalities associated with solid wastes—have a comparative advantage in converting some of their land into landfills and taking solid waste from cities in exchange for dumping fees.

This follows from what we already know about economic base theory and trade. Remember that economic base theory emphasizes the importance of bringing money into an area. From this standpoint, one can "follow the money trail" and identify the places that receive the fees as the location of an export industry. The solid waste and the dumping fees move in opposite directions. The places that receive the money are exporting the service of their land as landfill sites in return for the payments made by cities who agree to pay them for that service. Both Pennsylvania and Virginia have a comparative advantage in landfill sites because they have many rural areas with low population densities that can be used for waste disposal, and because they are relatively close to many urban areas that desperately need such a service. For the many cities that choose to use these landfills, it is cheaper—because of transportation costs—to send their waste to Pennsylvania and Virginia than it is to send them to sites in Wyoming or Arizona, where there is even more land available for such activity.

The issues of land availability and cost-efficiency that were emerging in the late nineteenth and early twentieth centuries also highlighted another aspect of waste management. Like the hypothetical island resident described earlier in this section who composted some of his waste, cities also thought about reuse and recycling. From the earliest municipal collection, there was awareness that under some circumstances waste could be reused, and that some material could be sold such that the proceeds could be used to offset some of the costs of collection. The 1880 census notes that the city of Boston collected ash and garbage separately, and then sold the food wastes to farmers for fertilizer and used ash as fill for low-lying land (U.S. Bureau of the Census 1886). Other cities used similar strategies, or let farmers use the dumps as feeding grounds for their pigs. As municipal solid waste collection further expanded in the twentieth century, the overall solid waste management system became one in which sophisticated pricing was needed to determine what wastes to recycle and which to dispose of in traditional ways. Recycling came into its own during World War II, when paper drives and scrap metal drives were instituted in most high schools to provide raw materials for the war effort.

Municipal strategies also were modified as awareness of previously unrecognized types of social costs emerged. Cost-benefit considerations and concern about previously unrecognized social costs shaped many of the changes in solid waste management in the twentieth century. Chief among these has been increasing public awareness of the dangers of air pollution and other environmental hazards (such as might be associated with incineration), and increasing regulation to reduce these hazards.

But the primary concern about solid waste management in the twenty-first century arises simply because consumers are generating more waste. According to the U.S. Environmental Protection Agency, the amount of solid waste generated in the nation increased sharply between 1960 and 1990 (U.S. Environmental Protection Agency 2005). In 1960, solid waste collection in the United States averaged 2.7 pounds per person per day. By the beginning of the twenty-first century, collection averaged 4.5 pounds per person per day. For a four-person family, that translates into more than 3 tons of waste per year. With both the per capita amount increasing and the population increasing, the amount of solid waste collected in the United States more than doubled during those thirty years—from 88 million tons to more than 200 million tons—and has since increased to 251 million tons in 2006 (see **Figure 10.1**). Using a different methodology, another study estimates that a total of almost 388 million tons was produced in 2004—the equivalent to a mountain comprised of 260 million full-size passenger cars (Simmons et al. 2006). Not surprisingly, cities across

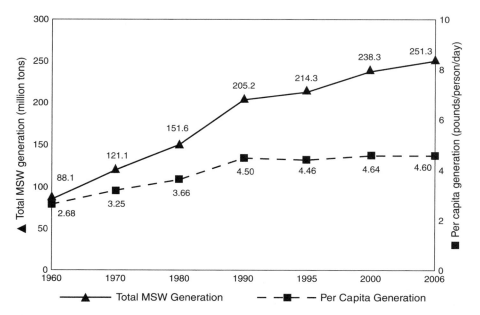

Figure 10.1 Municipal Solid Waste Generation (MSW), 1960–2006. *Source:* U.S. Environmental Protection Agency 2007.

the United States are now adopting recycling as an integral part of solid waste disposal in order to reduce the amount of material put into landfills, incinerated, or exported to ever more distant locations.

Urban Wastewater and Sewers

Disposing of liquid waste is still another matter for cities and towns. Sewer systems address two problems in urban areas. First, they move wastewater generated by households and commercial businesses—in today's society, water from sinks, washing machines, toilets, and tubs. Second, they provide a method for directing and removing the excess storm water that runs off streets and land during and after major downpours.

Despite their shared roots in efforts to promote public health and their similar use of underground pipes, the creation of municipal sewer systems lagged many decades behind the creation of water supply systems. While several cities had already planned and created water systems in the first half of the nineteenth century, the first planned sewer systems were not created until the late 1850s, when Brooklyn and Chicago constructed their systems. The difference in timing occurred for several reasons.

First, effective waterworks were a necessary preexisting condition for the creation of sewer systems, since sewer systems depend upon the existence of a dependable and substantial supply of water that can be relied upon to move the waste from homes and businesses to other areas. Second, in some cities, the previously existing system of privy vaults supplemented by privately built trenches and other disposal methods seemed to be meeting most needs, so there was less urgency about creating a new system for household wastewater. Nonetheless, as more people lived in ever closer proximity to each other, the privy vault system began to show its limitations. In most cases, there were no standards for construction of the privy vault, and some leaked or occasionally overflowed. The increasing amount of human waste had to be removed periodically and taken elsewhere. Enforcement of standards to safely dispose of this waste proved difficult.

Urban Sewer Systems

As the movement for greater sanitation grew stronger, other cities joined in the construction of planned sewer systems. Providence, Cincinnati, Indianapolis, New Haven, and Boston had extensive sewer systems by 1876. In 1880, the newly created federal public health entity, the National Board of Health, sent a specialist to study the sewer systems that were widely used in Europe. By the early 1880s, designers and builders of sewer systems were actively marketing their systems to city governments, carrying with them the arguments of the now widely accepted germ theory of disease. By the 1920s, the planning and construction of sewer systems was an established role for governments in most large cities.

Like water supply systems, sewer systems were natural monopolies with high fixed costs and huge economies of scale. Accordingly, they were typically built and managed by municipal governments.

Typically, sewer pipes carried wastewater to a body of water, into which it was then discharged through an open pipe. As the population and spatial dimensions of cities grew, however, this practice had two problems. The waterways into which the sewers emptied were often the same bodies of water from which drinking water for the cities was taken. If a relatively small amount of wastewater flowed into this water, city officials could count on dilution to reduce (but not eliminate) the amount of the raw sewage that returned through water intake pipes. However, as population increased, the amount of household and industrial wastewater increased such that satisfactory dilution could not occur.

Many cities dealt with this problem by installing wastewater pipes downstream from the intake pipes, so that the pipes drawing water into the city did not come into contact with the sewage-polluted water downstream. However, solving the intake problem for one city did not solve all of the problems generated by the water pollution. There were externalities. Often these same waterways continued downstream to other cities and towns, degrading the quality of the drinking water in these downstream communities. To reduce the impact of sewage on waterways flowing between municipalities, cities had two alternatives. The cities where the wastewater originated could treat it with filters and other methods to remove potentially harmful material before it was released into waterways. Cities could also filter water during the intake process, between the time that it was removed from the water source and its eventual release into pipes where it flowed to households. One of the major issues of the first half of the twentieth century was this question of whether water from upstream cities would be treated in wastewater treatment plants before being dumped back into waterways, or whether downstream cities would have to rely upon filtering of polluted water drawn from those waterways.

Essentially, such sewer systems mirrored the market failure dynamics of some solid waste systems. By sending the wastes to another area, the originating city exported the negative externalities, creating costs for other communities. As long as the originating city did not have to bear the cost of the negative externalities, it had no incentive to correct the problem. Meanwhile, the downstream cities had to bear the higher costs to maintain clean drinking water because of the need to remove the contamination from the raw sewage flowing to them from upstream. Several U.S. cities that were located downstream from other cities turned to state and federal courts to obtain legal intervention to force the upstream cities to initiate or improve sewage treatment processes.

Those who brought suit often had an important point. With substantial under-investment in treatment of raw sewage, many waterways became notoriously polluted, filthy, and smelly from the combination of household wastewater, industrial and commercial wastewater, and municipal solid waste. Although sewage treatment techniques were available in the early 1900s, until 1940, more than half of all urban dwellers lived in metro areas with sewage systems that discharged raw sewage into the environment (Melosi 2000; Burian et al. 2000). One of the most widely publicized cases was that of the Cuyahoga River, which flows through Cleveland. The river was so filled with solid and liquid waste that it actually caught fire and burned for eight days in 1952, causing damage estimated as high as $1.5 million (Adler 2002). The river caught fire again in 1969, further raising national awareness of the extent of pollution in many of the nation's waterways.

New Challenges to Urban Sewer Systems

The last half of the twentieth century was characterized by economic changes that presented several additional problems for urban sewage systems. The manufacture of new products introduced new chemicals into industrial wastewater (from production processes associated with the new products), household wastewater (from use of products such as modern detergents and cleaning fluids), and runoff water (from pesticides and petrochemicals). The introduction of such chemicals into the waste-water stream ultimately exceeded the ability of sewer pipes to withstand corrosion—and thus led to leaks in the pipes—and also challenged the ability of sewage treatment plants to remove the new chemicals before discharge into waterways. While the Federal Water Pollution Control Acts of 1948 and 1956 encouraged the building of sewage treatment plants, the problems inherent in wastewater often outpaced the technology used in the treatment plants.

Public attention was brought to the general environmental problems posed by some chemicals through Rachel Carson's widely read book *Silent Spring*, published in 1962. Greater public awareness of the potential dangers of chemicals in water led to many developments in the 1970s, including the creation of the Environmental Protection Agency (EPA) in 1970, and the passage of the Federal Water Pollution Control Act in 1972. After it was amended in 1977, this act became known more commonly as the Clean Water Act.

The Clean Water Act established new regulations for sewage treatment plants, and additional funding for building such plants. It established standards for pre-treatment of wastewater before it left industry sites, and gave the EPA authority to do inspections and monitor compliance with these standards. It also set aside billions of dollars in grants ($18 billion in the first three years alone) to assist in the construction of municipal sewage treatment facilities (including facilities that served more than one municipality) (Dolin 2004). This act continues to be key legislation for addressing the problems of wastewater's impact on lakes, rivers, and other waterways.

Without federal and state financial assistance, the cost of building sewage treatment facilities would have been very problematic for municipalities. The rapid out-migration of central city residents to less dense suburbs added to the problem. When houses and businesses are farther away from each other, it takes a greater length of pipe to reach each building, increasing the per-unit cost of providing and laying the pipes. Many of the new suburbs constituted political jurisdictions that were too small to finance their own sewage systems and treatment plants. In many metro areas, suburbs dealt with this problem by establishing agreements with central cities under which the central cities would extend their sewage pipes to the suburban communities and charge them user fees to cover the costs of constructing and managing the system. In other metro areas, central cities and suburbs agreed to create metropolitan sewer districts—independent of any one municipality—that would finance the expansion of sewers into suburbs and manage both suburban and central city sewer service.

Boston provides a good example of how regionwide sewer systems evolved (Massachusetts Water Resources Authority 2006). In 1876, a city commission appointed by the mayor recommended building what became known as the Boston Main Drainage System to address "the connection between decomposing matter from our sewers and disease" (Dolin 2004). The project took seven years to complete. Other municipalities and the State Board of Health subsequently advocated for expansion of this system into a system that would serve not only Boston, but several surrounding communities. Because this would involve moving waste across several jurisdictions, the state took authority for addressing the issue and created a Board of Metropolitan Sewerage Commissioners in 1889—which later became the Metropolitan District Commission—to build the system. The new interjurisdictional system was completed in 1904.

When it was fully in operation, it served eighteen cities and towns, diverting untreated sewerage to Moon Island in Boston Harbor, where it was left during the day and then released untreated into the ocean with the outgoing tide. This practice created major problems that lasted for decades, since some of the raw sewage came back into the harbor with the returning tide, fouling the harbor and the shoreline. The first regional sewage treatment plant was not built until 1952, with a second one constructed in 1968. These first treatment facilities were designed to remove and partially decompose most of the solids from the raw sewage, but then discharge the resulting material into the ocean. As the population of the region continued to grow, pollution levels in Boston Harbor continued to rise. Despite urging from many sources, including the federal government, to improve the treatment processes given to the sewage, the discharge of partially decomposed waste—called sludge— continued through the 1970s and into the 1980s.

The passage of the Federal Water Pollution Control Act in 1972 placed the facility in noncompliance with the new federal law. However, it was only after a federal court order in 1985 mandated the construction of a modern treatment plant in order to bring Boston's sewerage system into line with federal environmental protection laws that the new Massachusetts Water Resources Authority, which was established by the state to take over authority for the system, built the state-of-the-art Deer Island treatment facility in Boston Harbor. Completed in 2000 at a cost of $3.8 billion, the treatment plant serves 2.5 million residents and 5,500 large industrial users in the city of Boston and 60 other cities and towns in the region. Even with this Herculean effort, it will still take decades for Boston Harbor to be clear of man-made pollution.

As the pre-2000 Boston case makes clear, key parts of many sewage systems throughout the country began to reach their maximum capacity well before the dawn of the twenty-first century. Other parts of the older infrastructure reached stages of advanced deterioration due to age and/or lack of maintenance. Many metropolitan area sewage systems, therefore, had to choose between expanding existing systems into newer suburbs, augmenting major parts of the system to increase capacity for expected future growth, or replacing older pipes in central cities. Some cities adopted "fix it first" policies before extending their sewer systems to more distant suburbs.

City sewer systems that were not part of larger sewage districts faced even bigger challenges. The loss of businesses and the decreasing income profile of residents— as more well-to-do families moved to suburbs—left many cities with decreased business activity and property values and, consequently, with little ability to increase revenue because of the lower incomes and property values. For these cities, maintenance, repair, and replacement of deteriorating sewer lines and treatment plants was financially difficult or impossible.

Often, giving priority to sewage systems was not possible because of large opportunity costs. Providing needed financing for sewers would mean that other basic services (such as police, fire, education, and hospitals)—many of which might already be underfunded—would have to be cut. The outward movement of urban economic activity, and the consequent increasing poverty within many cities, ultimately affected the ability of older municipalities to provide vital waste treatment services just as the original systems began to wear out or were overwhelmed by demand. If it were not for federal and state courts ordering cities and towns to build modern up-to-date water treatment plants and sewers, it is doubtful that such basic infrastructure would win over the hearts, minds, and purse strings of city leaders, who were faced with so many other municipal functions that needed funding.

Urban Public Amenities: Public Libraries and Pastoral Parks

With the expansion of water, sewer, and sanitation systems in the nineteenth and early twentieth centuries, the threat to cities from disease and contagion began to subside even if pollution continued to threaten the environment in many regions. However, business leaders were often equally concerned about a different kind of threat, posed by social upheaval and labor activism. The development of public libraries and municipal parks was a response to this threat against the existing social order.

Public libraries and pastoral parks are part of a broader category of municipal services that may be called **urban public amenities** and includes municipally owned museums, zoos, swimming pools, tennis courts, golf courses, and skating rinks. Urban public amenities share these characteristics:

1. They developed during the latter half of the nineteenth century or early in the twentieth century, during the period of explosive urban growth.
2. Though these services may share with public education a purpose of moral, physical, and intellectual development—each may be seen as contributing to the ideal of *mens sana in corpore sano* (a sound mind in a sound body)—their use is entirely voluntary, in contrast with mandatory school attendance.
3. These services are relevant primarily to people's leisure time, in contrast with services that provide support to individuals and business firms in their roles as earners of income.
4. Compared with public health and safety services like police, fire, and sanitation, private-sector analogs are more readily available for these amenities, so more-privileged citizens can simply purchase them privately, rather than relying on the public sector.
5. Private philanthropy often preceded and may have stimulated municipal funding, helping to redefine the boundary between private and public.

The public libraries established by Andrew Carnegie, the nineteenth-century Pittsburgh steel magnate, are familiar examples of this last point. Carnegie Library funds essentially were matching grants for which municipalities, in order to be eligible, had to agree to spend annually on their libraries a sum no less than 10 percent of the amount of Carnegie's grant (Bobinski 1969). That sum had to come from tax revenues, not from other gifts. The late-nineteenth-century journalist Finley Peter Dunne (1906) has his fictional alter ego, the inestimable Mr. Dooley, mimic Andrew Carnegie expounding on this requirement:

> All I ask iv a city in rayturn f'r a fifty thousan' dollar libry is that it shall raise wan millyon dollars to maintain th' buildin' an' keep me name shiny, an' if it won't do that much f'r lithrachoor, th' divvle take it, it's onworthy iv th' name iv an American city. What ivry community needs is taxes an' lithrachoor. I give thim both. Three cheers f'r a libry an' a bonded debt! Lithrachoor, taxation, and Andhrew Carnaygie, wan an' insiprable, now an' firiver!

Social Unrest and the Provision of Urban Public Amenities

The provision of urban public amenities was a response to the explosive growth of cities and the concomitant growth of urban unrest during the late nineteenth century. This was Lewis Mumford's Paleotechnic Era: an economy powered by iron and coal, a period of intense industrialization and growth of manufacturing. Schlesinger's 1933 study of this period in U.S. history is aptly named *The Rise of the City*. It was a period of dramatic demographic change, as newcomers poured into the cities, the result of internal migration from rural areas as well as immigration from abroad. It was a period of vast improvements in infrastructure, including transportation and public works.

But it was also a period characterized by severe class conflict. There was a high degree of inequality, most pronounced in cities, where the richest of the rich and the poorest of the poor resided. Rising land values made housing expensive and created a housing crisis for the poor. Business cycles and periodic depressions amplified economic insecurity. In 1877, great labor upheavals focused on the railroads; in 1886, there was a nationwide wave of strike activity. In addition, it was an age of gross municipal corruption. James Bryce (1888), in an influential book of the time, made the pronouncement that "the government of cities is the one conspicuous failure of the United States."

In response to the corruption within cities, the late nineteenth century spawned a number of reform movements. Some were aimed at moral uplift and spearheaded by leaders within Protestant churches. These included the proliferation of the Young Men's Christian Association (YMCA), children's aid societies, and anti-vice and anti-prostitution movements.

The historian Melvin Holli (1969) has distinguished between two categories of late-nineteenth-century municipal reformers: the structural reformers and the social reformers. The structural reformers focused their efforts on achieving "good government"—efficient, businesslike procedures; economical government; non-partisan citywide elections to abolish the influence of parties and wards; shorter ballots; secret ballots; and an emphasis on professional expertise. These structural reformers, like Seth Low of New York City, were the forerunners of the Progressive Era reformers of the early twentieth century.

In contrast with the structural reformers, social reformers like Mayor Hazen Pingree of Detroit advocated for lower utility rates and shifting taxes to corporations. They promoted municipal ownership of streetcar lines and public utilities to address what they saw as the true source of corruption—bribery and graft in the awarding of public franchises to private transportation and utility companies. They tended to dismiss legislation that regulated morals as a distraction from the true problem of corruption, the awarding of municipal franchises. They also advocated for free public baths, and the expansion of parks, schools, and public relief.

Richard T. Ely, a founder of the American Economics Association, was active in the social reform movement and argued against the structural reform notion of drafting future mayors from the ranks of businessmen. In *The Coming City* (1902), he argued that businessmen would bring the wrong point of view to government, because of their "habit of looking at public questions from a private point of view." Businessmen, he said, would be too preoccupied with reducing spending. The expansion of the economic role of local government thus came out of this milieu of industrialization, urbanization, corruption, and reform.

While the establishment of urban public amenities was one response of the nineteenth-century elite to the turmoil of the cities, it was not the only response. Carnegie donated funds for libraries, but he also hired the infamous Pinkerton Agency to put a bloody end to a strike by his workers. The era that witnessed the development of libraries and parks also saw the construction of armories, those quintessential urban structures of the late nineteenth century (Fogelson 1989). The armories, which often resembled medieval fortresses up to their crenellated tops, were built as staging areas for the troops that were called in to quell urban unrest. Both the armory, on the one hand, and the public library and pastoral park, on the other, were responses to class tensions that emoted in the cities of the late nineteenth century. Each was a solution for the unease with which the elite viewed the lower classes. The public libraries and parks could be seen as the velvet glove, the public armories as the iron fist.

The privileged classes of the late nineteenth century could not isolate themselves from the lower classes in the city. Many of the elite lived inside city limits, but even those who moved their residences to the early upper-class suburbs continued to depend on the city and its workers for their livelihood. There were common themes in the way the privileged classes thought about the public libraries and pastoral parks they were providing for the lower classes. These were envisioned as large-scale single citywide units that were available to all, but they were meant especially to reach adult males of the lower classes. Ideally, the laboring husband would take his family to the park on a Sunday for a day to spend together in leisure, enjoying fresh air and relaxation away from their cramped hovel. The laboring man would use the library to teach himself the skills and knowledge necessary for self-improvement. Indeed, at the beginning of the public library era, one had to be over age 14 to use the library at all. The expectation was that parks and libraries would serve as alternatives to the saloon. The parks provided water fountains but prohibited alcohol; claims were made that where libraries were available, saloons lost business.

But there were contradictions. Advocates wanted to attract the lower classes, but did not want to be overrun by them; they wanted to serve the lower classes, but also wanted to enforce middle-class standards of behavior. In order to emphasize the pastoral experience, there were initially no organized activities, no facilities for sports and athletics, no restaurants or shops. Large areas of vacant land were expensive, so parks were often built at the outskirts of the city, requiring streetcar rides that were prohibitively expensive for poor families.

In the case of the public libraries, middle-class librarians could and did enforce strict rules for silence and cleanliness, and harsh punishment for petty thievery. Early librarians debated whether to stock fiction at all, and whether to stock foreign language books for non-native speakers of English. As a result, the use of parks and libraries by the lower classes was disappointingly sparse. Much to the chagrin of reformers, the lower classes chose more lively amusement parks and beer gardens over pastoral parks. Instead of using the library, they read newspapers, dime novels, and various publications of ethnic, labor, religious, and political groups.

A Failure of Expectations

As such, the public libraries and pastoral parks built in the late nineteenth century—no matter their grandiose and stately design—did not fulfill the expectations of their creators. It seems almost quaint now to think that the nineteenth-century elite believed in the power of these institutions to reduce class tensions and rechannel dissatisfaction into individual upward mobility. But they did believe it. At the dedication of the multiple-purpose institution comprised of a library, gymnasium, and music hall that Andrew Carnegie donated to Homestead, Pennsylvania, in 1898—six years after he broke a strike and destroyed the union there—he said, "How a man spends his hours of recreation is really the key of his progress in all the virtues." Similarly, Frederick Law Olmsted's expectations for Central Park in New York City are characterized by the historian Geoffrey Blodgett (1966), as follows: "the natural simplicity of pastoral landscape would, he hoped, inspire communal feelings among all urban classes, muting resentments over disparities of wealth and fashion. For an untrusting, watchful crown of urban strangers, the park would restore that 'communicativeness' which Olmsted prized as a central American need."

Failure to accomplish their original goals led to similar changes in both institutions: The emphasis shifted to a more active policy of outreach centered on smaller, neighborhood-based units that included branch libraries and neighborhood playgrounds. Similarly, with inspiration from the example of the settlement house workers, the focus shifted away from adult males to concentrate more on children, by providing organized activities run by trained personnel such as children's librarians and recreation workers. Now, in the twenty-first century, investment in large pastoral parks, as well as the refurbishing and expansion of museums, seems to be inspired as much by their potential contributions to an area's tourist economy as they are by a desire to improve the well-being of the resident population. They have become part of the economic development strategy of cities that are trying to retain and attract young workers to the central city.

Transportation: Roads and Rails in Metro Areas

Above the water mains and sewers, in front of the libraries, and beside the pastoral parks lies the urban transportation system. As we saw in Chapter 3, during the age of waterborne transportation, the first U.S. cities were located along rivers and harbors. It was the completion of the Erie Canal early in the nineteenth century that vaulted

New York City into its position of preeminence among U.S. cities—a position it has held unchallenged for nearly two centuries. Later, in the mid-nineteenth century, during the age of railroad construction, the location of the routes helped to determine the growth of places like Chicago. Rail transportation first connected one city with another; later, it became an important means of transportation within cities. In both instances, land values along the routes rose as those locations became more accessible and therefore more valuable for development. In the case of the intracity lines, the entrepreneurs prospered from the sale of land adjacent to the tracks more than from the transit lines themselves.

Transportation routes helped to channel the path of subsequent economic development. As cities grew, however, the need for improved transportation between established population centers also influenced subsequent patterns of investment in transportation. In New York State, for example, many of the largest cities, including Albany and Buffalo, originally grew because of their location along the Erie Canal. In later eras, railroad and highway routes connected these existing population centers, following the route of the canal. In this example, we can see both the interaction of public policy—the decision by New York State to build the canal—and market forces, in this case, the decisions of thousands of households and firms to locate in a place with good transportation, as well as the interaction between transportation decisions and land-use decisions. In an iterative process, decisions about transportation affect patterns of land use, but patterns of land use then affect subsequent transportation decisions.

A metropolitan area's transportation network is a crucial part of its physical infrastructure. If we were designing a city on a blank slate, our initial choices about where to place our investments in transportation infrastructure and how to balance rail networks with highways would have a profound impact on the shape of the resulting city. Once the city is built, however, our choices about subsequent transportation investment would be constrained by the existing patterns of land use. A transportation project such as a subway that would make sense in a highly centralized metropolitan area like New York is less likely to work in a more decentralized metropolitan area like Houston.

Unless we are building a fresh new city, we will need to take the "dead hand of history" into account. As the saying goes, "all roads lead to Rome." In the days of the Roman Empire, that is what the emperors wanted. More than 2,000 years later, many of the routes originally laid out by the Romans are still in use throughout Europe. That is a "dead hand" that extended its influence over two millennia.

In looking at the transportation problems that arise in metropolitan areas, we will need to concern ourselves with short-term issues (getting transportation prices right) versus long-term issues (guiding future transportation investment), externalities (pollution, congestion, and accidents), and conflicts between the criteria of efficiency and equity—for example, a new commuter rail link might reduce highway congestion in a metropolitan area, but would do nothing to solve the mobility problems of the area's poor.

What Consumers Want: The Demand Side of Metropolitan Transportation

Aspiring journalists are told that their news stories must include the *who*, *what*, *when*, *where*, *why*, and *how* of the situation. Similarly, with regard to the demand for transportation, we can ask: *who* is doing the traveling, *at what time* and *for what purpose, from what origin to what destination,* and *by what means?* How can a metropolitan area's transportation system—a network that might include airports, highways, heavy rail, light rail, ferries, buses, and streets that might or might not be attractive to pedestrians and bicyclists—serve the varied needs of the out-of-town business traveler or tourist, as well as the needs of residents who might be journeying to work or to a doctor's appointment, shopping for groceries, or going out for entertainment or for visits with friends and relatives? How does the demand for transportation differ between households who own cars and those who do not and between individuals who can drive cars and those who cannot?

Travel Trends

The U.S. Department of Transportation has been collecting data on personal travel through periodic surveys, starting with the 1969 *Nationwide Personal Transportation Survey (NPTS)*. Most recently, the *National Household Travel Survey (NHTS)* was conducted in 2001 (Hu and Reuscher 2004). Because of changes in methodology, some data can be compared over the entire period from 1969 to 2001, while others can be compared only for the period 1990–2001. Overall, the data show a nation ever more reliant on the private automobile to serve a greater portion of its transportation needs. Chapter 13 discusses in greater detail how the interaction between land-use patterns and modes of transportation has contributed greatly to this increased reliance on private vehicles. Even as average household size in the United States has declined from 3.16 people in 1969 to 2.58 in 2001, the number of vehicles per household has increased, from 1.16 to 1.89, so that by 2001, there were 1.06 vehicles per licensed driver—slightly *more* than one vehicle for every licensed driver in the household (see **Table 10.2**).

U.S. motorists typically drove many more miles at the beginning of the twenty-first century than they did back at the end of the 1960s. Overall, average annual miles driven per licensed driver increased by nearly 60 percent, from 8,685 miles in 1969 to 13,785 miles in 2001. While men drove half again as many miles in 2001 as in 1969 (16,920 versus 11,352, respectively), women drove nearly 90 percent more (10,233 miles in 2001 versus 5,411 miles in 1969) (see **Table 10.3**). By 2001, the average amount of time spent in a vehicle (as a driver or as a passenger) exceeded an hour a day for people between the ages of 19 and 64. People aged 65 and older spent nearly an hour a day inside a vehicle and even children less than five years old spent about three-quarters of an hour each day inside a vehicle (see **Figure 10.2**).

Where were we all going? Among women, about 15 percent of trips were for commuting to or from work or traveling on work-related business. Nearly half the trips were for family and personal business. Men's trips were more likely to involve commuting to work or traveling on work-related business and less likely to

Table 10.2 Auto Vehicle Use in the United States: Summary of Demographic Trends, 1969, 1977, 1983, 1990, 1995 *NPTS*, and 2001 *NHTS*

	1969	1977	1983	1990	1995	2001
Persons per household	3.16	2.83	2.69	2.56	2.63	2.58
Vehicles per household	1.16	1.59	1.68	1.77	1.78	1.89
Licensed drivers per household	1.65	1.69	1.72	1.75	1.78	1.77
Vehicles per licensed driver	0.70	0.94	0.98	1.01	1.00	1.06
Workers per household	1.21	1.23	1.21	1.27	1.33	1.35
Vehicles per worker	0.96	1.29	1.39	1.40	1.34	1.39

Note: The 1969 survey does not include pickups and other light trucks as household vehicles.
Source: Hu and Reuscher 2004, table 2, p. 11.

involve family and personal business. Men and women had similar proportions of trips to school or church (about 10%) and for social or recreational purposes (about 26%).

The amount of time that drivers spend behind the wheel varies across metropolitan areas of different sizes. As **Table 10.4** demonstrates, among drivers who were traveling on the day for which the data were collected, the average time they spent behind the wheel was 81.35 minutes in 2001, nearly 10 minutes more than the comparable figure for 1990. Drivers spent about 76 minutes behind the wheel in smaller metropolitan areas and about 85 minutes in the largest cities. That difference

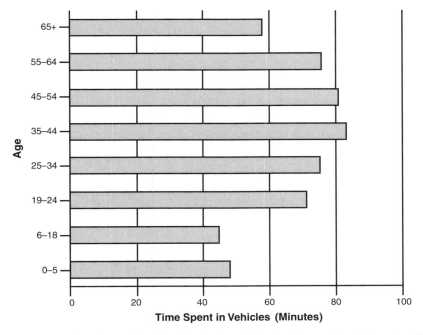

Figure 10.2 Time Spent in Auto Travel per Day by Age of Traveler. *Source:* Hu and Reuscher 2004, figure 5, p. 28.

Table 10.3 Average Annual Miles per Licensed Driver by Driver Age and Gender (Driver's Self-Estimate), 1969, 1977, 1983, 1990, 1995 *NPTS*, and 2001 *NHTS*

							Percent Change	
Driver Age	1969	1977	1983	1990	1995	2001	Annual Rate, 1969–2001	Total Change, 1969–2001
All								
16 to 19	4,633	5,662	4,986	8,485	7,624	7,331	1.44	58.23
20 to 34	9,348	11,063	11,531	14,776	15,098	15,650	1.62	67.42
35 to 54	9,771	11,539	12,627	14,836	15,291	15,627	1.48	59.93
55 to 64	8,611	9,196	9,611	11,436	11,972	13,177	1.34	53.03
65+	5,171	5,475	5,386	7,084	7,646	7,684	1.25	48.60
All	8,685	10,006	10,536	13,125	13,476	13,785	1.45	58.72
Men								
16 to 19	5,461	7,045	5,908	9,543	8,206	8,228	1.29	50.67
20 to 34	13,133	15,222	15,844	18,310	17,976	18,634	1.10	41.89
35 to 54	12,841	16,097	17,808	18,871	18,858	19,287	1.28	50.20
55 to 64	10,696	12,455	13,431	15,224	15,859	16,883	1.44	57.84
65+	5,919	6,795	7,198	9,162	10,304	10,163	1.70	71.70
All	11,352	13,397	13,962	16,536	16,550	16,920	1.26	49.05
Women								
16 to 19	3,586	4,036	3,874	7,387	6,873	6,106	1.68	70.27
20 to 34	5,512	6,571	7,121	11,174	12,004	12,266	2.53	122.53
35 to 54	6,003	6,534	7,347	10,539	11,464	11,590	2.08	93.07
55 to 64	5,375	5,097	5,432	7,211	7,780	8,795	1.55	63.63
65+	3,664	3,572	3,308	4,750	4,785	4,803	0.85	31.09
All	5,411	5,940	6,382	9,528	10,142	10,233	2.01	89.11

Notes: (1) All tables reporting totals could include some unreported characteristics. (2) In 1995, some drivers who indicated that they drove "no miles" for their average annual miles were changed to "miles not reported."
Source: Hu and Reuscher 2004, table 23, p. 41.

of 11 minutes a day may seem trivial, but when you multiply it by 365 days, it means that in the largest metro regions, drivers spent nearly 55 hours more per year in their cars than those who live in smaller regions. If we compare that to how much time the typical American spends on his or her job, it is equivalent to more than one and a half weeks.

According to the 2001 *NHTS*, the proportion of households without a vehicle has declined from 20.6 percent in 1969 to only 8.1 percent in 2001. As **Table 10.5** shows, the proportion of households without a vehicle has fallen over time, but increases with the size of the metropolitan area. Less than 6 percent of households in smaller metropolitan areas or outside of cities are without a vehicle. In the largest metropolitan areas, nearly 12 percent—more than one in nine households—do without.

In a nation so reliant on private vehicles, what does it mean to live in a household without one? A small number of these households might be "car-free" by choice—for example, relatively prosperous Manhattan residents who could afford to own a car but choose not to because of the hassles of traffic and parking in their dense

Table 10.4 Average Time Spent Driving a Private Vehicle in a Typical Day by MSA Size, Adjusted 1990 and 1995 *NPTS*, and 2001 *NHTS* (in Minutes)

	Only Persons Who Drove on Their Travel Day		
MSA Size	1990 Adj	1995	2001
All	71.88	73.24	81.35
Not in MSA	69.20	72.96	81.74
< 250,000	67.94	69.35	76.40
250,000 to 499,999	71.66	71.72	76.50
500,000 to 999,999	72.42	73.35	79.34
1 to 2.9 million	74.38	72.19	79.55
3+ million	71.08	75.02	85.12

Notes: (1) For 1990 and 1995, average time spent driving does not include any driving done in a segmented trip. Also excludes driving done as an "essential part of work." (2) Note that only the 1990 data have been adjusted to make them more comparable with the 1995 and 2001 data. Thus, there are limits on the conclusions that can be drawn in comparing travel with earlier survey years. The adjustments to 1990 data affect only person trips, vehicle trips, person miles of travel (PMT) and vehicle miles of travel (VMT).
Source: Hu and Reuscher 2004, table 15, p. 30.

neighborhoods. These households have many other travel modes easily available to them, including taxicabs. They also have the option of renting a car occasionally should the need arise.

For the vast majority of households without vehicles, though, it is not a matter of choice; these are households that are too poor to own a car. In an era in which the most robust job growth within metropolitan areas has occurred outside the central city in the suburbs, these households confront serious employment problems. They are also likely to find that their transportation needs are not addressed very well by existing public transit routes.

Table 10.5 Percent of Households without a Vehicle within MSA Size Group, 1977, 1983, 1990, 1995 *NPTS*, and 2001 *NHTS*

	Percent of Households within an Area without a Vehicle					
(S)MSA Size	1977	1983	1990	1995	2001	Percent Change, 1977–2001
Not in (S)MSA	12.2	10.5	7.7	5.3	5.8	−52
< 250,000	13.7	10.1	8.6	4.8	5.8	−58
250,000 to 499,999	12.2	8.1	5.7	7.3	5.2	−57
500,000 to 999,999	14.0	14.3	8.4	6.3	7.0	−50
1 to 2.9 million	14.2	12.1	8.2	6.9	6.4	−55
3+ million	26.1	25.4	12.4	11.2	11.9	−54
All	15.3	13.5	9.2	8.1	8.1	−47

Notes: (1) The population size groups for 1977–1983 NPTS are SMSA Size Groups and 1990–2001 are MSA Size Groups. (2) All tables reporting totals could include some unreported characteristics.
Source: Hu and Reuscher 2004, table 19, p. 36.

The Journey to Work

Although the demand for transportation—the need for mobility and access—encompasses far more than just the journey to work, it is there that some of the thorniest problems arise. Traveling from Point A to Point B involves costs—the expenses of owning and operating a car or paying a fare on public transportation, as well as the opportunity cost of one's time. If you are relocating from one metropolitan area to another because you have accepted a new job, you might look for housing that is conveniently located to your new workplace. Conversely, if you are committed to staying where you are, you might look for jobs in firms located within a reasonable commute from your home. However, there are likely to be trade-offs. You might have to accept a longer commute to be able to afford a larger house with more land in a metro area where housing is cheaper on the fringes of the region. In the case of the metropolitan areas with the hottest housing markets, you might need to move to a more distant suburb just to be able to afford anything at all. Alternatively, you might accept a long commute to take a job with better wages and working conditions or better chances for promotion. If there is more than one worker in the household, a delicate process of triangulation might ensue—a balancing act between home and two or more job destinations. With the typical family now having two working adults, this balancing job is more difficult than ever.

Once the questions of where to live and where to work have been resolved (at least for the time being), the next order of business for most commuters will be to figure out how to ease the pain of commuting. In getting from Point A to Point B, commuters face a complicated choice that is likely to involve speed, comfort, out-of-pocket cost, privacy, reliability, schedule flexibility, and protection from bad weather. On many of these criteria, traveling solo by private vehicle is a more attractive option than taking mass transit or carpooling. For many, a more comfortable door-to-door ride from home to work, or the need for trip-chaining—dropping kids off at school, picking them up at day care, stopping to get the groceries or the dry cleaning—will make commuters opt for the use of a private automobile rather than using a bus, subway, other mass transit, or a carpool.

In their pathbreaking book on urban transportation, Meyer, Kain, and Wohl (1965) point out that decentralization in mid-twentieth-century U.S. metropolitan areas was occurring as rapidly in places with well-developed public transportation systems as in places without them. Even in places where consumers had a choice between public transportation and the automobile, they overwhelmingly chose the automobile. Moreover, Meyer, Kain, and Wohl argue, as decentralization affected not only residential location but also the location of businesses, commuting patterns would continue to shift away from job destinations in the central city. Instead, a growing share of commuters would be cross-commuting (traveling from one suburb to another) or they would be reverse-commuting (traveling from homes in the central city to job destinations in the suburbs). Given the large economies of scale required to justify the creation of a fixed rail system, the authors argue that the shift

Table 10.6 Commuting to Work, 1960–2000: Percent Using Each Mode

	1960	1970	1980	1990	2000
Private Vehicle	69.5	80.6	85.9	88	87.9
Public Transit	12.6	8.5	6.2	5.1	4.7
Walked to Work .	10.4	7.4	5.6	3.9	2.9
Other	6.8	2.5	1.6	1.3	1.2
Worked at Home	7.5	3.5	2.3	3	3.3
Total	100	100	100	100	100

Notes: Private Vehicle includes cars, trucks, and vans; includes solo drivers and carpools; Public Transit includes bus, streetcar, subway, railroad, ferryboat, and taxicab.
Source: McGuckin and Srinivasan 2003, exhibit 1.1.

in commuting patterns would make new investment in fixed rail systems undesirable and that it would be a poor use of resources.

As **Table 10.6** indicates, the proportion of workers who commute by private vehicle rose dramatically between 1960 and 2000. Moreover, while carpooling accounted for about 20 percentage points of the 69.5 percent of those who commuted by private vehicle in 1960, it accounted for only 12.2 percentage points of the 87.9 percent of those who commuted by private automobile in 2000 (McGuckin and Srinivasan 2003). Data for 2003 (U.S. Department of Transportation 2005b) show that nearly nine out of ten commuters travel by private vehicle—79 percent of all commuters drive solo and an additional 9 percent carpool (see **Figure 10.3**). With so many people on the road, the 2005 *Urban Mobility Study* revealed that the number of hours a day in which commuters face congested roads increased from 4.5 hours in 1982 to 7.1 hours in 2003. This certainly gives new meaning to the term rush "hour." On the other hand, the increase in average commuting time has been far less dramatic: it rose from 21.7 minutes in 1980 to 25.5 minutes in 2000 (Pisarski 2006).

While these figures show the increasing role of solo driving among commuters, they should not be taken as a pure expression of consumer preferences. Changes in the location and types of workplaces, as well as the location and structure of households, have also played an important role in determining the transportation we select. The continued decentralization of residences and workplaces has made it likelier that workers will have fewer alternatives to commuting by private vehicle. The changing demographics of the workforce and the workplace—including the increase in the proportion of women workers since 1960 and the variability in work schedules—make carpooling less feasible for many. The more dispersed the location of firms and families, the less likely that mass transit will have the ridership to support regular bus service, let alone commuter rail or subway service.

Externalities and Mass-Transit Subsidies

If commuting motorists paid the full cost for opting to use their private autos for transit, we could leave the story here, noting simply that driving to work alone is an increasingly popular choice. But it is not as simple as that. Each individual who

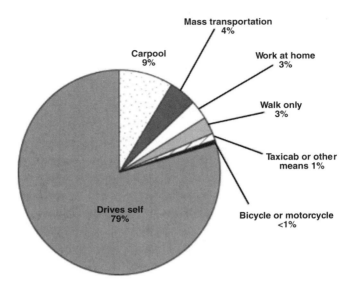

Figure 10.3 How People Get to Work, 2003. *Sources:* U.S. Department of Housing and Urban Development and U.S. Department of Commerce, U.S. Bureau of the Census, *American Housing Survey for the United States*, H150 (Washington, D.C., biennial issues), http://www.bts.gov/publications/transportation_statistics_annual_report/2005/html/chapter_02/figure_04_09.html.

drives to work alone imposes costs on other drivers and on the larger community. The more people who choose to use this transportation mode, the higher the external costs imposed on others. These externalities arise chiefly in the form of growing traffic congestion and, therefore, time-delayed trips; air and water pollution from the use of automobiles; and a growing incidence of accidents on the more congested highways. Like any negative externality, too many solo drivers will choose to drive during periods of congestion unless the cost of the externalities is somehow factored into the price of driving.

Essentially, the social cost of solo driving is higher—perhaps significantly higher—than the private cost. The private costs to the individual motorist—no matter how much it costs to own a car—do not include the spillover costs to other motorists or to the residents of the area. Generally speaking, the denser the region, the higher the social cost. Those who live in rural areas impose much lower social costs than those who drive their vehicles in downtown Manhattan or any large central city.

One interesting corollary of this phenomenon concerns the question of subsidies for mass transit. It is highly unlikely that a public transit authority would be able to charge a price that would cover the average cost of operating buses or subway systems. As the price of a bus or subway ride rises, the ridership normally declines, which would be the case for most goods or services. The higher the price, the lower the quantity of rides demanded. The new higher price multiplied by the new lower ridership yield a revenue that is below the full cost of providing the service. Yet, given the enormous fixed cost of operating a mass-transit system, charging a low

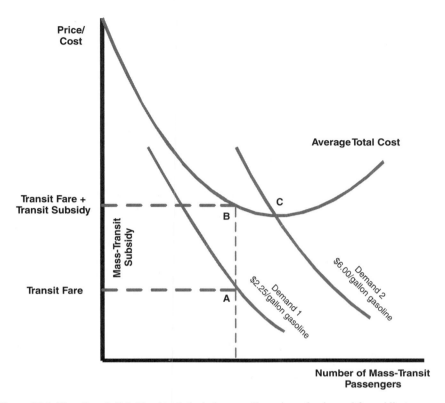

Figure 10.4 Mass-Transit Subsidy. At relatively low gasoline prices, the demand for public transportation is low and the system operates with excess capacity. Revenues do not cover costs. If the price of gasoline were to rise substantially, the demand for mass transit would rise, the system would operate at capacity, and revenues would cover costs.

price to attract more riders will not usually generate enough new ridership to cover total costs either.

This can be seen in **Figure 10.4**. With the price of gasoline at $2.25 per gallon, the demand curve for mass transit lies everywhere below the Average Total Cost curve for mass transit. If the transit authority sets the transit fare at A, a subsidy of AB is needed to cover the transit system's average total cost. If the authority were to raise the transit fare, the number of mass-transit passengers would decline, but at no price can the system survive without a subsidy. Essentially, the authority must consider how many mass-transit riders it would want to subsidize in order to encourage people to leave their cars at home and reduce auto congestion on the highways. Note that it is possible to operate the mass-transit system without a subsidy (at Point C on Demand Curve 2), but only if taxes on gasoline are raised so high as to discourage drivers from using their cars. In this case, presumably many more commuters would choose to use urban bus, trolley, and subway transport as the cheaper option, even at a transit fare that covered the entire average total cost of the public transit system.

Because gasoline prices (including federal and state taxes) are still at levels that do not force auto drivers to shift to mass transit, virtually all mass-transit systems in the United States require some form of subsidy from local, state, and federal government. These subsidies are quite large. According to data from the National Transit Database, revenue from fares covered only 33.5 percent of the operating expenses of transit systems in 2004 (Federal Transit Administration 2005).

Normally, this would suggest that automobile drivers are subsidizing mass-transit riders. But, given rising congestion costs on highways and roads and the added time and frustration needed to get from Point A to Point B by car, it can be argued that the real subsidy may go in the opposite direction. Those who use private cars to get to work or to do chores, especially during rush hour, are actually subsidized by mass-transit riders. The subsidy does not take the form of a cash allowance, but the form of less congestion and less time to get to work. In our busy lives, "time is money." The commuters who leave their cars behind and rely on mass transit reduce the amount of congestion and drive time for those who continue to use their cars. In this case, a "subsidy" goes from the mass-transit user to those who commute by auto.

Very few studies have actually attempted to measure these social benefits of mass transit. One, by Winston and Maheshri (2006), examines twenty-five urban rail systems and finds that social benefits, including reduced travel time for drivers, are greater than costs only for the San Francisco Bay Area system (Bay Area Rapid Transit, or BART). They argue that net benefits (benefits minus costs) are negative for all the other systems, including the two largest ones in New York City and in Washington, D.C. However, another study of the Washington, D.C. Metro system, using a different methodology, found the opposite: net social benefits were positive, with congestion-reduction benefits of the system far larger than the subsidies (Nelson et al. 2007). The controversy continues.

There are some interesting policy implications that we might consider based on this way of thinking about transit. But before we examine the various policy alternatives available for addressing the externalities caused by motorists, as well as the mobility needs of those without access to automobiles, we need to explore the supply side of urban transportation markets. How have past decisions affected the array of transportation options available to us today?

The Supply Side of Metropolitan Transportation

If transportation were like apples, we would have a highly competitive market in which there were many producers, each accounting for only a small amount of total output. It would be relatively easy for new producers to enter the market on a small scale if they were attracted by profitable opportunities. Economist Adam Smith's "invisible hand" (the assertion that a large number of independent producers interacting in a market with a large number of independent buyers results in a socially optimal outcome) would ensure that the result of each producer acting in his own self-interest would be low prices and a large array of choices for consumers.

But the transportation market is not at all like the apple market. Like other components of a metropolitan area's physical infrastructure, transportation networks are subject to huge economies of scale. Like the water and sewer systems we have already examined, transportation networks are yet another example of a natural monopoly in which it is more efficient for one large supplier to produce the entire output. In this case, we are not talking about the individual automobile or, for that matter, the individual bus, streetcar, or subway train. Rather, we refer to the highways, roads, and metro rail systems that have enormous economies of scale and therefore tend to be natural monopolies. Not surprisingly, in most cases—but not all—these are constructed, maintained, and run by the public sector. Therefore, in looking at the supply side of metropolitan area transportation, we are really examining the decisions about infrastructure investment made by past and present governments at the local, state, and federal levels.

Before the steam engine, the first large-scale public transportation systems took the form of canals, the most famous being the Erie Canal in New York State, first proposed in 1808 and completed in 1825. The canal systems of the early nineteenth century gave way to the railroads, whose construction began in the middle of that century. By the late nineteenth and early twentieth centuries, rail lines were built not only to facilitate transportation between cities but, most importantly, also within them. Before the advent of the automobile and truck and the construction of hardened road surfaces, rail was the fastest and most convenient form of transportation for passengers and freight within the city.

Because of the extraordinarily high fixed costs and large scale of these systems, state and local governments played a crucial role in their creation. In some instances, these were government projects; in others, private developers received franchise rights as well as some financial support from state and local governments. Eventually, most of these private systems were no longer profitable and were taken over by government agencies. Thus, the same transformation from private ownership to public we saw in the case of water and sewer systems also applied to transportation.

Although state and local governments were building roadways from the 1920s through the early part of the 1950s to accommodate the increasingly popular automobile, the passage of the federal government's 1956 National Interstate and Defense Highways Act profoundly changed the transportation and land-use patterns of U.S. metropolitan areas. This legislation created the Highway Trust Fund (HTF). All proceeds from the federal gasoline tax would go directly into this earmarked fund. Until the early 1970s, the fund could be used for one purpose only—to build interstate highways.

As the highway network grew, automobile travel became ever more attractive and feasible. With more drivers on the road and more miles driven, gasoline tax revenues continued to grow, the highway trust fund coffers were filled, and so it became easy to finance round after round of highway construction. Subsidies increase the demand for whatever is subsidized. Highways are perhaps America's best example.

The flip side of this positive reinforcement loop for motorists was that as commuters abandoned public transit for private automobiles, revenues from fare collections fell, transit agencies faced budget problems that necessitated cuts in service, and poorer-quality service drove more commuters away from transit and toward automobiles. The United States became more reliant on highways and on the low-density suburban expansion they spawned.

Issues in Contemporary Metropolitan Transportation Policy

So here we are, early in the twenty-first century, living with the transportation infrastructure decisions that were made 50, 100, and even 150 years ago. How can we make the best use of what we currently have, and how can we make wise decisions about transportation infrastructure investment now so that future generations will have a more reliable, environmentally friendly system for their use?

These are not easy questions to answer, and even in instances where there is substantial agreement about the nature of the problem, there is no clear agreement among policy makers about the best solution.

Short-Run Issues: Getting Prices Right.   Tomatoes are cheap and delicious in the summertime, when they are easy to grow in many parts of the country. They are more expensive and often not as tasty in the winter, when many are grown with greater effort and expense inside special hothouses. It is not surprising that consumers will buy more tomatoes when they are cheaper, fewer when they are more expensive. In the tomato market, the lower summer price and the higher winter price reflect the actual difference in production costs. The market works the way it is supposed to work. Prices, which reflect underlying production costs, send the right signals to consumers, who change their buying behavior accordingly and economize on their use of tomatoes in winter when the prices are higher.

In a market system, prices can play an extremely useful role in guiding consumer choice, but only if they reflect accurate cost information. If the price a consumer faces does not accurately reflect the cost of making that choice, decisions will be distorted. If a motorist's cost to drive his car does not reflect the full cost to society of his making that choice, he will make too many car trips, drive too many miles, and drive during the "wrong" time of day. One issue for getting prices right is that automobile transportation is generally priced too low, and the underpricing is even more extreme during the rush-hour commute. Another, as noted above, is that the actual—though often unacknowledged and implicit—subsidy to the rush-hour motorist is often greater than the explicit subsidy given to transit riders, thereby distorting the choice between automobile and transit. What would we need to do to get prices right?

Although the federal gasoline tax is often referred to as a "user tax" because motorists' payments are correlated with the amount of driving they do and the tax revenues are earmarked for transportation projects, it does not actually fit that description. A true **user tax** gets the consumer to confront the full cost of his activity.

In the case of the federal gasoline tax, there are many **cross-subsidies**. Drivers in some states receive far more from the HTF than they contribute. Over the period from 1956 to 2002, for example, Alaska received six and a half times as much funding from the HTF as its drivers contributed (Wachs 2005). Other cross-subsidies are said to favor drivers of heavy trucks over lighter vehicles and rush-hour motorists over drivers in off-peak times.

Similar cross-subsidies affect state gasoline tax receipts and expenditures as well. In Ohio, for example, some of the funds received from state fuel taxes are distributed equally across the state's eighty-eight counties, so that motorists in dense urban areas end up subsidizing the roadways of the state's rural areas. Funds generated in urban areas with greater road maintenance requirements are often siphoned off to rural areas with less pressing needs (Hill et al. 2005). Also, like the HTF before the 1970s, Ohio's receipts from fuel taxes may be used only for highways, not for public transit. These constraints occur in many other states as well, and are barriers to a more efficient use of transportation revenues and resources.

Economists are fond of reminding people that there is "no free lunch," meaning that everything has an opportunity cost, and that it is being paid by someone, somewhere, even if the good is provided free of charge to the consumer. Consider the case of free parking that is provided to employees who drive to work. There were costs involved in acquiring the land and building the parking structures or paving the parking lots. If business firms deduct these costs from their taxes as business expenses, it means that taxpayers in general are subsidizing those employees who drive to work. As Donald Shoup argues in *The High Cost of Free Parking* (2005, p. 2), "If drivers don't pay for parking, who does? Everyone does, even if they don't drive. Initially the developer pays for the required parking, but soon the tenants do, and then their customers, and so on, until the cost of parking has diffused everywhere in the economy."

Shoup argues that ubiquitous free parking distorts the consumers' choice of travel mode because of its implicit subsidy to motorists. In the case of employers' subsidizing parking for their workers, Shoup estimates that the total variable cost per day for a typical commuter—operating costs plus parking cost—would be $8.09, but with employer-provided free parking, it's only $2.32. Free parking subsidizes the commuting motorist for more than two-thirds of the variable costs of driving to work.

The externalities of congestion, pollution, and accidents are other ways that the motorist does not confront the actual cost of his behavior. As we demonstrated in Chapter 9, the question of what, if any, toll to charge for a car crossing a bridge depends in part on whether the bridge has reached its capacity. Once the bridge is congested, another driver trying to cross increases travel time not only for himself but also for other drivers.

There are many instances in which consumers will face higher prices for a given product, depending on the timing of their demand. In-season rates for airplane travel or resort hotels are higher than they would be for those who are willing to travel off-season. Movie theaters charge higher prices for their evening shows than for their matinees. Restaurants might offer "early bird specials" for diners who are willing to

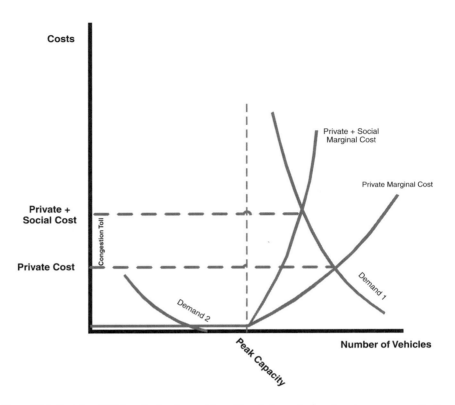

Figure 10.5 Peak Load Pricing. During times of low off-peak demand when there is excess capacity, the cost of allowing one additional driver on the road is minimal, and therefore there is no need to charge a congestion toll. However, once the road has reached its capacity, the cost of adding each additional driver rises. Some of these costs are borne by the driver, but others are spillover costs that the driver does not take into account. The purpose of the congestion toll is to have the driver take these spillover costs into account.

come in before the evening rush. In all of these instances, there is a fixed seating capacity, and building additional capacity would be difficult and expensive. There are times when the demand is higher than can be easily accommodated and other times when there is a good deal of excess capacity. Charging different prices for the peak load versus the off-peak demand helps to make better use of the existing capacity by shifting some of the demand to a time when it can more easily be handled.

Although peak-load pricing is common in the private sector, it has not been used as much in the public sector. Many economists argue that it should be, and that is their basis for endorsing **congestion pricing** for highways. As **Figure 10.5** shows, there is a greater and more inelastic demand (D_1) for highway travel during the morning rush hour, when many people need to arrive at work at the same time, and during the evening rush hours, when many people want to leave work at the same time. The demand is less elastic because unlike many other trips, going to work cannot be avoided or postponed. At other times of the day, the demand for highway use is much smaller and more elastic (D_2)—say, two to four o'clock in the morning, when most people are at home and asleep. On the cost side, the marginal cost of allowing one more car on the highway in the wee hours of the morning is trivial since the highway is not likely to be congested. Once congestion begins and cars slow down during rush hour, the marginal private cost (MPC) of having one extra car traveling on the highway begins to rise, and continues to climb as more cars try to travel at the same time. The individual driver experiences the increase in marginal private cost. It takes commuters more time to get to work, they use more gasoline, they bear the frustration of crawling along in traffic, and they are aware that this stop-and-go driving will mean extra maintenance expenses to keep their cars in good working order.

However, in addition to the increasing marginal private cost as congestion increases, there is also an even faster increasing marginal social cost (MSC): the sum of marginal private cost and the external cost imposed on others. For instance, the concentration of automobile exhaust fumes pollutes the neighborhoods in which the congestion is occurring, and their residents consequently will have higher levels of respiratory illnesses. In addition, employers will not operate as efficiently when workers are delayed by traffic, and emergency vehicles will not be able to make their way through traffic jams in a timely fashion.

The idea of congestion pricing is to charge a toll equivalent to these external costs. If solo motorists face a higher price for traveling during congested times, they might have the incentive to the change their behavior—to carpool or to select a different mode of transportation. Congestion pricing takes many specific forms. In Singapore and in London, cars are charged a price for entering downtown business districts during the day. In the United States, on some toll roads, higher tolls are charged during rush hours. Most recently, some areas have been expanding the use of special carpool lanes—High-Occupancy Vehicle (HOV) lanes, developed to encourage carpooling—to include single-occupancy vehicles willing to pay a toll. These lanes have been renamed HOT (High-Occupancy plus Toll) lanes. In the case of Interstate 15 in San Diego, for example, the price for single-occupancy vehicles to enter the HOT lane changes every few minutes with the level of congestion. Single-occupancy motorists then have a choice of whether to spend more time or more money to get to their destination. As the number of cars equipped with transponders continues to grow, it will be feasible to use congestion pricing in a wider variety of situations.

Even if automobile travel occurs under free-flow circumstances where there is no congestion, every additional driver adds to air pollution and the emission of greenhouse gases. These are externalities generated by motorists for which they are generally not forced to pay and, therefore, another way that automobile travel is underpriced. As we have seen during periods of gasoline price spikes, consumers will respond to higher prices with efforts to change their behavior. Sales of gas-guzzling vehicles fall off dramatically. Newspapers run feature articles about motorists switching to bicycles or public transit. There have even been reports of increased ridership on school buses as growing numbers of parents forgo the usual practice of driving their children to school. But unless gasoline prices are high, there is little incentive to switch to these modes of transit.

All of this implies that raising gasoline taxes would be an effective way to counteract the underpricing of automobile travel. Following good market principles, higher gasoline prices would do all of the following:

- More commuters would use mass transit, which produces fewer emissions per passenger.
- Motorists would purchase more fuel-efficient cars, reducing the amount of emissions and greenhouse gases per mile.
- Households would consider living closer to the central city or closer to their jobs in order to reduce the cost of commuting, thereby reducing emissions as well.

Getting prices right would encourage motorists to change their behavior and thereby lead to a more efficient use of existing resources. The problem is a political one—convincing voters, most of whom currently drive to work or use their cars most days of the year, to agree to a tax hike on gasoline. Most politicians are leery of going to their constituents with such a plan.

Long-Run Issues: Deciding on Future Transportation Infrastructure Investment. What about the future? What factors should policy makers consider in making decisions about new investment in transportation infrastructure?

The Interstate Highway System has been substantially complete since 1991, and a new agenda for transportation infrastructure investment is the subject of continuing debate. Should we continue to encourage dependence on private vehicles? How do we address the mobility and access needs of those who are unable to drive because of age, infirmity, or poverty? If we are to encourage other transportation modes including public transit, bicycles, and walking, what does that imply for changes in land-use policy? Although the interaction between land-use policy and transportation infrastructure investment will be explored more fully in Chapter 13, we will focus here on transportation policy initiatives and the controversies surrounding them.

One fundamental question is whether it is possible to solve traffic congestion problems by building more highway capacity. In his biography of Robert Moses, *The Power Broker: Robert Moses and the Fall of New York*, Robert Caro (1974) describes Moses's enthusiasm for highway construction spanning several decades in which he wielded extraordinary power in shaping the New York City metropolitan area's transportation network. Each time a new highway experienced congestion, Moses's solution was to build another. Decade after decade, new capacity was added, but congestion did not diminish. Caro reports that Moses also resisted the extension of public transit to the developing suburbs by rejecting proposals to build highway median strips that were capable of accommodating rail transit and by designing highway overpasses that were too low to allow clearance for buses.

Why does it seem so difficult to build our way out of congestion? The tendency of new road capacity to generate additional traffic is called "induced traffic," and according to Anthony Downs (2004) of the Brookings Institution, it is the result of a "triple convergence." First, when the new road initially opens, if it seems to offer a faster way to travel, commuters will be induced to shift the time they travel during the day. Off-peak travelers will return to traveling during peak hours. Second, commuters will switch their route from the road they are currently using to the new one. And, third, some mass-transit commuters will now shift their mode to highway use. In the end, congestion will occur soon after the additional highway is built. Supply creates its own demand.

In 1991, Congress made a dramatic change in federal transportation policy when it passed the Intermodal Surface Transportation Efficiency Act (ISTEA, pronounced "ice tea"). With the substantial completion of the Interstate Highway System, the new legislation focused on metropolitan transportation planning, development of alternatives to automobile transportation, linking transportation modes—such as bus–rail links—and making changes in transportation investment that would pro- mote greater compliance with the Clean Air Act. It allowed greater flexibility in how metropolitan areas used their federal transportation dollars and shifted the focus of lessening traffic congestion by reducing the necessity of travel via private auto- mobile rather than by vainly attempting to do so by increasing highway capacity (Vuchic 1999).

Although subsequent legislation—the 1998 Transportation Equity Act for the 21st Century (TEA-21) and the 2005 Safe, Accountable, Flexible, Efficient Trans- portation Equity Act: A Legacy for Users (SAFETEA-LU)—has preserved these policy shifts, this is a contentious area. Proponents of automobile transportation and highway construction oppose this new approach. They argue that most public transit requires high-density development along transportation corridors and that such investment is not justified in a nation that has voted with its feet for low-density development.

Transportation Equity Issues. Aside from the longer term efficiency issues, there are also a number of equity issues. How do we provide mobility for those who are too young, too old, too infirm, or too poor to drive? If there is a spatial mismatch between the poor who are concentrated in the central cities and the availability of new jobs located on the periphery of the metropolitan area, there are three logical alternatives for reducing the severity of the problem: (1) move jobs closer to the areas where poor people are concentrated (this is the aim of the enterprise zone and empowerment zone programs that provide incentives for firms to locate in low- income areas); (2) move people closer to where the new jobs are located (this is one of the aims of the Moving to Opportunity program that helps low-income families move to affordable housing in the suburbs); or (3) improve the transportation options available to the poor so that they can more easily overcome the barrier of spatial separation between home and workplace.

Because commuter rail systems were designed to transport suburban residents to jobs in the central city, the stations are located in residential areas. Therefore, these systems do not work well to satisfy the needs of "reverse commuters"—those who commute from central city homes to widely dispersed suburban job locations.

Programs that subsidize car ownership for inner-city residents have been viewed with promise. Other alternatives to solving the mobility needs of those who cannot drive focus on "para-transit"—the use of small vans that are responsive to demand and whose dispatchers devise flexible routes that depend on the origins and destinations of those who wish to travel at any given time on any given day.

Moreover, as life expectancies increase and as baby-boom drivers age, we will need to pay more attention to the mobility needs of the elderly. As Rosenbloom (2005) notes, we do not yet understand these needs very well because paradoxically, as some elders might become too infirm to drive, many others with limited ability to walk or climb steps are still fully capable of driving. For this latter group, driving is what allows them to maintain their independence.

Ultimately, for all the reasons we have explored in this chapter, to meet the transportation needs of cities and towns in the future, we will need to have a better understanding of externalities, subsidies, commuting needs, and land-use patterns, and how each of these affects mobility and independence—not just for the poor, the elderly, and infirm, but for all of us. With changing demographics, growing environmental concerns, and changing life styles, what kind of urban transportation system will be best for individual households as well as the entire planet in the years to come?

References

Adler, Jonathan H. 2002. "Fables of the Cuyahoga: Reconstructing a History of Environmental Protection." *Fordham Environmental Law Journal* 14, no. 1: 89–146. New York: Fordham University School of Law.

Baer, William C., Seong-Youn Choi, and Dowell Myers. 1996. "The Changing Problem of Overcrowded Housing." *Journal of the American Planning Association* 62, no. 1: 66–84.

Blodgett, Geoffrey. 1966. *The Gentle Reformers: Massachusetts Democrats in the Cleveland Era.* Cambridge, Mass.: Harvard University Press.

Bloom, Khaled J. 1993. *The Mississippi Valley's Great Yellow Fever Epidemic of 1878.* Baton Rouge: Louisiana State University Press.

Bobinski, George. 1969. *Carnegie Libraries: Their History and Impact on American Public Library Development.* Chicago: American Library Association.

Bryce, James. 1888. *The American Commonwealth.* New York: Macmillan.

Burian, Steven J., Stephan J. Nix, Robert E. Pitt, and S. Rocky Durrans. 2000. "Urban Wastewater Management in the United States: Past, Present, and Future." *Journal of Urban Technology* 7, no. 3 (December): 33–62.

Caro, Robert. 1974. *The Power Broker: Robert Moses and the Fall of New York.* New York: Knopf.

Carson, Rachel. 1962. *Silent Spring.* Boston: Houghton Mifflin.

Crosby, Alfred W. 1989. *America's Forgotten Pandemic: The Influenza of 1918.* New York: Cambridge University Press.

Cutler, David, and Grant Miller. 2006. "Water, Water Everywhere: Municipal Finance and Water Supply in American Cities." In Edward Glaeser and Claudia Goldin, eds., *Corruption and Reform: Lessons from America's History.* National Bureau of Economic Research Conference Report Series. Chicago: University of Chicago Press, pp. 153–186.

Dolin, Eric. 2004. *Political Waters.* Amherst: University of Massachusetts Press.

Downs, Anthony. 2004. *Still Stuck in Traffic.* Washington, D.C.: Brookings Institution Press.

Duffy, John. 1990. *The Sanitarians: A History of American Public Health.* Urbana: University of Illinois Press.

Dunne, Finley Peter. 1906. *Dissertations by Mr. Dooley*. New York: Harper & Brothers.

Ely, Richard T. 1902. *The Coming City*. New York: Thomas Y. Crowell.

Finder, Alan. 1991. "New York Eases Sanitation Code for Residents in Building Strike." *New York Times*, April 23, Late Edition (East Coast), p. B2.

Fogelson, Robert. 1989. *America's Armories: Architecture, Society, and Public Order*. Cambridge, Mass.: Harvard University Press.

Hill, Edward, Billie Geyer, Kevin O'Brien, Claudette Robey, John Brennan, and Robert Puentes. 2005. "Slanted Pavement: How Ohio's Highway Spending Shortchanges Cities and Suburbs." In Bruce Katz and Robert Puentes, eds., *Taking the High Road: A Metropolitan Agenda for Transportation Reform*. Washington, D.C.: Brookings Institution Press, pp. 101–138.

Holli, Melvin. 1969. *Reform in Detroit: Hazen S. Pingree and Urban Politics*. New York: Oxford University Press.

Hu, Patricia S., and Timothy R. Reuscher. 2004. *Summary of Travel Trends: 2001 National Household Travel Survey*. Washington, D.C.: U.S. Department of Transportation, Federal Highway Administration, December.

Humphreys, Margaret. 1992. *Yellow Fever and the South*. New Brunswick, N.J.: Rutgers University Press.

Massachusetts Water Resources Authority. 2006. www.mwra.state.ma.us/03sewer/html/swehist.htm.

McGuckin, Nancy A., and Nanda Srinivasan. 2003. *Journey to Work Trends in the United States and Its Major Metropolitan Areas 1960–2000*. Washington, D.C.: U.S. Department of Transportation, Federal Highway Administration, Office of Planning, June 30.

Melosi, Martin V. 2000. *The Sanitary City: Urban Infrastructure in America from Colonial Times to the Present*. Baltimore, Md.: Johns Hopkins University Press.

———. 2005. *Garbage in the Cities: Refuse, Reform, and the Environment*, rev. ed. Pittsburgh: University of Pittsburgh Press.

Meyer, John R., John F. Kain, and Martin Wohl. 1965. *The Urban Transportation Problem*. Cambridge, Mass.: Harvard University Press.

Nelson, Peter, Andrew Baglino, Winston Harrington, Elena Safirova, and Abram Lipman. 2007. "Transit in Washington, DC: Current Benefits and Optimal Level of Provision." *Journal of Urban Economics*, 62, no. 2: 231–251.

Pisarski, Alan E. 2006. *Commuting in America III*. Washington D.C.: Transportation Research Board of the National Academies.

Rosenberg, Charles E. 1962. *The Cholera Years*. Chicago: University of Chicago Press.

Rosenbloom, Sandra. 2005. "The Mobility Needs of Older Americans: Implications for Transportation Reauthorization." In Bruce Katz and Robert Puentes, eds., *Taking the High Road: A Metropolitan Agenda for Transportation Reform*. Washington, D.C.: Brookings Institution Press, pp. 227–256.

Schlesinger, Arthur M. 1933. *The Rise of the City, 1878–1898*. New York: Macmillan.

Schultz, Stanley K., and Clay McShane. 1978. "To Engineer the Metropolis: Sewers, Sanitation, and City Planning in Late-Nineteenth-Century America." *Journal of American History* 65, no. 2: 389–411. Bloomington, Ind.: Organization of American Historians.

Shoup, Donald. 2005. *The High Cost of Free Parking*. Chicago: American Planning Association.

Simmons, Phil, Nora Goldstein, Scott Kaufman, Nickolas Themelis, and James Thompson Jr. 2006. "The State of Garbage in America: 15th Nationwide Survey of Municipal Solid Waste Management in the United States." *BioCycle Magazine* (BioCycle and the Earth Engineering Center of Columbia University), 47, no. 4 (April): 26–43.

Tarr, Joel A. 1984. "The Evolution of the Urban Infrastructure in the Nineteenth and Twentieth Centuries." In Royce Hanson, ed., *Perspectives on Urban Infrastructure*. Washington, D.C.: National Academy Press.

Tomes, Nancy. 1998. *The Gospel of Germs: Men, Women, and the Microbe in American Life*. Cambridge, Mass.: Harvard University Press.

U.S. Bureau of the Census. 1886. "Report on the Social Statistics of Cities, Tenth Census, 1880." Washington, D.C.: Department of the Interior, U.S. Government Printing Office.

U.S. Department of Transportation. 2005a. "Report Year 2005 National Transit Summaries and Trends." Report from the Federal Transit Administration National Transit Database.

Washington, D.C.: U.S. Department of Transportation. http://www.ntdprogram.gov/ntdprogram/pubs/NTST/2005/2005/NTST.pdf.

————. 2005b. "Transportation Statistics Annual Report." Research and Innovative Technology Administration. Washington, D.C.: U.S. Department of Transportation. http://www.bts.gov/publications/transportation_statistics_annual_report/2005/html/chapter_02/figure_04_09.html.

U.S. Environmental Protection Agency. 2000. "Progress in Water Quality: An Evaluation of the National Investment in Municipal Wastewater Treatment." Report prepared by Tetra Tech, Inc. and Andrew Stoddard for the U.S. Environmental Protection Agency Office of Wastewater Management, June. http:// www.epa.gov/OW-OWM.html/wquality/benetifts.htm.

————. 2005. "Municipal Solid Waste Generation, Recycling, and Disposal in the United States: Facts and Figures for 2003." Report EPA530-F-05-003. Washington, D.C.: U.S. Environmental Protection Agency. http://www.epa.gov/msw/pubs/msw03rpt.pdf.

————. 2007. "Municipal Solid Waste Generation, Recycling, and Disposal in the United States: Facts and Figures for 2006," Report EPA530-F-07-030. Washington, D.C.: U.S. Environmental Protection Agency. http://www.epa.gov/epaoswer/non-hw/muncpl/pubs/msw06.pdf.

Vuchic, Vukan R. 1999. *Transportation for Livable Cities.* New Brunswick, N.J.: Center for Urban Policy Research, Rutgers University.

Wachs, Martin. 2005. "Improving Efficiency and Equity and Transportation Finance." In Bruce Katz and Robert Puentes, eds., *Taking the High Road: A Metropolitan Agenda for Transportation Reform.* Washington, D.C.: Brookings Institution Press, pp. 77–100.

Walsh, Donald C. 2002. "Urban Residential Refuse Composition and Generation Rates for the 20th Century." *Environmental Science and Technology* 36, no. 22 (October): 4936–4942.

Water Infrastructure Network. 2000. "Clean and Safe Water for the 21st Century: A Renewed National Commitment to Water and Wastewater Infrastructure." Washington, D.C. http://www.win-water.org/reports.

Wikipedia. 2006. John Lindsay. http://en.wikipedia.org/wiki/John_Lindsay.

Winston, Clifford, and Vikram Maheshri. 2006. "On the Social Desirability of Urban Rail Transit Systems." *Journal of Urban Economics,* 62, no. 2: 362–382.

Chapter 10 Questions and Exercises

1. As mentioned in the Chapter 9 exercises, the U.S. Bureau of the Census conducts a Census of Governments once every five years (in years ending in "2" and "7"), and one of the reports generated from this Census is "Finances of Municipal and Township Governments." The latest version of this report, released in 2005, is available on the Web at

http://www.census.gov/prod/2005pubs/gc024x4.pdf

Go to this report and scroll down to Table 18, "Finances of Individual Municipal Governments with a Population of 25,000 or More by State: 2001–02." Choose the city or town in which you live (or the one closest to you) and any three additional cities/towns of interest to you.

+ For each city/town you selected, what is the amount the municipal government spends on expenditures on sewerage and solid waste management (column 21)?

+ What is the amount each city/town spends on parks and recreation (column 19)?

+ What is the amount each city/town spends on highways (column 16)?

+ For each city/town, what percentage of total municipal government expenditures is devoted to each of these categories? (Divide the expenditure amounts found in columns 21, 19, and 16 by the total municipal expenditures given in column 10.)

- Do the percentages vary from one place to another? If so, what explanations might you offer?

2. The expenditures of municipal governments covered in the data for exercise 1 above represent only part of the expenditures on physical infrastructure within metropolitan areas because in many metropolitan areas expenditures on physical infrastructure are also made by other government entities, including the county governments of the counties comprising the metropolitan area. For example, in 2001–2002, the city of Miami (one of the cities in Miami-Dade County, Florida) spent $34 million on sewerage and solid waste management, while the Miami-Dade County government spent $467 million in this category. Expenditure data for each county government is available on the Web at

http://www.census.gov/prod/2005pubs/gc02x43.pdf

Go to this Web site and scroll down to Table 13, "Finances of Individual County Governments by State: 2001–02." Select four counties.

- For each county selected, what are the amounts of county government expenditures on sewerage and solid waste management (column 21), natural resources and parks and recreation (column 20), and highways (column 17)?
- What percentage of the total county government expenditures are devoted to each of these categories? (Divide each of the expenditure amounts in columns 21, 20, and 17 by the total expenditures given in column 10.)
- Do the percentages vary from one place to another?
- If so, what explanations might you offer?

3. As Chapter 10 points out, water supply and water flow are important issues for metropolitan areas. In 2007 there was a major drought in the Atlanta metropolitan area, causing a water shortage. The existence of a shortage, of course, depends upon the relationship between supply and demand. To shed a bit of light on the demand side of this issue, use the *Urban Experience* CD to determine how much the population and the number of housing units in the Atlanta metropolitan have increased since 1980. (*Note:* For instructions on how to use this CD, see examples in the exercises for Chapter 1.)

4. In response to the water shortage described in exercise 3 above, Atlanta officials urged the Army Corps of Engineers to use its authority over the water resources of the United States to make more water available from Lake Lanier and the Chattahoochee River, which provide Atlanta's water supply. However, these waterways also serve as sources of water for some towns in Alabama and for wetlands in Florida. Florida and Alabama officials objected because increasing the water supply to Atlanta would have meant less water for these two states. Explain how this situation is related to the concept of externalities. In what other ways discussed in Chapter 10 and previous chapters have waterways been related to externalities for urban areas?

5. The Environmental Protection Agency collects data on municipal solid waste and publishes its findings in a report titled "Municipal Solid Waste Generation, Recycling,

and Disposal in the United States." The report is updated every two years and can be found on the Web at

http://www.epa.gov/msw/msw99.htm

Go to this Web page. Scroll down one or two paragraphs and click on the most recent report (the latest report at the time this book went to press was subtitled "Facts and Figures for 2006"). Within this report, scroll down to Table 3, "Generation, Materials Recovery, Composting, Combustion with Energy Recovery and Discards of MSW, 1960–2006 (in millions of tons)."

- Of the 251.3 million tons of municipal waste generated in 2006, how many tons were discarded in landfills?
- How does this compare with 1960? And 1990?
- How do these three years compare in percentage terms? (Divide discard-to-landfill by generation.)
- How much of the solid waste that was generated was recovered for recycling in 1960 and in 2006 (or whatever year is most current)?
- Next, take a look at Table 4, "Generation, Materials Recovery, Composting, Combustion with Energy Recovery and Discards of MSW, 1960–2006 (in pounds per person per day)." How many pounds per person per day are we discarding to landfills, and how does this figure compare with previous years?
- How many pounds per person per day are recovered for recycling, and how does this figure compare with previous years?

6. As described in Chapter 10, many municipalities ship their solid waste to landfills located in other states. Data on the interstate movement of municipal solid waste (MSW) can be found in the Congressional Research Service report "Interstate Shipment of Municipal Solid Waste: 2007 Update," available on the Web at

http://www.ncseonline.org/NLE/CRSreports/07Jul/RL34043.pdf

Go to this report and scroll down to Table 1.

- Which states are the top five importers of municipal solid waste?
- Where does your state rank in terms of the import of municipal solid waste? See Table 2 on the next page.
- Which states are the top exporters of municipal solid waste?
- Where does your state rank among the exporters?
- Proceed to Table 4 and take a look at the third and fifth columns of the table. To which states does your state export MSW? From which states does your state import MSW?

7. As Chapter 10 articulates, one of the major issues facing metropolitan areas is the heavy traffic on their roadways, particularly during certain hours of the day. Data on traffic congestion for eighty-five U.S. cities can be found in the Texas Transportation Institute's *Urban Mobility Report*, available on the Web at

http://mobility.tamu.edu.

Included in the report is a table of the annual delays during peak period travel in 1982, 1995, and recent years. Go to the latest *Urban Mobility Report* and find this table in the report (in the 2007 report it is Table 4). You will note that the eighty-five urban areas are grouped by size, with "Very Large" urban areas listed first, followed by "Large," "Medium," and finally "Small" urban areas. Select two urban areas in each of these categories.

- ✦ What was the change in the annual delay per traveler for each of those cities between 1982 and the latest year available?
- ✦ Did most of this change occur between 1982 and 1995, or after 1995?

8. Continuing with the *Urban Mobility Report*, keep in mind the eight urban areas (two in each category) you selected for the question above and scroll up to a table titled "Components of the Congestion Problem" (in the 2007 report this is Table 2). For each of the eight urban areas you selected, how much excess fuel was consumed due to congestion delays? According to this table, what was the cost of congestion for travelers in each of those urban areas? Examine the explanation of the congestion cost estimates found in the notes at the bottom of the table. How, if at all, does the estimation consider each of the following types of costs: opportunity costs, private costs, and social costs? Explain.

9. As Chapter 10 discusses, public transportation is typically subsidized by local, state, and/or federal governments. The extent to which the operating expenses are subsidized varies from one metropolitan area to another. The pertinent data on the "recovery rate"—the percentage of operating funds that are recovered from fare revenues—are published by the Federal Transit Administration in its National Transit Database (NTD). These data can be accessed through the NTD's Web page at

    http://www.ntdprogram.gov/ntdprogram/data.htm#ntst

Go to this Web page. At the top of the page, click on "National Transit Summary and Trends." Next, click on the latest year available (you can choose either a pdf document or an html document). When the report appears, scroll down to the Table of Contents, and then scroll down within the Table of Contents to find the page number for a table titled "Transit Data by 2000 U.S. Census Urbanized Area." Advance to the relevant page. You will see that 150 urban areas are listed, appearing in order of population size, and that the recovery ratio is in the column on the far right.

- ✦ Which metropolitan areas have high recovery ratios?
- ✦ What do they have in common?
- ✦ How can you relate this to the reasons why governments subsidize public mass transportation?
- ✦ How can you relate this to government subsidy of private transportation by auto?

11 Urban Social Infrastructure

*Public Health, Public Safety, and
Public Welfare Policy*

As we have seen in previous chapters, in rural areas where there may be no more than a few people per acre or per square mile, externalities are not a major factor. However, as population density increases and people live in close proximity to each other, spillover effects can grow exponentially. As a result, cities and suburbs are where we need to be most concerned about public health, safety, and welfare.

These three elements of urban social infrastructure provide valuable contributions to the economic vitality and the quality of life in metropolitan areas. The social dynamics of cities and suburbs, as well as the specific location decisions of businesses and families, have been significantly shaped by health, safety, and welfare issues and by the effectiveness of the public infrastructure developed to deal with them. In addition, social infrastructure itself has spillover effects. The ways and extent to which cities provide public services affect the cohesiveness of communities, their norms and values, and their residents' sense of the opportunities available to them.

The Provision of Public Health Services

Most metro areas rely on a variety of local agencies to provide a battery of health-related services. As discussed in Chapter 10, water and sewer systems are essential parts of the health system. In addition, local health boards regulate eating and drinking establishments to give us some reasonable assurance that the food we eat will not make us ill. Emergency medical technicians (EMTs) and ambulance service are available 24/7 in the case of an accident or major illness. Local housing inspection services exist to make sure that children are protected from the dangers of lead paint; that smoke alarms are armed and ready to warn of fire; that a safe means of egress is available in homes and in commercial and industrial buildings; and that electrical systems are up to code to prevent the danger of fire or electrocution. Depending on where you live, these services are provided directly by the local government or by a regulated private agency and they are often subsidized to assure their availability to all. We take most of this for granted, even as we often complain about the taxes and fees we pay. But when it comes to urban life, all of these services are indispensable.

Local Public Health Departments

Treatment of illnesses, accidents, and other conditions that need medical intervention is an important activity in every metropolitan area, but medical treatment at doctors' offices, health clinics, and hospitals is only part of the urban health infrastructure. The other part focuses on keeping people healthy. This is the province of municipal health departments and other public health agencies.

As noted in Chapter 10, epidemics were once a major issue for urban areas. By the early nineteenth century, it was recognized that many diseases were contagious—passed from one person to another—although the exact means by which the diseases were transmitted had not been determined (Tomes 1998). While the wealthy could try to flee from cities that were in the early stages of epidemics, this was not an option for most residents. To protect the health of residents and the activities within cities, one of the early functions of city government was the quarantining of people with communicable diseases (Duffy 1990). This applied to city residents and their families, as well as to crew members from the ships and boats that frequently arrived in city ports (Humphreys 1992). Quarantining as an urban public health measure continued to be the basic defense against potential epidemics throughout most of the nineteenth century.

The establishment and enforcement of quarantines provided the genesis of modern municipal health departments. During the widespread outbreak of yellow fever between 1793 and 1805, volunteer health committees, the precursor to local health departments, enforced quarantines (Duffy 1990). Recognizing the need to establish legal authority for such efforts, state legislatures in Massachusetts and New York gave municipalities within their borders the authority to appoint local boards of health that had the unquestioned power to enforce quarantines during epidemics. Similar authority was subsequently given to local boards of health in the other states.

After the cholera epidemic of 1849–1854 raised public concern regarding sanitary conditions, many city governments commissioned surveys and reports on conditions that affected health in their cities; subsequently, between 1870 and 1890, they created permanent boards of health (Rosenberg 1987). These initial boards typically served in an advisory role to city government rather than having direct administrative authority for action. Support for the safety of water and sewer systems was one of the key responsibilities of these boards.

In addition to promoting water and sewer systems and inspecting sanitary conditions in the city, local health boards also were made responsible for preparing laboratory testing for evidence of bacteria and viruses, and educating the populace about the need for sanitary practices in and around the home. With these new roles, both municipal and state boards of health received additional administrative powers and achieved new prominence, not only influencing the government and individual families during outbreaks of major diseases, but also acting as a constant presence and source of action for public health education, inspection, and research (Duffy 1990).

While public health boards advocated for the development of hospitals and other institutions to provide for the care of the sick and injured, public health officials have over time focused on an ever broader set of initiatives to keep people healthy and safe. For more than 150 years, they have dealt with the quality of water and food being provided in their jurisdictions. They were originally concerned with how health was related to the physical and social environment, particularly in poor neighborhoods where thousands of families were crowded into tenements. More recently, they have drawn attention to lead paint poisoning, asthma, pollution, and violence—recognizing that place matters for health, as it does for many other urban issues (Kawachi and Berkman 2003). They also address lifestyle issues contributing to illnesses such as high blood pressure, diabetes, lung cancer, obesity, and kidney failure. Their concerns include the particular problems that are associated with substance abuse, the mentally ill, and individuals being released from prison (Cohen 2007). Today, the purview of public health covers ten different functions that can be grouped into four general categories (Institute of Medicine of the National Academies 2002):

Assessment

1. Monitor health status to identify community health problems.
2. Diagnose and investigate health problems and health hazards in the community.

Policy Development

3. Inform, educate, and empower people about health issues.
4. Mobilize community partnerships to identify and solve health problems.
5. Develop policies and plans that support individual and community health efforts.

Assurance

6. Enforce laws and regulations that protect health and ensure safety.
7. Link people to needed personal health services and assure the provision of health care when otherwise unavailable.
8. Assure a competent public health and personal health-care workforce.
9. Evaluate effectiveness, accessibility, and quality of personal and population-based health services.

Serving All Functions

10. Research for new insights and innovative solutions to health problems.

Personal Health Care: Hospitals and Health Centers

Unlike in many countries, personal health care in the United States is handled—for the most part—by the private sector. In today's cities, visits to private hospitals and other health centers are a familiar part of life. In 2002, the 100 largest cities in the United States had a total of more than 1,400 hospitals—an average of more than 14 hospitals each. Together, these 1,400 hospitals served 151 million patients that year, either through admission to hospital beds or through outpatient care (Andrulis and Duchon 2005). Most births take place in hospitals and most routine physical examinations are done in the smaller health centers or the clusters of doctors' offices that are also an intrinsic part of the urban health infrastructure. Physicians who still make house calls are very rare.

This system of care actually would have astonished residents of early U.S. cities. Like water and sewer systems, the hospitals and health centers that characterize urban communities today were nonexistent even as late as the early part of the nineteenth century. Births, illnesses, and deaths typically occurred at home rather than in clinics or hospitals, and that is where doctors treated their patients. Institutions for the sick were mainly places for the terminally ill poor people, or quarantine stations during outbreaks of major disease. There were some exceptions that served temporarily ill individuals—such as Massachusetts General Hospital in Boston, Bellevue Hospital in New York, the Philadelphia Hospital, and Charity Hospital in New Orleans—but, for the most part, these were seen as places to treat crews of ships that landed temporarily in port, as well as other travelers (Duffy 1990).

The first major expansion of hospital services occurred between 1840 and 1860 as a result of federal government interests in ship- and boat-based trade. To serve the crews of ships and boats engaged in trade and military activities away from their home ports, the U.S. Congress authorized the construction of twenty-seven hospitals in cities along the Mississippi and Ohio Rivers and on the Great Lakes. Further expansion of hospitals occurred during and after the Civil War (Duffy 1990). After antiseptic techniques and anesthesia were introduced, hospitals developed a new role as centers for surgery. As methods of fighting communicable diseases were developed, the number of hospitals in the United States increased from 100 in 1870 to more than 6,000 in 1920. Most of these were located in urban areas (Cassedy 1991). A number of them were "city hospitals," built and operated by municipal governments under the auspices of the new municipal health agencies.

The first federal funding for local health facilities was provided during the 1930s. Further increases in the number of urban hospitals occurred in the late 1940s, when Congress included federal funding for the construction of public and nonprofit hospitals in smaller cities under the National Hospital Survey and Construction Act, better known today as the Hill-Burton Act (Waagen 1948).

With these twentieth-century developments, hospitals became mainstays of the urban landscape and their role within the health infrastructure continued to grow—as centers that contain and treat communicable disease, repair injuries, provide surgery, and address other medically treatable conditions. Today, within metropolitan areas, one is likely to find city hospitals (built and operated under the auspices of the local government), for-profit private hospitals, university-based nonprofit hospitals (built and operated by the medical schools of major universities), and nonprofit hospitals (built and operated by religious groups or other organizations).

While we tend to take hospital care for granted, like the cities that house them, such economic factors as fixed costs, economies of scale, and agglomeration economies are critically important to their existence. Hospitals and health centers have developed as important sites, compared to medical treatment in the home, because they provide a common location for the aggregation of various health professionals who together can treat illnesses and injuries, as well as centers for costly medical devices such as X-ray machines and CAT scanners. It is a more efficient use of medical expertise to have patients visit the hospital than to have doctors and nurses spend enormous amounts of time traveling from one patient to another—just one more indication of the usefulness of the Weber models we first encountered in Chapter 3.

The activities conducted within hospitals involve high fixed costs for diagnostic and surgical equipment. Other medically related facilities—including doctors' offices and medical laboratories—tend to cluster around hospitals because of agglomeration economies (specifically, localization economies) that are associated with health services. The population density within metropolitan areas provides a stream of patients and revenue that allows health providers to specialize in particular diseases or procedures, thus contributing to the level of expertise in each specialty. For this reason, the quantity of medical facilities and the array of medical specialists available in major urban medical centers greatly exceed those available outside metropolitan areas. Not surprisingly, then, the physician-to-population ratio is highest in cities, especially those with wealthier populations. The highest ratio (one physician to eighty residents) is in Rochester, Minnesota, outside of Minneapolis-St. Paul, where the famous Mayo Clinic is located. In other large cities, as **Table 11.1** demonstrates, the ratio runs from 1:231 in San Francisco to 1:558 in Austin. In small towns like Brazonia, Texas, there is only one physician for every 1,339 residents (Benbow 2003).

Health Care for the Poor

Because the prevention of communicable disease is a major goal of the health-care infrastructure, and because disease prevention is a public good, public interest in the provision of a safety net of health services for those who cannot afford to pay the full cost of health care is of prime importance. As such, at the beginning of the twentieth century, many medical services for the poor were provided through "dispensaries," specifically established to provide medical aid, and through "settlement houses," which were established to deal with a range of health and related issues faced by new immigrant populations. By the 1930s, most of these facilities had been replaced—with the support of local health boards, the American Red Cross, and other health advocacy organizations—by more than 1,500 health centers that combined health treatment with outreach and health education (Duffy 1990). Such health centers continue to provide direct care and many other important services in urban communities.

Municipal health centers derive their mandates and funding from city governments. Nonetheless, to address the confluence of poor health care and poverty, Congress authorized the creation of federally funded "comprehensive community

Table 11.1 Physician-to-Population Ratio, Selected Metro Areas, 2000

Metropolitan Area	Physician-to-Population Ratio
Rochester, Minn. (home of the Mayo Clinic)	1:80 (Highest ratio in United States)
San Francisco	1:231
New York	1:255
Raleigh	1:276
Boston	1:291
Newark	1:343
Milwaukee	1:350
Buffalo	1:359
Tucson	1:360
Hartford	1:378
St. Louis	1:395
Portland, Ore.	1:407
Chicago	1:409
Los Angeles	1:412
Detroit	1:427
Jacksonville	1:453
Salt Lake City	1:463
Tacoma	1:504
Phoenix	1:505
Atlanta	1:506
Austin	1:558
Brazoria, Tex.	1:1,339 (Lowest ratio in United States)

Source: National Association of County and City Health Officials, Benbow, N., ed. 2003. "Big Cities Health Inventory, 2003." Reprinted by permission of National Association of County and City Health Officials, Washington, D.C.

health centers" in low-income neighborhoods as part of the War on Poverty in 1965. These health centers, funded through the Office of Economic Opportunity, were called "comprehensive" because they were intended to offer a wide range of medical services that extended beyond those provided by local health centers. The federally funded Community Health Center Program expanded rapidly between 1965 and 1980, and became another mainstay of health services in urban environments. In 2004, there were more than 900 such health centers that provided services in 5,500 neighborhoods, with half of these located in urban communities and the remainder serving rural populations (National Association of Community Health Centers 2005).

Health Disparities in the Metro Region

The provision of basic health care to all residents in urban areas is still a major issue. Low birth weight (infants weighing less than 5.5 pounds), infant mortality, asthma, high blood pressure, tuberculosis, and other medical diseases and conditions are much more prevalent in central cities than in suburban areas, and much greater among blacks and Latinos than among whites. The racial variation in just one of these health statistics—infant mortality rates—is displayed in **Figure 11.1** for a range of central cities (Benbow 2003). Of the cities depicted here, San Diego has the

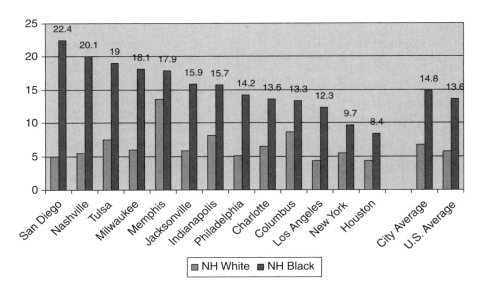

Figure 11.1 Infant Mortality Rates: Non-Hispanic Black versus Non-Hispanic White. *Note:* Data is for the year 2000. *Source:* National Association of County and City Health Officials, Benbow, N., ed. 2003. "Big Cities Health Inventory, 2003." Reprinted by permission of National Association of County and City Health Officials, Washington, D.C.

highest infant mortality rate for non-Hispanic blacks—22.4 deaths per thousand live births. This is more than twice as high as the rate in New York City or Houston and more than four times higher than the rate for non-Hispanic whites in San Diego. In each and every city in this figure, the black rate exceeds the white rate. Across all central cities, the black rate of 14.8 deaths per thousand live births is more than double the white rate. Similar or greater disparities across cities and between racial and ethnic groups would be found in the incidence of low birth weight, heart disease, lung cancer mortality, and HIV/AIDS mortality rates. For example, the rate of black babies born with low birth weight is double that for whites, while tuberculosis rates are seven times higher for blacks than whites. Overall, the rate of babies born with low birth weights in cities is 25 percent higher than in suburban areas.

Why Are Health Disparities So Prevalent?

Several factors contribute to differences in medical care. First, one underlying factor is associated with the location choices made by physicians. The benefits of working in a dense urban setting are greater for medical specialists than for physicians who provide basic medical care. If, for example, the incidence of congenital heart defects among infants is relatively rare, it will take an area with a large number of newborns to support a pediatric cardiologist. A much smaller population would be sufficient to support a general practitioner who treats sore throats. Consequently, the attractiveness of dense metropolitan areas for specialists is even greater than for physicians who provide general care. The high ratio of physicians to population in urban areas noted earlier does not necessarily represent the availability of physicians who provide basic health care.

Second, medical providers are more likely to choose to practice their craft in higher-income urban and suburban neighborhoods than in lower-income neighborhoods. In fact, in both central cities and in small towns, there is often a shortage of general practitioners. A 1994 study of health-care access for low-income neighborhoods in four metropolitan areas concluded that in these neighborhoods, physician-population ratios were as low as 1:10,000 to 1:15,000, in contrast to affluent neighborhoods with ratios of 1:300 or even higher (Ginzberg 1994). Given the recognition in 2006 that "primary care in general has lost popularity as a practice discipline" (Rosenblatt et al. 2006, p. 1046), the shortage that Ginzberg found in 1994 might be even greater if not for physicians who have received National Health Service Corps scholarships or low-interest-rate loans in exchange for agreeing to work a specific number of years in high-need areas, as well as for the number of graduates of foreign medical schools who receive visa waivers in return for agreeing to work in community health centers or inner-city hospitals in the United States. According to data for 2004, one-quarter of all physicians and dentists in community health centers are current participants in federally sponsored scholarship or loan programs, but many of these physicians leave the health centers after serving the required time. Even with a steady flow of such physicians, 24 percent of the community health centers had general practitioner openings that had not been filled for seven months or more (Rosenblatt et al. 2006).

A third reason for disparities in medical care stems from the financing of health services. Households without health insurance are less likely to have general medical checkups and tend to rely on city hospital emergency rooms only when they are desperately ill or injured. As **Table 11.2** reveals, in 2006, nearly 16 percent of the U.S. population had no health insurance whatsoever. This represents more than 47 million Americans out of a total population of 300 million. Of all those who do have health insurance, 84.2 percent are covered by their employer or have paid for private insurance. About one in eight Americans (12.9%) is covered by Medicaid, which serves low-income households and about the same proportion (13.6%) by Medicare, which serves seniors. But coverage differs significantly by race and ethnicity. While better than 89 percent of non-Hispanic whites are insured, only 79.5 percent of non-Hispanic blacks and 65.9 percent of Hispanics have any form of health insurance (U.S. Bureau of the Census 2007a). That means that more than one-fifth of all blacks and more than one-third of all Hispanics have no medical coverage whatsoever. Moreover, the type of insurance that individuals have also varies by race and ethnicity. While all but 24 percent of whites have private insurance and only 9 percent rely on Medicaid—the federal/state-funded program for indigent families—nearly 23 percent of blacks and 22 percent of Hispanics rely on this form of public health insurance for their medical care. Only 54 percent of blacks and 43 percent of Hispanics have private insurance paid for by employers or paid out of their own pockets.

The problem is that many medical providers refuse to take patients who have no insurance. As the Institute of Medicine of the National Academies (2003, p. 2)

Table 11.2 Health Insurance Coverage by Race/Ethnic Group, 2006 (Percent of Population)

	Total Insured	Type of Health Insurance			
		Private Insured	Medicaid	Medicare	Uninsured
Total Population	84.2	67.9	12.9	13.6	15.8
White Non-Hispanic	89.2	76.2	9.0	16.2	10.8
Black Non-Hispanic	79.5	53.6	22.8	10.9	20.5
Hispanic	65.9	43.3	21.5	6.1	34.1

Note: Percentages do not add to 100 because individuals can be covered by both Medicaid and Medicare.
Source: U.S. Bureau of the Census, *Current Population Survey* (Washington, D.C.: U.S. Government Printing Office, 2007), "2007 Annual Social and Economic Supplement," table HI01, "Health Insurance Coverage Status and Type of Coverage by Selected Characteristics."

reports, "Uninsured persons have much more trouble finding health-care providers who will see them, use health-care services much less often when they need care than do insured persons, and are more likely to incur high unreimbursed costs when they do obtain care."

This has repercussions for central cities, where poverty rates are higher and insurance coverage is less complete. The percentage of central city residents without health insurance (19.0%) is much greater than the corresponding percentages in suburban areas (12.8%) or rural areas (16.0%), as shown in **Table 11.3**.

A related problem, especially in central cities, is that health-care providers are more likely to avoid patients who are covered by Medicaid and Medicare because the amount that such insurance is willing to pay for specific services is often lower than the payments provided by private health insurance firms. There are some significant disparities even among those with private health insurance, since families that are stretched financially are more likely to opt for lower-cost plans with more limited coverage of health services and higher patient contributions (called "co-pays") for each service.

Transportation can also be a barrier that creates health disparities. Health-care centers may not be located in accessible locations for all residents of urban areas. Access to medical centers can be a problem for individuals who lack private transportation and live in areas where public transportation lines do not provide affordable and efficient access.

Race or cultural factors are sometimes an issue, too. Racial discrimination or class prejudice may lead some medical providers to avoid administering care to segments of the population, while language and cultural barriers may prevent effective communication about medical issues between medical providers and patients.

Health Disparities between Neighborhoods

Some health disparities are related to differences in the specific neighborhoods where people live. If different races, ethnicities, or income groups live in different sections of cities or metropolitan areas, we can expect that their health outcomes will

Table 11.3 Health Insurance Coverage by Type of Residence, 2006 (Percent of Population)

	Total Insured	**Uninsured**
Total Population	84.2	15.8
Central City	81.0	19.0
Suburb	86.2	13.8
Rural	84.0	16.0

Source: U.S. Bureau of the Census, *Income, Poverty, and Health Insurance Coverage in the United States: 2006* (Washington, D.C.: U.S. Government Printing Office, 2007), table 6, "People with and without Health Insurance by Selected Characteristics: 2005 and 2006."

be correlated with the health issues in their environment (Acevedo-Garcia and Lochner 2003). For example, neighborhoods with few grocery stores and many fast-food outlets will encourage the consumption of whatever foods are readily available and, in many cases, this leads to unbalanced, unhealthy diets. Communities with few recreational outlets limit the opportunities that children have for exercise and contribute to higher incidences of obesity and diabetes. Neighborhoods with street violence not only harm the health of those who are the direct victims but also force virtually all residents to spend inordinate amounts of time inside their homes to escape the possibility of being victimized. This limits exercise and contributes to a range of health problems.

In some neighborhoods, pollution from local sources contributes to the occurrence of asthma and other respiratory problems. Areas with housing that is poorly built or badly maintained may generate poor health among their residents due to the presence of rodents and vermin. Lead paint in older homes can cause severe health problems among young children. Stress—from poverty, racism, crowded surroundings, and violence—has many health repercussions. In general, economic circumstances, neighborhood conditions, and health outcomes are greatly intertwined (Link and Phelan 1995; Institute of Medicine of the National Academies 2003; Smedley, Stith, and Nelson 2003; Massey 2004). Addressing these issues often requires a concerted effort from a range of local government agencies that help to coordinate public health, housing, transportation, and recreation.

Urban Public Health in a Global Context: Epidemics, Bioterrorism, and Homeland Security

Previous chapters have discussed changes in the speed and cost of transportation and communication that make urban issues of the twenty-first century unlike those of the twentieth. This also applies to public health. The simple fact of increased business and tourist travel between countries means that there is more frequent contact between individuals from different countries who may have communicable diseases. The increased speed of transportation makes it more likely that people may be exposed to a disease and then travel to new destinations before the incubation period is over and the first noticeable symptoms appear. Consequently, urban areas are now more susceptible to the spread of international epidemics. In addition, as the dev-astating experience of Hurricane Katrina's impact on New Orleans in 2005 reveals, cities and their surrounding suburbs may also be subject to major natural disasters with substantial public health impacts.

It is impossible to tell when disaster might strike. Yet the spread of AIDS around the globe in the last two decades of the twentieth century, the international concern about avian flu in the early twenty-first century, the dissemination of anthrax-contaminated letters through the mail in 2001, the release of nerve gas in a subway in Japan, and other events show that public health officials face new challenges unlike any in the past. While the exact probability and timing of natural and man-made disasters may be unknown, it is certain that local public health institutions play an important role in preparing for such events, assessing them, providing immediate response, and com-municating with the public and other government agencies about them.

Even the rise of global terrorism is a new concern for cities, since most of the presumed terrorist targets are urban-based. Bioterrorism experts have emphasized that cities bear the brunt of any response to emergency disasters, and that the main federal role is to fund state and local health agencies to prepare and to respond (Institute of Medicine of the National Academies 2002; Noji, Goodwin, and Hop-meier 2005).

Creating the capacity for local authorities to fulfill this role is no small task, and requires that public health become a greater priority for government. After the anthrax scare of 2001, it became clear that communication capabilities in state and local public health departments were grossly insufficient; only half had full-time Internet connections, and among those who did, one-fifth lacked e-mail. Additional problems existed in laboratory facilities, workforce staffing and training levels, coordination between local public health agencies and other institutions, and in the capacity of local hospitals to deal with a sudden influx of patients (Institute of Medicine of the National Academies 2002; U.S. General Accounting Office 2003).

Efforts to increase the emergency disaster capacities of state and local public health agencies continue, with financial support from the Department of Homeland Security. Still, the challenge of preparing for major disasters remains one of the most important tasks of cities and their surrounding suburbs in the early twenty-first century. It joins the other ongoing efforts of the overall health system—to provide medical intervention when needed, and, in the larger context, to impact our sur-roundings and our activities in ways that keep us healthy.

Urban Police

"To protect and to serve"—this is how the title of a recent television show and a recent history of police in America summarize the functions of police forces (Wadman and Allison 2004). But while this is a simple slogan, the implementation of these ideas involves issues that are much more complex, particularly in urban settings.

Like many other functions of local government, municipal police forces originally arose in response to the challenges that grew from population density and urbanization (Monkkonen 1981). The link between formal police departments and urban problems was such that for much of the nineteenth century, police forces were found almost exclusively in urban settings, not rural areas (Hahn and Jeffries 2003). It is not surprising, therefore, that in the years since the first municipal police forces were established in cities, the scope of their responsibilities—and the ways in which they have addressed these responsibilities—have been shaped by the economic and social issues discussed throughout this book: demographic change, the spatial relocation of families and industries, and technological innovation.

According to Hickman and Reaves (2006), there were more than 12,600 individual local police forces in the United States in 2003, employing a total of more than 580,000 full-time personnel and 51,000 part-time employees. On a national basis, although cities with populations of 100,000 or more had just 2 percent of all the local police departments in the nation, they had more than half of all police employees. New York City alone had nearly 36,000 police officers with arrest powers, while Chicago had the second-largest municipal police force, with 13,500 such personnel. With operating budgets that totaled $24 billion, cities with populations larger than 100,000 were responsible for spending 54 percent of the total expenditures for local police forces in the entire country.

The Impact of Demographic Change on Police

Four basic questions are relevant to the role of the police: To protect and to serve whom? Protection *by* whom? Protection *from* what? And, to protect and to serve how? If you lived in cities in the United States before 1825 or so, the question of "protection by whom" was fairly simple, but varied by region. In the cities of the Northeast and the growing Midwest, the general needs of the populace for public order and protection were provided by an appointed constable with arrest powers, who relied on volunteers to carry out his orders (Monkkonen 1981; Gaines, Kappeler, and Vaughn 1999; Wadman and Allison 2004; Walker and Katz 2005). Typically, able-bodied males were expected to voluntarily serve "on watch" on a rotating basis, maintaining order through their capacity to summon the local militia (armed volunteers) in cases where force was needed, and—in less serious circumstances—through their familiarity with disorderly individuals. Major property owners addressed their specific needs by hiring private guards to watch and protect their property (Hahn and Jeffries 2003).

In the slaveholding cities of the Southeast and Deep South, including Richmond, Charleston, Raleigh, Mobile, and New Orleans, civilian structures were utilized, but "protection by whom" was firmly tied to the question of "whom to protect." Order and protection of the status quo were provided by urban slave patrols appointed by local officials from lists of able-bodied white males, whose primary functions were to discourage slave rebellions, to prevent runaways, and to prevent destruction of property (Wadman and Allison 2004; Walker and Katz 2005).

The spatial expansion of cities, along with their burgeoning population growth, made it harder to manage the volunteer systems. As they grew larger, the watch systems became more unwieldy. Moreover, the social cohesion and close communication upon which the watch systems were based began to fray. In the 1830s and 1840s, ethnic, racial, and workforce conflict led to serious urban riots in Boston, Philadelphia, Cincinnati, New York, Detroit, Indianapolis, and other cities in the Northeast and Midwest (Monkkonen 1981; Gaines, Kappeler, and Vaughn 1999; Wadman and Allison 2004; Walker and Katz 2005).

In response to these challenges to civil peace, American cities began to establish formal municipal police forces that contained full-time employees paid by city governments from municipal revenue. In establishing these forces, cities melded their experience with civilian watches and slave patrols with the example of municipal police forces that had recently been established in England. By the late 1800s, municipal police forces existed in cities throughout the United States (Monkkonen 1981).

Expanding urban population and growing demographic diversity in the nineteenth century instigated a change in the role of law enforcement in society. Advocates of self-policing, rotating-watch systems believed that the social embeddedness of watch members was an important aspect of law enforcement. Specifically, they believed that watch members were a part of the community of citizens, affected by the social context of the community, and could therefore be expected to apply the authority with which they had temporarily been entrusted more judiciously.

However, as metro areas expanded, familiarity, trust, and other social ties between residents across the city became more tenuous (Monkkonen 1981; Hahn and Jeffries 2003). As a result, the interaction between the police and the population became more anonymous. Ethnic and class interests played larger roles in urban socioeconomic and political dynamics. By the time regular municipal police forces were formed in the cities of the Northeast and Midwest, there was already antipathy toward the large number of immigrants arriving from Ireland and Germany, and suspicion about their culture and religion. For the native-born, the motivation for establishing formal police forces shifted from self-policing a common community to helping protect "us" against "them"—a conception that already existed in a much more intense racial form in the cities of the South (Hahn and Jeffries 2003).

The conflicting role of police departments continued right into and throughout the twentieth century. In southern cities like Birmingham and Montgomery, Alabama, and Jackson, Mississippi, newsreel footage of police turning high-pressure water hoses, billy clubs, and police dogs on civil rights marchers in the 1960s was memorably captured. As a result, during the civil rights struggles in the 1960s and 1970s, efforts to racially integrate police forces and to influence the actions and perceptions of police officers were among the important goals of the equal rights movement.

This was particularly important because the recruitment of police officers was often based upon family ties and neighborhood networks. Many officers working in the central city were recruited from the suburbs, which were predominantly white. Affirmative action hiring programs were introduced in many large cities, but only late in the twentieth century. These policies slowly changed the racial and ethnic composition of the police force in many communities and finally began to change the nature of the police force, as well as policing itself.

Transformation in the Structure and Responsibilities of Urban Police Departments

To understand the economic and public policy issues facing urban law enforcement today, it is important to understand the genesis of what is now regarded as the twentieth century's "traditional approach" to urban policing. In the early twentieth century, reformers set out to build a revised concept of the role of police forces that focused on creating professional crime-fighting specialists. These changes were part of a larger civic reform movement of the early century to reduce patronage in public administration (Walker and Katz 2005). Exams for hiring and promotion were introduced to reduce the number of politically motivated appointments and nepotism. Civil service status was granted to provide police with job security and reassure officers against arbitrary or sudden unwarranted loss of employment. Many inspection tasks were shifted to departments of health or other municipal offices. Most important, the new training was designed to reorient police away from service to powerful individuals—ward bosses and mayors—and to emphasize apprehension of criminals and the solving of criminal cases (Greene 2000).

These reforms became the dominant approach to policing for the rest of the century. Aided by improvements in automotive transportation and communication—including radio communication between police headquarters and patrol cars—and assisted by advances in investigation techniques, including the creation of police department crime laboratories, this approach to crime emphasized protection by rapid response, and deterrence by raising the probability of arrest.

As cities continued to grow, changes in technology and the increased scale of police operations also encouraged a growing division of labor within police departments. Some paperwork and communications tasks could be efficiently handled through centralized offices by individuals without extensive training. On the other end of the spectrum, the growing scientific sophistication of investigatory functions required centralized laboratories and more specialized expertise. Popular television shows including *CSI* (*Crime Scene Investigation*) convey these roles of specially trained personnel in law enforcement operations today.

Due to this growing division of labor and specialization, the composition of law enforcement personnel changed. By the last decades of the twentieth century, the typical urban police department included not only police officers but also numerous civilian employees working as telephone responders for the emergency 911 system, computer data-entry workers, and laboratory technicians. By the early twenty-first century, in local police departments serving populations of 100,000 or more, one-quarter of all full-time employees are civilian employees and even the job of the police officer on the beat has become highly professionalized (Hickman and Reaves 2006).

Crime Prevention in Urban Settings: From Twentieth- to Twenty-First-Century Paradigms

According to recent statistics, 18 percent of central city households experience a crime each year, while the corresponding percentage for suburban households is 13 percent (Klaus 2006). However, if you ask metropolitan area residents what should be done to reduce the crime that affects them, you are likely to get a variety of different answers. Some residents may advocate hiring more police, so that potential crimes are deterred and the likelihood of repeated crimes by the same person is reduced. Some residents may advocate longer sentences, thinking that if individuals face the prospect of longer jail terms, they are less likely to commit crimes. Others may advocate helping poor people find jobs, since a significant number of crimes are related to the economic desperation of individuals who find themselves in tough economic circumstances. Still others may want the creation of more substance abuse treatment programs, since a substantial number of crimes are committed by individuals who are addicted. Other residents may want funding for community groups, arguing that decreasing anonymity among neighbors is the most effective way to decrease crime.

Although a higher level of spending on law enforcement might reduce crime rates, communities must weigh the importance of crime prevention against other types of expenditures, given city budget constraints. If people value expenditures on law enforcement more than other public-sector expenditures, they will spend their money accordingly.

However, it is not purely a matter of the total amount of spending on law enforcement but also a question of *how* local public funds are spent on the range of services that can prevent crime or increase the likelihood of apprehending criminals once a crime has been committed. Should a municipality spend more on police officers, computer equipment, and jails? Should it spend more on youth programs, job search assistance, and overall job creation? Or should it focus its expenditures on demolishing abandoned buildings, installing more street lamps, and meetings with community groups? In a world without budget constraints, these approaches are not mutually exclusive. However, in the real world of fiscal constraints, the way that communities view the effectiveness of various crime-fighting strategies is important.

Community Policing versus Traditional Approaches

Current debate focuses on the viability of three different approaches to urban crime prevention: (1) the "traditional" approach of cracking down on crime, (2) the "broken-windows/zero tolerance" approach of fixing up a neighborhood and apprehending anyone who degrades it, and (3) "community-oriented policing."

Some law enforcement personnel and city officials start from the premise that crime originates with the inclinations of individuals who are outlaws by nature. In the early twentieth century, due to the influence of widespread racism, this idea was often combined with the inaccurate notion that some ethnic or racial groups were inherently more predisposed to crime than others (National Advisory Commission on Civil Disorders 1968; Hahn and Jeffries 2003). But whether linked to race or not, these beliefs in the importance of apprehending people who are inherently "the criminals" or "the bad guys" has had—and continues to have—a strong resonance in public thought today. Through this perspective, crime fighting is seen as protection against individuals. From the standpoint of those who emphasize this interpretation of the origins of crime, an effective crime-reduction strategy must focus on identifying and controlling the activities of those individuals. The "traditional" approach to crime—which focuses on rapid response, gathering information about and investigating individuals, and apprehension—is strongly tied to this concept of individual criminal motivation (Greene 2000).

The major alternatives to this way of understanding urban crime and crime reduction began by trying to understand various aspects of the urban environment. Drawing upon the work of the early twentieth-century Chicago School of Sociology, which emphasized the relationship between human behavior and the socioeconomic environment, a number of studies have focused on the relationship between crime and social conditions such as overcrowding, poverty, and rapid residential turnover. Rather than focusing on the origin of crime as the work of "criminal minds," this approach argues that while crime is committed by individuals, a substantial amount is spawned by socioeconomic conditions, and that levels of crime are best understood as manifestations of social conditions. At the core of the policy prescriptions arising from such studies is the idea that reductions in crime could occur by improving the socioeconomic environment (Cahill 2005).

Within this approach, some interpretations of the possibilities for crime reduction emphasize the direct relationship between crime and economic circumstances. The proponents of this view would say that if you reduce poverty and unemployment, you can substantially reduce crime. Another type of socioeconomic explanation emphasizes noneconomic variables. Many studies tie the incidence of crime to the absence of the social capital that would have provided formal and informal control of individual behavior. This approach explains why urban neighborhoods with similar levels of poverty or unemployment may have greatly dissimilar crime levels.

Included among the factors examined within this "systemic social disorganization" approach are neighborhood characteristics that create problems in the individual household's ability to nurture and guide the behavior of children and adolescents (such as family disruption); factors at the community level that inhibit the growth of shared norms, trust, communication, and neighborhood involvement (such as the level of residential turnover in a community); and lack of access to resources from public institutions that could contribute toward solutions to neighborhood problems (Wilcox et al. 2004). The social disorganization approach implies that crime can be substantially reduced by measures that change the pattern of social interaction among families—and between families and public institutions—within a community.

Another widely adopted perspective on urban crime argues that the key to crime reduction is to be found in the relationship between criminals' preexisting desire to commit crimes and urban circumstances that provide opportunities for crime—including isolated pedestrian pathways and the design of buildings. According to this view, urban crime can be substantially reduced by making changes in the urban environment that increase criminals' perceptions that their crimes will be observed and that attempted escapes from the site of the crime will be impeded. One variation on this approach is the "broken windows" form of policing, which was enacted with much media attention in New York City under Mayor Rudolph Giuliani. This policy follows the logic that if the citizens report broken windows and other signs of vandalism and disorder, and the police assure that the problem will be taken care of, criminals are more likely to believe that the residents and the city care about what happens in that location, and that people in the neighborhood are more likely to take note, quickly report, and physically react if a crime occurs (Wilson and Kelling 1982; Greene 2000; but see Sampson and Raudenbush 2001).

Community policing (also called **community-oriented policing**) is a reform that was first formally introduced in the mid-1980s (Forst 2000; Greene 2000). It built upon studies of crime and riots in major cities which concluded that the magnitude and intensity of poor relationships between urban police and urban residents constituted a real urban crisis. Proponents of community policing argued that the emphasis on apprehension rather than other forms of crime prevention, the growing racial separation within urban areas, and police hiring practices that tended to draw police recruits primarily from white neighborhoods and suburbia led to police work characterized by alienation from residents of many of the areas they covered, lack of familiarity with neighborhood dynamics, disrespect for residents, and an overemphasis on force (Forst 2000).

Community-policing advocates argued that the focus and operations of police could be changed in ways to create a better relationship between police and neighborhood residents, create more public support for police departments, help build neighborhood capacity to prevent crime, and strengthen the community's ability to recover from incidences of crime. As part of community policing, law officers emphasize crime prevention rather than just response and apprehension; they interact frequently with community residents in a problem-solving context; they strengthen and utilize their own communication and interaction skills; and they link crime-prevention efforts more closely with other municipal services.

Recognized by some as one of the most significant shifts of perspective for police work in the twentieth century (Greene 2000), community policing received a major boost in 1994, with federal funds for training in community policing and for allowing police departments to hire additional officers for this specific purpose. By 2003, more than half of all local police departments serving populations of more than 100,000 had formal, written community policing plans and 75 percent of the local police departments in these larger cities are training their new recruits in community policing, whether they have formal written plans or not (Hickman and Reaves 2006).

While the general concept of community-oriented policing focuses on the relationship between residents and the police, another relatively new approach focuses on changing the relationship between police and the events that get their attention.

This approach, called **problem-oriented policing**, states that instead of thinking in terms of responding to incidents, police should think in terms of underlying problems (Greene 2000; Scott 2000). Rather than react to individual events, police forces are encouraged to identify recurring problems, to analyze them systematically, and then have police officers use problem solving, planning, mediating, and neighborhood organizing skills (along with the improved relationship with the community developed through community-oriented policing) to develop and implement specific strategies to address underlying factors that cause or contribute to the problems. The results are then evaluated to determine their efficacy. Problem-oriented policing was first applied in 1981 in Madison, Wisconsin. Among the other early urban police departments to adopt this approach were Baltimore County, Newport News, San Diego, Tampa, and Jersey City (Scott 2000).

The question of how best to protect and serve continues to be a major topic of discussion and debate, and both police practices and the relationship between police and residents continue to be modified in urban police forces across the country.

Twenty-First-Century Public Safety Issues: Private Security, Internet-Based Crime, and Homeland Security

Today, if you go to a shopping mall, a hospital, a sports stadium, a large concert, or one of the many other kinds of activities open to the public, you are likely to see uniformed security guards—hired as employees by the business directly or as contract workers from firms that specialize in security services. Research prepared for the National Institute of Justice reveals that private security guards now outnumber the officers in public police forces (Forst 2000; Bayley and Shearing 2001). They provide screening at building entry points and monitoring of behavior through direct observation and the use of closed-circuit television cameras.

Summarizing the literature on private policing, Bayley and Shearing (2001) suggest that the rapid growth of this phenomenon constitutes a basic "restructuring of policing." While they note that private policing is generally more focused on prevention rather than the apprehension of criminals, the growth of market-provided security has many implications for justice, equity, and political stability. The reason for this is that the restructuring of policing through markets distorts the distribution of security in favor of those who can afford it and runs the risk of creating a dual system of policing, where the poor are protected by the public police and the rich are protected by private security officers.

Just as public safety in the early 1900s was faced with new challenges as cities grew rapidly with new migrants from rural areas and immigrants from many parts of the world, urban public safety in the twenty-first century is faced with several challenges that did not exist throughout most of the twentieth century. As noted by the National Institute of Justice, property crime rates stabilized early in the first decade of the new century and the rate of juvenile crime decreased in many cities. But, with the spread of information technology, new forms of crime are on the rise (National Institute of Justice 2005, 2006). Urban police are faced with an increase in the number of Internet predators and perpetrators of identity theft. In 2004 alone, identity theft affected 3.6 million households (National Institute of Justice 2006; Baum 2006).

Internet scams and fraud involving the transfer of funds through electronic means have not only increased within the United States, but also frequently involve links between the United States and criminal operations in other countries. According to the Federal Trade Commission, in 2004, more than half (53%) of all reported fraud cases (205,568 incidents) were Internet-related (Federal Trade Commission 2005). Transnational gang violence is also on the increase in cities like Los Angeles and Washington, D.C. (National Institute of Justice 2006). Metro areas in the United States have increasingly become destinations for groups involved in cross-national human trafficking that prey on children and women for many kinds of illegal activities (National Institute of Justice 2006).

Since the September 11, 2001, attacks on the World Trade Center in New York and the Pentagon just outside of Washington, D.C., there has also been greater awareness of the need to prevent terrorism. In 2003, formal written plans for an urban response to terrorist attacks were in place in 90 percent of local police departments serving populations of 250,000 or more, and in nearly 80 percent of police forces serving populations of between 50,000 and 249,999 (Hickman and Reaves 2006).

According to police experts, the threat of terrorism not only presents a physical threat to cities but also challenges recent advances in new approaches to policing. Murray (2005) notes the tendency among some police officers and some politicians to abandon community-oriented policing and instead revert to traditional policing models in order to prevent terrorist acts. This is despite the fact, Murray argues, that the community-police relationship, based on mutual trust, is more likely to help identify prospective terrorists.

These new challenges will continue to redefine the scope and meaning of public safety and the role of urban policing in the twenty-first century.

Fire Departments and Emergency Medical Services

Throughout the nineteenth century and into the twentieth, the threat of fire was a major source of fear for urban residents. The crowded wood-frame housing in which most people lived made it easy for flames to pass quickly from one residence to another, while the use of wood stoves and open fireplaces for warmth and cooking provided the opportunity for wayward sparks to ignite. Cities suffering from "Great Fires" that left many dead and thousands of others homeless included Detroit, New York, Pittsburgh, Chicago, Boston, Seattle, Jacksonville, Baltimore, San Francisco, and Atlanta.

As in policing, the threat of fire in early U.S. cities was initially addressed by volunteers, some of whom acted as lookouts, while others responded to emergencies when summoned (Rothenberg and Giglierano 2006). However, by the mid-nineteenth century, as increased city size reduced the efficacy of the volunteer system, the largest cities turned to full-time municipally paid fire departments, just as they had done in the case of police (Hashagan 2006).

Among the major factors in fighting fire are the speed of response and the availability of water. Advances in technology during the nineteenth century moved firefighting from bucket brigades in the early 1800s to horse-drawn steam-powered pumps by mid-century, and to trucks specifically designed for quick response to fires in the early twentieth century (Calderone 2006). But the threat of fires could not be addressed by quick response alone, so cities instituted a combination of fire safety education and new regulations to address hazardous situations.

Regulations that addressed potential sources of fire—chimneys and particular types of building materials—were introduced as early as colonial times, with tragedy often being the impetus for new policies (Brannigan and Carter 2006). In 1903, a fire in Chicago's Iroquois Theater, a venue with poorly marked exits, left 602 dead. In 1911, despite pleas by the New York fire chief for more regulation of conditions in factories, the Triangle Shirtwaist Factory caught fire, killing 146 workers. In 1942, a fire broke out at Boston's Cocoanut Grove Nightclub, killing 491. Studies of each of these fires pointed to the importance of building construction guidelines; occupancy limits; clear, unfettered paths to exits; and overall fire-safety plans that could be utilized to decrease the toll from fire, smoke, and trampling during rushes toward the exits. Nevertheless, lapses in inspection and enforcement continue. A fire at the Station Nightclub in West Warwick, Rhode Island, on February 20, 2003, resulted in 100 deaths and more than 200 injuries (*Boston Globe* 2003).

While new regulations could be incorporated into the construction of new buildings, the renovation of older buildings to include such measures was more complicated. In many cities, some older buildings were renovated, some were demolished, some were abandoned, and others became targets of arson. As the stock of housing and commercial buildings within central cities aged, fighting fires in such older buildings presented hazards for firefighters and for nearby residents.

Changes in manufacturing also affected firefighting. New types of plastics and new chemicals created hazardous fumes as they burned. The use of these new materials in manufacturing challenged firefighting techniques, and led to an expansion of expertise within fire departments. Firefighting training expanded to include the treatment of hazardous materials, and many large cities are now equipped with "Hazmat" trucks that are fully equipped to deal with a range of hazardous materials.

As was the case with police departments, in many cities, the social context of firefighting and the racial composition of fire departments became an issue. In the early twentieth century, fire departments were frequently part of the political machinery of urban areas, providing patronage jobs and support for political figures. Race and ethnicity also played a direct part in firefighting. By the mid-twentieth century (again echoing events in police departments), hiring and recruitment of firefighters became an area of contention for cities that were becoming increasingly black and Hispanic. During the urban riots of the 1960s, the mainly white firefighting forces that arrived to put out blazes were sometimes seen as symbols of the gap that existed between urban power structures and the feelings of disempowerment in black and Latino neighborhoods; in some cases, rocks and bricks were thrown at the fire trucks as they arrived (National Advisory Commission on Civil Disorders 1968).

Today, fire departments are more racially diverse and more highly trained than they were half a century ago. However, they also face new challenges. Continual changes in materials used in manufacturing, the presence of abandoned and structurally unsound buildings, and the threat of arson and terrorism make metro areas ever more dependent on effective firefighting as an essential part of public safety and the quality of life. The expanding number of high-rise office towers adds new challenges to firefighting in the largest cities, as was so tragically evident in the terrorist attacks on the World Trade Center in 2001.

Emergency Medical Services

One of the key roles of firefighting is to rescue individuals who might be trapped, rendered unconscious, or injured by flame, smoke, or lack of oxygen. This was a major factor in the creation of Emergency Medical Services (EMS) in the 1960s (National Highway Traffic Safety Administration 1996). Before this time, ambulance drivers and the attendants who rode with them were relatively unskilled. Many public health officials thought that more lives could be saved if effective intervention could be done before patients reached hospitals. In 1960, studies showed that cardiopulmonary resuscitation (CPR)—a combination of mouth-to-mouth breathing assistance and rhythmic chest compressions—could help save lives after accidents.

The first systematic implementation of CPR occurred among firefighters during rescues, and the positive results from this use led Congress to approve funds for the development of regional emergency medical services as part of the Highway Safety Act of 1966 (National Highway Traffic Safety Administration 1996). Federal funding for further development of EMS and for the training of emergency service technicians (EMTs) was expanded in 1973 with the Emergency Medical Services Systems Act. Today, such systems have become a basic part of the public health and safety infrastructure in virtually all metro areas.

Urban Social Welfare

As we saw in Chapter 3, the development of steam power in the middle of the nineteenth century allowed factories to relocate from the fall lines of powerful rivers to the large cities where they could more easily assemble a workforce from the hordes of new arrivals. As a result, the social problems inherent in industrialization became specifically urban problems. The economic insecurity of the late-nineteenth-century factory age—the risk of unemployment as well as the risk of death or disability from industrial accidents—was felt most acutely in the cities, where the industrial workforce was concentrated. As city populations continued to swell, the problem of urban poverty intensified.

Even before the late nineteenth century, local communities had provided alms-houses, orphanages, charity hospitals, and insane asylums (Chudacoff and Smith 2000). These institutions developed during an era in which poverty was viewed primarily as a personal failing. In the wake of the dramatic business-cycle fluctuations that produced the Panic of 1873 and the massive economic depression of the mid-1890s, the notion that poverty and unemployment were primarily the result of individual failings was challenged. One aspect of that challenge was the recognition that economic insecurity was a by-product of the industrial age and was endemic to a capitalist system.

The recognition that a family could become poor through no fault of its own— that a worker could become unemployed as a result of adverse economic conditions causing massive layoffs and that industrial accidents causing death or disability could deprive a family of its breadwinner—led to a spate of state legislation intended to protect families from the grimmer side of industrialization. In the late nineteenth and early twentieth centuries, a number of industrial states created programs that included unemployment insurance and workmen's compensation to provide at least a partial replacement for workers' wages.

At a time when married women were generally expected to engage in unpaid work within the home rather than paid work in the labor force, states created widows' pensions and mothers' pensions to transfer income to households lacking an adult male breadwinner. They enacted protective legislation that regulated working conditions for those women who did enter the workforce, as well as laws that prohibited child labor. In the wake of the 1911 Triangle Shirtwaist Factory fire in which 146 workers died, most of whom were young immigrant women, states enacted workplace safety codes.

Early twentieth-century Supreme Court justice Louis Brandeis referred to the states as "laboratories of democracy" for their willingness to enact innovative solutions to the problems of an industrial society. With the advent of the New Deal in the 1930s—in another period of severe economic depression—the federal government took over major responsibility for many of these state obligations, and greatly expanded their scope. Current programs such as Social Security (retirement income and income for surviving spouses and children of deceased workers), Supplementary Security Income (SSI, income support for the elderly and disabled poor), Temporary Assistance for Needy Families (TANF, income support mainly for single-parent, mostly female-headed, families with dependent children), and Unemployment Compensation (partial wage replacement for workers who lose their jobs) date back to this period. Federal legislation for regulating wages and hours that established a minimum wage rate and defined a standard work week of forty hours also originated with the New Deal. Federal responsibility for workplace safety began in 1971 with the passage of the Occupational Safety and Health Act.

Ameliorating Living Conditions in Poor Neighborhoods

In the late nineteenth and early twentieth centuries, as the notion took hold that individuals were poor not primarily because of personal failings but because of the dire conditions in which they lived, the role of private philanthropy also evolved from focusing on individuals to focusing on communities. This is best exemplified in the settlement house movement, in which young, idealistic, well-educated volunteers from the middle class moved into community centers in poor neighborhoods and lived there full-time in an effort to reach out to residents and help them improve their circumstances.

Similarly, as the focus shifted from the individual to the neighborhood, a greater emphasis on the documentation of living conditions and systematic data collection also emerged. The publication in 1890 of Jacob Riis's *How the Other Half Lives* had a profound impact on public awareness of slum conditions, not only from Riis's narrative but also from his use of photography, which provided compelling documentary evidence. Settlement house workers collected systematic data on living conditions in their neighborhoods. In 1907–1908, the Russell Sage Foundation funded *The Pittsburgh Survey*, a comprehensive pathbreaking examination of social and economic conditions in that steelmaking city. The development of sociology as a field of study in the United States and the development of social work as a profession also have their origins in this period of intense urbanization of the very late nineteenth and early twentieth centuries.

Earlier in the nineteenth century, reformers such as Charles Loring Brace and his Children's Aid Society tried to improve the lives of urban poor children by removing them from their environment and sending them off to live with other families in small towns and rural areas. By the early twentieth century, through the efforts of the settlement houses and other child welfare agencies, the focus shifted to improving the urban environment in which these children lived. Efforts to create more nurturing environments for children were pursued through the movement to establish community playgrounds and other urban outlets for healthy recreation. Some of the services first created through the settlement house movement, such as playgrounds, public baths, and kindergartens, were then taken on as responsibilities of local government. However, as the historian Jon Teaford (1984) suggests, U.S. cities lagged far behind those of Germany and Britain in the municipal provision of several types of services, including public bathhouses and lodging houses for the poor.

Early in the twentieth century, municipal public welfare departments were established to coordinate with private agencies in funding and delivering social services to the poor. Such arrangements continue to the present day and are the vehicle for dealing with such contemporary social service needs as sheltering those who are homeless or who are victims of domestic violence. Private charities that deal with homelessness and domestic violence continue in the tradition of their early twentieth-century forebears in which middle-class professionals seek to ameliorate the problems of the poor. Over the last forty years, they have been joined by another type of nonprofit—the **community-based organization** (CBO)—working on a different model of community change. In CBOs, residents of poor neighborhoods are themselves the decision makers who guide the policies that will affect the environment in which they live. **Community development corporations** (CDCs) (to which we give greater attention in Chapter 15) have played an integral role in neighborhood improvement in many cities. Their activities range from cleaning up neighborhood eyesores (such as vacant lots and illegal dumping sites) to developing jobs, housing, and retail establishments needed in the community.

Thus, by the early twenty-first century the roles of the public health department, the police and fire departments, and the social welfare infrastructure of the modern city continued to evolve from the forms and functions they first were assigned in the nineteenth and early twentieth centuries. As the nature of the city changes and as the demographic composition of urban areas evolves, other new social services undoubtedly will be needed to assure that urban residents are well-protected in terms of health, physical security, and the vagaries of the modern economy.

References

Acevedo-Garcia, Dolores, and Kimberly Lochner. 2003. "Residential Segregation and Health." In Ichiro Kawachi and Lisa Berkman, eds., *Neighborhoods and Health*. New York: Oxford University Press, pp. 265–287.

Andrulis, Dennis P., and Lisa M. Duchon. 2005. *Hospital Care in the 100 Largest Cities and Their Suburbs, 1996–2002: Implications for the Future of the Hospital Safety Net in Metropolitan America*. Report prepared for the Social and Health Landscape of Urban and Suburban America Report Series, SUNY Downstate Medical Center, Brooklyn, N.Y.

Baum, Katrina. 2006. "Identity Theft, 2004." Bureau of Justice Statistics Bulletin NCJ 212213. Washington, D.C.: U.S. Department of Justice, Office of Justice Programs.

Bayley, David, and Clifford D. Shearing. 2001. "The New Structure of Policing: Description, Conceptualization, and Research Agenda." National Institute of Justice Research Report NCJ 187083. Washington, D.C.: U.S. Department of Justice, Office of Justice Programs.

Benbow, Nanette, ed. 2003. *Big Cities Health Inventory*. Washington, D.C.: National Association of County and City Health Officials.

Boston Globe. 2003. "First Victims ID'd; Tales of Lives Lost for Families, Shock Slowly Fades to a Grim Reality." *Boston Globe*, February 23, p. A1.

Brannigan, Francis, and Harry Carter. 2006. "Fire Disasters: What Have We Learned?" http://www.firefightercentral.com/history/learned_from_fire_disaster.htm.

Cahill, Meagan E. 2005. "Geographies of Urban Crime: An Intraurban Study of Crime in Nashville, Tennessee; Portland, Oregon; and Tucson, Arizona." Report to the U.S. Department of Justice, Document #209263. http://www.ncjrs.gov/pdffiles1/nij/grants/209263.pdf.

Calderone, John. 2006. "Fire Apparatus: Past and Present." http://www.firefightercentral.com/history/fire_appartus_past_and_present.htm.

Cassedy, James H. 1991. *Medicine in America: A Short History*. Baltimore, Md.: Johns Hopkins University Press.

Chudacoff, Howard, and Judith Smith. 2000. *The Evolution of American Urban Society*, 5th ed. Upper Saddle River, N.J.: Prentice Hall.

Cohen, Bruce. 2007. E-mail communication with the authors, June.

Duffy, John. 1990. *The Sanitarians: A History of American Public Health*. Urbana: University of Illinois Press.

Federal Trade Commission. 2005. "National and State Trends in Fraud and Identity Theft: January–December 2004." http://www.ftc.gov/bcp/edu/microsites/idtheft/downloads/clearinghouse_2004.pdf.

Forst, Brian. 2000. "The Privatization and Civilianization of Policing." In *Criminal Justice 2000: Boundary Changes in Criminal Justice Organizations*, vol. 2. Washington, D.C.: U.S. Department of Justice, National Institute of Justice, pp. 19–79.

Gaines, Larry K., Victor Kappeler, and Joseph Vaughn. 1999. *Policing in America*, 3rd ed. Cincinnati, Ohio: Anderson Publishing.

Ginzberg, E. 1994. "Improving Health Care for the Poor: Lessons from the 1980s." *Journal of the American Medical Association* 271, no. 6: 464–467.

Greene, Jack R. 2000. "Community Policing in America: Changing the Nature, Structure, and Function of the Police." In *Criminal Justice 2000: Policies, Processes, and Decisions of the Criminal Justice System*. Washington, D.C.: U.S. Department of Justice, National Institute of Justice.

Hahn, Harlan, and Judson Jeffries. 2003. *Urban America and Its Police*. Boulder: University Press of Colorado.

Hashagan, Paul. 2006. "Firefighting in Colonial America." http://www.firefightercentral.com/firefighter_history.htm.

Hickman, Matthew J., and Brian Reaves. 2006. "Local Police Departments, 2003." National Institute of Justice Research Report NCJ 210118. Washington, D.C.: U.S. Department of Justice, Bureau of Justice Statistics.

Humphreys, Margaret. 1992. *Yellow Fever and the South*. New Brunswick, N.J.: Rutgers University Press.

Institute of Medicine of the National Academies. 2002. *The Future of the Public's Health in the 21st Century*. National Academy of Sciences. Washington, D.C.: National Academies Press.
———. 2003. *A Shared Destiny: Community Effects of Uninsurance*. National Academy of Sciences. Washington, D.C.: National Academies Press.

Kawachi, Ichiro, and Lisa Berkman, eds. 2003. *Neighborhoods and Health*. New York: Oxford University Press.

Klaus, Patsy. 2006. "Crime and the Nation's Households, 2004." National Institute of Justice Research Report NCJ 211511. Washington, D.C.: U.S. Department of Justice, Bureau of Justice Statistics.

Link, Bruge G., and Jo Phelan. 1995. "Social Conditions as Fundamental Causes of Disease." *Journal of Health and Social Behavior* 35 (Extra Issue): 80–94.

Massey, Douglas. 2004. "Segregation and Stratification: A Biosocial Perspective." *Du Bois Review* 1, no. 1: 7–25.

Monkkonen, Eric. 1981. *Police in Urban America, 1860–1920*. New York: Cambridge University Press.

Murray, John. 2005. "Policing Terrorism: A Threat to Community Policing or Just a Shift in Priorities?" *Police Practice and Research* 6, no. 4: 347–361.

National Advisory Commission on Civil Disorders. 1968. *Report of the National Advisory Commission on Civil Disorders*. New York: Bantam Books.

National Association of Community Health Centers. 2005. "Health Center Fact Sheet: United States." Bethesda, MD, June. http://www.chnwa.org/Policyadvocacy/ResearchAndReports/HealthCenterFactSheetUnitedStates.pdf.

National Highway Traffic Safety Administration. 1996. "Emergency Medical Services Agenda for the Future." Washington D.C.: National Highway Traffic Safety Administration, Office of Emergency Medical Services.

National Institute of Justice. 2005. *2004 Annual Report*. NCJ 209274. Washington, D.C.: U.S. Department of Justice, Office of Justice Programs.
———. 2006. *2005 Annual Report*. NCJ 213267. Washington, D.C.: U.S. Department of Justice, Office of Justice Programs.

Noji, Eric, Tress Goodwin, and Michael Hopmeier. 2005. "Demystifying Bioterrorism: Misinformation and Misperceptions." *Prehospital and Disaster Medicine* 20, no. 1: 3–6.

Riis, Jacob. 1890. *How the Other Half Lives*. New York: Charles Scribner's Sons.

Rosenberg, Charles E. 1987. *The Cholera Years: The United States in 1832, 1849 and 1866*, 2nd ed. Chicago: University of Chicago Press.

Rosenblatt, Roger A., C. Holly Andrilla, Thomas Curtin, and L. Gary Hart. 2006. "Shortages of Medical Personnel at Community Health Centers: Implications for Planned Expansion." *Journal of the American Medical Association* 295, no. 9: 1042–1049.

Rothenberg, Peter, and Geoff Giglierano. 2006. "A Quick History of the FDNY." http://www.nycfiremuseum.org/education/history/chapter1.php.

Sampson, Robert, and Stephen Raudenbush. 2001. "Disorder in Urban Neighborhoods—Does It Lead to Crime?" *National Institute of Justice Research in Brief* (February): 1–6.

Scott, Michael S. 2000. "Problem-Oriented Policing: Reflections on the First 20 Years." Washington D.C.: U.S. Department of Justice, Office of Community Oriented Policing Services.

Smedley, Brian D., Adrienne Y. Stith, and Alan R. Nelson, eds. 2003. "Unequal Treatment: Confronting Racial and Ethnic Disparities in Health Care." National Academy of Sciences. Washington, D.C.: National Academies Press.

Teaford, Jon C. 1984. *The Unheralded Triumph: City Government in America, 1870–1900*. Baltimore, Md.: Johns Hopkins University Press.

Tomes, Nancy. 1998. *The Gospel of Germs: Men, Women and the Microbe in American Life*. Cambridge, Mass.: Harvard University Press.

U.S. Bureau of the Census. 2007a. *Current Population Survey*. "2007 Annual Social and Economic Supplement." Washington, D.C.: U.S. Government Printing Office.

———. 2007b. *Income, Poverty, and Health Insurance Coverage in the United States: 2006*. Washington, D.C.: U.S. Government Printing Office, August.

U.S. General Accounting Office. 2003. "Bioterrorism: Public Health Response to Anthrax Incidents of 2001," Report to the Honorable Bill Frist, Majority Leader, U.S. Senate, GAO-04-152. Washington, D.C., October.

Waagen, Louise O. 1948. "The Hospital Survey and Construction Act." *American Journal of Nursing* 48, no. 6 (June): 361–363.

Wadman, Robert, and William Allison. 2004. *To Protect and to Serve: A History of Police in America*. Upper Saddle River, N.J.: Pearson/Prentice Hall.

Walker, Samuel, and Charles Katz. 2005. *The Police in America*. New York: McGraw-Hill.

Wilcox, Pamela, Neil Quisenberry, Debra Cabrera, and Shayne Jones. 2004. "Busy Places and Broken Windows: Toward Defining the Role of Physical Structure and Process in Community Crime Models." *Sociological Quarterly* 45, no. 2: 185–207. Berkeley: University of California Press.

Wilson, James Q., and George Kelling. 1982. "Broken Windows: The Police and Neighborhood Public Safety." *Atlantic Monthly* (March): 29–38.

Chapter 11 Questions and Exercises

1. As mentioned in the exercises for Chapters 9 and 10, the U.S. Bureau of the Census conducts a Census of Governments every five years. One of the reports generated from this census is "Finances of Municipal and Township Governments," and the latest version of this report is available on the Web at

http://www.census.gov/prod/2005pubs/gc024x4.pdf

Go to this report and scroll down to Table 18, "Finances of Individual Municipal Governments with a Population of 25,000 or More by State: 2001–02." Choose the city or town in which you live (or the one closest to you) and any three additional cities/towns of interest to you.

+ For each city/town you selected, what is the amount (if any) each city/town spends on public welfare (column 14), health and hospitals (column 15), and police protection (column 17)?

+ For each city/town, what percentage of total municipal government expenditures is devoted to each of these categories? (Divide the expenditure amounts found in columns 14, 15, and 17 by the total municipal government expenditures given in column 10.)

  + Do the percentages vary from one place to another?
  + If so, what explanations might you offer?

2. The expenditures of municipal governments covered in exercise 1 above represent only part of the expenditures on social infrastructure within metropolitan areas because in many metropolitan areas expenditures on social infrastructure are also made by other government entities, including the county governments of the counties comprising the metropolitan area. Expenditure data for each county government is available in the Census of Government's report, "Finances of County Governments: 2002," on the Web at

http://www.census.gov/prod/2005pubs/gc02x43.pdf

Go to this Web site and scroll down to Table 13, "Finances of Individual County Governments by State: 2001–02." Select four counties.

  + For each county selected, what are the amounts of county government expenditures on public welfare (column 14), hospitals (column 15), health (column 16), police protection (column 18), and correctional facilities (column 19)?
  + What percentage of the total county government expenditures are devoted to each of these categories? (Divide each of the expenditure amounts in columns 14, 15, 16, 18, and 19 by the total county government expenditures given in column 10.)
  + Do these percentages vary from one place to another?
  + If so, what explanations might you offer?

3. The National Association of County and City Health Officials (NACCHO) publishes "Big Cities Health Inventory," a compilation of health data covering the fifty-four largest cities in the United States. This report is available on the Web at

http://www.naccho.org/topics/crosscutting/documents/bchi07colorfinal.pdf

Go to this report and scroll down to the map titled "Cities Represented in This Report." Select four of the cities shown. Then scroll down through the tables and, for each of these cities, determine whether they are above or below the city average for heart disease mortality rate (Table 1.10), lung cancer mortality rate (Table 1.12), diabetes mortality rate (Table 1.20), and the infant mortality rate (Table 1.21). Note that, as shown at the bottom of each table, the average for cities is greater than the average for the United States as a whole. Why do you think that the city mortality rate is greater than that for the nation?

4. As Chapter 11 discusses, in many cases a disparity exists between the health of white city residents and black city residents. In the "Big Cities Health Inventory" introduced above in exercise 3, scroll down through the tables into section 2 and examine the figures for non-Hispanic whites (NH White Alone) and non-Hispanic blacks (NH Black Alone) and, if data are available, for Hispanics in each of the four cities you selected. For each of the cities you selected (if data are available), does a disparity exist for heart disease mortality rate (Table 2.10), lung cancer mortality rate

(Table 2.12), diabetes mortality rate (Table 2.20), or the infant mortality rate (Table 2.21)? If so, how large is it? How large is the disparity for the "City Average"? What explanations might you offer for these disparities?

5. Data on crime is collected by the U.S. Federal Bureau of Investigation and is available in the annual FBI report, "Crime in the United States," on the Web at

http://www.fbi.gov/ucr/ucr.htm#cius

Go to this Web site and ascertain the crime rates for three MSAs and three principal cities of your choice. To obtain these data, follow the directions below:

- Scroll down to "Crime in the United States" and click on the latest report (do not use "Preliminary Data" reports because they do not provide the detail necessary for this exercise).
- A screen may appear urging caution in the use of these statistics; click on "Continue to Crime in the United States."
- When this caution screen is gone and a new screen appears, look on the left side under "Offenses Known" and click on "Go to Offense Tables."
- On the right side, under "Browse by," scroll down to "Browse by Links" and click on "Metropolitan Statistical Areas." You will note that the names of the MSAs are on the left (in alphabetical order), that each principal city within the MSA is listed, and that the last row for each MSA is the crime rate per 100,000 residents within the MSA. (*Note:* Crime rates are not given if less than 100% of the MSA submitted data to the FBI.)

When you have reached the table, select any three MSAs.

- ✦ How many violent crimes were there per 100,000 residents in each of the MSAs? What was the property crime rate per 100,000 residents?
- ✦ Choose one principal city within each of the three MSAs you selected. Although the crime rates are not explicitly given for the principal cities, they can be calculated from the data shown. For each principal city, divide the number of violent crimes by the city population to get the number of violent crimes per capita and then multiply by 100,000. Similarly, divide the number of property crimes by the city population to get the number of property crimes per capita, and then multiply by 100,000. How do the crime rates in the principal cities compare with the crime rates in the MSA as a whole?

6. Using the *Urban Experience* CD, find out how official poverty rates have changed between 1970 and 2005 within three CBSAs (metropolitan or micropolitan areas) for a principal city and for the suburbs. Include among the three CBSAs you select the one in which you live (or the one closest to you) and two other CBSAs of interest to you. To obtain these data in the *Urban Experience* CD, go to the "Get Data" screen and follow these directions:

- In the "Choose Data Items" section, click on the arrow immediately to the right and choose "Percentages."
- Check the box next to "Percentages" when it appears under "Choose Data Items" and a drop-down list of data categories will appear.
- Check the box next to "Income and Poverty."

- Another drop-down list will appear; check the box next to "In Poverty."
- Move on to the "Choose Locations" section of the screen.
- Double-click on "By CBSA Name" and a drop-down list of all CBSAs will appear.
- Scroll down until you locate the first of the three CBSAs you have selected.
- Double-click on the name of the CBSA and a list will appear. Note that the first item in this list is the sum for all principal cities of the CBSA (the identifying name ends with ("CBSA-Prin Cities"). The second item in the list is the sum for all suburbs in the CBSA (the identifying name ends with "CBSA-suburbs"). The next items in the list are each of the individual principal cities in alphabetical order (there may be one or more than one). After all principal cities have been listed, the list continues with each of the individual suburbs in alphabetical order. For this exercise, check the box for the sum of all suburbs (the second item in the drop-down list) and a box next to any one of your choices among the principal cities.
- Proceed to the next CBSAs you have chosen (one at a time) and repeat checking the boxes for the sum of suburbs and a principal city in those CBSAs.
- Finally, in the "Choose Years" section of the screen, check the boxes for all of the years that are available.
- Click on "Go," and then, on the far left side of the screen, click on "Chart" (or if you prefer seeing the results in a table, click on "Table").

  - How have the poverty rates changed between 1970 and 2005 for each of the principal cities you selected?
  - How have the poverty rates changed within the suburban area of each of the CBSAs? How do the patterns between 1970 and 2005 differ (if at all) when you compare all three principal cities?
  - How do the patterns differ (if at all) when you compare the suburban areas of the three CBSAs?

Urban Housing Markets, Residential Location, and Housing Policy

12

It should now be clear that how well you live depends in part on where you live. Some urban areas have plenty of jobs, while others are losing employers and jobs. Some cities and suburbs have better schools than others and you—or at least your children—therefore have a better chance of gaining the human capital needed to succeed in the labor market.

How well you live also depends on a city or suburb's physical and social infrastructure. Better city services and transportation, better health care, and safer streets can make life a lot more pleasant. Housing is important not only because it affects residents' living standards but its price and quality also may affect the municipality's ability to attract workers and their families, as well as business investment.

To understand the housing market, we need to examine a range of important issues. Why do housing prices and apartment rents vary so much within and across metropolitan areas? What determines whether a family will want to rent rather than own a home? How do housing prices affect a metro area's ability to attract young families and new business ventures? And, how have federal—and state and local government—policies affected the housing market over time?

The Housing Consumer: The Price of an Individual Home

To begin with, it is important to note that a great deal of our wealth is tied up in housing. The total value of residential structures in the United States represents more than one-third of our total net tangible wealth. As **Table 12.1** indicates, the value of housing stock is more than 50 percent higher than the value of all factories, commercial buildings, retail establishments, and other nonresidential structures combined. The nation's housing stock is nearly four times as valuable as all other consumer durables, including the value of all motor vehicles on the road and all the furniture and household equipment that families own. In the year 2000, the asset value of the total U.S. housing stock was nearly $11 trillion, with three-fourths of this in owner-occupied housing and a quarter in rental units. That is a lot of wealth wrapped up in housing.

In many ways, housing is a unique commodity. In almost all cases, it is highly durable, provides service for decades or even centuries, and unlike most other goods,

Table 12.1 Net U.S. Stock of Fixed Tangible Wealth, 2000

	Billions of Dollars	Percent of Total Wealth	Percent of Total Residential Fixed Assets
Total Net Tangible Wealth	$31,022	100.0	
Private	22,190	71.5	
Nonresidential Structures	6,767	21.8	
Nonresidential Equipment	4,355	14.0	
All Residential Structures	11,012	35.5	
Consumer Durable Goods	2,830	9.1	
Motor Vehicles	849	2.7	
Furniture, Household Equipment, Other	1,981	6.4	
Public (Defense and Nondefense)	6,002	19.3	
Total Residential Fixed Assets	10,719		100.0
Owner Occupied	$8,123		75.8
Renter Occupied	$2,596		24.2

Note: Total Residential Fixed Assets excludes nonfarm residential assets such as dormitories and fraternity and sorority houses.
Source: U.S. Bureau of the Census 2003, table 711, p. 470, and table 978, p. 631.

it is spatially fixed. Where housing is located makes a great deal of difference in terms of its value, unlike an automobile or a television set.

Housing is also a very complex good, and many factors go into both its use value to the homeowner or renter and its market price. Imagine a consumer, Gail, who has a hankering for ice cream. Her favorite flavor is butter pecan and her favorite ice cream parlor is close by, so she stops on her way home from work and leaves the store enjoying her purchase. When asked why she picked butter pecan, she replies, "I think it tastes the best." Later that week, and certainly after weeks, months, or even years of shopping around, Gail buys a house. When asked why she picked that particular house, she gives a lengthy answer: "It wasn't quite the design I would have preferred, but it was closer to public transportation than the other houses that were available, so I'll have a shorter commute to work. The kitchen is small, but it has a good backyard for the kids, it's only a short bus ride for them to school, and it's in a good neighborhood."

The difference in the length of Gail's explanation is indicative of an important characteristic of complex goods. While Gail could evaluate ice cream with regard to a single source of pleasure—taste—and its price, the house that she chose to buy had to fulfill a wide range of preferences.

The characteristics of both the dwelling itself and its site are important. Several of the attributes of interest to Gail depend upon the existence of other goods and services, so that the full value perceived in the house is not exclusively internal to the house itself. Instead, the value of the house comes from its use in *conjunction* with external goods and services, including the local school and mass-transit system. As such, municipal government actually plays a considerable role in the prices that housing fetches on the market.

Attributes Theory and Hedonic Prices

Recognition of goods and situations like this led to the development of the **attributes theory of consumer behavior**. As articulated by one of the pioneers of this approach, Kelvin Lancaster (1972), the theory eschews the idea "that goods are the direct objects of utility," and instead states that "it is the properties or characteristics of the goods from which utility is derived." This might seem obvious, but it has profound implications for how we value things.

Because a good with numerous attributes may involve different types of value, consumers' choices about these goods must involve the trade-offs between these different types of value. For example, Gail implicitly chose certain attributes—like the size of the backyard, access to transportation, and her ideas about what a "good neighborhood" is—over the size of the kitchen and the design of the house. Importantly, the attributes theory recognizes that utility obtained from a good (the house, in this case) may change over time as the internal characteristics of the good change (e.g., as the house gets older) or as the external attributes change (e.g., if the city decides to discontinue the nearest public transit route, or if homes nearby are either renovated or left to deteriorate).

Because of the many attributes considered in the choice of housing, economists often resort to a **hedonic price index** to measure the value of one house against another. In theory, any given house can have hundreds of attributes, each of which can be given a value. For expositional purposes, however, assume that Gail considered only the six characteristics we mentioned above: overall house design, size of kitchen, size of backyard, proximity to public transportation, the quality of the schools in the district, and the nature of the neighborhood.

In the city where Gail bought her home, the average house might sell for $210,000; Gail, however, paid $245,000 for hers. On average, her ranch-type home on a slab was worth $30,000 less than the average home that comes with two floors and a full basement, and the size of the kitchen reduced the value by another $10,000. However, the large backyard she wanted for her kids added $25,000 to the value of the home, the proximity to public transportation added another $20,000, and the good reputation of the neighborhood school where Gail will send her two children added still another $30,000. Calculate these figures and you get the $245,000 value of Gail's new home. Just such a hedonic price for Gail's house suggests that there is only partial truth in the old maxim: "the three things that matter most in real estate are location, location, and location."

In developing a hedonic price index, researchers usually generate an equation where price is on the left-hand side and all of the relevant characteristics of housing are on the right. This is somewhat analogous to the human capital equation shown in Chapter 7 on urban labor markets. The equation here might look as follows:

$$\text{Price}_i = a_0 + b_1 * \text{Sq. Ft.}_i + b_2 * \text{Year Built}_i + b_3 * \text{Number of Bedrooms}_i + b_4 * \text{Garage}_i + b_5 * \text{Central Air}_i + b_6 * \text{Number of Bathrooms}_i + b_7 * \text{Average High School SAT Score}_j + b_8 * \text{Number of Burglaries per 100,000 in neighborhood}_j$$

where a_0 refers to the value of an undeveloped piece of land with no house on it, b_1, $b_2 \ldots b_8$ refers to the change in price due to each characteristic, and i refers to an individual housing unit and j refers to a particular neighborhood.

For instance, if we ran this equation on a set of 1,000 house sales in a metro area, the coefficient (b_i) on Sq. Ft might be something like 61.0, meaning that a home with 3,000 square feet would sell for $61,000 more than a 2,000-square-foot home, all other things equal. Similarly, if the coefficient on Year Built was positive, this would show that newer homes were more highly valued than older ones. The value of the coefficient would tell us whether the age of the house contributed a great deal to its price or if it was relatively unimportant. If the coefficient were negative and statistically significant, it would tell us that in this community, ceteris paribus, older homes are valued more highly.

Note that other factors—like the perceived quality of the school district j where $house_i$ is located (measured here as the average SAT score of high school students)—also enter the equation. One suspects that this coefficient would be positive, while the coefficient on number of burglaries per 100,000 residents in the neighborhood would be negative.

Just such an analysis was carried out by Kain and Quigley (1975) using real data for St. Louis. In the 1970s when housing was much less expensive, they found that a home with four extra years of roof life was worth $400 more, a longer commute time was worth $2,000 less, and being in a neighborhood with relatively low pollution added $1,200 to the value of a home.

If one had all this information and it was up to date, it could be used for house hunting. One could estimate the value of a particular house based on the equation, check it against the asking price, and conclude that the price was way too high, just about right, or—lucky for you—a real steal. You could counteroffer based on this analysis. Of course, in real life, it is rare that someone has so much information. But each rational home buyer does a mental back-of-the-envelope calculation that mimics this process when deciding whether to purchase a particular home. Gail did such a hedonic calculation, evaluating a whole bundle of housing characteristics, even if she did not fully comprehend the process.

Budget Constraints and Housing Preferences

The reason Gail had to make trade-offs—for example, the smaller kitchen for the backyard—is that she, like everyone else (except for a few billionaires like Bill Gates and Donald Trump), faces a **budget constraint** when it comes to buying a home. We can see how preferences as represented by **indifference curves** and a budget constraint interact to determine what type of home someone will likely buy (see **Appendix A** for a brief explanation of this technique).

Figure 12.1 depicts the trade-off between house size and the quality of the local schools. Essentially, it suggests that if there is a given budget constraint—a fixed amount of money to buy a house—as shown by either of the straight lines in the drawing, you can choose to buy a small home in a high-quality school district or a

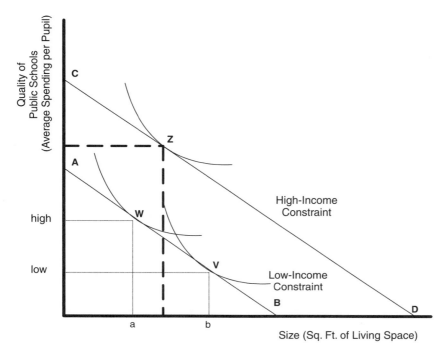

Figure 12.1 Housing Choice: Budget Constraints and Indifference Curves. The lines AB and CD represent the income constraints for low- and high-income households, respectively. Each point on these lines represents a combination of school quality and size of home that can be purchased given the budget constraint, revealing the trade-off between these two housing attributes. The two indifference curves, W and V, show the preferences for two different households, with the former choosing to buy a smaller home in a district with better schools and the latter choosing a larger home in a district where less is spent per pupil. Compared with household W, household Z purchases a larger home in a district that spends more on its students.

larger home in a district where the schools are reputed to be not quite as good. The straight line AB represents the combination of size and school quality that a low-income family can buy—or a family that wishes to spend no more than what a low-income family could afford.

Superimposed on this low-income budget constraint are two indifference curves that represent the preferences of two different families. The family to the left is willing to live in a smaller home (size "a") in order to be in a district with quality schools. The family to the right chooses to live in a spacious home (size "b") in a district where homes are larger but the schools are reputed to be of somewhat lower quality. A third family, which has more money to pay for housing plus a strong desire for a good school, is shown in the figure as well. While this family can afford to live in a larger home than family "a," even with its higher income constraint, it chooses to live in a smaller home than family "b" in order to be located in a school district that is known for its superior schools.

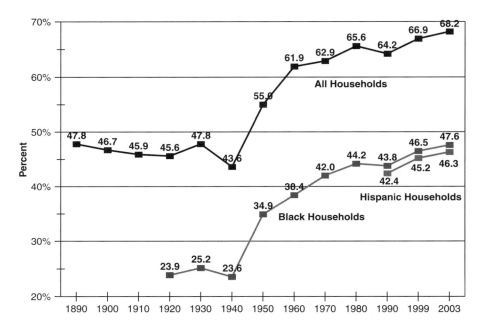

Figure 12.2 U.S. Home Ownership Rate, 1890–2003. *Source:* U.S. Bureau of the Census, *Statistical Abstract of the United States* (Washington, D.C.: U.S. Government Printing Office, 1950–2005).

Because of the huge number of factors that go into the home buying (or renting) decision, the wide variety of preferences for different housing attributes, and the great variance in household incomes, we can begin to appreciate the diverse pattern of housing one finds in any city or metropolitan area. The distribution of housing— where it is located and its style and size—reflects all of this diversity. As we will see later in this chapter, other factors also play a role, including racial discrimination and the business practices of mortgage companies and real estate agents. These factors also affect the way households are distributed by community and neighborhood across a metropolitan area's stock of housing.

Home Ownership versus Rental Housing

Gail chose to purchase her home rather than rent. But it was not until after World War II that a majority of American households owned their own homes. Indeed, from 1890 through 1940, the home ownership rate remained between 44 and 48 percent (see **Figure 12.2**). A slight long-term decline during this period is partially due to the huge number of immigrants who came to the United States after 1890. Many lived in tenement housing when they first arrived and rented homes until they had built up enough savings to afford a down payment. During the Great Depression, many families were forced to rent after they lost their homes and their farms due to foreclosure. Consequently, by the end of the 1930s, the home ownership rate was down to 43.6 percent, the lowest rate of the twentieth century (U.S. Bureau of the Census 2007).

It was during the brief period between 1940 and 1960 that the proportion of households owning their own homes increased by nearly half (from 43.6% to 61.9%). Since then, the ownership rate has increased, but only slowly. Today, about two-thirds (68%) of all occupied housing units are owner-occupied, with the remainder being rental units. The ownership rate among black and Hispanic households has continued to lag behind that of whites. In 2003, 72.2 percent of white households were home owners, compared with just 47.6 percent of black and 46.3 percent of Hispanics.

The Role of Government Incentives for Home Ownership

The great postwar home ownership boom was spurred by several factors. During World War II, families built up large savings accounts. Virtually everyone who wanted to work during the war could find a job and often earned overtime pay. Since there was wartime rationing, there was little to buy, including housing. Thus, at the end of the war, households were flush with savings and had—often for the first time—the wherewithal for a down payment.

Adding to the housing momentum were federal government policies explicitly aimed at encouraging ownership. The Federal Housing Administration (FHA), first established in 1934 as part of President Franklin Roosevelt's New Deal, provided insurance to mortgage lenders that permitted them to lower the down payment for potential home owners and extend home loan repayment for up to thirty years. The longer term allowed lower monthly payments and provided home owners with the ability to pay back some of the principal as well as interest, so they owned their homes outright at the end of the mortgage period. These are fully **amortized** mortgages. When mortgage rates were higher, mortgages were often **nonamortizing**, meaning that only the interest on the loan was paid during the mortgage period. At the end of the mortgage, a family had to secure another mortgage if they wanted to continue to live in their home, or they could pay for the entire cost of the house if they wanted to buy it outright. The Veterans Housing Administration (VHA) also provided mortgage insurance that served the same purpose of substituting amortized mortgages for those that were nonamortized.

Even more important for fostering home ownership was the mortgage deduction under the federal personal income tax. By making the interest charges on a home mortgage deductible on the home owner's federal personal income tax return—thus reducing taxable income—the effective monthly cost of buying a home was often less than the monthly cost of renting. If a household pays $1,400 per month in mortgage interest payments and is in the 25 percent federal income tax bracket, the household's $1,400 monthly mortgage interest payment is equal *after-tax* to a monthly payment of only $1,050. Being able to deduct local residential property taxes in addition to mortgage interest against the federal tax gave an added incentive to buy rather than rent. No other consumer good has been as tax-favored as home ownership.

Given this circumstance, why would anyone rent? A large part of the answer is that low-income households do not have the means for a down payment, nor possibly a credit rating that permits them to obtain a conventional mortgage. Another part has to do with the competitiveness of the rental market. If there is a sufficiently high vacancy rate to keep landlords' economic profit close to zero, some of the benefits that home owners receive are received by renters as well. Since landlords can also deduct their mortgage interest, this will translate into lower rental rates in a competitive rental market. In addition, landlords can use **accelerated depreciation** to deduct maintenance expenses from their federal income tax. Under the accelerated depreciation provision of the federal income tax, landlords can deduct a large proportion of the cost of maintenance in the early years of such an investment rather than spreading out the deduction in equal shares over the full expected life of the property-improvement investment. This reduces their after-tax costs, which, in a competitive market, will be passed along to renters. Using our example above, this might translate into a rent of $800 per month, not $1,050. In this case, for equal amounts of housing, renting can be competitive with buying. This is particularly true if the renter can invest the monthly savings in an asset that is appreciating faster than housing.

Trends in Home Ownership

It is not surprising that ownership rises steadily with age and with income, as **Table 12.2** demonstrates. The decision to buy a home is often made between the ages of 25 and 34. Only about 23 percent of those under age 25 own their own homes, but by the time they reach 30–34, well more than half (57%) are home owners. The ownership rate continues to rise until it peaks among sixty-five- to sixty-nine-year-olds. After that, some elders sell their homes and move into apartments or some form of senior rental housing.

There is a monotonic—continually rising—relationship between household income and home ownership. Fewer than half of households with less than $15,000 annual incomes are home owners. Many of these are older householders, whose retirement incomes are low but who bought their homes when their income was much higher. By the time a household is making in excess of $100,000 a year, the probability of owning a home is close to 90 percent.

This is not surprising, since the tax advantages of owning a home rise with income. Referring to our previous example, at the 25 percent federal personal income tax bracket for a family with $50,000 in adjusted gross income (AGI), $1,400 spent on monthly mortgage interest payments translates into an after-tax payment of $1,050, taking into account the tax savings of $350. But for a higher- income household with $330,000 in AGI in the 35 percent tax bracket, the tax savings on the same $1,400 monthly mortgage interest payment are $490, and the after-tax monthly payment is only $910. In effect, the federal government assists home owners in paying their mortgage interest, and the higher the tax bracket, the larger the amount of monthly mortgage interest paid by the federal government.

Table 12.2 Home Ownership Rates by Age and Income, 2003

	Home Ownership Rate
Age of Householder	
< 25	22.8
25–29	39.8
30–34	56.5
35–39	65.1
40–44	71.3
45–49	75.4
50–54	77.9
55–59	80.9
60–64	81.9
65–69	82.5
70–74	82.0
75+	78.7
Household Income	
< $15,000	46.7
$15,000–$24,999	56.3
$25,000–$34,999	60.3
$35,000–$49,999	66.8
$50,000–$74,999	76.4
$75,000–$99,999	83.4
$100,000 +	89.4

Source: U.S. Bureau of the Census 2005b, table 951, p. 612 and table 667, p. 444.

Household Income and the Individual's Housing Demand

How *much* housing a household purchases is also a function of income. Using data from the *American Housing Survey* for 1989, DiPasquale and Wheaton (1996) calculate the average value of homes owned by married couples as a function of their income. **Table 12.3** reproduces part of their results. At every stage in a household's life, there is the expected positive correlation between income and housing consumption as measured by the dollar value of the homes they own. Moreover, generally, as the head of the household ages, there is a modest increase in housing consumption, perhaps reflecting the desire for more housing as children age and are often given their own bedrooms.

Using the data from Table 12.3, it is possible to estimate the **income elasticity** of housing demand. This elasticity measures, in percentage terms, how the consumption of housing varies with income. Mathematically, this is equal to an estimated percentage change in consumption (C) with respect to a 1 percent change in income (Y)—or mathematically (log C/log Y). The "log-log" regression equation that reflects this relationship between two percentage changes and is generated by using the data in Table 12.3 for twenty-five- to thirty-four-year-olds is:

$$\log C = 1.31 + .78 \log (Y)$$

$$R^2 = 0.94, N = 6$$

Table 12.3 Average Value of Home Owned by Married Couples with Children as a Function of Income, 1989

| | Age of Household Head | | |
	25–34	35–44	45–54
Household Income			
Less than $20,000	$43,822	$70,817	$65,407
$20,000–$29,999	51,145	73,206	77,353
$30,000–$39,999	61,964	75,588	77,720
$40,000–$49,999	93,814	98,544	111,975
$50,000–$74,999	109,679	122,282	114,804
$75,000 +	182,377	190,244	196,848

Source: DiPasquale and Wheaton 1996, table 9.1, p. 218.

Thus, the income elasticity is estimated to be 0.78, which suggests that a doubling of income (+100%) typically leads to a 78 percent increase in housing consumption, measured by the value of a household's primary residence. The R^2 of 0.94 suggests that more than 90 percent of the variance in housing consumption can be explained by the variance in family income.

As a family's income grows, it tends to buy "more" housing—a bigger home or one in a better neighborhood—but as its income continues to grow, its "consumption" of housing slows down relative to the rise in its income. Note from Table 12.3 that the typical household of thirty-five- to forty-four-year-olds with an income of less than $20,000 lives in a home whose value is more than *triple* their income, while comparably aged households with more than $75,000 in income will live in a home valued at a little more than *double* their income.

Overall, the demand for housing by individual households is influenced by household income and the age of the householder. Between the ages of 25 and 54, the value of housing consumed tends to increase, as individual earnings (and thus household incomes) tend to rise over time, peaking for most heads of households when they are in their fifties. Perhaps surprisingly, DiPasquale and Wheaton (1996) find that the level of housing expenditures does not change very much with the presence and then departure of children. What changes are the attributes of the house. Families with children may opt for somewhat larger homes in better school districts, but ones in outer suburbs with lower prices. Once they become "empty nesters," couples may opt for smaller homes, but ones in pricier neighborhoods or with greater amenities. Only with retirement do households seem to reduce their housing expenditures, giving up their larger homes for smaller ones, condominiums, or apartments. Total household spending on housing is kept from falling even further in the retirement years because older, wealthier families often have the ability to purchase multiple homes, including a second home or apartment in a warmer clime where they might spend the winter months.

For at least the past fifty years, the demand for housing units has increased faster than population growth—indeed, much faster. This is not so much because families are buying second homes, but because average household size has fallen so dramatically. In 1950, the average household contained almost 3.6 people. By the 2000 census, the average household size was already down to 2.7. This came about because of the decline in the number of married couples, a growing delay in the age at which families had their first child, and an explosion in the number of people living by themselves. Of all households in 1950, more than three-fourths (78.1%) contained a married couple, compared to only about half (51.7%), fifty years later. One-person households—comprised of larger numbers of young people on the one hand and the elderly on the other—increased from less than one in ten households (9.5%) to more than one in four (25.8%) (Hobbs and Stoops 2002). Thus, even in metro areas such as those in New England, where the total population is growing quite slowly, the demand for housing, given the growing number of households, is still brisk.

The Urban/Metro Housing Market

As we noted in Chapter 2, the cost of living differs significantly across metro areas. The primary driving force behind this phenomenon is the cost of housing. Identical households in terms of income, age, and family composition can afford a lot more house in one region than another. **Figure 12.3** makes this case convincingly. Across the twenty metro regions we have been tracking, the median price of a single-family house in 2005 varied from a staggering $655,000 in San Francisco to just $100,000

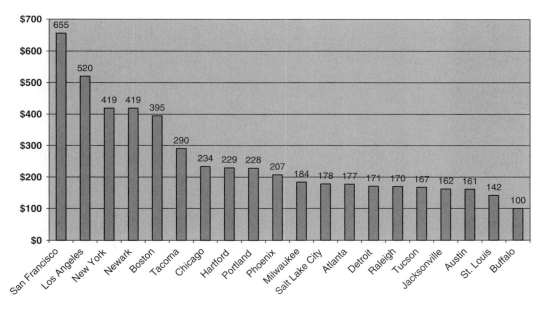

Figure 12.3 Median House Value, Metro Region, 2005 (Thousands of Dollars). *Source:* U.S. Department of Housing and Urban Development, HUD User Policy Development and Research Information Service, SOCDS data set, 2007, http://socds.huduser.org.

in Buffalo. Even if we eliminate San Francisco as a special case, the median-priced house in Los Angeles is more than three times the price in Tucson, Jacksonville, or Austin.

In general, one can find the "best" prices for housing in older industrial regions as well as in many of the new southern and southwestern metro areas. Note that all the cities in the lower half of Figure 12.3 are in the Midwest, the South, or the Southwest. As we shall see, this primarily reflects *demand* conditions in the older regions and *supply* conditions in the newer ones.

A first hint at the importance of demand conditions is provided in **Figure 12.4**, which reflects the increase in housing prices between 1970 and 2005 (in inflation-adjusted 2005 dollars). Again, San Francisco leads the pack—this time by an extraordinary margin. Controlling for normal inflation, the cost of the median-priced home in San Francisco increased over this thirty-five-year period by nearly 400 percent. Los Angeles, Boston, New York, and Newark (which includes some prosperous New Jersey suburbs of the Greater New York region) all saw their inflation-adjusted prices rise by more than 200 percent over the same period. On the other hand, after controlling for normal inflation, you would have had to pay only 10 percent more in 2005 than in 1970 for a median-priced home in Buffalo. In addition to Buffalo, the next four metro regions experiencing the slowest growth in home prices were also traditional manufacturing cities—Milwaukee, Detroit, St. Louis, and Hartford. Moreover, the central cities in these metro areas experienced only modest increases in housing values, and Buffalo actually saw the median price for a house fall by 7 percent (see **Figure 12.5**).

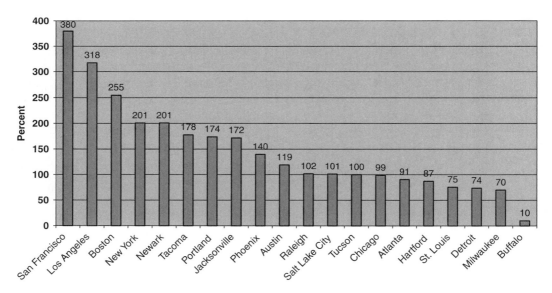

Figure 12.4 Increase in Median House Value, Metro Region, 1970–2005 (2005 Dollars). *Source:* U.S. Department of Housing and Urban Development, HUD User Policy Development and Research Information Service, SOCDS data set, 2007, http://socds.huduser.org.

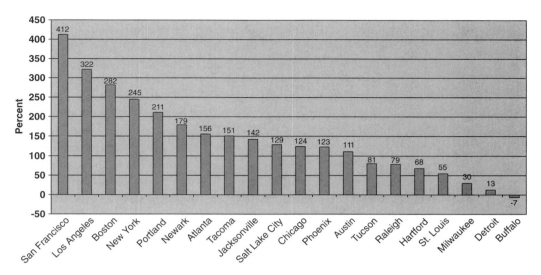

Figure 12.5 Increase in Median House Value, Central City, 1970–2005 (2005 Dollars). *Source:* U.S. Department of Housing and Urban Development, HUD User Policy Development and Research Information Service, SOCDS data set, 2007, http://socds.huduser.org.

One might expect that high-priced housing would translate into higher-priced rents. This is generally true, as shown in **Figure 12.6**, but there are some anomalies. Renting the typical apartment in San Francisco will cost you nearly twice as much as the typical apartment in Buffalo. But rents are also relatively high in Atlanta and Jacksonville, despite the fact that their house prices placed them in the bottom half of the median housing value distribution. What could account for this? In Atlanta,

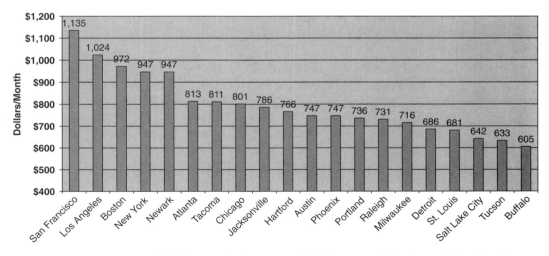

Figure 12.6 Gross Monthly Rent in 2005, Metro Region. *Source:* U.S. Department of Housing and Urban Development, HUD User Policy Development and Research Information Service, SOCDS data set, 2007, http://socds.huduser.org.

the widespread conversion of rental units to owner-occupied condominiums, thus reducing the stock of rental units, may help explain the relatively high rents in this southern city. In Jacksonville, the demand for short-term rentals for northerners trying to escape cold winters may be responsible for this phenomenon.

What Drives Metro Area Housing Prices: Supply and Demand

Demand for housing in a particular city or suburb is determined by many factors. We already mentioned one when we noted that Gail was willing to pay more for a home in a municipality with a reputation for good schools. Communities with many amenities ranging from public parks and museums to a wealth of recreational activities will attract families who have a strong affinity for such things. Cities situated in a warm climate will attract retirees and others who are weary of wintry months of snow and ice.

Of course, perhaps the most important factor that drives housing demand is the state of a region's economy. Metro areas with rapidly growing businesses and strong labor markets will attract workers and their families, naturally increasing the demand for housing. Regions losing large numbers of jobs are likely to see substantial losses in population, and this means a reduction in housing demand. The loss of manufacturing jobs and residents in central cities like Buffalo, Milwaukee, Detroit, St. Louis, and Hartford is clearly the leading cause of the very low appreciation in real median housing values we saw in Figure 12.5.

The supply of housing is also a function of many factors. To be sure, an area that experiences rapid population growth because new jobs are being created or because older households are seeking a retirement home will be a prime location for housing developers who wish to satisfy the increased demand. But the ability of developers to acquire land for housing construction is constrained by the amount of vacant land still available, zoning restrictions imposed by cities and towns to limit the type or amount of new housing, and environmental considerations.

In the short run—which can actually last a number of years if any of the above limitations are in place—the supply of housing in a given city or suburb is relatively fixed and even modest increases in demand can lead to a sharp increase in housing prices and rents. This condition is depicted in **Figure 12.7**. With supply fixed in the short run—equivalent to a **price elasticity of supply** equal to zero—the increase in demand results in the average house price rising sharply from A to B. A zero price elasticity of supply means that an increase in price does not elicit any increase in the quantity supplied, at least in the short run.

In the long run, if developers can produce the housing demanded, supply increases, as in **Figure 12.8**, and housing prices moderate. With the increase in supply, the new price is found at C rather than at B. It turns out that in newer cities and particularly those where there is still a lot of undeveloped land and few zoning restrictions, developers have been able to build housing almost as soon as it is demanded, and sometimes in anticipation of increased demand. In these metro areas, housing prices have risen at a rate not much faster than overall inflation—3 to 4

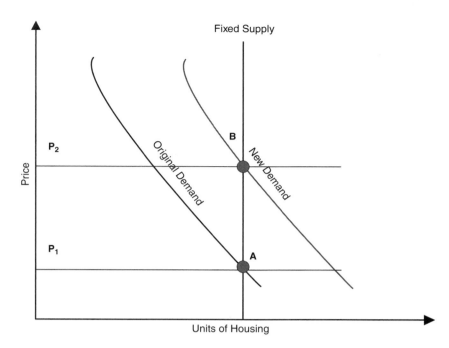

Figure 12.7 Housing Prices with Fixed Housing Supply. Curve A represents the original demand for housing. When the demand increases to curve B, the price of housing rises sharply from P_1 to P_2 due to a fixed housing supply in the short run.

percent a year. But in those metro areas where barriers to new development are high, housing prices have often risen by more than 10 percent a year.

The Greater Boston metropolitan statistical area (MSA) is a good example of a region with high barriers to new development. Recall from Figure 12.4 that between 1970 and 2005 the Greater Boston region experienced a 255 percent increase in the median price of a home—compared to, say, Tucson, where prices rose by only 101 percent. The pace of housing price appreciation in Boston actually accelerated in the late 1990s and continued at a red hot pace for six years running. Between 1998 and 2004, the median price of a single-family home grew from $186,000 to more than $375,000—an increase that averaged more than 12 percent a year (Heudorfer and Bluestone 2006). In the face of a strong economy with a substantial increase in employment, there was little new housing construction in the region. Glaeser, Schuetz, and Ward (2006) found the sluggish growth in housing development was due primarily to local land-use regulations, not a lack of land, per se. Minimum lot sizes of one acre or more, strict wetlands regulations, and the ability to use the court system to delay building permits all contributed to forestalling further housing construction in the region. The median lot size for a new single-family home went from an average of .76 acres between 1990 and 1998 to an average of .91 acres between 1998 and 2002, with much of this a response to municipal zoning

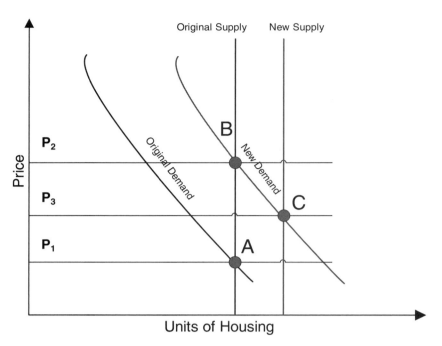

Figure 12.8 Housing Prices with Additional Supply. With additional housing supply, the supply curve shifts to the right. Now, the final price of a housing unit declines from P_2 to P_3, where the new supply curve intersects the new demand curve (at C).

(Jakabovics 2006). As a result, housing prices increased dramatically—as shown in the movement from A to B in Figure 12.7.

Breaking down these barriers to new housing construction is not easy because existing residents raise many arguments whenever a new development is planned. There is the fear that more housing means more traffic congestion. The possibility of young families with children moving in means the municipality must find the resources to pay for additional schooling. The additional property tax receipts from the new housing may not be sufficient to cover these additional expenditures. Deeper fears, often not expressed, have to do with the value of their homes and possible changes in the "character" of their neighborhoods (Fischel 2001). If sufficient housing is built, a sellers' market—where the seller has pricing leverage over potential buyers—can turn into a buyers' market in which sellers must consider whether to reduce their asking price. With more homes available at more affordable prices, some current residents fear that families with lower incomes or from a different racial or ethnic group might move in and change the "middle-class" nature or racial composition of their neighborhood. Politically, those opposed to liberalized zoning and deregulation often have a great deal of power over local municipal leaders, making it difficult for any reform to occur. In this case, existing residents exert the equivalent of monopoly power in the housing market, eliminating much of the competition that would come from additional housing production. As in any monopoly, this results in higher prices and lower output than would occur in a competitive market.

Housing "Affordability"

Particularly where housing supply is constrained, many families trying to buy into the market will find housing "unaffordable." The U.S. Department of Housing and Urban Development (HUD) considers housing to be affordable if a family need not spend more than 30 percent of its gross annual income to cover its mortgage payments, real estate taxes, and home owners' insurance or to pay their rent and utilities. Families who spend more than this are considered **cost-burdened** in the sense that they need to skimp on other necessities including food, clothing, transportation, and medical care (U.S. Department of Housing and Urban Development 2007a).

Using this definition of affordability, the National Low Income Housing Coalition estimates that at the beginning of 2007, 35 percent of American households were cost-burdened, an increase from the 27 percent who had an affordability problem in 2000 (Favro 2007). The problem is much worse for the 15 percent of all households who are **severely cost-burdened**, those paying 50 percent or more of their pretax household income on housing (Joint Center for Housing Studies 2007). In 2005, it is estimated that more than one in ten home owners (11%) and nearly a quarter of all renters (24%) paid this much or more of their income to cover their housing costs. Among the cities with the highest rates of severe cost burden for home owners were Miami (35.8%), Boston (27.1%), and Los Angeles (26.5%) (Miller 2006).

Housing costs are now so high in many cities that individuals and families cannot afford any housing at all, and they end up homeless. According to the U.S. Department of Housing and Urban Development (2007b), there were more than 750,000 persons homeless on any given night in 2005. The government agency found that 65 percent of the homeless are men, the largest segment are thirty-one to fifty years old, 34 percent are in families with children, and 59 percent are from a racial minority. Three-quarters of the homeless are found in central cities; one-quarter are found on suburban streets.

Housing Prices and Vacancy Rates

In labor economics, there is a well-known relationship between the rate of unemployment and inflation. This relationship is captured in the notion of the **Phillips Curve**, first discovered by the British economist A. W. Phillips (1958) in the late 1950s. Phillips observed that there was a nonlinear inverse relationship between the rate of increase in money wage rates and the unemployment rate in England over the period 1861–1957. He found that, in general, wage inflation increased at an ever faster rate the further unemployment fell below 2.5 percent. Above that rate, money wage rates would decline, but only modestly. In the 1980s and 1990s, those who

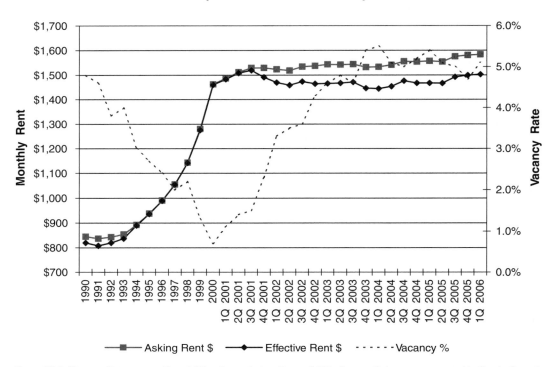

Figure 12.9 Vacancy Rates versus Rental Price Appreciation, Boston MSA. *Source:* Reis.com, as reported in Heudorfer and Bluestone 2006.

believed the Phillips Curve still held suggested that the noninflationary rate of unemployment was closer to 6 percent. Richard Lipsey, writing in 1960, found that this empirical relationship could be explained by noting that the level of wage inflation was a function of the degree of excess demand in the labor market. When there was a lot of "excess demand," wages were bid up. When unemployment was high, indicating an absence of excess demand, wages stabilized or even fell.

We can apply this same logic to the housing market, using housing vacancy rates—the percentage of housing stock available to new owners or tenants—as a measure of "excess demand" for homes. Vacancy rates will always be greater than zero because of housing market friction and imperfect information (Belsky 2006). Renters and potential home buyers take time to search for housing that meets their needs and their budget. Landlords and home sellers attempt to maximize the rent or price they receive and therefore often set prices above what the market will absorb immediately. A vacancy exists until a buyer and a seller (or renter and landlord) can come to terms. As Belsky points out, the landlord (or home seller) is in much the

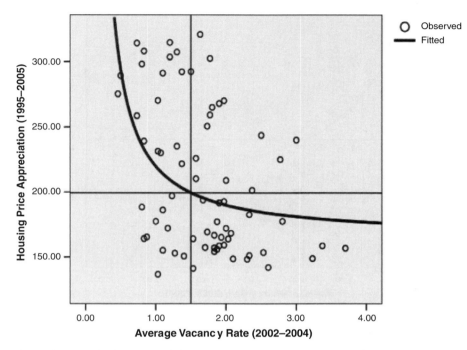

Figure 12.10 Housing Price Appreciation versus Vacancy Rates: Low to Modest Vacancy Rates. At very low vacancy rates, below 1 percent, housing prices rise sharply. At vacancy rates above 1.5 percent, prices fall slowly. *Source:* Bluestone 2006, figure 24.

same position as a retailer who receives periodic shipments of goods. It is more profitable for him to maintain an inventory than to set prices so low that the merchandise is sold as soon as it is placed on the shelves. Testing the waters to see "what the market will bear" requires time and therefore creates vacancies in the short run.

We would expect that when vacancy rates are in the normal range for owner-occupied housing—about 1.5 to 2 percent—housing price appreciation will not be much greater than general inflation. The normal range for rental units is considered to be in the 5 to 6 percent range. As vacancy rates rise above the normal range, prices will tend to stabilize and ultimately may decline. In the short run, housing prices will not decline very much, as sellers either hold out for the price they had hoped to get or perhaps take their homes off the market altogether. As vacancy rates fall below the normal rate, housing prices will tend to rise, like the Phillips Curve, at a faster and faster rate the more the vacancy rate falls below normal. The home market becomes a sellers' market, much like the game of musical chairs with people running ever faster to find an empty chair and bidding prices up in the process. Ultimately, this leads to a housing price spiral.

Figure 12.9 provides a simple picture of how rents are related to vacancy rates. In this case, we have data on both **asking rents** (what is advertised) and **effective rents** (asking rents plus any special charges or discounts) for the Greater Boston metro

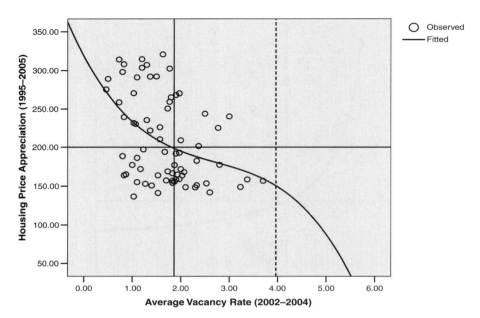

Figure 12.11 Housing Price Appreciation versus Vacancy Rates: Low to High Vacancy Rates. At vacancy rates above 4 percent, housing prices begin to fall sharply. *Source:* Bluestone 2006, figure 24.

area from 1990 through the first quarter of 2006, superimposed on the rental vacancy rate (Heudorfer and Bluestone 2006). Note that in 1990, the vacancy rate was in the normal range (5–6 percent) and rents were stable. As the vacancy rate fell, rents began to rise and the more the rate declined, the higher rents went. By the time the vacancy rate fell to an almost negligible 0.5 percent, the average rent in the region had reached nearly $1,500, almost double what it had been just six years earlier. As Boston's economy began to weaken in 2000 and employment declined, demand for rental units decreased and the vacancy rate climbed back to near 5 percent over the course of just two years. Rent increases slowed to a crawl and rents remained nearly constant for five years.

We find the same kind of relationship for owner-occupied housing using vacancy data for the seventy-five largest MSAs, averaged over the period 2002 to 2004, and data on housing price appreciation between 1995 and 2005 (see **Figure 12.10**). The fitted curve provides just the kind of Phillips Curve relationship expected. At vacancy rates *above* 1.5 percent, home prices rose on average by less than 100 percent (Index Value = 200). At vacancy rates below 1.5 percent, home prices appreciated at higher and higher rates, depending on how low the vacancy rate declined below "normal." At an average vacancy rate of just 0.5 percent—no more than a third to a quarter of the normal rate—price appreciation was 175 percent (Index Value = 275.35).

Refitting the same data using a more complex statistical function provides some insight as to what happens when vacancy rates rise to even higher levels (see **Figure 12.11**). Note that at vacancy rates above 3.5 percent, price appreciation falls off more rapidly. This suggests that when the number of housing units available far

Table 12.4 Housing Price Depreciation

	Peak Quarter	Housing Price Index	Trough Quarter	Housing Price Index	Percent Change	Years to Recovery
Gary, IN	1981:I	63.42	1984:III	56.68	−10.6	7
Boston, MA	1988:IV	112.95	1992:II	99.2	−12.2	9
Duluth, MN	1988:II	114.18	1991:III	99.27	−13.1	11
Worcester, MA	1989:IV	117.26	1995:I	100	−14.7	9
Springfield, MA	1989:iv	117.43	1995:i	100	−14.8	11
Honolulu, HI	1993:II	101.55	1999:III	84.69	−16.6	9
Detroit, MI	1981:IV	61.29	1982:IV	49.69	−18.9	5
Hartford, CT	1988:III	126.4	1995:I	100	−20.9	13
Los Angeles, CA	1990:III	127.16	1996:III	99.7	−21.6	12
Lafayette, LA	1982:III	115.27	1988:IV	65.53	−43.2	15

Source: Bluestone 2006, table 7.

outstrips the number that households want to buy, there can be a housing bubble effect and prices deflate quickly.

There is ample historical evidence of both overheated housing markets and the bursting of a housing bubble. Between 1995 and 2004, with an owner-occupied housing vacancy rate hovering in the 0.5 percent range, the median price of a house in the Boston metropolitan region increased from $154,000 to $395,000—an increase of 156 percent in less than a decade. On the other hand, with vacancy rates rising—in some cases, to double digits—home prices have fallen sharply in some markets and prices have not necessarily recovered very quickly. **Table 12.4** provides a few examples of this phenomenon. Reasonably mild downturns occurred in Gary, Indiana, in the early 1980s, and in Boston from 1988 to 1992. Prices fell between 10 and 12 percent and did not recover to their previous peaks for up to nine years. Much more serious downturns occurred in Detroit, Hartford, Los Angeles, and Lafayette, Louisiana. Prices plummeted by 19 percent to more than 43 percent and did not return to their previous peak for as long as fifteen years. While not as volatile as the stock market, housing prices can become quite unstable when vacancy rates change dramatically. Following the trend in vacancy rates in a given city or metro area can provide a pretty accurate forecast of how prices and rents are likely to move in the local housing market.

The Impact of Housing Prices on Local Employment and Population Growth

While a city or metro area undergoing rapid economic expansion with strong job growth will normally experience appreciating housing prices and rents, it is possible that if housing supply does not expand to match demand, prices and rents can rise high enough to choke off further economic expansion. In this way, at least in theory, an economic boom can lead to an economic bust creating something of a roller-coaster local economy.

At least circumstantially, there is evidence of such a phenomenon. In a number of metro areas across America, but particularly in the Northeast and on the West Coast, housing prices appreciated during the 1980s and early 1990s and then rose even more sharply from the middle of the 1990s through at least 2005 as demand for housing increased much more than supply. Since 1980, New England as a whole has seen house prices increase more than fivefold (528%), while the Pacific region has witnessed increases almost as large (475%). Just between 2001 and 2006, these regions saw average house prices increase by 66 and 96 percent, respectively. By way of contrast, the farther inland you retreat from the coasts, the less housing prices have appreciated (see **Figure 12.12**). Since 1980, the West South Central region saw housing prices increase only 113 percent, while the East South Central states averaged 172 percent—and both experienced no more than a 26 percent increase in prices over the five years ending in 2006 (Office of Federal Housing Enterprise Oversight 2006).

Data on urban labor markets for the regions experiencing the fastest growth in housing prices reveal that a number of these metro areas suffered net domestic out-migration beginning in 2000 and experienced inordinately slow employment growth or an absolute loss in jobs. In the Boston MSA between 2000 and 2004, the net number of nonforeign residents who moved to other MSAs or states amounted to 5.2 percent of its population. Other high-housing-cost communities that suffered a similar fate of net out-migration include the Pacific region's San Jose (10.4%), San Francisco (8.8%), and Los Angeles-Long Beach (4.2%), while net out-migrants from the mid-Atlantic's New York MSA amounted to 7.1 percent of that metro area's population.

Over the same period of time, Boston lost 4.9 percent of its job base. San Jose did much worse, losing 15.4 percent, while San Francisco experienced a 10 percent drop

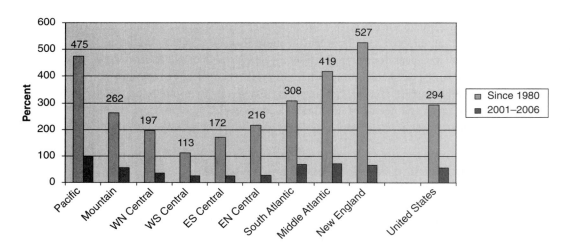

Figure 12.12 Percent Change in Housing Prices, U.S. Census Divisions. *Source:* Based on data from U.S. Department of Housing and Urban Development, Office of Federal Housing Enterprise Oversight, HPI data, http://www.ofheo.gov/media/hpi/3q07_hpi_reg.csv.

in employment. New York lost 3 percent of its jobs, while Los Angeles-Long Beach lost 1 percent. Presumably, housing prices had risen so high that firms thought twice about locating new facilities in these high-cost-of-living metro areas and older firms considered leaving for other areas where the cost of living (and presumably labor cost) was lower.

Compelling as such statistics might seem to be, it is certainly possible that the recent dearth of new jobs in these high-housing-cost metro areas is attributable to factors other than housing prices and that the loss of population is due to either older residents retiring to sunnier climes or younger residents leaving because of a lack of jobs *unrelated* to the high cost of living. Remember, a correlation between two trends does not necessarily imply causation. In this case, there might be a housing affordability problem in these communities, but not necessarily a concern about placing economic development or continued prosperity at risk. Indeed, the high cost of housing might be an indication of just how good things have become in these cities and suburbs. After all, places like Flint, Michigan, have a great deal of affordable housing, but few businesses and people are moving there.

To test the proposition that housing prices can affect economic development, Bluestone (2006) relied on housing cost data collected by the Economic Policy Institute (EPI) in Washington, D.C., and census data on internal net migration and employment growth for hundreds of metro areas. The EPI data provide a comparable measure of housing costs across MSAs.

Across 304 MSAs, it turns out that housing is particularly expensive in the top decile, as **Figure 12.13** reveals. The average monthly housing cost of $1,045 among these thirty-one metro areas is 36 percent higher than the second decile average. Typical of this top decile are Boston, San Francisco, San Jose, Washington, D.C.,

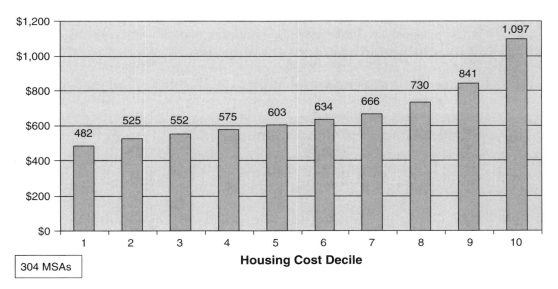

Figure 12.13 Average Monthly Housing Cost by Housing Cost Decile, 2004. *Source:* Economic Policy Institute 2005.

Fort Lauderdale, and New York. Housing costs in the remaining deciles vary by much less. The mean in the second-highest decile is only 43 percent higher than in the tenth (lowest cost) decile. Hence, the cost gap between the first and second deciles is nearly as large as the gap between the second and the tenth. Typical of MSAs with the lowest-cost housing are Johnstown, Pennsylvania; Decatur, Illinois; Lafayette, Louisiana; and Altoona, Pennsylvania.

Housing Prices and Employment Growth

Bluestone (2006) hypothesizes that the relationship between employment growth and housing prices across metro areas, if one existed at all, would be nonlinear. Those MSAs with the highest housing costs should have slower growth in employment than those with more modest home prices and rents. At the same time, those areas with the lowest housing costs might also experience slow growth or even job loss to the extent that low housing prices and rents reflect a weak economy. In this case, the poor employment outlook induces out-migration, which causes a surplus in housing units and a consequent reduction in housing prices.

Following this logic, Bluestone (2006) uses a **quadratic regression equation** that relies on housing cost and housing cost squared from the 2005 EPI data as the independent variables and the percentage change in employment between 2000 and 2004 as the dependent variable (for the 245 MSAs with U.S. Bureau of Labor Statistics employment data). A quadratic equation uses a squared term in order to control for nonlinearity (i.e., curvature) in a function.

The results, as shown in **Regression Equation 1**, indicate that while only about 6 percent of the total variance in employment growth can be accounted for by housing costs alone, both independent variables are highly significant with t-statistics in excess of 4.0, which suggests that housing costs do indeed have something to do with job growth. The signs on the independent variables are as expected, with the linear term positive and the squared term negative. This means that in those metro areas with the very highest housing costs, the negative coefficient on the housing cost squared term dominates the positive coefficient on the linear term—indicating slower growth in employment in these cities or an outright loss of jobs.

Regression Equation 1

$$\% \ \Delta \ \text{Employment}_i = -.1466 + .0000396 \ \text{Housing Cost}_i$$
$$(4.07)$$

$$- 2.291\text{E-}007 \ \text{Housing Cost Squared}_i$$
$$(4.04)$$

$$R^2 = .056, \ N = 245 \ \text{MSAs}$$

A graph for this equation is found in **Figure 12.14**. One notes that despite the broad scatter plot (reflecting the low R^2), which indicates a great deal of "unexplained"

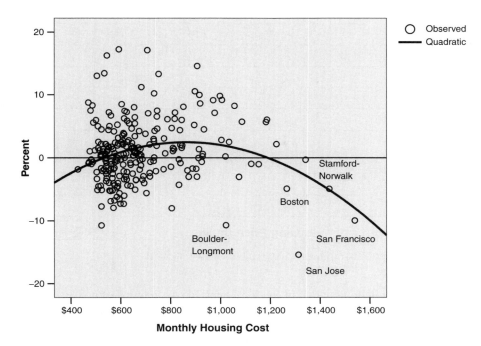

Figure 12.14 Employment Change, 2000–2004 (Percent). This quadratic regression line suggests that employment growth is negative in metro areas with extremely low housing costs, but also negative for metro areas with very high housing costs. The negative employment growth in the low-housing-cost regions reflects the fact that housing costs have fallen as jobs and workers have left the region, increasing the gap between housing demand and housing supply. The negative employment growth in the high-housing-cost regions presumably reflects the adverse impact of high housing costs on business investment and net domestic out-migration of workers and their families. *Source:* Bluestone 2006.

variance in employment growth across metro areas, the regression line reveals that employment actually declines almost universally for the MSAs with the very highest-priced housing ($1,200 per month and above). There is also job loss in the lowest-cost regions.

Something that resembles these findings can be depicted by simply dividing the 245 MSAs into housing cost deciles and plotting the average employment growth in each of them. This can be seen in **Figure 12.15.** Note that 2000–2004 employment growth in the top (tenth) decile representing the twenty-five MSAs with the highest housing costs is less than 1 percent. Dropping back to the ninth housing cost decile more than triples the job growth rate, while job growth in the eighth decile is more than twice as strong. In the lower housing cost deciles, employment growth is close to zero or negative, with the anomalous exception of the very lowest cost decile. The metro areas in the lowest cost of living decile include places like Provo, Utah; Texarkana, Texas; Fort Smith, Arkansas; Biloxi, Mississippi; and Browns-ville, Texas. It is possible that the higher employment growth in such MSAs is partially due to the influx of migrant labor. Otherwise, the decile chart follows the curve of the quadratic regression equation.

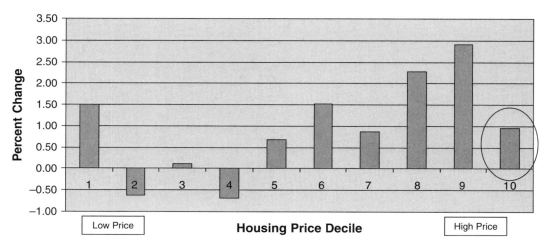

Figure 12.15 Employment Growth, 2000–2004 (Percent). *Source:* Bluestone 2006, figure 19.

It is worthwhile to note that of the top fifteen MSAs in terms of housing costs, nine (60%) experienced actual job loss between 2000 and 2004. Only twenty-eight (33%) of the next eighty-five MSAs suffered a similar fate.

At the other end of the housing cost continuum, a good number of MSAs lost jobs as well. Decatur, Illinois, led in this department, losing 10.7 percent of its jobs, followed by Youngstown, Ohio (–7.7%), Flint, Michigan (–7.3%), Ft. Wayne, Indiana (–5.2%), and Binghamton, New York (–5.1%). Each of these old manufacturing cities has suffered significant "deindustrialization" over the past three decades, which has led to employment loss and out-migration of business and population. The result has been a surplus of housing units that has extended over a long period of time and forced housing prices down.

Housing Prices and Population Migration

Bluestone (2006) performed a similar analysis on internal net population migration in 304 MSAs. Once again, the regression equation fit the data with the expected signs and explained nearly three times as much variance.

Regression Equation 2

$$\% \, \Delta \text{ Internal Migration}_i = -.1541 + .000430 \text{ Housing Cost}_i$$
$$(7.03)$$

$$- \, 2.6580E\text{-}007 \text{ Housing Cost Squared}_i$$
$$(7.39)$$

$$R^2 = .153, \, N = 304 \text{ MSAs}$$

Figure 12.16 provides a graph of the regression results. With fifty-nine more observations in the regression, we have a number of additional high-housing-price

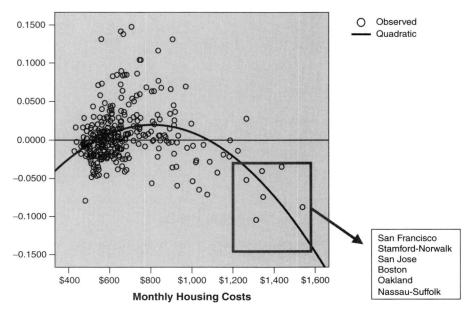

Figure 12.16 Internal Migration (Percent Change). The quadratic regression equation reveals that net out-migration is especially severe in the highest housing cost regions. *Source*: Bluestone 2006, figure 22.

MSAs and nearly all of them have experienced net out-migration. The curve is somewhat more bowed upward than that for employment growth, which suggests that housing costs have a greater impact on migration than on employment levels when those costs are very high.

The big migration losers in addition to Boston are San Francisco, Stamford-Norwalk, San Jose, Oakland, and Nassau-Suffolk, New York. These are generally the same communities that lost jobs.

When the MSAs are divided into housing-cost deciles, as shown in **Figure 12.17,** we find that the top decile lost population between 2000 and 2004 due to net internal out-migration. The top decile has an average negative migration rate of –2.25 percent; deciles 9 through 3 all have a positive in-migration rate, with the highest being in decile 8 (+3.05%), decile 7 (+2.72%), and decile 9 (+2.45%); and the two lowest cost deciles have average net *out*-migration rates like the top decile. This U-shaped pattern is so strong and consistent that it suggests a highly robust relationship between housing costs and migration rates, with both the highest-cost and lowest-cost regions losing population to migration.

Further analysis of the data, using more sophisticated regressions, demonstrated that this phenomenon is independent of other forces responsible for job trends and population dynamics. Even after controlling for job growth in an MSA, the highest housing cost regions lost population to out-migration, which indicates that house-holds move to lower-cost regions, even when jobs are available in the cities or suburbs they are leaving.

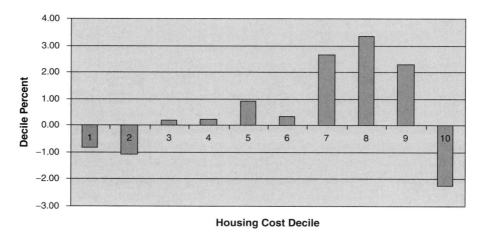

Figure 12.17 Internal Net Migration, 2000–2004. *Source*: Bluestone 2006, figure 23.

In a powerful way, this analysis underscores the more general economic notion of how prices affect both consumer and business behavior. Responding to high housing prices, households tend to move to regions with somewhat lower costs and plenty of job opportunities. In response to the difficulty of retaining and attracting workers in high-housing-cost regions, businesses move to metro areas with lower costs expecting to find a ready supply of labor at wage rates not inflated by the need to cover high living costs. Not surprisingly, both firms and people seem to be moving from high-cost areas like Boston to lower-cost areas like Raleigh-Durham-Chapel Hill. Hence, the economic development of individual metro areas is tied not only to the success of their industries but also to the price of their housing.

Post–World War II Suburbanization and Residential Segregation

When most households in metropolitan areas still lived inside the central city, racial and ethnic segregation was not as extreme. Black families and white families might not have lived on the same block or even in the same neighborhood, but they still lived in the same municipality. With the growth of suburbs after World War II, residential segregation became more prevalent.

Clearly, part of the reason for residential segregation by race was related to social class and income. White families could more easily afford to move to the suburbs where housing prices were higher, while black families remained economically segregated in the denser central city, where rents and home prices were lower—and perhaps falling as a result of whites leaving the central city and thereby creating a surplus in the housing stock. White flight to the suburbs was reinforced as central cities lost population and therefore municipal revenue, making it more difficult for them to support good public services—including public schools and well-equipped police forces—that could reduce crime. In a matter of decades, many American metro areas became "chocolate cities with vanilla suburbs," to use the phrase coined by demographer Reynolds Farley and his colleagues (1978).

Measuring Segregation

Residential or housing segregation is normally measured using the **dissimilarity index**, which reflects the proportion of one racial or ethnic group that must relocate to achieve a spatial configuration where each census tract or neighborhood replicates the racial composition of the metropolitan region as a whole. There are actually as many as twenty different indicators of segregation as identified by Massey and Denton (1988) that measure the evenness of a distribution; exposure or isolation from other groups; or the concentration, centralization, or clustering of a particular sub-group of a population. Nonetheless, the dissimilarity index is the measure most widely used.

According to the U.S. Bureau of the Census (2005), across 300 metropolitan areas, the average dissimilarity index in 1980 for African Americans was 0.727. In the "average" MSA, nearly 73 percent of African Americans would have had to relocate to census tracts where other racial and ethnic groups dominated—particularly white neighborhoods—in order to achieve full racial integration. Slow progress occurred over the next two decades, but still by 2000, almost two-thirds (64%) of African Americans would have to have moved to nonblack areas for racial parity. Contrary to some conventional wisdom, the highest degree of housing segregation was in the Northeast metro areas, where the dissimilarity index in 2000 was 0.739; the lowest was in the West (0.559) followed by the South (0.581). In that year, the most segregated MSA among the forty-three metro areas with at least 3 percent black population and 1 million or more in total population was Detroit, with a dissimilarity index of 0.846. Detroit was followed by Milwaukee, New York City, and Newark, New Jersey. African Americans in the least segregated MSAs were living in Orange County, California; San Jose, California; Phoenix; Riverside, California; and Norfolk-Virginia Beach, Virginia.

In general, Hispanics and Asians are much less segregated. The average dissimilarity index in 2000 across all MSAs was 0.509 for Latinos and 0.411 for Asians and Pacific Islanders. Of the largest MSAs with 20,000 or more Hispanics, St. Louis, Missouri, had the lowest degree of dissimilarity (0.273) while Providence, Rhode Island was the most segregated for this ethic group (0.676). The most segregated large cities for Asians were New York (0.505) and San Francisco (0.484), both famous for their large and ethnically concentrated Chinatowns.

The Causes of Housing Segregation

Housing segregation has many causes. As noted above, social class as measured by income is one, but it is surprisingly less important than one might think. Using data from Los Angeles County for 1990, Camille Charles (2000) calculates the predicted index of dissimilarity for blacks, Latinos, and Asians and compares it with the actual index. The predicted index controls for household income and household structure including family type, age of head, and number of household members. The predicted index for blacks was 0.110, more than five and half times lower than the actual index. For Latinos, the predicted index was 0.191, less than half the actual 0.458. For Asians, the predicted dissimilarity index was only 0.087, one-fourth the actual 0.344.

This suggests that other factors besides income and family structure must be responsible for much of the segregation we find in major metro areas. One factor, of course, is racial preferences. In Los Angeles, more than 70 percent of whites express comfort with a neighborhood that is one-third black. However, when asked to consider living in a neighborhood that is 53 percent black and 47 percent white, the percentage of whites expressing comfort drops to just 46 percent. Using a similar technique for assessing preferences, Bluestone and Stevenson (2000) find that in the Boston metro area, whites felt the "ideal" neighborhood was one in which they represented 62 percent of the households, blacks represented 15 percent, Hispanics 10 percent, and Asians 13 percent. This would make for a fairly integrated neighborhood. When blacks were asked the same set of questions about their preferences, their "ideal" neighborhood turned out to be 41 percent black, 23 percent white, 19 percent Hispanic, and 17 percent Asian. Again, this is a fairly integrated neighborhood. The same was true for Hispanics, whose ideal community was 40 percent Latino, 25 percent white, 19 percent black, and 16 percent Asian. This sounds like nearly everyone is in favor of living in a racially and ethnically diverse neighborhood.

But there is one problem. The math simply does not add up. Combining the three "ideals" from the perspective of each racial/ethnic group, the perfect community is 62 percent white, 41 percent black, and 40 percent Hispanic. Unfortunately, a community cannot have more than 100 percent population! Therefore, part of the reason segregation persists is that few whites, blacks, Hispanics, and Asians want to live in a community where they are a distinct minority. As a result, there appears to be a good deal of self-segregation, as well as segregation due to income differentials.

Beyond income and personal preferences is the role of government policy in encouraging residential segregation. In 1938, the Federal Housing Administration (FHA) explicitly asserted in its underwriting manual that "if a neighborhood is to retain stability, it is necessary that properties shall continue to be occupied by the same social and racial classes. A change in social or racial occupancy generally contributes to instability or a decline in values" (Squires 1994). The agency encouraged the use of racially restrictive covenants in sales contracts and deeds. While the Supreme Court ruled that such covenants were unenforceable in 1948, the FHA continued to redline or refuse mortgage insurance to minority-dominated inner-city areas until 1965 (Colman 1975). By building public housing almost exclusively in central cities, the federal and state governments concentrated poorer families—many of them racial and ethnic minorities—into central city locations.

Even after the civil rights laws of the 1960s barred the federal government from racial discrimination, real estate brokers and banks contributed to racial and ethnic segregation by deliberate racial "steering"—showing white families housing only in white areas and blacks only in black. Commercial banks and mortgage companies discriminated against black families who were trying to obtain mortgages, as shown in matched-pair studies where a black borrower in the same financial position as a white borrower both approached the same bank for a housing loan. In many cases, the white borrower was more likely to obtain the mortgage.

The combination of unequal incomes, racial and ethnic preferences, and the legacy of implicit as well as explicit government policies is powerful enough to have kept segregation indices at well over 50 percent for most U.S. metropolitan areas. Adding to this problem is that it has proven difficult to maintain integrated neighborhoods once they achieve a low dissimilarity index. As a racial or ethnic minority begins to move into a neighborhood that was previously nearly all-white, there is normally only a small change in the racial or ethnic composition of the community. But in many cities, as more minority members move in, there appears to be a **tipping point** when the pace of white flight suddenly accelerates and a neighborhood becomes a majority minority in just a few years. This is consistent with the residential preferences mentioned earlier, which revealed that white residents, on average, are satisfied with having some minority neighbors, but prefer not to live in a neighborhood where they no longer comprise at least three-fifths of the residents.

Segregation and Social-Class Structure

In some cities, as the racial or ethnic composition of a particular neighborhood changed, there was also a change in the social-class structure of the community. The first African Americans who moved into the northwest section of Detroit in the 1960s—an area that had been comprised overwhelmingly of middle-class whites— were solidly middle class themselves and often had incomes equal to or greater than the whites who sold them their homes. Over time, however, as both middle-class white and middle-class black families moved to the suburbs, lower-income black families moved in behind them. The result was **downward filtering**, with the housing stock moving from medium quality to lower quality because the new families had less money to maintain these properties.

The opposite can occur as well. As we saw in Chapter 5, in a number of metro areas, central city neighborhoods have been rejuvenated as middle-class "pioneers" choose to move back to the city to take advantage of short commutes to downtown office jobs and the cultural and social amenities offered in dense communities. When these upper-income households begin to move into a dilapidated inner-city neighborhood, they help to improve the community. But as more middle-class households choose to buy into the community, they bid up rents and home prices, which leads to the displacement of the original residents. Such **gentrification** leads to **upward filtering**, and the consequent loss of affordable housing units is difficult to stop once a neighborhood's property values begin to rise.

The passing of the tipping point in previously white neighborhoods that transition toward a majority or almost exclusive minority presence and gentrification of formerly rundown inner-city locations to white middle-class enclaves helps explain why the dissimilarity index in most metro areas declined only slightly between 1980 and 2000.

Concentrated Poverty in the Inner City

The combination of upward and downward filtering combined with racial segregation has intensified the spatial dimension of poverty in most metro areas. By the 1960s, social scientists were using the term **urban ghetto** to refer to sections of the city that contained high proportions of desperately poor households, most of them people of color. The term **urban slum** was also used to describe these neighborhoods, where the concentration of poor people leads to a concentration of social ills that cause or are caused by poverty. Just between 1970 and 1990, the number of people living in high-poverty areas doubled, as we noted in Chapter 2. The probability that a poor black child would be trapped in a high-poverty neighborhood increased from one in four to one in three (Jargowsky 2003). This occurred during a time when the poverty rate—the proportion of families living under the official U.S. poverty threshold—did not increase at all. What changed was the growing physical isolation of the poor in America. The social distance between the poor inner city and the more prosperous suburbs grew dramatically.

Such a concentration of disadvantaged households, especially in the inner city, tends to make poverty even more difficult to eradicate. As we noted in Chapter 7, with jobs moving to the suburbs, there is a tendency for **spatial mismatch** to occur where those trapped in the city are unable to reach the jobs that are increasingly located in more distant suburbs. The lack of good public transportation to the suburbs makes this problem even worse. In studying Atlanta, Katz and Allen (2001) find that three-fourths of new entry-level jobs are located at least 10 miles away from the inner city, where many poor unemployed workers live. Ihlanfeldt and Sjoquist (1990) estimate that about a quarter of the gap between black and white youth employment rates can be explained simply by the lack of access to employment opportunities afforded those living in inner-city poor neighborhoods.

Areas of concentrated poverty are also places where you will often find a proliferation of abandoned and boarded-up housing—even where there may be a shortage of housing units. In 2000, more than 16 percent of all the housing units in the central city of St. Louis were vacant. More than 10 percent were vacant in Buffalo, Hartford, and Detroit (U.S. Department of Housing and Urban Development 2007c). Low-income families can only afford to pay minimal rent. Landlords may find that the rent they can charge is insufficient to maintain their properties and still make the profit they expect. In general, the older the building, the greater the maintenance cost. If maintenance costs rise faster than revenue from rent, landlords will have little incentive to take care of their properties (unless they believe maintenance will permit them to sell these units at a sufficiently high price to compensate for the improvements, or unless local building inspectors or public health authorities insist on such investment). If the cost of maintaining the property is prohibitive—where total revenue minus total cost is less than required profit—landlords will allow their property to deteriorate to the point that it becomes uninhabitable and, ultimately, abandoned. This will happen particularly in areas where housing demand has dropped so much that the highest rent a landlord can charge is below the cost of maintaining the property.

For those who have studied concentrated poverty, a high-poverty neighborhood is considered one in which 40 percent or more of its residents fall below the official poverty line (Danziger and Gottschalk 1987; Jargowsky and Bane 1991; and Kasarda 1993). Between 1970 and 1990, the number of concentrated poverty census tracts more than doubled across the country so that by the end of this period, 10.4 million people were living in concentrated poverty neighborhoods, most in inner cities.

One might have expected this trend toward concentrated poverty to continue beyond 1990. But, indeed, just the opposite occurred. The combination of rapid economic growth during the late 1990s, the growing ability of poorer families to seek housing in close-in suburbs, and the reemergence of the central city as a prime location for young urban professionals led to a dramatic reduction of concentrated poverty in many metro areas. According to Jargowsky (2003), of the 331 metro areas in the United States, 227 of them (69%) saw a decrease in concentrated poverty between 1990 and 2000; only 55 (17%) experienced an increase.

Overall, the population of high-poverty neighborhoods declined from 10.4 million in 1990 to 7.9 million in 2000. Almost all of this decline took place in central cities and in rural areas. In contrast, there was virtually no decline in concentrated poverty in the suburbs—mostly those close to the central city—where at least some of the poor had moved. By the beginning of the twenty-first century, there was growing concern that the inner-ring suburbs were becoming the new locus of concentrated poverty, with more affluent households concentrated in the new gentrified central city areas and in the outer suburbs. As such, the spatial deconcentration of poverty is leading to a new, doughnut-shaped geography of metro areas. Upward filtering is removing the poor from the inner city, while the outer suburbs remain blocked to low-income families through high housing prices and/or outright discrimination.

The result is a tendency toward an inner ring of growing poverty at the fringes of the central city and in the close-in suburbs. Yonkers, a close-in suburb of New York City, has seen its poverty rate increase from 9.8 to 15.5 percent—as its minority population increased from 21 percent in 1980 to 49 percent in 2000. Similarly, the poverty rate in Oak Park, Michigan, a close-in suburb of Detroit, increased from just 3.9 percent in 1970 to 9.4 percent in 2000. Over the same thirty years, the poverty rate in Brockton, Massachusetts—just south of Boston—rose from 8.5 to 14.5 percent. Although the poverty rate rose in each of these inner-ring suburbs, the increase in each case has been less severe than it might otherwise have been, presumably as a result of being closer to suburban jobs.

Federal Housing Policy

While housing would seem to be the quintessential local good, an array of national policies dictated by the federal government has an enormous influence on the supply of housing, the type of housing demanded, and the price households pay to live where they do. The reason why government is involved at all in housing is that shelter is considered a **merit good**, whose consumption is deemed to be intrinsically beneficial and therefore worth encouraging. Decent shelter is seen as important to a household's well-being, not only for keeping its members warm and dry during inclement weather but because it also contributes to better health, very likely improves the chances of education success for young children, and provides a place for families to have some quiet refuge from the rest of the community. Just as they are encouraged to pay attention to proper nutrition and health care, families are also encouraged to live in decent homes.

Subsidizing Housing Demand

In fiscal year (FY) 2006, the U.S. Department of Housing and Urban Development (2006) provided a total of $25.5 billion in housing assistance through a variety of rental assistance programs and funds for public housing. The vast majority of these funds went to low-income tenants. The federal government provided even more housing assistance—more than four times as much—through **tax expenditures**, most of which went to middle- and upper-income home owners. Tax expenditures are defined by the government as "revenue losses attributable to provisions of the Federal tax laws which allow a special exclusion, exemption, or deduction from gross income or which provide a special credit, a preferential rate of tax, or a deferral of tax liability" (U.S. Congress Committee on Ways and Means and the Committee on Finance 2003). In FY 2006, tax expenditures for housing amounted to $114 billion—including $76 billion for the tax deductibility of home mortgage interest, $15 billion for the residential property tax deduction, and $18 billion for the exclusion of capital gains on the sale of a home owner's principal residence. As we saw earlier in this chapter, these tax policies encourage home ownership by reducing the cost of owning versus renting. The higher the tax bracket of the home owner and the greater the value of the home, the more valuable the deduction.

As we also noted earlier in this chapter, the creation of the Federal Housing Administration (FHA) in 1934 has played a critical role in increasing the home ownership rate in the United States. Under FHA, the Federal National Mortgage Association, better known as Fannie Mae, was created to help reduce mortgage risk by assisting financial institutions to diversify their portfolios. Fannie Mae runs a **secondary mortgage market** so that private banks can sell a portion of their primary mortgages sold to home owners for other types of securities. Fannie Mae and its newer federal mortgage cousin, Freddie Mac, aid the home owner by providing funds for mortgage lending and permitting local banks to limit their default risk and, therefore, offer lower interest rates. Freddie Mac claims that it saves the typical home owner $18,000 in interest charges over the thirty-year life of a $150,000 mortgage (Freddie Mac 2007).

Tax expenditures and the expanded availability of mortgage money increase the consumption of housing by augmenting the demand side of the housing market. The same has been true of a number of federal mortgage and rent subsidy programs.

The Section 221(d)(3) program, introduced in 1961 under President John F. Kennedy, provided a mortgage subsidy for low-income home buyers, increasing their demand for housing. The Housing Act of 1974 was famous for creating the Section 8 **housing allowance** or voucher, which is equivalent to a cash grant to a low-income household that can only be used to help pay rent. Under Section 8, a qualifying household receives a monthly grant for the difference between the "fair market rent" for a particular housing unit (as determined by a hedonic index similar to one discussed earlier in this chapter) and the amount that the low-income renter can "afford." In this case, a household is assumed to be able to afford a contribution toward rent equal to 30 percent of its monthly income, with the remaining 70 percent needed for other necessities. Hence, if a household has a monthly income of $1,500, its expected contribution is $450 (.30 × $1,500). If the household finds an approved Section 8 apartment with a fair market value of $800 per month, the Section 8 allowance will equal $350, the difference between the $800 rent and the household's $450 expected contribution.

Only households with incomes of less than 80 percent of the "area median income" are eligible for Section 8. Since this housing subsidy is not an **entitlement** that is available automatically to all qualifying households, only a fraction of those eligible for Section 8 actually receive allowances—based on the amount of funds committed by Congress. In some communities, the Section 8 program is so over-subscribed that a household can wait for years to become eligible for assistance.

Subsidizing Housing Supply

If we are concerned about improving housing conditions for low-income families, the irony of federal government intervention on the demand side is that, as we have just seen, more than 80 percent of the demand-side subsidies go to better-off families through the tax expenditures that result from the deductibility of mortgage interest. What about the federal government's interventions on the supply side of the housing market? There is an irony here as well. As we demonstrated in Figure 12.8, increasing the supply of housing is one way to reduce its price. Therefore, the logic of a supply-side intervention to improve housing conditions for low-income families would require that we increase the number of housing units. However, neither of the two major federal supply-side interventions of the mid-twentieth century actually resulted in an expansion of the housing stock. How can that be?

The Public Housing Act of 1937 provided federal subsidies to local housing authorities that wanted to clear out slums. It is the program under which many of the large-scale high-rise projects were constructed—including the notorious and since-demolished Pruitt-Igoe Houses in St. Louis and the Cabrini Green Houses in Chicago. These projects tended to exacerbate the social isolation of the poor. This proved to be a disastrous social experiment, where the concentration of poverty in these "projects" often led to dilapidation and high crime rates. Based on this adverse experience, very few new units of public housing have been built since the 1970s. What is left of public housing provision by the federal government is the HOPE VI (Housing Opportunities for People Everywhere) program, which provides government funds to rehabilitate existing housing projects that are badly in need of renovation and repair. Under this program that began in the early 1990s, older high-rise buildings have been razed and, in their place, the government has constructed low-rise units and town houses. Public housing tenants are given temporary housing while the new units are being built and then have an opportunity to establish residency in the new units.

According to the noted urban historian Kenneth Jackson (1985), the purpose of the 1937 law was primarily to create construction jobs as a way of stimulating economic activity during the Great Depression of the 1930s. In order to protect real estate interests at a time when private housing markets were already weak, the law required that one housing unit—presumably a unit of low-quality slum housing—be destroyed for every new housing unit created by the program. Thus, on net, this intervention left the total supply of housing units unchanged.

The next major federal intervention on the supply side occurred with passage of the Housing Act of 1949. The preamble of this law stated that every American family deserves a "decent home and a suitable living environment" (Lang and Sohmer 2000). This act established the urban renewal program that cleared large swaths through many low-income urban neighborhoods and often used the cleared land to house a smaller number of higher-income households (as in the development of the upscale Charles River Park in the old working-class West End of Boston) or converted it to a nonresidential use (as in the Lincoln Center Performing Arts complex that replaced a Hispanic neighborhood on Manhattan's West Side). As Rothenberg (1972) points out, the many goals of the urban renewal program were often incompatible with each other. Efforts to revitalize cities and bring back middle- and higher-income residents often played a greater role than improving housing standards for the poor. The program destroyed more housing units than it created, and many of those who were displaced wound up paying higher rents for poorer-quality units—the outcome we would expect, knowing that the program actually reduced the number of housing units available.

A more recent federal housing supply program, begun in 1986, is the Low Income Housing Tax Credit (LIHTC) targeted at encouraging affordable housing construction by private developers. By 2000, nearly 1 million housing units had been built under this program, which offers federally tax-exempt bonds to lower interest rates plus tax credits equal to 70 percent of the construction costs for privately developed housing projects that include a proportion of units reserved for low-income households. Developers can use the tax credits to offset losses to their after-tax profit that occurs as a result of offering housing to low-income households at below-market prices or rents. Today, the LIHTC is used to build more low-income housing than any other single federal program.

State and Local Housing Policy

While the federal government has played a substantial role—albeit one that has its paradoxes—on both the supply and demand sides of the housing market, states and local communities are still responsible for most housing policies. As we noted above, the zoning decisions of local municipalities can reduce the supply of land available for housing, which increases the cost of producing new housing units. Without spending a penny, local jurisdictions can exert a powerful influence on both the rental and the home-ownership markets through such land regulation. Glaeser et al. (2006) estimate that increasing minimum lot size by one acre results in anywhere from an 11.5 to 13.8 percent increase in median home prices, after controlling for the size, age, and number of rooms in the house.

As state governments begin to better understand the impact of high housing prices on their own economic development, a number of states have begun to develop policies to influence local land regulations and to provide incentives for housing construction, particularly aimed at building housing for low- and moderate-income households. A number of states have created **housing trust funds**, which provide developers with low-cost loans if they agree to set aside a minimum number of units in their projects that can be rented or sold at below-market prices.

Some cities, including Boston and Cambridge, Massachusetts, have passed **inclusionary zoning laws**, which encourage builders to include a number of affordable housing units in their developments in return for the municipality permitting them to construct more units per acre and therefore lower their land costs. Alternatively, the developer of such a dense housing project can pay into a municipal fund that is then used to underwrite the housing trust fund, which can encourage the building of affordable units in other locations within the community.

Other municipalities have instituted **linkage programs**, which require developers of commercial and industrial property to pay into a housing fund in order to offset pressure on the housing market caused by the hiring of new employees in the businesses that occupy these properties and who presumably need housing themselves.

In a unique program, Massachusetts passed a Smart Growth Overlay Zoning law in 2005 that provides its cities and towns with monetary incentives if they rezone land around town centers, transit stops, and where abandoned industrial property is located so that denser, more affordable housing can be built (Carman, Bluestone, and White 2004). The new law complements older legislation passed in 1969, which required cities and towns to assure that 10 percent of their housing stock is affordable to low- and moderate-income households. If municipalities under the 10 percent threshold balk at permitting developers to build new housing in their communities, the developer can bypass local zoning and obtain a "comprehensive permit" from the state. In Massachusetts, where local home rule is so powerful in terms of zoning, this state law has been the single most potent instrument for assuring the production of low- and moderate-income housing. Even so, more than thirty-five years after passage of the law, only forty-seven of the state's 351 cities and towns are in full compliance with its requirements.

The Massachusetts law enacted in 1969, providing sanctions on municipalities that do not move aggressively to assure a minimum of 10 percent affordable housing, spawned action in other states. In 1975, the New Jersey Supreme Court held that every city and town in the state has the constitutional obligation to provide for the "regional general welfare" by, in part, helping to meet the region's affordable housing needs (Haar 1996; Kirp, Dwyer, and Rosenthal 1996). The state court's now famous *Mt. Laurel* decision came in response to a group of low-income black residents in that New Jersey town, who tried to replace a local slum with thirty-six units of modestly priced garden apartments. The town refused to permit the small development, by maintaining zoning only for single-family houses. The court struck down the use of zoning to exclude low-income housing, but in the ensuing years, Mt. Laurel and virtually all other suburbs in the state found ways to evade the court's intent by establishing other barriers to development that included minimum lot sizes, building setback rules, and extraordinarily rigid environmental regulations.

Angered by the municipal response to its original ruling, the state supreme court came back in 1983 in *Mt. Laurel II* with a much more powerful set of sanctions like those in Massachusetts, which permitted a "builder's remedy" such that developers could circumvent local town regulations. While the state legislature in New Jersey, under great pressure from suburban voters, weakened the impact of *Mt. Laurel II* by permitting municipalities to meet their obligations through age-restricted housing for the elderly and through regional contribution agreements, the court's rulings have brought some positive results. In the town of Mt. Laurel itself, 140 town houses for low- and moderate-income renters were constructed and, throughout the state, more than 15,000 units of affordable housing were produced in the decade following the court's reaffirmation of the original *Mt. Laurel* decision.

Rent Control

In the face of escalating housing prices and rents, increasing the supply of housing should eventually bring the cost down and make decent shelter affordable to more families. But because of the range of barriers to producing more housing units, some advocates for low-income families have suggested the need to go back to some form of price control on rents. During World War II, as factory after factory switched from the production of civilian goods to military products, the U.S. Office of Price Administration established wage and price controls to combat inflationary pressure in the civilian sector. At the same time, to prevent landlords from gouging renters on what were now fixed incomes, it instituted a national system of rent control. After the war, New York City retained the controls and, during the 1970s, a number of cities—including Boston and Cambridge in Massachusetts and Los Angeles, Berkeley, and Santa Monica in California—reinstituted various forms of rent stabilization.

The Unintended Short-Run Consequences of Rent Control

On the surface, such controls seem warranted and low-income households who find rent-controlled apartments benefit from them. Nonetheless, there is considerable evidence that while rent control may provide some price relief in the short run, there are consequences that build up over time and prove counterproductive to prospective tenants, perhaps even more so than to landlords. There are at least six reasons for this:

1. By reducing the profitability of rental housing and increasing the possibility of expensive, time-consuming litigation over rent increases or evictions, the supply of rental housing tends to shrink in the long run.
2. Owners of existing rental housing are less likely and, in some cases, unable to afford to maintain their properties, which accelerates the *deterioration* of existing rental stock.
3. If not explicitly prohibited from doing so, landlords will *convert* their rental units to condominiums or other land uses, further reducing the supply of rental property to those who cannot afford to buy.
4. The existence of rent controls *discourages* developers from building new housing, even if the new housing is initially exempt from the rent-control statute. Possible future control of these properties is factored into the calculation of the rate of return, which reduces the expected value of the development.
5. Where only one municipality passes rent control, there is every inducement for developers to go elsewhere if they wish to remain in the housing production business.
6. In the long run, deterioration of the existing housing stock and the discouragement of new production lead to lower property tax revenue for the city and greater difficulty in funding city services—including those for low-income households.

These unintended consequences are not simply theoretical. An early study of rent control in New York City conducted by the RAND Corporation found that between 1960 and 1967, the inventory of "sound" housing increased by only 2.4 percent, while the inventory of "dilapidated" housing increased by 44 percent and the inventory of "deteriorating" housing increased by 37 percent. The same RAND study found that between 1965 and 1967, 111,400 units in the city were simply retired from the housing stock by landlords, converting them to other uses or abandoning them (Lowry et. al. 1971). A more recent study in Cambridge, Massachusetts, found that maintenance expenditure per rental unit declined by $50 per year as the result of rent control, which led to growing deterioration over time (Navarro 1985).

The impact of rent control on the monthly rent that tenants pay and on the supply of rental housing is summarized diagrammatically in **Figure 12.18**. Point A represents the monthly rent that a tenant pays before rent control is instituted. With the supply of housing fixed in the short run (given the time it takes to build more housing or to have existing housing deteriorate in quality), the monthly rent drops to B—the price set under the rent-control statute. The tenant benefits by the difference between A and B, which is exactly what the landlord is forced to sacrifice. This short-run effect is what the advocates of rent control desire.

The Unintended Long-Run Consequences of Rent Control

The problem is that over the longer run—defined as the time when new housing can actually be built or existing housing can deteriorate—developers who expect lower

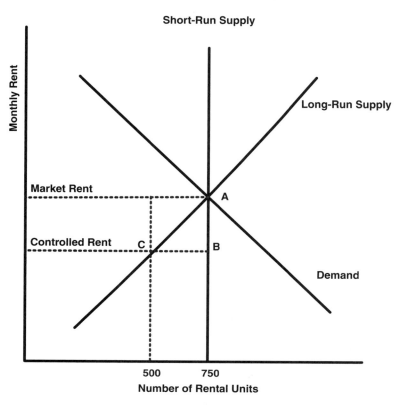

Figure 12.18 Short-Run and Long-Run Effects of Rent Control. In the absence of rent control, the
market rent will be at point A, where housing supply and demand are equal. If rent control sets rent at B,
landlords will begin to reduce the supply of rental units. This can occur as landlords convert existing
rental units into owner-occupied condominiums, reduce the value of rental units by failing to maintain
their properties, or as developers refuse to build new housing units in rent-controlled municipalities.

rents refuse to build as much housing as they might otherwise, and landlords either
convert their units to condominiums for sale or allow existing units to deteriorate to
the point where the real supply of decent housing declines. In the hypothetical
example illustrated in Figure 12.18, the number of units declines from 750 to 500. In
the long run, existing tenants continue to benefit from rent control, but low-income
households looking for housing now find it even more difficult to find.

In practice, because of these unintended consequences, municipalities with rent
control were often forced to consider "vacancy decontrol" in order to maintain some
incentive for developers to build new units and for existing landlords to maintain
their properties. Rent-control statutes were amended so that rents remained fixed
only as long as the current tenant lived in the unit. When the tenant moved out of the
apartment, the landlord was allowed to seek the market rate rent for the next tenant,

where the rent would be fixed again. This, however, created a strong incentive for landlords to evict tenants in order to hike the rent periodically. To counter this response, rent control needed further tinkering, which created rent-control boards where tenants could appeal their evictions. In order to evict a tenant, the landlord would have to prove that the tenant violated the lease in some way.

As rent control became increasingly burdensome with more and more rules to follow, landlords sought other ways to avoid it. By turning their rental units into condominiums and selling these units to home buyers, the supply of rental property declined even faster. In a number of municipalities, this led—in a continuing series of legal gambits and countergambits—to the inclusion of anticondominium conversion amendments in the rent-control statutes. In trying to deal with the landlords' ability to circumvent rent control, the entire rent-control machinery became more and more complex and more difficult to implement.

Beyond the deleterious effect on housing supply, rent control often ended up with unintended "distribution" effects. Those who are most in need of affordable rental housing are not the ones who always obtain it when rent control is instituted. Landlords have every incentive to select higher-income tenants who have the means to maintain their properties and do the routine upkeep that normally would be the responsibility of the owner. This means that landlords are less likely under rent control to lease units to low-income families, especially those with children. Also, once in a rent-controlled unit, renters are less likely to move even when "over-housed," so that one- and two-person households end up living in units that would be much better suited to larger families.

Essentially, rent control or "stabilization" creates a form of rationing that benefits those already in controlled housing yet harms those who need it most, exacerbating inequity in the housing market. In addition, if rent control lasts very long, it is common for a "black market" to be established in which landlords may ask for—or be urged to accept from potential tenants who are desperate for a rent-controlled apartment—illegal or quasi-legal, under-the-table payments. Without a great deal of monitoring, this activity will take place along with renter subletting that allows the renter to charge a fee in excess of the rent-controlled price. The longer rent control is in force, the greater the certainty that all of these unintended consequences will arise, undermining the stated objective of rent control. Not surprisingly, by the late 1990s, rent control had disappeared in most cities.

Indeed, there are only a few rare circumstances when economists conclude that the benefits of rent control can outweigh its adverse consequences. During World War II, when nearly everything was rationed or subject to price controls, it made sense to impose temporary limits on rent increases as well. It probably also made sense during the oil boom in Alaska, but only as a short-term measure, where it was expected that after construction of the pipeline there would no longer be the need for a large permanent housing stock. In these cases, there was no concern about the impact of rent control on discouraging future supply or of displacing low-income families in favor of richer ones.

Intervening in Housing Markets: A Word of Caution

Given the importance of housing to social well-being, only those who hold the strongest free market conservative philosophy are against any and all interventions in the housing market. For those who favor deliberate policy, it is critical to understand that the variety of interventions confer a range of benefits and costs and produce both winners and losers. The federal tax deductions for mortgage interest and local property taxes cost the federal government more than $100 billion a year in forgone tax revenue that could be used for all manner of other public goods and services. These tax expenditures benefit home owners while conferring little advantage to renters and almost surely lead to the "overconsumption" of housing in the form of bigger and plusher accommodations than would be the case if such tax forgiveness did not exist.

Public subsidies to developers of affordable housing increase the supply of housing, particularly for lower-income households, making it possible for such families to afford better housing than they would otherwise. But, once again, these housing subsidies have an opportunity cost because the revenue for such publicly provided subsidies could have been used for other public goods and services or returned to the taxpayers for their own use. Public subsidies that are provided to renters—and, in some cases, home owners—such as Section 8 vouchers, permit low-income households to purchase more and better housing than they would otherwise (and often benefit landlords), but in expanding the demand for housing, these vouchers most likely raise the rents for those who do not qualify for them.

Rent control, as we have seen, provides immediate relief for low-income renters—and others who somehow can take advantage of rent-controlled units—but the long-term implications for housing supply and prices are adverse.

Programs to limit zoning restrictions or to provide incentives for zoning reform that favors more housing probably have the fewest unintended consequences, but even here there are winners and losers. Increasing the supply of housing reduces the rate of housing price appreciation, which benefits those entering the housing market but reduces the price premium that existing home owners can charge.

There is a simple lesson here. As long as we believe that a particular good is a merit good, there can be a case for subsidizing its production and consumption. However, care must be taken to assure that both efficiency and equity are served by intervention in the market. This takes a thorough examination of various policies and even more careful implementation.

Appendix A

Indifference Curves and Budget Constraints

Many students who have taken introductory microeconomics will be familiar with the basic model and assumptions used to understand an individual's choices among various goods and services. In the basic model, the individual chooses a bundle of goods from the combinations permitted within his or her budget (including any available credit). Assuming unencumbered choice and availability, it can be inferred that this individual will choose the combination of items that maximizes his well-being. No other combination within his budget would make him any better off.

This type of behavior is normally depicted in a diagram that incorporates a **budget constraint** and a set of **indifference curves**. **Figure A12.1** shows a simple diagram with two goods (ice cream and beer) and a set of indifference curves for a single individual. The budget constraint is depicted by the straight line AB, which shows that this particular consumer has sufficient funds after all other consumer goods are purchased to buy fifteen ice cream cones a month if he buys no beer, or eighteen bottles of beer if he buys no ice cream. If the individual is willing to give up some beer, he can buy some more ice cream and if he is willing to give up some ice cream, he can buy some more beer.

This particular consumer likes both. The trade-off between his desire for ice cream and beer is shown in the set of indifference curves in the diagram. The points along each individual indifference curve show each of the combinations of ice cream and beer that leaves the individual absolutely "indifferent" in terms of utility or satisfaction. Thus, on the lowest indifference curve, our consumer is equally satisfied with six ice cream cones and two beers a month OR with three ice cream cones and three beers. The shape of the indifference curve suggests that when you have a large amount of one good and a small amount of another, you would normally be willing to give up a lot of the first good in order to get just a little more of the second.

To find out where this consumer ends up, you keep plotting individual indifference curves until you find the highest one that is just tangent to the budget constraint. At this point, X, the consumer with the budget constraint AB, is purchasing a monthly ration of ice cream and beer that provides maximum satisfaction. At any other point along the budget constraint, the consumer would be less satisfied—he or she would be on a lower indifference curve.

The key point is that the decision over the purchase of any combination of goods and services is based on two factors: the consumer's budget constraint and the

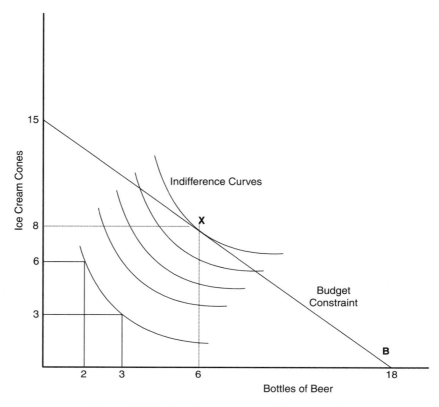

Figure A12.1 Budget Constraints and Indifference Curves.

consumer's preference function. By considering both of these, we can begin to understand what consumers purchase and why.

References

Belsky, Eric S. 2006. "Rental Vacancy Rates: A Policy Primer." *Housing Policy Debate* 3, no. 3: 793–813.

Bluestone, Barry. 2006. "Sustaining the Mass Economy: Housing Costs, Population Dynamics, and Employment." Paper prepared for the Federal Reserve Bank of Boston and the Rappaport Institute for Greater Boston at Harvard University, May.

Bluestone, Barry, and Mary Huff Stevenson. 2000. *The Boston Renaissance: Race, Space, and Economic Change in an American Metropolis*. New York: Russell Sage.

Carman, Ted, Barry Bluestone, and Eleanor White. 2004. *Building on Our Heritage: A Housing Strategy for Smart Growth and Economic Development*. Boston: The Boston Foundation.

Charles, Camille Z. 2000. "Residential Segregation in Los Angeles." In Lawrence Bobo, Melvin Oliver, James Johnson, and Abel Valenzuela Jr., eds., *Prismatic Metropolis: Inequality in Los Angeles*. New York: Russell Sage, pp. 167–219.

Cisneros, Henry G., Jack F. Kemp, Nicolas P. Retsinas, and Kent W. Colton. 2004. *Opportunity and Progress: A Bipartisan Platform for National Housing Policy.* Cambridge, Mass.: Joint Center for Housing Studies of Harvard University.

Colman, William G. 1975. *Cities, Suburbs and States: Governing and Financing Urban America.* New York: Free Press.

Danziger, Sheldon, and Peter Gottschalk. 1987. "Earnings Inequality, the Spatial Concentration of Poverty, and the Underclass." *American Economic Review Papers and Proceedings* 77, no. 2 (May): 211–215.

DiPasquale, Denise, and William C. Wheaton. 1996. *Urban Economics and Real Estate Markets.* Englewood Cliffs, N.J.: Prentice Hall.

Economic Policy Institute. 2005. "Family Budget Calculator." http://www.epinet.org.

Farley, Reynolds, Howard Shuman, Suzanne Bianchi, Diane Colasanto, and Shirley Hatchett. 1978. "Chocolate City, Vanilla Suburbs: Will the Trend toward Racially Separate Communities Continue?" *Social Science Research* 7 (December): 319–344.

Favro, Tony. 2007. "Affordable Housing Crisis Casts a Shadow over the American Dream." January 20. http://www.citymayors.com/society/housing_usa.html.

Fischel, William A. 2001. *The Homevoter Hypothesis: How Home Values Influence Local Government Taxation, School Finance, and Land-Use Policies.* Cambridge, Mass.: Harvard University Press.

Freddie Mac. 2007. "Just the Facts: How We Make Home Possible." Pamplet. McLean, Va.: Freddie Mac, September.

Glaeser, Edward L., Jenny Schuetz, and Bryce Ward. 2006. "Regulation and the Rise of Housing Prices in Greater Boston: A Study Based on New Data from 187 Communities in Eastern Massachusetts." Rappaport Institute for Greater Boston at Harvard University, January.

Harr, Charles M. 1996. *Suburbs under Siege.* Princeton, N.J.: Princeton University Press.

Heilbrun, James. 1987. *Urban Economics and Public Policy.* New York: St. Martin's Press.

Heudorfer, Bonnie, and Barry Bluestone. 2006. *The Greater Boston Housing Report Card.* Boston: The Boston Foundation, September.

Hobbs, Frank, and Nicole Stoops. 2002. *Demographic Trends in the 20th Century.* Washington, D.C.: U.S. Bureau of the Census, November.

Ihlanfeldt, Keith, and David Sjoquist. 1990. "Job Accessibility and Racial Differences in Youth Employment Rates." *American Economic Review* 80, no. 1: 266–276.

Jackson, Kenneth. 1985. *Crabgrass Frontier: The Suburbanization of the United States.* New York: Oxford University Press.

Jakabovics, Andrew. 2006. "Housing Affordability Initiative: Land Use Research Findings." http://web.mit.edu/cre/research/hai/land-use.html.

Jargowsky, Paul. 2003. "Stunning Progress, Hidden Problems: The Dramatic Decline of Concentrated Poverty in the 1990s." *Center for Urban and Metropolitan Policy.* Washington, D.C.: Brookings Institution, May.

Jargowsky, Paul, and Mary Jo Bane. 1991. "Ghetto Poverty: Basic Questions." In L. E. Lynn and M. G. H. McGeary, eds., *Inner-City Poverty in the United States.* Washington, D.C.: National Academy Press.

Joint Center for Housing Studies. 2007. *The State of the Nation's Housing.* Cambridge, Mass.: Harvard University Press.

Kain, John, and John Quigley. 1975. *Housing Markets and Racial Discrimination: A Microeconomic Analysis.* Cambridge, Mass.: National Bureau of Economic Research.

Kasarda, John. 1993. "Inner City Poverty and Economic Access." In J. Sommer and D. A. Hicks, eds., *Rediscovering Urban America: Perspectives on the 1980s.* Washington, D.C.: U.S. Department of Housing and Economic Development.

Katz, Bruce, and Katherine Allen. 2001. "Cities Matter: Shifting the Focus of Welfare Reform." *Brookings Review* 19, no. 3 (Summer): 30–33.

Kirp, David L., John P. Dwyer, and Larry Rosenthal. 1996. *Our Town: Race, Housing, and the Soul of Suburbia.* New Brunswick, N.J.: Rutgers University Press.

Lancaster, Kevin. 1972. *Consumer Demand: A New Approach.* New York: Columbia University Press.

Lang, Robert E., and Rebecca R. Sohmer. 2000. "Legacy of the Housing Act of 1949: The Past, Present, and Future of Housing and Urban Policy." *Housing Policy Debate* 11, no. 2: 291–298.

Levenson, Michael. 2006. "Most Who Left State Don't Plan to Return: Jobs, Housing Inspired Moves, Survey Finds." *Boston Sunday Globe*, May 14, p. 1.

Lipsey, Richard. 1960. "The Relation between Unemployment and the Rate of Change of Money Wage Rates in the United Kingdom, 1862–1957: A Further Analysis." *Economica* 26, no. 105 (February): 1–31.

Lowrey, Ira S., Joseph S. De Salvo, and Barbara M. Woodfill. 1971. *Rental Housing in New York City*. Publication No. RM-6190. Santa Monica, Calif.: RAND Corporation.

Massey, Douglas S., and Nancy A. Denton. 1988. "The Dimensions of Residential Segregation." *Social Forces* 67, no. 2: 281–315.

Miller, Sara L. 2006. "Homeowners Stretched Perilously." March. http://www.csmonitor.com.

Navarro, Peter. 1985. "Rent Control in Cambridge, Massachusetts." *Public Interest* 91 (Spring): 83–100.

Office of Federal Housing Enterprise Oversight (OFHEO). 2006. "House Price Increases Continue; Some Deceleration Evident." Washington, D.C.: OFHEO, June.

Phillips, A. W. 1958. "The Relation between Unemployment and the Rate of Change of Money Wage Rates in the United Kingdom, 1861–1957." *Economica* 25, no. 100 (November): 283–299.

Rothenberg, Jerome. 1972. "The Nature of Redevelopment Benefits." In Matthew Edel and Jerome Rothenberg, eds., *Readings in Urban Economics.* New York: Macmillan.

Squires, Gregory. 1994. *Capital and Communities in Black and White: The Intersection of Race, Class and Uneven Development*. Albany: State University of New York Press.

U.S. Bureau of the Census. 2003. *Statistical Abstract of the United States, 2003.* Washington, D.C.: U.S. Government Printing Office.

———. 2005a. *Racial and Ethnic Segregation in the United States: 1980–2000.* Washington, D.C.: U.S. Government Printing Office.

———. 2005b. *Statistical Abstract of the United States, 2004-5.* Washington, D.C.: U.S. Government Printing Office.

———. 2007. "Homeownership 1900–2000." http://www.census.gov./hhes/www/housing/census/historic/owner.html.

U.S. Congress. Committee on Ways and Means and the Committee on Finance. 2003. "Estimates of Federal Tax Expenditures for Fiscal Years 2004–2008." Report. Washington, D.C.: U.S. Government Printing Office, December 22.

U.S. Department of Housing and Urban Development. 2006. *Fiscal Year 2006 Budget Summary.* Appendix A. Washington, D.C.: U.S. Government Printing Office.

———. 2007a. "Affordable Housing." http://www.hud.gov/offices/cpd/affordablehousing.

———. 2007b. *Annual Homeless Assessment Report to Congress.* Washington, D.C.: U.S. Government Printing Office, February 28.

———. 2007c. HUD User Policy Development and Research Information Service. SOCDS (State of the Cities Data Systems) data set. http://socds.huduser.org.

Chapter 12 Questions and Exercises

1. As Chapter 12 discusses, the housing market is a key aspect of the metropolitan economic and social environment. What is the housing market like in the metropolitan (or micropolitan) areas of interest to you? To explore this question, let's look first at how housing in those areas is divided among owner-occupied housing, renter-occupied housing, and vacancies in three CBSAs of your choice and in one principal city within each of those three CBSAs.To obtain these data in the *Urban Experience* CD, go to the "Get Data" screen and follow these directions:

- In the "Choose Data Items" section, click on the arrow immediately to the right and choose "Percentages."
- Check the box next to "Percentages" when it appears under "Choose Data Items" and a drop-down list of data categories will appear.
- Check the box next to "Housing." Another drop-down list will appear; check the boxes next to "Vacant Units" and "Occupied Units."
- Move on to the "Choose Locations" section of the screen. Double-click on "By CBSA Name" and a drop-down list of all CBSAs will appear. Scroll down until you locate the first of the three CBSAs you have decided upon. Double-click on the name of the CBSA and a drop-down list will appear underneath the name of the CBSA. Note that the first item in this list is the sum for all principal cities of the CBSA (the identifying name ends with ("CBSA-Prin Cities"). The second item in the list is the sum for all suburbs in the CBSA (the identifying name ends with "CBSA-suburbs"). The next items in the list are each of the individual principal cities in alphabetical order (there may be one or more than one). After all principal cities have been listed, the list continues with each of the individual suburbs in alphabetical order. For this exercise, check the box for the CBSA (the top box that is offset to the left) and then check a box next to any one of your choices among the principal cities. Proceed to the next two CBSAs you have chosen (one at a time) and repeat checking the boxes for the overall CBSA and for a principal city in the CBSA.
- Finally, in the "Choose Years" section of the screen, check the box for 2005.
- Click on "Go," and then, on the far left side of the screen, click on "Chart" (or if you prefer seeing the results in a table, click on "Table").

  - Among the areas you chose, which have the highest vacancy rates?
  - Which factors might account for the variation in the vacancy rates?

2. Cities and metropolitan areas may vary a great deal in the proportions of their occupied housing that are owner occupied and renter occupied. This aspect constitutes the next inquiry we will make into the housing market in the CBSAs you have chosen.

   To obtain these data in the *Urban Experience* CD, follow these steps:

- Click on "Get Data" to return to the main screen.
- Remove the checks in the boxes next to "Vacant Units" and "Occupied Units" and check the boxes next to "Owner Occupied" and "Renter Occupied." Leave everything else the same as in the previous exercise.
- Click on "Go," and then, on the far left side of the screen, click on "Chart" (or if you prefer seeing the results in a table, click on "Table").

  - Among the CBSAs you selected, which have the highest proportion of owner-occupied housing?
  - Among the principal cities you selected, which have the highest proportion of owner-occupied housing?
  - Within each CBSA, how does the proportion of owner-occupied housing differ between the CBSA as a whole and the principal city you selected?

3. Cities and metropolitan areas also may vary considerably in the cost of housing. Investigate this aspect of the market in the areas you selected by considering the median cost of rental housing.

To get these data in the *Urban Experience* CD, follow these steps:

- Click on "Get Data" to return to the main screen.
- In the "Choose Data Items" section, click on the arrow immediately to the right and choose "Counts." Check the box next to "Counts" when it appears under "Choose Data Items" and a drop-down list of data categories will appear.
- Check the box next to "Household Rent/Owner's Value." Another drop-down list will appear.
- Check the box next to "Median Household Gross Rent." Leave everything else the same as in the previous two exercises.
- Click on "Go," and then, on the far left side of the screen, click on "Table."

  - In 2005, among the CBSAs you selected, which have the highest median household gross rent and which have the lowest?
  - Among the principal cities you selected, which have the highest and lowest median household gross rent?
  - Within each CBSA, how does the median household gross rent differ between the CBSA as a whole and the principal city you selected?
  - Which factors might account for the variation in the median rent levels?

4. As Chapter 12 discusses, the cost of housing changes in response to conditions affecting demand and supply. As the next step in your investigation of the housing markets in the CBSAs you selected, take a look at how median household gross rent has changed between 1970 and 2005. (Note that the dollar amounts used for this exercise are "real dollars"—they have been adjusted to take inflation into account.)

To get these data in the *Urban Experience* CD, follow these steps:

- Click on "Get Data" to return to the main screen. Make sure that the screen has "Counts" immediately to the right of "Choose Data Items" and that the box next to "Median Household Gross Rent" is checked.
- In the "Choose Years" segment of the screen, check the boxes for all of the available years. Leave everything else the same as in the previous two exercises.
- Click on "Go," and then, on the far left side of the screen, click on "Table."

  - Among the CBSAs you selected, which one has the largest change in dollar value between 1970 and 2005?
  - Which CBSA has the largest percentage change? Calculate the percentage change for each CBSA by dividing the 2005 dollar amount by the 1970 dollar amount.
  - Among the principal cities you selected, which one has the largest change in dollar value and which has the largest percentage change?

♦ Which factors might account for the variation (if any) in the change of the median gross rent that you found?

5. Housing affordability depends upon the size of the housing unit, which depends in turn upon the size of the household seeking housing. You can investigate the expected housing costs for various sizes of families in different metropolitan areas through the Economic Policy Institute's (EPI) "Family Budget Calculator" (micropolitan areas are not included in the EPI's calculator). To access this calculator, go to

http://www.epi.org/content.cfm/datazone_fambud_budget

Click on "One parent, two children," and then enter the state and one metro area of your choice.

♦ What is the expected cost of monthly housing for a family of that size in that metro area?
♦ Return to the Family Budget Calculator Web page (refreshing the screen if necessary) and this time click on "Two parents, three children." What is the expected cost of monthly housing for a family of this size?
♦ Repeat this investigation for two other metro areas of your choice. In which metro areas are the expected housing costs for each of these two sizes of family the highest and the lowest?

6. As Chapter 12 discusses, residential segregation is an important socioeconomic issue in metropolitan areas. The U.S. Bureau of the Census publishes a report, "Racial and Ethnic Residential Segregation in the United States: 1980–2000," available on the Web at

http://www.census.gov/hhes/www/housing/housing_patterns/pdftoc.html

The report contains dissimilarity indexes for a number of metropolitan areas, calculated from U.S. Census data in 1980, 1990, and 2000. Go to this Web site and click on the link for "Residential Segregation of Blacks or African Americans: 1980–2000" to access the chapter on dissimilarity indexes for black/white (non-Hispanic) metro area residents. Advance to Table 5-4.

♦ Among the metropolitan areas listed, which five had the highest black/white dissimilarity indexes in 2000? Which five had the lowest indexes?
♦ Pick any three of the metro areas listed. Referring back to the discussion of dissimilarity indexes in Chapter 12, how would you interpret the dissimilarity indexes in 2000 for each of these metro areas?
♦ For each of these three metro areas, how did their dissimilarity indexes change between 1980 and 2000?

Return to the main Web page of the aforementioned report and click on the link for "Residential Segregation of Hispanics or Latinos: 1980–2000" to access the chapter on dissimilarity indexes for Hispanic/white (non-Hispanic) metro area residents. Advance to Table 6.4.

♦ Among the metro areas listed, which five had the highest Hispanic/white dissimilarity indexes? Which had the lowest?

+ Picking three of the metro areas, how did their dissimilarity indexes change between 1980 and 2000?

Repeat these questions, if you so desire, for the chapters on "Residential Segregation of Asians and Pacific-Islanders" and "Residential Segregation of Native Americans and Alaska Natives" by returning to the main Web page and choosing the relevant chapters of the report.

Land-Use Controls, Sprawl, and Smart Growth

13

Industrial Age cities were never pleasant places in which to work or live. The smell, the smoke, and the noise; the foulness that permeated air and water; the filth in the streets; and the soot and grime that defeated even the most vigorous attempts to maintain a clean home were not only an assault on the senses but also a danger to health and life itself. Urban historian Lewis Mumford (1961) describes nineteenth-century cities, dominated by factory and railroad, as places where rivers served as open sewers for the by-products of the cotton, chemical, and iron industries that did not wind up in the slag heaps piled up around town. In *The City in History*, he points out:

> Workers' houses, often those of the middle classes, too, would be built smack up against a steelworks, a dye plant, a gas works, or a railroad cutting. They would be built, often enough, on land filled in with ashes and broken glass and rubbish, where even the grass could not take root; they might be on the edge of a dump or a vast permanent pile of coal and slag; day in and day out the stench of the refuse, the murky outpouring of chimneys, the noise of hammering or of whirring machinery, accompanied the household routine.

In 1906, Upton Sinclair published his muckraking novel *The Jungle*, an indictment of the living and working conditions of the immigrant workforce in Chicago's meatpacking plants. The "Back-of-the-Yards" neighborhood next to the plants, which reeked of packinghouse decay, and overflowing garbage dumps and sewage pits, had high rates of infectious diseases like tuberculosis and numerous cases of infant mortality. Similarly, George Orwell's *The Road to Wigan Pier*, published in 1937, gives this bleak description of the northern England steelmaking town of Sheffield:

> And the stench! If at rare moments you stop smelling sulphur it is because you have begun smelling gas. Even the shallow river that runs through the town is usually bright yellow with some chemical or other.... One scene especially lingers in my mind. A frightful patch of waste ground (somehow, up there, a patch of waste ground attains a squalor that would be impossible even in London) trampled bare of grass and littered with newspapers and old saucepans. To the right an isolated row of gaunt four-roomed houses, dark red, blackened by smoke. To the left an interminable vista of factory chimneys, chimney beyond chimney, fading away into a dim blackish haze. Behind me a railway embankment made of the slag from furnaces. In front, across the patch of

451

waste ground, a cubical building of red and yellow brick, with the sign, "Thomas Grocock, Haulage Contractor."

As industrial cities grew throughout the nineteenth and early twentieth centuries, the completely unfettered land market contributed to sanitation and public health problems that ultimately threatened further growth. One response to these negative externalities was the public health reform movement and the development of municipal sanitation systems that we discussed in Chapter 10. Another was the development of land-use controls.

Land-Use Restrictions and Zoning

While location restrictions of some economic activities—particularly those officially recognized as posing a threat to the well-being of the general populace—extend back to colonial periods, citywide planning through land-use restrictions is of more recent vintage. A growing awareness of the need for city planning emerged during the explosive urban growth of the late 1800s and early 1900s, when factories were being built in cities at a feverish pace. In the span of one year alone (1906–1907), New York saw 3,060 new factories established, most in Manhattan and in close proximity to where hundreds of thousands of residents lived (Boyer 1994).

There were a number of problems with unregulated location. Newly established industries with offensive aromas or with water and air pollution as by-products could create devastating externalities for retail businesses. Crowded tenement housing in the alleys of industrial areas contributed to crime, disastrous fires, and other public safety problems. The uncertainty of the future uses of adjacent land could preclude investment in a business or create unwanted risk for real estate speculators. Families who sought to remove themselves from the dynamics of the central city might find their new locations encroached upon by the same social and economic factors they had sought to escape.

Hence, by the early 1900s, various residential, business, real estate, environmental, social reform, and public-sector interests began to coalesce into a widespread movement for the adoption of citywide regulations to control land use (Boyer 1994). William Fischel (1999), a Dartmouth College economist who has written extensively about government-imposed land-use controls, offers the possibility that they were necessary, like sewer systems, for industrial era cities to continue to take advantage of agglomeration economies and counteract the disadvantages hazardous to health and to life.

The legal authority for local governments to exercise some control over the use of private property includes the rights of **eminent domain** and **police power**. The former refers to the power of local government to take private land for public use, the latter to the local government's right to protect the health, safety, and general well-being of its citizens by imposing enforceable regulations. The legitimacy of zoning—public restrictions on how private (and public) land can be used—derives from these local government police powers.

The Power of Eminent Domain

In the legal tradition followed by the United States, real estate exists as a right conferred to individuals and to private entities by government under an ownership classification called **fee simple**. The right to own property is transferable to other parties, but remains fundamentally a right conferred by government. It has long been established that a local government has the right to take private land to serve a public purpose, so long as the owner is paid the property's fair market value. Through the middle of the twentieth century, the power of eminent domain was used to transfer land from the private sector back to the public sector in order to build public schools, courthouses, or highways. Under the Housing Act of 1949—which, among other provisions, established the nation's urban renewal program—the definition of public purpose was expanded to include slum clearance. The urban renewal program often used the power of eminent domain to transfer property from one group of private owners to another, who would then agree to erase blighted areas by redeveloping the land. Based on the expectation at the time that private developers would shun the city and instead build only in the suburbs, the program subsidized these developers by buying the land, clearing it, and then selling it to them far below its cost.

In the latest of many court cases that have challenged the power of eminent domain, the Supreme Court in June 2005 ruled in *Kelo v. City of New London* that local economic development was itself a legitimate public purpose for which a city could use eminent domain even when an area was not a slum or blighted area. The court opined that improving the climate for private investment and job creation in a municipality hard hit by disinvestment and job loss could serve as a legal rationale for a local community to seize land under eminent domain, as long as the owners were fairly compensated.

For the plaintiffs, however, fair compensation was beside the point. The issue for them was not about their homes' objective value—their **market value**—but about their homes' subjective value—their **use value**. Even with fair compensation for her house, it would be difficult for Susette Kelo to replicate the distinctive water views she cherished. But it would be impossible for Wilhelmina Dery to replicate what she lost; the house had been in her family for more than a hundred years, she was born there in 1918 and had lived there ever since. As Logan and Molotch (1987) point out, those who acquire land for its potential future market value are often more savvy about the uses of political power than those who want to retain the land for its use value.

The *Kelo* case was decided by a vote of 5–4 and has generated enormous controversy. In its wake, many states have sought to pass their own laws that restrict the use of eminent domain, especially in those instances when the local government transfers land from one group of private owners to another. In her dissenting opinion, Justice Sandra Day O'Connor wrote, "The specter of condemnation hangs over all property. Nothing is to prevent the State from replacing any Motel 6 with a Ritz-Carlton, any home with a shopping mall, or any farm with a factory."

O'Connor's statement raises an intriguing puzzle. If, in a market economy such as ours, land is usually sold to the highest bidder, why would the state need to intervene at all? Why would the market itself not replace a Motel 6 with a Ritz-Carlton? That is the logic behind the bid rent curves we discussed in Chapter 4. We see the result of that bidding process every time a drive-in movie theater gives way to an industrial park or an apple orchard is sold off to become a residential subdivision. The concept of **highest and best use** refers to the normal situation in which the market mechanism itself determines the most productive use for any given plot of land. Therefore, why would the state need to use its power of eminent domain?

Remember how the game Monopoly proceeds? Players can buy property they land on, but they can build houses and hotels only if they own all the properties of the same color. Say you own two of the three yellow properties—Atlantic and Ventnor—but another player owns Marvin Gardens. Maybe you can negotiate to buy it from him. He might hold out for a high price, but it still might be worth it, just to be able to build and collect higher rents. However, that other player might be your kid brother and he might refuse to sell just because yellow is his favorite color, or maybe just to spite you. Now you have a **site assembly problem**. In Monopoly, the site assembly problem means you cannot build at all. In the real world, the site assembly problem—the prospect of dealing with holdouts who believe they can ransom their properties or those who just plain refuse to sell—is a powerful deterrent to redevelopment. A municipality's ability to use eminent domain solves the developer's site assembly problem.

The Power to Enact Zoning Regulations

Like eminent domain, zoning may also involve a change in circumstances for the landowner. In this case, the government places limits on how a parcel of land may be used. But, unlike the power of eminent domain, the land is not taken from its owner, and zoning does not normally require that the owner be compensated for any loss in value. The power to zone was ultimately affirmed in a 1926 U.S. Supreme Court decision, *Village of Euclid, Ohio v. Ambler Realty Co.* Although some large cities already had zoning ordinances prior to 1926, these regulations proliferated among municipalities of all sizes after the Supreme Court made its ruling. Today, because of the Standard State Zoning Enabling Act passed by the U.S. Congress two years later, in 1928, there is a good deal of uniformity in zoning laws nationwide.

While recent cases have reaffirmed the court's decision in the *Euclid* case—arguing compensation for loss in value is not required if a legitimate public purpose is being served and if the land retains some value—it remains an area of great legal contention. The Fifth Amendment to the U.S. Constitution states, in part, "nor shall private property be taken for public use, without just compensation." The issue in contention is whether loss in property value as a result of zoning or other environmental regulations—such as wetlands protection—is a "taking" under the Fifth Amendment that requires compensation for the owner. According to Jerold Kayden (2001), an expert on property rights, the Supreme Court established the broad principle that "although owners are not entitled to the most profitable use of their property, they are entitled not to be denied all economically viable use." Beyond that, the

Supreme Court has left it to lower courts to adjudicate the issue on a case-by-case basis.

The main economic justification offered for zoning and used to support the original 1926 Supreme Court case is the need to prevent negative externalities that result from incompatible land uses. Thus, it is an argument based on the criterion of promoting efficiency by reducing real private or social costs or enhancing real private or social value.

There are four principal motives for zoning. **Externality zoning** separates land uses to deal with the fact that land used for some purposes creates negative externalities for other uses. Early factories, for example, poured filth into the air and nearby rivers, which affected the value of nearby housing. The first citywide externality zoning plan in the United States was adopted by Los Angeles in 1908, and limited industrial location to twenty-five designated areas of the city. The Los Angeles plan was followed by a more comprehensive zoning plan in New York. The New York plan, adopted in 1916, created separate residential, business, and industrial districts—in the process, forcing hundreds of factories to move from central Manhattan—reserved two-thirds of the city for residential purposes, and regulated building heights throughout the city. The practice quickly spread. After their adoption in New York, zoning regulations spread to seventy-six U.S. cities by 1926, and to more than 1,300 cities by 1936 (Boyer 1994).

Today, externality zoning is typically addressed through one of three means: (1) prescriptive approaches to externality zoning that identify a specific use for each plot of land in a city; (2) cumulative approaches that identify a range of specific allowable uses for each plot; and (3) performance approaches that focus on the intensity of the externality—for example, the amount of noise, glare, or fumes. Standards are set for the externality and instead of restricting a particular type of use, allow usage of the land by any entity that produces externalities below the maximum intensity permitted.

Design zoning restricts land use with the goal of promoting efficient use of the city's infrastructure or conserving open spaces. Through the zoning process, new development can be limited to areas that have compatible transportation, water, and sewer systems. Green spaces that include parks, riverfronts, and other open spaces for plazas and fields can also be preserved in this way.

Fiscal zoning attempts to bar changes that would have an adverse effect on the municipal budget. The central motivation of fiscal zoning is an effort to stabilize city expenditures relative to its revenues; it takes the position that the additional municipal costs associated with a change should not be greater than the additional revenues coming from that change. For example, some cities and towns may want to discourage increased population density because the additional tax revenues would be less than the cost of providing city services, especially schooling, to the increased population.

Finally, **exclusionary zoning** attempts to bar one or more subsets of the urban population from sections of the city. Efforts to exclude on the basis of race represented one of the primary goals of early citywide zoning. In the 1880s, San Francisco adopted laws that segregated its Chinese population. In 1910, Baltimore adopted a citywide regulation that mandated the separation of white and African American residences. By 1914, racial zoning regulations had also been adopted in nine southern cities—Richmond, Norfolk, Portsmouth, Roanoke, Winston-Salem, Greenville, Atlanta, Louisville, and Birmingham. The U.S. Supreme Court ruled such laws unconstitutional in 1917, but many southern cities attempted to establish new racial zoning laws in the decades that followed. Birmingham enforced a racial zoning law until 1951, despite the Supreme Court ruling. Throughout the 1900s, some cities in both the North and the South engaged in "racially informed zoning," in which goals of racial separation were not explicitly mentioned, but were nonetheless advanced through the use of externality, design, and fiscal zoning as tools (Silver 1997).

Exclusionary zoning has also been used to maintain the income and wealth character of some suburban areas. Minimum lot sizes, for example, may be set forth as a fiscal zoning concern or as a design zoning issue, when the underlying motivation that drives the regulation is to prevent the encroachment of families who cannot afford large lots. In practice, it is often difficult to disentangle the legitimate role of zoning to reduce the negative externalities that would accompany incompatible land use from its "hidden agenda" of promoting exclusion on the basis of race, ethnicity, or income (Boyer 1994; Silver 1997).

Land-use regulations are often a source of conflict in metropolitan areas because citywide and suburban zoning affect the entire metropolitan economy, because different interest groups within metropolitan areas may be in conflict over specific zoning plans, and because exclusionary motives can often be presented as externality, design, or fiscal zoning plans. They pit developers against local communities, businesses against home owners, and often one social class against another. They affect decisions about transportation and limit the growth of "urban sprawl." Whenever limits are placed on land use through zoning, there is bound to be some conflict. But without zoning, one can imagine that cities might be much more unpleasant places in which to live and work.

Houston's Alternative to Zoning

There are alternatives to zoning, however, and Houston is a city with no zoning at all. One would naturally think that Houston would have a hodgepodge of activities throughout the city and would therefore experience a high level of negative externalities. Yet, there is no stark contrast between land-use patterns in Houston and other cities. In the absence of zoning, how has Houston avoided a return to the nightmare landscapes of an earlier age, such as the ones with which we began this chapter? Although land in Houston is not zoned, its use is nevertheless regulated, through private arrangements called deed restrictions, or restrictive covenants (Siegan 1972).

For example, two individuals purchasing property in Houston, Smith and Jones, have to decide whether to buy into a subdivision with restrictive covenants. Smith decides that restrictions on his own property, such as the color he is allowed to paint the exterior of his home or the type of fence he can erect in his yard—which limit his ability to impose negative externalities on his neighbors—would reduce its value to him by $10,000. But Smith also calculates that restrictions on what his immediate neighbors can do—which limit their ability to impose negative externalities on him—would increase the value of his own home by $15,000. Smith therefore buys the property. Jones calculates that the restrictions on him would reduce his value by $15,000, while restrictions on his neighbors would increase it by only $10,000, so he does not buy the property. To the extent that more households see the situation in the same way as Smith, the subdivision will be successful.

Much of Houston's land was built up in big subdivisions owned by large-scale developers. These developers established rules, enforceable by the city, which governed the use of the property through its sale and resale to subsequent owners. This ability to avoid negative externalities through negotiations in the private market is consistent with the limited-government orientation of the noted economist Ronald Coase, recipient of the 1991 Nobel Prize in Economics.

In his landmark 1960 article, "The Problem of Social Cost," Coase argues that externalities do not necessarily require government intervention and that private bargaining will lead to the optimal outcome if three conditions hold: (1) property rights are clearly specified, (2) the number of parties involved is small, and (3) the costs of bargaining (transaction costs) are negligible. Using this line of argument, the **Coase theorem** begins from the presumption that the problem of externalities is reciprocal. For example, I might be harmed if you add another story to your house, thereby casting a shadow that causes my landscaped garden to wither; but you might be harmed if I prevent you from doing so, even though your family is expanding and you need another bedroom.

Coase argues that as long as property rights are completely specified, it does not matter who initially possesses them. If the garden owner possesses the property right, and thus the power to veto a building project, the builder and the garden owner should be willing to arrange compensation for the externality that affects the garden owner, as long as the value to the builder exceeds the value of the garden owner's loss. An outcome that maximizes total value to the parties taken as a whole will occur in either case.

Say the new room will add $10,000 to the value of your house above the cost of building it. Moreover, let's assume that it would cost me $6,000 for alternative landscaping with shrubs that thrive in shadow and are as pleasing to me as my current landscaping. If *you* have the property right to build, you will do so, since I will not be willing to pay you enough to get you to change your mind. I will not pay you $10,000 to save my garden, which is worth only $6,000 to me. However, if *I* have the right to prevent you from building, you can still negotiate a side payment of $6,000 to me that pays for the new landscaping, thereby compensating me for my loss. Whether or not I receive compensation will be determined by which of us possesses the property right, but it will not determine whether the bedroom is built. In either case, you wind up building your new bedroom: in the first case, without having to pay me; and in the latter, by making the $6,000 side payment. In both cases, the total value to the two parties together is $10,000. If you have the right to build, you will gain the total $10,000 benefit. If I have the right to prevent you from building, you can pay me the $6,000 and you have a net gain of $4,000—a total benefit again of $10,000.

On the other hand, if the new room adds $10,000 to the value of your house but causes $20,000 in damages to my landscaping, the optimal outcome in terms of our total benefits would be not to build, and that is what will occur. In this case, if I have the right to prevent you from building, I will, since it would not be worth it for you to try to compensate me for the value of my loss. If you have the right to build, I will negotiate a payment that makes it worth your while not to do so. You could use that payment to purchase a larger house elsewhere or figure out some other way to create more space, perhaps by waterproofing your basement. Whether or not you get paid (for not building) depends on which of us possesses the property right, but in either case, the additional story will not be built.

Where it can be applied, the Coase theorem is an elegant private-market solution to the problem of externalities. However, in many real world instances of externalities, property rights cannot be completely specified, a large number of parties are affected, or transaction costs are significant. If the pattern of land development in Houston had not involved big subdivisions developed by a small number of large companies that got to specify the terms of purchase, it is unlikely that such a nonzoning alternative would have been possible. No other major U.S. city has even attempted this. Moreover, although Houston does not have a zoning board, it does have a Planning Department, as well as a Deed Restriction Enforcement Team within the city's Legal Department. Though more reliant on private markets to determine land use, Houston is still a significant departure from the notion of an unfettered free market where property owners can do as they please with regard to the unrestricted use of their land.

Underzoning and Overzoning

It is one thing to say that the justification for zoning is the reduction of negative externalities that result from incompatible land uses, and quite another to determine the optimal amount of zoning. Under what circumstances do zoning laws fail to effectively reduce negative externalities? Under what circumstances do zoning regulations go beyond the point of meeting the efficiency criteria for which they were intended?

In Niagara Falls, New York, land was excavated for a canal in the 1890s. However, the Love Canal (the builder, Love, named it after himself) was never completed. Beginning in the 1920s and up until 1952, several chemical companies used the site as a waste dump. The area was covered over in 1953 and was subsequently the site of an elementary school and many homes. The water table in the area rose throughout the 1960s and 1970s, causing contaminated groundwater to come to the surface. By 1978, air samples showed dangerously high levels of toxic wastes, including benzene, a known human carcinogen. The area was found to have a higher than normal incidence of cancer, miscarriages, and birth defects. Ultimately, all of the residents in a ten-square-block area were relocated and the elementary school was demolished (Beck 1979).

In 1980, in response to the environmental tragedy at Love Canal, the U.S. Congress enacted the Superfund program to clean up hazardous waste sites. Under the terms of this law, the U.S. Environmental Protection Agency (EPA) had, by April 2004, relocated more than 45,000 people who were living on or near Superfund cleanup sites and provided alternative sources of drinking water to more than 600,000 people living on or near these sites (U.S. Environmental Protection Agency 2004). In many instances, the nature and severity of the hazard was not known until long after the damage was done, and therefore would not have been prevented by zoning. However, the *Washington Post* reported in 2002 that hundreds of public schools are located within one-half mile of Superfund sites and that while many had been built decades earlier, some were relatively new (Pianin and Fletcher 2002). They also described instances in which parents and other community members were successful in blocking attempts to site new schools on former waste sites. Zoning regulations do not necessarily deal with such environmental hazards. Land formerly used for waste sites is relatively cheap and therefore attractive, from a cost perspective, for development.

The issue of underzoning, or failure to prevent negative externalities that arise from incompatible land use, is also central to the concept of **environmental justice.** The EPA's definition of environmental justice includes this criterion for fair treatment: "no group of people, including racial, ethnic, or socioeconomic groups, should bear a disproportionate share of negative consequences resulting from industrial, municipal, and commercial operations or the execution of federal, state, local, and tribal environmental programs and policies" (U.S. Environmental Protection Agency 2007).

Yale Rabin (1989), an urban planning expert, argues that many municipalities have used zoning ordinances to protect white residential areas from incompatible land uses, but have denied black residential areas the same protection. He uses the term **expulsive zoning** to describe local governments' use of zoning ordinances to protect white residential areas, while zoning black residential areas for industrial or other **locally unwanted land uses (LULUs).**

A study completed for the EPA by the National Academy of Public Administration (2003) reports that even though minorities were far more likely than white residents to live near hazardous waste sites, enforcement of the law was stronger in white areas. The study found that the penalties imposed on environmentally compromised sites were greater in white areas; it took longer to place sites in minority areas on the hazardous waste site National Priorities List. It took one to three and a half years longer for the EPA to begin cleanups at sites in minority areas, and the EPA chose containment rather than permanent treatment more often in minority areas, while choosing permanent treatment more often in white areas.

The issue of environmental justice combines problems of efficiency (the failure to prevent negative externalities) and equity (disparate treatment of whites and minorities) that arise when areas are underzoned. As we shall see, other equity issues arise from instances where areas are overzoned rather than underzoned. Many jurisdictions engage in overzoning: They use zoning ordinances for purposes that have little or nothing to do with preventing the negative externalities that arise from incompatible land use. Often, the goal of such zoning is to keep any further development from occurring in the community.

Equity Issues in Zoning

As Fischel (1999) points out, "Zoning is the product of a political process, and it serves the interests of those who control that process." In many jurisdictions, those interests are served through the use of fiscal zoning, as noted earlier in this chapter, in which land uses that bring in more property tax revenue than they cost in local expenditures are sought after, while land uses that do the opposite are excluded. Similarly, in those jurisdictions that collect local sales taxes, there is a powerful incentive to zone land for retail use.

As we saw in Chapter 9, municipalities are heavily dependent on the property tax as a source of revenue to fund local public-sector functions, the largest category being primary and secondary education. Existing property owners within a jurisdiction know that they will be able to get more and/or better quality public services in return for their own contribution to tax revenues to the extent that they are successful in practicing fiscal zoning. Attracting office parks, regional headquarters, or other forms of clean, nonpolluting business activity will generate high property tax revenue that is more than sufficient to pay for the additional roads and public safety expenditures they might require. On the other hand, allowing the construction of homes worth less than the current median house value will dilute the public-sector benefits that existing property owners receive in return for their property tax payments. If those homes contain school-age children, the town will often incur additional expenditures that are not fully offset by additional revenues. Therefore, it is in the interest of existing residents to repel low- or moderate-income families with children, while welcoming higher-income families and older households without children.

If current residents want to ensure that the value of new homes will be above that of the existing housing stock, they can use zoning laws to exclude trailer parks, garden apartments, two-family houses, and even one-family houses on small lots. Large-lot, single-family zoning ensures that the area will be low density and therefore beyond the price range of families who would cost local government more than they contribute.

While low- and moderate-income families are shunned, clean industry is sought after for its contribution to the fiscal health of a community. The motives for fiscal zoning are economic, but the result is exclusion based on income. Since minorities tend to have lower incomes than whites, exclusion on the basis of income will also exclude a disproportionate number of minority families.

In addition to the economic motives behind fiscal zoning, there may be other motives to exclude households, not only on the basis of income but also on the basis of race and ethnicity. In Chapter 7, we saw how employers who practice statistical discrimination would exclude qualified minority workers from desirable jobs. Similarly, white property owners who believe that the incidence of crime is higher among low-income minority households with young adults can use carefully constructed exclusionary zoning to keep such households out of the area. Zoning for age-restricted housing where only those over age 55 are allowed to rent or buy is just one type of such zoning. Restricting the minimum lot size for housing construction is another. In the end, residential segregation by income results in fiscal disparities between communities. The winners in the fiscal zoning competition are able to provide high-quality public-sector services at relatively low tax rates; the losers tax themselves more heavily but are still unable to fund public-sector services of comparable quality.

Edwin S. Mills (1979), a noted urban economist, points out that exclusion based on race or ethnicity was the hidden agenda behind some of the nation's earliest zoning laws. As mentioned earlier in this chapter, in the 1880s, a time of virulent discrimination against Asians, San Francisco passed a law excluding them from living in some parts of the city. California courts judged that law unconstitutional, so the city instead passed a law that excluded laundries from those areas. Since many laundries were operated by Asians who lived close to where they worked, the new law served the same purpose as the old, but without running afoul of the state's constitution. Similarly, New York City's early twentieth-century zoning laws used districting and height limits to keep garment manufacturers and their low-income Eastern European immigrant female workforce segregated from the city's fashionable shopping areas and their more prosperous clientele. Mills argues that the ability to determine their own zoning laws was an important motivation for suburban jurisdictions to reject central city attempts at annexation.

In a similar vein, urban economist John M. Levy (1985) argues that the powers of local zoning boards to rezone or to grant **variances** can be applied selectively to enforce exclusionary goals without blatantly violating the law. Rezoning changes the land-use restrictions in a given area; granting a variance keeps the restrictions in place but gives permission to a nonconforming use that would otherwise be in violation of the ordinance. An area zoned for single-family housing might be rezoned if a company wanted to build its corporate headquarters there, or if a developer wanted to build apartments for affluent retirees, but not if the developer wanted to build affordable housing for young families. Levy notes that many of the corporate headquarters in Westchester County, New York (the county just north of New York City), have been built on land that was originally zoned for large-lot, single-family homes.

In the face of these economic and discriminatory motives, efforts to get suburban jurisdictions to accept even small amounts of affordable housing have had very limited success. Judicial decisions like that in the 1975 New Jersey case, *Southern Burlington County NAACP v. Township of Mount Laurel* (*Mount Laurel* I) and the subsequent 1983 ruling (*Mount Laurel* II), and legislative efforts like in the 1969 Massachusetts passage of Chapter 40B, the "anti-snob-zoning" act, require that every jurisdiction in the state provide some affordable housing units as a proportion of its total housing stock. While these requirements have led to the construction of a modest amount of affordable units in the suburbs, the overall impact has been small, leading to a continuation of income and racial/ethnic segregation.

Thus, while the fundamental economic justification for zoning to reduce negative externalities is still widely accepted, concerns about the motives behind its implementation in many municipalities raise important issues of social equity. From a public policy perspective, the conundrum is how to craft zoning laws that limit true adverse externalities but do not blatantly or even subtly create insurmountable hurdles to those who are striving for a better place to live.

Zoning and Metropolitan Sprawl

Particular forms of suburban development raise an additional set of efficiency and equity questions. If you walk out the front door of your house and you do not have access to an automobile, what opportunities are available to you? Can you borrow a cup of sugar from a neighbor? Can you walk to the store to buy a container of milk? Can you bicycle down to the local coffee shop? Can you get on a bus, light-rail, or other "fixed guideway" vehicle (e.g., a trolley, subway, or monorail) that will take you to another part of town? If you live inside a city or in one of the older suburbs built before World War II, it is likely that at least some of the preceding options will be available to you. However, if you live in a newer suburb at the edge of the metropolitan area, the exclusive-use zoning and the complete separation of land use that it requires makes it more likely that you will depend on an automobile for most, or even all, of these activities. The tendency to build newer suburbs at lower density, to segregate land use more completely, and to be more dependent on automobiles than cities or older suburbs is part of the phenomenon called **urban sprawl**. It is one reason for our love-hate relationship with cities and suburbs that we described in Chapter 1.

William H. Whyte is credited with coining the term "urban sprawl" in a 1958 essay in which he warns, "Already huge patches of once green countryside have been turned into vast, smog-filled deserts that are neither city, suburb, nor country, and each day—at a rate of some 3,000 acres a day—more countryside is being bulldozed under." Although there is no commonly accepted definition of sprawl, figuring prominently in many descriptions are low density, separation of land uses, and automobile dependency. A relatively dispassionate discussion of the costs and benefits of sprawl is available in Burchell et al. (2002).

As we saw in Chapter 4, decentralization has been occurring since the latter part of the nineteenth century. Its pace increased after the 1920s and accelerated further after the 1950s. Sprawl is not synonymous with decentralization, although it is sometimes used this way, sowing much confusion. Sprawl refers to a specific form of decentralization that is characterized by much of the late-twentieth-century metropolitan growth in which single-use developments—housing subdivisions, shopping malls, office parks, and industrial parks—are segregated from each other and are accessible primarily by automobiles traveling on arterial roads. This pattern of land use differs not only from that of cities but also from that of older suburbs. In the debate over sprawl, the dichotomy is not between city and suburb, but between pre–World War II patterns of city and suburban growth and development patterns adopted after World War II. The concern is not primarily about the continuation of decentralization per se, but the form that decentralization has taken in recent decades.

What's Wrong with Sprawl?

Critics of sprawl raise a number of concerns. Some architectural critics find it aesthetically undesirable. For example, Dolores Hayden (2003) of Yale University describes Tyson's Corner, Virginia (a quintessential edge city), as resembling "a model with all the building blocks for both suburb and city thrown on the ground by a two-year-old having a tantrum."

Other criticisms of sprawl fall more comfortably into the economists' domain of efficiency and equity. The list of efficiency concerns includes those that are specifically related to environmental degradation, as well as a more general set of negative externalities that affect various subgroups of the population.

A sprawling pattern of growth consumes large areas of land. **Figure 13.1** shows U.S. Geological Survey maps for the Washington, D.C. area, which track urban growth over more than 200 years and make projections for possible scenarios by 2025. The expansion of metropolitan area boundaries is disproportionate to the area's population growth. Similar expansion occurs even in metropolitan areas whose populations are shrinking.

Large-lot, low-density development may contribute to the pollution of soil and groundwater through the use of septic systems instead of sewers, as well as through the use of pesticides and fertilizers on large expanses of lawn. In some regions of the country, the use of scarce water supplies to nourish parched lawns and other non-indigenous plants and shrubs places further strain on natural resources. Moreover, new infrastructure such as streets and highways, communication networks, and other public utilities are extended out to the fringe of the metropolitan area only at great expense, while some of the existing infrastructure in depopulated areas within the central city remains underutilized.

Urban Sprawl and Commuting Times

Although average commuting time has increased by only a few minutes each way each day over the period from 1980 to 2000, as we pointed out in Chapter 10, reliance on the automobile for virtually all trips to all destinations raises its own set of concerns, only some of which are related to environmental issues. Increases in gasoline consumption as automobile ownership rises and an increase in total per capita miles driven accelerates the depletion of a nonrenewable resource. With increased road congestion due to the total number of trips taken each day, overall

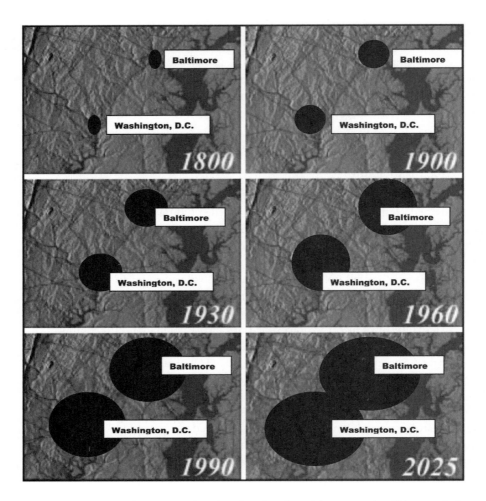

Figure 13.1 Washington, D.C.-Baltimore Metro Growth. This series of maps shows more than 200 years of urban growth in and around the Washington area. The background in each map is a shaded-relief image. The darkness of the shading represents population density. *Source:* U.S. Department of the Interior, U.S. Geological Survey, "Analyzing Land Use Change in Urban Environments," USGS Fact Sheet 188–99 (Washington, D.C.: U.S. Government Printing Office, November 1999), p. 3.

travel times continue to grow, which reduces the amount of time people can spend at work, with family, or simply enjoying leisure.

This can represent a huge **opportunity cost**: the time that could have been spent in other pursuits. In some metropolitan areas, the number of hours spent in congested traffic every year is the equivalent of several workweeks. If you add in the time spent in commuting to work as work time, an increase in traffic congestion reduces labor productivity—that is, output per hour of work. For the nation, this shows up in the form of a reduction in potential national gross domestic product. For the individual worker, it shows up as a lower realized hourly wage. Some critics of sprawl also argue that there is a social cost to congestion. The inordinate amounts of time that people spend inside their cars have cut into the time available for civic activities, and thereby reduced the level of civic engagement.

The Texas Transportation Institute issues an annual report on traffic congestion (Schrank and Lomax 2005). As part of that report, the authors calculate a travel time index, which is the ratio of travel time in peak periods to travel time under free-flow conditions—which they define as 60 miles per hour on freeways and 35 miles per hour on principal arterial roads. A travel time index of 1.5, for example, would mean that a 20-minute free-flow trip would take 30 minutes during congested times. **Table 13.1** shows the trends in the travel time index from 1982 to 2003 for four different categories of urban areas: Very Large (population over 3 million), Large (population over 1 million but less than 3 million), Medium (population over 500,000 but less than 1 million), and Small (population less than 500,000). The ratio increased in each category, with congestion taking its greatest toll in the very large urban areas. Overall, the travel time index increased from 1.12 in 1982 to 1.37 in 2003 (a 20-minute free-flow trip took 22.4 minutes at 1982 congestion levels but 27.4 minutes at 2003 congestion levels). However, in the most congested area—Los Angeles-Long Beach-Santa Ana, California—the 20-minute free-flow trip took 26 minutes at 1982 congestion levels (travel time index 1.3) but 35 minutes at 2003 levels (travel time index 1.75). That extra 15 minutes per congested trip used up 2.5 hours per week for each driver who was stuck in traffic during his weekday morning and evening commutes. Multiply that by 50 weeks (give the poor wretch a well-deserved, two-week vacation!) and it amounts to an extra 125 hours per year—just a bit more than three 40-hour workweeks each year—spent at the wheel during rush hour.

Attempts to reduce traffic congestion due to sprawl—and thus increase efficiency—impose other costs on society. Adding additional lanes to highways in order to speed the flow of traffic is very expensive in its own right. The resources used in highway construction could potentially be used for other purposes. For the federal, state, or local government, taxes spent on widening roads could, at least in theory, have been used for building schools or parks. For the individual taxpayer, more road construction ultimately means higher taxes and less after-tax disposable income. So sprawl can be seen as imposing all kinds of opportunity costs on society.

Moving farther away from central cities explicitly involves decentralization. However, as we pointed out earlier, decentralization is not necessarily synonymous with sprawl; the specific manner in which a suburban development is designed can turn decentralization into sprawl. In *A Better Place to Live*, Philip Langdon (1994) shows how the design of many modern residential subdivisions not only makes it impossible to provide public transportation but also actually discourages residents from walking or riding bicycles. The development of residential "pods" that are accessible from an external arterial road and contain long, curving internal routes and cul-de-sacs that lack easy connections between sites makes it difficult to navigate even *within* the pod by any means other than automobile. The result for residents is that the automobile is indispensable for even the simplest of errands. The corollary for nondrivers—the young, the old, and some of the disabled—is that there

Table 13.1 Travel Time Index, 1982–2003: Point Change in Peak-Period Time Penalty

Urban Area	2003	2002	1993	1982	Points	Rank
85-Area Average	1.37	1.37	1.28	1.12	25	
Very Large Area Average	1.48	1.49	1.38	1.18	30	
Very Large (13 areas):						
Los Angeles-Long Beach-Santa Ana, CA	1.75	1.77	1.73	1.30	45	1
Chicago, IL-IN	1.57	1.54	1.34	1.18	39	2
Atlanta, GA	1.46	1.42	1.18	1.08	38	3
San Francisco-Oakland, CA	1.54	1.55	1.44	1.21	33	5
Washington, DC-VA-MD	1.51	1.50	1.38	1.18	33	5
Miami, FL	1.42	1.40	1.26	1.09	33	5
Dallas-Fort Worth-Arlington, TX	1.36	1.35	1.20	1.07	29	16
New York-Newark, NY-NJ-CT	1.39	1.40	1.28	1.13	26	17
Detroit, MI	1.38	1.36	1.36	1.12	26	17
Boston, MA-NH-RI	1.34	1.35	1.26	1.10	24	22
Phoenix, AZ	1.35	1.35	1.27	1.13	22	25
Philadelphia, PA-NJ-DE-MD	1.32	1.35	1.20	1.13	19	28
Houston, TX	1.42	1.41	1.24	1.28	14	39
Large (26 areas):						
San Diego, CA	1.41	1.40	1.22	1.06	35	4
Riverside-San Bernardino, CA	1.37	1.34	1.27	1.04	33	5
Las Vegas, NV	1.39	1.36	1.24	1.07	32	9
Portland, OR-WA	1.37	1.38	1.24	1.05	32	9
Seattle, WA	1.38	1.36	1.35	1.07	31	11
Minneapolis-St. Paul, MN	1.34	1.34	1.16	1.03	31	11
Denver-Aurora, CO	1.40	1.40	1.24	1.10	30	13
Sacramento, CA	1.37	1.34	1.19	1.07	30	13
Baltimore, MD	1.37	1.35	1.20	1.07	30	13
Orlando, FL	1.30	1.31	1.21	1.09	21	26
Indianapolis, IN	1.24	1.24	1.16	1.03	21	26
San Jose, CA	1.37	1.39	1.34	1.18	19	28
Cincinnati, OH-KY-IN	1.22	1.22	1.15	1.04	18	32
San Antonio, TX	1.22	1.23	1.07	1.05	17	33
Milwaukee, WI	1.21	1.23	1.17	1.05	16	35
Columbus, OH	1.19	1.19	1.14	1.03	16	35
Tampa-St. Petersburg, FL	1.33	1.31	1.30	1.19	14	39
Providence, RI-MA	1.19	1.18	1.11	1.05	14	39
St. Louis, MO-IL	1.22	1.24	1.18	1.09	13	46
Virginia Beach, VA	1.21	1.20	1.13	1.08	13	46
Kansas City, MO-KS	1.11	1.10	1.06	1.01	10	54
New Orleans, LA	1.19	1.18	1.16	1.10	9	56
Oklahoma City, OK	1.10	1.11	1.04	1.02	8	62
Buffalo, NY	1.10	1.08	1.04	1.03	7	67
Cleveland, OH	1.09	1.10	1.08	1.02	7	67
Pittsburgh, PA	1.10	1.10	1.09	1.08	2	82

Notes: Very Large Urban Areas: population over 3 million. Large Urban Areas: population more than 1 million and less than 3 million. Travel Time Index: The ratio of travel time in the peak period to the travel time at free-flow conditions. A value of 1.35 indicates that a 20-minute free-flow trip takes 27 minutes in the peak. Free-flow speeds (60 mph on freeways and 35 mph on principal arterials) are used as the comparison threshold. The effects of operational treatments are included in 2002 and 2003 data. Users of this data are cautioned to avoid placing too much value on the rankings of all 85 urban areas. Often, there is little difference between being sixth on the list and being twelfth, for example. Furthermore, these rankings compare all urban areas without respect to population or other differences that can significantly influence the ranking outcomes. Rankings should be used to make broad, general comparisons only and not distinguish between urban areas based on small differences in ranking outcomes.
Source: Schrank and Lomax 2005, table 5, "Trends—Travel Time Index, 1982–2003," p. 24.

is a significant loss of autonomy, since even the simplest of errands requires that they depend on someone else who can drive them to their destinations.

Recently, the extreme dependence on automobiles and the disappearance of opportunities to walk simply as part of one's normal way of being out in the world has been linked to increases in obesity and other illnesses related to sedentary lifestyles (Frumkin, Frank, and Jackson 2004). Health experts tell us that we should be getting exercise equivalent to walking 30 minutes each day. A generation or two ago, that could be achieved effortlessly in the course of living one's life: going to work or school, stopping for a container of milk, getting to a doctor's appointment, mailing a letter, getting a haircut or manicure. Nowadays, for many of us, that exercise has to be scheduled in, because it no longer occurs in the normal course of our daily lives. In a real sense, the rise of the modern health club can trace its roots to urban sprawl.

The Debate about Sprawl

Critics of sprawl argue that it is undesirable because of its concomitant inefficiencies and inequities. They support a range of public policies at the federal, state, and local levels that would curb sprawl. In contrast, defenders of sprawl argue that current land-use patterns reflect consumer choice. If the fastest-growing counties in the United States are characterized by large houses on large lots and populated by adults who drive sport-utility vehicles (SUVs), it is simply a reflection of people voting with their feet and evidence that a growing number of households have been successful in achieving the American Dream of single-family home ownership.

The defenders of sprawl maintain that the automobile has allowed an unprecedented degree of geographic mobility, which has expanded the range of choices for household members in their roles as workers, consumers, and citizens. They argue that suburb-to-suburb commuting patterns reduce the pressure on downtown roads and relieve congestion. Concerns over the loss of farmland and open space are misplaced or overblown. After all, productivity per acre has increased dramatically so that less farmland is needed, and areas of open space are increasing in the United States as the rural population continues to dwindle.

Moreover, defenders of sprawl like Gordon and Richardson (1998) point out that the Los Angeles metropolitan area, the proverbial "poster child" of sprawl, actually has a higher population density than many eastern metropolitan areas such as Boston or Philadelphia. They argue that the critics of sprawl tend to be intellectuals who prefer to live in cities and who are imposing their own tastes on an unreceptive population. In this view, policies to curb sprawl would be unwise, unwarranted, and unworkable.

Robert Bruegmann (2005), an art historian, argues that current decentralization is simply the continuation of a worldwide process that has been going on for centuries, facilitated by economic growth and affluence that give people more choice about where to locate their homes and businesses. In comparing older and newer U.S. metropolitan areas, he argues that settlement patterns seem to be converging, as density falls in the older, higher-density places and rises in the newer, lower-density ones. While a desire for mobility, privacy, and choice will cause some households to choose the high-density core of the metropolitan area, many will seek lower densities as a way to achieve these goals. Ultimately, he argues, sprawl is the product of increasing affluence and political democracy.

Jan Brueckner (2000), an urban economist, observes that while sprawl could be accompanied by several types of market failure, remedies should address those specific forms of market failure, rather than deterring sprawl itself. He recognizes that market failure could arise in three ways: (1) failure to account for the social value of open space near cities—in which case, at least theoretically, a development tax could be imposed on agricultural land that is being converted to urban use; (2) failure to account for the social costs of highway congestion—in which case, a congestion toll (like the one we discussed in Chapter 10) could be charged; and (3) failure to fully account for the infrastructure costs of new development—in which case, impact fees could be assessed on the developer who would then need to take these costs into account. Glaeser and Kahn (2004) concur with Brueckner's arguments. They add that the major social problem caused by sprawl is the inability of poor families without cars to participate in an automobile-based economy. The remedy, they say, is not to enact a policy to limit sprawl but to subsidize automobile ownership for the poor.

To get a better handle on this debate, we need to understand how current land-use patterns developed, and the extent to which they were shaped by market forces and public policy. But first, we need a way to measure sprawl and to assess its effects. As we shall see, even this seemingly straightforward task turns out to be controversial.

Measuring Sprawl

Some attempts to measure sprawl focus solely on population density; others account for a set of additional attributes. A Brookings Institution study on density (Fulton et al. 2001) compared population growth against the expansion in urbanized land area between 1982 and 1997 for 281 metropolitan areas. The study found that for the nation as a whole, while population grew by 17 percent, the amount of land that had been "urbanized" had grown by 47 percent.

What does "urbanized land" mean? The U.S. Bureau of the Census defines **urban areas** as those portions of the metropolitan area with population densities of at least 1,000 persons per square mile. As Fulton and his colleagues at Brookings note, the *U.S. National Resources Inventory* uses a more refined definition of "urban area" that is based on actual land use:

> residential, industrial, commercial, and institutional land; construction sites; public administrative sites; railroad yards; cemeteries; airports; golf courses; sanitary land-fills; sewage treatment plants; water control structures and spillways; other land used for such purposes; small parks (less than ten acres) within urban and built-up areas; and highways, railroads, and other transportation facilities if they are surrounded by urban areas.

The Brookings study uses this latter definition. In both instances, the area of urbanization is highly likely to be smaller than the metropolitan area. Remember from Chapter 2 that counties are the basis of metropolitan area boundaries and that entire counties are included in metropolitan areas even if portions of the counties are rural.

What the Brookings study found is that even metropolitan areas that lost population added to their urbanized land area. For example, the Pittsburgh metropolitan area added 43 percent to its urbanized land area even while it was losing 8 percent of its population. During this 15-year period, 264 of the 281 metropolitan areas experienced reductions in population density. Those few metropolitan areas that actually gained in density tended to be located in the West. Las Vegas, Phoenix, and Los Angeles, often thought of as sprawling, were among the few already urbanized areas that experienced substantial increases in their populations. Surprisingly, some of the densest metropolitan areas are in the western states of California, Nevada, and Arizona (see **Table 13.2**). Fulton and his colleagues explain that topographic features such as coastlines and/or mountains, the presence of large land areas owned by the federal government, and the heavy reliance on public water and sewer systems in arid climates all serve as constraints on the outward expansion of metropolitan areas in the West.

Others who have attempted to measure sprawl argue that population density as measured above—a metropolitan area's population divided by its urbanized land area—is not by itself an accurate indicator of sprawl (Galster et al. 2001; Lopez and Hynes 2003). Ewing, Pendall, and Chen (2002) present a more extensive approach to measuring sprawl. For eighty-three metropolitan areas, they created an index score based on four factors: (1) residential density; (2) neighborhood mix of homes, jobs, and services; (3) strength of activity centers and downtowns; and (4) accessibility of the street network. Using a variety of data sources, they define twenty-two variables to operationalize the components of their four-factor sprawl index. A score of 100 on the sprawl index represents the average, while scores over 100 represent less-than-average sprawl, and scores under 100 represent greater-than-average sprawl.

The overall sprawl score combines the scores on the four factors. These scores are then standardized again to control for any effects of population size so that the results are not biased by size, per se. Given this second stage of standardization, overall scores can be below (or above) the average of the four-factor scores.

Table 13.3 provides a ranked list of the eighty-three areas—primary metropolitan statistical areas (PMSAs) or metropolitan statistical areas (MSAs)—along with their overall four-factor sprawl score. Those regions that appear as the most sprawling include Riverside-San Bernardino, California; Greensboro–Winston-Salem–High Point, North Carolina; Raleigh-Durham, North Carolina; Atlanta, Georgia; and Greenville-Spartanburg, South Carolina. Those that have sprawled the least include New York; Jersey City; Providence-Pawtucket-Woonsocket, Rhode Island; and San Francisco, California.

The Jersey City PMSA and the New York PMSA, along with the New York consolidated metropolitan statistical area (CMSA) of which they both are a part, are

Table 13.2 Persons per Urbanized Acre, Metro Areas, 1997

Rank	Persons per Urbanized Acre
1 Honolulu, HI	12.36
2 Los Angeles-Anaheim-Riverside, CA	8.31
3 New York-Northern New Jersey-Long Island, NY-NJ-CT	7.99
4 Reno, NV	7.99
5 San Francisco-Oakland-San Jose, CA	7.96
6 Miami-Fort Lauderdale, FL	7.93
7 Provo-Orem, UT	7.78
8 San Diego, CA	7.50
9 Visalia-Tulare-Porterville, CA	7.39
10 Modesto, CA	7.31
11 Phoenix, AZ	7.20
12 Salinas-Seaside-Monterey, CA	7.08
13 Stockton, CA	6.82
14 Las Vegas, NV	6.67
15 Chicago-Gary-Lake County, IL-IN-WI	6.02
16 Providence-Pawtucket-Woonsocket, RI	5.93
17 Washington, DC-MD-VA	5.88
18 Buffalo-Niagara Falls, NY	5.74
19 Boston-Lawrence-Salem-Lowell-Brockton, MA	5.65
20 Santa Barbara-Santa Maria-Lompoc, CA	5.65

Source: Fulton et al. 2001, table 2.

scored as among the least sprawling in both rankings, as is the San Francisco metropolitan area. On the other hand, Los Angeles and Las Vegas, while scoring well on measures that emphasize density, do not score as well on the four-factor index. As we examine the results of studies that measure the impact of sprawl, it is a good idea to remember that at least for some cities, their sprawl rankings depend on the way that sprawl is measured.

Using the four-factor sprawl index (density, mixed use, centeredness, and street connectivity) as reported in Table 13.3, Ewing, Pendall, and Chen (2002) find that more sprawling areas had higher rates of mileage driven per person; higher rates of automobile ownership, even after controlling for household income; increased levels of ozone pollution, even after controlling for per capita income and employment levels; greater risk of fatal car crashes; and lower rates of commuting by methods other than automobiles, such as public transit or walking. They found that delays caused by traffic congestion were at the same level in more sprawling areas as in less sprawling ones, thereby refuting the notion that sprawl can be a way to reduce congestion. Using the same four-factor sprawl index, Sturm and Cohen (2004) find not only that higher levels of sprawl were associated with a greater risk of being overweight or obese, but that they were also associated with higher rates of chronic diseases such as high blood pressure, arthritis, headaches, and breathing difficulties. These findings were attributed to the high degree of automobile dependency in sprawling areas and the consequent reduction in physical activities that included walking or bicycling.

Table 13.3 Sprawl Scores for Eighty-Three Metropolitan Regions

Metropolitan Region	Overall Sprawl Score	Street Connectivity Score	Centeredness Score	Mixed-Use Score	Density Score
Riverside-San Bernardino, CA PMSA	14.2	80.5	41.4	41.5	93.5
Greensboro–Winston-Salem–High Point, NC MSA	46.8	66.3	69.1	46.7	74.2
Raleigh-Durham, NC MSA	54.2	80.8	77.2	39.5	76.2
Atlanta, GA MSA	57.7	57.0	82.3	73.7	84.5
Greenville-Spartanburg, SC MSA	58.6	62.1	98.5	50.4	71.9
West Palm Beach-Boca Raton-Delray Beach, FL MSA	67.7	104.7	53.9	54.7	94.0
Bridgeport-Stamford-Norwalk-Danbury, CT NECMA	68.4	80.7	94.8	137.5	92.5
Knoxville, TN MSA	68.7	75.5	97.8	62.9	71.2
Oxnard-Ventura, CA PMSA	75.1	106.5	55.5	139.4	103.9
Fort Worth-Arlington, TX PMSA	77.2	97.5	73.9	89.1	90.3
Gary-Hammond, IN PMSA	77.4	100.5	61.2	123.7	86.4
Rochester, NY MSA	77.9	37.2	120.7	82.3	91.4
Vallejo-Fairfield-Napa, CA PMSA	78.4	109.7	40.9	116.3	97.4
Detroit, MI PMSA	79.5	93.0	63.0	102.5	97.3
Syracuse, NY MSA	80.3	52.6	124.9	72.0	85.8
Newark, NJ PMSA	81.3	115.4	82.2	120.4	118.9
Little Rock-North Little Rock, AR MSA	82.3	88.2	105.9	68.3	77.5
Albany-Schenectady-Troy, NY MSA	83.3	73.2	98.5	89.3	82.9
Hartford-New Britain-Middletown-Bristol, CT NEC	85.2	59.6	84.6	119.4	86.3
Oklahoma City, OK MSA	85.6	69.1	95.6	101.3	84.5
Tampa-St. Petersburg-Clearwater, FL MSA	86.3	133.6	51.9	80.0	93.6
Birmingham, AL MSA	88.0	104.0	112.5	62.2	77.1
Baton Rouge, LA MSA	90.1	76.2	106.2	95.9	80.8
Worcester-Fitchburg-Leominster, MA NECMA	90.5	74.5	122.7	82.3	81.2
Washington, DC-MD-VA MSA	90.8	98.0	97.8	78.7	106.9
Columbus, OH MSA	91.1	97.2	101.5	76.5	91.5
Jacksonville, FL MSA	91.6	104.6	102.1	72.9	85.6
Kansas City, MO-KS MSA	91.6	88.8	89.0	100.0	90.9
Cleveland, OH PMSA	91.8	66.8	100.9	107.4	99.7
Memphis, TN-AR-MS MSA	92.2	76.5	104.2	97.0	88.9
Houston, TX PMSA	93.3	95.6	87.0	110.1	95.3
Indianapolis, IN MSA	93.7	84.5	102.4	96.2	89.3
Columbia, SC MSA	94.2	79.5	147.3	67.1	74.6
St. Louis, MO-IL MSA	94.5	106.0	76.2	107.4	90.3
Grand Rapids, MI MSA	95.2	63.7	110.3	115.7	82.7

(*continued*)

Table 13.3 (*continued*)

Metropolitan Region	Overall Sprawl Score	Street Connectivity Score	Centeredness Score	Mixed-Use Score	Density Score
Norfolk-Virginia Beach-Newport News, VA MSA	95.6	113.1	82.0	87.2	95.0
Minneapolis-St. Paul, MN-WI MSA	95.9	87.7	107.8	94.7	94.7
Cincinnati, OH-KY-IN PMSA	96.0	85.4	110.2	95.8	88.8
Orlando, FL MSA	96.4	120.6	103.5	60.8	93.8
Anaheim-Santa Ana, CA PMSA	97.1	136.4	72.1	121.5	128.8
Oakland, CA PMSA	98.8	133.4	57.6	106.3	116.6
Tulsa, OK MSA	99.1	96.2	115.0	88.0	82.7
Seattle, WA PMSA	100.9	117.1	98.0	79.4	103.6
Los Angeles-Long Beach, CA PMSA	101.8	123.3	72.4	123.1	151.5
San Diego, CA MSA	101.9	106.0	74.4	105.4	113.4
Sacramento, CA MSA	102.6	98.4	87.4	110.9	99.1
Las Vegas, NV MSA	104.7	108.8	99.8	80.1	110.0
Akron, OH PMSA	105.9	84.2	119.5	118.7	86.8
Tacoma, WA PMSA	105.9	111.2	122.7	85.6	90.8
Pittsburgh, PA PMSA	105.9	124.2	104.5	86.8	90.4
New Haven-Waterbury-Meriden, CT NECMA	107.0	86.5	78.9	144.3	91.6
Toledo, OH MSA	107.2	77.6	112.2	119.6	91.3
San Antonio, TX MSA	107.8	103.0	108.4	100.1	95.0
Fort Lauderdale-Hollywood-Pompano Beach, FL PMSA	108.4	137.2	75.0	94.7	113.9
Tucson, AZ MSA	109.1	88.0	106.4	121.8	90.4
San Jose, CA PMSA	109.7	125.2	93.9	96.6	124.8
Wichita, KS MSA	110.1	78.6	131.4	113.1	84.4
Austin, TX MSA	110.3	94.4	115.8	111.9	89.0
Fresno, CA MSA	110.3	73.0	112.6	130.1	93.5
Salt Lake City-Ogden, UT MSA	110.9	117.0	93.8	103.2	99.5
Phoenix, AZ MSA	110.9	107.2	92.6	116.0	106.8
Philadelphia, PA-NJ PMSA	112.6	113.0	95.9	119.5	114.7
Baltimore, MD MSA	115.9	105.2	115.6	106.8	104.3
El Paso, TX MSA	117.2	102.3	119.5	103.4	100.1
Milwaukee, WI PMSA	117.3	93.9	117.7	117.9	101.4
Buffalo, NY PMSA	119.1	70.6	135.2	124.7	102.1
Chicago, IL PMSA	121.2	134.9	85.8	115.1	142.9
Springfield, MA NECMA	122.5	87.3	148.6	115.7	86.3
Allentown-Bethlehem-Easton, PA-NJ MSA	124.0	131.0	91.7	133.4	86.2
Colorado Springs, CO MSA	124.4	96.7	135.2	119.0	91.2
Albuquerque, NM MSA	124.5	117.8	124.0	103.7	97.0
Denver, CO PMSA	125.2	125.7	108.9	115.7	103.7
New Orleans, LA MSA	125.4	138.6	123.7	80.4	105.9
Miami-Hialeah, FL PMSA	125.7	136.4	92.7	104.7	129.1
Portland, OR PMSA	126.1	128.0	121.8	102.3	101.3

Table 13.3 (*continued*)

Metropolitan Region	Overall Sprawl Score	Street Connectivity Score	Centeredness Score	Mixed-Use Score	Density Score
Boston-Lawrence-Salem-Lowell-Brockton, MA NECM	126.9	119.1	109.4	124.4	113.6
Omaha, NE-IA MSA	128.4	104.6	132.3	119.3	96.4
Honolulu, HI MSA	140.2	114.3	167.3	84.3	116.5
San Francisco, CA PMSA	146.8	139.8	128.6	107.3	155.2
Providence-Pawtucket-Woonsocket, RI NECMA	153.7	135.9	140.3	140.5	99.1
Jersey City, NJ PMSA	162.3	166.8	98.7	172.9	195.7
New York, NY PMSA	177.8	154.9	144.6	129.8	242.5

Note: The average score for each factor is 100. The table is ranked in order from most sprawling to least sprawling on the overall four-factor sprawl index.
Source: Ewing, Pendall, and Chen 2002, pp. 15–16.

Recent research has questioned the notion that there is a causal relationship between sprawl and obesity. While acknowledging that there is a strong correlation between sprawl and obesity, Eid et al. (2006) remind us that correlation does not imply causation. They argue that the correlation is explained by self-selection: Individuals who do not like to walk choose locations where it is more convenient to travel by car, while those who do like to walk choose less sprawling environments. They track a large number of individuals over time and find that once they control for self-selection, the correlation between sprawl and obesity disappears. They argue that changing the built environment would not be an effective strategy for reducing obesity.

Generating Sprawl: Market Forces and Public Policy

Recently, the fastest-growing counties in the United States have been those outside of major cities in the South and West. If households can be said to vote with their feet, the vast majority are voting in such a way as to exacerbate sprawl. As we saw in Chapter 4, land values often decline with distance from the center of the metropolitan area. Hence, households that locate at the edge of the metropolitan area benefit from cheaper land prices, which makes bigger houses on larger lots more affordable than they would be if they were closer to the core city. To the extent that these communities practice fiscal zoning, the consequent exclusion of lower-income households also means the exclusion of lower-income children from the community's public schools.

Consumer sovereignty, the notion that the consumer is "king" and knows best what goods and services will yield the most satisfaction, implies that suburban sprawl has occurred because it best satisfies consumers' desires for low-density living along with the flexibility and convenience of automobile-based transportation. The decentralization of jobs also makes it desirable for households to move to the edge of the metropolitan area without necessarily increasing commuting time. Thus, market forces have played an important role in promoting sprawl, especially for families with children—the quintessential suburbanites.

However, a variety of public policies at the federal, state, and local levels have also contributed to this pattern of development. Chapter 4 discussed how the federal government subsidized the migration of households to the suburbs through the Federal Housing Administration (FHA) mortgage insurance program, the deductibility of mortgage interest and property taxes from the federal personal income tax, and the construction of the interstate highway system.

At the state level, the infrastructure to support households moving into new developments at the periphery is heavily subsidized. Residents of these areas do not pay the full costs of the new roads, schools, and water and sewer systems that are required to serve them. At the local level, the ability to zone out small-lot, single-family housing, or any other land use that is perceived to require a higher expenditure on public services than it generates in tax revenues, ensures that the density in new areas will be low while older urban jurisdictions will bear the burden of housing the region's lower-income households.

As we saw in Chapter 9, proper allocation of resources requires that individuals and households take into account all of the costs and all of the benefits of their choices. While proponents of sprawl place their emphasis on the degree to which this outcome is a result of consumer choice, critics argue that consumers do not, in fact, face the full cost of their choice and that the subsidies given to households at the periphery are unwarranted. Consumer sovereignty only yields an efficient outcome when all the costs of consumption, including externalities, are fully borne by the consumer. With all kinds of tax and subsidy programs either explicitly or implicitly encouraging sprawl, one cannot be assured that consumer sovereignty will lead to an efficient use of land.

Reducing Sprawl: Market Forces and Public Policy

Recent demographic changes in the United States may have reduced the attractiveness of large-lot, single-family houses in automobile-dependent suburbs, at least among some growing subgroups of the population. An increasing proportion of households do not have school-age children: some empty nesters with grown children no longer want to maintain large homes and lawns; the very old among the elderly are no longer willing or able to drive; and many recent college graduates find better job opportunities and better entertainment options closer to or within the central city. Many new immigrants value access to their community's institutions, including churches, cultural centers, ethnic restaurants and food stores more highly than they value low-density living.

Growing numbers in all of these segments of the population would indicate an increasing demand for higher-density patterns of development such as those found in central cities and older suburbs. Moreover, the sustainability of sprawling development has also been called into question by physical and geographical limits. As we noted earlier, some metropolitan areas in the West have already encountered natural limits to continued low-density development because of topographical features like coastlines or mountain ranges, federally owned land not available for development, or limited water supplies already strained to capacity.

However, if sprawl has been caused in part by public policies that have subsidized this form of development, either directly or indirectly, then its reduction requires that these policies be changed. Implicit subsidies would need to be removed, whether in the form of below-cost extension of infrastructure or gasoline prices that do not reflect the full costs of driving, including the social costs of pollution and congestion. States might finance a larger share of per-pupil spending as a way to remove one of the strongest incentives for localities to practice fiscal zoning. Higher-density patterns of development would need to be encouraged on efficiency grounds, and this is what the **smart growth** initiatives in several states have tried to do. Essentially, consumers respond to incentives, and when the incentives are made right—through the appropriate pricing of public services—decisions about where to live change.

Smart Growth

The suburbs that were developed *before* World War II exhibit many of the characteristics admired by smart growth proponents. Compared with newer developments, the older suburbs tended to be served by mass-transit routes, had mixed-use development, included multifamily and small-lot, single-family housing, and were more conducive to walking and bicycling. A variety of housing options existed in close proximity to each other. Apartments were built over storefronts. Accessory apartments—sometimes called "mother-in-law" apartments—were built into single-family homes. These places reflect the human scale and the lively streets that Jane Jacobs (1961) wrote about so eloquently.

Today, smart growth initiatives—and there are quite a variety—try to replicate some of these features, rather than prohibiting them, as most current zoning laws would do. **Transit-oriented development** (TOD) emphasizes alternatives to the exclusive reliance on automobiles by locating higher-density housing and mixed-use development near transit routes. Peter Calthorpe (1993), one of its original proponents, argues that a minimum density of ten households per acre is necessary to achieve the critical mass to support transit routes. A social concept known as **new urbanism** places emphasis on architecture and design elements that restore the importance of lively streets, front porches, and higher-density housing in order to recreate more vibrant civic life. In their 2007 book, *Visualizing Density,* Campoli and MacLean emphasize that density need not mean ugly tenements, overcrowding, or congestion. They try to overcome the negative connotations of higher density with myriad examples of well-designed dense neighborhoods.

Location-efficient mortgages—currently available only in Seattle, San Francisco, Los Angeles, and Chicago—allow households that locate in areas where driving is less of a requirement to qualify for larger loans on the theory that more of the household's income can be used for housing. If a growing area wants to change its current zoning practices in which, say, 100 acres of farmland are zoned for 100 single-family homes each on one-acre lots, and in which the owners of the land would ordinarily reap profits only if the land is sold for development, it can instead use **transferable development rights** to preserve a portion of that farmland, while granting the owners the ability to sell those rights to developers who will use them to build at higher density within only a portion of the area that is set aside for new construction. An **urban growth boundary** can be used to contain development within a certain radius of the core city. Keeping density constant, places with growth boundaries would find that limiting the supply of land would make housing more expensive than in places without such a boundary. However, one of the purposes of the boundary is specifically to encourage higher-density development, so that the land is used more intensively and permits more affordable housing. Many of these tools are being considered by communities across the country.

Barriers to Smart Growth Implementation

As urban expert Anthony Downs (2005) points out, even when there is sentiment in favor of smart growth initiatives, these programs are often difficult to implement. He argues that the pressure to adopt smart growth policies typically comes from environmentalists, urban planners, and other local public officials, and some innovative real estate developers, rather than from ordinary citizens. Some of the obstacles encountered in persuading ordinary citizens to support smart growth policies include: a shift in the distribution of the costs and benefits of development (which creates new categories of winners and losers); a need to shift power from local to regional authorities (often resisted because of the loss of local autonomy); and an increase in residential density that might threaten the property values of existing homes, given Fischel's homevoter hypothesis (2001) that home owners' primary motivation is to protect the value of their single most important asset. Although these latter fears might be mitigated to the extent that limits on growth might actually raise housing prices, this possibility is at odds with one of the often-stated goals of smart growth, to increase the supply of affordable housing.

In a similar vein, political scientist David Luberoff (2007) argues that strict policies to enforce smart growth goals (such as Portland, Oregon's growth boundary) are more likely to create a backlash that ultimately undermines those goals. Policies that merely offer incentives are less likely to cause a backlash, but they are also less likely to have a dramatic impact on changing settlement patterns.

In the Portland case, the state of Oregon adopted urban growth boundaries for its cities in 1973. The boundary around Portland was intended to provide enough undeveloped land to accommodate twenty years of future growth and has been successful in confining growth to areas within the boundary. However, since land outside the boundary could not be developed, there was a huge discrepancy in land values between the land just inside versus the land just outside. In a hotly contested election in 2004, voters approved Measure 37, which allowed landowners outside the boundary to request full compensation from their local government for the loss in value caused by the growth boundary's restrictions on development. Local governments could choose either to pay full compensation or to grant a waiver that allowed development in accordance with whatever use would have been permitted before the boundary went into effect.

As Anthony Flint (2006) points out, there were very few restrictions on land use before the boundary was imposed. Since local governments generally cannot afford to pay full compensation to the claimants, Measure 37 could mean an end to the growth boundary. As of 2007, efforts were under way to present Oregon voters with another measure that would modify the impact of Measure 37 by allowing some ability to build a limited number of homes on land outside the boundary while still prohibiting other uses, thereby restoring the growth boundary as a meaningful restriction on sprawl.

Equity and Efficiency Considerations in Alternative Metropolitan Growth Scenarios

What will metropolitan areas look like in the year 2020? In an article written for a Federal National Mortgage Association (Fannie Mae) publication in 2000, architecture and planning professor Lance Freeman outlined four possible scenarios: (1) *Sprawlville*, a continuation of current practices with regard to sprawl and social equity, (2) *Smart Town*, adoption of practices to combat sprawl without thought to equity implications, (3) *Equitopia*, programs to address equity issues like affordable housing but without any attention to sprawl, and (4) *Milleniumburg*, smart growth initiatives that include a concern for social equity.

In *Sprawlville*, the relocation of workplaces to the expanding metropolitan fringe, along with total reliance on automobiles and their attendant traffic jams, make workplaces inaccessible to a growing proportion of the potential labor pool. Poor central city and inner-ring suburban residents are unable to relocate closer to jobs because of the continuing lack of affordable housing and because of zoning laws that effectively exclude the poor. Income segregation increases, as do fiscal disparities between communities. Differences in the quality of public school systems reinforce existing inequalities and perpetuate them through the next generation.

Smart Town establishes an urban growth boundary so that farmlands and woodlands outside the boundary are preserved. As the area grows, underutilized land within the boundary is developed through infill projects. Transit-oriented development projects are undertaken, and the resulting new urbanism-style higher density and mixed land-use patterns attract high-earning professionals. However, an unintended consequence of this success is the disappearance of affordable housing as neighborhoods become gentrified. With few alternatives available to them, families of the low-paid service workers in the area double and triple up in units that were meant for one family, while single individuals live in overcrowded conditions in rooming houses.

Equitopia is in the forefront of enacting affordable-housing initiatives, and it has been able to implement its plans because it has a single government for the entire metropolitan area. It scatters affordable housing throughout the metropolitan area, thus avoiding concentrations of the poor in any single location. However, the lack of a workable transit system that is necessary to improve job opportunities for the poor and the competing demands to use funds to finance the infrastructure required by unabated sprawl undermine support for affordable housing.

In *Milleniumburg*, attention is given both to smart growth initiatives and to equity issues. There is a regional authority that has responsibility for planning. Open space is set aside to protect the most ecologically sensitive lands, but there are greenbelts and watersheds that meander through the region rather than a fixed growth boundary. Transit-oriented development is encouraged, as is central city redevelopment—the latter through the expedition of permits and reduction of red tape. Zoning is based on performance standards to encourage mixed land use while preventing negative externalities. Inclusionary zoning requires that 10 percent of the units in new developments are affordable. Location-efficient mortgages help to bring home ownership to families who would not be able to afford the combination of transportation and housing expenses required of exurbanites.

Freeman's scenarios remind us that current patterns of metropolitan growth are inefficient and inequitable. However, alternative scenarios that focus only on efficiency without regard to equity or vice versa are also problematic. The challenge is to find ways to promote metropolitan growth that are both equitable and efficient and make Milleniumburg more than just an imaginary place.

Land-Use Controls and Spatial Form

The contours of metropolitan areas continue to grow and change over time. Market forces and public policies each play a role in influencing spatial form. While the economic justification for zoning laws is based on reducing negative externalities, actual zoning practices may deviate from that goal. If the area is underzoned, significant negative externalities may persist. If it is overzoned, the motivation might be primarily to exclude rather than to reduce negative externalities. In many suburbs, contemporary zoning regulations, with their extreme separation of land uses, along with large-lot, single-family zoning, have contributed to metropolitan sprawl. Changes in public policy, including changes in zoning regulations, are important elements in smart growth efforts to promote higher-density development.

Massachusetts's Chapter 40R Smart Growth Overlay Zoning Law, enacted in 2005, provides just one example of how smart growth and affordable housing can be encouraged through well-engineered public policy (Carman, Bluestone, and White 2004). Under the Chapter 40R zoning law, the state government pays towns and cities in Massachusetts "density bonuses" if they rezone land near transit stops, town centers, or where there are abandoned industrial and commercial buildings. The new zoning "overlays" any existing zoning, which allows developers to build housing on smaller lots with the provision that they set aside at least 20 percent of the units for low-income households.

To add to the incentive plan, the state enacted Chapter 40S in 2006 to insure municipalities against the possibility that building smaller, more affordable family housing would cost the town or city more in school costs than they would collect on the new housing units (Carman, Bluestone, and White 2005). By getting the incentives right, the state hopes to relieve the pressure of high housing prices while reducing auto traffic congestion and making sure that a portion of the new housing stock is affordable to families on limited income. Other states—including Connecticut and New Jersey—are now considering following Massachusetts's lead toward using a range of incentives that encourage municipalities to alter their zoning laws and permit denser, smarter growth with guaranteed affordable housing. In this way, regions desperate for housing may be able to obtain it while reducing urban sprawl, not encouraging it.

It will not be easy to overcome the combination of market forces and public policy that has produced sprawl over the last fifty years of U.S. metropolitan growth, but with a combination of innovative public policies, sprawl can be contained over the next fifty years.

References

Beck, Eckardt C. 1979. "The Love Canal Tragedy." *Environmental Protection Agency Journal* (January). http://www.epa.gov/history/topics/lovecanal/01.htm.

Boyer, M. Christine. 1994. *Dreaming the Rational City: The Myth of American City Planning.* Cambridge, Mass.: MIT Press.

Brueckner, Jan. 2000. "Urban Sprawl: Diagnosis and Remedies." *International Regional Science Review* 23, no. 2: 160–171.

Bruegmann, Robert. 2005. *Sprawl: A Compact History.* Chicago: University of Chicago Press.

Burchell, Robert W., George Lowenstein, William R. Dolphin, Catherine C. Galley, Anthony Downs, Samuel Seskin, Catherine Gray Still, and Terry Moore. 2002. *Costs of Sprawl—2000.* Washington D.C.: Transportation Research Board, National Research Council.

Calthorpe, Peter. 1993. *The Next American Metropolis: Ecology, Community, and the American Dream.* Princeton N.J.: Princeton Architectural Press.

Campoli, Julie, and Alex S. MacLean. 2007. *Visualizing Density.* Cambridge, Mass.: Lincoln Institute of Land Policy.

Carman, Ted, Barry Bluestone, and Eleanor White. 2004. "Building on Our Heritage: A Housing Strategy for Smart Growth and Economic Development." Report. Boston: The Boston Foundation.

———. 2005. "Chapter 40R School Cost Analysis and Proposed Smart Growth School Cost Insurance Supplement." Report. Boston: The Boston Foundation.

Coase, Ronald. 1960. "The Problem of Social Cost." *Journal of Law and Economics* 3 (October): 1–44.

Downs, Anthony. 2005. "Smart Growth: Why We Discuss It More than We Do It." *Journal of the American Planning Association* 71, no. 4 (Autumn): 367–380.

Duany, Andres, Elizabeth Plater-Zyberk, and Jeff Speck. 2001. *Suburban Nation: The Rise of Sprawl and the Decline of the American Dream.* New York: North Point Press.

Eid, Jean, Henry G. Overman, Diego Puga, and Matthew A. Turner. 2006. "Fat City: Questioning the Relationship between Urban Sprawl and Obesity." Working Paper, University of Toronto Department of Economics, October 30.

Ewing, Reid, Rolf Pendall, and Don Chen. 2002. *Measuring Sprawl and Its Impact.* Washington, D.C.: Smart Growth America.

Fischel, William A. 1999. "Zoning and Land Use Regulation." http://encyclo.findlaw.com/2200book.pdf.

————. 2001. *The Homevoter Hypothesis: How Home Values Influence Local Government Taxation, School Finance, and Land-Use Policies.* Cambridge, Mass.: Harvard University Press.

Flint, Anthony. 2006. *This Land.* Baltimore, Md.: Johns Hopkins University Press.

Freeman, Lance. 2000. "Fair Growth 2020: A Tale of Four Futures." Fannie Mae Foundation. *Housing Facts & Findings* 2, no. 4: 1, 6–14.

Frumkin, Howard, Lawrence Frank, and Richard Jackson. 2004. *Urban Sprawl and Public Health: Designing, Planning, and Building for Healthy Communities.* Washington, D.C.: Island Press.

Fulton, William, Rolf Pendall, Mai Nguyen, and Alicia Harrison. 2001. *Who Sprawls the Most? How Growth Patterns Differ across the U.S.* Washington, D.C.: Brookings Institution, Center for Urban and Metropolitan Policy, July.

Galster, George, Royce Hanson, Hal Wolman, Stephen Coleman, and Jason Freihage. 2001. "Wrestling Sprawl to the Ground: Defining and Measuring an Elusive Concept." *Housing Policy Debate* 12, no. 4: 681–717.

Glaeser, Edward L., and Matthew E. Kahn. 2004. "Sprawl and Urban Growth." In J. Vernon Henderson and Jacques F. Thisse, eds., *Handbook of Regional and Urban Economics*, vol. 4, *Cities and Geography.* New York: Reed Elsevier, pp. 2481–2527.

Gordon, Peter, and Harry W. Richardson. 1998. "Prove It: The Costs and Benefits of Sprawl." *Brookings Review,* September 22, pp. 23–26.

Hayden, Dolores. 2003. *Building Suburbia: Greenfields and Urban Growth.* New York: Pantheon.

Jacobs, Jane. 1961. *The Death and Life of Great American Cities.* New York: Random House.

Kayden, Jerold S. 2001. "National Land-Use Planning and Regulation in the United States:Understanding its Fundamental Importance." In Rachel Alterman, ed., *National-Level Spatial Planning in Democratic Countries: An International Comparison of City and Regional Policy-Making.* Liverpool, England: Liverpool University Press, pp. 43–64.

Langdon, Philip. 1994. *A Better Place to Live: Reshaping the American Suburb.* Boston: University of Massachusetts Press.

Levy, John M. 1985. *Urban and Metropolitan Economics.* New York: McGraw-Hill.

Logan, John R., and Harvey L. Molotch. 1987. *Urban Fortunes.* Berkeley: University of California Press.

Lopez, Russ, and H. Patricia Hynes. 2003. "Sprawl in the 1990s, Measurement, Distribution, and Trends." *Urban Affairs Review* 38, no. 3: 325–355.

Luberoff, David. 2007. "Getting Smart." *Commonwealth Magazine* (Winter). http://www.mass inc.org/.

Mills, Edwin. 1979. "Economic Analysis of Land Use Controls." In Peter Mieszkowski and Mahlon Straszheim, eds., *Current Issues in Urban Economics.* Baltimore, Md.: Johns Hopkins University Press, pp. 511–541.

Mumford, Lewis. 1961. *The City in History.* New York: Harcourt Brace Jovanovich.

National Academy of Public Administration. 2003. "Addressing Community Concerns: How Environmental Justice Relates to Land Use Planning and Zoning." Report. Washington D.C.: National Academy of Public Administration, July.

Orwell, George. 1937. *The Road to Wigan Pier.* London: Victor Gollancz.

Pianin, Eric, and Michael A. Fletcher. 2002. "Many Schools Built Near Toxic Sites, Study Finds." *Washington Post,* January 21, p. A2.

Rabin, Yale. 1989. "Expulsive Zoning: The Inequitable Legacy of Euclid." In Charles Harr and Jerold Kayden, eds., *Zoning and the American Dream: Promises Still to Keep.* Washington, D.C.: American Planning Association Press, pp. 101–121.

Schrank, David, and Tim Lomax. 2005. *The 2005 Urban Mobility Report.* Texas Transportation Institute, Texas A&M University System, May. http://mobility.tamu.edu.

Siegan, Bernard H. 1972. *Land Use without Zoning.* Lexington, Mass.: Lexington Books.

Silver, Christopher. 1997. "The Racial Origins of Zoning in American Cities." In June Manning Thomas and Marsha Ritzdorf, eds., *Urban Planning and the African American Community.* Thousand Oaks, Calif.: Sage Publications, pp. 23–42.

Sinclair, Upton. 1906. *The Jungle.* New York: Doubleday, Page.

Sturm, Roland, and Deborah Cohen. 2004. "Suburban Sprawl and Physical and Mental Health." *Public Health* 118, no. 7 (October): 488–496.

U.S. Environmental Protection Agency. 2004. "Populations Protected." Superfund Environmental Indicators, September. http://www.epa.gov/superfund/accomp/ei/ind_a.htm.
———. 2007. "Environmental Justice." http://www.epa.gov/compliance/environmentaljustice.
Whyte, William H. 1958. "Urban Sprawl." In William H. Whyte, ed., *The Exploding Metropolis.* New York: Doubleday, pp. 133–156.

Chapter 13 Questions and Exercises

1. Imagine that a supermarket chain announces plans to open a store very near where you live, drawing customers from a wide area. What externalities, positive and negative, would this store impose on you? How might the issues of eminent domain, design zoning, fiscal zoning, and exclusionary zoning appear in discussions by neighbors or in city government as they discuss the store's plans?

2. In 2004, the U.S. Geological Survey (USGS), part of the U.S. Department of the Interior, produced a report, "Urban Growth in American Cities: Glimpses of U.S. Urbanization" by Auch, Taylor, and Acevedo. This report is available on the Web at

   http://pubs.usgs.gov/circ/2004/circ1252/

   and presents images of urban growth and descriptions of growth-related issues for sixteen U.S. cities. Go to this Web site and scroll down to the Table of Contents. Within the Table of Contents you will see a list of the sixteen cities, which also serves as links for each of those cities and their surrounding areas. (*Note:* The areas analyzed within the maps in this report typically cover a wider area than the official U.S. Census metropolitan area boundaries.) Choose Pittsburgh and three other cities, and click on their names one at a time to access the underlying maps and related information about the cities and their growth in the years between the 1970s and the 1990s.

   ✦ How would you describe the visual images of the spatial growth of each area? Was the growth small or extensive? Was it more extensive in some directions than in others?
   ✦ What was the population change for the areas shown between 1970 and 1990, and how does it compare to the change in developed land area? See the left side of the narrative.
   ✦ How do the dynamics of physical growth vary from one place to another?
   ✦ What were the major issues, identified by the authors of this report, facing each area as a result of this growth?

3. Another series of images and accompanying information sheets produced through the USGS Urban Dynamics Research program can be found at

   http://landcover.usgs.gov/LCI/urban/info_sheets.php

   Take a look at the images for the Willamette Valley (depicting the growth of the Portland Oregon metropolitan area) for 1970 and 1990 and compare them with the images (covering similar years) for the Detroit River Corridor (Detroit, Michigan), the Middle Rio Grande Basin (Albuquerque, New Mexico), and Sioux Falls, South Dakota.

    ✦ How is the Willamette Valley growth different from the other areas?

    ✦ According to the information sheet, what land-use policy exists in the Willamette Valley Region that might explain the difference?

4. The Lincoln Institute of Land Policy has a Web site devoted to increasing awareness and understanding of architectural, urban design, and other visual issues associated with population density. Associated with the award-winning book *Visualizing Density* (Campoli and MacLean 2007), the Web site can be found at

    http://www.lincolninst.edu/subcenters/VD

Go to this Web site. To begin, click on "A Bird's Eye View of Density." A screen will come up asking you to register before using the site. Fill out the form to register and click on "Submit." The first screen for "A Bird's Eye View of Density" will come up. Proceed from Screen 1 to Screen 2, and then to Screen 3. After reading these three screens, click on the "Quick Quiz: How Dense Can You Be?" (listed on the left side of the screen). Take the quiz and submit your answers. The correct answers and explanations will appear. How many questions did you answer correctly?

5. According to the National Wildlife Federation, urban sprawl threatens a number of wildlife species found in and around metropolitan areas. A recent report, "Endangered by Sprawl: How Runaway Development Threatens America's Wildlife" (Ewing et al. 2005), published jointly by the National Wildlife Federation, Smart Growth America, and NatureServe, is available on the Web at

    http://www.nwf.org/nwfwebadmin/binaryVault/EndangeredBySprawlFinal.pdf

This site presents findings about threatened species in thirty-five metropolitan areas. Go to this Web site and scroll down to the Metropolitan Area Data in Appendix B. Pick any three of the metropolitan areas that are listed. According to the National Wildlife Federation, how many species are imperiled within each of the metro areas you have selected?

Urban Economic Development Strategies

14

Just for a moment, consider that you are the mayor or city manager of a midsized city that has been hemorrhaging jobs and revenue for some years. The unemployment rate in your community is double the state average, some of the commercial and industrial buildings in town have been closed and boarded up, and younger people are beginning to move to other locations to find work. You have read about what has happened to older industrial cities like Detroit and Flint, Michigan; Youngstown, Ohio; and Wilkes Barre, Pennsylvania, and worry that the same kind of deindustrialization and economic deterioration could happen to yours. What do you recommend to the city council? What economic development tools should you use to keep businesses from moving out, and how can you attract some new ones to set up shop? These questions are, in fact, faced every day by mayors, city managers, and city planners across the country.

While the provision of public services and the drafting and enforcement of city and town laws and regulations constitute the chief functions of local government, state and municipal officials also face the task of keeping companies and jobs in their communities and attracting new ones. Because of the continual turnover in business enterprise in any one city or town, few metro areas can rest on their laurels, celebrating the investments they attracted yesterday. Local leaders try to promulgate a "good business climate" by resorting to a range of policies from property tax abatements and public subsidies to government investments in infrastructure, worker training, sports facilities, and cultural amenities. It is a high-stakes game that few cities can choose not to play. In doing so, they have to work with private developers, bankers, and neighborhood associations, trying to balance the demands of the business community with the needs of the broader population.

Deindustrialization and Firm Relocation

To provide some idea of just how much business turnover exists during a relatively short time period, we can turn to **Table 14.1**, which tracks employment change between 1969 and 1976 throughout the United States. This was a period that began with a buoyant national economy for the first four years, followed by a recession in 1975 and the beginning of a recovery in 1976. It is also a period for which we have

483

Table 14.1 Jobs Created and Destroyed as a Result of Openings, Closings, Relocations, Expansions, and Contractions of Private Business Establishments in the United States, 1969–1976 (in Thousands of Jobs)

Region	Number of Jobs in 1969	Jobs Created		Jobs Destroyed		Net Job Change
		By Openings and Immigrations	Expansions	By Closures and Out-Migrations	Contractions	
United States as a whole	57,936	25,281	19,056	22,302	13,183	8,852
Frostbelt	32,701	11,322	9,470	11,352	7,212	2,228
Northeast	15,825	4,940	4,348	5,882	3,589	−183
New England	3,905	1,251	1,131	1,437	952	−7.1
Mid-Atlantic	11,919	3,689	3,217	4,444	2,637	−176
Midwest	16,877	6,381	5,123	5,470	3,623	2,411
East North Central	12,564	4,671	3,582	3,963	2,652	1,638
West North Central	4,313	1,710	1,541	1,507	972	773
Sunbelt	25,235	13,960	9,586	10,951	5,971	6,624
South	16,045	8,934	5,965	6,824	3,803	4,271
South Atlantic	8,204	4,651	2,913	3,548	2,014	2,002
East South Central	3,065	1,518	1,090	1,211	632	765
West South Central	4,775	2,765	1,962	2,065	1,157	1,504
West	9,190	5,026	3,621	4,126	2,168	2,353
Mountain	1,942	1,226	954	978	481	721
Pacific	7,249	3,800	2,668	3,148	1,687	1,632

Note: New England: Connecticut, Maine, Massachusetts, New Hampshire, Rhode Island, Vermont; Mid-Atlantic: New Jersey, New York, Pennsylvania; East North Central: Illinois, Indiana, Michigan, Ohio, Wisconsin; West North Central: Iowa, Kansas, Minnesota, Missouri, Nebraska, North Dakota, South Dakota; South Atlantic: Delaware, D.C., Florida, Georgia, Maryland, N. Carolina, S. Carolina, Virginia, W. Virginia; East South Central: Alabama, Kentucky, Mississippi, Tennessee; West South Central: Arkansas, Louisiana, Oklahoma, Texas; Mountain: Arizona, Colorado, Idaho, Montana, Nevada, New Mexico, Utah, Wyoming; Pacific: Alaska, California, Hawaii, Oregon, Washington.
Source: Bluestone and Harrison 1982; table 2.1; based on Birch 1979, appendix A.

uniquely rich and reasonably complete data on the **gross flows of employment**, not simply the net change in the number of jobs. Gross flows measure both the creation of new jobs (through the expansion of existing establishments and employment in new start-ups) and the destruction of existing jobs (the result of company contractions; out-of-state relocations; and plant, store, and office closings). The original data for this table come from Dun & Bradstreet and were compiled by David Birch for his research on *The Job Generation Process* (1979). Bluestone and Harrison (1982) carefully reassembled these data by region.

Deindustrialization in the 1970s

Nationwide, between 1969 and 1976, investment in brand new private-sector facilities—from large manufacturing plants to small retail establishments—was responsible for creating 25 million jobs, an average of 3.6 million new jobs each year. Over the same period, however, 22 million jobs—or 3.2 million per year—disappeared as a result of establishment closings. This "churning" of employment is part of a process the early twentieth-century economist Joseph Schumpeter termed **creative destruction**—out with the old, in with the new.

In addition, during the same time period, firms created more than 19 million jobs in existing facilities in the cities, towns, and rural areas where they already had establishments. Offsetting this good news for workers and communities was the loss of more than 13 million jobs due to the downsizing of companies.

Overall, between new facilities and expanding ones, the nation boasted nearly 9 million more jobs in 1976 than had existed just seven years before. But certain states and metro areas were great winners in the job game and others were big losers. The biggest net losers were states in the Northeast—the six New England states plus New York, New Jersey, and Pennsylvania. More than 4.9 million new jobs were created in these nine states through establishment openings and through firms moving into the region from other places in the country or from abroad. But this gain was more than offset by the loss of nearly 5.9 million jobs, as thousands of establishments closed or relocated across state lines. Many of these Frostbelt jobs went to the Sunbelt—the South and the West. Even though expansions of existing facilities created more jobs than contractions destroyed, on net across the entire national labor market, the Northeast lost more jobs than it created.

The states of the Midwest fared somewhat better than those in the Northeast, with a net addition of 2.4 million jobs, but there, too, millions of jobs were lost to plant closings and contractions—indeed, more than 9 million. Auto plants were closing or moving to the South. Some companies were beginning to experiment with plants in Mexico. Similarly, steel mills were closing, along with all kinds of other manufacturing concerns. When these anchor institutions moved, thousands of local smaller plants, retail shops, and service companies also went out of business as part of a ripple effect throughout the region.

However, even the emerging South and West were not immune to deindustrialization (that is, the massive loss of jobs to plant closings and contractions).

Throughout the South, almost 7 million jobs were lost to shutdowns, with another 3.8 million lost through cutbacks in existing operations. Altogether, the West lost more than 6 million jobs. What made these Sunbelt regions so successful is that for every job lost, more than 1.4 new jobs were created. In the Frostbelt regions, for every job lost, only 1.1 new jobs took its place.

Continuing Deindustrialization

In the great scheme of things, this churning may not call for national attention because a job lost in one location (if it stays in the United States) can be a job gained somewhere else. But the addition of a job in Springhill, Tennessee, at the expense of a job lost in Flint, Michigan, is certainly a cause of concern for the mayor of Flint, while the job gained in Springhill is cause for celebration among local officials there. If the loss or gain is numbered in the hundreds or thousands, it is a major political issue and not just an economic one.

Because job turnover affects every region of the country, no community can expect that its industries will continue to create jobs for its citizens and generate tax revenues to pay for public services. At one time, Detroit felt that its economic success was assured by the presence of the auto industry. Pittsburgh felt the same way because of steel.

Between 1995 and 2003, when the nation as a whole saw the creation of more than 13 million jobs, a gain of nearly 11 percent, the Springfield, Massachusetts metro area lost 3 percent of its job base, while the Youngtown, Ohio region lost 5 percent. Today, even the cities and regions that are leaders in growth industries like information technology know that they could suddenly lose their economic base because of changing technology, changes in demand, or the opening of new competing firms elsewhere in the United States or abroad. Even California, with its burgeoning population, lost one out of six of its existing manufacturing jobs between 1990 and 2002 (State of California 2003).

Consequently, cities and towns—as well as states—have found themselves in the business of constantly trying to attract new capital in order to secure jobs and revenue, and striving just as hard to hold on to the businesses they currently have. In this competitive battleground for jobs and investment, municipalities and states have relied on an arsenal of economic development strategies, instruments, and tools. One reasonably reliable estimate suggests that states and local governments spend nearly $50 billion a year on local economic development programs (Thomas 2000).

Goals of Economic Development

Local public officials have three major objectives when they consider ways to encourage economic investment in their municipalities. The *first* is to produce jobs that can provide wages, salaries, and benefits for local citizens (Blair, Fictenbaum, and Swaney 1984; Furdell 1994). Obviously, if the number of jobs in a locale is declining quickly or not keeping up with population growth, there will be an increase in unemployment. If joblessness is prolonged, the result can be increased poverty and ultimately out-migration, as the unemployed seek work elsewhere. This can lead to a **vicious cycle** in which an initial increase in unemployment leads to a loss in prime-age workers, making the community less likely to attract new investment and more likely to sink ever further into decline and disrepair. This has been the story of many Rustbelt cities in the Northeast and Midwest, with the most extreme case being the old-fashioned, western "ghost town," abandoned when the gold mine went bust or the railroad passed it by.

The *second* objective for local officials is to maintain or increase the local tax base by attracting private-sector investment (Jones and Bachelor 1993; Pagano and Bowman 1995). To provide for roads, parks, libraries, public schools, and other public services, towns and cities must have sufficient tax revenue. Some of this can be raised from home owners through the local residential property tax. In a limited number of larger cities, revenue also comes from a general sales tax, levies on specific services (e.g., hotel or meal taxes), or a local income tax.

Most municipalities also rely on the taxation of industrial and commercial properties to help pay for local public services. A suburban strip mall or downtown commercial district teeming with office towers, restaurants, hotels, and a bevy of service firms often can provide tax revenues in excess of the expense incurred from the municipality's requirement to supply these business ventures with police and fire protection, road maintenance, and other public services. The surplus can be used to improve local schools, provide subsidized housing for low-income families, beautify a park, or improve a city's waterfront. Likewise, a large factory can generate property tax revenue that can be used for the same purposes.

In many cases, a town or city would rather have a developer build a new office tower, construct a new sprawling mall, or lay out a large factory than see the construction of a hundred new small homes, many of which house school-age children who require large outlays for school buildings, teachers, and books. While some municipalities have tried to zone against the construction of a large Wal-Mart or other megamall for fear that it will compete against smaller downtown retailers and drive them out of business, other communities desperate for tax revenue welcome the arrival of such revenue-producing establishments. Building up a large nonresidential tax base by attracting businesses to a community can solve a thorny revenue problem for municipal leaders.

The *third* objective is to raise the local economic multiplier by substituting local services and production for imported ones. If municipal leaders can encourage entrepreneurs to set up local operations, dollars that would have quickly left the community can be recirculated, which would increase the incomes of residents and thereby produce greater local prosperity.

For these reasons—jobs, tax revenue, and an increased local multiplier—most local public officials work hard to attract private-sector investment to their own towns and cities. As we examine the strategies that local governments have pursued toward this end, it is important to keep two questions in mind. First, to what extent have these strategies achieved their goals; that is, have new jobs actually been created and, if so, at what cost? Second, even when these strategies work, does it mean a net gain of jobs for the nation or merely a relocation of jobs from more efficient sites to ones that are less efficient? Recall from Chapter 3 that agglomeration economies are positive externalities in production that provide an efficient use of resources. If firms are lured away from their most efficient sites, the loss to the society as a whole may outweigh the gain to the municipality with the winning bid. With these caveats in mind, we can examine the options available to local governments.

Location from the Business Perspective

Whether a firm will choose to locate in a particular city or town depends on a wide array of factors, some of which are susceptible to influence by state and local public policy. To understand this variety of factors, it is useful to look at a simple model of the firm. We can assume that the primary objective of a firm is to make a profit. The profit of a firm over any discrete period of time is the difference between its total revenue and its total costs, as we noted in Chapter 4 when we looked at the basic Alonso model. The equation for a firm's profit is therefore:

$$\pi = TR - TC \tag{14a}$$

where π = profits, TR = total revenue, and TC = total cost.

Total revenue (TR) is equal to the price of each of the products or services that the firm sells times the quantity sold, or $p \times Q$, where p = price and Q = quantity. Total costs are a bit more complicated, but can be reduced to the cost of the three primary inputs used in production: physical capital (K), labor (L), and raw materials (N). Thus, rewriting equation 14a, we obtain the following equation:

$$\pi = (p \times Q) - (r \times K) - (w \times L) - (p_n \times N) \tag{14b}$$

where r = interest rate on capital, K = plant and equipment, w = wage and benefit cost per worker, L = number of employees, p_n = price of raw materials, and N = raw materials.

In a world with transportation costs, taxes, and regulations, this equation becomes even more complex. Since firms are interested in maximizing their *after-tax* profits, we need to subtract out their transportation costs, as well as any taxes they pay and any regulatory costs they face. That makes our final equation the following:

$$\pi_{AT} = (p \times Q) - (r \times K) - (w \times L) - (p_n \times N) - C_s - T - R \tag{14c}$$

$$\left[\begin{array}{c} \text{Total} \\ \text{Revenue} \end{array} \right] \quad [\ldots\ldots\ldots\ldots \text{ Total Costs } \ldots\ldots\ldots\ldots]$$

where π_{AT} = after-tax profits, C_s = shipping/transportation costs, T = taxes and public fees, and R = costs of complying with public-sector regulations.

Based on this equation, we can begin to see what firms must do to maximize profits and how municipal officials might try to influence companies to remain in their communities, expand their operations, or entice new companies to move in.

In a reasonably competitive marketplace, firms can only increase their total revenue by improving their product or differentiating it from others so that they can sell a larger quantity. Highly competitive firms have little leeway to change the price they charge; if they raise their prices above the level set by their competitors, they lose customers. In this case, p might go up, but Q falls so much in response that the product of the two, TR, actually declines. This is the case where the **price elasticity of demand** has a value smaller than negative 1. A 1 percent *increase* in price leads to more than a 1 percent *decrease* in quantity sold.

On the other hand, if a firm lowers its price a great deal in an attempt to attract customers, it may not even be able to cover its costs and will likewise take a loss. Moreover, if its competitors lower their prices in response, this reduces any price advantage. The only thing a firm in a competitive market can do to raise revenue is try to differentiate its product from those of its competitors. This is what drives most firms to continually attempt to innovate and advertise in order to stay one jump ahead of the competition. This takes investment and time.

Because of the short-term barriers to increasing total revenue, most firms are in a constant battle to find ways to reduce their total costs. Given the fact that the interest rate (r) on loanable funds used to purchase plant and equipment (K) is set by banks or other lending institutions, most firms can do little about lowering their capital costs—unless they can obtain an interest-subsidized loan through some government program. Finding cheaper sources of labor (L) is possible, especially if the firm can move its operations. During the nineteenth century, textile manufacturers in the highly competitive market in New England turned to one immigrant group after another seeking out workers who were willing to accept ever-lower wages (w). When Irish immigrants who fled the potato famine demanded higher wages, the textile mill owners turned to French Canadians and, in rapid succession, Italians, Russian Jews, Poles, and other Eastern Europeans to keep their wage costs down. At the end of the nineteenth century and throughout the first half of the twentieth, the mill owners found they could find even cheaper labor by moving their operations to the South. By 1922, the majority of U.S. textile production was found outside New England. Other industries, including steel and auto, followed suit and left their original midwestern locations for cheaper labor in the South and later in Mexico. With cheaper transportation available via rail and interstate highway, it was possible to move industrial inputs to wherever they were needed and ship final products to wherever they were demanded.

As for raw materials (N)—which ranged from agricultural products, minerals, and energy sources to finished inputs purchased for assembly into final products—firms also scouted out different locations to assure lowest cost. The early textile mills were built in cities like Lawrence and Lowell, Massachusetts, because there was a ready supply of low-cost waterpower in towns situated along rivers. With the introduction and perfection of the steam engine, companies no longer needed to be situated in riverside towns. Many landlocked towns and cities became cost-effective options for industrial production. Today, with low-cost, high-speed communications and transportation (C_s) available by telephone, fax, and Internet—which permit economically efficient management of far-flung industrial empires—an ever-expanding number of locations have become viable alternatives for production. As noted in Chapter 5, the United States now imports goods and services equal in value to 15 percent of national gross domestic product (GDP). Shoes, once made by the millions in Maine and Massachusetts towns are now made in Indonesia, Mexico, and Sri Lanka. Before the 1990s, we imported virtually nothing from China. Yet, by 2004, more than 10 percent of U.S. imports—including a very high proportion of sophisticated American company products—were being manufactured in China, where labor and energy costs are low by almost any international standard. Cities in India are now home to call centers that serve U.S. customers who need technical assistance with America Online (AOL) or their Dell computers. All of this reduces labor cost for U.S. producers, but it means the export of jobs from American cities and towns and real concerns for mayors and other municipal officials.

The final factors on the cost side of any firm's financial accounts are taxes (T) and regulatory costs (R). While usually small in relation to capital, labor, and natural resource costs, firms try to find locations for their operations that, other things equal, impose lower taxes and a smaller regulatory burden. City and town officials often try to influence firm location by offering favorable tax treatment, but there are a host of other economic development strategies that they can pursue in an effort to provide jobs for their citizens, augment local tax revenues, and increase the local multiplier.

Public Policy, Economic Development, and Firm Location

A review of equation 14c helps us to develop a taxonomy of local economic development strategies. There is not a great deal that local or state governments can do to attract or retain investment by assisting firms in their drive to increase their total revenue (p × Q). There are no simple direct ways to increase the price of a firm's products or services or increase the quantity sold, short of the local community or state guaranteeing the purchase of a share of the firm's output. In a few cases, it might be able to influence where a bank places its branches if the local or state government agrees to use the bank to hold its deposits, but this is extremely rare. When Michael Dukakis was governor of Massachusetts, he helped keep open a General Motors assembly plant in his state by agreeing to buy cars built in that plant to replace older vehicles in the state's agency fleet.

More common is the use of lobbying by local and state government officials to encourage the federal government to contract with firms in their communities (Leonard and Walder 2000). This is especially true with regard to defense procurement and spending by the National Aeronautics and Space Administration (NASA). Local government officials in Seattle have long helped lobby members of

Congress and procurement officers at the Department of Defense to assure that Boeing receives contracts for military aircraft built in the state of Washington. President Lyndon Johnson was famous for steering business to firms in his home state of Texas with contracts to build equipment for NASA and the space program. Such lobbying pays off in terms of local jobs and increased local tax revenue, although the overall result can be thought of as a zero-sum game. What cities like Houston received in the way of federal contracts simply reduces the amount of revenue that could have flowed to localities with less political clout.

Reducing Capital Costs (r × K)

Much more can be done by government with respect to assisting firms to reduce their total costs rather than by trying to boost their revenue. We can begin with the cost of capital. States have a variety of tools available to them to help reduce the cost of capital for firms that consider relocating or starting up new operations. The state can issue private-purpose **industrial revenue bonds**. Typically, these bonds carry a lower interest rate than can be obtained in the private sector because their interest is exempt from federal and state taxes and because the bonds are considered low risk, backed by the full faith and credit of the state. Before the mid-1980s, the federal government placed little restriction on the issuance of these bonds and they were generously used by communities across the nation. Some $66 billion in industrial revenue bonds were floated in 1984, the proceeds of which were loaned to private businesses at lower interest rates (Sbraglia 1996). This produced a drain on the U.S. Treasury, which Congress ultimately moved to limit.

The Tax Reform Act, passed by the Congress in 1986, established a cap on the total amount of federal tax–exempt borrowing that states and localities could undertake and restricted the types of projects that could be funded with them. Under the new law, industrial parks, sports stadiums, convention centers, most private office buildings, and most parking facilities could not be funded through this mechanism. Still, more than $14 billion in such bonds were authorized in 1989 to help states and localities attract manufacturing facilities and other businesses. Offering capital to firms at these discounted interest rates can make a particular community location more appealing.

An alternative development tool to industrial revenue bonds was established by the Urban Development Action Grant (UDAG) program, enacted into federal law in 1977 as part of President Jimmy Carter's urban policy (Stephenson 1987; Pelissero 2003). The purpose of UDAGs was to alleviate central city decay by offering local communities direct subsidies for real estate development that they could use in combination with private capital to redevelop distressed neighborhoods. The ratio of private capital to UDAG subsidy was set at 2.5 to 1, and the locality was required to prove to the federal government that the development project would be financially infeasible without the subsidy.

Research on economic development policies undertaken by Richard Bingham (2003) provides a good example of the use of a UDAG. In redeveloping its riverfront in an effort to become a prime location for conventions, the mayor and city council of San Antonio wanted a 600-room luxury convention hotel built along its projected "Riverwalk." Using the lure of a $14 million UDAG grant to restore nearby historic properties, develop a small commercial shopping mall, and construct a 500-car parking garage, the city was able to coax the Hyatt Corporation to build the luxury hotel it wanted at a cost of $37 million in private funds—which satisfied the federal government's 2.5:1 private capital/subsidy ratio. Without the federal grant, it is unlikely that any private developer would have taken the gamble of putting up such a hotel in a community whose convention potential was not readily apparent. Today, San Antonio boasts a $4 billion per year visitor industry based on national and regional conventions and tourism.

At its peak, the UDAG program provided $675 million annually in public grants to communities. Over its twelve-year existence, before it was killed off by Congress in order to use the funds to pay for a NASA space station, the program awarded $4.6 billion to communities for investment in physical infrastructure projects. Nearly 3,000 projects in more than 1,200 cities were funded under the program. While this program did not directly reduce the cost of capital to the private sector, it did the equivalent by paying for surrounding physical improvements that presumably made the private investments more profitable.

UDAGs were not without their critics. Conservatives claimed that the program was simply a new form of **pork barrel politics**—awarding billions of federal dollars to city mayors to dole out on the pet projects of private developers in return for their political support. Community activists often criticized the UDAG program for focusing development on downtown office projects rather than on projects that would serve the neighborhoods (Chalkley 2003). Clearly, many UDAG projects served the broader interests of the community, while some no doubt ended up mainly serving the profit needs of locally influential developers. The real key to their success was in the ability of city leaders to bargain aggressively with private developers to assure that the community benefited from the projects underwritten with public subsidies (Sagalyn 1997).

A number of states have experimented with the provision of venture capital, especially for high-tech start-ups (Florida and Smith 1992). In this case, the state has an economic stake in the companies it helps to finance. Two notable examples are found in the Massachusetts Technology Development Corporation (MTDC) and the Connecticut Product Development Corporation (CPDC). Public entities like these generally function as passive limited partners in a consortium of funders. Often, these quasi-public corporations use pension fund reserves to capitalize these ventures.

One of the most creative development tools available to local communities to affect capital costs is **tax increment financing (TIF)** (Bingham 2003). California, the first state to use TIFs, introduced them in 1962. They grew in popularity in the late 1970s, and their use has increased steadily ever since. Today, they are available to local communities in forty-nine states (Weber 2003a).

Unlike UDAGs funded by the federal government, TIF emanates from state government. Under a TIF, a city designates a specific neighborhood for improvement, making it a TIF district. The central idea behind this development instrument is to use all or a substantial share of expected *future increments* in local property tax revenue to underwrite *currently* issued general obligation bonds. Essentially, new development in TIF districts should increase property values and, therefore, property tax revenue. Future increments in property tax revenues made possible by a TIF-backed development can then be used to pay the principal and interest on the original bonds. The amount of property tax revenue that goes to the local community over the period of the TIF-backed bonds is fixed at or just above its predevelopment level. Then, all or at least most of the increase in real estate taxes tied to increased property values in the TIF district go to pay off the bonds until the full principal and interest is paid off. Only then can the community use increased property tax revenue inside the TIF district to pay for city services.

The proceeds from the bond sales can be used for land assembly, site clearance, utility installation, street construction and repair, and subsidies to businesses and developers. As such, TIFs cover many of the ancillary costs of new projects and reduce the capital costs for private firms that are willing to locate in depressed areas where TIF districts are permitted. In theory, all these development tools aimed at assisting firms with their capital costs can help steer investment and jobs into communities willing to use them.

Reducing Labor Costs (w × L)

State and local communities have also weighed in on labor costs, hoping to attract firms by helping to keep wage costs down or contributing to the cost of training employees so as to improve the productivity of the workers hired by firms. To keep wages low, many southern states have long supported so-called right-to-work statutes that make it difficult for unions to organize workers. They have done this to signal firms that they are more likely to avoid unionization if they locate in communities within these states. The strategy seems to have worked given the data in Table 14.1. The amount of job creation in the South has far outstripped that in the North.

Besides attempting to influence the actual price of labor, state and local communities have tried to attract firms by promising to pay for the training of their employees. This directly reduces the cost of labor by substituting publicly provided training for what would have been paid for by the private sector. This training presumably improves the quality of the labor force, boosts a firm's productivity, and likely increases its profits.

States and local communities work to improve the quality of the labor force in two ways. One is by investments in their public schools, community colleges, and state universities. A well-educated labor force, learned in general skills, is easier and less expensive to train for the specific jobs that firms need to fill. Going beyond general training, state and local governments have established community colleges with competency-based curricula, providing skilled labor that can be immediately absorbed into jobs within local firms. Community colleges offer a wide range of specific occupational training for a broad range of workers, from licensed practical nurses to Class A machinists and accountants. Communities with good schools and a rich array of community colleges and state universities trumpet these assets in marketing campaigns aimed at attracting firms.

States and even some local communities have also experimented with subsidies to private firms to cover the training of their own employees. As Fitzgerald (1993) has noted, the Ohio Department of Development's Industrial Training Program (OITP), created in 1980, invested more than $70 million in training for 500,000 Ohio workers. Much of this training was customized to fit the needs of specific firms. In Massachusetts, the Machine Action Project (MAP) was established by the state government to help meet the skill needs of small, specialized metalworking firms that remained in a region of the state where towns and cities had suffered from a high level of deindustrialization. With federal and state grants and small fees from local firms, the MAP worked with a local technical community college to provide training in setting up and operating new tools for computerized numerical cutting (CNC). If the MAP had not intervened, claims Fitzgerald, the small firms would have begun closing their doors and moving to locations where labor trained in the new technologies was more readily available.

Remedying the skills mismatch between the existing training of the local labor force and the evolving needs of local business is now considered a standard development policy in virtually all regions of the country. For companies, subsidized training is equivalent to lowering its labor costs. Still, firms that are considering a new location prefer areas where there is access to an already trained labor force, making early job training of existing residents a priority in development.

Reducing Raw Materials, Natural Resources, and Transportation Costs ($p_n \times N$), C_s

Not much opportunity exists for municipalities to affect the quantity or price of raw materials or natural resources that private firms use, except for the provision of water and sewerage and of land. However, by using bond financing to pay for this basic infrastructure, local communities can help to reduce company costs. To coax new large developments into their regions, cities and towns will often underwrite the cost of making changes to existing roads and highways to accommodate a company's needs. In its bid to win the new General Motors (GM) Saturn plant in the mid-1980s, in a competition that involved sites in seven different states, Tennessee offered a package of inducements that included $30 million for a highway project that connected the proposed plant in Spring Hill to Interstate 65. This, along with funds for a subsidized training program and property tax subsidies, helped the state win the competition in 1985 (Bartik et al. 1987). Since its inception, GM has spent $5.5 billion on the Spring Hill plant, including $1.5 billion pledged in 2000 to add products and expand the facility (Eldridge 2003). As of 2003, the Spring Hill Saturn plant employed more than 6,300 workers, with thousands of other jobs at Saturn suppliers in the area (Bernard 2003).

Many cities and suburbs have developed industrial parks, providing subsidized land to private firms in the hopes of attracting new investment. In older cities, this often means assembling parcels of land large enough for industrial or commercial use. One of the most spectacular examples of this strategy involved the city of Detroit and General Motors. With auto factories closing down and fleeing the Motor City in the early 1980s, GM informed Detroit's mayor that it would agree to build a new ultramodern, single-story Cadillac assembly facility right in the middle of the city in an area called "Poletown"(due to its once-heavy Polish immigrant population). But to get the company to do this rather than move out of state, the city would have to meet its demands for land assembly, site preparation, and a substantial property tax abatement. With little bargaining power, Detroit ultimately agreed to use its power of eminent domain to clear more than 400 acres of land, in the process displacing 3,200 residents, dozens of churches, nursing homes, and 160 community businesses. It paid for the relocation of on-off ramps for two of the city's expressways, paid for clearing the land to the point where it was ready for construction, and added a $240 million, twelve-year property tax abatement to the bargain. In return, the city retained about 3,000 autoworker jobs (Bluestone and Harrison 1982).

In a more modern version of this story, the three older industrial cities of Malden, Everett, and Medford, Massachusetts, pooled their resources to take more than 200 acres of land by eminent domain to create "Telecom City," with the hope of transforming this area into a modern high-tech industrial park. But just as the land was being readied for construction in 2001, the telecommunications industry went into a tailspin and the land still remains vacant. In 2004, recognizing the problem of targeting too limited a set of industries, the cities renamed the project "River's Edge," and they are now actively marketing it to a broader spectrum of industries and to housing developers.

Reducing Taxes (T)

Obviously, the two factors that states and municipalities have the greatest control over are taxes and business regulation. The *types* of income streams and wealth subject to tax affect the cost of doing business in any particular location. The same is true of the income, sales, and property tax rates levied on businesses and households. States like New Hampshire have no income tax and no sales tax, relying almost exclusively on property taxes to pay for public services. Other states like Massachusetts—once dubbed "Taxachusetts"—levy a state income tax, a state capital gains tax, a statewide sales tax, a local excise tax on motor vehicles, and property taxes on both residences and businesses in each of its 351 towns and cities. An entire array of incentives is used to attract industry to a particular state or community including low taxes on business, providing abatements on taxes in the form of lower rates or tax holidays for new businesses, and limiting taxes on highly paid executives.

Robert Lynch (2004) notes there are five common arguments that politicians and special-interest groups make for cutting state and local taxes to induce economic development. The first is the *tax burden* argument. Simply stated, lowering the tax burden on companies increases their after-tax profits. Ceteris paribus, communities that help companies improve the bottom line are the communities where businesses want to set up operations. For cities and towns, this means more jobs.

The second, the *supply-side* argument, is actually a variant of the tax burden claim. It holds that tax cuts for individuals and for businesses provide incentives that encourage people to work more and to increase their savings and investment, thereby stimulating economic activity. A reduction in the individual income tax, for example, supposedly will encourage workers to work harder and longer because they can keep more of every dollar they earn. Workers substitute more work for leisure because the opportunity cost—the implicit price—of leisure goes up when the after-tax value of an hour's work goes up. For businesses, a tax cut provides an incentive to invest both because it boosts their after-tax profit rate, which makes investment more profitable, and because it leaves them with more funds for investment.

The third argument, this one on the *demand side*, is another variant of the tax burden claim. When taxes are reduced, consumers and businesses will spend part of their tax savings on goods and services, leading to a higher volume of business sales. This, in turn, will help create jobs and additional income.

Still a fourth argument rests on the effect of taxes on the so-called *business climate*. A state, a metro region, or a city's business climate is usually defined in terms of a combination of factors that makes an area a good place in which to invest. This includes everything from the area's social and physical infrastructure and the quality of life for employees to indicators of how local government deals with business in terms of zoning, building codes, and taxes; essentially, how the local government accommodates the needs of business. Those who promote tax cuts suggest that businesses judge the business climate first and foremost on the basis of the local tax burden. The tax burden here is seen as less important in terms of after-tax profit per se and more important as a general indicator or sign of a local community's attitude toward business. Thus, even if the tax burden is a tiny fraction of a company's costs, a lower tax is seen as beneficial to economic development because it sends a signal that a local community is hungry for business and is working hard to attract it.

Finally, there is the *competitiveness* argument. It is, in some sense, the argument of last resort for tax cut proponents. Even if taxes have little impact on corporate profits, and even if companies do not explicitly demand lower taxes or special tax treatment, cities and towns must offer tax relief to compete with other locales that do. Those communities that refuse to play the tax-cut game are presumably doomed to lose. Jurisdictions that actively court business with low taxes and other monetary incentives will allegedly have a leg up when it comes to attracting footloose industry.

In practice, states, cities, and towns have a broad array of tax weapons to use as part of an economic development strategy. Tax cuts generally refer to reductions in income, sales, or property tax rates. But taxes can also be manipulated by changes in the tax base. For example, excluding certain forms of capital from the property tax can reduce the property tax burden without changing the tax rate. A local property tax can be changed, for instance, by deciding to include or exclude physical equipment inside a plant as "property." Changes in tax burdens can also be accomplished by manipulating income thresholds on a graduated income tax or by changing the level and types of exemptions.

Local tax policy can also be targeted. *General tax incentives*, according to Lynch, are "entitlements automatically provided to all firms meeting the qualifications specified in the tax law" (Lynch 2004, p. 14). Alternatively, a city or town might provide a *special* tax cut or a tax credit to specific firms, keyed to the number of new workers they hired. Such incentives can also be targeted geographically, so that only specified neighborhoods within a municipality are eligible for favorable treatment. There are also many cases, such as the Saturn and GM examples, where special tax treatment is offered to a single firm in order to encourage it to stay in town, move to town, or expand its operations. The problem, of course, is that by reducing taxes on selected firms, a wedge is driven between their tax burden and that of all other firms in the area. This may appear to be inequitable and may dissuade, or at least not encourage, other firms from increasing their employment levels.

Municipalities have direct control over a broad range of tax gambits to play in the development game. Nearly all states offer sales and/or use tax abatements on firms' new equipment in order to encourage them to invest in new capital and new technology. All but six states offer a jobs tax credit that provides tax relief based on the number of new jobs created. All but one permit an exemption for raw materials purchased by their manufacturing enterprises. The tax incentives spreading most quickly to other states are job-creation tax credits and the research and development tax exemption (Chi and Leatherby 1997). As a result of increased credits and exemptions, the state corporate income tax as a percentage of total state revenue collected has declined, nationally, from 9.5 percent in 1977 to 6 percent in 1998 (Schweke 2004). As of 2007, it represented 6.1 percent of total state tax collections—about one-sixth of what states collected from general sales taxes and from the personal income tax.

Streamlining Regulations (R)

The other factor over which states and municipalities have direct control is the set of business regulations that govern zoning, building code enforcement, pollution control, and local minimum wage rates. These regulations were put in place to control the use of land, to assure that buildings are safe for occupancy, to control air and water contamination, and to limit downward pressure on wages and family incomes. These objectives of government policy are now widely accepted.

Each of them, however, imposes costs on business. Like taxes, if they are too onerous, they can dissuade firms from establishing operations in a city or town and, in some cases, may encourage companies to close up shop and move to a location where the regulatory burden is lower. Moreover, it is not simply the level of regulation that matters but also the uncertainty that sometimes attends its implementation. A firm that needs a zoning variance to construct its building may be frustrated for months as its request works its way through the local bureaucracy and any community review process that is stipulated in the zoning law. Fulfilling the letter of the law with regard to building codes and passing muster with the local building inspector can also add a great deal of uncertainty to the investment process. Developers refer to the legal costs and time delays due to regulation as *soft costs*, but these can be as much a burden as the *hard costs* of capital, labor, and taxes.

In making investment decisions, firms differentiate between **risk** and **uncertainty**, and worry particularly about the latter. Risk involves the calculation of probabilities. A developer may not know for sure whether it will receive a municipal zoning variance that will permit it to build on a specified site, but if it knows that in 80 percent of cases in this city or town, zoning relief is granted, it can take this risk into account in making its location decision. Uncertainly exists where the probabilities of something occurring are not known because the process is truly random or arbitrary. A city that develops a reputation for making zoning decisions that seem haphazard or indiscriminate will soon find that few businesses are willing to locate there.

Soule, Fitzgerald, and Bluestone (2004) found anecdotal evidence—from developers and location specialists who are charged with the responsibility of finding appropriate sites for business development—that regulatory costs are generally more burdensome in older industrial cities, where the volume of zoning laws and building codes tend to be greater simply because they have evolved over many decades. Similarly, there is a widespread belief that communities in older cities have a stronger network of organizations that can resist new development through social pressure and legal action. This presents an unacceptable level of uncertainty to firms and developers. As such, establishing a business in the suburbs, especially in younger areas farthest from the central city, is seen as less costly on regulatory grounds and on the basis of less uncertainty. Nonetheless, as newer suburbs mature with more residents and more firms, they too often add regulations that, according to some developers, are nearly as burdensome as those in older cities. This is especially true when it comes to zoning and the granting of building permits.

One particular approach to reducing the tax and regulatory burden in distressed areas is found in the concept of the **enterprise zone** (EZ). The original idea was borrowed from the Margaret Thatcher government in Britain and gained adherents in this country under the Reagan administration during the 1980s. Businesses that agree to locate in an economically distressed area that is designated as an enterprise zone are eligible for tax and regulatory relief. This relief can take many forms that include state sales tax exemptions, real estate assessment freezes, local property tax waivers, and waivers of building permit fees. In some cases, subsidies are provided to firms that hire workers in designated EZs. Although a federal enterprise zone law was not enacted until 1993 under the Clinton administration's **empowerment zone** program, at least forty states implemented some form of the legislation beginning as early as 1981 (Bingham 2003). Theoretically, other things held constant, firms can increase their after-tax profits by choosing to locate in an enterprise zone. In doing so, jobs are supposedly created where they are most needed—in depressed communities with high unemployment.

Increasing Social Amenities

Beyond what municipal leaders can do to augment the profits of companies that are willing to remain or settle in their city or town is a set of policies aimed at making their communities physically and culturally attractive to business leaders and employees. Most business leaders would rather live in communities where there is a bevy of cultural attractions, natural beauty, a wide availability of retail services, and sports franchises. A city rich in museums and parks, professional sports teams, and close to recreational areas often can use these amenities to attract business firms. That is why cities often bid for major-league teams by offering free land and subsidies for stadium construction. Since 1991, Phoenix, Arizona, has spent almost $1 billion on the construction of cultural and sporting attractions in the downtown area with the explicit goal of increasing business investment and boosting tourist trade (Bogart 1998). Phoenix is not alone. Since 1985, seventy-one major performing arts centers and museums have been built, renovated, or substantially expanded in cities that range from Baltimore, Newark, and Pittsburgh in the East to Atlanta, Charlotte, Miami, Nashville, and New Orleans in the South to Albuquerque, Denver, Dallas, and Seattle in the West. In 2001 alone, nearly $450 million was allocated by states across the country to help subsidize the construction of museums and art galleries, performing arts centers, and symphony halls (Strom 2002).

As we saw in Chapter 5, Richard Florida's seminal work in *The Rise of the Creative Class* (Florida 2002) suggests still another way of looking at cultural amenities as a spur to regional economic growth. He argues that at one time, cities and towns grew prosperous because they were located near transportation routes or because they were endowed with valuable natural resources. Today, however, modern business turns less on physical forms of capital and more on human capital. The human capital theory of economic development argues that "the key to regional growth lies not in reducing the costs of doing business, but in endowments of highly educated and productive people" (Florida 2002, p. 221). Even cities with a high cost of doing business, like Boston and San Diego, survive and prosper because they can attract members of the "creative class"—those who work in such fields as science and engineering, computers and mathematics, education, arts and design, and entertainment. Florida calculates that roughly 30 percent of the U.S. workforce is now part of this *class* that drives economic growth in an information age.

Presumably, those metro areas that can attract a disproportionate share of the creative class are destined for greater prosperity in very much the same way that older industrial cities in the late nineteenth and early twentieth centuries grew prosperous if they had access to transportation and natural resources. According to Florida, what draws the creative class to places like Washington, D.C., Raleigh-Durham, Boston, Austin, San Francisco, Minneapolis, Denver, and Seattle is lifestyle, diversity, and social interaction. The best places offer a combination of a built environment and a natural environment conducive to indoor cultural attractions and outdoor recreation; culturally diverse neighborhoods that offer a variety of food, entertainment, and lifestyle; and a "vibrancy of street life, café culture, arts, music, and people engaging in outdoor activity—altogether a lot of active, exciting, creative endeavors" (Florida 2002, p. 232).

If this model of the new economy is roughly correct, then cities can do little to attract business by helping it to boost revenue or to cut the costs of capital, labor, raw materials, transportation, or taxes and regulations. Instead, a region that wishes to attract business must find ways to attract the creative class. This involves sizable investments in cultural amenities and improvements in the natural ecology of a region. In Florida's words, the winning municipalities of the future are going to be the ones that develop a world-class *people climate* rather than simply trying to create the best *business climate*. The former requires significant public-sector investments; the latter has historically required significant cuts in the revenues needed for those very investments.

What Works?

So far, we have laid out an extremely broad array of possible public policies to help attract investment and jobs. **Table 14.2** summarizes all of these policies in a simple taxonomy. But which of these work best and what are the costs of implementing them? Let us take a look at what we seem to know about the efficacy of all these strategies aimed at retaining or attracting businesses to a local community.

Once again, the concept of opportunity costs is central to any evaluation of these strategies. Pursuing a given strategy almost always reduces the funds available for pursuing something else. If implementing a particular strategy were truly costless— and it was not inherently counterproductive—then there would be little reason not to implement that strategy, even if the payoff in terms of investment and employment were minimal. But since every strategy has at least some opportunity costs, it needs to be weighed in some form of **cost-benefit analysis**. (For more information on cost-benefit analysis, see **Appendix A**.)

Without taking into account the direct costs (including opportunity costs) of a particular development strategy as well as its benefits, it is possible and even likely to engage in strategies that are quite inefficient. By this, we mean that the goals of the strategy could have been met using fewer resources.

Those who have studied public policy have developed what has been called the "rational model" of policy implementation (Howlett and Ramesh 2003). It assumes that a "rational individual," in this case a mayor or city manager or a designated city planner or policy analyst, undertakes the following sequential set of activities:

1. A goal for solving a problem is established.
2. All alternative strategies of achieving the goal are explored and listed.
3. All significant consequences of each alternative strategy are predicted and the probability that those consequences will occur is estimated.
4. Finally, the strategy that most nearly solves the problem or offers the least costly solution is selected.

Table 14.2 A Taxonomy of Local and State Economic Development Strategies

Assisting Firms in Boosting Their Total Revenue	Direct purchases of firm's product or service by local or state municipality
	State or local lobbying of federal government for federal contracts for local firms to produce goods or services for the federal government
Assisting Firms in Reducing Their Capital Costs	State issuance of tax-exempt industrial revenue bonds with the proceeds used to provide low-interest loans to private firms
	Urban Development Action Grant (UDAGs) to subsidize private capital investments in distressed neighborhoods
	State provision of venture capital to new start-up firms
	Tax increment financing to underwrite cost of infrastructure in neighborhoods
Assisting Firms in Reducing Their Labor Costs	State passage of right-to-work laws
	State and local investments in primary, secondary, and postsecondary education
	State and local investments in community colleges and technical training
	State subsidies for specialized training for individual firms or industries
Assisting Firms in Reducing Their Raw Materials, Natural Resources, and Transportation Costs	Local provision of water and sewer systems
	State or local investment in highways and on-off expressway ramps to meet individual company needs
	State and local investment in airports, seaport facilities
	Local development of industrial parks for the siting of new business
Reductions in State and Local Taxes	Limit the number and type of state and local taxes on business
	Reductions in income and sales tax rates
	Local property tax abatements
Streamlining Regulations	Reduce the time for zoning variances
	Speed up the building code review process
	Create enterprise zones/empowerment zones in economically distressed areas within which the tax and regulatory burden is reduced
Increasing Social Amenities	Subsidize construction of cultural venues and sports stadiums
	Public investment in parks, waterfronts, and festival areas

For various reasons, the pure rational model is seldom followed. The Nobel Prize–winning economist Herbert Simon (1997) has studied the problem of public administration and policy implementation and concludes that "pure comprehensive rationality" is impossible because of two primary factors. *First*, there are cognitive limits to the decision makers' ability to consider all options, forcing them to consider alternatives selectively. The number of possible options facing a city or town that wishes to attract investment and jobs is so great that only a few options can actually be analyzed with any rigor.

Second, each policy entails a bundle of favorable and adverse consequences that makes comparisons among them difficult. One policy may create more jobs than another, but the jobs may pay lower wages. Another may be more efficient, but have distribution implications that are not favored. Therefore, there is no unambiguous "best" policy. No matter what strategy is contemplated by a mayor or city manager, one will find both winners and losers among his or her constituencies, especially when there are large opportunity costs attached to any single strategy.

As a result, it is nearly impossible in practice to pursue the pure rational model. At best, we get public decisions that do not necessarily maximize benefits over costs, but merely tend to be satisfactory outcomes given the goals and criteria established by decision makers. Simon concludes that this "satisficing" criterion is a realistic one given the bounded rationality with which human beings are endowed. It represents "the best we can do."

With this as prologue, let us finally turn to examining the benefits and costs of the local development strategies outlined above.

Increasing a Firm's Total Revenue

As noted above, there is little a municipality can do to add to corporate profitability on the revenue side of the company's accounts. Consequently, there are few cases like the one involving the GM plant in Massachusetts, which remained open after the state guaranteed purchase of autos produced there. What appears from anecdotal evidence is that this strategy only works as a "sweetener" when a company has already come close to selecting a location. Its cost to the government may be quite small if the product would have been purchased in any case.

More important, perhaps, is the belief on the part of corporate executives that local and state leaders will take an active role in lobbying for federal contracts. Knowing that a mayor, a governor, or a House or Senate member can be counted on to use political leverage to win contracts can help attract certain firms to a particular state or city. That is one reason why, regardless of political party, incumbents in the Congress, in state legislatures, and on city councils, have an inherent advantage in elections. Their seniority is seen as giving them political clout when it comes to the allocation of federal, state, and municipal contracts. Economic advantage often has deep political roots. Local political leaders understand that in the real world, successful economic development strategies rely on many tactics.

Most local development strategies focus, of course, on the cost side of the company's ledger. Here we can look at the existing evidence regarding the efficiency and efficacy of these strategies. Again, returning to equation 14c, we can review these in order, beginning with incentives to assist a firm with its capital investments.

Reducing a Firm's Capital Costs

The evidence regarding *public subsidy of private-sector capital costs* is hardly conclusive, despite the widespread use of industrial development bonds and, for at least a decade, UDAGs. Little is known about how important such subsidies have been to increasing the level of capital investment or redirecting investment into depressed cities, towns, older suburbs, and neighborhoods. It seems clearer that such subsidies are an expensive way to generate new jobs.

One example is provided by economic journalists Donald Bartlett and James Steele (1998), who have chronicled what has been dubbed **corporate welfare**—direct and indirect subsidies to corporations. They note as just one example that in 1997, the city of Philadelphia and the state of Pennsylvania provided $307 million in incentives, including capital subsidies, to a Norwegian company to encourage it to reopen a portion of the closed Philadelphia naval yard. The project was a success from the point of view of restoring an important business in the city. However, given the level of incentives, the 950 jobs that were created "cost" $323,000 each. For the most part, these were good jobs that paid around $50,000 a year. Yet, given local and state tax rates, it will take forty-eight years for the city and state to earn back its investment.

The question one should ask is whether that $307 million could have been spent in another way that would have created just as many or more good jobs at less than $323,000 each. In theory, there may have been a lot of possibilities for using that pool of public funds, but in practice, the city fathers of Philadelphia were presented with a company willing to reopen the city's naval yard and the decision had to be made whether to take the bird in hand or wait for the two that might be hidden in the bush. City managers would love the opportunity to make choices among a set of equally viable strategies, but they rarely have a chance to compare one strategy against another given the sequencing of available options and the fear that passing up one option to pursue another eliminates the possibility of coming back to the first if subsequent options prove illusory or more expensive. So, despite the fact that public-sector subsidies of private-sector investment often appear economically inefficient, city and town officials find themselves in the political bind of being obligated to offer them, especially if jobs are desperately needed for their unemployed citizens.

Public venture funds, in theory, should be more cost efficient. If the private venture assisted through public investment proves profitable, the state or local venture capital program should earn back its investment plus a capital gain. The return could be used as part of a revolving credit system to assist additional start-ups or used to pay for normal public services. MassDevelopment is the quasi-public agency charged with this responsibility in Massachusetts. In 2003, this statewide development agency financed $860 million in projects across the state using development funds, tax-exempt bonds, and a variety of loan and guarantee programs. These ventures ranged from a $75,000 loan to a Boston-based community development corporation to do a brownfield site assessment for a possible new retail business establishment in the inner city to a $4 million tax-exempt bond refinancing for a manufacturing company in the middle of the state (MassDevelopment 2003).

MassDevelopment has a fine reputation, yet existing evaluations seem to show that public venture funds are likely to be effective only in a very limited number of metropolitan areas. These are locations where there is already a supply of the other inputs needed to make such risky new enterprise successful: a rich array of technologically savvy entrepreneurs and a technologically skilled labor force such as is found in Silicon Valley in California, the Route 128 ring in Massachusetts, or the Research Triangle of Durham, Chapel Hill, and Raleigh, North Carolina. In most other cases, few jobs are generated as a result of public investment and the gains tend to be of a zero-sum variety, where jurisdictions compete for investment in a manner that benefits private investors with little return to the community (Florida and Smith 1992).

Local communities that offer such capital subsidies and then carefully negotiate with private businesses over the conditions governing their granting are more likely to attain public benefits that would not otherwise be forthcoming. Robert Meir (1984) notes that one of the early UDAGs used by the city of Oakland, California, garnered gains for inner-city businesses and minority residents. In return for providing 12.5 percent of the development costs of a new Hyatt Hotel in that city, the city council required the private developers to assure that at least a quarter of the construction expenditures went to minority contractors, that half the construction workforce should be minority, and that at least two-fifths of the professional work associated with the construction (e.g., architecture, engineering, legal) should be with minority firms.

The difficult questions that need to be answered by city leaders in deciding whether to grant a capital subsidy or other investment incentive should be: How many jobs will the project actually produce? Are they permanent or temporary? Who gets the jobs—city residents or suburbanites, the technically skilled or the unskilled (Krumholz 1984)? Without having good answers to these questions and reasonable assurance from the private venture that certain job goals will be met, it is likely that any form of public subsidy to a private concern will end up failing any straightforward cost-benefit test.

Tax increment financing (TIF) seems to be a better targeted and more efficient investment instrument, particularly in blighted areas, but it is not without its costs or risks. Chicago provides a good example (Fitzgerald and Leigh 2002). The Windy City has created more than 110 TIF districts that cover a total land area with a 1995 assessed property tax value of more than $2 billion—nearly 7 percent of the total equalized assessed property valuation of the entire city. Chicago uses TIF financing to float bonds that are used to underwrite both private and public investment in these deteriorating areas. It combines up-front financing for public infrastructure with a "pay-as-you-go" system for private development, whereby the private developers put up the initial cash for investment, but then are partly reimbursed by the city over time as the tax revenues are realized. Essentially, this links public-sector investment in infrastructure to a property tax rebate for firms that invest in TIF districts. In the three newest Chicago TIFs, the city estimates that between 5,750 and 8,000 new jobs will be created on property that should rise in value to $315 million by 2015 from the undeveloped value of $135 million in 1998. What the city is risking, however, is that an increasing share of future tax revenues will be diverted to paying off bonds or reimbursing businesses rather than being available for improving public schools, repairing roads, cleaning up parks, and doing the thousands of other things cities need to do.

Reducing Labor Costs/Increasing Skills and Education

Public investment in people rather than enterprises is generally considered a much better use of a city's or town's resources. This is particularly true in an information age, when a larger proportion of a firm's workers need an advanced education in order to perform their jobs. As such, the leaders of local communities with good public schools trumpet this fact when they are trying to attract new investment. Nonetheless, the best research into the impact of public school spending levels on employment growth yields mixed results. Of nineteen research studies reviewed by Luce (1994) regarding the impact of various forms of public-sector spending on local employment growth, only six revealed a significant positive relationship between education spending and employment creation. Hence, while everyone will acknowledge that education is important, it is not clear that spending an additional $10 million or $100 million on schooling will result in more companies remaining in a community or additional companies choosing to locate there. Public spending on schools may be absolutely crucial to attracting private investment, but differences in spending among communities does not seem to be critical, at least in a preponderance of studies.

College and university education may be much more important in attracting industry. Given the emergence of an information-age society, one would think that state governments and local municipalities would be moving aggressively to expand their two-year community colleges and their state colleges and universities. These are training grounds for local workers and crucibles for developing new technology, and they seem to pay off in terms of local output and employment. Timothy Bartik (1996), who has evaluated a variety of state incentives aimed at increasing local development, finds that public-service spending in general provides only a modest boost to economic development. But spending on public universities and colleges pays off handsomely. He finds that an increase in higher education spending equal to 1 percent of a state's personal income and financed by an increase in property taxes increases state manufacturing output in the long run by 8.3 percent. In earlier research that compared education spending across forty-eight states between 1973 and 1980, Michael Wasylenko (1986) found that a 1 percentage point increase in the ratio of public education spending to state personal income was associated with a 0.72 percent increase in total employment.

Nonetheless, state funding for public higher education as a percent of state tax revenue has been on a roller coaster, especially after 1990 (Feller 2004). In 1980, states spent 9.82 percent of their revenue on higher education; by 1990, they were spending 8.85 percent; and by 2000, only 6.94 percent—before recovering to 9.3 percent in 2004–2005 (U.S. Bureau of the Census 2007). Feller notes that the funding trend reflects the fact that public university officials have to compete with the growing demands on state budgets for elementary and secondary education, Medicaid and prisons, and shifting perspectives regarding whether the benefits from public universities and colleges accrue to society as a whole or just to the students who take advantage of subsidized higher education. If students and their families are willing to pay ever higher tuitions and fees, why should the state subsidize higher education at all? In this case, the private benefits are apparently so high that state and local communities receive the public benefits from advanced education at little or no public cost.

Still, when one looks at the metropolitan regions growing the fastest, a common denominator seems to be the presence of one or more nationally prominent universities. Boston, Austin, Ann Arbor, Durham-Chapel Hill, and the region around Stanford University are just the most noteworthy of these communities. What is likely true, however, is less the pedagogical value of these schools per se than their research value. Each of these regions boasts universities that are heavily research-based with powerful laboratories and graduate programs producing scientific, engineering, and medical technology that can be transferred to viable private-sector firms in the community or provide the core ideas for new start-up ventures. Unfortunately, for those communities without such institutions of higher education, there is little that can be done. It is hard to imagine how such communities could contribute to the creation of a major research university where none now exists. State governments can play a larger role as they have in Michigan, Texas, and North Carolina in continuing to fund the likes of the University of Michigan, Michigan State University, the University of Texas, and the University of North Carolina. Such state universities, well-endowed with public funds, find it easier to attract leading research scientists and engineers.

Programs that are directly aimed at reducing labor cost by providing job tax credits and specific training receive mixed reviews in the evaluation literature. Cost-benefit studies often show that tax credits linked to hiring and retraining disadvantaged individuals are not efficient or particularly effective. A U.S. General Accounting Office (1991) study of the federal Targeted Jobs Tax Credit (TJTC) that compensates employers for hiring and retraining young workers, welfare clients, and the disabled found that more than half (55%) of employers actually hired a disadvantaged worker first and then found out they were eligible for a tax credit. Similarly, a U.S. Department of Labor (1993) audit of the TJTC program found that for every dollar in program costs, there were only 37 cents in benefits to recipients and the public sector.

These high cost-benefit ratios are apparently commonplace. Ultimately, they may point to the weakness in existing job credit and training programs rather than the failure of a link between human capital investment and local economic development. Better and more finely targeted programs with real performance criteria might yield greater benefits.

Public Provision of Transportation and Land

Like the support for public investment in education and training as a local economic development strategy, most economists and policy planners agree that metropolitan regions must supply an adequate amount of public infrastructure to meet the needs of business enterprise—even if the empirical evidence is not always strong. This includes provision of sufficient water and sewerage capacity; roads, highways, rail, air, and mass transit to transport goods, workers, and customers; fair-priced electric and gas utilities, and land suitably zoned for industrial or commercial uses.

Separate research completed in the late 1980s and early 1990s by David Aschauer (1989) and Alicia Munnell (1990, 1992) suggested that public infrastructure investment was so critical to economic development that much of the decline in U.S. productivity experienced in the 1970s could be traced to declining rates of public capital investment. According to Aschauer, a $1 increase in public capital stock raises private output by 60 cents. Munnell found a smaller impact, but by no means trivial: a 1 percent increase in public-sector capital investment yields a .34 percent increase in national output. While these precise estimates have been challenged by other economists (Holtz-Eakin 1993), there is no doubt that businesses demand high-quality infrastructure to remain in a location, and they are especially demanding when choosing a new location.

Eberts and Fogarty (1987), in earlier research using data from 1904 to 1978 for forty metropolitan areas, found that public investment led to private investment in cities—but primarily in those that experienced most of their growth before the 1950s. Those cities that grew fastest *after* 1950—mostly southern cities—seemed to demonstrate a reverse causation. In these metro regions, rapid private economic growth permitted sufficient local tax revenue to boost public infrastructure investment. With such a chicken-and-egg problem, it is hard to discern cause and effect without very powerful statistical tools. Therefore, the importance of an additional infusion of public capital in roads or other infrastructure for local private investment and employment growth has not yet been fully assessed.

There is also the problem of determining what types of infrastructure make the most sense economically. With a fixed amount of pubic investment dollars for transportation, for example, how much should be placed into improving the road system versus improving mass transit? When does it make sense to build a light-rail system or even make the heavy investment in a full-scale subway system? From the perspective of the individual business enterprise, having surplus infrastructure capacity is beneficial for transporting its products and employees (and even its waste materials through the local water and sewer systems). If workers and raw materials can get to the firm without long delays due to congestion, it reduces the amount of tardiness and absenteeism, as well as the need to carry large inventories. Thus, metro areas with high-capacity infrastructure often advertise this in their quest for business investment. But, as we saw in Chapter 10, a careful cost-benefit analysis is required to determine the amount of investment and into which mode of public infrastructure it should be made.

Industrial Parks and Eminent Domain

Providing land for business enterprise is still another matter. In the case of public subsidies to build *industrial parks*, the use of eminent domain for private enterprise is a departure from its earlier use. Originally, states and cities used their eminent domain powers to secure land for public use, most importantly for obtaining the rights of way for new roads and highways. Clearly, such a purpose could be justified. From an equity perspective, the justification for taking land from one set of private citizens (with presumably fair compensation) to reallocate to other private parties is not as obvious. Moreover, even from an efficiency perspective, it is not necessarily true that the new uses of the land will yield a higher return than the original uses. Remember, the GM plant in Detroit displaced 160 existing community businesses, plus a number of churches and nursing homes that employed other workers as well. Telecom City in Massachusetts also displaced existing companies. Mayors and city managers often feel they have to take such gambles in the hope that they will pay off in terms of more jobs and ultimately more revenue, but the creation of an industrial park in an area with existing businesses is usually somewhat risky.

Again, measuring the opportunity costs is critical. If the area to be turned into an industrial park is essentially vacant, then the cost to the city is equal to the price of securing the land from the current owners and rehabilitating the space for new tenants. City leaders need to calculate whether these direct costs will be recouped in the long run. This will depend on whether business tenants will set up operations in the new industrial park, how many jobs will be created and at what wages, and how much additional property tax will be generated by these new businesses. When a municipality begins to consider such an investment, it is unlikely that they have all the information they need to make a fully rational choice.

Reducing State and Local Taxes

More than forty years of economic research has been devoted to assessing the impact of state and local taxes on the business location decision since the early work of Due (1961); Mueller, Wilken, and Woods (1961); and Greenhut and Goldberg (1962). Nearly all of this research concludes that state and local taxes are not a significant factor that affects firms' location decisions. Once a firm is satisfied that a community offers it a cost-effective combination of labor, transportation, raw materials, and quality-of-life factors, state and local taxes have little significance. Interview studies during the 1970s and early 1980s confirmed the early research in this regard.

Yet, more recent surveys taken as markets have become more competitive both nationally and internationally suggest that while other factors remain more important, tax rates and tax incentives can sometimes be decisive factors in firm location decisions. A survey by Walker and Greenstreet (1989) found that 37 percent of new manufacturing plants that had accepted tax and financial incentives to locate in Appalachia would not, according to their owners, have set up operations in this region without them. Similarly, a study of firms that moved into a New Jersey enterprise zone found the zone's tax incentives were the sole or major factor in their location decision (Rubin 1991).

From the confusing array of tax-incentive studies, policy makers unfortunately receive little guidance in what to do in any particular case. As Terry Buss has concluded, "Taxes should matter to states (and local communities), but researchers cannot say how, when, and where with much certainty. Firms may need tax incentives to increase their viability in some locations, but researchers cannot definitively say which businesses or which locations" (Buss 2001, p. 101). Here again, we need to ask whether the job gain to the locality that offers a tax incentive is offset by the loss of jobs to another municipality. When firms are induced to move from more viable locations to less viable ones in response to tax incentives, the result, even if beneficial to the winning locality, may well be a society that uses its resources less efficiently.

Streamlining Regulations and Enterprise Zones

There is little evidence in the literature concerning the usefulness of streamlining state and local regulations in attracting investment and jobs. Nonetheless, anecdotal evidence from developers and location specialists who advise firms on where to locate their operations suggests that with the spread of other incentives across so many jurisdictions, firms are now looking to such factors as the speed of building inspections and the difficulty of obtaining zoning variances in order to differentiate among possible sites. How important such bureaucratic factors are varies from industry to industry based on the complexity of the building inspection process (e.g., for biotech firms using dangerous microorganisms versus a plastics extrusion plant) and the market necessity for a speedy transition from building a new plant to actual occupancy and production.

Much more evidence exists regarding the efficacy of enterprise and empowerment zones. On the surface, the establishment of an enterprise or empowerment zone would seem to provide obvious benefits to a community. In practice, it is harder to make a strong case for them. When an EZ is limited to a small, severely depressed area, as was the original intent, the economic limitations of such areas—locations with high crime, poor schools, and environmental distress—render it unlikely that private investment will respond to tax or regulatory relief. There are simply too many other factors that make such locations a high cost from the firm's point of view. If, on the other hand, the EZ covers a large area, then the tax and regulatory relief is likely to be diluted, providing little incentive to firms. In either case, unless the EZ actually induces additional economic activity rather than redistributing existing activity from outside an EZ into it, then the overall result is a "zero-sum game" (Erickson 1992). In addition, if the incentives induce capital-intensive firms to enter the EZ, the result may be very little job creation in areas with high unemployment (Jacobs and Wasylenko 1981). Alternatively, if the EZ permits local minimum wage laws to be circumvented, more jobs may result, but at "sweatshop" wage levels.

In his assessment of enterprise zones at the beginning of the 1990s, Rodney Erickson concluded that while EZ programs were not a panacea for economic distress, notable economic improvement occurred in many zones (Erickson 1992). On average, nearly nine new establishments were developed in each zone with another nine firms expanding operations. According to Erickson's analysis, the mean investment in a zone exceeded $23 million and created or saved an average of 464 jobs. More than 60 percent of the jobs went to EZ residents and more than half went to low-income persons. On the other hand, the cost was not trivial: in excess of $106,000 per job created or saved. Still, the added local tax revenues derived from greater EZ investments were apparently sufficient to offset the estimated tax losses.

Other researchers have come to less optimistic conclusions about the efficacy of empowerment zones. A 1999 study by the U.S. Department of Housing and Urban Development (HUD) claims that EZs and so-called enterprise communities (ECs) have created 20,000 new jobs based on $4 billion of new private-sector investment (U.S. Department of Housing and Urban Development 1999). But when University of Michigan planning professor Margaret Dewar (2000) reviewed the HUD study, she found that the assumptions behind this research were hard to maintain. Essentially, the study assumed that all new development in a zone was due to the EZ or EC incentives. This was in sharp contrast to the results in Dewar's own, more detailed studies of employer behavior in three business districts in the Detroit EZ, where she found that the official EZ incentives had no impact on business investment, enterprise expansion, or firm location decisions.

Building Convention Centers and Sports Stadiums

Cities desperately compete to be prime destinations for conventions and trade shows and even more for professional sports franchises. Any mayor who sat back while his baseball, football, or basketball team was snatched away to another city would certainly find local fans cursing his name. Yet, virtually every study evaluating the economic gains from public underwriting of convention centers and public subsidies to sports franchises has concluded that the economic benefits fall far short of the public costs.

As for convention arenas, the problem lies in the number of cities that rely on this development strategy. With so many cities building convention centers and expanding them, total convention capacity exceeds total convention demand. As a result, convention and hotel occupancy rates are almost always lower than the rosy predictions conjured up by the consultants hired by cities to justify spending public dollars on convention center construction, expansion, and remodeling (Sanders 2002). The only big winners in the convention game appear to be Las Vegas, Orlando, and pre-Katrina New Orleans. The gambling capital has seen its number of top 200 trade show events increase from seventeen in 1989 to thirty-four in 1999, while the city known as the Big Easy hosted seventeen of these massive trade show/conventions, up from eight. Based on the successes of Walt Disney World, Universal Studios, and SeaWorld, Orlando parlayed its reputation as a tourist destination into a tourist plus conventioneer city, hosting eighteen major trade shows in 1999. Over the same period, Chicago was down from twenty-nine to twenty-three; New York, despite its massive investment in the Jacob Javits Convention Center, was down to sixteen from twenty-eight; and Dallas was down from twenty to eleven (Sanders 2002). The story seems to be that if you are not already a tourist-based city, the chances of attracting major convention traffic is very low. Detroit is just one example of this principle: The city spent $200 million in 1989 to expand its Cobo Arena and erect new highway ramps leading to it. But after a successful launch, its convention business has continued to flag to the point where trade show attendance was 120,500 in 2000, down from more than 370,000 in 1990 (Sanders 2002).

The data on sports stadiums are even more damaging. According to Noll and Zimbalist (1997), who have examined virtually every stadium project in recent history, "building a stadium is good for the local economy only if a stadium is the most productive way to make capital investments and use its workers." But the opportunity costs almost always exceed the benefits. They find that no recent facility, including the extremely popular Camden Yards in Baltimore, has earned anything that approaches a reasonable rate of return on public investment.

The problem is that a sports stadium does not even have the export base potential of a convention arena. Most of the fans who come to games are from the locality and therefore do not generate any new revenue in the community. Essentially, stadiums serve the purpose of redistributing income from fans to owners and players, but produce little new output or tax revenue. Camden Yards produces about $3 million a year in tax revenues on a public investment of $200 million. Essentially, Baltimore baseball fans are being subsidized to come to games by those who pay taxes but have little interest in the Orioles.

Worse yet, because professional sports operate within monopolized—or more accurately, oligopolized—leagues that keep the number of franchises below what might otherwise be created, cities find themselves in bidding wars for the few franchises up for sale (Zimbalist 2003). The result is that local and state governments have ended up paying more than $100 million in individual stadium subsidies to land a team. The added subsidy becomes pure profit to the owners and players.

Why Do Cities Pursue Economic Development Strategies with Such Low Payoffs?

If most of the economic development strategies pursued by state governments and local communities have cost-benefit ratios that are greater than one, why do most states, cities, and towns pursue them? There are a number of answers to this question.

The first is simply that governments are run by politicians who need to demonstrate to their constituencies that they are working hard to solve problems like unemployment and the poverty that afflicts disadvantaged groups within their jurisdictions. If issuing a tax-exempt industrial revenue bond, subsidizing a training program, building a new on-off ramp to a freeway, providing a business property tax abatement, creating an enterprise zone, or subsidizing the construction of a convention center provides some jobs or targets some of those jobs for disadvantaged workers, the subtleties of a poor cost-benefit ratio will often be overlooked. This is particularly true in communities that have long suffered deindustrialization. Because "something has to be done" to arrest economic decline and deterioration, many mayors, city councils, and governors grasp at straws to assuage their constituencies.

A closely related second reason is found in the literature on *stakeholders*. Even if the real cost-benefit ratio associated with a particular incentive is greater than one and even if a majority of constituents—if mobilized—would urge denial of the development scheme, a small group of powerful stakeholders can carry the day because of the real gain accruing to them. Thus, for example, team owners, local business leaders, and sports fans can exert so much pressure on local political leaders that mayors and city councillors find it difficult not to support an exorbitant demand for a publicly subsidized stadium. One good example is recounted by Friedman and Mason (2004, p. 248), based on the research of Blair and Swindell (1997) and Brown and Paul (1999):

> In 1994, owners of the (Cincinnati) Reds (Major League Baseball) and Bengals (National Football League) requested subsidies for two new single-use facilities while threatening possible relocation to other cities. After a year in which competing proposals were considered, the Hamilton County Commission approved a $544-million plan in 1995, funded by a 1-cent sales tax increase, despite a referendum to roll back the tax increase by collecting more than 90,000 signatures on petitions. However, stadium proponents, consisting of Cincinnati business leaders, leading politicians, and sports fans, also organized by creating Citizens for a Major League Future and spent more than $1.1 million, including more than $300,000 from the team owners, promoting the project to voters. That compared to just $30,000 spent by opponents. When the referendum was held in March 1996, proponents won 61% to 39%. In Cincinnati, the efforts of definitive stakeholders were decisive.

A third reason has to do with what is known as the **prisoner's dilemma**. Cities are not in isolation when they are urged to consider stakeholder requests for location subsidies. In practice, a firm will play off one city against another in an attempt to win the best set of incentives it can muster. For example, let us say that a firm has considered three cities for a new branch office, and City A is found to be the lowest-cost option. The firm will still pursue City B and City C—or at least communicate to City A that it is considering doing so—to see what these cities will offer in the form of a property tax abatement or some other subsidy or to see if City A will make an offer itself. Not knowing definitively about any possible secret negotiations with B and C, City A will often offer a subsidy itself, fearing it could lose the firm to one of its competitor municipalities. Instead of being the exceptional case, this type of prisoner's dilemma is routinely faced by local governments. Individual cities would all fare better in this game if they could trust each other not to offer cost-ineffective subsidies. But the pressure to attract investment and jobs is so great that cities and states rarely trust each other in this high-stakes game.

Finally, there is the question of how to measure the opportunity costs of any given location incentive. In the best of all possible worlds, a city would be faced simultaneously with a large array of economic development policy options and then have the time and resources to make a careful assessment of the costs and benefits of each one. But this is rarely the case. Individual firms approach a municipality one at a time, which forces local leaders to make choices without having the full array of options. If you pass up pursuing a given firm that is considering the possibility of locating in your community, you have no idea when the next opportunity will arise and whether this opportunity is better or worse than what the first firm offered in terms of investment and jobs. Essentially, firms contemplating a location decision benefit from being in a monopoly position vis-à-vis cities and towns. Monopolists win when they can play one customer off against another.

In addition, simply measuring the opportunity costs is not at all easy. If a firm demands the equivalent of a $1 million tax subsidy, it is not easy to measure what the benefits would be if, instead of offering the subsidy, the city were to use these funds to improve their public schools, add an addition to a branch library, or invest in a public health program. The benefits from all of these investments seem so amorphous when compared with the alleged benefits that take the form of promised real investment and real jobs. Hence, although most mayors and city managers will tell you that they know the location subsidy game is rigged against them, they will nevertheless play the game because they feel they have little economic or political option.

What Should City Leaders and Policy Makers Do to Play the Economic Development Game Better?

In Chapter 6 we concluded that the quality and quantity of an area's productive resources are the real key to its long-term prosperity. To the extent that local policy makers are able to augment and improve their social and physical infrastructure through investment in education as well as in transportation and communication networks, they can create places that are attractive to business firms because of their inherent productivity—their ability to generate external economies. Nevertheless, for cities that face job loss and economic stagnation, the pressure to offer location incentives can be overwhelming. While few cities can opt out from actively encouraging economic development to retain firms and attract new ones, there are at least some basic principals that local officials and state agencies should follow. Terry Buss (2001, pp. 101–102) provides an excellent summary of them, as follows:

1. Require cost-benefit studies prior to making large incentive awards to individual firms or inaugurating new or revised tax incentive programs.
2. Require periodic evaluations of all tax incentive programs.

3. Require sunset provisions for all economic development legislation, and terminate programs after a set period of time unless explicitly reauthorized by new legislation.

4. Require truth and disclosure in financing provisions, rendering all aspects of a public subsidy program transparent to all constituencies.

5. Require legally binding performance contracts, penalizing firms for not meeting the goals established in exchange for incentives.

6. Embed specific incentive programs within broader cohesive strategic plans so that any incentives offered have maximum impact.

7. Eliminate entitlements to just any business that wants incentive programs. Do not be overgenerous, and negotiate hard with firms to reduce unneeded public expenditures.

8. Award incentives only if they do not put other businesses in a less competitive position.

9. Avoid redistributing wealth by using incentives. Be careful not to tax low-income families in order to award wealthy interests with large economic gains.

10. Encourage public participation in debates over the issuing of location incentives.

All of these are good suggestions for when you decide to run for mayor; the hard part will be putting them into practice once you win.

Appendix A
Cost-Benefit Analysis

A city councillor introduces a bill under which the city would create a riverfront park. Should the other councillors vote for or against this bill? Issues involving the expenditure of public funds, like this one, come up frequently in urban areas. But, assuming that the goal is to do something good for the city, how do we determine whether a particular project is worthwhile? This is the question that cost-benefit analysis attempts to answer.

As its name implies, the evaluation undertaken in cost-benefit analysis is not just a matter of determining whether benefits ensue from a project. After all, we would probably not want to gain $10 worth of pleasure from something that we had to spend $100 to get. Benefits must be weighed against the costs incurred to gain those benefits. Cost-benefit analysis differs from **cost-effectiveness analysis** because the latter does not include any evaluation of whether the ultimate benefits of the project are worthwhile. Instead, cost-effectiveness analysis simply takes a given objective and asks how it can be achieved at the least cost.

Doing a full cost-benefit analysis is not easy. It first involves trying to make sure that all the benefits from a particular project are actually measured. The same is true for costs. In terms of public policy, there are often hidden benefits and costs that are easily overlooked. If these turn out to be important, the cost-benefit analysis can give policy makers the wrong answer when they are deciding to go ahead with a project or to reject it. Moreover, since the stream of costs and the stream of benefits of most projects extend over time, and the two streams are often not coterminous, it is necessary to "discount" both of them because benefits and costs incurred now are typically considered more important than those experienced later.

The general mathematical framework in which cost-benefit analysis occurs is:

$$\Sigma \ (\text{Benefits}_t - \text{Costs}_t) \ / \ (1 + r)^t$$

evaluated over the meaningful life of the project, with t representing time and r representing a discount rate for time. To elucidate the ideas behind this mathematical expression, let's examine some issues involved in the conceptualization and measurement of cost-benefit analysis.

Time Discounts in Cost-Benefit Analysis

One of the most important characteristics of a major project is the time span over which costs and benefits occur. In many initiatives, costs and benefits extend over many years, decades, or even longer. Projects like school buildings may last for decades, while some may last indefinitely—like San Francisco's Golden Gate Bridge, constructed in 1937, and the Brooklyn Bridge, completed in 1883. Cost-benefit analysis must be prepared not only to identify specific costs and benefits, but also to specify when they can be expected to occur, and to evaluate how the timing of the costs and benefits affect the overall value of the project.

The most common way to evaluate future costs and benefits builds upon the idea that a benefit in the present is perceived as more valuable than the same benefit in the future. Consequently, under this approach, future benefits must be "discounted" to establish their "present value." Arguments in support of the present value approach include the ideas that:

- People are "myopic," that is, predisposed to value things that are experienced now more highly than things that are farther away in the future.
- The future is more uncertain than the present. The longer that one extends expectations of costs and/or benefits into the future, the less certain they are. It is appropriate, therefore, to weight expectations about the future less heavily because of this uncertainty.
- Benefits obtained should be weighed against the returns that would have occurred in the financial market from lending the money at market interest rates rather than spending it on the project.

Typically, the present value is calculated by determining the net benefits (benefits minus costs) expected in each time period, discounting each period's net benefits to its value in the present, and then summing the net benefits over the meaningful life of the project. It is easy to see how discounting works mathematically.

Let's suppose that an individual, who we will call Elaine, has the choice of spending a sum of money now or in the future. If she does not spend the money, it earns interest, so that at the end of the year, she would have a greater sum than at the beginning of the year. The sum at the end of one year, S_1, would, in fact, be the original sum, P, plus the interest earned on that sum "iP." Thus, $S_1 = P + iP$. Stated another way, $S_1 = P(1 + i)$.

If Elaine continues to invest this sum of money at a given interest rate, the sum builds up over time. Since the interest rate is now applied to the amount she has accumulated going into the second year, the sum at the end of the second year would be $S_2 = P + iP + i(P + iP)$ or $S_2 = P + 2iP + i^2P = P(1 + 2i + i^2)$.

Noting that $1 + 2i + i^2 = (1 + i)^2$, we can rewrite the above as

$$S_2 = P(1 + i)^2.$$

Similarly, at the end of the third year, the returns through the financial market would be

$$S_3 = P + iP + i(P + iP) + i[P + iP + i(P + iP)].$$

Simplifying this equation, we obtain

$$S_3 = P + iP + iP + i^2P + iP + i^2P + i^2P + i^3P = P + 3iP + 3 \ i^2P + i^3P$$

which can be expressed as

$$S_3 = P \ (1 + i)^3.$$

In fact, generalizing for the returns through any time period, t,

$$S_t = P \ (1 + i)^t.$$

This equation can be reorganized in the following form:

$$P = S_t \ /(1 + i)^t.$$

In this form, P is the **present discounted value** of the sum S_t at time t. From the previous equations we can notice that S_t is larger than P, but due to the previously mentioned concept that benefits in the future are worth less than current benefits, S_t has been discounted by a factor of $1/(1 + i)^t$, where i is the "time discount rate." Alternatively stated, we can say that one unit of S_t is worth a fraction $1/(1 + i)^t$ of a unit of the present value P.

The above example uses the interest rates faced by individuals in the financial market as the source of the time discount rate. Several other sources of time discount have been proposed for cost-benefit analysis. They include the interest rate faced by producers (which may not be the same as the interest rate faced by consumers) and a weighted average of the interest rates faced by producers and consumers.

Measuring Benefits and Costs

Let's go back to our initial mathematical expression for cost-benefit analysis:

$$\Sigma \ (\text{Benefits}_t - \text{Costs}_t) \ / \ (1 + r)^t,$$

and focus now upon the numerator of this expression. Within the cost-benefit framework, there are several aspects of benefits and costs that should be considered (Layard and Glaister 1994; Adler and Posner 2001). Among these are:

1. Benefits may accrue to some people, but not to others. Alternatively, benefits to one part of the public may be substantial, while another segment of the population receives only small benefits. Therefore, an important part of cost-benefit analysis is determining which groups benefit, to what degree each benefits, and how to compare benefits for different groups. For example, should benefits for one group be weighted more heavily than benefits for another group?
2. Benefits may not be all of the same type. For example, residents' access to recreation is a different type of benefit than a change in businesses' access to customers. Cost-benefit analysis seeks to identify the different types of benefits and costs, and to place a dollar valuation on each.

3. The valuation of benefits and costs cannot rely strictly upon market values in all cases, since various forms of market failure may result in market values differing from their social costs and social benefits.

Once costs and benefits have been determined, and appropriate adjustments have been made for the time periods in which they occur, the task of cost-benefit analysis is still not complete. For an economically proper analysis, another key aspect remains to be taken into consideration—opportunity costs. The economic costs that are incurred in creating the benefits are not just the direct costs associated with the project, but the opportunity costs (forgone benefits) from other projects that could be undertaken with the same money. Accordingly, once it is determined whether benefits outweigh costs for a particular project, this project must be weighed against other projects that could be undertaken with the same resources. The relevant question for decision makers is not simply: Does this project's benefits outweigh their costs? Instead, given our limited resources: Does this project provide greater benefits than any of the alternatives we could pursue instead?

Thorough cost-benefit analysis involves skilled use of time discounting, calculation of costs and benefits, aggregation of different types of benefits and different types of costs, a consideration of various groups that might be impacted, and a weighing of opportunity costs. Because of these complexities, some critics argue that a flawed cost-benefit analysis is worse than none at all and, therefore, should be used with the greatest caution. Supporters note that despite its potential flaws, this tool provides greater transparency about the reasoning and assumptions that contribute to a conclusion about a project's worth.

References

Adler, Matthew, and Eric Posner, eds. 2001. *Cost-Benefit Analysis: Economic, Philosophical and Legal Perspectives*. Chicago: University of Chicago Press.

Aschauer, David Alan. 1989. "Is Public Expenditure Productive?" *Journal of Monetary Economics* 23, no. 2 (March): 177–200.

Bartik, Timothy J. 1996. *Growing State Economies: How Taxes and Public Services Affect Private-Sector Performance*. Washington, D.C.: Economic Policy Institute.

Bartik, Timothy J., Charles Becker, Steve Lake, and Josh Bush. 1987. "Saturn and State Economic Development." *Forum for Applied Research and Public Policy* 2, no. 1 (Spring).

Bartlett, David, and James Steele. 1998. "Corporate Welfare." Part One. *Time*, November 8 (Reprint).

Bernard, Bush. 2003. "Saturn's Role in Flux as Division of GM." Tennessean.com, accessed December 8.

Bingham, Richard D. 2003. "Economic Development Policies." In John P. Pelissero, ed., *Cities, Politics, and Policy*. Washington, D.C.: CQ Press, pp. 237–253.

Birch, David L. 1979. *The Job Generation Process*. Cambridge, Mass.: MIT Program on Neighborhood and Regional Change.

Blair, John P., Rudy H. Fictenbaum, and James A. Swaney. 1984. "The Market for Jobs: Locational Decisions and the Competition for Economic Development." *Urban Affairs Quarterly* 20 (September).

Blair, John P., and D. Swindell. 1997. "Sports, Politics, and Economics: The Cincinnati Story." In Richard Noll and Andrew Zimbalist, eds. *Sports, Jobs and Taxes*. Washington, D.C.: The Brookings Institution, pp. 282–323.

Bluestone, Barry, and Bennett Harrison. 1982. *The Deindustrialization of America: Plant Closings, Community Abandonment, and the Dismantling of Basic Industry.* New York: Basic Books.

Bogart, William Thomas. 1998. *The Economics of Cities and Suburbs.* Upper Saddle River, N.J.: Prentice Hall.

Brown, C., and D. Paul. 1999. "Local Organized Interests and the 1996 Cincinnati Sports Stadia Tax Referendum." *Journal of Sport and Social Issues* 23, no. 1: 218–237.

Buss, Terry. 2001. "The Effect of State Tax Incentives on Economic Growth and Firm Location Decisions: An Overview of the Literature." *Economic Development Quarterly* 15, no. 1 (February): 90–105.

Chalkley, Tom. 2003. "The City That Builds: From the Inner Harbor to the Hippodrome, 30-Plus Years of Baltimore Development." *City Paper*, November 12. http://www.citypaper.com/news/story.asp?id=3314.

Chi, K. S., and D. Leatherby. 1997. *State Business Incentives.* Lexington, Ky.: Council of State Governments.

Dewar, Margaret. 2000. "The Detroit Empowerment Zone's Effect on Economic Opportunity: Employers' Responses to the Zone's Programs and Incentives." Report. Ann Arbor: University of Michigan Urban and Planning Program.

Due, John. 1961. "Studies of State and Local Tax Incentives on Location of Industry." *National Tax Journal* 14 (June).

Eberts, Randall W., and Michael S. Fogarty. 1987. "Estimating the Relationship between Local Public and Private Investment." Working Paper No. 8703, Federal Reserve Bank of Cleveland, May.

Eldridge, Earle. 2003. "Is Beaten-Up Saturn GM's Falling Star?" *USA Today*, December 4, p. 1.

Erickson, Rodney A. 1992. "Enterprise Zones: Lessons from the State Government Experience." In Edwin S. Mills and John F. McDonald, eds., *Source of Metropolitan Growth.* New Brunswick, N.J.: Center for Urban Policy Research, pp. 161–182.

Feller, Irwin. 2004. "Virtuous and Vicious Cycles in the Contributions of Public Research Universities to State Economic Development Objectives." *Economic Development Quarterly* 18, no. 2: 138–150.

Fitzgerald, Joan. 1993. "Labor Force, Education, and Work." In Richard D. Bingham and Robert Mier, eds., *Theories of Local Economic Development: Perspectives from across the Disciplines.* Newbury Park, Calif.: Sage, pp. 125–146.

Fitzgerald, Joan, and Nancey Green Leigh. 2002. *Economic Revitalization: Cases and Strategies for City and Suburb.* Thousand Oaks, Calif.: Sage.

Florida, Richard. 2002. *The Rise of the Creative Class.* New York: Basic Books.

Florida, Richard, and Donald F. Smith Jr. 1992. "Venture Capital's Role in Economic Development: An Empirical Analysis." In Edwin S. Mills and John F. McDonald, eds., *Sources of Metropolitan Growth.* New Brunswick, N.J.: Center for Urban Policy Research, pp. 183–209.

Friedman, Michael T., and Daniel S. Mason. 2004. "A Stakeholder Approach to Understanding Economic Development Decision Making: Public Subsidies for Professional Sport Facilities." *Economic Development Quarterly* 18, no. 3 (August): 236–254.

Furdell, Phylis A. 1994. *Poverty and Economic Development: Views of City Hall.* Washington, D.C.: National League of Cities.

Greenhut, M., and M. Goldberg. 1962. *Factors in the Location of Florida Industry.* Tallahassee: Florida State University Press.

Holtz-Eakin, Douglas. 1993. "Correspondence: Public Investment in Infrastructure." *Journal of Economic Perspectives* 7, no. 4 (Fall): 231–234.

Howlett, Michael, and M. Ramesh. 2003. *Studying Public Policy.* New York: Oxford University Press.

Jacobs, S., and M. Wasylenko. 1981. "Government Policy to Stimulate Economic Development: Enterprise Zones." In N. Walzer and D. L. Chicoine, eds., *Financing State and Local Governments in the 1980s: Issues and Trends.* Cambridge, Mass.: Oelgeschlager, Gunn, and Hain.

Jones, Brian, and Lynn W. Bachelor. 1993. *The Sustaining Hand*, 2nd ed. Lawrence: University of Kansas Press.

Krumholz, Norman. 1984. "Recovery of Cities: An Alternate View." In Paul R. Porter and David C. Sweet, eds., *Rebuilding America's Cities: Roads to Recovery.* New Brunswick, N.J.: Center for Urban Policy Research, pp. 173–190.

Layard, Richard, and Stephen Glaister, eds. 1994. *Cost-Benefit Analysis.* Cambridge, Mass.: Cambridge University Press.

Leonard, Herman P., and Jay H. Walder. 2000. *The Federal Budget and the States,* 24th ed. Cambridge, Mass.: Taubman Center for State and Local Government, John F. Kennedy School of Government, December 15.

Luce, T. F. 1994. "Local Taxes, Public Services, and Firm Location." *Public Finance Quarterly* 22, no. 2 (April): 139–168.

Lynch, Robert G. 2004. *Rethinking Growth Strategies: How State and Local Taxes and Services Affect Economic Development.* Washington, D.C.: Economic Policy Institute.

MassDevelopment. 2003. *Annual Report 2003.* Boston: MassDevelopment.

Meir, Robert. 1984. "Job Generation as a Road to Recovery." In Paul R. Porter and David C. Sweet, eds., *Rebuilding America's Cities: Roads to Recovery.* New Brunswick, N.J.: Center for Urban Policy Research, pp. 160–172.

Mueller, E., A. Wilken, and M. Woods. 1961. "Location Decisions and Industrial Mobility in Michigan." Report. Ann Arbor, Mich.: Institute for Social Research.

Munnell, Alicia. 1990. "Why Has Productivity Declined? Productivity and Public Investment." Federal Reserve Bank of Boston, *New England Economic Review* (January/February).

———. 1992. "Policy Watch: Infrastructure Investment and Economic Growth." *Journal of Economic Perspectives* 6, no. 4 (Fall): 189–198.

Noll, Roger G., and Andrew Zimbalist. 1997. *Sports, Jobs, and Taxes: The Economic Impact of Sports Teams and Stadiums.* Washington, D.C.: The Brookings Institution.

Pagano, Michael A., and Ann Bowman. 1995. *Cityscapes and Capital.* Baltimore, Md.: Johns Hopkins University Press.

Pelissero, John P., ed. 2003. *Cities, Politics, and Policy: A Comparative Analysis.* Washington, D.C.: CQ Press.

Rubin, M. 1991. "Urban Enterprise Zones in New Jersey: Have They Made a Difference?" In R. Green, ed., *Enterprise Zones.* Newbury Park, Calif.: Sage.

Sagalyn, Lynne B. 1997. "Negotiating for Public Benefits: The Bargaining Calculus of Public-Private Development." *Urban Studies* 34, no. 12 (December): 1955–1971.

Sanders, Heywood T. 2002. "Convention Myths and Markets: A Critical Review of Convention Center Feasibility Studies." *Economic Development Quarterly* 16, no. 3 (August): 195–210.

Sbraglia, Alberta M. 1996. *Debt Wish: Entrepreneurial Cities, U.S. Federalism, and Economic Development.* Pittsburgh: University of Pittsburgh Press.

Schweke, William. 2004. *Smart Money: Education and Economic Development.* Washington, D.C.: Economic Policy Institute.

Simon, Herbert A. 1997. *Administrative Behavior,* 4th ed. New York: Free Press.

Soule, David, Joan Fitzgerald, and Barry Bluestone. 2004. "The Rebirth of Older Industrial Cities: Exciting Opportunities for Private Sector Investment." Boston: Center for Urban and Regional Policy.

State of California. 2003. *California State Abstract.* Sacramento: California Department of Finance, December, table C-3.

Stephenson, Max O. 1987. "The Policy and Premises of Urban Development Action Grant Program Implementation: A Comprehensive Analysis of the Carter and Reagan Presidencies." *Journal of Urban Affairs* 9, no. 1 (Winter): 19–35.

Strom, Elizabeth. 2002. "Converting Pork into Porcelain: Cultural Institutions and Downtown Development." *Urban Affairs Quarterly* 38, no. 1 (September): 3–22.

Thomas, Kenneth. 2000. *Competing for Capital: Europe and North America in a Global Era.* Washington, D.C.: Georgetown University Press.

U.S. Bureau of the Census. 2007. "State and Local Government Finances by Level of Government and by State: 2004–05." May, table 1. http://www.census.gov/govs.

U.S. Department of Housing and Urban Development. 1999. *Now Is the Time: Places Left Behind in the New Economy.* Washington, D.C.: U.S. Government Printing Office.

U.S Department of Labor, Office of Inspector General. 1993. *Targeted Jobs Tax Credit Program*. Washington, D.C.: U.S. Government Printing Office.

U.S. General Accounting Office. 1991. *Targeted Jobs Tax Credit*. Washington, D.C.: U.S. Government Printing Office.

Walker, R., and D. Greenstreet. 1989. "Public Policy and Job Growth in Manufacturing: An Analysis of Incentive and Assistance Programs." Paper presented at the 36th North American Meetings of the Regional Science Association. Santa Barbara, Calif., November.

Wasylenko, Michael. 1986. *The Effect of Business Employment on Employment Growth*, vol. 2. Minneapolis: Minnesota Tax Study Commission Staff Papers.

Weber, Rachel. 2003a. "Equity and Entrepreneurialism: The Impact of Tax Increment Financing on School Finance." *Urban Affairs Review* 38, no. 5 (May): 619–645.

———. 2003b. *May the Best Team Win: Baseball Economics and Public Policy*. Washington, D.C.: Brookings Institution Press.

Chapter 14 Questions and Exercises

1. As discussed in Chapter 14, one of the factors affecting economic development and the economic development strategies chosen by local and state governments is de-industrialization. Two maps of the United States, showing the percentage of manufacturing jobs in each county in 1960 and 1990, respectively, are contained in the U.S. Department of Commerce Economic Development Administration's publication, "EDA and U.S. Economic Distress: 1965– 2000," available on the Web at

    http://www.eda.gov/ImageCache/EDAPublic/documents/
    pdfdocs/2004julyedaandu_2es_2eeconomicdistressreport_2epdf/
    v1/2004julyedaandu.s.economicdistressreport.pdf

    Go to this report. Scroll down to figures 2.13 and 2.14. Comparing the two maps, what trends do you see in the location patterns of manufacturing jobs between 1960 and 1990?

2. In February 2007, Toyota announced that it would build a new automobile plant in Tupelo, Mississippi. A newspaper article about the agreement ("Mississippi Officials Welcome Toyota to Tupelo") appeared in *The Chattanoogan* on February 27, 2007, and is available on the Web at

    http://www.chattanoogan.com/articles/article_102563.asp

    Another article, emphasizing somewhat different aspects of the benefits to Toyota ("SUV Plant Strengthens Toyota's Foothold in U.S."), appeared in the *Washington Post* on February 28, 2007, and is available on the Web at

    www.washingtonpost.com/wp-dyn/content/article/2007/
    02/27/AR2007022702038.html

    Read both of these articles. What were the incentives for Toyota to build a plant in Tupelo? How do these incentives relate to the types of economic development strategies discussed in Chapter 14?

3. Explain how the Tupelo automobile plant is expected to have economic multiplier effects beyond the job creation at the plant and the sales of automobiles from the plant.

4. Many cities and metro areas try to attract the attention of prospective companies through the information conveyed on their Web sites. Go to one of those Web sites—the site of the Metro Denver Economic Development Corporation—at

http://www.metrodenver.org

Read the content under "Mile High Advantages." What are the aspects of the Denver area that this part of the Web site promotes? Next, move your cursor over "Site Selection" and a drop-down menu will appear. Click on "Incentives." On the first page that comes up, under "Incentives," what additional inducements are listed? How do the "Mile High Advantages" and the "Incentives" relate to the types of economic development strategies discussed in Chapter 14?

Urban Well-Being, Civility, and Civic Engagement in the Twenty-First Century

15

Chicago suffered a brutal heat wave in July 1995, during which there were more than 700 heat-related deaths. Those likeliest to die were elderly poor people who lived alone. Yet, as Eric Klinenberg (2002) discovered in *Heat Wave*, his "social autopsy" of the event, two equally poor neighborhoods experienced strikingly different death rates for their most vulnerable residents. He found that a person's chance of surviving depended not only on individual characteristics like age and income but also on the characteristics of the neighborhood in which that person lived.

Why are some neighborhoods better able than others to protect their most vulnerable residents? What constitutes a good neighborhood? As a society, what can we do to promote healthy neighborhoods? As we have done throughout this book, we use the criteria of equity and efficiency to examine these questions, and look closely at issues of consumer sovereignty and positive and negative externalities.

What Do We Want from Our Neighborhoods and How Do We Get It?

If we asked a thousand different individuals to describe their ideal neighborhood, we would likely get a thousand different and conflicting answers. One person might say his ideal neighborhood must contain a skateboard park, while another thinks that skateboarding should be prohibited; one might say that it should be an area where pets can roam freely, and another might want pets to be closely confined. Nevertheless, there are some fundamental characteristics of "a good neighborhood" on which we would expect wide agreement. A good neighborhood is a place where people feel safe and secure, whether they are inside their own homes or out and about. It is a place where the most vulnerable residents—children, the elderly, the infirm— are protected. A good neighborhood facilitates good health for its residents and is free of environmental hazards that pollute the earth, air, and water. A good neighborhood minimizes intrusions such as noise, garbage, and other assaults on the senses. It is a place where people are respectful both of common areas and of other peoples' property. A good neighborhood is a place where schoolchildren can flourish and all people—not just children—can continue to grow and to learn. A good neighborhood provides access to transportation beyond its boundaries for employment, shopping, and a myriad of other purposes. A good neighborhood is responsive to the needs and desires of its residents. It is a place where people feel a civic responsibility to the community and to each other. A good neighborhood is a place where people care.

Since some elements of a good neighborhood are widely shared beliefs, while others may vary from one individual to another, the ability of households to sort themselves according to their preferences—to "vote with their feet" and move to an area populated with like-minded individuals who share their preferences with regard to local taxing and spending patterns—would seem to maximize satisfaction and epitomize efficiency in the use of resources. This, of course, is the Tiebout hypothesis we examined so closely in Chapter 9. Tiebout used this approach to argue that the division of a metropolitan area into many small and varied jurisdictions was desirable precisely because it allowed each household to choose the public-sector package that maximized its satisfaction.

The Tiebout Hypothesis and the Privatization of Public Space

Tiebout was theorizing about how to maximize satisfaction from the collective consumption of goods provided by local government. In recent decades, private organizations have been formed with the same purpose in mind. These **common interest developments** refer to ways in which individual households or business firms form associations to pursue common goals through shared consumption. In some respects, these associations have taken on some of the traditional roles of local government. A **business improvement district (BID)**, for example, is comprised of businesses within an area that form an association and assess fees from their members to provide services such as additional street cleaning or private security patrols beyond the level of service provided by the municipality. The association might provide sidewalk amenities such as plantings of trees and flowering bushes. It might also engage in marketing and promotional activities, and some BIDs have even more ambitious capital improvement and social service programs.

However, several questions have been raised about the way BIDs operate. For example, since BIDs give large property owners disproportionate weight in decision making, are they democratic? Since BIDs operate with a high degree of autonomy, are they accountable to the citizens of the jurisdiction? Since BIDs provide extra security within their boundaries, do they actually reduce crime or do they simply displace it to neighboring areas, thereby causing negative spillovers (Briffault 1999; Hoyt and Gopal-Agge 2007)?

Home owners have also formed associations to provide themselves with services over and above those provided by the municipality. Like the business improvement districts, fees assessed by the home owners' association might cover private security patrols, street cleaning, and snow removal. If the home owners' association precedes the development's construction, which is usually the case, streets inside the development might be wholly owned and maintained by the association.

When households buy property that is part of a home owners' association, they must agree to join the association and abide by its rules. These might include a lengthy list of restrictions: no outside clotheslines, exterior paint choice limited to a handful of acceptable shades, no garbage cans visible from the street, no multi-colored Christmas lighting, and a host of other restrictions. A household that moves into such a development gives up its right to place an unregistered car on cinder blocks in its driveway in return for the assurance that none of its neighbors will be able to do so either. Essentially, the household surrenders some of its consumer sovereignty in order to reduce the possibility of suffering a negative externality.

While a municipality is limited in its ability to place restrictions on household behavior through zoning laws, a home owners' association can accomplish a far greater degree of control through its contractual bylaws. Whatever amenities the home owners' association agrees to provide—a swimming pool, a golf course, tennis courts—will be paid for by association members, and their use will be limited to members only. In this sense, it is, though usually on a smaller scale, a private-sector analog to the local public-sector theory developed by Tiebout.

In *Private Neighborhoods and the Transformation of Local Government,* economist Robert H. Nelson (2005) points out that in the years between 1965 and 2005, the proportion of the U.S. population living in private community associations including home owners' associations, condominiums, or cooperatives has risen from less than 1 percent to 18 percent. Moreover, private community associations account for roughly half of all new U.S. residential construction built within the last twenty-five years and most of the new developments in the rapidly growing areas of the South and West. In some instances, home owners' associations beyond the boundaries of growing cities provide services in the absence of local government and continue to provide these services even after annexation has occurred.

Nelson argues that while municipal zoning represents one response to dealing with externalities, these private associations represent another response, through the establishment of private property rights. This is analogous to the Coasean solutions we discussed in Chapter 13. Arguing within this framework of maximizing the role of the market and minimizing the role of government, Nelson posits that it would be desirable to allow neighborhood-size private communities to replace local government, even to the extent of replacing the "one-person one-vote" process of decision making in the public sector with the "one-share one-vote" process of decision making among stockholders in private corporations.

Of course, such a proposal flies directly in the face of long-standing democratic principles. The principle that each citizen is entitled to equal representation was reaffirmed in the landmark 1967 U.S. Supreme Court decision, *Avery v. Midland County*—referred to at the time as the principle of "one man, one vote." Moreover, as eminent economist Arthur Okun warns in his examination of the balance between political rights and economic rights, although there is a place for the market, we must also know when to "keep the market in its place," and not impinge on basic human rights in a free society (Okun 1975).

Gated Communities and the Avoidance of Disamenities

In some instances, home owners' associations have gone beyond the step of creating developments in which everything, including the streets, is privately owned and maintained: They have erected walls, fences, and gates to exclude those who do not own property within. These gated communities have been growing in popularity over the last few decades. According to the 2001 *American Housing Survey*, 11 percent of the population in the West, 6.8 percent in the South, and 3 percent in other U.S. regions now live in gated communities.

Blakely and Snyder (1997) identify three different types of gated communities: (1) the recreation and retirement communities organized around leisure lifestyle activities such as golf and tennis; (2) the elite communities of the rich and famous, including celebrities who wish to maintain their privacy and noncelebrities who wish to enjoy the prestige of living in such an expensive and exclusive area; and (3) the embattled zone areas in which barriers are retrofitted onto vulnerable communities in an effort to reduce high crime rates. Many of the communities in this last category have little in common with the previous two categories in which boundaries are intended to be impermeable and space is privately owned. They include neighborhoods in which road barriers prevent the passage of automobiles, but pedestrians can move freely. They also include public housing projects in which gates were installed despite residents' objections. Notwithstanding this last category, the majority of gated communities attract households that have a great deal of choice about where to live and intentionally choose to withdraw into a private realm.

While the Tiebout hypothesis emphasizes maximization of household choice with regard to a community's spending and taxing patterns, the flip side of associating with those whose preferences most closely match one's own is the aversion to associating with those who are different. In *Behind the Gates*, sociologist Setha Low (2003) interviewed residents of several gated communities. Some of these communities were in the West and Southwest, others in the Northeast; some were middle income, others were upper middle income or high income. Some fell into the "lifestyle" category described by Blakely and Snyder, while others were in their "elite" category. The common theme that emerged in all of these communities was a concern for safety and security and, in some instances, fear of others who were of different races, ethnicities, or income classes. Low argues that the focus on safety and security may be unwarranted, given that the nongated alternatives generally available to this group are comprised of other neighborhoods in which crime rates are already quite low.

In a few instances, gated communities in California and Florida have actually incorporated as municipalities, taking privatization of public space to its logical conclusion. While Nelson might see this as a triumph of private property rights, Blakely and Snyder view it as secession from civic responsibility. In the context of a rapid growth in the number of gated communities, Blakely and Snyder ask, "Can this nation fulfill its social contract in the absence of social contact?"

Dissatisfied Citizens and Their Choices: Exit versus Voice

As we demonstrated in Chapter 9, the Tiebout hypothesis is the public-sector analog to the theory of competition in the private sector: Households vote with their feet to choose the jurisdiction that best satisfies their local public-sector taxing and spending preferences, just like they maximize satisfaction in the private sector by choosing from an array of alternatives for restaurant meals, shoes, or deodorants. The larger the number of alternatives from which one can choose, the likelier it is that every household will maximize its well-being. Or so the theory goes. If the service or the quality of the food in your favorite restaurant begins to deteriorate, you will go elsewhere. Similarly, if the dry cleaners botched your last batch of clothes, you will take your business elsewhere. If the employer down the block is paying higher wages, you may well quit your current job to take a new one. And in the public realm, if the public schools in one jurisdiction start to decline, households might move to another jurisdiction or send their children to private schools instead.

In *Exit, Voice, and Loyalty,* the noted economist Albert O. Hirschman (1970) referred to these choices as "exit"—if one is dissatisfied with a good or service, and if alternatives are readily available, it is easy enough to choose an alternative, and that is what we would expect people to do. Through competition, the restaurants that do not please their customers will close; those that do will flourish. The market outcome will be efficient. This assumes, of course, that there are no economies of scale and no externalities to cloud the sunny outcome predicted by the workings of the competitive marketplace.

But exit is not the only choice, nor is it always available—or desirable. Say you have accumulated a substantial number of frequent flyer miles with one airline. The airline adopts a new policy stating the frequent flyer miles can only be used to book travel during times in which there is a full moon. You are very unhappy with the new policy but exit is not a real option here, since your frequent flyer miles have no value on another airline. Instead, you are likely to complain, in an effort to change the airline's new policy. As an individual, you might send angry notes to the customer service department. You might call your congressional representative. You might also band together with other individuals to picket the company's offices or otherwise embarrass them. The group might consult an attorney to see if legal action is warranted. In Hirschman's terminology, you would be exercising "voice," rather than "exit." You would try to remedy or improve the existing situation instead of withdrawing from it.

To the extent that individuals perceive that voice has been successful, their sense of loyalty to the organization will grow. Those individuals who would otherwise exit might similarly be induced to remain if they perceive that the concerns they have expressed have been addressed. Thus, voice, if acknowledged, can be a powerful way to build loyalty.

Under what circumstances would individuals choose voice rather than exit? Consider the case of the employer down the block who is paying higher wages. If you have not been working for your current employer for very long, the cost of exit is low, and you are likely to leave in response to higher wages elsewhere. However, if you have been with your current employer for many years, you may have accumulated some valuable seniority rights—more weeks of vacation, priority in being able to select the vacation time of your choice, and/or protection against being laid off if the company downsizes. In this case, the cost of exit is high, and you might decide to exercise voice instead by requesting a raise or promotion to a better paid job category, joining with other coworkers to form a union or lobby management, or writing letters to the corporate board of directors, asking them to review their personnel policies. Similarly, as Fischel (2001) points out in his homevoter hypothesis, many home owners might choose voice rather than exit because their single most important asset, the value of their homes, is tied to a specific place.

In other circumstances, there is no choice because exit is impossible. What happens when exit is an option for some, but not for all? Going back to our frequent flyer example, what if rival airlines decide to honor your airline's frequent flyer miles, but only for those who have accumulated more than 500,000 miles (these individuals might be particularly desirable as a source of future business, given how much they travel). In this instance, the individuals with the greatest motivation to exercise voice, those who perceive themselves to have the most at stake, will be siphoned off. The remaining individuals will lose their most powerful and well-connected spokespeople and advocates; their chances of improving their situation by using voice will have been greatly reduced. The airline might get its comeuppance sometime in the future, when it fails to attract new customers to its frequent flyer program, but that will not remedy the situation for the existing group of frequent flyers who cannot exit.

And what if we were discussing public education, rather than frequent flyer miles? What if, in response to a decline in the quality of an area's public schools, exit could be chosen only by households wealthy enough to pay private school tuition or move to a jurisdiction with better public schools? With exit an option for the favored segment of the population, voice becomes a less effective strategy for those who remain and who lack the exit option. Initial inequality breeds even greater inequality and the disparity in education resources across the income spectrum grows wider.

In this case, competition does not improve the outcome for everyone—those who can exit may be better off, but those who cannot are even worse off than they were before. In this context, it is easy to understand why parents in poor-performing school districts often support voucher programs that would provide them with the exit option they currently lack. Political scientist Terry Moe (2001) found that while 60 percent of the general population expresses support for vouchers, 77 percent of inner-city public school parents do; while 63 percent of white parents support vouchers, 75 percent of black parents and 71 percent of Hispanic parents do.

Former secretary of labor Robert Reich (1991) has written about the "secession of the successful," and why it is potentially so problematic. He argues that growing income disparities are one result of the structural changes in the economy. With the increase in globalization, those U.S. workers whose skills command a high value in the international marketplace find their incomes growing, while other U.S. workers, typically those with less education, find that they cannot compete against lower-paid workers in other parts of the world. As manufacturing jobs continue to be lost, the supply of workers to the remaining low-paid service jobs grows, and this additional supply puts pressure on wages, keeping them from rising as fast as they otherwise would. The resulting growth in income disparities has exacerbated an already high degree of residential segregation by income levels. Sharing public services within communities now means sharing resources within a relatively homogeneous group, firmly bounded by the town's borders.

Reich argues that as the income gap between the most prosperous 20 percent of the population and the other 80 percent grows ever wider, those at the top are less inclined to share resources with those below. Their exit takes many forms, moving into expensive suburbs or into city enclaves in which privately provided schools, clubs, and other recreational activities supplant those provided through the public sector. Even the charitable offerings of this group are more likely to support institutions whose services they themselves consume (e.g., private educational or cultural institutions) rather than those that help to ameliorate the situation of those who are less fortunate.

The devolution of many federal government responsibilities—the shift of responsibility from the federal level to lower levels of government—has amplified the fiscal disparities between local jurisdictions. Even as poor jurisdictions face a greater need to provide more services to their residents, they have fewer resources from higher levels of government to support them. In Reich's view, this is yet another form of exit, and one that raises fundamental questions about the responsibility of one citizen to another.

Reich's "secession of the successful" can be seen as the triumph of exit over voice. As we saw when we first examined the Tiebout hypothesis in Chapter 9, it is possible for exit to purchase efficient outcomes only if there are no economies of scale and no externalities between jurisdictions, neither of which is a likely scenario. In addition, if exit can be employed only by the more privileged, its use will widen income disparities and worsen conditions for those who must remain.

How Do We Create Better Communities?

More than 600 years ago, Ambrogio Lorenzetti, a painter in Siena, Italy, created murals for its town hall. These murals were titled "Allegories of Good and Bad Government and Their Effects in the City and in the Countryside." In the case of good government, guided by wisdom and justice, the outcome was peace, prosperity, happiness, a vibrant life in the city, and abundance and well-tended crops in the countryside. In the case of bad government, the forces of tyranny, betrayal, and fraud resulted in a city destroyed by war, famine, hatred, and idleness, and a countryside that was barren. In these murals, created from 1338 to 1340, Lorenzetti believed that the fate of the city and the countryside were intertwined. Do we still believe that today? What are the elements of "good government" that will lead to peace and prosperity for communities, city and countryside alike?

The Role of Social Capital and Civic Engagement

As the poet John Donne famously said, "No man is an island, entire of itself." We are all connected to other individuals through networks of family and friends, concentric rings of those who are closest to us, as well as those to whom we are connected in increasingly more marginal ways. We might rely on the people in our networks for advice, information, support, leads on promising jobs or apartments, or even introductions to potential mates. New high school graduates might rely on their networks to find entry-level jobs; new college graduates might do the same. But networks can work for you or against you—it all depends on who is in your network. New college graduates whose friends' parents—or parents' friends—are successful and well-connected might have access to better opportunities than they could come up with on their own; new high school graduates living in low-income communities among poorly educated adults are likely to find only dead-end jobs through their networks. They would be better off searching on their own.

Social capital refers to the ability of individuals to harness the resources they need through their network of friends and relatives. It may be as trivial as knowing which friend to call to get the name of a moving company that is quick, reliable, and relatively inexpensive. Or it may literally be a matter of life and death. As we learned in the aftermath of Hurricane Katrina, most of those who perished during the flooding of New Orleans were very poor, elderly, or infirm African Americans, who did not own cars and could not ask for help from anyone who did. The circumstances of extreme racial and income segregation under which they lived meant that many residents of severely flooded neighborhoods only knew other people whose situation was as bad as their own.

In his pathbreaking book *Bowling Alone*, Robert Putnam (2000) explains the importance of social capital, both for the individual and for the larger society. In a neighborhood where friends will watch your house while you are away and you will do the same for them, your house is safer and so is theirs. But by making this a safer area, even those families who are not part of this reciprocal arrangement will benefit. In this way, social capital yields positive externalities. In a larger sense, building social capital means building trust. This may take time and effort, but once trust has been established, many benefits flow. It is much easier to do business with others if you are confident that they deserve your trust. It also turns out that people who live in areas where trust is warranted have greater life expectancies, presumably because their day-to-day encounters are less stressful.

Putnam distinguishes between specific reciprocity, in which the donor of a good deed is paid in kind by the recipient ("I'll buy the first round of drinks, you'll buy the next one") and general reciprocity, in which the donor might expect to be rewarded in some cosmic sense, but not necessarily by the recipient. There are many catchphrases that embody this notion of general reciprocity: "one good turn deserves another," "what goes around comes around," "practice random kindness and senseless acts of beauty," or the notion of "creating good karma." There are also many instances in which fortunate people from humble beginnings describe their charitable acts as "giving back" to the community. It is this general reciprocity that is crucial in establishing trust and that consequently makes everyone better off.

Putnam also distinguishes between "bonding" social capital (making firmer connections with people who share some fundamental identities—for example, immigrants who live in the same ethnic enclave) and "bridging" social capital (making firmer connections with those who may come from very different backgrounds but seek some common purpose—for example, an environmentalist group). Bonding social capital is based on homogeneity and exclusion; bridging social capital is based on heterogeneity and inclusion.

While it is more difficult to build bridging social capital, it may also be more useful, both to the individual and to society. Sociologist Mark Granovetter (1973) describes the "strength of weak ties," in which an individual's best opportunities come not from the people closest to him, whose networks already overlap his own, but from acquaintances outside his inner circle, whose networks are more likely to augment his and provide entirely new contacts ("Need some help with this? I know a guy who knows a guy . . ."). Moreover, bridging social capital expands horizons and fosters tolerance and empathy. Without it, bonding social capital alone can produce gangs and ethnic hatreds, where trust and reciprocity are limited only to those within the group, while those outside are treated with contempt or, in the extreme, might even be subject to annihilation.

Social capital is an important component of vibrant communities. In areas where people know each other, not only are they more likely to live in greater safety but they also are apt to live longer and healthier lives. In addition, they are more likely to be able to advocate effectively for the changes they seek—whether it be the installation of a traffic light at a busy intersection or the establishment of an on-site, after-school day-care program in the area's elementary schools. Social capital is therefore crucial for "voice" to be a viable alternative to "exit."

Just as in Lorenzetti's murals in Siena, good government begets happiness and prosperity and bad government begets famine and strife. It is therefore a matter of great concern that, according to Putnam, levels of social capital and civic engagement have been falling in the United States since the late 1960s. A recent study by McPherson, Smith-Lovin, and Brashears, "Social Isolation in America" (2006), provides additional confirmation of this decline. In the last twenty years, the average number of people whom Americans say they turn to when they want to discuss serious matters in their lives has fallen from three to two, and the likelihood that they will discuss these matters only with family members has risen. In addition, in the 2004 General Social Survey (GSS), about one-quarter said that they have no one in whom to confide, an increase from only 10 percent who responded this way in the 1985 GSS.

Why has social capital declined? The reasons are complex, and they include such disparate factors as generational change (the dying off of the generation whose high degree of public spiritedness was shaped by the Depression and World War II), increases in television viewing (which promotes passivity rather than engagement), and the increase in work hours among women as well as men (which reduces the amount of time and energy available for other activities). In addition to these changes, however, the growth of suburbs and the increasingly sprawling pattern of suburban development have also played a role.

Social Capital, Suburbanization, and Sprawl

As we saw in Chapter 4, newer suburbs are oriented around the automobile, in contrast to the transit-oriented suburbs of the pre–World War II era. As residences and workplaces have shifted farther out, and as the extreme segregation of land use between residential, commercial, and industrial structures has grown, the amount of time Americans spend in their cars has risen, and in the majority of car trips, the driver is alone.

Other aspects of suburban development have also had adverse effects on the development of social capital. Income segregation and the consequent growth of homogeneous communities have reduced opportunities for creating bridging social capital. Segregation of land use through zoning and the prohibition against building neighborhood stores, restaurants, or bars in residential suburban neighborhoods reduces the serendipitous encounters that help neighbors to get to know each other.

Earlier in this chapter, we discussed the privatization of public spaces, but along with this privatization there has also been a withdrawal from public spaces and public life. As newly constructed homes grow ever larger, suburbanites spend more time within their own houses and yards, in a completely private sphere with a small, inner circle of intimates. The grandest of the new houses, which encompass thousands of square feet and are equipped with specialized rooms for exercising or viewing media make it easier for families to turn inward, to be more self-sufficient, and to require fewer outside contacts. As the proportion of the population living in the newer suburbs continues to grow, it is not surprising that, according to McPherson, Smith-Lovin, and Brashears (2006), the percentage of those who confide only in family members rose from 57 percent in 1985 to 80 percent in 2004.

Social Capital and Neighborhood Form

A clear implication of the previous section on social capital, suburbanization, and sprawl is that a person's physical environment affects his or her behavior. The spatial configuration of newly built suburbs makes it more difficult to foster the interactions through which social capital is created. The housing reform pioneers of the previous century also believed in this cause-and-effect relationship between physical environment and social environment. Reformers such as Catherine Bauer, who was instrumental in drafting the Housing Act of 1937—the law that created the public housing program—believed that the way to eliminate the antisocial behavior found in poor slums was to eliminate the slums themselves (Oberlander and Newbrun 1999).

Slum clearance and the replacement of poor-quality housing with newly built public housing of better quality would create the necessary changes in the physical environment. It was expected that when the physical environment changed, the social environment would also change. People living in better housing, it was believed, would change their behavior and stop engaging in violent and unlawful acts. Of course, this did not happen. Many public housing projects became as dangerous as the slums they replaced; many became even more dangerous. The reformers were ridiculed for their naiveté in thinking that merely changing peoples' surroundings would change their behavior.

Yet nowadays, we are once again exploring the relationship between physical environment and social environment. The housing reformers of the early twentieth century may well have had the right idea in thinking that one's physical environment mattered. Where they went wrong was in the way they executed that idea.

In her seminal 1961 book, *The Death and Life of Great American Cities,* Jane Jacobs offered a scathing critique of the then-current conventional wisdom on how to rebuild cities. She argued that the typical urban renewal project of the time—in which small city blocks were consolidated into megablocks and in which mixed-use streets were replaced with single-use, large-scale developments—sucked the energy out of cities, killing off vibrant street life. For Jacobs, the public housing projects of the 1950s epitomized everything that was wrong with contemporary urban development. Their isolation from the surrounding urban fabric, and their pattern of high-rise buildings separated by large swaths of poorly maintained and often useless grounds were antithetical to her ideal of building "on a human scale."

For Jacobs, what mattered was a physical environment that fostered human contact: small blocks, mixed uses, clear distinctions between public space and private space, and serendipitous meetings of neighbors. What Jacobs described was a neighborhood conducive to building social capital. She argued that the best way to control crime was to have lively streets—that "eyes on the street" would provide fewer opportunities to criminals, and that the best way to promote "eyes on the street" was to have many reasons for people to be out and about throughout the day and evening. Although hers was a voice in the wilderness for many years, her ideas have now taken hold and are reflected in many of the precepts of the **new urbanism**. This approach to architecture and design, as noted in Chapter 13, emphasizes walkable neighborhoods that contain a mixture of commercial and residential properties, a mixture of residential types (single-family homes, apartments, and town houses), a connected network of narrow streets (no cul-de-sacs), and the placement of buildings (often with porches) close to the sidewalk.

Areas in which people have a reason to walk around, where there are well-designed public spaces, and areas characterized by mixed use, tend to promote the formation of social capital. Conversely, areas where people are more dependent on automobiles, those that are devoid of public spaces and occupied by low-density residential development are not as conducive to the development of social capital.

Recent Empirical Work on Communities and Social Capital

What is the impact of a community's racial and ethnic diversity on its civic life? As Robert Putnam (2007) points out, previous work on this question falls into two categories: contact theory (more interaction between groups leads to more harmony) or conflict theory (more interaction leads to more discord). What Putnam found instead was that communities with greater racial and ethnic diversity had lower levels of civic engagement and a general withdrawal from civic life. "Diversity, at least in the short run, seems to bring out the turtle in all of us," he concluded.

Paradoxically, while diversity in residential communities seems to reduce civic engagement, diversity in the workplace increases productivity and innovation. Putnam tries to resolve the issue by arguing that in the long run, differences that seemed all-important to a previous generation become less germane over time. Taking this long view, while the current wave of immigration seems to pose great challenges, previous waves of immigrants have been assimilated into the United States and have thereby contributed to our strength as a nation.

And what can be said about the relationship between social capital and smart growth? Putnam (2000) himself found that each additional ten minutes spent commuting reduces community involvement by 10 percent. To the extent that sprawl increases commuting time, we would expect a negative relationship like this between sprawl and social capital. Similarly, political scientist Thad Williamson (2002) found that communities with higher percentages of single-occupancy vehicle commuters had lower civic and social participation. Conversely, it is reasonable to think that communities designed to facilitate interaction through walkability and mixed land use would do just that. What does the evidence actually show? One study of a community built on new urbanist principles, Orenco Station in Portland, Oregon, shows higher levels of social cohesion and community interaction than two other comparison communities that are also part of Portland.

However, two caveats must be mentioned. First, the other two communities were not really control groups, since they differed on many other characteristics, not just on neighborhood design. Moreover, even if there is a genuine correlation between social capital and neighborhood design, it would not necessarily mean that neighborhood design *caused* higher amounts of social capital, although it might facilitate it. If people who want more civic engagement are attracted to communities that tout their ability to deliver it, then self-selection, rather than design itself, could explain the correlation. Recall that we encountered a similar argument in Chapter 13 with regard to the correlation between obesity and sprawl.

A recent study that examines social capital as a function of population density finds a negative relationship—social interaction is higher in low population density census tracts and declines as population density increases (Brueckner and Largey 2007). However, as we pointed out in Chapter 13, sprawl is not simply a matter of density but also a matter of design. Areas with the same population density can differ dramatically in terms of walkability and mixed uses of land.

A review by Thomas Sander (2002), executive director of the Saguaro Seminar on Civic Engagement in America, utilizes the old proverb "You can bring a horse to water but you can't make him drink." Sander views smart growth principles and new urbanism design as leading the proverbial horse to water by creating an environment that would facilitate social interaction. Achieving that goal, however, may ultimately prove to be more elusive than simply changing neighborhood design. Sander's review of the existing studies implies that so far, the results are equivocal—neither a rousing endorsement nor a failure with regard to the efficacy of these designs.

Neighborhood Form and Crime Reduction

The fear of crime is a potent force, and it has self-reinforcing effects. If people perceive an area to be unsafe, they will avoid it, and the now-abandoned area will, in fact, be a more dangerous place. While many factors affect an area's crime rate, our focus here is to expand a bit farther beyond our discussion in Chapter 11 on the link between physical design and social capital, and the impact of that link on crime prevention.

In the early 1970s, criminologist C. Ray Jeffery (1971) developed the approach known as Crime Prevention Through Environmental Design (CPTED). Architect Oscar Newman's approach, termed **defensible space**, fits within this framework. Building on the ideas of observers like Jane Jacobs, this framework examines how the physical design of an area can be used to deter crime by changing the behavior of both the potential criminal and the area's residents. The idea is to discourage the potential perpetrator from committing the crime in the first place by raising the likelihood that any such crime will be seen and reported. This is achieved through maximizing visibility in an area (e.g., replacing high fences or bushes that can serve as hiding places with lower ones; making sure that outdoor areas are well-lit) and through creating public spaces that foster a sense of ownership and responsibility among residents (e.g., small areas used by relatively few households rather than broad swaths of ground that become, literally, "no man's land"). These steps foster social capital, which keeps the area safer and encourages residents to watch for and report suspicious behavior.

Poorly maintained areas reduce social capital formation, while well-maintained areas encourage it. Therefore, the CPTED approach has expanded from its original formulation in the 1970s to include the "broken windows" theory expounded by Kelling and Wilson in 1982. This theory also is based on the notion that changing the physical environment will change behavior. If small problems in an area like a broken window, graffiti, litter, or panhandling are tolerated, the theory says, it sends a message that no one cares, no one will take action, and, therefore, more serious offenses also will be tolerated.

New York City implemented the broken windows theory in its "zero tolerance" approach to subway fare jumpers, squeegee men, and graffiti artists. Although its crime rate dropped, there is controversy over the extent to which broken windows policies should be credited. Other factors, such as demographic change (e.g., fewer young men), economic change (e.g., an improved economy and lower unemployment in the late 1990s), as well as additional resources for law enforcement agencies and improvements in the criminal justice system and in other social service agencies also played extremely important roles. Unlike in a physical science laboratory, we cannot run controlled experiments in the messy real world, so it is extraordinarily difficult to isolate the actual contribution, if any, of broken windows policies.

The Effect of Social Capital on the Lives of the Most Vulnerable

Individuals in low-income communities do not own large stocks of physical capital (such as valuable buildings) or human capital (such as postsecondary education). Therefore, the presence or absence of social capital is particularly important to the quality of their lives. In this respect, the overall decline of social capital may have its worst impact in these communities. Vulnerable individuals in low-income communities are like the proverbial canaries in the coal mine. If, as a society, we cannot protect our most vulnerable citizens, it does not bode well for the rest of us either. As Franklin Delano Roosevelt said in his second inaugural address in 1937, "The test of our progress is not whether we add more to the abundance of those who have much, it is whether we provide enough for those who have too little."

The preamble to the Housing Act of 1949 states as a national goal the provision of "a decent home and a suitable living environment for every American family." Despite the fact that this has been an explicit national goal for more than half a century, governments at all levels—federal, state, and local—have failed to achieve it. In too many instances, those who are poor have neither, especially if they are also elderly, infirm, or part of a racial or ethnic minority group. During times of crisis, these vulnerable groups are also at greater risk of dying and are less likely to receive the protection that governments are expected to provide for their citizens during public emergencies.

More than 1,800 people died as a result of Hurricane Katrina in 2005; more than 700 people died in a severe Chicago heat wave in 1995. In both instances, those who were at greatest risk of dying were poor, elderly, and infirm. Being African American compounded the risk. In both instances, there were scandalous failures on the part of government agencies. In both instances, existing disaster plans were seriously deficient. And in both instances, government agencies failed to follow even these deficient plans.

As the twenty-first century unfolds, we are experiencing the phenomena of dramatic climate change—global warming—as well as dramatic demographic change in terms of the growth in life expectancies. Therefore, we can expect to see more heat waves and destructive hurricanes; we can expect to see a U.S. population with a higher proportion of elders, including a higher proportion of the very old (those over age 85), who tend to be frailer. A closer examination of the tragedies that occurred in

Chicago in 1995 and in New Orleans in 2005 might help us to understand how to avoid similar tragedies in the future, not only through better planning and implementation of plans at the government agency level but also by building more social capital at the community level—by delivering on the 1949 promise of not only a "decent home" but also of a "suitable living environment."

Every major city has its low-income areas, but it is a mistake to think that they are all alike. Jane Jacobs (1961) recognized this when she described an old neighborhood in Boston, the North End, in which incomes were low and in which banks, viewing the area as a slum, would not grant mortgages or home-improvement loans. Yet the area was safe. In addition to its low crime rate, social indicators that measured health status and school attendance and completion rates also showed that this was a healthy community, despite its very modest physical surroundings. This was an area that had all the characteristics she valued: short blocks, mixed residential and commercial land use, high residential density, a vibrant street life, and surroundings attuned to a "human scale." She contrasted this with the sterile design of public housing projects that, although much newer and built to higher construction standards, were areas with much higher crime rates and other forms of social dysfunction.

Recent work in urban public health (e.g., see Kawachi and Berkman 2003) shows that an individual's health status depends in part on that individual's own characteristics, including age and income, but also depends on the characteristics of the neighborhood in which the individual resides. In other words, an individual who is seventy-five years old and living below the poverty line will fare better if he lives in a neighborhood with a low crime rate than an otherwise identical person who lives in a more crime-ridden area, even if he is not a crime victim himself.

This is also what Klinenberg found in his study of the 1995 Chicago heat wave. Two neighborhoods in the same part of Chicago, Little Village and North Lawndale, had similar proportions of their elderly populations who were poor and who lived alone—demographic factors that put people at higher risk of dying during a heat wave. Yet, the death rate in North Lawndale was ten times higher than the death rate in Little Village. The contrast, Klinenberg argues, was not due to the differences between individuals, but the differences between the neighborhoods in which they lived. Little Village is a low-income neighborhood that exemplifies the healthy urban environment described by Jane Jacobs. It has a busy street life, lots of commercial establishments mixed in with high-density residential development, and a low crime rate. It is currently a Latino area with a growing population. Many of the elderly residents are remnants of a previous generation of white ethnics who once lived there. Even though they did not share the culture or language of the current residents, the fact that they routinely left their homes to walk on the safe streets or to buy items from the local merchants meant that they were less isolated and that they had easy and regular access to places that were air-conditioned. In contrast, North Lawndale was a high crime rate area that had lost population and in which there were many abandoned lots and hardly any stores. Older people in this neighborhood were not as likely to venture outside their homes—it was too dangerous, and besides, there was no place to go. Poor elderly people living alone in Little Village had the "suitable living environment" promised in the 1949 Housing Act; similarly situated elders in North Lawndale did not, and for some, it was the difference between life and death.

While Little Village was a low-income neighborhood, North Lawndale was an area in which circumstances were far more severe—it was an area of concentrated poverty—defined as a neighborhood in which more than 40 percent of the residents live below the poverty line. In concentrated poverty areas, poor people are likely to interact only with others who are also poor. The extreme segregation and isolation from the world of the nonpoor has toxic effects on residents of these areas. These are high-crime areas in which everyday life is full of stress, which affects mental and physical health. Poor health affects children's performance in school and adults' prospects on the job market. These self-reinforcing effects make it difficult for people in the circumstances to improve their situations.

According to Jargowsky (2003), 10.3 percent of those who live below the poverty line in the United States reside in neighborhoods with concentrated poverty. In New Orleans, however, 37.7 percent of the poor lived in these circumstances—the second-highest rate of concentrated poverty among large cities. Only Fresno, California, had a higher rate, at 43.5 percent. In New Orleans, while 10.9 percent of poor whites and 18 percent of poor Hispanics lived in neighborhoods with concentrated poverty, 42.6 percent of the city's African Americans lived in these dire circumstances.

This high degree of concentrated poverty was, in part, a result of government decisions about where to relocate tenants of condemned public housing projects. According to historian Douglas Brinkley (2006), the condemned projects were close to downtown and accessible by public transportation; the new locations in the Seventh Ward and New Orleans East were more isolated. As Brinkley says, "Many of those new to the neighborhood had worked in what blacks called the 'servant industry,' toiling as hotel maids, parking attendants, or domestic help for well-to-do whites. It was an honest living. Suddenly, with their relocation, they had no easy way to get to work downtown." The geographical and social isolation of these communities left their residents, too poor to own cars, without access to any of the resources that might have allowed them to escape to safer places.

Being poor in America is no picnic, but it does not have to be a death sentence, either. Misguided government policies contributed to the growth in concentrated poverty in the late twentieth century, especially during the 1970s and 1980s. The economic prosperity of the 1990s, with its high employment rates and low unemployment, spurred some reduction in the extent of concentrated poverty. We can also attempt to reduce its impact through better neighborhood design.

Central City Renaissance

In recent years, many central cities have undergone a renaissance. Crime rates have fallen, population has risen, and many central city locations are newly attractive to young professionals, empty nesters, and new waves of immigrants. This was not necessarily what one might have expected as late as the 1970s, when cities like New York were almost considered relics. With so many families fleeing to the suburbs and with the city government virtually bankrupt as properties were abandoned and property tax revenue plummeted, many thought that New York, along with other older cities, would continue to lose population and the people who were left in the city would be increasingly poor.

This has certainly happened in some cities, but the cataclysmic depopulation of some has slowed or even reversed. Indeed, some central cities that were growing very rapidly between 1970 and 2000 have seen a slowdown in population growth, while others have actually reversed their population loss. As **Figure 15.1** reveals, Austin, Texas, for example, grew faster than any of the other twenty central cities we have tracked in this book. Between 1970 and 2000, its population expanded at an annual rate of 3.25 percent. Since 2000, it has continued to grow, but at a much more modest rate—0.85 percent per year. Other cities that have seen their rapid growth slow down (but are still growing) include Phoenix; Tucson; Portland, Oregon; and Tacoma, Washington.

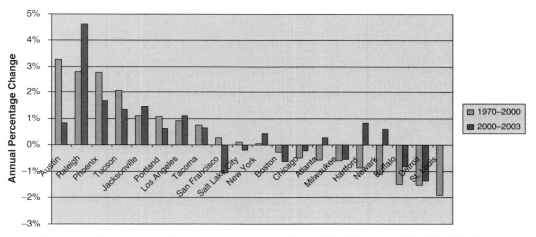

Figure 15.1 Central City Population Growth Annual Percentage Rate, 1970–2000 versus 2000–2003. This figure arrays central city population growth for the twenty cities we have followed throughout the book. Central cities with the largest population growth *increases* (measured in percentages) per year between 1970 and 2000 (Austin, Raleigh, and Phoenix) are on the left, and those with the largest annual population growth *decreases* during that time period (St. Louis, Detroit, and Buffalo) are on the right. As the darker shaded bars show, annual population growth between 2000 and 2003 is, in many cases, very different from the patterns for the previous three decades. For example, annual growth in the central city of Austin dropped from more than 3 percent per year for 1970–2000 to less than 1 percent per year for the period from 2000 to 2003, while growth in Raleigh climbed from just below 3 percent to more than 4.5 percent. Similarly, while the central city population of San Francisco grew slightly during 1970–2000, it dropped by 1 percent per year from 1970 to 2000. Atlanta, Newark, and Buffalo each experienced declining population from 1970 to 2000, but had population increases from 2000 to 2003. St. Louis's population remained constant between 2000 and 2003 and therefore shows no bar for this period. *Source:* U.S. Department of Housing and Urban Development, HUD User Policy Development and Research Information Service, SOCDS data set, 2007, http://socds.huduser.org.

Even though their metropolitan area suburban populations have been growing faster, it is still noteworthy that several central cities have shown increases in their populations after long periods of decline. New York City has actually seen its population growth rate increase since 2000. It had virtually no annual growth between 1970 and 2000 (+0.05%). Since then, it has been growing eight times faster—0.42 percent per year. Atlanta, having seen its population decline from 497,000 in 1970 to 416,000 in 2000, has stopped hemorrhaging. This is also true of Hartford, Newark, and St. Louis. The Missouri central city saw its population plunge from 622,000 in 1970 to only 348,000 in 2000; since then, the population has been nearly constant.

To be sure, there are central cities that have continued their population demise. Milwaukee, Buffalo, and Detroit fall into these ranks. But clearly, the ability to stem population decline in some older cities suggests that a loss in population is not inevitable.

It is also clear that population growth is not necessary for economic success. According to research by Weissbourd and Berry (2004), there was a reasonably high and statistically significant positive correlation between population growth and metro area income growth from at least 1969 through 1991. After that time, the correlation declined in value and was no longer statistically significant. The two researchers concluded that "cities do not need to grow big to become wealthy, and growing big will not necessarily lead to wealth." **Table 15.1**, compiled from their data on population growth from 1990 to 2000, compared with per capita income growth for the largest 100 central cities, demonstrates this conclusion quite clearly— yielding some interesting results in the process.

The table divides the 100 central cities into quartiles on both population growth and income growth. Seven of the cities fall into the top quartile in both population and income. Among these are Austin, Texas; Charlotte, North Carolina; Denver, Colorado; and Portland, Oregon. All of these are cities that have been able to attract large numbers of young professionals who are moving there for good jobs and presumably a pleasant lifestyle. No surprises here. But note that there are also a set of central cities that are in the bottom twenty-five in population growth, but in the top twenty-five in terms of per capita income growth. These include Birmingham, Alabama; Cincinnati; Cleveland; and Dayton, Ohio. These are all cities that experienced substantial deindustrialization with the loss of much of their manufacturing base. Nonetheless, the dramatic loss in population has not automatically translated into stagnant income. Indeed, each of these cities has been able to attract middle-class individuals and some families back to the city to take advantage of highly affordable housing. Other cities like New York have attracted both young professionals and many new immigrants so that their population has grown, but average per capita income saw little improvement in the 1990s. Finally, there is a set of central cities near the bottom in terms of both population and income growth. These include Newark, Philadelphia, Toledo, Milwaukee, and Buffalo. Presumably, these central cities continue to lose middle-class households at a rate faster than most other cities. But if other central cities provide any lesson at all, even they have a chance to become "comeback cities."

Table 15.1 Income Growth versus Population Growth in Central Cities, 1990–2000

		Population Growth, 1990–2000			
		Top 25	**Second 25**	**Third 25**	**Bottom 25**
Per Capita Income Growth, 1990–2000	Top 25	Austin, TX Charlotte, NC Colorado Springs, CO Denver, CO Fremont, CA Portland, OR San Antonio, TX	Columbus, OH Lexington, KY Madison, WI Omaha, NE San Jose, CA Seattle, WA Tacoma, WA Tampa, FL	Atlanta, GA Chicago, IL San Francisco, CA	Birmingham, AL Cincinnati, OH Cleveland, OH Dayton, OH Detroit, MI Louisville, KY Miami, FL
	Second 25	Las Vegas, NV Lincoln, NE Raleigh, NC	Albuquerque, NM El Paso, TX Jacksonville, FL Nashville, TN Spokane, WA	Baton Rouge, LA Boston, MA Indianapolis, IN Jersey City, NJ Little Rock, AR Memphis, TN Minneapolis, MN Oakland, CA St. Petersburg, FL	Kansas City, MO New Orleans, LA Norfolk, VA Pittsburgh, PA Richmond, VA Shreveport, LA St. Louis, MO Washington, DC
	Third 25	Fort Wayne, IN Greensboro, NC Houston, TX Mesa, AZ Phoenix, AZ Tucson, AZ	Arlington, VA Oklahoma, OK San Diego, CA Virginia Beach, VA Wichita, KS	Corpus Christi, TX Des Moines, IA Grand Rapids, MI Lubbock, TX St. Paul, MN	Akron, OH Baltimore, MD Buffalo, NY Milwaukee, WI Mobile, AL Toledo, OH
	Bottom 25	Anaheim, CA Arlington, TX Aurora, CO Bakersfield, CA Dallas, TX Fresno, CA Garland, TX Hialeah, FL	Anchorage, AK Glendale, CA New York, NY Riverside, CA Sacramento, CA Santa Ana, CA Stockton, CA	Huntington Beach, CA Long Beach, CA Los Angeles, CA Newport News, VA Tulsa, OK Yonkers, NY	Honolulu, HI Jackson, MS Newark, NJ Philadelphia, PA Rochester, NY

Note: In this table, cities that were in the top 25 percent (statisticians refer to the top 25 percent as the top "quartile") of population growth *and* in the top quartile of per capita income growth are in the top left corner of the figure (Austin, Charlotte, Colorado Springs, etc.). Cities that were in the top quartile of income growth and the second quartile (ranking from the 26th percentile to the 50th percentile) of population growth are in the top row, second column (Columbus, Lexington, etc.). Cities that were in the top quartile of population growth but the second quartile of per capita income growth are in the first column, second row (Las Vegas, Lincoln, and Raleigh). Cities that were in the bottom quartile of both per capita income and population growth are in the bottom right-hand corner (Honolulu, Jackson, etc.).
Source: Adapted from Weissbourd and Berry 2004, appendix C.

Regeneration for Whom? Rebuilding Central City Neighborhoods

In some cities, low-income residents who have worked hard to make their neighborhoods safer now find that they have been priced out of once-affordable housing. What are the challenges of building desirable communities within central cities? In *When Work Disappears*, William Julius Wilson (1996) describes the hopelessness of many African American Chicago neighborhoods where crime and drug trafficking ran rampant, many adults were locked into low-wage jobs, and others were disconnected from the world of work altogether. In this urban dystopia, communities were depopulated, local stores could not survive, and vacant lots and abandoned buildings were common. School dropout rates were high, academic achievement scores were low, and the next generation was doomed to continue the pattern. Between 1970 and 1990, most large U.S. cities had similar areas of despair and concentrated poverty, particularly affecting African Americans because they are more highly segregated than other low-income minorities. Then, during the 1990s, many inner cities, once designated as areas of concentrated poverty, began to experience a comeback. While severe problems persist in many areas, some neighborhoods were able to improve the circumstances under which their residents lived. What accounts for the turnaround that some places were able to achieve?

The Role of Community Development Corporations

Starting in the late 1960s in some areas, local residents and merchants, often joined by local religious organizations and other stakeholders, formed nonprofit groups—**community development corporations** (**CDCs**)—to improve conditions in their low- and moderate-income neighborhoods, primarily through housing construction and job creation. The Ford Foundation created the Local Initiatives Support Corporation (LISC) in 1980 to provide technical and financial support to many of these organizations. According to the National Congress for Community Economic Development, CDCs across the United States had created 550,000 units of affordable housing and 247,000 private-sector jobs by 1998.

However, CDCs have been the subject of controversy. In a widely disseminated *New York Times Sunday Magazine* article, the journalist Nicholas Lemann (1994) questions the entire strategy of ghetto job development, including the role played by CDCs. He argues that offering economic inducements to get major firms that operate in national or international markets to locate in inner-city neighborhoods that they would otherwise avoid simply does not work. He points out that the emphasis on job development inside the ghetto through these inducements is misplaced, as long as jobs can be found elsewhere. After all, most people do not live and work in the same neighborhood.

He concludes that for political reasons, it is more acceptable for CDCs to emphasize their role in job creation, even though their major contributions have been in the creation of housing. While criticizing what is, in his view, a futile effort focused on economic development, Lemann nevertheless lauds the social service role that CDCs play in delivering affordable housing, health services, child care, and education and training programs.

In *Comeback Cities*, Paul Grogan (a former president of LISC) and Tony Proscio (2000) describe the four ingredients they view as necessary to transform inner-city neighborhoods. CDCs are one of them; they are the agencies through which housing, small business, and social capital can be rebuilt in places where it has been destroyed. Through CDCs, residents and other local stakeholders develop their own leadership to respond to the needs of the existing community.

The second ingredient is private investment. As social capital is accumulated, as depopulation is halted, and as new housing is built, the area becomes more inviting to local businesses. When merchants are willing to invest in the area, a virtuous cycle begins—more jobs and housing are created, abandoned buildings are recycled, and vacant lots are filled in. "Exit" gives way to "voice," and some residents who have the option of leaving choose to stay and work toward further improvement.

Retail trade is one of the areas for private investment where inner cities actually have an advantage. While the average household income in central city neighborhoods, particularly those with large numbers of low-income families, is well below the average household income of suburban residents, the much greater density of housing in the inner city means that the average retail demand *per square mile* in central city neighborhoods is usually much higher than in the suburbs. According to a 1998 study by the Boston Consulting Group (BCS), retail demand per square mile for food and apparel was an estimated $116 million in Harlem, New York, compared with $53 million across the rest of the New York metropolitan area. In other cities, similar disparities in retail demand per mile were found: In Chicago, the BCS estimated that households' combined retail demand per square mile was $57 million, compared with $27 million across the entire metro area. In Boston, the inner city to metro region ratio was $71 million to $12 million per square mile (Boston Consulting Group 1998).

Based on such studies and the proselytizing by the Initiative for a Competitive Inner City, an organization formed by Harvard University's Michael Porter, a number of inner-city retail malls have been established in cities, including New York and Boston. Those like the South Cove Mall in the Dorchester neighborhood of Boston have attracted national chain stores that include Home Depot, Stop & Shop Supermarkets, and Staples. They generally report higher sales volume per square foot of retail space than their suburban outlets because of the density of the demand per square mile and the general absence of competition in the inner-city communities where they have built stores. By diversifying their product lines to appeal to inner-city multiracial and multiethnic communities, many of these stores are prospering. In 2007, Wal-Mart decided to build fifty stores in low-income urban neighborhoods to take advantage of the retail opportunities there (Miara 2007).

In addition to the role of CDCs and the role of private markets, Grogan and Proscio argue that the two other necessary ingredients for the renaissance of low-income, inner-city neighborhoods are the reduction of crime rates—part of which automatically occurs as the virtuous circle begins to increase the liveliness of the area's streets and provides jobs for local residents—and a reduction in the monolithic force of the welfare, public housing, and public school bureaucracies. Local, state, and federal governments have important roles to play in facilitating these reforms: a shift to community policing, an income maintenance system that promotes independence and supports work effort, a redesign of public housing that avoids large-scale high-rise buildings, and a school system that offers more choice and is more accountable for its outcomes.

Citing the failure of the 1960s War on Poverty to eliminate poverty altogether and the recognition that the elimination of poverty is not a goal likely to be reached in the foreseeable future, the real task, say Grogan and Proscio, is to create decent neighborhoods for low- and moderate-income households today. With these four ingredients in place, they argue that it is possible for low-income households to live in decent circumstances despite their poverty.

Demographic Change and Low-Income Communities

One important demographic change in central cities cited by Grogan and Proscio (2000) is the recent large wave of immigration. They argue that although changes in the legislation that affect immigration—whether it is the restrictions put in place in the 1920s or their removal in 1965—never had the explicit purpose of affecting the well-being of urban areas, they have nevertheless had an important unintended consequence for central cities. The roughly forty-year period in the mid-twentieth century in which immigration was severely reduced coincided with the decline in central city fortunes. As residents of central city neighborhoods departed for the suburbs, there was no one to replace them, and thus the depopulation trend commenced. With the flow of new immigrants restored after 1965, depopulation in the gateway cities was finally halted. Those cities that are not destinations for immigrants continue to suffer.

College students and young professionals are another source of new residents. Urban-based institutions of higher learning, once viewed primarily in an adversarial role by their host cities, have also stabilized neighborhood economies in many low-income areas. Though tensions persist, universities and the communities in which they are located have tried to find common ground in pursuing mutually beneficial outcomes.

Along with immigrants, students, and young professionals, artists have long been attracted to areas with cheap housing and available loft space. New York and Boston are not the only places that have benefited from artists helping to stabilize an area. Even smaller cities, such as the very old industrial mill town of Pawtucket, Rhode Island, have tried to attract artists to converted mill space as a strategy for regeneration.

The Perils of Success

What happens when a neighborhood is successful in regenerating itself? What are the rewards for the hard efforts of those who survived the bad times to share in the newfound safety and stability? In some instances, the area becomes so attractive that real estate values soar and residents are victims of their own success. Property owners might reap the windfall of higher values, but residential renters and small business owners who lease retail or commercial space may find that they are priced out of the area.

Neighborhoods that are initially attractive to higher-income households because of their economic and racial diversity become less diverse over time as property values soar. Similarly, small business owners in successful retail districts are succeeded by franchises of national companies who can afford to outbid them for retail space. As demonstrated in Chapter 5, a process of gentrification takes hold.

This can be a double-edged sword. On the one hand, cities benefit from higher tax receipts and all neighborhood residents stand to benefit from the economic and political power of higher-income residents who have committed themselves to city living and who demand, and often receive, better public services. To the extent that an influx of more privileged families means cleaner and safer streets, better public schools, and more frequent bus service for everyone in the neighborhood, the longer-term residents who preceded the gentrification wave may be better off.

On the other hand, without some protection against soaring rent increases, there is a "killing the goose that laid the golden egg" aspect to this process. The initially attractive features of the area as someplace unique begin to disappear as the one-of-a-kind funky stores and restaurants are displaced by the more standardized fare available in any generic shopping mall. The longer-term residents who gave the place its character and stability and who endured when the area suffered through hard times are replaced by new arrivals who are generally younger and better educated. The area has become less diverse—more segregated—not only by race and income, but also by age.

As a society, we have been effective in fulfilling the desires of those who seek segregation. Through market forces reinforced by public policy decisions, we have created communities segregated by race and/or income. We have been far less effective in fulfilling the desires of those who seek diversity. Our record in creating and sustaining communities integrated both by race and by income has been disappointing.

Over the next few decades, the influx of new immigrants and their children will continue to change the racial and ethnic mix of our society. As the baby-boom generation ages and as life expectancies grow, the age composition of our nation will also change. Long-term economic changes in our industrial structure—the impact of globalization and new technologies—will affect how and where we work, and the nature of work itself. If present trends continue, the earnings gap between those who are highly educated and those who are not will continue to grow, and economic inequality will be even more pronounced. In a society that is demographically more diverse but also more unequal with respect to income and wealth, will we be able to move any closer toward achieving the goal of providing "a decent home and a suitable living environment for every American family," which was set more than half a century ago? It is one of the great challenges we will need to address in shaping the U.S. metropolitan areas of the twenty-first century.

References

Berube, Alan, and Bruce Katz. 2005. "Katrina's Window: Confronting Concentrated Poverty across America." Special Analysis in Metropolitan Policy. Washington, D.C.: Brookings Institution, October. http://www.brookings.edu/metro/pubs/20051012_Concentratedpoverty.pdf.

Blakely, Edward J., and Mary Gail Snyder. 1997. *Fortress America: Gated Communities in the United States.* Washington, D.C.: Brookings Institution.

Boston Consulting Group. 1998. "The Business Case for Pursuing Retail Opportunities in the Inner City." June. http://imaps.indygov.org/ed_portal/studies/bcg_inner_city_retail.pdf.

Briffault, Richard. 1999. "A Government for Our Time? Business Improvement Districts and Urban Governance." *Columbia Law Review* 99, no. 2: 365–477.

Brinkley, Douglas. 2006. *The Great Deluge: Hurricane Katrina, New Orleans, and the Mississippi Gulf Coast.* New York: HarperCollins.

Brueckner, Jan K., and Ann G. Largey. 2007. "Social Interaction and Urban Sprawl." University of California Irvine Working Paper Series, August.

Fischel, William. 2001. *The Homevoter Hypothesis: How Home Values Influence Local Government Taxation, School Finance, and Land-Use Policy.* Cambridge, Mass.: Harvard University Press.

Granovetter, Mark. 1973. "The Strength of Weak Ties." *American Journal of Sociology* 78, no. 6 (May): 1360–1380.

Grogan, Paul S., and Tony Proscio. 2000. *Comeback Cities: A Blueprint for Urban Neighborhood Revival.* Boulder, Colo.: Westview Press.

Hirschman, Albert O. 1970. *Exit, Voice, and Loyalty: Responses to Decline in Firms, Organizations, and States.* Cambridge, Mass.: Harvard University Press.

Hoyt, Lorlene, and Devika Gopal-Agge. 2007. "The Business Improvement District Model: A Balanced Review of Contemporary Debates." *Geography Compass* 1, no. 4: 946–958.

Jacobs, Jane. 1961. *The Death and Life of Great American Cities.* New York: Random House.

Jargowsky, Paul A. 2003. "Stunning Progress, Hidden Problems: The Dramatic Decline of Concentrated Poverty in the 1990s." Living Cities Census Series. Washington, D.C.: Brookings Institution, May. http://www.brookings.edu/~/media/Files/rc/reports/2003/05demo graphics_jargowsky/jargowskypoverty.pdf.

Jeffery, C. Ray. 1971. *Crime Prevention through Environmental Design.* Beverly Hills, Calif.: Sage.

Kawachi, Ichiro, and Lisa F. Berkman. 2003. *Neighborhoods and Health.* New York: Oxford University Press.

Kelling, George L., and James Q. Wilson. 1982. "Broken Windows." *Atlantic Monthly* 249, no. 3 (March): 29–38.

Klinenberg, Eric. 2002. *Heat Wave: A Social Autopsy of Disaster in Chicago.* Chicago: University of Chicago Press.

Lemann, Nicholas. 1994. "The Myth of Community Development." *New York Times Sunday Magazine*, January 9, pp. 27–31, 50, 54, 60.

Low, Setha. 2003. *Behind the Gates: Life, Security, and the Pursuit of Happiness in Fortress America.* New York: Routledge.

McPherson, Miller, Lynn Smith-Lovin, and Matthew E. Brashears. 2006. "Social Isolation in America: Changes in Core Discussion Networks over Two Decades." *American Sociological Review* 71, no. 3 (June): 353–375.

Miara, James. 2007. "Retail in Inner Cities." *Urban Land* (January): 98–105.

Moe, Terry M. 2001. *Schools, Vouchers, and the American Public.* Washington, D.C.: Brookings Institution Press.

Nelson, Robert H. 2005. *Private Neighborhoods and the Transformation of Local Government.* Washington, D.C.: Urban Institute Press.

Newman, Oscar. 1972. *Defensible Space: Crime Prevention through Urban Design.* New York: Macmillan.

Oberlander, N. Peter, and Eva Newbrun. 1999. *Houser: The Life and Work of Catherine Bauer.* Vancouver: University of British Columbia Press.

Okun, Arthur M. 1975. *Equality and Efficiency: The Big Tradeoff.* Washington, D.C.: Brookings Institution Press.

Podobnik, Bruce. 2002. "New Urbanism and the Generation of Social Capital: Evidence from Orenco Station." *National Civic Review* 91, no. 3 (Fall): 245–255.

Putnam, Robert D. 2000. *Bowling Alone: The Collapse and Revival of American Community.* New York: Simon & Schuster.

———. 2007. "*E Pluribus Unum:* Diversity and Community in the Twenty-First Century. The 2006 Johan Skytte Prize Lecture." *Scandinavian Political Studies* 30, no. 2: 137–174.

Putnam, Robert D., and Lewis M. Feldstein, with Don Cohen. 2003. *Better Together: Restoring the American Community.* New York: Simon & Schuster.

Reich, Robert B. 1991. *The Work of Nations: Preparing Ourselves for 21st-Century Capitalism.* New York: Alfred A. Knopf.

Sander, Thomas H. 2002. "Social Capital and New Urbanism: Leading a Civic Horse to Water?" *National Civic Review* 91, no. 3 (Fall): 213–234.

Tiebout, Charles. 1956. "A Pure Theory of Local Expenditures." *Journal of Political Economy* 64, no. 5 (October): 416–424.

U.S. Department of Housing and Urban Development. 2007. HUD User Policy Development and Research Information Service. SOCDS (State of the Cities Data Systems) data set. http://socds.huduser.org.

Weissbourd, Robert, and Christopher Berry. 2004. *The Changing Dynamics of Urban America.* Chicago: CEOs for Cities, March 30.

Williamson, Thad. 2002. "Sprawl, Politics, and Participation: A Preliminary Analysis." *National Civic Review* 91, no. 3 (Fall): 235–244.

Wilson, William J. 1996. *When Work Disappears: The World of the New Urban Poor.* New York: Alfred A. Knopf.

Chapter 15 Questions and Exercises

1. The U.S. Bureau of the Census tracks changes in housing patterns through the American Housing Survey. Data is collected for forty-seven metro areas on a revolving basis, with each of these metro areas surveyed at least once every six years. The data for specific metro areas is available on the Web at

    http://www.census.gov/hhes/www/housing/ahs/metropolitandata.html

    Go to this Web site and pick one of the metro areas that have been surveyed since 2000. Click on the latest year for that metro area. When the report appears, scroll down to Table 2.8. You will note that the total number of occupied units is given in the first row. On the second page of the table you will see a section titled "Secured Communities," with a row titled "Community access secured with walls or fences." (*Note:* these are also known as gated communities.)

    + What is the total number of occupied units in this category for the metro area you selected?
    + What percentage of the total number of occupied units does this represent? (Divide by the total occupied units in the first row of the table.)
    + How many of the occupied houses in these "gated neighborhoods" had been built in the previous four years? (See the column titled "New construction 4 years.")
    + What percentage do these recently built units in gated neighborhoods rep-

resent of all occupied units built in the past four years? (See this same column in the top row of the table.)

2. Repeat the above inquiry for two other metro areas from regions of the United States different from the metro area you picked above. What similarities or differences do you see in the data among the three metro areas you selected?

3. Where are the places, if any, in which you talk about important issues with other people? (Do not include school.) In what ways are the people with whom you talk similar to you, and in what ways are they different?

Glossary

absolute advantage: The ability of one firm, region, or country to produce a commodity using fewer resources per unit of output than any other firm, region, or country.

accelerated depreciation: Under this provision of the federal income tax, firms (or landlords) can deduct a large proportion of the cost of maintenance in the early years of such an investment rather than spreading out the deduction in equal shares over the full expected life of the property improvement. This reduces the amount of income tax paid by the firm or landlord.

affordable housing: According to the U.S. Department of Housing and Urban Development, housing for which the household pays no more than 30 percent of its own income in rent including utilities or in mortgage payments.

agglomeration economies: Reduced costs in an economic activity that result from enterprises or activities locating near one another. There are two types of agglomeration economies: localization economies and urbanization economies.

allocation role of government: The role that governments play when they change the amount of goods and services that would otherwise be produced in a market economy.

allocative efficiency: The use of resources to produce the particular combination of goods and services that maximizes consumer satisfaction.

amortize: To pay off a debt (e.g., a mortgage) through periodic agreed-upon installments, gradually reducing the balance owed.

annexation: The extension of the geographic boundaries of a city or town by adding a neighboring area or municipality to its jurisdiction.

asking rent: The rent advertised for a house or apartment as the owner seeks a tenant.

asymmetric information: Unequal information held by the buyer and seller in a market exchange. For example, a used car dealer may know more than the prospective buyer about the quality of a car being sold.

attributes theory of consumer behavior: An approach to understanding consumer behavior emphasizing that a good is actually a combination of attributes (characteristics), and that these attributes hold value for a consumer. From this perspective, the source of consumer demand for a specific good (e.g., a house or a car) is the demand for a specific combination of attributes exhibited by that good.

average-cost curve: A curve that depicts the cost per unit of output, where the cost of all inputs—fixed and variable—are included. The typical average-cost curve is U-shaped, which reflects the fact that at low levels of output, fixed costs must be spread over a small number of units of output, raising average cost per unit. At some medium level of output, average costs are minimized. At high levels of output, shortages of some inputs require paying a higher price for these, raising the average cost per unit.

average total cost curve (long run): The average total cost curve during a time period sufficiently long that increases in plant and equipment can occur. Thus, the long-run average cost curve depicts production costs when all inputs can be increased.

average total cost curve (short run): The average total cost curve during a short enough time period that no changes in plant and equipment can take place. Any increase in output is due only to increased use of labor and raw materials.

basic/nonbasic approach: An approach to understanding urban economic growth in which production is divided into two sectors. "Basic production" and related "basic jobs" pertain to firms that produce goods and/or services for export to other regions in return for payments from consumers from those other regions. Export can refer to sales to other municipalities, states, or nations. "Nonbasic production" and "nonbasic jobs" pertain to firms whose goods/services are not exported, but instead are only sold locally.

bid rent: The amount renters or buyers are willing to offer in order to gain access to and use of a specific parcel of land.

bid rent curve: A graph that shows the maximum amounts (represented on the vertical axis) that a type of land user (e.g., commercial businesses) would be willing to pay for land, as the distance from the city center increases (represented on the horizontal axis).

bioterrorism: The use of disease-causing microorganisms (such as bacteria, fungi, or viruses) to create panic arising from health crises within a civilian population.

boards of health: Individuals appointed by state or local governments to oversee the quality of public health in an area, to pursue initiatives designed to increase health-related services, promote healthy behavior, and prevent disease and injury.

broken windows/zero tolerance: An approach to crime prevention that emphasizes police response to vandalism and minor disorder. The underlying reasoning is that if potential criminals notice such response, they are likely to believe that residents and city government care about what happens in those locations, that criminal activity is more likely to be observed and reported in that area, and that arrest is more likely.

budget constraint: The limit on a household's purchasing power due to the limited money the household has available to spend. In graphs, the budget constraint is a line that represents the various combinations of goods and services a household can buy with a given income.

building codes: Standards and specifications contained in government regulations, designed to establish minimum safeguards for the construction of buildings, and to protect the people who live and work in them from fire, threats to health, and other hazards.

building code violations: Failure to comply with government regulations pertaining to the construction, design, maintenance, or maximum capacity (the number of people allowed inside) of buildings.

building construction guidelines: Regulations covering the type and quality of materials used, design, size, height, or other aspects of building construction.

bump rate: The frequency with which two or more parties come into contact with each other and share ideas.

business cycle: A fluctuation in the level of economic activity where output expands and then contracts or vice versa.

business improvement district (BID): An association formed by businesses within an area to provide services (such as street cleaning or security patrols) beyond the level of services provided by the municipal government.

capital resources: Buildings (e.g., factories, offices) and equipment (e.g., tools, machinery) used in the production of goods and services.

census tract: An official small census unit that usually contains between 2,500 and 8,000 persons who are more or less homogeneous with respect to population characteristics, economic status, and living conditions.

central business district (CBD): A densely developed center of a city, used primarily for business activities.

central city: The largest municipality, containing more than 50,000 population, in a metropolitan area. Under certain conditions regarding size and commuting patterns, there can be more than one central city in a given metropolitan area. Also known as a "principal city."

central place theory: A theory asserting that there is a hierarchy of size and function among cities and towns within any given region, based upon the market areas of different types of firms located in each city or town. At the top of the hierarchy are cities that contain industries producing goods and services for export widely throughout a region, nation, or the globe. Lower in the hierarchy are municipalities that produce goods and services for local consumption or for consumption in those cities at the top of the central place hierarchy.

centrifugal force: Factors that encourage dispersal of activities away from a center toward the outskirts.

centripetal force: Factors that encourage locational choice toward the center of a city.

ceteris paribus: Latin for "other things being equal"; a theoretical condition used frequently in economic explanations. To focus attention upon a limited number of factors, other things that could change are assumed to be held constant.

charter schools: Schools established by private groups that provide publicly funded education under contracts (charters) with designated government educational authorities.

circular causation with cumulative effect: The theory that a small change in one direction leads to a large effect in that direction, while a small change in another direction leads to a large effect in that direction. As an example, small differences in initial schooling can lead to large changes in life opportunities.

Coase theorem: The theory that externalities do not necessarily require government intervention and that private bargaining between those producing externalities and those that they potentially affect will lead to optimal outcomes if three conditions hold. These conditions are that property rights are clearly specified, the number of parties involved is small, and the costs of bargaining are negligible.

cognitive maps: Mental "maps" of a community created by employers and other decision makers that reflect their beliefs about the strengths and weaknesses of each location as a place to live, establish a business, or from which to hire new employees. Cognitive maps can be based on impressions and beliefs rather than objective reality and can lead to certain forms of discrimination.

combined statistical area (CSA): As defined by the U.S. Bureau of the Census, a large urbanized area that links together metropolitan statistical areas (MSAs) where there is a substantial amount of commuting between individual metropolitan areas. These combined statistical areas can cover hundreds of square miles.

common interest developments: Private organizations formed by individual households or business firms to pursue common goals through shared consumption of goods and services.

communicable diseases: Diseases that can be transmitted through contact with other humans or contact with other living organisms. Communicable diseases can be contrasted with noncommunicable diseases, such as scurvy, which arise because of nutritional or other deficiencies, and are not transmittable.

community-based organizations (CBOs): Any of a broad range of nonprofit organizations based in urban neighborhoods and dedicated to improving the quality of life for their residents.

community development corporations (CDCs): Nonprofit groups formed to improve conditions in low- and moderate-income neighborhoods, primarily through housing construction and job creation.

community-oriented policing: An approach toward crime that emphasizes the creation of a close relationship between police and neighborhood residents, with the objective of building neighborhood residents' capacity to prevent crime, solving neighborhood problems that may be related to crime levels, and linking crime prevention by police and residents with other municipal services.

comparative advantage: A country or region has a comparative advantage in producing a good or service, relative to another region or country, if the relative cost of producing the good or service—its opportunity cost in terms of other goods forgone—is lower than it is in the other region. Even if one region has an absolute advantage in the production of two goods, the region without absolute advantage has comparative advantage in the production of the good whose opportunity cost is less than the opportunity cost of the region with absolute advantage. Under comparative advantage, maximum output and maximum utility is achieved when each region concentrates its resources in the production of the good or service for which its opportunity cost of production is lowest and then trades some of this good or service for some of the good or service produced in the other region.

competitive advantage: A firm's (or region's, or nation's) success in a particular industry against rival firms (or regions or nations) producing the same, or a similar, product. Competitive advantage can be gained either through low-cost production or product differentiation—producing a unique product or one that is considered to be of higher quality or more innovative.

complex good: A good that embodies several different characteristics of importance to a consumer. Because the characteristics of a complex good typically involve several types of value, consumers' choices about such goods involve trade-offs between the different types of value. For example, housing may be valued for its size, layout, amenities, proximity to work, and the quality of the school district where the house is located. The choice of a particular house depends upon how much the home buyer values each of these different aspects relative to each other and the trade-offs that he or she is willing to make in terms of these varied attributes.

comprehensive community health centers: Centers funded by the U.S. Congress to provide a wide array of medical services and health outreach in urban and rural low-income areas.

congestion pricing: Varying the tolls on a roadway, bridge, or tunnel so that motorists are charged the most during periods of heaviest traffic (congestion).

consolidated metropolitan statistical area (CMSA): As defined by the U.S. Bureau of the Census and used until 2003 for what is now termed a combined statistical area (CSA).

constrained maximization: Maximizing a particular goal given a set of limits on resources. For example, a consumer seeks to maximize the utility he or she gets from the consumption of a set of goods and services subject to a budget constraint, that is, a limit on the amount he or she can spend.

consumer markets: The sale of goods and services from firms to households, or the locations in which such sale takes place.

consumer sovereignty: The idea that the desires of individual consumers either (1) are paramount in an economy, or (2) that they should be paramount. The first way of using the term asserts that what consumers want actually determines what is produced in a society. The second way of using the term is an assertion about how things should be: that consumers should decide for themselves what to buy, rather than having their purchases affected by government regulations that influence production or choice.

consumption: Spending by households on goods and services.

contagious diseases: Diseases that can be passed from one person to another. Contagious diseases are one category of communicable diseases (diseases that can be either passed from human to human or contracted through contact with other living organisms).

co-pays: The amount from a bill for medical services that a person with health insurance is required to pay out of pocket; the portion of the medical bill that remains after the health insurance company has paid its share.

core-based statistical area (CBSA): As defined by the U.S. Bureau of the Census, a term in use since 2003, to refer either to a metropolitan or micropolitan statistical area.

corporate welfare: A term used by some journalists to describe the public provision of direct and indirect subsidies for capital and other costs as incentives to businesses.

correspondence principle: The theory that the school system is established in order to provide the labor market with the number of skilled and unskilled workers it requires.

cost-benefit analysis: A study to determine whether a proposed project is worthwhile, by assessing current and future costs and benefits from the project. The general mathematical framework in which cost-benefit analysis occurs expresses the present value of the difference between the stream of current and future benefits and the stream of current and future costs: Σ (Benefits$_t$ − Costs$_t$) / (1 + r)$_t$.

cost-burdened housing: Housing costs that exceed 30 percent of a household's pretax annual income (see "affordable housing").

cost-effectiveness analysis: A technique closely related to cost-benefit analysis that attempts to find the least cost method for obtaining a particular objective even when the value of the objective cannot be judged against the cost of obtaining it.

cost-of-living index: An index of the cost of maintaining a given standard of living. This is found by measuring the total cost of a specified set of goods and services commonly bought by consumers and measuring the change in the cost of purchasing this market basket of goods and services over time.

county: One of the geographic areas established as a primary legal division of most states. Outside of New England, each metropolitan area is a collection of counties.

creative class: As defined by Richard Florida, the group of workers in science and engineering, architecture and design, education, arts, and music and entertainment whose economic function is to create new ideas, new technology, and/or new creative content.

creative destruction: The replacement of older industries and economic activity in a region with new industries and economic activities.

cross hauling: The simultaneous shipment of the same (or similar) goods between two (or more) cities or regions. For example, a brand of yogurt produced in New England might be sold in New York, while another brand of yogurt produced in New York is sold in New England.

cross-subsidies: Paying for services that operate at a loss using the revenue derived from other services that operate at a profit.

cultural/tourism/recreation centers: Cities (or metropolitan areas) where activities tied to recreation, culturally significant venues, and historically important sites constitute a large part of the economic base, or where such activities are the dominant source of economic growth.

decision accretion: The gradual, uncoordinated buildup of small actions and small decisions from different offices within an organization without consideration and analysis of the implications of these changes.

de facto: A Latin term meaning "from reality." De facto is often used to indicate that a phenomenon is occurring without formal legal authorization (in other words, not "de jure"). For example, de facto segregation is segregation that exists due to economic factors or social behavior, not imposed by law.

defensible space: An architectural term referring to design elements that deter crime. This can be accomplished through the physical design of an area by raising the likelihood that a crime will be seen and reported, reducing the number of places in which a perpetrator could hide, and creating public spaces that foster a sense of ownership and responsibility among residents.

deindustrialization: The rapid loss of factories and factory-related jobs to other parts of the country or to other nations or to the cessation or sharp reduction of production activities in key industries for any reason.

de jure: A Latin term meaning "from law." For example, de jure segregation is segregation that is written into law and maintained through the enforcement of such law.

demand: The quantity of a good or service that an individual, group, or nation is willing and able to buy at a specified price.

demerit good: A good whose consumption is deemed intrinsically harmful (or harmful beyond a certain amount of consumption), but which, due to imperfect knowledge or unaccounted-for externalities, individuals would nevertheless choose to consume in excessive amounts. The consumption of demerit goods (such as cigarettes) is often discouraged by government—through regulation or taxation—because of the known or alleged negative consequences to society.

demographics: Statistical data about the characteristics of the population within a specified geographic area.

demographic shifts: Changes in the population characteristics of a city, suburb, or other geographic area. These would include changes in the racial and ethnic composition of the population, as well as changes in its age structure, its nativity, or number of people per household.

design zoning: Regulating the use of land to promote efficient use of a city's infrastructure or to conserve open spaces.

diseconomies of scale: Factors that cause long-run average cost to increase as a firm attempts to increase its output. For example, diseconomies of scale may arise from problems in communication or coordination as a large organization continues to grow.

disembodied knowledge: Knowledge that has been written down by people with skills and insight, so that it can be learned by others rather than only learned only through experience.

dissimilarity index: A measure of the difference in the patterns in which two population groups are spread across a geographic area. Used in studies of housing markets and social dynamics, the dissimilarity index shows the extent to which each census tract or neighborhood within the geographic area replicates the racial composition of the area as a whole.

distribution costs (transportation): The costs of taking finished products to be sold from the production site to the place where they will be sold (the market).

distribution of income and wealth: The share of income or wealth received by different segments of a community or nation.

division of labor: A system of production in which different people are assigned different types of work.

downward filtering: A succession of ownership (or rental residency) that moves down income levels from higher-income families to middle-income families to lower-income families.

dual labor market: A labor market in which there is a "primary" sector, containing jobs that pay relatively high wages, provide good working conditions and reasonable employment stability, and offer chances of advancement; and a "secondary" sector, containing jobs that tend to be low-paying with poor working conditions and considerable instability, little chance for advancement, and high turnover.

economic base: Economic activities that produce goods and services that can be sold outside the metropolitan area, generating income for those in the metro area from those residing in other regions. Economic base theory states that such firms are the primary determining factor in the economic growth of a town or region.

economic profit: The return that a business owner receives over and above what is necessary to keep him or her willingly in business. This is typically thought of as the amount above the return the owner would receive in the owner's next-best business alternative.

economies of scale: Factors that cause a firm's long-run average cost to decrease as the firm's output increases. For example, large-scale production permits specialization in the use of labor, buying in bulk, and other ways of acquiring and using resources, all of which may help to lower costs.

edge cities: A term used to describe a pattern of urban growth where there are concentrations of economic activity and residences in the outer rings of metropolitan areas. Edge cities are typically built around large retail malls or the intersection of two major highways. According to Joel Garreau, who introduced the term in the early 1990s, an edge city must include at least 5 million square feet of leasable office space and 600,000 square feet of retail space.

education management organizations (EMOs): Private firms that specialize in the management of schools. Such firms operate under contract with municipal governments or other school authorities, replacing the previous management structure of the schools, while using the existing teachers and other school staff.

education production function: A mathematical representation of the relationship between inputs in the educational process, such as the teacher/student ratio in a school or the number of library books, and educational outcomes, such as graduation rates or scores on standardized tests.

education vouchers: Educational systems in which households are entitled to a certain amount of public funding for a child's education, regardless of whether the child attends public, private, or parochial (religiously oriented) schools. Parents of school-age children typically receive a document (called a voucher) that can be used toward the payment of tuition at any school within the voucher system.

effective rent: The rent that is actually paid by a tenant. The effective rent is the asking rent adjusted for any special charges or discounts.

efficiency: Using resources in the most optimal way. This entails either maximizing output (being as productive as possible) with a given set of inputs, or minimizing the amount of inputs needed to produce a given amount of output.

elitism: The belief that public-sector decision making reflects the interests and values of powerful individuals or groups, rather than the interests of the public at large.

emergency medical services: The provision of emergency services, such as cardiopulmonary resuscitation, control of bleeding, administration of lifesaving drugs, and other potentially lifesaving techniques, by trained personnel from the public or private sectors, who specialize in on-the-scene medical interventions for injured or ill people prior to and during transportation to hospitals.

emergency medical technicians (EMTs): Trained personnel who travel to a scene in ambulances to provide emergency medical services.

eminent domain: The power of local government to take private land for public use.

empowerment zone: An economically distressed area eligible for tax and regulatory relief under the Federal Empowerment Zone program, initiated in 1993.

enterprise zone (EZ): An economically distressed area eligible for tax and regulatory relief (e.g., sales tax exemptions, tax waivers, building permit fee waivers, subsidies) under state enterprise zone laws.

entitlement: A benefit available by law automatically to all qualifying individuals or households.

envelope curve: In the study of cost curves, an envelope curve depicts the minimum cost production process for any level of output, given all the possible production processes available.

environmental justice: Fairness to all racial, ethnic, or socioeconomic groups, with respect to the environmental impacts of industrial, municipal, and commercial activities and with respect to the environmental impacts of government policies and programs.

epidemics: Diseases that affect many more people than usual, and rapidly spread to others.

equity: Fairness in the distribution of resources or income.

excludable: Capable of being provided to one person and not to others. Excludable goods/services can be purchased and consumed by one person, without others having access to the good/service that has been purchased. This contrasts with nonexcludable goods, which, once they are provided, are accessible to everyone. For example, most privately purchased goods (e.g., an ice cream cone) are excludable. A good like national defense is nonexcludable since, if it is provided, all presumably benefit from it.

exclusionary zoning: Regulating the use of land to bar one or more demographic groups (e.g., racial groups, ethnic groups, or income groups) from areas of a city or town.

export: A good or service that is produced in one metropolitan area (or region, or country) and sold to consumers from another metropolitan area (or region, or country).

export base theory: A theory which states that the demand from other regions for an area's exports is the key driving force in that area's economic prosperity.

expulsive zoning: The use of local zoning ordinances to bar use of land for activities that produce negative externalities in areas populated by a particular race/ ethnicity group, while allowing those activities in areas populated by other race/ ethnicities. The unwanted externalities are essentially expelled from the former areas into the nonprotected areas.

external diseconomies: A cost that arises from an economic activity that does not fall on the person or firm producing or consuming the goods or services produced by that activity.

external economies: A benefit that arises from an economic activity that does not accrue to the person or firm producing or consuming the goods or services produced by that activity.

externalities: A cost or benefit in production or consumption that does not accrue to the producer or consumer of the commodity.

externality zoning: Regulating the use of land to separate activities that create negative externalities from other activities that may be adversely affected by those externalities.

exurban regions: Areas or towns that are located in the rural areas beyond what are considered to be the suburbs of a city.

fee: A fixed amount of money charged for a service or privilege.

fee simple: A legal tradition in which, at the most fundamental level, land is owned by government, and the ownership of private property by individuals and other private entities is a right conferred by government. The implication of fee simple is that governments can revoke the right of ownership. This is the legal underpinning for eminent domain.

finance cities (centers): Cities (or metropolitan areas) where access and expertise that link firms and individuals to financial services (such as potential investors, sources of loans, accounting, wealth management and/or insurance) constitute a large part of the economic base, or where such activities are the dominant source of growth.

first-mover advantage: The benefit from being first into a market with a new product.

fiscal zoning: Regulating the use of land to bar changes that would adversely affect tax revenue or the municipal budget.

fixed costs: Costs that do not vary with the level of output.

free rider problem: The ability of individuals or firms to legally enjoy consumer goods or services without having to pay for them. This phenomenon exists in the case of nonexcludable goods where no provision for payment through taxes or special user fees is established.

gated communities: Privately owned residential areas created by home owners' associations where fences, gates, and walls exclude those who do not own property within.

gentrification: The displacement of low- and moderate-income residents from an area due to rising housing values, and their replacement with higher-income families.

globalization: The increased integration of economic activity (including trade, investment, production, technological change, and other activities) across national boundaries.

gross flows of employment: Measures of the creation of new jobs (through the expansion of existing establishments and employment in new start-ups) and the destruction of existing jobs (the result of company contractions; out-of-state relocations; and plant, store, and office closings). Gross flows can be contrasted with net changes in employment, which do not capture the separate dynamics of creation and destruction of jobs.

growth machine: A concept that emphasizes the role of real estate investors, bankers, and other local business interests acting out of self-interest to promote intensification of land use as their primary objective.

hazmat trucks: Trucks that carry industrial waste, nuclear waste, chemicals, or other materials that are potentially hazardous to humans.

hedonic price index: A statistical technique that seeks to quantify the value of each of the various attributes of a complex good.

highest and best use: The use of market competition to determine the most productive use for land or other goods.

household: All the people who occupy an individual housing unit. A household includes all related family members and all unrelated individuals, if any—such as lodgers, foster children, wards, or employees—who share a single housing unit. A household unit can contain as few as one person, unlike a family, which requires two or more related individuals.

housing allowance: The amount of money represented by a housing voucher, given to a low-income household to help cover the costs of renting an apartment or house. The allowance or voucher can only be used for paying for housing. See "vouchers (housing)."

housing trust funds: Low-cost loans made available to housing developers if they agree to set aside a minimum number to be rented or sold at prices affordable to low- and/or moderate-income households.

human capital: Skills, knowledge, or other attributes that render a worker more productive.

import substitution: A strategy for increasing output and employment in a region by producing goods or services for local consumption that were once imported into the region from other locations. The strategy of import substitution can be contrasted with that of export promotion, where industrial effort is focused on the production and goods and services that can be sold to other regions to generate local income.

inclusionary zoning laws: Municipal laws that provide housing developers with waivers of previously existing limits on the number of units per acre in return for the developer building a number of affordable housing units in the development or contributing to an affordable housing trust fund used for building low-income housing.

income: The amount of funds received by an individual, corporation, or economy in a given time period.

income elasticity: A measure of how much a specified variable changes in response to changes in income (both expressed in percentage terms). For example, the income elasticity of demand for food is the percentage increase in demand for food divided by the percentage increase in income. An income elasticity of 0.2 would mean that if income rises by 1 percent, the demand for food rises by 0.2 percent.

income inequality: Differences in income between demographic groups.

incrementalism: The building of public policy through small successive steps in which decision makers agree about particular measures to be taken in the short term, without fully exploring or agreeing about long-term goals.

indifference curves: A line or curve that shows all combinations of consumption goods that yield the same level of total satisfaction (utility) for an individual. Because they each yield the same level of satisfaction, the individual would be indifferent as to which combination was received.

industrial composition: The set of extractive, construction, manufacturing, trade, service, and government enterprises in a city, metro area, state, or nation.

industrial revenue bonds: Bonds issued by municipal governments to raise funds to provide land, buildings, and/or equipment that will be leased by a private industrial company for a set number of years. Such bonds are often used to attract companies to an area, or to provide funding for expansion of companies that already exist in the area.

industrial transformation: The prosperity and growth of some industries, while others become obsolete (see also "creative destruction").

industry: A set of firms that sell a specified product or closely related set of products.

industry clusters: Groups of firms located near each other, that are in the same industry, or that are in related industries (through their roles as suppliers or purchasers of each other's products, or through their reliance upon the same set of inputs).

industry sectors (primary-secondary-tertiary): Industries are generally divided into primary, secondary, and tertiary sectors. Primary industries refer to such extractive industries as mining and forestry, as well as farming. Secondary sector industries are generally manufacturing industries such as auto and steel. Tertiary sector industries refer to trade and services industries such as retail trade and business services.

inelastic demand: Demand for a good or service for which consumers are not highly sensitive to changes in price. Often, these are commodities without good substitutes, so many consumers will continue to purchase them despite higher prices.

infant mortality rate: The proportion of deaths among children during their first year of life. The infant mortality rate is calculated by taking the number of deaths of children before their first birthday during a year, and dividing it by the number of live births during that same year.

informal economy: See "underground economy."

infrastructure: The basic underlying capital equipment (such as pipes, roads, cables, etc.) used to provide services to the general public (such as transport, telecommunications, water, and sanitation).

innovation cities (centers): Cities (or metropolitan areas) where activities (such as research and development, universities, and medical facilities) related to the discovery of new ideas and new products constitute a large part of the economic base, or where such activities are the dominant source of growth.

input: Any resource used in the production process to produce output.

input-output analysis: A technique for studying the interdependence in production among the entire array of industrial sectors of an economy. An input-output table calculates all flows of goods and services between sectors of origin (and factor services) and sectors of destination. As an example, an input-output analysis will show how much steel is consumed in the production functions of each industry (including the steel industry itself).

institutional factors: Institutions such as government, trade unions, and community organizations that affect social and economic outcomes. For example, unions help establish wage rates paid by individual firms to their employees.

interdistrict choice: An educational system in which families are allowed to select and send their children to public schools in school districts other than the ones in which they reside.

interest-group theory: The belief that public-sector decision making can best be understood through the realization that decision makers face competing pressures and demands from formal and informal groups of individuals, with each group trying to persuade the decision makers to make decisions favorable to that group. Also known as "pluralist theory."

intergenerational equity: Fairness with regard to how the costs of providing a service are divided across generations. Intergenerational equity is an issue in financing major projects for which services and payments will continue across generations.

internal economies of scale: Economies of scale that result from factors within the firm. Internal economies of scale contrast with external economies of scale (such as agglomeration economies), which result from factors outside the firm.

Internet scams: Fraudulent messages sent over the Internet, designed to convince the recipients to send money or take other action to benefit the sender under false pretences.

intradistrict choice: An educational system in which families are allowed to select and send their children to any public school within the boundaries of the school district in which they reside.

iso-access lines: Lines on a map or on a graph of an area, which indicate various points that are an equal time away from a destination.

jobless rate: The proportion of working-age individuals (ages 16–64) who are not employed. This includes those who are officially unemployed (see "unemployment rate") plus those who are not working and not seeking work.

job multiplier: The relationship between employment in economic base (basic) industries and employment in the economy as a whole. The job multiplier is calculated as total employment divided by export employment in the economic base industries. Economic base theory states that the job multiplier is a measure of the number of jobs in the overall economy of an area that will be created as the result of each additional job in basic industries. Also known as "employment multiplier."

knowledge spillovers: The spread of new skills, insights, and information from one application to another or from one firm to another. Knowledge spillovers can occur through formal arrangements, such as industry symposia designed to spread new knowledge, or through informal channels, such as when workers from different firms within a field socialize with each other.

labor market segmentation: A labor market containing two or more segments that provide very different wages and working conditions (see "dual labor market").

linkage programs: Municipal laws that require developers of commercial and industrial property to make payments to a housing fund for the construction of affordable housing to offset pressure on the housing market that presumably will be caused by the hiring of new employees in the businesses occupying those properties.

localization economies: Agglomeration economies that result from firms in the same industry locating near one another (see "agglomeration economies").

locally unwanted land uses (LULUs): Land uses that residents do not want to have nearby (such as industrial plants and hazardous waste sites).

location-efficient mortgages: Mortgages that offer better terms for home purchases in areas where there is less need to commute by private automobile. Such mortgages are currently available in only a few cities.

location quotient: A statistical measure of the extent to which a particular economic activity is over- or underrepresented in the economy of a region, compared to its representation in the economy as a whole.

log-log regression: A statistical regression analysis in which the logarithm of the dependent variable is regressed against the logarithm of the independent (or explanatory) variables (see "regression").

low birth weight: The weight of a newborn who is less than 2,500 grams (about five and a half pounds). Babies with low birth weights are more likely to be at risk for life-threatening complications.

macroeconomics: The study of the behavior of a national economy as a whole, including the study of gross domestic product, inflation, unemployment, and economic growth.

magnet schools: Public schools with a specialized curriculum or a distinctive approach to learning that are open to students throughout a school district, regardless of the school to which they would normally be assigned.

manufacturing cities (centers): Cities (or metropolitan areas) where the production of finished consumer goods or components for use as inputs in further manufacture constitute a large part of the economic base, or where such activities are the dominant source of growth.

marginal product: The additional quantity of output that is generated by one more unit of a single input. For example, the marginal product of labor is the increase in the amount of output that comes from one more worker.

market: Any setting in which the sale and purchase of goods and services takes place. In many contexts, the term "market" may also refer to the exchange of goods and services without alluding to a particular place.

market-oriented firms: Firms for which transportation costs are the primary determinant of location, and in which those costs are minimized by locating production close to the market where the final consumer is located.

market power: The ability to influence the terms on which a market exchange is made. As most commonly used, the term market power describes the ability of a monopoly or oligopoly to raise prices. A firm with no market power has to sell at the same price that other sellers of the same good are charging.

market value: The price that a good would receive if sold on the open market.

materials-oriented firms: Firms for which transportation costs are the primary determinant of location, and in which those costs are minimized by locating production close to the source of raw materials.

median family income: After arraying all families according to income from lowest to highest, the income that divides the distribution in half. Fifty percent of all families have an income lower than the median; 50 percent have an income above it.

median household income: After arraying all households according to income from lowest to highest, the income that divides the distribution in half. Fifty percent of all households have an income lower than the median; 50 percent have an income above it.

Medicaid: A joint state/federal health insurance program to fund health care for individuals with low income and few resources. Created in 1965, in the same legislation that created Medicare, Medicaid is managed by the states, and is available only to individuals who fall under specified income and resource criteria.

Medicare: A federal health insurance program to fund health care to individuals who are over age 65 or who have disabilities. Initiated in 1965, Medicare is funded, in part, by payroll deductions from employed persons. Everybody who meets the age or disability requirements is eligible for Medicare; there are no income criteria.

merit good: Also called "merit wants." A good whose consumption is deemed to be intrinsically beneficial, but which, due to imperfect knowledge or unaccounted-for externalities, is purchased by consumers in insufficient quantities. The consumption of merit goods (such as basic education or housing) is often encouraged by government through public provision or subsidy because of the beneficial results that presumably ensue to society.

merit pay: In the education sector, providing bonuses to teachers whose students meet certain criteria (e.g., if students' test scores significantly improve from one year to the next).

merit wants: See "merit good."

metropolitan areas: A geographic area containing a large population nucleus, together with adjacent communities that have a high degree of economic and social integration with that nucleus (some metropolitan areas are defined around two or more nuclei). Metropolitan areas are designated by the federal Office of Management and Budget in terms of one or more counties or, in New England, county subdivisions (primarily cities and towns).

metropolitanism: Cooperation between central cities and their surrounding suburbs to work toward common goals.

metropolitan statistical areas (MSAs): Defined by the U.S. Office of Management and Budget as an area that includes a city of at least 50,000 population or an urbanized area of at least 50,000 with a total metropolitan area population of at least 100,000. Generally, an MSA consists of one or more counties, except in New England, where MSAs are defined in terms of county subdivisions (primarily cities and towns).

microeconomics: The study of the behavior of individual consumers and firms, including the study of how prices are determined in markets for specific goods or services, how goods are distributed among the population, and how income from market exchange is distributed.

micropolitan area: As defined by the U.S. Office of Management and Budget, urban areas too small to be classified as metropolitan areas, but having at least one urban cluster of between 10,000 and 50,000 inhabitants.

minimum wage: A minimum level of pay established by law for workers in general. The federal minimum wage law covers the vast majority of U.S. workers; many states have minimum wage laws that supersede federal law.

monetary weight: The monetary cost of transporting a product times the weight of that product. Monetary weights are used in the determination of the most cost-effective location for a transportation-cost-oriented firm.

monocentric model: The concept found in many early models of cities in which there is a single central district with population and employment density declining as distance from the central location increases.

monocentrism: The characteristic of having one center of activity. (See "monocentric model").

mononuclearity: Having one, and only one, center of key activity, with other parts of the urban area dependent upon this one central area.

monopolist: A business that is the only seller of a particular good or service for which there is no close substitute.

monopoly: The existence of only one seller for a given product for which there is no close substitute.

monotonic: A sequence of numbers or values that either consistently increase or consistently decrease. A monotonically increasing series has no number that is lower than the preceding number. A monotonically decreasing series has no number that is higher than the preceding number.

morphology: The form or structure of an organism, city, or region.

multiple identities: A situation in which an individual may have one persona within a specific group at one time and a completely different persona with another group at another time.

municipal health centers: Centers established and funded by municipal governments to provide medical services, health education, health-related outreach, and other services. The extent of services provided is determined by individual city governments.

municipalities: Legally established cities or towns, usually pursuant to state legislation.

municipal public welfare departments: Municipal offices established to help coordinate and deliver publicly and privately financed social services to poor people.

National Health Service Corps scholarship: A federally sponsored scholarship and loan program, that provides financial aid to individuals who are training in primary care health professions (medicine, dentistry, and mental health) in return for their commitment to spend a specified number of years providing services in communities with shortages of health professionals.

natural monopoly: The existence of a monopoly in which economies of scale are so large that no entry by competitors is possible once an incumbent firm is established.

natural resource cities (centers): Cities (or metropolitan areas) where activities related to nearby natural resources (such as minerals, timber, soil quality for agriculture, lakes, and mountain slopes) constitute a large part of the economic base, or where natural resource-based activities are the dominant source of growth.

natural resources: Factors of production provided by nature, including land, mineral deposits, and water.

new growth theory: A theory of economic growth that emphasizes the role of education and technology in the growth process. Within new growth theory, education not only has direct effects on productivity, but also has spillover effects that enhance a region's competitive advantage.

new trade theory: An approach to understanding trade between countries or regions that emphasizes the effect of economies of scale in production and the barriers that existing large-scale production pose for the entry of new firms to an industry.

new urbanism: An approach to urban planning that seeks to recreate more vibrant civic life through architectural and design elements, such as higher-density housing, front porches, and other elements that encourage interaction along lively streets.

No Child Left Behind Act (NCLB): The name given to the reauthorization of the federal Elementary and Secondary Education Act in 2001. This legislation included new provisions pertaining to standardized testing, accountability for school outcomes, and the creation of alternatives (such as "charter schools") to existing public schools.

nominal wages: The dollar amount of the pay received; the amount shown on a paycheck (contrast with "real wages").

nonamortizing mortgages: Mortgages in which only the interest is paid during the term of the mortgage, and a large payment, consisting of the entire principal, is due at the end of the mortgage. This contrasts with amortized mortgages, where the amount of the principal is gradually reduced through payments during the mortgage term.

nonbasic sector: In the basic/nonbasic approach to understanding urban economic growth, the nonbasic sector refers to firms whose output is not exported, but instead is only sold locally.

nonexcludable: A characteristic of a good or service that, once provided, is available to everybody.

nonrival: A characteristic of a good or service such that consumption or use by one person does not diminish the amount of that good or service available for other individuals. An example would be a less than fully utilized highway in which one person's use does not diminish the use of another.

Occupational Safety and Health Act: A federal law, passed in 1970, which requires employers to provide workers with safe and sanitary workplaces.

offshoring: The relocation of a production center, or some other part of a firm, to another country, using a central office in the original country simply to coordinate production and distribution. Offshoring is particularly notable in recent decades, as some firms have moved part of their operations to areas with cheaper labor or better access to other inputs.

oligopolist: A firm that is one of only a few producers in its industry.

oligopoly: The existence of only a few producers in an industry.

operating costs: The costs of materials, labor, energy, and other inputs (not including the costs of the land and physical plant) used in the operation of the firm.

opportunity cost: The value of the best alternative given up (forgone) when income or time is used to consume something else.

opportunity structures: The access to resources and institutions that individuals possess. Access is affected by where individuals live, as well as by race, ethnicity, income, wealth, and other factors, and is continuously shaped by government policies, private-sector decisions, and the choices of individuals.

option value: The value that consumers who do not usually use a good or service place on the standby availability of that good/service (that is, its availability), should they want or need to use it in the future. An example would be a city park that may be seldom used by a particular resident but is still available to that resident if he or she chooses to visit it. Also refers to the value of completing a given education degree in terms of the completion permitting one to go on to a higher level of schooling.

output: Goods or services produced as part of an economic process.

outsourcing: Moving functions originally performed within a company to another firm that performs the function and sells the resulting parts or services to the original firm. It is called outsourcing because after the functions have been moved, the source of the parts or services is outside the original firm.

Pareto optimality: The condition of an allocation of goods such that no shift of resources is possible without reducing the satisfaction of at least one consumer.

paternalism: Governmental action where the judgment of government decision makers is substituted for the judgment of individual citizens or consumers.

path dependency: The situation that occurs when elements of the past and/ or present affect future conditions; historical circumstances or choices made by individuals open up some possibilities for the future, while closing off other possibilities.

per capita income: The average income per person for a particular group, calculated by dividing the total income of a particular group by the total population in that group.

permanent income: The average annual income received by an individual or household over a specified period of years. The concept of permanent income is frequently used when trying to explain how consumers plan their spending over a lifetime, or over a shorter multiyear period during which consumers have formed income expectations.

Phillips Curve: Statistical observation by A. W. Phillips of an inverse relationship between the rate of inflation and the unemployment rate.

pluralism: Another name for interest-group theory; the belief that public-sector decision making can best be understood through the realization that decision makers face competing pressures and demands from formal and informal groups of individuals, with each group trying to persuade the decision makers to make decisions favorable to that group.

police power: The right of local government to protect the health, safety, and general well-being of its citizens by imposing appropriate regulations. This is the legal basis for building codes, zoning, health regulations, and other measures that restrict the activities that occur within a government's jurisdiction.

political jurisdiction: A geographic area covered by a particular unit of government. The key political jurisdictions in the United States are towns, cities, counties, and states.

polycentric city form: A model of a city that depicts more than one center. This contrasts with the monocentric city form, which depicts a city as having only one center surrounded by suburbs.

population density: A statistical measure of the number of people who live within a certain land area (total population divided by area). Also, a descriptive attribute meaning large numbers of people living in close proximity to each other.

pork barrel politics: Government spending that is intended to benefit constituents of a politician, such as private urban developers or defense contractors in return for their political support, either in the form of campaign contributions or votes.

poverty rate: The proportion of the population in a given area with income below the poverty thresholds (which differ according to family size) established by the U.S. government.

poverty trap: Dynamics arising from markets, institutions, or both, that act to perpetuate poverty, and that are self-reinforcing.

present discounted value: The value now of a stream of future income payments, taking into account that payments made in the future are worth less than payments made today because a current payment can accumulate interest.

prevailing wages: Wages that would be considered customary for a certain type of job. In practice, prevailing wages are usually synonymous with union wage scales.

price elasticity of demand: The percentage change in quantity demanded resulting from a 1 percent change in price.

price elasticity of supply: The percentage change in quantity supplied resulting from a 1 percent change in price.

primary metropolitan statistical area (PMSA): Now obsolete, this term was defined by the U.S. Bureau of the Census to refer to a metropolitan statistical area (MSA) that was part of a larger consolidated metropolitan statistical area (CMSA).

primary mortgage market: The market in which banks and other financial institutions are offering (selling) mortgages to households.

primary sector industries: Agriculture, timber, mining, and fishing industries (see also "secondary sector industries" and "tertiary sector industries").

principal-agent problem: The problem that exists when the interests of an agent acting on behalf of a client (the principal) diverge from the interests of the client. For example, the interests of the manager of a corporation may differ from the interests of the stockholders who hired the manager.

principal city: The largest city in a metropolitan area, along with any cities in a metro area with a population of at least 250,000 or in which 100,000 or more persons work, and other cities in the metro area that meet specified official standards of population size and employment. This term is often a synonym for "central city."

prisoner's dilemma: A situation where the pursuit of self-interest by separate individuals without regard for the well-being of others keeps all individuals from reaching goals that actually maximize their self-interest.

private security guards: Individuals hired by private groups to provide screening, monitoring, and control of behavior, and other activities related to the security of the people or firms who have hired them.

privatization: The transfer of operations originally carried out by public agencies to the private sector.

problem-oriented policing: An approach to crime prevention that relies on the police attempting to systematically understand the causes of recurring crime and react with a concerted effort of problem solving, planning, mediating, and organizing the community to fight it.

procurement costs (transportation): The costs of bringing raw materials and/or other inputs needed for production of a good to a firm.

product differentiation: The process by which producers create real or apparent differences between products that perform the same general function. Examples of real differences are better quality and unique characteristics; examples of apparent differences often include brand names and endorsements.

production: Combining inputs and technology to produce output in the form of goods and services.

production costs: The costs incurred in the manufacture of a good, including the cost of labor, raw material, machinery, rental property, energy, and taxes and fees.

productive efficiency: Producing goods at the lowest possible cost per unit.

product life cycle theory: An approach to understanding firm location and urban prosperity which emphasizes that the location of production for a particular good may change over time due to changes in production and marketing needs and competitive forces as the product moves from initial introduction into the market to widespread market circulation.

profit: The difference between a firm's total revenue and its total costs.

public choice theory: A branch of economics concerned with the application of economics to the analysis of nonmarket public decision making. One assumption of public choice theory is that public employees will seek to maximize personal utility, and in the absence of adequate monitoring by government, decisions may be made that benefit the employees' interests rather than the interests of the overall public.

public health: Efforts by local, state, and national governments, and other institutions, to provide health-related services, to promote healthy behavior, and to prevent disease and injury.

pull factors: Positive characteristics of an area that attract migration of residents or firms from other regions or nations.

pure public goods: Goods that are nonexcludable (once they are provided, they are available to everybody), and nonrival (consumption or use by one person does not diminish the amount of that good or service available for other individuals).

push factors: Negative characteristics of an area that encourage migration of residents or firms to other regions or nations.

quadratic regression equation: An equation or regression with a squared term in order to account for nonlinearity or curvature in a function. Functions like the standard average cost curve can be represented by such an equation.

real wages: The dollar amount of the pay received adjusted for changes in prices over time; the purchasing power of wages compared to the purchasing power of the same nominal wage in the past.

redlining: A practice where banks (or other lenders) refuse to make mortgage and/or home repair loans for specific areas in a city. Historically associated with racial discrimination, the practice is known as redlining because some lenders drew red lines on maps to indicate the areas that were not to be given loans.

refuse: Also known as solid waste, refuse is leftover material that has been thrown away by households, businesses, and other parties (see "solid waste").

regime theory: An approach to understanding the relationships between government and private sectors as decisions are made that affect urban areas. Regimes are informal coalitions that represent business, government, and others who are working toward a goal that requires the participation of both private and public sectors. Parties within the coalition may not have the same exact interests but are willing to participate in movement toward a goal because of the benefits that are expected from achieving the goal, or because of promises that have been made from other members of the coalition to acquire their cooperation.

regression analysis: A statistical technique that seeks to explain changes in an outcome (a dependent variable) in terms of changes in other variables (independent variables) that are, based on theory, believed to be causes of the outcome.

regulatory costs: Costs incurred by businesses in the course of complying with local, state, and federal laws.

rent: In discussion of housing (or commercial property), rent is the price paid to the owner of a property for use of the home (or commercial space). In microeconomics, "rent" is sometimes used to refer to the amount paid for an input (e.g., to a worker with unique talents) above the amount of that input's opportunity cost (its next-best-paying alternative use).

repurposing: Adapting buildings, workforces, transportation facilities, and other productive resources so that they can fit into a changing national economy in new ways.

residential paradox: The situation in which lower-income families tend to live closer to the central parts of cities on more expensive land and where higher-income families live in the suburbs on less expensive land. The paradox is explained by the high-density living conditions of lower-income families so that the price per square foot per person is lower in the "higher-priced" central city than in "less expensive" suburbs.

residential segregation: A residential pattern where households of different races or members of particular ethnic groups live in separate neighborhoods within a city or metro area.

retirement centers: Cities (or metropolitan areas) that attract large numbers of individuals retiring from their former jobs, and where income from retirement earnings and activities related to retirement constitutes a large part of the economic base, or where such activities are the dominant source of growth.

right-to-work states: States that have adopted laws that bar unions and firms from requiring union membership as a condition of employment. Firms in right-to-work states are said to have "open shops" where employees have the right to work, regardless of whether they join a union or not. "Open shops" contrast with "closed shops," where only individuals who have previously joined a union can work, and with "union shops" where employees do not need to be union members before being hired, but are required to join the union within a specified period after being hired.

risk: The situation that exists when future outcomes are not known but probabilities of various outcomes can be calculated from data.

rival: The characteristic of a good or service where consumption or use by one person diminishes the amount of that good or service available for other individuals.

scale economies: See "economies of scale."

school choice: An educational system in which parents can decide which school their children attend, rather than having schools assigned by residential address or other criteria.

secondary mortgage market: The market in which banks or other financial institutions sell their existing mortgage contracts with households to other parties (such as other financial institutions and pension funds). The secondary mortgage market provides cash (or other short-term assets) to the bank that originally sold the loan, while providing a longer term flow of funds (from the household) to the new mortgage holder.

secondary sector industries: Construction and manufacturing industries (see also "primary sector industries" and "tertiary sector industries").

selective migration: Migration in which those who leave an area come disproportionately from specific demographic groups. For example, the migration away from depressed areas tends to be composed disproportionately of younger, better educated individuals.

settlement houses: Organizations (and the buildings out of which they operated) that were established to provide social, educational, and health services to immigrants and to low-income residents of cities in the late 1800s and early 1900s. The most widely known settlement house was Hull House, founded in Chicago by Jane Addams.

severely cost-burdened housing: Housing costs that exceed 50 percent of a household's pretax annual income.

shadow economy: See "underground economy."

site assembly problem: The problem confronted by developers when a certain amount of land is needed for a development project but parts of the needed land are owned by a variety of individuals, some of whom are willing to sell to the developer and others who are not.

site costs: Costs incurred to procure—and make any necessary adjustments to—the land and buildings that a business occupies.

skills mismatch: A gap between the education or skills of residents of a geographic area, and the education or skills needed for employment in that geographic area (or in a specific industry within that geographic area).

smart growth: Planned development to limit suburban sprawl through measures that increase density. Among current smart growth initiatives are transit-oriented development, urban growth boundaries, location-efficient mortgages, transferable development rights, and new urbanism. Proponents of smart growth development believe that it can improve central cities, promote environmental quality, save public resources, lower energy consumption, and preserve rural land and open space.

social benefit: The sum of the gains or benefits to society as a whole from an activity or project. This includes benefits accrued both by the particular consumers of the activity or project and by others who are not directly party to the consumption. A common example is the social benefit that derives from the education of other people's children.

social capital: The ability of individuals to harness the resources they need through a network of friends and relatives. Social capital depends upon intangible things with economic value that either are contained within or are transmitted through social relationships. Examples of social capital include trust, information, and obligations.

social cost: The full opportunity cost to society of using resources to produce a particular good or service rather than using the resources for some other purpose.

social network: A social structure made of nodes (which are generally individuals or organizations) that are tied together by one or more specific types of relations, including kinship, employment, or business links. Social networks play a critical role in determining the way problems are solved, organizations are run, and the degree to which individuals succeed in achieving their goals.

Social Security: A federal program to provide retirement income, disability income, and income for surviving spouses and children of deceased workers.

solid waste: Leftover nonliquid material that has been thrown away by households, businesses, and other actors. Also known as refuse, solid waste includes garbage, trash, dead vegetation, and/or debris from building construction/repair.

spatial mismatch: A situation where lack of access to suburban housing (due to housing discrimination or to high prices for houses) and lack of access to transportation prevent jobseekers in cities from reaching jobs that are located in the suburbs.

spatial relocation: The movement of households, businesses, and other activities from one geographic area to another. Spatial relocation includes movement from one country to another, from one metro area to another, or from city to suburb (and vice versa).

specialization: Dividing up production tasks so that people (or places) concentrate on tasks in which they have an advantage—that is, that they can perform more efficiently than other people (or places). Specialization normally results in higher levels of output, and/or improved quality of output.

spillover effects: The positive or negative impact of an exchange on third parties who are neither the buyers nor the sellers involved in the transaction.

standard deviation: A statistic used for measuring the variation in a set of numbers.

standard metropolitan statistical areas (SMSAs): As defined by the U.S. Office of Management and Budget, a term used between 1959 and 1983 to refer to large metro areas. In 1983, the term "standard" was dropped, and large metro areas were subsequently referred to simply as "metropolitan statistical areas" (MSAs).

standards movement: Initiatives to reform schooling based upon the belief that one of the fundamental problems with traditional schools is their lack of accountability for student outcomes. Among the measures introduced by the standards movement are test-based criteria for measuring student progress, criteria for assessing the quality of teachers, and sanctions imposed on schools for failing to meet goals related to student progress.

statistical discrimination: Judging an individual not on his or her own credentials, but on beliefs about the characteristics of the average or typical member of a demographic group to which the individual belongs.

steering: The practice by real estate agents of limiting housing options by showing to prospective home buyers only the housing in neighborhoods with population characteristics similar to their own (e.g., showing white households properties only in white areas and showing minority households properties only in minority areas).

suburbs: The communities lying outside and around a city.

Supplementary Security Income: A federal program to provide income support for low-income elderly and disabled individuals.

supply: The amount of a good or service offered for sale at any given price.

supply chains: The systems of firms, processes, and transportation that are involved in producing a good and making it available for purchase. Supply chains can extend from extraction of the basic raw materials from which the good is made, through all steps in manufacturing, and end with final sale of the finished product.

sustained competitive advantage: The ability of firms and regions to innovate in order to successfully maintain a competitive advantage over an extended period of time.

systemic social disorganization approach to urban crime: An approach to crime that emphasizes the ability of neighborhood residents to build social capital (such as trust and shared norms) that will increase their influence on the behavior of individual residents. Adherents of this approach try to change patterns of social interaction among families in ways that will build social capital.

tax: Financial obligation imposed by a government upon individuals, businesses, and other entities to provide funds used to support government activities.

tax effort: The tax rate per dollar of assessed property value; the total property tax collected by local governments divided by the total value of assessed property in their jurisdictions.

tax expenditures: Preferential tax treatment that reduces revenue flowing to government, and increases the income retained by a particular group of households or firms. Essentially, it is the cost to government of tax exclusions, exemptions, deductions and deferrals provided to particular groups of households or firms. An example of a tax expenditure is the provision in federal tax laws that allows home owners to reduce their taxable income by the amount of their home mortgage interest.

tax increment financing (TIF): The financing of local development projects through the issuance of municipal bonds backed by the expected increase (increments) in tax revenue from future increases in property values within the designated TIF area. The proceeds from the bond sales can be used for site clearance, utility installation, street construction and repair, and other purposes that reduce costs for private businesses willing to locate in depressed areas where TIF districts are permitted.

tax revolt: Initiatives by voters to limit the tax rates that governments can charge on property and/or other taxable items.

technological progress: The use of new or recent scientific knowledge in ways that lead to new innovations, inventions, and insights.

telecommuting: Performing a job from home, rather than coming into a central workplace, and communicating with the employer and other workers in the office or elsewhere through use of the Internet or telephone.

teleconferencing: Using telecommunications equipment (such as conferencing telephones or the Internet) to conduct live meetings among three or more people in different locations.

Temporary Assistance for Needy Families (TANF): A federal program to provide income support mainly for single-parent families with dependent children. In place since 1995, it replaced the older Aid to Families with Dependent Children (AFCD).

tertiary sector industries: Wholesale and retail trade and business and personal service industries (see also "primary sector industries" and "secondary sector industries").

tipping point: The small action in the course of a series of actions that leads to a major change in a trend or behavior. For example, when a new racial group begins to reside in what was once a segregated neighborhood, there may be little change in racial composition until the proportion of the new racial group reaches a critical point and then the racial composition of the neighborhood changes dramatically.

total cost (TC): The sum of a firm's fixed costs and variable costs.

total revenue (TR): The total receipts that a firm takes in from selling its goods and/or services.

trade: The exchange of goods and services for money, or for other goods and services.

traditional approach to urban crime: A police department approach to crime that emphasizes rapid response and raising the probability of arrest through the use of crime laboratories and investigatory techniques. This was the dominant police department approach to crime throughout most of the twentieth century.

transferable development rights (TDRs): Government programs that use market forces to promote conservation in agricultural land and open space areas while encouraging smart growth in developed or rapidly developing sections of a community. In a TDR program, a community identifies a local area it would like to see protected from development (the "sending zone") and another area where it desires more concentrated development (the "receiving zone"). Landowners in the sending zone are allocated a number of development credits that can be sold to developers, speculators, or the community itself to help compensate for the loss of market value that preservation entails. Meanwhile, the purchaser of the development credits can apply them to develop at a higher density than otherwise allowed on property within the receiving zone.

transit-oriented development: An approach to urban planning that emphasizes locating higher-density housing and mixed-use development near transit routes, to reduce an area's reliance upon automobiles.

transportation-cost-oriented firms: Firms for which transportation costs are the key factor determining where the firm should be located. The two basic types of transportation-cost-oriented firms are market-oriented firms and materials-oriented firms (sometimes called "resource-oriented firms").

transportation costs: Costs incurred in moving inputs to producers (procurement) and shipping the output to points of sale (distribution).

transportation hubs: Cities where activities related to transportation lines (such as switching goods or people from one mode of transportation to another, redirecting goods or people in new directions, or breaking large shipments of goods into smaller shipments) constitute a large part of the economic base, or where such transportation-related activities are the dominant source of growth.

travel distance: The measurement of distance between two places along existing travel routes (which typically involve twists and turns) rather than as a straight line between the two places.

uncertainty: The situation that exists when future outcomes are not known and probabilities of various outcomes cannot be calculated because the process leading to the outcome is random or arbitrary. This contrasts with "risk," a term used when it is possible to calculate the probabilities of various outcomes.

underground economy: This unregulated and poorly measured part of the economy consists of both legal activities (with the exception that taxes are usually not paid on their proceeds) and a range of illegal activities, from unsanctioned gambling and prostitution to the sale of drugs.

Unemployment Compensation: A federal/state program to provide temporary partial wage replacement for workers who lose their jobs.

unemployment rate: The number of people who are without a job but actively seeking work divided by the number of people in the labor force—those who are either working or actively seeking work.

unincorporated area: A geographic area that is not part of a legally established town or city.

unintended consequences: Unforeseen impacts of actions consciously taken by an individual, business, or government. Unintended consequences can be either positive or negative.

union density: The rate of unionization (the ratio of union members to all workers) within a geographic area, industry, or occupation.

union shop: Places of employment where, under the contract with the employees' union, new employees are required to join the union within a specified period after being hired. In contrast to a "closed shop," new hires in a union shop do not need to be union members before being hired.

unit costs: The cost associated with producing one additional unit of a good or service.

upward filtering: A succession of ownership (or rental residency) that moves up income levels from lower-income families to middle-income families to higher-income families.

urban area: All territory located within an urban cluster or urbanized area (see "urban cluster" and "urbanized area").

urban cluster: A smaller version of an urban area. As defined by the U.S. Bureau of the Census, an urban cluster has a census population of 2,500 to 49,999, at least one core of blocks with a population density of at least 1,000 people per square mile, and adjacent block groups and blocks with at least 500 people per square mile.

urban economics: A field within economics that focuses on the causes and consequences of the location decisions made by households and business firms located in urban areas.

urban ghetto: A term used by social scientists to refer to sections of the city that contain high proportions of very poor households. It often refers to neighborhoods that contain poor minority households.

urban growth boundary: A geographic area within which future growth will occur, as established by legislation that limits future development to within a certain radius of the core city.

urbanization economies: Agglomeration economies that result from economic activities being concentrated in urban areas. As an example, having a concentration of accounting, advertising, and marketing services available in a central business district reduces the cost to businesses that require all of these services.

urbanized area: As defined by the U.S. Bureau of the Census, a densely settled area that has an overall population of at least 50,000, at least one core of blocks with a population density of at least 1,000 people per square mile, and adjacent block groups and blocks with at least 500 people per square mile.

urban population: As defined by the U.S. Bureau of the Census, all people living in official urbanized areas plus people outside of urbanized areas who live in urban clusters (i.e., towns with more than 2,500 inhabitants).

urban public amenities: Municipal services intended for voluntary leisure use by the public.

urban slum: Sections of a city where a concentration of poor people leads to a concentration of poverty-related social problems.

urban sprawl: Land-use patterns characterized by low density, clusters of activity with only one use (such as housing subdivisions, malls, and industrial parks), and automobile dependency, with resulting negative effects upon a variety of issues that may be of concern to environmentalists, urban planners, and others.

user fees: Fees charged to the actual users of government-provided goods or services, in contrast to paying for these items out of general tax revenue. Examples of user fees include charging tolls to cross a bridge, metering households for the amount of water they use, and adopting admission prices for city zoos.

user tax: A tax that is charged only to individuals who use a good or service, but which may not, as in the case of a user fee, be prorated on the amount of good or service consumed.

use value: The subjective value that an individual places upon using or owning a good.

vacancy rate: The percentage of housing stock in a neighborhood, city, or metro area that is available for purchase or rental.

variable costs: The part of a firm's costs that vary with the level of output. For example, labor costs usually vary with the level of output, since producing more requires hiring more workers.

variances: Decisions by city government to approve a specific application for land use that would otherwise be barred by zoning laws. Variances do not change the zoning laws, but give permission for the single nonconforming application.

vicious cycle: A course of events where predictable factors perpetuate and reinforce an undesirable outcome.

virtuous cycle: A course of events where predictable factors perpetuate and reinforce a desirable outcome.

vouchers (housing): A document issued by government to low-income families that can be used to pay a portion of the costs of housing, schooling, or other needs.

zero-sum game: A game where the sum of the gains to winners equals the sum of the losses to losers. Zero-sum games are contrasted with positive-sum games, where gains for all participants are possible and negative-sum games, where all parties may be worse off as a result of some joint activity.

zoning: The system of specifying that certain uses of land can only be carried on in particular areas within a given jurisdiction and that other uses are prohibited.

Index

Note: Page numbers followed by *f* and *t* indicate figures and tables.

Absolute advantage, 174–175

Affordable housing. *See* Housing

African Americans: internal migration, 88–90, 121–123, 122*t*; metro area rankings, 26–27. *See also* Race and ethnicity; Segregation

Age, home ownership and, 410, 410*t*, 461

Agglomeration economies: central city growth, 65, 66–68, 67*f*, 73, 82–85; health, 376; land-use restrictions, 452; technology, 86

Agriculture, internal migration and, 87–89, 93–94

Akron, OH, 75, 78–80

Alabama, 132, 259

Alaska, 361, 441

Allen, Katherine, 432

Allocation role of government, 288

Allocative efficiency: failure to achieve, 291–298; as market's role, 288–291; pricing of government services, 311–313

Alonso, William, 103–104. *See also* Alonso model

Alonso model, 103–104; bid rent curves, 104–108, 105*t*, 107*f*, 109*f*; bid rent curves applied to metropolitan development, 108–110; edge cities, 126–128, 127*f*; gentrification, 128–129, 129*f*; polycentric cities with income-differentiated neighborhoods, 137; reduced costs and twenty-first-century cities, 150–153, 152*t*; residential paradox, 110–111, 110*f*, 111*t*; sectoral growth patterns, 137–138; street layout, 134, 135*f*; travel speed, 135–137, 136*f*

Altshuler, Alan, 320

Amenities. *See* Cultural amenities

American Childhood, An (Dillard), 7

American Housing Survey, 526

Annexation, 9, 37, 94

Antitrust laws, 292

Arkansas, 259

Armories, 347

Aschauer, David, 507

Asking rents, 419

Asymmetric information, market failure and public policy, 289, 293–294, 335; Tiebout hypothesis and, 314–315

Atlanta, GA: changing fortunes, 132; earnings, 214; as metropolitan statistical area, 29; population change, 119*f*, 120, 540; poverty, 49; race and ethnicity, 38–39, 39*f*; as transportation hub, 130; union density, 233

Attributes theory of consumer behavior, 403

Austin, TX: education levels, 254; median family income, 47; trade and prosperity, 173–174, 178, 195–196; union density, 233

Automobiles. *See Transportation entries*

Average total cost curve, 224

Avery v. Midland County, 525

Baltimore, MD: economic development strategies, 511; poverty, 49; purchasing power, 50; school reform, 274

Barnett, W. S., 266

Bartik, Timothy, 505

Bartlett, Donald, 503

Basic/nonbasic approach, to economic measurement, 184–187

Bauer, Catherine, 532

Bayley, David, 389

Becker, Gary S., 223–224

Behind the Gates (Low), 526
Belsky, Eric, 418–419
Berra, Yogi, 18–19
Berry, Christopher, 155–156, 547
Better Place to Live, A (Langdon), 465
Beyers, William, 157
Bid rent, 105, 105*t*
Bid rent curve, 104–108, 107*f*, 109*f*; applied
    to metropolitan development, 108–110;
    edge cities, 126–128, 127*f*; gentrification,
    128–129, 129*f*; polycentric cities with
    income-differentiated neighborhoods,
    137; reduced costs and twenty-first-
    century cities, 150–153, 152*t*; residential
    paradox, 110–111, 110*f*, 111*t*; sectoral
    growth patterns, 137–138; street layout,
    134, 135*f*; travel speed, 135–137, 136*f*
Bingham, Richard, 491–492
Bioterrorism, 382
Birch, David, 485
Birch, Eugenie, 152
Birmingham, AL, 132
Blair, John P., 256, 512
Blakely, Edward, 526
Blodgett, Geoffrey, 348
Bluestone, Barry, 116, 230–231, 237–238,
    423–428, 430, 485, 498
Bogosian, Eric, 7
Bonding social capital, 531
Booza, Jason C., 163
Boston, MA: affordable housing, 52;
    annexation avoided, 94; crime, 54;
    demographic changes, 124; earnings, 211,
    213; education levels, 251, 254;
    establishment and early role, 63; housing,
    415–416; metropolitan dynamics, 11,
    13; poverty, 49–50; purchasing power, 51,
    51*t*; regional sewer systems, 343–344;
    retail demand, 543; school reform, 273;
    trade and prosperity, 181, 189, 194–195;
    vacancy rates, 421
Boston Consulting Group, 543
Bowles, Samuel, 263
Bowling Alone (Putnam), 530–531
Boyd, Donald, 262
Brandeis, Louis, 393
Brashears, Matthew, 531, 532
Bridges, economics of building and paying
    for, 310–313
Bridging social capital, 531
Brinkley, Douglas, 538
Brockton, MA, 433

"Broken windows" theory of crime
    prevention, 387–388, 535–536
Brookings Institution, 191, 194, 468–469
Brookline Early Education Project (BEEP),
    266–267
Brooks, David, 6
Brown, C., 512
Brown v. Board of Education, 268, 270
Brueckner, Jan, 468
Bruegmann, Robert, 467–468
Bryce, James, 346
Buchanan, James, 317
Buddin, Richard, 278
Budget constraints, of individuals, housing
    choice and, 404–406, 405*f*,
    443–444, 444*f*
Buffalo, NY: housing, 412; immigrants,
    236; trade and prosperity, 174, 178,
    195; unemployment rate, 207; union
    density, 233
Bump rate, 256
Burchell, Robert, 462
Burgess, Ernest, 101, 103*f*
Business climate, tax reduction and, 496
Business cycle, employment and, 207
Business improvement districts (BIDs), 524
Business locations. *See* Economic
    development strategies; Urban location
    dynamics
Buss, Terry, 509, 513–514

Calthorpe, Peter, 475
Campoli, Julie, 475
Capital costs, of businesses, economic
    development strategies to reduce,
    491–493, 501*t*, 503–505
Capital resources, of businesses, sustained
    competitive advantage and, 181
Carnegie, Andrew, 345, 347, 348
Carnoy, Martin, 278
Caro, Robert, 364
Carson, Rachel, 342–343
Carter, Jimmy, 491
Census tract, defined, 49
Central business district (CBD), 65
Central cities: defined, 29; income disparity
    and inequality, 53; low and high growth,
    32–37, 35–36*t*; median family income,
    41–48, 44*f*, 46–48*f*; population and
    income growth, in twenty-first century,
    538–545, 539*f*, 541*t*; population decrease
    in, 118, 119*f*, 120, 120*t*; poverty, 49–50;

segregation, 121–123, 122*t*, 125*t*. *See also*
    Metropolitan areas (MAs)
Central place theory, 68
Centripetal/centrifugal forces, city
    populations and, 62–65, 85–86
Charles, Camille, 429
Charlotte, NC: affordable housing, 52–53; as
    finance city, 131, 158–159
Charter schools, 273–274, 275, 277–279
Chattanooga, TN, 322–323
Chen, Don, 469, 470
Chicago, IL: economic development
    strategies, 504–505; as finance city,
    158–159; heat wave in 1995, 523,
    536–537; median family income, 42;
    metropolitan dynamics, 12; poverty, 49,
    50; retail demand, 543; spatial mismatch,
    226–229; trade and prosperity, 173, 195;
    transportation costs and growth of, 75;
    as transportation hub, 130; union density,
    233
Chicago School of Sociology, 387
Child welfare agencies, 394
China: emigration, 91; offshoring,
    144–145
Chinitz, Benjamin, 190
Cincinnati, OH, 132
Circular causation with cumulative effect, 266
Cities. *See* Central cities; Metropolitan areas
    (MAs)
City in History, The (Mumford), 451
Clean Air Act, 365
Clean Water Act, 343
Cleveland, OH: changing fortunes, 132;
    school reform, 277; sewer systems, 342
Coase, Ronald, 457
Coase theorem, 457–458
Cognitive maps, 27, 224, 230
Cohen, Deborah, 470
Cohen, Natalie, 256
Coleman, James S., 261, 264
Columbus, OH, 26–27
Combined statistical area (CSAs), 29, 31–32,
    31*t*, 33*f*, 34*t*
Comeback Cities (Grogan), 542
Coming City, The (Ely), 346–347
Common interest developments, 524
Communication: business location, 115;
    central city growth, 64–65; changing
    fortunes of cities, 132; edge cities, 128;
    twenty-first-century cities, 143–165

Community-based organizations (CBOs),
    294–295
Community development corporations
    (CDCs), 295, 542–543
Community-oriented policing, 388, 390
Community processes, metropolitan
    dynamics, 10, 10*f*
Commuting: social capital, 534; sprawl,
    463–467, 466*t*; trends, 354–355, 355*t*,
    356*f*. *See also* Transportation, physical
    infrastructure
Comparative advantage, 18, 175–177, 176*f*;
    demand and supply sides and, 188; static
    nature of, 177–178
Competitive advantage, 179–182; inner-city
    neighborhoods, 192; supply-side
    perspective, 188–192
Competitiveness argument, for tax reduction,
    496
Complex good, 402
Concentric zone model, of urban land use,
    101, 102–103*f*. *See also* Alonso model
Conflict theory of diversity, 534
Congestion pricing, transportation and,
    361–363, 362*f*
Connecticut: Danbury, 49; economic
    development strategies, 492; school
    spending, 259. *See also* Hartford, CT
Consolidated metropolitan statistical areas
    (CMSAs), 28
Constrained choice: land values, 112–113;
    Tiebout hypothesis, 315
Constrained maximization, 177
Consumer markets: central city growth, 65,
    70, 73; transportation costs, 75
Consumer sovereignty, 473–474
Contact theory of diversity, 534
Contracting out, of public services, 302–303,
    305–306
Convention centers, economic development
    strategies and, 501*t*, 510–511
Core-based statistical areas (CBSAs),
    28–29
"Corporate welfare," 503. *See also*
    Economic development strategies
Correspondence principle, schools and, 263
Cortright, Joseph, 154
Cost-benefit analysis, of economic
    development strategies, 500; calculation
    of, 515–518
Cost-burdened home owners, 417

Cost containment. *See* Economic development strategies

Cost of living: affordable housing and home ownership, 52–53; purchasing power, 50–51, 51*t*, 52*f*

Creative class, 155, 164, 499–500

Creative destruction, 86, 485

"Creative edge of capitalism," 86

Crime: center city regeneration, 543; metro area rankings, 54–55; neighborhood form, 535–536; prosperity, 191–192; students' performance, 265–266

Crime Prevention Through Environmental Design (CPTED), 535

Cross-subsidies, transportation user fees, 361

Cultural amenities: characteristics of, 345; economic development strategies, 499–500, 501*t*, 510–511, 512; versus economic incentives, 154–156; social unrest and, 345–348

Cultural/tourism/recreation centers, 159–160

Cutler, David, 335

Cutsinger, Jackie, 163

Cuyahoga River, 342

Danbury, CT, 49

Data, wise use of, 55

Dayton, OH, 273

Death and Life of Great American Cities, The (Jacobs), 533

Decentralization: business location, 151; commuting trends, 354–355, 355*t*, 356*f*; of public school system in the United States, 248–249, 249*t*; sprawl, 462–466

Decision accretion, 319

Deed restrictions, 456

De facto segregation, 271

Defensible space, 535

Deindustrialization, 113–116, 145–146, 426; employment changes, 483–486, 484*t*

Deindustrialization of America, The (Bluestone and Harrison), 116

De jure segregation, 268, 270–271

Demand-side perspective: export base theory, 182–187; housing prices, 411–417, 411–413*f*; input-output analysis, 187–189, 199–201, 202*t*; interaction with supply side, 190–191; metropolitan transportation, 350–358; subsidized housing, 434–435; tax reduction, 496

Demographic shifts: central city growth, 90*t*, 92–93*t*; historical growth, 86–94, 88*t*, 92*f*; late twentieth century, 121–129, 122*t*, 125*t*, 127*f*, 129*f*; metropolitan dynamics, 10, 10*f*; police departments, 383–385; twenty-first-century cities, 162–165, 163*t*

Density. *See* Population density; Urban growth, dynamics of historical

Denton, Nancy, 429

Denver, CO, 274–275

Design zoning, 455

Detroit, MI: business locations, 114–115; changing fortunes, 132; earnings, 211, 212–213; economic development strategies, 495, 508, 511; education levels, 254; immigrants, 236; metropolitan dynamics, 27; population change, 36, 119*f*, 120; poverty, 49, 50; race and ethnicity, 37, 38*f*, 39, 41; spatial mismatch, 226–229; trade and prosperity, 173–174, 179, 180, 188, 193; unemployment rate, 207; union density, 233; wage differentials, 222

Dewar, Margaret, 510

Dillard, Annie, 7

DiPasquale, Denise, 409, 410

Discrimination. *See* Race and ethnicity; Segregation

Diseconomies of scale, 69, 73

Disembodied knowledge, 256

Dissimilarity index, 429

Distribution costs, 74–75; in Weber model, 76–77*f*, 77–78

Division of labor, 66, 174

Donne, John, 530

Downs, Anthony, 364–365

Downtown areas, 152–153

Downward filtering, housing and, 430

Dreiser, Theodore, 5

Dual labor market, 221

Due, John, 508

Dukakis, Michael, 490

Dulles, Foster Rhea, 95

Duluth, MN, 132

Dunne, Finley Peter, 345

Dye, Thomas, 318

Eberts, Randall, 507

Economic development strategies, 483–522; basic principles, suggested, 513–514; cost factor reduction, 488–500, 501*t*; cost factor reduction, outcomes, 500, 502–511;

deindustrialization, 483–486, 484*t*; goals, 486–488; low payoffs and decision process, 511–513

Economic multiplier, economic development goals and, 487

Economic Policy Institute's "Family Budget Calculator," 50–51

Economic profit, 104. *See also* Bid rent curve

Economics: concepts of, 18–22; concepts underlying urban growth, 65–73; of trade, 174–182; urban issues and, 3–5; urban paradoxes and, 15–16. *See also* Public policy, government versus market role in

Economies of scale: central city growth, 65, 68–70, 69*f*; new trade theory, 178–179; transportation networks, 359

Economy of Cities, The (Jacobs), 61, 79

Edge cities, 126–128, 127*f*

Edison, Thomas, 65

Edison Schools, 274

Education: central city growth, 95; changing fortunes of cities, 132; debate over government distribution of well-being, 299–300; economic development strategies, 493–494, 501*t*, 505–507; employment, 207, 209, 210*t*, 211; employment figures for sector, 303–305, 303*t*; externalities, 21; as key public policy issue, 16; metro area rankings, 53; as positive externality, 289, 295–296, 324–325, 325–326*f*. *See also* Education, prosperity and; Human capital theory

Education, prosperity and, 191–192, 195–196, 247–284; decentralized public education in the United States, 248–249, 249*t*; education levels in metro areas, 250–254, 251–253*f*; education production functions and school quality, 254–264; new growth theory and, 254–256; public schooling's importance, 249–250, 256–257; public school structure reforms, 271–279; segregation and public school challenges, 267–271, 269–270*t*; wage differentials, 219–220, 221*f*, 237–238

Education management organizations (EMOs), 274

Education production function, 257–264; curriculum choice and, 263–264; preschool and home influences, 264–267; spending impacts, 261–262; spending variations, 257–262

Education Trust, 260

Education vouchers, 275, 276–279, 300, 302, 528

Effective rents, 419

Efficiency: alternative growth scenarios, 477–478; criteria of, 20; equity versus, in public pricing, 309–316; transportation infrastructure investment, 364–365

Eid, Jean, 473

Electricity: central city growth, 64–65, 94–95; markets for, 301–302

Elitism, 15, 317–318

Ely, Richard T., 346–347

Emergency Medical Services, 392

Eminent domain, 452–454, 495, 508

Employment: deindustrialization and changes in, 483–486, 484*t*; housing prices and, 421–426, 422–423*f*, 425–426*f*; in public sector, 303–305, 303–304*t*. *See also* Economic development strategies; Labor markets

Empowerment zones, 498, 509–510

Engler, John, 260

Enterprise communities (ECs), 510

Enterprise zones (EZs), 498, 509–510

Envelope curve, 68

Environmental justice, 458–459

Environmental Protection Agency (EPA), 343, 459

Environmental quality: metro area rankings, 54; pollution as negative externality, 21, 294–295, 322–323, 323*f*

Epidemics, 332–334, 333*t*, 373, 381–382

"Equitopia," 477–478

Equity: alternative growth scenarios, 477–478; criteria of, 20; efficiency versus, in public pricing, 309–316; transportation infrastructure investment, 365–366; zoning and, 459–462

Erickson, Rodney, 510

Erie Canal, 12, 348–349, 359

Etzioni, Amitai, 318

Euclid case, 454

Ewing, Reid, 469, 470

Excludable goods, 296–298

Exclusionary zoning, 112, 455–456, 460–462

Exit versus voice, neighborhoods and, 527–529, 543

Exit, Voice, and Loyalty (Hirschman), 527

Export base theory, 182–187

Expulsive zoning, 459

External diseconomies, 67–68, 67*f*

External economies of production, 67, 67*f*

Externalities: definition and examples of, 20–21; market failure and public policy, 289, 294–296, 322–325, 323*f*, 325–326*f*; Tiebout hypothesis and, 315–316; transportation pricing, 361–364. *See also* Negative externalities; Positive externalities

Externality zoning, 455

Exurban regions, 12

Fainstein, Norman and Susan, 15, 319

"Family Budget Calculator," of Economic Policy Institute, 50–51

Fannie Mae, 434

Federal Housing Authority (FHA), 118, 407, 434; residential segregation, 122–123, 430; sprawl, 474

Fee simple property ownership, 453

Finance cities, 131, 158–159

Fire departments, 390–392

First-mover advantage, 179

"Fiscal equivalence," Olson's principle of, 315

Fiscal zoning, 455, 460–462

Fischel, William A., 94, 296, 452, 460, 476, 528

Fitzgerald, Joan, 494, 498

"Flat" world, metro areas' changing role in, 17–18, 143–144

Fleming, Lee, 197–198

Flint, Anthony, 477

Florida, Richard, 155, 159, 164, 190, 192, 499–500

Fogarty, Michael, 507

Freddie Mac, 434

Freeman, Lance, 477–478

Free parking, cost of, 361

Free rider problem, 296–297

Friedman, Michael, 512

Friedman, Milton, 299–300, 302

Friedman, Thomas, 18, 143–144

Frost, Robert, 18–19

Fulton, William, 468–469

Gaebler, Ted, 305–306

Galbraith, John Kenneth, 300

Galster, George, 13, 163

Gans, Herbert, 6

Garbage. *See* Solid waste management

Garreau, Joel, 126

Gasoline prices: commuting and mass-transit subsidies, 355–358, 357*f*; transportation policies and, 360–364

Gated communities, 526

GDP, imports as percent of, 143–144, 144*f*, 490

General reciprocity, 530–531

Gentrification, 544–546; income segregation, 137, 162–164, 163*t*; residential paradox, 128–129, 129*f*; social class, 431

Geographic boundary definitions, 27–32

Geography of Nowhere, The (Kunstler), 7

Gilder, George, 153

Gintis, Herbert, 263

Ginzberg, E., 379

Giuliani, Rudolph, 388

Glaeser, Edward, 115–116, 154, 162, 190–191, 226, 257, 415, 437, 468

Globalization: dynamics of, 143–146; health risks, 381–382; outsourcing, 144–145, 490

Goldberg, M., 508

Gordon, Peter, 153, 467

Granovetter, Mark, 531

Greenhut, M., 508

Greenstreet, D., 509

Grogan, Paul, 542–545

Gross flows, of employment, 484–485, 484*t*

Growth: as key public policy issue, 17; metro area rankings, 32–37, 34–36*t*. *See also* Urban growth, dynamics of historical

"Growth machines," 319–320

Hanushek, Eric, 261

Harkavy, Ira, 159

Harris, Chauncy, 101

Harrison, Bennett, 116, 485

Hartford, CT: earnings, 211; education levels, 254; median family income, 42, 45, 47; trade and prosperity, 173, 174, 193–194

Hayden, Dolores, 463

Health. *See* Public health issues

Health centers, 376–377, 379

Health insurance, disparities in care and, 379–381, 380–381*t*

Heat Wave (Klinenberg), 523

Hedonic price index, housing value and, 403–404

Hefetz, Amir, 306

Hickman, Matthew, 383

High Cost of Free Parking, The (Shoup), 361
Highest and best use of land concept, 454
Highways. *See Transportation entries*
Highway Trust Fund (HTF), 359, 361
Hirschman, Albert O., 527
Holli, Melvin, 346
Homeland security, 382, 390
Home owners' associations, 524–526
Home Owners Loan Corporation (HOLC), 118, 122–123
Homevoter hypothesis, 476, 528
HOPE VI (Housing Opportunities for People Everywhere), 435–436
Horn, Jerry, 278
Hospitals, 374–376, 377t
HOT (High-Occupancy plus Toll) lanes, 363
Household income. *See* Income
Housing, 401–450; affordable, defined, 52; economic factors of price and value, 401–406; employment and population growth, 421–428, 422–423f, 425–426f; equity and efficiency, 477–478; federal policies, 433–436; as key public policy issue, 16–17; owned versus rented, 52–53, 406f, 406–411; policy cautions, 442; purchasing power and, 50; rent control, 438–441, 440f; segregation, 428–433; state and local policies, 436–438; supply and demand factors of price, 411–417, 411–413f; vacancy rates and price, 417–421, 418–420f, 421t
Housing Act of 1937, 532
Housing Act of 1947, 435
Housing Act of 1949, 436, 453, 536
Housing allowance, 302
Housing and Urban Development (HUD), Department of, 434; Section 8 housing allowances, 435, 442
Housing trust funds, 437
Houston, TX: alternatives to zoning, 456–458; metropolitan dynamics, 12; school reform, 273
Howlett, Michael, 318
How the Other Half Lives (Riis), 394
Hoxby, Caroline, 261, 277
Hoyt, Homer, 101
Hub cities, 130–131, 158
Human capital theory, 219–220, 499–500. *See also Education entries*
Human resources, sustained competitive advantage and, 181
Hurricane Katrina, 382, 530, 536–538

Ihlanfeldt, Keith, 225, 432
Illinois, 260. *See also* Chicago, IL
Immigration: central city growth and, 90–94, 92f, 92–93t, 121, 123–124, 125t, 544, 545; police departments and, 384; in twenty-first-century cities, 164–165; wage differentials and, 235–237, 235f
Imports, as percent of GDP, 143–144, 144f
Import substitution, 185
Inclusionary zoning laws, 437, 478
Income: education levels, 253f, 254; growth, 540, 541t; home ownership, 408–411, 409–410t; income-differentiated neighborhoods, in Alonso model, 137; median changes in, and prosperity, 171–174, 172–173f; metro area rankings, 41–48, 42f, 44f, 46–48f, 53; personal income per student (PIPS), 259
Income elasticity of housing demand, 409–410, 410t
Income taxes, 309
Incrementalism, 318–319
Indianapolis, IN, 52, 94
Indifference curves, housing choice and, 404–406, 405f, 443–444, 444f
Individuals: influence on public decision making, 316–321; multiple identities in cities, 7
Industrialization: industrial parks and economic development, 494–495, 508; metropolitan dynamics, 10, 10f; sectors of industries, 125; social welfare, 392–393
Industrial revenue bonds, 491
Industry clusters, 180, 191
Inelastic demand, wage differentials and, 224
Infant mortality rates, 377–378, 378f
Informal economy, 221
Information problems. *See* Asymmetric information, market failure and public policy
Infrastructure, sustained competitive advantage and, 181. *See also* Physical infrastructure; Social infrastructure
Initiative for a Competitive Inner City, 543
Inner-city neighborhoods: competitive advantage, 192; poverty concentration, 432–433
Innovation cities, 131, 157, 159
Input-output analysis, 187–189, 199–201, 202t
Institute of Medicine of the National Academies, 379–380

Intangible assets, taxation and, 309
Interdistrict school choice, 276
Interest groups, metropolitan dynamics and, 13–15
Interest-group theory, 317–318
Intergenerational equity, 310
Intermodel Surface Transportation Efficiency Act (ISTEA), 365
Internal economies of scale, 65, 68–70, 69f, 73
Internal migration, city growth and, 87–90, 88t, 90t
International City/County Management Association (ICMA) data, 305, 306
Internet-based crime, 389–390
Interstate Highway System. *See Transportation entries*
Intradistrict school choice, 276
"Invisible hand," of market, 288
Isard, Walter, 80, 81f
Iso-access lines, in Alonso model, 134–137, 135–136f, 150

Jackson, Kenneth, 436
Jacksonville, FL: annexation, 94; earnings, 214; union density, 233
Jacobs, Jane, 5, 61, 79, 158, 179, 191, 475, 533, 537
Jargowsky, Paul, 433, 538
Jefferson, Thomas, 5, 87
Jeffrey, C. Ray, 535–536
Job creation, 386, 453, 542–543. *See also* Economic development strategies; Labor markets
Job Generation Process, The (Birch), 485
Jobless rates. *See* Unemployment
Job multipliers, 184–185, 186
Job tax credits, 506
Johnson, Lyndon, 12, 261, 491
Jungle, The (Sinclair), 451
Kahn, Matthew E., 226, 468
Kain, John, 225, 354, 404
Katz, Bruce, 432
Kayden, Jerold, 454
Kelling, George, 535
Kelo v. City of New London, 453–454
Kirschenman, Joleen, 224
Klinenberg, Eric, 523, 537
Knowledge resources, sustained competitive advantage and, 181

Knowledge spillovers: demand and supply sides, 190–191; education, 255; industry clusters, 180. *See also* Externalities
Kohlhase, Janet, 115–116
Kozol, Jonathan, 262
Kreuger, Alan, 261
Krugman, Paul, 154
Kunstler, James, 7

Labor costs: economic development strategies to reduce, 493–494, 501t, 505–507; transportation and, 80; Weber model and twenty-first-century cities, 146, 147–148f, 148–150
Labor markets, 206–246: earning by metro area, 211–218, 212–216f, 218t; earnings differential by metro area, 236–238, 237t; education levels and, 207, 209, 210t, 211; employment and unemployment, 207, 208–209f, 209; household income and, 206, 239–241; as key public policy issue, 16; marginal revenue product curve, 242–243, 242f; segmentation of, 220–221; wage differentials, 218–236, 221f, 223f, 227f, 228–229t, 232–233f, 235f. *See also* Demographic shifts
Labor unions: politics and, 96; union shops, 234; wage differentials and, 222, 232–237, 232–233f
Lancaster, Kevin, 403
Land-use controls, 451–482; equity and efficiency in alternative growth, 477–478; smart growth, 475–477; spatial form, 478–479; sprawl, 462–475, 464f, 466t, 471–473t; zoning, 452–462
Land values, 100; Alonso model and bid rent curve, 103–112; Alonso model and reduced costs, 150–151; constrained choice and political factors, 112–113
Lang, Robert E., 151
Langdon, Philip, 465
Las Vegas, NV: economic development strategies, 510–511; race and ethnicity, 37, 38f, 39; school reform, 274; tourism and growth, 126, 160
Latham, Earl, 318
Launhardt, Wilhelm, 76
Lazarus, Emma, 91
Lemann, Nicholas, 542
Levine, Robert, 5
Levittown, NY, 6, 117, 123
Levy, John M., 461

Libraries, 345–348

Lindblom, Charles, 318–319

Linkage programs, housing and, 437

Lipsey, Richard, 418

Lobbying, economic development and, 490–491

Local Initiatives Support Corporation (LISC), 542

Localization economies, 83. *See also* Agglomeration economies

Locally unwanted land uses (LULUs), 459

Local service jobs, 190–192. *See also* Export base theory

Location-efficient mortgages, 475–476, 478

Location quotients, 185–186

Logan, John R., 14, 320, 454

Long Beach, CA, 132

Long-run average cost curve, 68–70, 69*f*

Lorenzetti, Ambrogio, 529

Los Angeles, CA: annexation, 94; education levels, 252, 254; immigrants, 236; metropolitan dynamics, 12; race and ethnicity, 39, 40*f*; spatial mismatch, 226–229; wage differentials, 222; zoning, 455

Louisiana, 259. *See also* Hurricane Katrina; New Orleans, LA

Louisville, KY, 158

Love Canal, 294, 458–459

Low, Seth, 346

Low, Setha, 526

Low-cost production, competitive advantage and, 179–180

Low Income Housing Tax Credit (LIHTC), 436

Luberoff, David, 320, 476

Lucas, Robert, 254

Luce, T. F., 505

Lynch, Robert, 495–497

MacLean, Alex, 475

Macroeconomics, 4

Magnet schools, 273, 275

Maheshri, Vikram, 358

Manufacturing cities, 63–64, 130, 157–158

Marginal costs: negative externalities, 322–323, 323*f*; positive externalities, 324–325, 325–326*f*; supply and demand in private sector, 289–291, 290–291*f*, 294

Marginal private cost (MPC), traffic and, 363

Marginal revenue product, wage differentials and, 207, 218–219, 242–243, 242*f*

Marginal social cost (MSC), traffic and, 363

Market failure, 291–298; information and transportation pricing, 360–364, 362*f*; sewer systems, 341–345; sprawl, 468; water supply systems, 334–336

Market forces/market power: competitive advantage and inner-city neighborhoods, 192; market failure and public policy, 288, 291–293, 293*f*; metropolitan dynamics, 10, 10*f*; wage differentials, 224

Market-oriented firms, 74–75, 77*f*, 81*f*

Market price, supply and demand in private sector and, 289–291, 294

Markets, theoretical role of, 288–291. *See also* Market failure; Market forces/market power

Marx, Matt, 197–198

Mason, Daniel, 512

Massachusetts: Brockton, 433; economic development strategies, 490, 492, 494, 495, 503–504, 508; housing policy, 437; school spending, 260; Smart Growth Overlay Zoning law, 437, 478–479; zoning and, 461–462. *See also* Boston, MA

Massey, Douglas, 429

Mass transit. *See Transportation entries*

Materials-oriented firms, 74, 76*f*

McPherson, Miller, 531, 532

McShane, Clay, 335

Median household income. *See* Income

Medicare/Medicaid, 380–381

Meinig, David W., 130

Meir, Robert, 504

Memphis, TN, 54, 158

Merit pay system, for teachers, 274–275

Merit wants, government distribution of well-being and, 300

Metropolitan areas (MAs): changing fortunes of, 131–133; changing role in "flat" world, 17–18, 143–144; classified by income-generating activities, 129–131; defined, 28; high school graduation rates, 268–271, 269–270*t*; love/hate relationship with, 5, 7–8; map of major, 43. *See also* Rankings, of metro areas

Metropolitan dynamics, 9–16, 10*f*. *See also* Metropolitan expansion; Urban growth; Urban location dynamics

Metropolitan expansion, 100–142; business
    location decentralization, 113–116;
    changing fortunes of cities, 131–133;
    cities classified by income-generating
    activities, 129–131; land values and bid
    rent curve, 103–112; land values and
    constrained choice and political factors,
    112–113; models of growth and
    development, 101, 102–103*f*; segregation
    in cities, 121–124, 122*t*, 125*t*; suburban
    residential development, 116–121, 119*f*,
    120*t*; Sunbelt cities, edge cities, and
    gentrification, 125–129
Metropolitanism, 316
Metropolitan statistical areas (MSAs),
    defined, 28
Meyer, John, 354
Miami, FL, 49, 54
Michigan, 260. *See also* Detroit, MI
Microeconomics, 4
Micropolitan statistical areas, defined, 28
Migration: immigration to cities, 90–94,
    92*f*, 92–93*t*; from rural to urban areas,
    87–90, 88*t*, 90*t*; segregation/racism and,
    121–124, 122*t*; selective, 11, 183–184
"Milleniumburg," 477, 478
Miller, Grant, 335
Milliken v. Bradley, 271
Mills, Edwin S., 461
Milwaukee, WI: earnings, 215; immigrants,
    236; school reform, 273, 276–277; trade
    and prosperity, 173, 174, 178, 195
Minneapolis, MN, 273
Miron, Gary, 278
Mississippi, 259
Moe, Terry, 528
Molotch, Harvey L., 14, 320, 454
Monetary weight of transportation, 75–78
Monocentric model, 104
Monopoly advantage: market failure and
    public policy, 292; wage differentials
    and, 224
Moral Dimension, The (Etzioni), 318
Mortgages, government incentives and,
    118, 407
Moses, Leon, 82
Moses, Robert, 364
Moss, Mitchell, 153–154
Moss, Philip, 230
"Most Liveable Large Cities," 26
Mt. Laurel I and II zoning decisions, 438, 461
Mueller, E., 508

Multifamily housing, 112
Multiple identities, of individuals in cities, 7
Multiple nuclei model, of urban land use,
    101, 102–103*f*
Mumford, Lewis, 5, 346, 451
Municipalities, definitions pertaining to,
    27–32
Munnell, Alicia, 507
Murray, John, 390
Musgrave, Richard, 317

National Assessment of Educational
    Progress (NAEP), 267
National Health Service Corps scholarship,
    379
National Household Travel Survey (*NHTS*),
    350–353
National Labor Relations Act (NLRA),
    233–234
Nation at Risk, A (National Commission on
    Excellence in Education), 271–272
Natural monopolies: public utilities as,
    292–293, 293*f*; regulated private
    markets, 301–302; transportation
    networks, 359; water provision, 334
Natural resource cities, 130, 157
Natural resource costs, economic
    development strategies to reduce,
    494–495, 501*t*, 507–508
Neckerman, Kathryn, 224
NECTA (New England City and Town
    Area), 29
Negative externalities: commuting and
    mass-transit subsidies, 355–358, 357*f*;
    marginal costs and, 322–323, 323*f*;
    pollution as, 21, 294–295, 322–323, 323*f*;
    sewer systems, 341–343; zoning and,
    455–462
Neighborhood associations, 14
Neighborhoods, 523–545; central city
    renaissance, 538–545, 539*f*, 541*t*; crime
    reduction, 535–536; fundamental
    characteristics of "good," 523–524; social
    capital, 529–535; Tiebout hypothesis and
    privatization of public space, 524–529;
    vulnerable persons in, 536–538
Nelson, Robert H., 525
Newark, NJ: earnings, 211; education levels,
    254; trade and prosperity, 174, 196–197;
    union density, 233
New England City and Town Area
    (NECTA), 29

New growth theory, 254–256
New Hampshire, 260
New Jersey: housing policy, 437–438; school spending, 260. *See also* Newark, NJ
Newman, Oscar, 535
New Orleans, LA, 511. *See also* Hurricane Katrina
New trade theory, 178–179
New Urbanism movement, 161–162, 475, 533, 535
New York, NY: combined statistical area, 31–32, 31*t*; crime, 54, 535–536; earnings, 211, 214; establishment and early role of, 63; as finance city, 131; immigrants, 90, 236; population growth, 540; poverty, 49, 95; rent control, 438, 439; retail demand, 543; transportation, 55; union density, 233; zoning, 455, 461
New York State: combined statistical areas, 32, 33*f*; metropolitan dynamics, 12; school spending, 260; Yonkers, 433. *See also* New York, NY
No Child Left Behind Act (NCLB), 275
Noll, Roger, 511
Nominal wages, 212
Nonexcludable goods, 313
Norfolk, VA, 63
North Dakota, 260

Oakland, CA, 504
Oak Park, MI, 433
Occupational Safety and Health Act (OSHA), 393
O'Connor, Sandra Day, 454
Offshoring, 145
Ohio: Akron, 75, 78–80; Cincinnati, 132; Cleveland, 132, 277, 342; Columbus, 26–27; Cuyahoga River, 342; Dayton, 273; economic development strategies, 494; transportation pricing, 361
Oklahoma, 259
Okun, Arthur, 525
Oligopoly advantage: market failure and public policy, 292; wage differentials and, 224
Olmsted, Frederick Law, 348
Olson, Mancur, 315
Opportunity cost: commuting time, 464–465; comparative advantage, 175–177; definition and examples of, 18–20; economic development strategies, 513

Opportunity structures, 13
Option value: public education, 249; pure public good, 297–298
Orlando, FL: economic development strategies, 510–511; tourism and growth, 126, 160
Orwell, George, 451–452
Osborne, David, 305–306
Outsourcing, 144–145, 490
Overcrowding, contrasted to population density, 332
Overzoning, 459–462, 478

Pager, Devah, 224
Pareto optimality, 290–291
Parks: industrial, 494–495, 508; pastoral public, 345–348
Paternalism, government distribution of well-being and, 300
Path dependency, 79
Paul, D., 512
Peak load pricing. *See* Congestion pricing
Peer pressure, students' performance and, 265
Pendall, Rolf, 469, 470
People of color. *See* African Americans; Race and ethnicity; Segregation
Perfect competition: key assumptions of, 288–289; market's role in public policy, 288–298; school choice, 276
Perry Preschool Program, 266
Personal income per student (PIPS), 259
Philadelphia, PA: annexation, 94; as cultural/tourism/recreation center, 160; economic development strategies, 503; establishment and early role of, 63; immigration, 90; poverty, 49; school reform, 274; water supply systems, 334
Phillips, A. W., 417
Phillips, D., 266
Phillips Curve, 417–421
Phoenix, AZ: economic development strategies, 499; spatial mismatch, 226–229; union density, 233
Physical infrastructure, 331–371; combating disease, 331–334, 333*t*; economic development strategies, 494–495, 501*t*, 507–508; public amenities and urban unrest, 345–348; solid waste management, 336–340, 340*f*; transportation issues, 346–366; wastewater and sewer systems, 340–345; water supply systems, 334–336

Physical resources, sustained competitive
    advantage and, 181
Physician-to-population ratio, 376–379,
    377*t*
Pingree, Hazen, 346
Pittsburgh, PA, 11, 36
Pittsburgh, Survey, The, 394
Place, importance of, 3, 12–13, 18
Plessy v. Ferguson, 268, 270
Pluralism, 15
Police departments, 382–390; changing
    approaches to policing, 385–389;
    demographic change and, 383–385; police
    power and regulation enforcement, 452;
    twenty-first-century issues, 389–390
Political science: paradoxes of, 15–16; urban
    issues and, 3–5
Politics/political factors: city growth, 96;
    economic development decisions, 512;
    immigration, 93; labor unions, 96; land
    values, 112–113; metropolitan dynamics,
    13–15. *See also* Public policy
Pollution, as negative externality, 21,
    294–295, 322–323, 323*f*
Polycentric cities, 137
Population density: contrasted to
    overcrowding, 332; importance of, 8;
    physician-to-population ratio, 376, 377*t*,
    378–379; public sector versus market
    roles, 287–288; pure public versus pure
    private goods, 297; residential paradox,
    110–112, 110*f*, 111*t*; social capital,
    534–535. *See also* Population size
Population size, 62*f*, 83*t*; housing prices and,
    426–428, 427–428*f*; metro area rankings,
    32–37, 34–36*t*; urban, 1830–1921, 71–72*f*,
    84; urban, 1970–2000, 538–540, 539*f*,
    541*t*. *See also* Population density
Pork barrel politics, 492
Porter, Michael, 18, 179–181, 190–191, 543
Portland, OR: earnings, 214; education
    levels, 251, 254; urban growth boundaries,
    476–477
Positive externalities: education as, 289,
    295–296, 324–325, 325–326*f*; marginal
    costs and, 324–325, 325–326*f*
Poverty: central city growth, 95; health care,
    376–381, 378*f*, 380–381*t*; inner-city
    housing, 432–433; metro area rankings,
    48–50; police approaches to crime, 387;
    school performance, 264–265; school
    spending variations, 259–260; social

capital and safety, 536–538; welfare
    services, 392–395. *See also* Residential
    paradox
*Power Broker: Robert Moses and the Fall of
    New York* (Caro), 364
Premus, Robert, 256
Preschool influences, performance and,
    264–267
Price elasticity of demand: business location,
    489; wage differentials, 224
Pricing: equity and efficiency of government
    services, 309–316; metropolitan
    transportation issues, 360–364, 362*f*
Primary metropolitan statistical areas
    (PMSAs), defined, 28
Primary sector industries, 125
Principal-agent problem, 335
Principal city, defined, 29
"Prisoner's dilemma," economic
    development decisions and, 512–513
Private investment, center city regeneration
    and, 543
*Private Neighborhoods and the
    Transformations of Local Government*
    (Nelson), 525
Private security guards, 389
Privatization, 302–303, 305–306
"Problem of Social Cost, The" (Coase),
    457
Problem-oriented policing, 388–389
Procurement costs, 74–75; in Weber model,
    76–77*f*, 77–78
Product differentiation, comparative
    advantage and, 179–180
Productive efficiency, 292
Product life cycle theory, 179
Property tax revenue, 307–309, 307*t*, 308*f*
Proscio, Tony, 542–545
Prosperity: labor markets' role in, 206–246;
    public education's role in, 247–284;
    trade's role in, 171–205
Public choice theory, 317
Public decision making: challenges of,
    320–321; influences on, 316–320
Public funding/private provision, of public
    services, 302
Public health issues: combating disease,
    331–334, 333*t*; disparities in care,
    377–381, 378*f*, 380–381*t*; health centers,
    376–377; health departments, 372,
    373–374; hospitals, 374–376, 377*t*;
    neighborhood form, 537; solid waste

management, 336–340, 340*f*; sprawl, 467, 473; student performance, 265, 267; twenty-first-century issues, 381–382; water supply systems, 334–336

Public health movement, 95–96

Public Housing Act of 1937, 435–436

Public policy, 4–5; federal, and housing, 433–436; federal, and suburban residential development, 117–118; immigration and cities, 123–125; incentives for home ownership, 407–408; influence on supply side, 188–192; key issues of, 16–17; metropolitan dynamics, 10, 10*f*, 11–13; paradoxes of, 15–16; residential segregation, 430; sprawl, 473–475; state and local policies, 436–438. *See also* Economic development strategies; Public policy, government versus market role in

Public policy, government versus market role in, 287–330; distribution of well-being debate, 298–301; government revenues, 307–309; government's role, 287–291; influences on, 316–321; local government employment and spending, 303–305; market failure, 291–298; market failure and service provision alternatives, 301–303; metropolitan transportation, 360–366; pricing of public services, 309–316

Public provision, privatization and, 302–303, 305–306

Public safety: Emergency Medical Services, 392; fire departments, 390–392; police departments, 382–390

Public-sector unions, 14

Public utilities, monopolies and regulation, 292–293

Public venture funds, 492, 503–504

Pull and push factors, 87; internal migration and, 87–90, 88*t*, 90*t*

Purchasing power, metro area rankings and, 50–51, 51*t*, 52*f*

Pure public goods, market failure and public policy, 296–298

Push and pull factors, 87; internal migration and, 87–90, 88*t*, 90*t*

Putnam, Robert, 530–531, 534

"Quality of Living" index, 26. *See also* Well-being

Quarantines, 373

Quasi-public corporations, 492

Quigley, John, 404

Quillian, Lincoln, 224

Rabin, Yale, 459

Race and ethnicity: center city regeneration, 541–545; civic engagement, 534; educational achievement, 267–271, 269–270*t*; firefighting, 391–392; health care disparities, 377–380, 378*f*, 380–381*t*; home ownership, 406–407; housing segregation, 428–433; metro area rankings, 37–41, 38–41*f*; police departments, 385–387; segregation and cities, 121–124, 122*t*, 125*t*; wage differentials, 222–224, 223*f*, 230–232, 237–238; zoning, 455–456, 459, 460–462. *See also* African Americans; Segregation

Rae, Douglas, 86

Railroads. *See Transportation entries*

Raleigh-Durham-Chapel Hill, NC: earnings, 215; education levels, 251, 252, 254; purchasing power, 51, 51*t*; trade and prosperity, 173–174, 178, 196; unemployment rate, 207; union density, 233

Ramesh, A., 318

RAND Corporation studies, 278, 439

Rankings, of metro areas, 25–58; affordable housing and home ownership, 52–53; cities and reputations, 25–27; crime, 54–55; education, 53; environmental quality, 54; geographic boundary definitions, 27–32; income disparity and inequality, 53; median income, 41–42, 42*f*, 44*f*, 45; median income changes, 45–48, 46–48*f*; population size, 32–37, 34–36*t*; poverty, 48–50; purchasing power, 50–51, 51*t*, 52*f*; race and ethnicity, 37–41, 38–41*f*; transportation, 55

Raw materials costs, economic development strategies to reduce, 494–495, 501*t*, 507–508

Real wages, 212

Reaves, Brian, 383

Reciprocity, specific versus general, 530–531

Recycling and reuse, 336–340

Redlining, 122–123

Refuse. *See* Solid waste management

Regime theory, 15, 319–320

Regulated private markets, as alternative for providing goods and services, 301–302

Regulation streamlining, economic development strategies for, 497–498, 501*t*, 509–510

Regulatory costs, business location and, 114

Reich, Robert, 528–529

Reinventing Government (Osborne and Gaebler), 305–306

Rent, 100. *See also* Land values

Rental housing: versus owned, 406–411, 406*f*; subsidies, 434–435; vacancy rates, 418–420, 418*f*

Rent control, consequences of, 438–441, 440*f*, 442

Repurposing, of cities, 157

Residential locations: Alonso model and reduced costs, 150–153; cultural amenities versus economic factors, 154–156; income segregation in twenty-first-century cities, 162–164, 163*t*

Residential paradox, 110–112, 110*f*, 111*t*; gentrification, 128–129, 129*f*; polycentric cities with income-differentiated neighborhoods, 137

Residential segregation, income and, 224–225, 461, 529

Restrictive covenants, 456

Retail businesses: central city growth and, 64, 543; competitive advantage and inner-city neighborhoods, 192

Retirement centers, 160–161

Revenues, of businesses, economic development strategies, 488–489, 501*t*, 502–503

Revenues, of government: pricing of services and, 309–316; taxation, 307–309, 307*t*, 308*f*

Ricardo, David, 175

Richardson, Harry W., 153, 467

"Right-to-Work" movement, 233*f*, 234

Riis, Jacob, 394

Rise of the City, The (Schlesinger), 346

Rise of the Creative Class, The (Florida), 159, 499

Risk, contrasted to uncertainty, 498

Rival goods, 296–298

"Road Not Taken, The" (Frost), 19

Road to Wigan Pier, The (Orwell), 451–452

Roger and Me (film), 183

Romer, Paul, 254

Roosevelt, Franklin Delano, 536

Rosenbloom, Sandra, 366

Rothenberg, Jerome, 436

Rothstein, Richard, 258–259, 260, 264

Russell Sage Foundation, 394

Safe, Accountable, Flexible, Efficient Transportation Equity Act (SAFETEA), 365

Safety. *See* Public safety

Saiz, Albert, 191

Sales taxes, 309

Salt Lake City, UT: education levels, 251; unemployment rate, 207; union density, 233

San Antonio, TX: economic development strategies, 492; race and ethnicity, 39, 40*f*, 41

San Antonio Independent School District v. Rodriguez, 260

Sander, Thomas, 535

San Diego, CA, 52

San Francisco, CA, 52; earnings, 211–212, 214, 215; education levels, 254; as finance city, 131; housing, 52, 411–412; immigrants, 91, 236; median family income, 42, 47–48; population change, 119*f*, 120; race and ethnicity, 39, 41, 41*f*; trade and prosperity, 174, 197–198; zoning, 461

San Jose, CA, 37, 132

Sassen, Saskia, 157

"Satisficing" criterion, 502

Saxenian, AnnaLee, 197

Scale economies, 68

Schlesinger, Arthur M., 346

School choice, 276–277. *See also Education entries*

Schuetz, Jenny, 415

Schultz, Stanley, 335

Schumpeter, Joseph, 86, 485

"Secession of the successful," 528–529

Secondary mortgage market, 434

Secondary sector industries, 125

Section 8 housing allowances, 435, 442

Sector model, of urban land use, 101, 102–103*f*, 110; Alonso model and, 137–138

Segregation: American cities and, 121–123, 122*t*, 125*t*; center city regeneration, 544–545; educational achievement, 267–271, 269–270*t*; housing, 428–433; by income in twenty-first-century cities,

162–164, 163*t*; residential and wage differentials, 224–225, 461, 529. *See also* Race and ethnicity

Selective migration, 11, 183–184

Self-interest, public decisions and, 318

Semiconductor industry, negative externalities and, 294–295

Service Employees International Union (SEIU), 235

Settlement house movement, 394

Sewer systems, 340–345

Shadow economy, 221

Shearing, Clifford, 389

Shonkoff, J. P., 266

Short-run average costs, 67–68, 67*f*, 69*f*

Shoup, Donald, 361

Sieberling, Frank, 80

Silent Spring (Carson), 342–343

Simon, Herbert, 502

Sinclair, Upton, 451

Sister Carrie (Dreiser), 5

Site assembly problem, 454

Site costs, Weber model and twenty-first-century cities, 146, 147–148*f*, 148–150. *See also* Urban location dynamics

Sjoquist, David, 432

Skills mismatch: economic development strategies, 493–494, 501*t*, 505–507; wage differentials, 228–232, 229*t*

Smart growth: barriers to implementation, 476–477; Smart Growth movement, 161, 475–477; social capital and, 534–535

Smart Growth Overlay Zoning law, 437, 478–479

"Smart Town," 477

Smith, Adam, 288

Smith-Lovin, Lynn, 531, 532

Snyder, Mary Gail, 526

Social amenities. *See* Cultural amenities

Social benefit: differs from private benefit, 324–325, 325–326*f*; market price and, 289–294. *See also* Positive externalities

Social capital: crime, 387; neighborhood form, 532–533; role in civic engagement, 529–532; smart growth, 534–535; suburbanization, 532; vulnerable persons, 536–538

Social-class structure, housing segregation and, 431

Social cost: marginal costs and, 289–294, 518; private costs and, 322–326, 323*f*. *See also* Negative externalities

Social disorganization approach, to policing, 387

Social infrastructure, 372–400; Emergency Medical Services, 392; fire departments, 390–392; health services, 372–382; police departments, 382–390; welfare services, 392–395

"Social Isolation in America" (McPherson, Smith-Lovin, and Brashears), 532

Social networks: central city growth, 83, 85; metropolitan dynamics, 10, 10*f*

Social reformers, 346–348

Social science, urban issues and, 3–9

Social Security, 393

Social unrest, public amenities and, 346–348

Sociology: paradoxes of, 15–16; urban issues and, 3–5

Solid waste management, 336–340, 340*f*

Soule, David, 498

South Dakota, 259, 260

Southern Burlington County NAACP v. Township of Mount Laurel. See Mt. Laurel I and II zoning decisions

Spatial mismatch: transportation infrastructure investment, 365–366, 432; wage differentials, 222, 224–232, 227*f*, 230, 237

Spatial relocation, metropolitan dynamics, 10, 10*f*. *See also* Urban location dynamics

Specialization, 66, 174–177, 176*f*

Specific reciprocity, 530–531

Spending patterns, of public sector, 303–305, 303–304*t*

Spillover effects, of metro areas, 8–9. *See also* Externalities; Knowledge spillovers

Sports stadiums, economic development strategies and, 501*t*, 510–511

Sprawl. *See* Urban sprawl

"Sprawlville," 477

"Sprinkler Cities," 6

Stakeholders, economic development decisions and, 512

Standard deviation, in real median income, 48

Standard metropolitan statistical areas (SMSAs), defined, 28

Standards movement, school reform and, 275

Statistical discrimination, 224

Statistics, wise use of, 55
Statue of Liberty, 91
Steele, James, 503
Stevenson, Mary Huff, 230–231, 237–238, 430
St. Louis, MO: earnings, 214–215; immigrants, 236; peer metro regions, 50–55; population growth, 540; poverty, 49; union density, 233
Stoll, Michael, 226
Stone, Clarence N., 15, 319
Street layout, in Alonso model, 134
Structural reformers, 346–348
Strumsky, Deborah, 197
Studying Public Policy (Howlett and Ramesh), 318
Sturm, Roland, 470
SubUrbia (Bogosian), 7
Suburbs: high school graduation rates in, 268–271, 269–270*t*; income disparity and inequality, 53; independence of, 94; love/hate relationship with, 6–8; low and high growth, 32, 34, 35–36*t*, 36; median family income, 44*f*; median family income changes, 45, 46*f*, 47–48; population growth, 35–36*t*; poverty and inner-ring, 433; public policy, 117–118; social capital, 532. *See also* Metropolitan expansion
Sunbelt cities, 125–126, 156
Superfund program, 294, 459
Supplementary Security Income (SSI), 393
Supply and demand: housing prices and, 411–417, 411–413*f*; private sector, 289–291, 290–291*f*
Supply chains, management of, 145
Supply-side perspective: metropolitan transportation, 358–366; prosperity, 189–192; subsidized housing, 435–436; tax reduction, 496
Sustained competitive advantage, 180
Swindell, Rudy, 512
Systemic social disorganization approach, to policing, 387

Tacoma, WA: education levels, 251; school reform, 273; as transportation hub, 130–131
Taft-Hartley Act, 234
"Takings." *See* Eminent domain
Tannenwald, Robert, 308–309
Targeted Jobs Tax Credit (TJTC), 506

Tax increment financing (TIF), 492–493, 504–505
Tax issues: business location, 114; economic development strategies, 487, 495–497, 501*t*, 508–509; government revenues, 307–309, 307*t*, 308*f*, 316; housing policy, 407–408, 434, 442; metropolitan dynamics, 14; school spending variations, 259–260; sprawl, 474; suburban residential development, 117–118
Teachers, education quality and, 262–263, 274–275
Teaford, Jon, 394
Technology, central city growth and, 65, 73, 85–86, 94–95
Telecom City, 495, 508
Telecommunications, 64–65, 145–146, 153–154, 159, 495
Temporary Assistance for Needy Families (TANF), 393
Tennessee, 494; Chattanooga, 322–323
Terrorism, 382, 390
Tertiary sector industries, 125
Texas Transportation Institute, 465
Thompson, Wilbur, 313
Tiebout, Charles, pricing hypothesis of, 313–316; privatization of public space and, 524–529
Tilly, Chris, 230–231
Tourism, as foundation of growth, 125–126, 159–160
Trade, prosperity and role of, 171–205; absolute advantage, 174–175; comparative advantage, 175–178, 176*f*; competitive advantage, 179–182; demand-side perspective, 182–189; household incomes, 171–174, 172–173*f*; new trade theory, 178–179; specific cases, 192–198; supply-side perspective, 188–192
Traditional approach, to policing, 385–387
Training, economic development strategies and, 493–494, 501*t*, 505–507. *See also Education entries*; Human capital theory
Transferable development rights, 476
Transit-oriented development (TOD), 475, 477–478
Transportation: central city growth, 64–65; changing fortunes of cities, 131–133; global health, 381–382; health care disparities, 380; hospital development, 375; as key public policy issue, 17; metro area rankings, 55; option value, 297–298;

spatial mismatch, 225; suburban residential development, 116–117

Transportation, physical infrastructure, 346–366; automobile travel trends, 96, 350–353, 351*f*, 351–353*t*; commuting trends, 354–355, 355*t*, 356*f*; equity issues, 365–366; investment and efficiency, 364–365; mass-transit subsidies, 355–358, 357*f*; pricing issues, 360–364; transportation planning history, 358–360

Transportation-cost-oriented firms, 74

Transportation costs: business location and, 114–116; central city growth, 65, 66; economic development strategies to reduce, 494–495, 501*t*, 507–508; gentrification, 128–129, 129*f*; land value in Alonso model, 104–112, 105*t*, 107*f*, 109–110*f*, 111*t*; in nineteenth-century cities, 73–82, 76*f*; in twenty-first-century cities, 143–165

Transportation Equity Act for the 21st Century (TEA-21), 365

Transportation hub cities, 130–131, 158

Trash. *See* Solid waste management

Travel distance, in Alonso model, 134

Travel speed, in Alonso model, 135–137, 136*f*

Travel time. *See* Commuting; Transportation, physical infrastructure

Truman, David, 318

Tucson, AZ: earnings, 211–212, 214; union density, 233; wage differentials, 222

Tyson's Corner, VA, 126–127, 463

Ullman, Edward, 101

Uncertainty, economic development strategies and, 498

Underground economy, 221

Underzoning, 458–459, 478

Unemployment, 207–209, 208–209*f*; approaches to crime and, 387; social welfare issues, 392–395. *See also* Labor markets

Unintended consequences, definition and examples of, 21–22

Unions. *See* Labor unions

UNITE HERE, 235

Upward filtering, housing and, 431

Urban areas, defined, 468–469

Urban cluster, defined, 28

Urban Development Action Grant (UDAG) program, 491–492, 503, 504

Urban economics, 4

Urban Frontier, The (Wade), 61

Urban ghetto/urban slum, 432

Urban growth, dynamics of historical, 61–99; agglomeration economies, 65, 66–68, 67*f*, 73, 82–85; centripetal and centrifugal forces, 62–65; changing patterns of, 94–96; consumer markets, 65, 70, 73; demographic growth, 86–94, 88*t*, 90*t*, 92*f*, 92–93*t*; early rural versus urban, 61–62; internal economies of scale, 65, 68–70, 69*f*, 73; technological progress, 65, 73, 85–86; transportation costs, 65, 66, 73–82, 76*f*, 79*f*, 81*f*

Urban growth boundary, 476

Urbanization economies, 85. *See also* Agglomeration economies

Urbanized area, defined, 28

Urban location dynamics, 143–168; Alonso model, 150–153, 152*t*; changing demographics, 162–165, 163*t*; changing role of cities, 153–161; decentralization of, 113–116, 117; globalization dynamics, 143–146; Smart Growth and New Urbanism, 161–162; Weber model, 146, 147–148*f*, 148–150

Urban population, defined, 28

Urban renewal programs, 436, 453, 532–533

Urban sprawl: commuting and, 463–467, 466*t*; debates about, 463, 467–468; defined, 462–463; market forces and public policy, 473–475; measurement of, 468–473, 471–473*t*. *See also* Smart growth

User fees/charges: as government revenue, 308; transportation policies and, 313, 360–364

U.S. National Resources Inventory, 468–469

Vacancy rates, housing prices and, 417–421, 418–420*f*, 421*t*

Venture capital, economic development strategies, 492, 503–504

Vernon, Raymond, 85

Veterans Administration (VA), 118

Village of Euclid, Ohio v. Ambler Realty Co., 454

Visualizing Density (Campoli and MacLean), 475

Voice versus exit, neighborhoods and, 527–529, 543
Voluntary organizations, metropolitan dynamics and, 14
"Voting with their feet" (Tiebout hypothesis), 313–316, 527–529
Vouchers: for education, 275, 276–279, 300, 302, 528; for food and housing, 302

Wade, Richard C., 61
Wage differentials: barriers to mobility, 220–222; education, 209, 210*t*, 211; human capital investment, 219–220, 221*f*; immigrants, 235–237, 235*f*; marginal revenue product curve, 218–219, 242–243, 242*f*; by metro area, 211–218, 212–216*f*, 218*t*; racial and ethnic discrimination, 222–224, 223*f*; skills mismatch, 228–232, 229*t*; spatial mismatch, 222, 224–232, 227*f*; unions and, 232–233*f*, 232–235, 236–237
Walker, R., 509
Wal-Mart, 543
Ward, Bryce, 415
Warner, Mildred, 306
Washington, D.C.: poverty, 49; school reform, 273; sprawl, 463, 464*f*
Waste management. *See* Solid waste management
Wastewater systems, 340–345
Wasylenko, Michael, 505
Water: power from, and city growth, 63–64; quality of, 54; supply systems, 334–336; wastewater systems, 340–345
Weber, Alfred, 76
Weber's graphical model of transportation costs, 76–81, 76–77*f*, 79*f*, 81*f*; reduced costs and twenty-first-century cities, 146, 147–148*f*, 148–150

"Weight-gaining" firm, 78
"Weight-losing" firm, 77–78
Weiss, Carol, 319
Weissbourd, Robert, 155–156, 547
Welfare services, 392–395
Well-being: government distribution of, 298–301, 311; industrial and social welfare, 293–295; public policy and, 12–13
Wheaton, William, 409, 410
When Work Disappears (Wilson), 541–542
Whyte, William H., 5, 462
Wilken, A., 508
Williamson, Harold F., Jr., 82
Williamson, Thad, 534
Wilson, James Q., 535
Wilson, William Julius, 541–542
Winston, Clifford, 358
Wohl, Martin, 354
Woods, M., 508
Wyly, Elvin K., 226
Wyoming, 260

Yonkers, NY, 433

Zeigler, Harmon, 318
Zimbalist, Andrew, 511
Zimmer, Ron, 278
Zoning regulations, 16–17, 442; economic development strategies, 497–498, 509; eminent domain, 452–454, 495, 508; environmental justice, 458–459; equity issues, 459–462; exclusionary, 112; Houston's alternative to, 456–458; land-use restrictions, 452–462; principal motives for, 455–456; as public policy, 436–437; race and, 455–456, 459, 460–462; urban sprawl and, 462–475, 464*f*, 466*t*, 471–473*t*
Zuckerman, Harmon, 159

CD-ROM Instructions

Important: This CD is engineered for Windows; it is not configured for MAC OS.

To install the Urban Experience (UE) Resource Kit on your PC:

1. Insert the CD in your CD/DVD drive. In a few seconds the InstallShield will appear.
2. Follow the InstallShield instructions on your screen.
3. Within a few minutes, the UE icon shortcut will be placed on your desktop, along with a UE tutorial.
4. Click on the UE icon to start the program.
5. After installation, you will not need to insert the CD to use the program.